M000307140

THE
CONVERSATION
CONTINUES

THE
CONVERSATION
CONTINUES

STUDIES
IN PAUL
& JOHN

In Honor of J. Louis Martyn

ROBERT T. FORTNA

AND

BEVERLY R. GAVENTA

EDITORS

Abingdon Press
NASHVILLE

THE CONVERSATION CONTINUES

This book is printed on acid-free paper.

The Conversation continues: studies in Paul and John in honor of J. Louis Martyn / Robert T. Fortna and Beverly R. Gaventa, editors.
    p.   cm
    Includes bibliographical references.
    ISBN 0-687-09634-0 (alk. paper)
    1. Martyn, J. Louis (James Louis), 1925-   . 2. Bible. N.T. Epistles of Paul—Criticism, interpretation, etc. 3. Bible. N.T. John—Criticism, interpretation, etc. I. Martyn, J. Louis (James Louis), 1925-   . II. Fortna, Robert Tomson. III. Gaventa, Beverly Roberts.
    BS2650.2.C65   1990
    226.5″06—dc20   90-33294
                                                                                  CIP

MANUFACTURED IN THE UNITED STATES OF AMERICA

AN OPEN LETTER TO J. LOUIS MARTYN

Dear Lou,

Although we address you, we are aware that others who read this letter may be puzzled by the use of the term *conversation* in our title. No one who has studied or worked with you will have a similar problem. For several decades now, your conversations—with the biblical text and with colleagues—have enriched us. From your inaugural lecture, with its striking image of an interpretive round table of discussion, from the imaginative conversations that enliven *History and Theology* and so forcefully reveal the Johannine church, from your more recent conversations with Paul, we have learned both to value and to cultivate the art of conversation. Your many colleagues and students have repeatedly identified their conversations with you as occasions marked by insight, honesty, and grace. This volume, then, seeks to continue those conversations.

You will not be surprised to learn that we are indebted to many people for their assistance. John Knox, Leander E. Keck, Raymond E. Brown, and—not least—Dorothy Martyn offered suggestions and advice at important points in the evolution of this work. Davis Perkins, now of Westminster/John Knox, eagerly accepted our proposal and prepared its way with Abingdon Press. Rex Matthews, his successor as academic editor, has sought in every way to make this volume deserving of you.

Together with all whose contributions appear in the book, we salute you on your sixty-fifth birthday and offer you these essays with thanks and deep affection.

Cordially yours,
Beverly and Bob

October 11, 1990

CONTENTS

CONTENTS

PART TWO. JOHN

CONTENTS

CONTRIBUTORS

William Baird
Professor of New Testament
Brite Divinity School, Texas
Christian University

J. Christiaan Beker
Professor of Biblical Theology
Princeton Theological
Seminary

Raymond E. Brown, S. S.
Auburn Distinguished
Professor of Biblical Studies
Union Theological Seminary

Schuyler Brown
Professor of New Testament
University of St. Michael's
College

Oscar Cullmann
Professor Emeritus
Universities of Basel and Paris

Nils A. Dahl
Buckingham Professor of New
Testament Criticism and
Interpretation (Emeritus)
The Divinity School, Yale
University

W. D. Davies
Professor Emeritus
Duke University

Marinus de Jonge
Professor of New Testament
and Early Christian Literature
University of Leiden

Robert T. Fortna
Professor of Religion
Vassar College

Reginald H. Fuller
Professor Emeritus
Protestant Episcopal Theologi-
cal Seminary in Virginia

11

Victor Paul Furnish
University Distinguished
Professor of New Testament
Perkins School of Theology,
Southern Methodist University

Beverly R. Gaventa
Professor of New Testament
Columbia Theological Seminary

Barbara Hall
Professor of New Testament
Protestant Episcopal Theological Seminary in Virginia

Robert Hamerton-Kelly
Senior Research Associate
Center for International
Security and Arms Control
Stanford University

Leander E. Keck
Winkley Professor of Biblical
Theology
The Divinity School, Yale
University

John Knox
Professor Emeritus of
New Testament
Union Theological Seminary and
The Episcopal Theological
Seminary of the Southwest

John Koenig
Professor of New Testament
General Theological Seminary

Abraham J. Malherbe
Buckingham Professor of New
Testament Criticism and
Interpretation
The Divinity School, Yale
University

Wayne A. Meeks
Woolsey Professor of Biblical
Studies
Yale University

Paul W. Meyer
Helen H. P. Manson Professor
of New Testament Literature
and Exegesis (Emeritus)
Princeton Theological
Seminary and
Adjunct Professor
University of North Carolina at
Chapel Hill

Paul S. Minear
Winkley Professor of Biblical
Theology (Emeritus)
The Divinity School, Yale
University

E. P. Sanders
Dean Ireland's Professor of
Exegesis of Holy Scripture
University of Oxford and
Fellow of The Queen's College

James A. Sanders
Professor of Biblical Studies
School of Theology at Claremont and Claremont Graduate
School and President, Ancient
Biblical Manuscript Center for
Preservation and Research

D. Moody Smith
George Washington Ivey
Professor of New Testament
The Divinity School, Duke
University

Kiyoshi Tsuchido
Professor of New Testament
Studies and Dean of Depart-
ment of Christian Studies
Tohuku Gakuin University

Walter Wink
Professor of Biblical
Interpretation
Auburn Theological Seminary

ABBREVIATIONS

AB	Anchor Bible
AGJU	Arbeiten zur Geschichte des antiken Judentums und des Urchristentums
ANRW	*Aufstieg und Niedergang des römischen Welt*
ATR	*Anglican Theological Review*
AUSS	*Andrews University Seminary Studies*
BA	*Biblical Archaeologist*
BAGD	W. Bauer, W. F. Arndt, F. W. Gingrich, and F. W. Danker, *Greek-English Lexicon of the NT*
BDF	F. Blass, A. Debrunner, and R. W. Funk, *A Greek Grammar of the NT*
BETL	Bibliotheca ephemeridum theologicarum lovaniensium
BEvT	Beiträge zur evangelischen Theologie
BHT	Beiträge zur historischen Theologie
Bib	*Biblica*
BZ	*Biblische Zeitschrift*
BZNW	Beihefte zur *ZNW*
CBQ	*Catholic Biblical Quarterly*

15

CJT	*Canadian Journal of Theology*
CNT	Commentaire du Nouveau Testament
CurTM	*Currents in Theology and Mission*
Ebib	Études bibliques
EKKNT	Evangelisch-katholischer Kommentar zum Neuen Testament
ETL	*Ephemerides theologicae lovanienses*
EvQ	*Evangelical Quarterly*
ExpTim	*Expository Times*
FRLANT	Forschungen zur Religion und Literatur des Alten und Neuen Testaments
Greg	*Gregorianum*
HeyJ	*Heythrop Journal*
HNT	Handbuch zum Neuen Testament
HNTC	Harper's NT Commentaries
HTR	*Harvard Theological Review*
HTS	Harvard Theological Studies
IB	*Interpreter's Bible*
ICC	International Critical Commentary
IDB	*Interpreter's Dictionary of the Bible*
IDBSup	Supplementary Volume to *IDB*
Int	*Interpretation*
JAC	Jahrbuch für Antike und Christentum
JBL	*Journal of Biblical Literature*
JJS	*Journal of Jewish Studies*
JR	*Journal of Religion*
JSNT	*Journal for the Study of the New Testament*
JSNTSup	Journal for the Study of the New Testament—Supplement Series

16

JTS	*Journal of Theological Studies*
LCC	Library of Christian Classics
LCL	Loeb Classical Library
LS	*Louvain Studies*
LSJ	Liddell-Scott-Jones, *Greek English Lexicon*
MeyerK	H. A. W. Meyer, Kritisch-exegetischer Kommentar über das Neue Testament
NCB	New Century Bible
NICNT	New International Commentary on the NT
NIGTC	New International Greek Testament Commentary
NovT	*Novum Testamentum*
NovTSup	Novum Testamentum, Supplements
NTD	Das Neue Testament Deutsch
NTS	*New Testament Studies*
OBT	Overtures to Biblical Theology
RB	*Revue biblique*
RelS	*Religious Studies*
RGG	*Religion in Geschichte und Gegenwart*
RHPR	*Revue d'histoire et de philosophies religieuses*
SBLDS	Society of Biblical Literature Dissertation Series
SBLSBS	Society of Biblical Literature Sources for Biblical Study
SBM	Stuttgarter biblische Monographien
SBT	Studies in Biblical Theology
SE	*Studia Evangelica*
SJLA	Studies in Judaism in Late Antiquity
SJT	*Scottish Journal of Theology*
SNTSMS	Society for New Testament Studies Monograph Series

Str-B	H. Strack and P. Billerbeck, *Kommentar zum Neuen Testament*
TDNT	G. Kittel and G. Friedrich (eds.), *Theological Dictionary of the New Testament*
THKNT	Theologische Handkommentar zum Neuen Testament
TLZ	*Theologische Literaturzeitung*
TRu	*Theologische Rundschau*
TS	*Theological Studies*
TU	Texte und Untersuchungen
TZ	*Theologische Zeitschrift*
USQR	*Union Seminary Quarterly Review*
WMANT	Wissenschaftliche Monographien zum Alten und Neuen Testament
WTJ	*Westminster Theological Journal*
WUNT	Wissenschaftliche Untersuchungen zum Neuen Testament
ZNW	*Zeitschrift für die neutestamentliche Wissenschaft*
ZTK	*Zeitschrift für Theologie und Kirche*

Abbreviations for biblical and other ancient texts may be found in "Instructions for Contributors," *Journal of Biblical Literature* 107 (1988) 579-96 and in Liddell-Scott-Jones, *A Greek-English Lexicon with Supplement* (Oxford: Clarendon, 1968) xvi-xlv.

PAUL THE THEOLOGIAN

Victor Paul Furnish

W as Paul a theologian in any meaningful sense, and if so how does one go about the task of uncovering and understanding his theology? An examination of some representative studies published over the last several decades leaves the impression that there is no clear consensus on these matters. This impression is confirmed by the papers prepared by various members of a group organized within the Society of Biblical Literature for the express purpose of discussing "Pauline theology."[1] Since by his membership in that group, as well as in his published work, Lou Martyn has made important contributions to an understanding of Paul's thought, it may not be inappropriate in a volume published in his honor to offer some prolegomena to the topic as a whole.

Questions about Pauline theology are, of course, inseparable from older and more fundamental questions about the meaning and aims of "biblical theology" and "New Testament theology." Within the necessarily limited scope of this essay, however, I must restrict my attention primarily to the matter of Pauline theology.[2] First, to illustrate the varied ways this has been defined and approached, I will survey the work of several representative scholars.[3] Then I will offer a few comments of my own on the two questions that were posed at the outset: Was Paul in some sense a theologian? If he was, what is required to understand his theology?

I

Rudolf Bultmann's treatment of Paul, in his *Theology of the New Testament,* continues to stand as a landmark among twentieth-century expositions of Pauline theology.[4] There the overall task of New

Testament theology was understood to consist "in the unfolding of those ideas by means of which Christian faith makes sure of its own object, basis, and consequences."[5] More specifically, Bultmann held that *"the theological thoughts of the New Testament writings"* are to be *"conceived and explicated as thoughts of faith, that is: as thoughts in which faith's understanding of God, the world, and man is unfolding itself."*[6] These statements reflect Bultmann's principled adherence to a distinction between the kerygma itself and the *interpretation* of that to which the "theological thoughts" of the New Testament give expression.[7] They also reflect his belief that New Testament theology, properly conceived, does not just collect and organize these theological thoughts, but seeks to render them meaningful for the present.[8]

For Bultmann, the most important theological thinking in the New Testament is to be found in the Pauline letters and in the Fourth Gospel. But when he referred to Paul as "a real theologian," he did not mean that the apostle had developed a coherent theological system. Rather, he meant that Paul, time and again, "reduces specific acute questions to a basic theological question" and makes concrete decisions "on the basis of fundamental theological considerations." In this, he held, Paul is not speculating in an "objectifying" way about God, the world, and so on, but is simply lifting "the knowledge inherent in faith itself into the clarity of conscious knowing." Although Bultmann believed that the apostle's "basic theological position . . . is more or less completely set forth in Romans,"[9] his own presentation of Pauline theology does not seem to have been controlled in any special way by the course of the argument in that letter. Rather, his presentation was controlled by the judgment that Paul spoke of God only as God is significant for human beings, their responsibilities, and their salvation—so that "every assertion about God is simultaneously an assertion about man and vice versa." Bultmann therefore quite deliberately presented Pauline "theology" as if it were a "doctrine of man," organizing his discussion under the two main headings, "Man Prior to the Revelation of Faith," and "Man Under Faith." For Bultmann, "Paul's theology is, at the same time, anthropology."[10]

This bold proposition has been either rejected or in some way qualified by almost every subsequent interpreter of Pauline theology.[11] Among the latter is Hans Conzelmann,[12] who shares with Bultmann the view that Pauline theology must be approached with reference to the apostle's understanding of faith and human existence. But Conzelmann is concerned that in Bultmann's two-part schematization "man before faith" is "given a significance which he does not have" in Paul's own letters, that "man, instead of faith, becomes the subject of theology,"[13] and that scant attention is paid to the form of Paul's thought.

Accordingly, most of the themes and anthropological terms which Bultmann had dealt with under the heading of "Man Prior to the Revelation of Faith" (e.g., body, flesh, sin, world) are treated by Conzelmann in a preliminary section.[14] The remainder of his discussion is then organized with reference to the *revelation* of God's *righteousness* and faith's reception of that.[15] It is apparent that Conzelmann wants to avoid the problems that he sees in Bultmann's anthropological approach, while at the same time retaining what he believes to be right about it, because for him as for Bultmann, "Pauline theology" involves the interpretation of the apostle's own interpretation of the meaning of faith.[16]

In contrast to Conzelmann, Herman Ridderbos specifically rejects the anthropological orientation of Bultmann's presentation, arguing that it produces "a great narrowing" of the apostle's thought whereby "all of the divine redemptive activity in Christ is regarded *sub specie hominis.*"[17] For Ridderbos, Pauline theology is clearly "redemptive-historical" and "eschatological" in character,[18] because it is oriented to "the Christocentric fulfillment of the redemptive promise given to Israel."[19] Within "this great redemptive-historical framework," which includes the ultimate consummation of God's saving work in Christ's return and the coming of the kingdom, all of the "subordinate parts" of Paul's preaching "receive their place and organically cohere."[20] Contrary to what one might expect, however, Ridderbos does not organize his exposition of Pauline thought according to the *heilsgeschichtlich* pattern of promise, fulfillment, and consummation. Instead, he follows in general the traditional topics of systematic theology, taking up in turn Paul's views of sin, the revelation of God's righteousness, reconciliation, the new life, church and sacraments, and eschatology. It is clear, however, that Ridderbos identifies Pauline theology with the apostle's understanding of how God has acted and is acting in history, not with his reflection on the meaning of what faith has received (Bultmann, Conzelmann). For Ridderbos, the presentation of Paul's theology apparently involves what he once refers to as "the unfolding of the Pauline doctrine of salvation."[21]

Leonhard Goppelt is critical not only of Bultmann for reducing Paul's theology to a one-sided "kerygmatic anthropology," but also of the kind of salvation-historical interpretation to which Ridderbos subscribes.[22] Although Goppelt, too, understands Paul's theological orientation as salvation-historical, he does not mean that the apostle was familiar with "a universal-historical master plan," but that his concern was for "the history of election, promise, and calling."[23] Specifically, Paul's theology "sought to put into words the promising address of God that had gone forth through Christ" and to evoke a "trusting acceptance toward

God."[24] As Goppelt understands it, then, Paul's focus is more christological than salvation-historical. In accord with this, he sets about "to develop Pauline theology from the reception of the tradition about Christ," an approach for which he finds support in the way Romans is organized.[25] It is probably at least as important, however, that Goppelt's arrangement conforms to his understanding of the "intrinsic structure" of all New Testament theology. As he sees it, this structure derives from the Easter *kerygma,* of which New Testament theology is the "interpretive explication." Since the kerygma had at "its base . . . the recounting of the earthly ministry of Jesus," New Testament theology explicates the christological tradition specifically.[26]

Joseph Fitzmyer similarly claims that "Paul's theology is predominantly a christology . . . ,"[27] but—unlike Goppelt—he does not stress the role of the earthly Jesus in Paul's thought,[28] and he believes that the apostle conceives of Christ's role in specifically salvation-historical terms.[29] Because he is convinced that "all else in Paul's teaching has to be oriented to [the apostle's] christocentric soteriology,"[30] that is the topic taken up first. Only in the second place does Fitzmyer discuss Paul's anthropology ("Humanity before Christ" and "Humanity in Christ"), and only after that Paul's ethics. Although he warns that one must not impose categories foreign to Paul, Fitzmyer has no qualms about providing "a systematization of the Apostle's thought in a form in which he himself did not present it."[31] Indeed, this is the proper task of the "biblical theologian," who "is not content merely with the interpretation of individual passages in their immediate context (i.e., with exegesis). One seeks to express the total Pauline message, which transcends the contextual situation and embraces also the relational meaning of Pauline utterances."[32]

In the opinion of Georg Eichholz, however, Paul's theological views are so wedded to "the contextual situation" of his mission that no comprehensive theology can be extracted from his letters.[33] For this reason one must take the title of Eichholz's book very seriously; he offers Paul's theology only "in outline" because he believes that our sources yield no more than that.[34] Since Paul's letters are dialogic in character, theology can be found there only in "fragmentary form,"[35] in *ad hoc* formulations embedded within the context of proclamation "as concrete exhortation, as concrete instruction, as a word addressed directly to those who received [the letters] back then."[36] If this is so, how can one present Paul's theology even in outline? Although Eichholz is of the opinion that the argument in Romans has more unity and is more often grounded christologically than that in any other letter, he insists that Romans, too, has the character of a dialogue and should therefore not be used as a model.[37] All that is left is to deal exegetically with specific passages, which is what Eichholz sets out to do.[38] Unfortunately, he does not say why he chooses certain passages and not others, how he has arrived at the nine topical headings under which he discusses them,[39] or what has determined the order in which he introduces the topics and passages. These are crucial matters, because Eichholz has ended up with a synthesis of texts and topics that goes substantially beyond the kind of exegesis to which, he believes, the interpreter of Pauline theology is necessarily restricted.

Leon Morris is also of the opinion that the nature of our sources precludes writing "a theology . . . of Paul."[40] While he is confident that the apostle has a "profound and well-thought-out" theology, he does not think it possible to arrange this "in a coherent system,"[41] or even to summarize "in orderly fashion" the "important theological ideas" to which Paul gives expression.[42] Nevertheless, Morris is confident that one can uncover "the theological truth" which lies behind and informs all of the New Testament writings.[43] In the particular case of the Pauline letters, he suggests that we are dealing with "a God-intoxicated man" who "spoke constantly about the One who was central in his thinking."[44] Therefore, rejecting Bultmann's anthropological starting point,[45] Morris starts out with a section on Paul's doctrine of God.[46] However, his judgment that Pauline theology is theocentric in character is scarcely in evidence when, in subsequent sections, he discusses the topics of christology, salvation, and life in the Spirit.[47]

Even though Ralph P. Martin does not describe the apostle's thought as theocentric, he does believe that "any statement of the centre of Paul's theology should set the sovereign design of God in his initiative and grace at the heart of the matter."[48] Beyond this, however, Martin argues that any presentation of Pauline thought should take account of (a) the apostle's view of the "cosmic predicament" and of humanity's alienation and sin, (b) his view of salvation as restoration and the reclaiming of the universe by its creator, and (c) his own experience of Christ.[49] In Martin's judgment, all of these elements are embraced within the concept of "reconciliation," which he therefore proposes as "an interpretive key"[50] and "an organising principle"[51] for the understanding of Pauline theology. This proposal would have greater appeal if the terminology of reconciliation were present in more than just three of the seven indisputably authentic letters (Romans and 1, 2 Corinthians—although Martin attributes Colossians to Paul and treats Ephesians as the work of a "Pauline theologian").[52] It is more important, however, to notice that Martin combines this thematic organization with a historical organization, as he deals in turn with the idea of reconciliation in the Corinthian letters, Colossians, Romans, and Ephesians. His book, therefore, stands as an interesting example of how one may operate simultaneously with a conception of some "center" in Paul's theology and a regard for the situational orientation of the sources.

J. Christiaan Beker's study, published in the same year as Martin's, probes the questions of method and presentation more explicitly and deeply.[53] Beker is equally critical of Bultmann for having so little to say about the "content" of the kerygma and of those who (like Martin) propose some theme as the "doctrinal center" of Paul's theology.[54] He himself prefers to speak of the "coherent center" of Paul's gospel[55]—or even to set aside the notion of any "fixed core" or "specific center" in order to view Paul's theology as a more "fluid and flexible structure."[56] According to Beker, Paul is to be regarded primarily as "a hermeneutic theologian,"[57] an interpreter (both of scripture and of Christian tradition) whose hermeneutic is characterized by "the reciprocal and circular interaction of coherence and contingency."[58] By "coherence" he means "the stable constant element which expresses the convictional basis of Paul's proclamation of the gospel," and by "contingency" he means "the variety and particularity of sociological, economic and psychological situations which Paul faces in his churches and on the mission-field."[59]

Beker identifies the "stable constant element" in Paul's gospel as the "apocalyptic interpretation of the death and resurrection of Christ."[60] This does not lead him to the conclusion that Pauline theology is christocentric, however. On the contrary, he describes Paul's interpretation as apocalyptic precisely because he is convinced that its "ultimate point of reference" is "the imminent apocalyptic triumph *of God*."[61] Indeed, Beker argues that the coherence of Pauline theology derives from its apocalyptic "substratum," to be understood as "a network of symbolic relations which nourishes Paul's thought and constitutes its 'linguistic world.' "[62]

Finally, account needs to be taken of Heinrich Schlier's book on Pauline theology, even though it is offered not as a historical but as a systematic study, not as a description of Paul's thought but as "theological reflection" based on the Pauline kerygma. Schlier conceives this "reflection" as involving the kind of discussion (*Auseinandersetzung*) with the Pauline texts that leads to understanding and that enables them to be translated into a "language" that is meaningful for the present.[63] In accordance with his stated interests—and in striking contrast to Beker's work, especially—Schlier gives no specific attention to the contingent aspects of Paul's thought, or even of his letters. The exposition is organized topically,[64] and citations (from all thirteen letters of the Pauline corpus) are melded together without explicit regard for the varying contexts from which they have been drawn. It must be stressed, however, that Schlier's objective is a special one. As signalled already by the title of his book, which refers to *a* Pauline theology, the aim is not to reproduce Paul's thought, but to produce a theology based on his thought.

II

Even this brief and partial survey should be sufficient to show that recent discussions of Pauline theology exhibit no common understanding of the sense in which Paul was a theologian. One cannot appeal to Paul himself for help in this matter, since the term *theologia* (literally, "an account of the gods [or God]") does not occur in his letters—or, for that matter, anywhere in the New Testament (or in the Septuagint). Its earliest Christian use is by the second century apologists, by whom it is employed in a number of different ways, including "teaching about the gods," "teaching about divine things," or even more generally, "religious speech." Although Origen (and others) began to employ the word more restrictively, of the Christian doctrine of God, that was by no means its only use. Thus Athanasius refers to the authors of scripture as "the theologians" because he regards their writings as divinely-inspired (see *On the Incarnation* 56.6-10; see also *Against the Pagans* 1.9-10). He means just that when he says that Paul was one of them—the earliest reference to Paul as a theologian known to me (*Against the Pagans* 35.18-20; see also 10.11ff. [written prior to 337 CE]). Not until much later—first of all among the twelfth-century scholastics (Abelard, Peter Lombard)—does "theology" come to mean the systematic arrangement of Christian doctrine as a whole.[65]

That Paul cannot be called a "theologian" if theology is conceived in the scholastic sense, is not disputed. Some, to be sure, have sought to construct a comprehensive theological system informed by the apostle's thought.[66] But even if it could be demonstrated that most, or perhaps all, of the terms and ideas of such a system had been derived in some way from Paul's letters, would it be "Pauline" theology in any proper sense? One certainly could not say that it was *Paul's*—any more than one could say, for example, that an automobile designed and constructed in the United States was a product of Japan simply because most or even all of its components were of Japanese origin.

It is preferable to understand theology less restrictively, with reference not to some end product but to a task—namely, as *critical reflection on the beliefs, rites, and social structures in which an experience of ultimate reality has found expression.*[67] This definition is more in keeping with the concept as it has come to be employed in current discussion. And in a certain sense it is also more in keeping with the broader, generic use of the term *theologia* in Paul's day—among the Stoics, for example, who applied it not only to mythical accounts of the gods, but also to knowledge about their rites and ceremonies and to rational inquiry into their nature.[68] If theology is to be understood as critical reflection, then it necessarily operates at a certain distance from the subject matter, since that has become, however deliberately, an object of inquiry and of analysis. But critical reflection may proceed more or less systematically, it may be more or less discerning, and it may or may not aim at some comprehensive result.

We can now define Christian theology as critical reflection on the beliefs and rites of the Christian tradition and on the social structures within which these beliefs and rites are continued. Where this critical reflection takes place with a significant measure of intentionality it is apt to proceed more systematically and with more specific aims than where it occurs more spontaneously. Yet, wherever Christian faith has become the object of critical inquiry, there one may speak of Christian theology. If concepts or statements are formulated independently of a system in the scholastic sense, that makes them no less "theological," even though to be credible they will have to cohere in some meaningful way.

When Christian theology is understood as I have suggested, one need not hesitate to regard Paul as a theologian. In each of his letters he is giving thoughtful attention, to be sure in different ways, to what he calls "the truth of the gospel" (Gal 2:5, 14). He does not just make assertions and express his personal convictions about this, but seeks to show how and why the gospel is true and to elucidate its significance. He does this by demonstrating how the gospel accords with the testimony of scripture and of tradition, with what reasonable people can recognize as credible, and with what his readers themselves have encountered in the process of coming to faith. His various statements about the truth of the gospel are, therefore, appropriately described as theological, even though they may occur in passages that by reason of their overall form and function must be described in other ways (as polemical, hortatory, apologetic, and so on).

Although Paul's theological statements are intended to expose and clarify the truth of the gospel, it would not be in accord with his thought to regard them as *constituting* that gospel. For Paul, the gospel is first and fundamentally *an event,* not a message. It is the event of God's powerful working for salvation, the unveiling of God's righteousness to everyone who has faith (Rom 1:16-17; see also 1 Thess 1:5). Paul's apostolic service, which includes but is by no means restricted to his preaching (*euangelizein* or *kēryssein*), bears witness to this event and is thus in its own way eventful.[69] His "theology," however, precisely because it is critical reflection on the truth and the meaning of the gospel, must necessarily stand apart from the event that is the object of its reflection.[70]

In the same way, Paul's theology is also to be distinguished from his *proclamation (kērygma)*.[71] While these are perforce closely related to each other, they are related to the gospel in distinctly different ways. Paul's kerygma is direct address; as proclamation it constitutes a direct summons to the gospel. His theology, however, takes the form of discourse; as explication it aims to unfold the truth of the gospel. The kerygma can finally be grasped only by faith, which Paul understands primarily as obedience. Theology has fulfilled its task when it has nurtured understanding. To be sure, because all kerygmatic formulations both imply and require an understanding of the gospel, they are implicitly theological; and because all theological formulations seek to foster an understanding of the gospel, they may be said to constitute an indirect summons to it. But kerygma and theology remain distinct in their primary function as well as in form, and one must not be confused with the other.

III

If Paul qualifies as "a real theologian" because he not only proclaimed the gospel but also reflected critically on its truth, what is involved in studying his theology? While Eichholz is surely correct in insisting that one must "engage the texts,"[72] the question remains just how that is to be done. What are the appropriate "rules of engagement"? My own ideas about these have been prompted by questions of method that are raised by, if not always in, the studies of Pauline theology surveyed above, as well as by the papers and discussions of the SBL group on Pauline theology. Each of the following proposals requires more elaboration and justification than is possible here, but that in itself may help to make it clear that they are offered only to further discussion of important procedural issues.

1. An understanding of Paul's theology must be based exclusively on primary sources, which in Paul's case means on his own letters. Moreover, it is better to risk excluding letters of possible authenticity than to include letters whose authenticity is in serious question. Thus Ephesians, Colossians, 2 Thessalonians, and the Pastoral Epistles are to be regarded as only secondary sources, at least until the "base line" of the apostle's thought has been established.

2. As documents of history, Paul's letters must be studied according to the canons of critical historical research. This applies no less when the object of one's inquiry is Paul's theology than it does when the object of one's inquiry is, for example, how often he visited Corinth. Thus Paul's claim that his gospel came to him "through a revelation of Jesus Christ" (Gal 1:11-12) must itself be critically assessed and by no means does it

invalidate the attempt to determine how his understanding of the gospel is indebted to historical factors.

3. Paul's theology is, at least in principle, understandable because his letters have been written thoughtfully, not frivolously. This is not to rule out the possibility that he may sometimes fail to express himself clearly or that he may on occasion wish to be unclear, to mislead, or even to deceive. Nevertheless, one must assume that Paul expects that his readers will be able to make some kind of sense out of what he has written, that they will be able to arrive at some understanding of it (see, for example, 2 Cor 1:13).

4. Understanding Paul's theology necessarily involves reconceiving it because understanding takes place only where the subject matter has been rendered intelligible. This rendering intelligible is an act of interpretation (*hermēneia*), which is exactly what Paul himself has in mind when he writes about the interpretation of tongues (1 Cor 12:10; 14:26; and so on). There are many reasons why interpreting Paul's thought is a more complicated task for twentieth-century readers, say in New York or Marburg, than it was for the members of Paul's own congregations, say in the towns of Galatia or Philippi. In principle, however, what is required in the two cases is exactly the same: translating Paul's thought into the conceptual categories that have currency in the interpreter's own cultural setting. This entails no responsibility for making Paul's theology acceptable, only for making it intelligible.

5. The interpretation of Paul's theology must proceed exegetically, and exegesis, like understanding itself, is essentially an analytical process—that is, exegesis seeks to release (*analyein*) the meaning of what a text contains by distinguishing and examining the constituent parts. Because the parts are examined not only as they exist in themselves but also as they relate to one another and to the whole, one might say that exegesis involves a certain amount of synthesis as well as analysis. In this case, however, "synthesis" does not mean combining distinct elements into a whole, but demonstrating whatever wholeness is already present. The important thing is to recognize that when exegesis is properly conceived and executed, its rigorously analytical procedures do not violate the integrity of a text or of Paul's thought, but lead rather to a clearer perception and understanding of them.

6. Critical historical analysis requires that, initially, each of Paul's letters be examined as if it were the sole surviving documentation of the apostle's thought. If in the process one concludes that the letter is a composite, then its parts must be examined individually. At this stage, nothing should be presupposed about the place of a letter (or a fragment thereof) in the sequence of Paul's letters, and nothing should be presumed about its relative theological importance. One's concern

should be to identify and to understand the theological aspects of Paul's argumentation within that specific letter (or fragment), taking account of whatever can be determined about its occasion and purpose.

7. Theological statements or discussions that serve apologetic or polemical ends are not to be discounted, even though like all other kinds of statements and discussions they are to be evaluated in the light of their specific contexts and purposes.[73]

8. Special attention should be accorded to: (a) passages in which Paul is with some deliberateness developing or explicating one or more theological conceptions (Rom 1:18–3:20; 5:12-21; 9–11; 1 Cor 12–14; 15; Gal 3:19–4:11; 5:2-11; 1 Thess 4:13-17); (b) passages in which Paul appears to be using kerygmatic formulations, especially when his own interpretation of them is discernible (Rom 3:21-31; 1 Cor 11:17-34; 15:1-11; 2 Cor 5:11-21; Phil 1:27–2:18; 1 Thess 1:2-10); (c) Paul's interpretation of passages from scripture (Rom 4; 2 Cor 3:7ff.); (d) statements in which Paul summarizes or in some other way refers to his own preaching or teaching (1 Cor 1:23-24; 2:1-5; 15:1ff.; 2 Cor 1:19; 4:5; Gal 3:1-5); (e) theological statements that have been formulated as generalizations or convictions (Rom 8:38-39; 14:14; 1 Cor 7:19; 8:1-3; Gal 6:14, 15; Phil 1:6); (f) theological statements that sanction appeals or warnings (Rom 13:11-12a; 15:3, 7b-9; 1 Cor 3:21b-23; 7:29-31; 2 Cor 8:9; 13:4; Gal 5:17-24).[74]

9. Once the letters have been examined individually, any theological conceptions or arguments that appear in more than one letter should be noted and compared. Not only those recurrent theological conceptions and arguments, but also any apparent inconsistencies in Paul's thought should be identified and analyzed. At this stage, whatever can be determined about the sequence of the letters (and other kinds of relationships among them) should be taken into account.

10. No "synthesis" of Pauline theology, if by that one means the construction of a comprehensive theology in the scholastic sense, can adequately represent his thought. Paul's theological conceptions and statements are not the structural fragments of some imposing theological edifice,[75] whether that be thought of as one already built but hidden from view or as one still under construction. No blueprint for such an edifice can be extrapolated from the Pauline letters. Rather, what these sources yield are comments about the meaning of the gospel as the apostle wishes that to be discerned by particular readers and acted on in their particular circumstances. It is, of course, important to try to ascertain whether these are the strictly *ad hoc* comments of an unreflective, "practical" man,[76] or whether—as I believe the evidence will show—they are the comments of one who has reflected with some care on the meaning and implications of the gospel he bears. This,

however, remains an essentially exegetical, and therefore *analytical*, task. One cannot find Paul the theologian in any synthesis of this theological affirmation, no matter how carefully and discerningly constructed, but only in those affirmations themselves.

Notes

1. The group began meeting in 1986 under the chairmanship of Robert Jewett. Certain of the essays prepared for it have appeared in volumes of the SBL Seminar Papers Series, while others are so far unpublished.
2. On the broader questions, see, for example, Hendrikus Boers, *What Is New Testament Theology? The Rise of Criticism and the Problem of a Theology of the New Testament* (Guides to Biblical Scholarship, New Testament Series; Philadelphia: Fortress, 1979). To Boers's annotated bibliography, one may add, *inter alia:* Robert Morgan, *The Nature of New Testament Theology: The Contributions of William Wrede and Adolf Schlatter* (Studies in Biblical Theology; 2nd series, 25; London: SCM Press, 1973); Georg Strecker, *Das Problem der Theologie des Neuen Testaments* (Wege der Forschung, 367; Darmstadt: Wissenschaftliche Buchgesellschaft, 1975); " 'Biblische Theologie'? Kritische Bemerkungen zu den Entwürfen von Hartmut Gese und Peter Stuhlmacher," in *Kirche. Festschrift für Günther Bornkamm zum 75. Geburtstag* (eds. Dieter Lührmann and Georg Strecker; Tübingen: Mohr-Siebeck, 1980) 425-45; Gerhard Hasel, *New Testament Theology: Basic Issues in the Current Debate* (Grand Rapids: Eerdmans, 1978), with an extensive bibliography; Ben C. Ollenburger, "Biblical Theology: Situating the Discipline," in *Understanding the Word: Essays in Honor of Bernhard W. Anderson* (eds. James T. Butler et al.; Sheffield: JSOT Press, 1987) 37-62; James Barr, "The Theological Case Against Biblical Theology," in *Canon, Theology, and Old Testament Interpretation: Essays in Honor of Brevard S. Childs* (eds. Gene M. Tucker et al.; Philadelphia: Fortress, 1988) 3-19.
3. Donald Guthrie's *New Testament Theology* (Downers Grove: Inter-Varsity Press, 1981) falls outside the purview of my survey, since it includes no discussion of Pauline theology specifically. That is only partly because the subject matter of the apostle's letters, aside from Romans, is regarded as essentially "practical" (31). Primarily the book falls outside my purview because the teachings of the whole New Testament are understood as divinely revealed truth, and therefore as essentially unified and "non-self-contradictory" (see 29-30, 56-59). Given this view of scripture, and also the author's interest in providing "a handbook to Christian doctrine" (17), it is little wonder that his whole discussion is organized under the topics and sub-topics of systematic theology. The fact that the one brief summary of Paul's preaching conforms by and large to the "kerygma" that C. H. Dodd extracted from the speeches in Acts (57-58) accords with Gutherie's concern "to demonstrate in a substantial way the unity of NT thought" (59). Compare Alan Richardson's topically-arranged *An Introduction to the Theology of the New Testament* (New York: Harper, 1958).
4. Rudolf Bultmann, *Theology of the New Testament* (2 vols.; trans. Kendrick Grobel; New York: Scribner's, 1951 [vol. 1, 1st German ed.; 1948] and 1955 [vol. 2, 1st German ed., 1951/1953]). In addition to the section on Paul (1.187-352), the epilogue is also important for our topic (2.236-51).
5. Ibid., 1.3; see also 2.251.
6. Ibid., 2.237.
7. Ibid., 2.237-41. See also Bultmann's important discussion of "kerygma" and "theology" in his essay on "Church and Teaching in the New Testament" (first published in 1929), in *Faith and Understanding* (vol. 1; ed. Robert W. Funk; trans. Louise Pettibone Smith; New York: Harper, 1969) esp. 218-19.
8. See Bultmann, *Theology of the New Testament*, 2.251.
9. Ibid., 1.190—where Romans is also described as exceptional among Paul's letters in that thoughts about God, Christ, the world, etc. are there developed "connectedly."

10. Ibid., 1.191.
11. One notable exception is D. E. H. Whiteley, whose study of *The Theology of St. Paul* (Philadelphia: Fortress, 1963) proceeds almost as if Bultmann's *Theology of the New Testament* had not been written. Because Whiteley is convinced that Paul's theology is "very closely integrated" and that its themes " 'coinhere' in such a way that it can be made to centre equally well upon the doctrines of, e.g., Christ, the Cross, the Church, and the Last Things," his discussion follows "the traditional 'chronological' order" (xiv), beginning with a chapter on creation and ending with one on eschatology. In the process there are a few references to Bultmann's views on particular points (as often favorable as unfavorable), but no account is taken of the fundamentally different way that Bultmann's discussion had been organized.
12. Hans Conzelmann, *Grundriss der Theologie des Neuen Testaments* (4th ed.; rev. by Andreas Lindemann; Tübingen: Mohr-Siebeck, 1987 [1st German ed., 1967]). Where it is possible to do so, I will cite as well John Bowden's English translation of the (unaltered) 2nd German ed., *An Outline of the Theology of the New Testament* (London: SCM Press, 1969).
13. Conzelmann, *Grundriss*, 169 (*Outline*, 159-60).
14. Ibid., 163-220 (*Outline*, 155-98).
15. Conzelmann's headings are "The Revelation of the Righteousness of Faith" and "Revelation in the Present" (*Grundriss*, 222-326). The organization is slightly different in the first two editions, and thus in the English translation.
16. One may compare Georg Strecker's judgment that a responsible New Testament hermeneutic must be oriented both to the Christ-event attested by the respective writers and to their anthropological perspective, for it is only the latter that provides access to the former (" 'Biblische Theologie'?" 444-45).
17. Herman Ridderbos, *Paul: An Outline of His Theology* (trans. John Richard de Witt; Grand Rapids: Eerdmans, 1975 [1st Dutch ed., 1967]) 42; see also 89.
18. Ibid., 39; see also 44.
19. Ibid., 27.
20. Ibid., 39. Compare Werner G. Kümmel, *The Theology of the New Testament According to Its Major Witnesses, Jesus-Paul-John* (Nashville: Abingdon, 1973 [1st German ed., 1969]) 137-254. Kümmel believes that the whole of Pauline theology is rooted in the conviction that "all the lines of divine activity since the creation [are] running toward Christ" so that "for him the Christ event represents the beginning of the divine eschatological salvation that has been planned from time immemorial" (149). Note as well the view of Daniel Patte, that Paul developed "a theology based upon reflections about history. Thus his theology is a sacred history, that is, a history of the acts of God, understood in terms of their continuity and of their cause and effect relations" (*Paul's Faith and the Power of the Gospel: A Structural Introduction to the Pauline Letters* [Philadelphia: Fortress, 1983] 200). However, Patte believes that it is important to distinguish between Paul's theology (his ideas) and his faith (*"being held by a system of convictions"* [11]), and apart from one chapter (190-231), he deals exclusively with the latter.
21. Ridderbos, *Paul*, 91.
22. Leonhard Goppelt, *Theology of the New Testament* (2 vols.; trans. John E. Alsup; Grand Rapids: Eerdmans, 1981 and 1982 [1st German ed., 1975 and 1976]) 2.61, 63. Ridderbos (*Paul*, 42-43) specifically associates his views with those of Oscar Cullmann, whose notion of "a universal plan of salvation" Goppelt rejects (*Theology*, 2.60; see also the brief reference to Ridderbos on 63).
23. Goppelt, *Theology*, 2.61.
24. Ibid., 2.62.
25. Ibid., 2.63. In an initial chapter on christology, Goppelt discusses Paul's use of various titles and formulas; the sub-section entitled "The Course of Christ's Life as Saving Revelation: The Cross" is his interpretation of Jesus' death (65-106). The following chapter deals with Paul's understanding of "the continued ministry of Jesus" in proclamation, the work of the Spirit, and faith (107-34); and two further, but substantially shorter, chapters discuss in turn "The Saving Effect of the Christ Event:

The Gospel as the Revelation of God's Righteousness" (135-41) and "The Emergence of the Gospel as Visible Form in the Church" (143-50).

26. Goppelt, *Theology*, 1.7; see also 9-11.

27. Joseph Fitzmyer, *Paul and His Theology: A Brief Sketch* (2nd ed.; Englewood Cliffs, N.J.: Prentice-Hall, 1989) 38.

28. Ibid., 33-34.

29. Ibid., 41-58.

30. Ibid., 38.

31. Ibid., 25.

32. Ibid., 26. In this respect, at least, Fitzmyer is a representative of the Roman Catholic tradition within which he stands. Compare the aim of Ferdinand Prat, who by careful synthesis hoped to reconstruct the unity of "the doctrinal elements" that "by the chance of historical circumstances" are "dispersed" throughout Paul's letters (Prat, *The Theology of Saint Paul* (2 vols.; trans. John L. Stoddard; Westminster, Md.: Newman, 1926 and 1927) 1.1. Prat acknowledged that "in order to reduce [Paul's] thought to a system, it will be sometimes needful to fill up the gaps, establish connections, and draw some conclusions," but he saw this as the proper role of biblical theology (2.12).

33. Georg Eichholtz, *Die Theologie des Paulus in Umriss* (2nd ed.; Neukirchen-Vluyn: Nuekirchener Verlag, 1977 [1st German ed., 1972]).

34. The word *outline* (Dutch: *Ontwerp*) in the subtitle of Ridderbos's book (see n. 17 above) cannot be taken with the same seriousness, however, because Ridderbos really does aim at a comprehensive presentation.

35. Eichholtz, *Theologie*, v.

36. Ibid., 11-12.

37. Ibid., 8, 12-13.

38. Ibid., 13. See also his call to "engage the texts" ("Wir müssen den Texten begegnen"), 7.

39. These are Paul's apostolic task, humanity's confrontation with the gospel, the Gentile as a defendant before God, the Jew as a defendant before God, christological emphases, justification and faith, the law, ethics, the church, and Israel.

40. Leon Morris, *New Testament Theology* (Grand Rapids: Academie Books [Zondervan] 1986).

41. Ibid., 90.

42. Ibid., 22.

43. Ibid., 11, 17, 22.

44. Ibid., 25.

45. Ibid., n. 2, but with no discussion of the issues involved.

46. Ibid., 25-28.

47. Ibid., 39-55, 56-75, and 76-90, respectively.

48. Ralph P. Martin, *Reconciliation: A Study of Paul's Theology* (New Foundations Theological Library; Atlanta: John Knox, 1980) 2.

49. Ibid., 46-47.

50. Ibid., 5.

51. Ibid., 46.

52. Ibid., 111-26 and 157-98, respectively.

53. J. Christiaan Beker, *Paul the Apostle: The Triumph of God in Life and Thought* (Philadelphia: Fortress, 1980). Beker clarifies and somewhat modifies his views in several subsequent essays, two of which are cited below.

54. Ibid., 13-14.

55. See ibid., 11.

56. J. Christiaan Beker, "The Method of Recasting Pauline Theology: The Coherence-Contingency Scheme as Interpretive Model," in *Society of Biblical Literature 1986 Seminar Papers* (SBL Seminar Papers Series, 25; ed. Kent Harold Richards; Atlanta: Scholars Press, 1986) 597-98. Contrast the way Riddberos writes of his quest to find the "main entrance" to "the imposing edifice of Paul's theology" (*Paul the Apostle*, 13).

57. J. Christiaan Beker, "The Faithfulness of God and the Priority of Israel in Paul's Letter

to the Romans," in *Christians Among Jews and Gentiles: Essays in Honor of Krister Stendahl on His Sixty-fifth Birthday* (ed. G. W. E. Nickelsburg with G. W. MacRae; Philadelphia: Fortress, 1986) 10. See also Beker, "Method," 596, and *Paul the Apostle,* 109-31.

58. Beker, "Method," 602.

59. Ibid., 596; see also 602, and Beker, "Faithfulness," 10-11.

60. Ibid., 598.

61. Ibid., 598, italics added. There is a full discussion in Beker, *Paul the Apostle,* 351-67.

62. Ibid., 598. Here, as Beker himself notes, he is backing off from his earlier view that the specific theme of God's coming triumph constitutes the "center" of Paul's thought, and thereby assures its coherence.

63. Heinrich Schlier, *Grundzüge einer paulinischen Theologie* (Freiburg/Basel/Wien: Herder, 1978) 9-12, 14, 15.

64. The five chapters deal in turn with God, the world, the appearance of God's righteousness in Jesus Christ, the Spirit and the gospel, and faith.

65. For surveys of the background and Christian development of the term see, for example, Gerhard Ebeling, "Theologie. I. Begrifsgeschichtlich," in *Die Religion in Geschichte und Gegenwart* (3rd ed.; eds. H. Frhr. von Campenhausen et al.; Tübingen: Mohr-Siebeck, 1962) 6.754-69; and Frank Whaling, "The Development of the Word 'Theology,' " *SJT* 34 (1981) 289-312.

66. It is not surprising that Roman Catholic interpreters have been the most explicit about their interest in constructing such a system out of Paul's letters (see the comments above about Fitzmyer, Prat [n. 32], and Schlier), while even those Protestant interpreters who come close to doing so often deny that it is possible (see Ridderbos, *Paul,* 39). See also the comments of George B. Stevens in his influential and often reprinted work *The Pauline Theology: A Study of the Origin and Correlation of the Doctrinal Teachings of the Apostle Paul* (rev. ed.; New York: Scribner's, 1892). Although Stevens set out "to present a systematic account of [Paul's] teaching upon the great themes which he considers," he sought only to determine "*how far* that set of convictions which [Paul] so firmly cherished and defended may be regarded as furnishing the materials for a theological system" (viii; italics added). Stevens was nevertheless confident that the apostle himself had provided "a full elaboration of those principles and truths which were the staple of [his] teaching" (25).

67. For this definition of theology, as for much of what follows in this section, I am deeply indebted to my colleague, Schubert M. Ogden. Although I cannot presume to represent his views, my own thinking about these matters has been greatly assisted by his writings, both published (see especially the essays collected in his book *On Theology* [San Francisco: Harper & Row, 1986]) and unpublished, and by conversations with him. I owe him thanks, as well, for drawing my attention to Bultmann's important essay on "Church and Teaching in the New Testament" (see above, n. 7).

68. See Whaling, "The Development of the Word 'Theology,' " 290. Note, too, that Philo refers to Moses as *ho theologos* simply because he speaks of divine things (*On Rewards and Punishments,* 53).

69. See my essay "Paul the ΜΑΡΤΥΣ," in *Witness and Existence: The Point of Christian Theology* (FS Schubert M. Ogden; eds. Philip Devenish and Larry Goodwin; Chicago: University of Chicago Press, 1989) 73-88.

70. Because I believe this distinction between the gospel event and theological reflection upon the event is an important one, I am hesitant to follow J. Louis Martyn in speaking of the theological event that occurs when the Galatians, for example, are confronted by the message of a letter from their apostle (see "Human Entry into the Covenant Community on the Original Conditions," an unpublished response to a paper by J. D. G. Dunn on the theology of Galatians [1988] esp. 10, 11, 27, 28). For similar reasons, I am unable to accept N. Thomas Wright's identification of Pauline theology with "that integrated *set of beliefs* which may be supposed to inform and undergird Paul's life, mission and writing . . . " ("Towards a Synthesis of Pauline Theology" [an unpublished paper, 1987] 2; italics added).

71. The distinction is Bultmann's (see his "Church and Teaching in the New Testament," 208, 213-14, 218-29), but the formulation of it that follows is my own.

72. See above, n. 38.
73. A similar judgment is offered by Robin Scroggs, "A Synthesis of Paul's Thought in 1 Thessalonians, Philippians, and Galatians" (an unpublished paper, 1988) 3.
74. The differences between this list and a comparable one offered by J. Paul Sampley ("Overcoming Traditional Methods by Synthesizing the Theology of Individual Letters," in *Society of Biblical Literature Seminar Papers Series*, 25 [ed. Kent Harold Richards; Atlanta: Scholars Press, 1986] 608-11) are explained by our differing views of Paul as a theologian. My list seeks to identify those points at which Paul's theology, understood as his *critical reflection on the meaning of the gospel*, is most apparent. Sampley's list, however, is aimed at a reconstruction of Paul's *proclamation of the gospel*, because he is convinced that the apostle "is not a theologian" (604).
75. The image is Ridderbos's (*Paul*, 13).
76. Heikki Räisänen (*Paul and the Law* [Philadelphia: Fortress Press, 1986]) comes close to this view when he depicts Paul as an "impulsive and flexible thinker [who] often shifted his ground" (9), leaving his letters strewn with "contradictions and tensions" (11), and as "a man of practical religion" whose theological statements are but "rationalizations" contrived to support his "intuition" (266-69).

SACRED VIOLENCE AND SINFUL DESIRE: PAUL'S INTERPRETATION OF ADAM'S SIN IN THE LETTER TO THE ROMANS

Robert Hamerton-Kelly

Give me that man
That is not passion's slave, and I will wear him
In my heart's core, ay, in my heart of heart.
(HAMLET 3.2.75-78)

C urrent Anglo-American fashion in the interpretation of Paul emphasizes the sociological aspects of his criticism of the Mosaic law, focusing on the problem of the requirements for the admission of the Gentiles to the Christian community.[1] J. L. Martyn has contributed impressively to the setting of this new style in two recent articles on Galatians and its background, but he remains essentially a theological interpreter, in the sense that he tries to understand Paul's account of the significance of the events of the gospel for human nature and destiny.[2] He seems well positioned between the kind of theological interpretation associated with the names of Bultmann and Käsemann on the one hand and the new approach on the other. In a recent article, for instance, Martyn illuminates Paul's theology by comparing the way he formulates antinomies in Galatians with a pattern of opposites in ancient thinking that Paul deliberately modifies. Historically the most pressing antinomy in Galatia was between those demanding circumcision and those defending uncircumcision, but Paul does not approach the problem historically, or "sociologically," by taking the side of uncircumcision against circumcision. Rather, he deals with it theologically by declaring the whole historical antinomy to be irrelevant (Gal 6:14-15; see also 5:6) in the light of the advent of the new creation. By pointing this out, Martyn reminds us of Paul's theological concern and the fact that historical and sociological interpretation fulfills an agenda appropriate to our scientific curiosity but alien to Paul's interest, an agenda that sometimes leads to doubtful results when, for instance, a too narrow empiricism is used to allege that Paul's thought is tendentious and confused.[3]

It is difficult to distinguish clearly between exegesis and hermeneutics in the field of Pauline studies for two reasons: first, because of the role the apostle plays in Lutheran theology and the magisterial interpretations of Lutherans like Bultmann and Käsemann; and, second, because Paul's theology is hermeneutical itself, insofar as it is a reading of other texts.[4] Our present interest is precisely one such reading—namely, the Pauline reading of the account of the first sin in Gen 2:15-17 and 3:1-7.

The method we shall use is based on the assumption that the apostle intends to give a true account of the human condition in the light of God's revelation in Christ, and that he proceeds hermeneutically by reading an authoritative text in the light of current circumstances and convictions. Like every author, he believes that, just as he shares enough of a common consciousness with the writers of Genesis to make it possible for him to understand their text, so also his readers share enough with him to make it possible for them to understand his text. Since we, too, share that consciousness, we can *mutatis mutandis* understand his message by entering imaginatively into his text and thinking with him about the problem he is addressing. In attempting to do this, we have used what is probably to be called a hermeneutical method, although it could be called exegesis as well because it does not violate the canons of historicity but rather, in view of a common human consciousness, shows the power of Paul's thought to interpret human life in our time by bringing out its implications in his. We are especially interested in his view of sin,[5] as it comes to light in his reading of the account of the sin of Adam.

His reading of the Adam story is controlled by general and particular criteria, the fundamental presuppositions of his world-view and the circumstances in which a particular text arises, the ontological and the rhetorical determinants. The ontologically fundamental presupposition of Paul's view of reality is the cross of Jesus. It stands at the center of his heremeneutical vision and discloses the truth about human nature and culture.[6] Whatever the wider ramifications of this disclosure might be, it is essentially a revelation of violence in the form of the murder of an innocent victim. The death of Jesus was not merely the unfortunate by-product of an otherwise benign civilization; it was the deliberate outcome of its wisest deliberation and most auspicious institutions. The law cursed and killed Christ and so revealed the violent basis of the order that it served (Gal 3:12).[7] This became evident to Paul through his experience on the Damascus road,[8] which revealed to him the violence not only in the order but also in himself.[9] He was on a mission of persecution when he experienced the revelation, and it brought together the anticipation of persecution and the memory of execution in a disclosure of the violence at the heart of religious order. Such a disclosure meant that there is now a new order antinomous to the old, which is sustained by a new transcendentally grounded power of nonviolence, called love, and that the old order now appears to be in thrall to "powers" of the kind that killed Jesus, the powers of violence. Paul's concept of sin is shaped by this disclosure. Sin is no longer merely the transgression of law, either its ritual or its moral injunctions, but the plight of human nature in an order based on violence, whose emblem and epitome are the law and the sacrificial system. This is the force of the apocalyptic imagery of the "powers" that rule over the "old" age (1 Cor 2:6-8; Rom 8:35-39; Gal 3:19-22, 4:8-11).[10] This discovery also entails the paradoxical conclusion that it is possible to do harm by doing good, that religiously righteous people are morally dangerous because they act within the old order where religion is one of the powers of violence.

Paul brings this vision of the cross as an act of violence to a reading of the traditional accounts of the origin and nature of sin in Genesis 2–3, and he uses it to interpret the element of desire in that etiology. The key to his understanding of sin as a human act rather than a cosmic event (as in the apocalyptic representations) is Rom 7:7-8:

> I would not have known sin, excepting through the law; I would not have known envy if the law had not said, "Thou shalt not envy." But taking the opportunity provided by the commandment, sin produced in me every kind of desire. (Author's trans.)

Sin is the impulse that corrupts desire, and the law is the means by which that corruption is accomplished. The evidence of sin's presence is that the law produces the very attitudes and actions that it intends to proscribe; it should guard the purity of desire, but instead it corrupts desire. What might Paul's reasoning have been in arriving at this conclusion? The ingredients of his reflection, in addition to the observation that the law produces the opposite of what it intends, are violence (the cross), desire (the self), and religion (the Mosaic law),[11] three elements that are also central to René Girard's theory of religion.[12] For this reason his theory can help us to understand the structure and ramifications of Paul's thought on this matter, and we set it out here at the beginning of our quest for the Pauline reading of Adam because within the hermeneutical circle it must guide us heuristically.

According to Girard, human nature is constitutionally imitative or mimetic,[13] and this propensity causes violence in the form of rivalry; he defines violence as mimetic rivalry. We are all in imitative thrall to one another's desire, an enthrallment that soon becomes mimetic as we learn what we should desire from the desires of others, and so become their rivals. Society, therefore, is a network of mimetic desire that produces rivalry in proportion to the scarcity of the objects and/or the proximity of the model.[14] In the beginning, at the level of the primal horde, such mimetic rivalry made order impossible, until at a moment of maximum disorder there emerged from within the turmoil of the group's mimesis the mechanism of the surrogate victim. A small swerve in the direction of desire, comparable to Democritus's swerve of the atoms, caused violent rivalry to change to violent co-operation in the killing of a surrogate victim. At the moment of the killing the group experienced unanimity, and in the deafening silence of that first reconciliation its members misattributed the cause of reconciliation to the victim. The victim was, in fact, only the catalyst for the shift from disordering to ordering violence, but the group identified the victim as the cause. Thus it concealed from itself the fact that its own unanimous violence is the basis of order, and began the process of deifying the victim by transferring to it its own mimetic rivalry and its own achievement of order through unanimous violence. The victim became the center of the primitive sacred with its double valency of threat and succor, threat corresponding to transferred mimetic rivalry and succor to the reconciling death, to the bad violence of disorder and the good violence of order. Thus, too, the group split off its violence from consciousness and transferred it not to the unconscious but to religious institutions, in a sociological rather than a psychological move. Religion is, therefore, an illusion in a clearer sense than Freud thought, and our hypothesis is preferable to his by the stroke of Occam's razor.

The nimbus of the sacred that clings to the idolized victim is essentially this transfigured violence, and from it issued the powers of cultural organization in the form of prohibition and ritual. Prohibition forbade all activity that threatened the new structure of differentiation and made the outbreak of mimetic rivalry likely, and ritual represented the moment of the surrogate victim's death as an attempt to renew its power of reconciliation. The essence of the prohibition is the threat of the vengeance of the god—vengeance being simply a form of mimetic violence—and the essence of ritual is sacrifice, the constant rekilling of the surrogate victim. Myth came later as the narrative retelling of the founding events that perpetuated the concealment of the group's violence from itself. Religion is, therefore, a system of self-deception that conceals our individual violence as well as the violent generation and sustenance of all our institutions; it is a shared self-delusion.

Girard calls this religious engine of culture the founding mechanism. It engendered all the cultural artifacts, including texts, and so can be used as a hermeneutical tool. It constitutes the deep structure of culture, and once revealed can be used to interpret cultural artifacts, especially the artifacts of religion. Paul's Judaism and the Pauline text itself are, therefore, susceptible to analysis by it. As a religion his Judaism, like all religion, is essentially a cloak for human violence, a system of self-deception that lives by scapegoating. Paul experienced the death of

Jesus at the hands of the religious establishment as a revelation of this violent heart of the primitive sacred in the Judaism of his time. The law represented this violent apparatus, and Jesus represented the innocent victim who, because of Paul's experience on the Damascus road, unveiled the mechanism and became the basis of a new creation. The law and the system of ritual sacrifice that characterized Judaism at the time of Paul are simply culturally specific manifestations of the generative mechanism. This should be clear at the outset, if only to preempt suspicions of anti-semitism, and, of course, one should not overlook the fact that Paul's own teaching might fall under the same indictment.

The preponderance of ritual prescriptions in the Mosaic law and the close association between observance of the law and observance of the temple ritual show that law and temple belong together. However, since the letter to the Romans wrestles with the law rather than with the ritual of the temple, although the two are always mutually entailed, we must for our present purposes be especially clear about the phenomenology of law as seen by Girardian theory. Law originates in the primal prohibition against mimetic desire, and its sanction is the vengeance of the god. Vengeance is essentially mimetic, driven by the irrational need to imitate the violence of the other and to inflict like damage. It is the supreme example of the fallacy that "two wrongs make a right," and it can spiral out of control in an open-ended system of violent reciprocity. It is a return to the violence of disorder prior to the discovery of the order of the surrogate victim. The threat of the vengeance of the god is, however, only the religiously dissembled threat of the outbreak of mimetic violence amongst ourselves. The god is the distorting mirror of our unacknowledged violence—not the source of it, but only the repository and representation of something that begins and ends with us. Because the sacred prohibition is thus really a denial of the true source and nature of mimetic desire, it achieves the opposite of what it intends. It stimulates rivalry and so makes the killing of new victims necessary, in a bloody symbiosis with the sacrificial system behind the curtain of the sacred. This explains why the Mosaic law provokes the very envy that it intends to proscribe—it is part of the system of the sacred. How something originally and essentially good became a part of such a system is the puzzle Paul is trying to solve. In his apocalyptic terms it is the question of how the law became the instrument of the powers of the age in service of their intention to enslave humanity. He approaches an answer via a reading of the story of Adam's sin, which we shall now attempt to reconstruct out of the text of Romans.

The generative mechanism of the letter to the Romans,[15] which produces the themes that interpreters of the text's surface find so difficult to expound with unanimity—sin, law, faith, justification—is the cross. The cross tears the curtain away from the vengeance and victimage of the old mechanism and reveals the generative violence of the sacred. The themes of the letter illuminate each other in a tightly constructed argument that arises out of the conflict between the new founding mechanism of the cross and the old mechanism of the surrogate victim. Ideally, therefore, we should present not a treatment of individual ideas or themes, but rather a reading of the whole text in the light of the generative roles of the rival mechanisms. They are the hermeneutical analogues of the apocalyptic antinomies that Martyn points out to us, the hermeneutical equivalents of the old and new creations. In this brief compass, however, we can read only selected passages that give us the clues we need to reconstruct Paul's reading of Adam. Romans 1:18–3:20, 5:12-21, 7:7-13, and 8:18-25 are the texts in question. The first and last passages are point and counterpoint, expounding the problem and the solution respectively, while 5:12-21, at the center of the argument, reveals its oppositional structure, and 7:7-13 begins the presentation of the solution that culminates in chap. 8. We shall discuss only 1:18–3:20 and 7:7-13.

In Romans 1, 5, and 7 Adam is in the background as the symbol of the human condition, seen from the point of view of faith in the death of Christ.[16] While the death of Christ revealed the human condition to be in thrall to desire as violence, the Jewish tradition saw it as enthralled by desire as sensuality. Taking its cue from the shame that Adam and Eve felt after their transgression, the tradition emphasized the erotic, rather than the mimetic, aspect of desire.[17] According to the Genesis text, however, sexual shame and its concomitant concupiscence were the results of transgression, not the transgression itself. This misplacing of the emphasis is probably due to the influence of the account of the fall of the "Watchers" in Genesis 6 upon general reflection about the origin of sin. The "Watchers" fell primarily because of lust—their very name suggests voyeurism—but even in this version of the fall the link between sin and violence is close because lust leads directly to violence.[18] The giants produced by these illicit unions teach humanity the eating of flesh and the making of weapons and warfare.[19] This story brings concupiscence to the center of the reflection, with the result that the Adamic tradition was mistakenly read as putting lust before violence in the order of sin. Paul sees that, in fact, the Adamic tradition in Genesis puts violence before lust: sin is neither constituted by nor the result of sexual concupiscence, but rather it is the desire to be as God, a desire that is mimetically driven and, by the Girardian definition, violent. The usual analysis of Paul's reading, of which C. K. Barrett's is a good example, comes very close to seeing that violence is the essence of Adam's sin, but does not quite reach that insight. Adam is said to wish to supplant God, to "be as God," in the sense of ruling over his own life, to be "marked by a will-to-power, an impatience with a position suggesting any kind of inferiority."[20]

If the Adam story is read in the light of the violence of the cross, as Paul read it, then the disobedience alone does not strike the reader, but the violence of the disobedience; its unrestrained and merciless nature. Terms like ἁρπαγμόν (Phil 2:6), with the connotation of something snatched and dragged away, and ἐξηπάτησέν με καὶ . . .ἀπέκτεινεν (Rom 7:11), "deceived and killed," and the account of vice in Rom 1:24-32, culminating in the sentence of death, all suggest that the violence of the transaction played an important part in Paul's interpretation of the story. If he, in fact, reads the Adam story this way, as an account of the corruption and deformation of desire into mimetic violence, it would elucidate not only the obvious elements of rivalry with the divine in Genesis 2-3, reflected in Phil 2:5-11, but also why the law causes the very actions that it intends to prohibit—because it is in thrall to the powers, which, in turn, must be seen as the mythological representations of the violence of the primitive sacred, whose coming into being the Genesis story presents symbolically.

Romans 1:18–3:20[21]

The keynote of the letter is that Jew and Gentile can be saved only by faith in the gospel, because the righteousness of God is given to this faith alone (1:16-17). Faith in the gospel has the death of Christ at its center (3:25), and so it is not important that the terms *cross* and *crucify* (σταυρός and σταυρόω respectively) do not occur in Romans. 3:21-26 is the hinge on which the argument of the letter turns,[22] and there Paul presents the death of Christ as the revelation of the two orders and faith as the way to pass from the one to the other. The whole argument unfolds from this faith in the death of Christ as the foundation of the new order of the righteousness of God.[23] From the vantage point of the new order Paul sees the old under the curse of Adam and interprets sin and the law accordingly, demythifying sin by means of the cross—it is violent desire—and desacralizing the Mosaic law by revealing how its basic intention has been corrupted. As he reads it, the story of Adam's sin is a symbolic account of the deviation of desire to violence by means of the law.

If we take 5:12—that sin and death entered the world through Adam's transgression—as a general rubric and 1:18–3:20 as a lens through which to read Paul's interpretation of Genesis 2 and 3, we might reconstruct his reading of it as follows: The characters in the story are the self (or desire) played by Adam and Eve, the self's propensity for

41

mimesis played by the serpent, and the Mosaic law played by the primal prohibition. The original state was one in which desire was structured by the pole of true transcendence, but idolatry deformed that structure into one based on the spurious transcendence of the human other (1:21-23). This corruption of desire took place in two stages, each of which is an element in idolatry. The first stage is the turning from the creator to the creature, symbolized by Eve's turning to the serpent (which is really the turning to oneself);[24] and the second stage is the desire to be like God (to enter into mimetic rivalry with the divine). The note of mimetic rivalry sounds right at the beginning of the story, when the serpent exaggerates the prohibition by extending it to all the trees (Gen 3:1, see also 2:16-17). We know that Eve has been affected when in her reply she, in turn, exaggerates the prohibition even as she corrects the serpent's exaggeration. On her own initiative she adds the prohibition on touching the tree to God's prohibition on eating from it and thus intensifies her own feeling of exclusion, ever so slightly: "This tree is so important to God that we are not allowed even to touch, let alone eat from it." Now she has the idea firmly lodged in her mind that she is being excluded from something valuable, and having lodged that idea of lack, the serpent develops it by suggesting that God threatened the ultimate sanction disingenuously because he wished to keep us from making up that deficiency. The fruit was ultimately valuable because it gave God something that we do not have, and to take it would be to see through his ruse and to succeed in the game of rivalry. Thus desire transforms God from creator, to whom one should be related in gratitude, into rival, to whom one is related by envy; desire corrupts itself to envy by persuading itself that God is envious first;[25] and so it comes unmasked upon the stage. We hear that the woman "saw that the tree was good for food, and that it was a delight to the eyes, and that the tree was to be desired to make one wise" (v. 6 RSV).[26] Only after the serpent had persuaded her by this deception to imitate God's desire for the fruit did it become desirable to her; she learned rivalry from mimesis's misprision of the divine desire. Thus desire idolized God by turning God into the primitive sacred and the prohibition into an envious exclusion.

The pivot on which the action turns is learning rivalry. The serpent, which is the symbol of desire's propensity for rivalry, teaches this, and in heeding the serpent's advice Eve in fact realizes the negative possibility of imitation. Symbolically we are told that the human race freely chose to allow desire, which is constitutionally imitative, to intensify the imitative bond to the point where the one pole had to displace or absorb the other. The human pole had to become the divine. In the course of this the human attributed to the divine the characteristics of its own rivalry and thus turned God into an idol. The idolization of God is, in turn, the presupposition of the idolization of my fellow human beings (1:24-32). I enter into the same mimetic rivalry with them and am "given over" to three forms of mimetic desire: the "desires of our hearts," "disgraceful passions," and the "failed mind" (ἀδόκιμος νοῦς). These are the pathologies of deviated desire in descending order, signalled by the experience of shame on the part of the first couple. Sexuality is infected by rivalry, and the first form of abandoned desire is sexual transgression in general, the dishonoring of the body through fornication, exhibitionism, or sado-masochism of all kinds. Paul probably has in mind not only sexual license but also the spectacles of the arena—gladiatorial combats, naked athletes, and the general vulgarity of professional sports, as well as the nude statues of the pagan gods and goddesses—anything that might appear to a Jewish sensibility to dishonor the human body by violating its modesty. The next stage in this Gadarene descent is homosexuality, understood as an explicit rather than an incidental perversion of the order of nature. The incidental violation of the body's modesty escalates into its intentional humiliation by perversion. The "desires of the heart" are those untrammelled by inhibition, but "disgraceful desires" are those that arise from deliberate perversion; thus corruption progresses from absence of restraint to active deformation, from passive to active corruption. Physical abuse is, however, merely symptomatic of a deeper corruption of desire that contaminates all human interactions, the murderous strife of the "failed mind" (ἀδόκιμος νοῦς). The "failed mind" is the third stage of corruption, and from it come the deeply destructive forces of disorder, the vices that destroy human community: "wickedness, evil, covetousness, malice. . . envy, murder, strife, deceit, malignity . . . gossips, slanderers, haters of God, insolent, haughty, boastful, inventors of evil, disobedient to parents, foolish, faithless, heartless, ruthless" (1:29-31).[27] It is not difficult to see how all of these vices stem from mimetic rivalry.[28] "The failed mind" is a mind enslaved to the deviated transcendence of mimetic rivalry in its most acute form, in which the object of desire is not merely physical but the intangible prizes of prestige and power.

The conclusion that the δικαίωμα of God decrees that those who do such things must die (1:32) returns us to the prohibition of Gen 2:15-17 as the first commandment that carries an explicit sanction of death.[29] Paul assumes that it is universally recognized; the failed mind of both Jew and Gentile intuits it (2:15),[30] and suppresses it by unrighteousness (1:18). The divinity of God that can be known from the created world is, therefore, essentially the prohibition on mimetic rivalry in the form of the demand for the recognition of true transcendence, expressed in Gen 2:15-17.

If something like this reading of the Adam story is behind 1:18-32, then Paul reckons with one fundamental commandment—namely, the primal prohibition—that has been corrupted along with desire; as desire became rivalry, so the prohibition became the expression of a jealous exclusiveness. This is the key to Paul's understanding of the Mosaic law. The Mosaic law is a corrupt expression of the primal prohibition, deformed by mimetic desire to the service of the primitive sacred. The true prohibition, on the other hand, is the one that we accept prior to the double transference onto the surrogate victim. It is the pre-sacralized prohibition that arises from personal responsibility, which has been corrupted by being transferred to the sacred and sanctioned by vengeance. The sanction of death that the true prohibition carries is not vengeful but minatory; if we transgress it we remove the proper limit that defines our creaturehood and open the way to rivalry not only with God but also with all other human beings. The refusal to give honor and thanks to God is the archetypal instance of the refusal to relate to one another in terms of respect and gratitude, and it results in the unleashing of mimetic rivalry with the ultimate outcome being death. There is, therefore, originally only the one prohibition that can be dissembled within the nexus of the sacred into a law that provokes the envy it proscribes, because within that nexus we refuse to take responsibility for our mimesis but transfer it to the idolized god. Paul understands this configuration by reason of the cross; he sees that in the hands of mimetic desire the prohibition can be made to transfer our violence to God and so to stimulate rather than prevent rivalry, and to promote the killing of surrogate victims in symbiosis with the sacrificial system. The individual expression of this pathology is the zealotry that he himself practised.

This unfolding of the consequences of idolatry in Rom 1:18–3:20 is described as the revelation of the "wrath of God" (1:18). Paul refers to the wrath (ὀργή) ten times in Romans (1:18; 2:5, 8; 3:5; 4:15; 5:9; 9:22; 12:19; 13:4, 5), and only once outside this epistle, in 1 Thess 2:16. The last text is a bitter indictment of the Jews, which many commentators find impossible to attribute to Paul for the reason of its bitterness. There is no reason, however, to deny the statement to Paul and consequently no reason not to use 1 Thess 2:14-16 to illuminate Rom 1:18ff.[31] In 1 Thess 2:14-16 Paul uses traditional material from the theme of the persecution of the prophets to blame the Jews for the death of Christ. In Rom 1:18ff. he develops the consequences of idolatry under the rubric "the Jew first and also the Greek" (1:16; 2:9-10; 3:9).[32] The rubric "the Jew first and also the Greek" applies not only to the order of salvation but also to the order of sin. The whole letter expounds how the transgression of the Jews in killing Christ produced "wealth for the cosmos" (11:12).[33] Therefore at the outset he argues that the Jews are first in sin! For the sake of the argument, however, which is directed primarily to Jews, he begins by making the point that salvation and sin encompass the whole world and there is no difference between Jew and Greek in these regards. All this world, in both its Jewish and Gentile manifestations, is under the wrath of God, shut up in disobedience (Rom 11:32; Gal 3:22), because of the sin of Adam (Rom 5:12; 1 Cor 15:22).

This wrath of God is revealed in the gospel, not just in the preaching but in the events on which the preaching is based.[34] This is clearly the sense of 1:18, which must be taken as carrying on the thought of 1:17, which identifies the gospel as the locus of revelation. The sense in which the wrath is revealed in the gospel is not, however, that the divine punishment that should have fallen on us fell on Jesus instead, but rather that the cross is the revelation of the wrath in as much as it is the disclosure of the violence of mimetic desire in the structure of Judaism, which, in turn serves as the critical instance of religion as violence. Wrath is religion as violence in its aspect of vengeance. The Jews are the "vessels of wrath created for destruction," whose function is to reveal the wrath and power of God (9:22).[35] That is why God has "borne them with patience" (9:22). Their very existence down through the ages as a structure of violence was a testimony to the wrath, seen most clearly in their killing of the prophets.

The wrath of God takes the form of the violence of men and women, dissembled through the forms of religion. It is the permission granted us by God to afflict ourselves unknowingly; it is the divine nonresistance to human evil. This is the meaning of the term *wrath* when it is thought of as being present in the world before the end. In Rom 13:4-5 Paul sees the wrath present in the institutions of the state, which are clearly analogous to the institutions of religion. In 4:15 he states explicitly that the law works wrath, which we take to mean that it is the basis of the Jewish religion as a violent system.

The passages in which wrath is a present phenomenon refer, therefore, to institutionalized violence in the form of religious and civil vengeance (4:15, 9:22, 13:4-5) and to the abandonment to deformed desire that culminates in the violence of the failed mind, whose prime instance is Jewish boasting (1:18–3:20). But the passages in which wrath is a future phenomenon understand it as the eschatological divine vengeance (Rom 12:19; 2:5, 8; 3:5; 5:9; and to some extent 9:22). Paul seems, therefore, himself not to be free of the sentiments of the primitive sacred, especially in the apocalyptic formulation that he coins or borrows. This may be, but in any case, the fact must be interpreted within the larger context of his thought as a symbolic expression of the moral nature of God in traditional terms that he no longer understands in the traditional (vengeful) way.

Paul indicts the whole world but singles out the Jews as an acute example of the pathology of sin. The phrase "those who do such things" (οἱ τὰ τοιαῦτα πράσσοντες), which he repeats three times (1:32; 2:2-3), is the transition to an explicit reference to the Jews. The "such things" that they do are chiefly the deeds of the "failed mind" (ἀδόκιμος νοῦς, 1:28-32), and those who do them are now explicitly both Jews and Gentiles (2:1). It is especially significant that Paul introduces the Jews explicitly only when the exposition of the development of sin has reached a climax in the "failed mind," although their presence has been implied all along. The erotic transgressions of the Gentile world are relatively harmless compared to the mimetic ferocity of the "failed mind," and it is the deeds of the latter that he uses as the occasion to introduce the Jew. "The Jew first!"—first in sin, first in salvation, and first in the heart of darkness! This is not to invent sins of which the Jewish way of life was innocent. It would be fatuous to believe that any human community could be free of theft and adultery, let alone the strife, duplicity, gossip, and other excesses of the awful list, with envy, strife, and murder at its center.[36]

We cannot solve the problem of Romans 2 here, but if the law in question is not the Mosaic law but the primal prohibition that everyone knows—namely, "that those who do such things are worthy of death" (1:32; 2:2-3)[37]—then there is at least the possibility of a new reading of the well-known puzzle of 2:13. There is, in fact, a law that everyone justified must have obeyed, the δικαίωμα. If the Adam story provides the categories by which Paul validates the argument that there is no difference between Jews 'and Gentiles (see 2 Cor 11:3, 1 Cor 6:16; 15:45-47), then the phrase "work of the Law written in their hearts" (τὸ ἔργον τοῦ νόμου, 2:15) must refer to the δικαίωμα also, and to the desire shared by all people to do the "good" (2:7, 10). It must refer to the evidence of the primal prohibition persisting in the human heart, however distorted by sin. The very fact that one can recognize that something is wrong shows that one has an intuition of the right, a trace of the Adamic prohibition.

In conclusion, as he reaffirms the equality of Jew and Gentile in sin, Paul says that the law, now in the sense of the Old Testament in general, speaks especially to those under the law (3:19-20) so that the Jews should be especially aware of the fact that the purpose of the law in the present circumstances is to uncover the hidden work of sin. The present circumstances are those revealed by the gospel. The old age in general and the way of life based on the Mosaic law in particular are being viewed *sub specie Crucis,* and this reveals them to be interlocking systems of mimetic violence. The concluding emphatic statement that the law speaks to those under the law (3:19) confirms that the Jew is first in sin. Jew and Gentile are equal in sin, but the Jew is more equal than the Gentile! Judaism is the acute example of the pathology of sacred violence consequent to Adam's sin of mimetic rivalry with the divine.

Romans 7:7-13

Paul applies the consequences of this reading of Adam's sin for the doctrine of the Mosaic law more pointedly in Rom 7:7-13, where he continues the distinction between the law of Moses and the δικαίωμα τοῦ θεοῦ (1:32, see also 8:4). Consonant with Jewish tradition Paul identifies the fundamental thrust of the Mosaic law with the tenth commandment of the Decalogue, the proscription against envy,[38] which in turn corresponds, by reason of its place as the last commandment, with the first commandment, the prohibition on idolatry. In Romans 1 Paul seems to have had both commandments in mind as he wrote, while in 7:7-13 he focuses on the last, taking it as the δικαίωμα τοῦ θεοῦ (νόμου). This can be seen from the way he uses the terms νόμος and ἐντολή in 7:7-13 as he reads the Decalogue in terms of the primal prohibition and vice versa;[39] νόμος is the Mosaic law and ἐντολή is the δικαίωμα (the primal prohibition). The Mosaic law is not the same as sin because it expresses the δικαίωμα (the prohibition on mimetic desire—οὐκ ἐπιθυμήσεις), but it has been hijacked to the sphere of the sacred and so its presentation of the δικαίωμα achieves the opposite of what it intends (τὴν ἁμαρτίαν οὐκ ἔγνων εἰ μὴ διὰ νόμου), serving the interests of the sacral order rather than the need of humanity to curb mimetic rivalry. Apart from the sacral order sin is dead and Adam alive (χωρὶς νόμου, vv. 8-9, compare 3:21), but the prohibition (ἐντολή) and the serpent arrived together, and I (desire) was deceived into using that arrival as an opportunity for mimetic rivalry (vv. 9-11).[40] Thus the order of the sacred came into being, and the Mosaic law as an expression of the primal prohibition within that order serves violence and achieves the opposite of what it intends—the chief evidence of this is not legalism but exclusionism, "boasting" (3:27-31).[41] The Decalogue, therefore, is holy, and the prohibition is "holy, just, and good" (v. 11) initially, but they have both been sacralized by desire's deception that transferred my violence to God and turned God into an idol.

Paul, therefore, reads the story of the Fall as a study in the nature and origin of mimetic desire and of the order of sacred violence. In this hermeneutical method he follows the lead of Hellenistic Jews like Philo, who internalized the story and read it as a psychological representation. Adam stands for the mind (νοῦς), Eve the senses (αἴσθησις), and the

47

serpent either pleasure (ἡδονή) or desire (ἐπιθυμία).[42] Paul seems to see these forces in the same way as capacities of the ego (or libido), but this is an illusion because his fundamental understanding of the ego differs from Philo's. The ego is not the stable and self-sufficient entity that a theory like Philo's demands, but is constituted mimetically by interaction.[43] The fact that I would not have known sin if the prohibition had not confronted me shows that for Paul the "other" is essential to the constitution of the ego. This does not mean that self-consciousness comes only through sin, but simply that this negative experience shows the dialogical structure of the self. The address of the other constitutes the possibilities of the ego, and thus the ego is constituted mimetically. A possibility within desire itself took the prohibition as an opportunity to corrupt gratitude into envy and thus produce what the prohibition seeks to prevent. On the level of ontogeny the voice of the serpent is the voice of the mimetic other, constituting the ego as deviating desire. Paul says that it "deceived me" (7:11). On the level of phylogeny the fundamental deception occurred when we mislocated the cause of the order brought by surrogate victimage, in the victim rather than in our unanimous violence, committed the fraud of the double transference and erected the order of sacred violence. Paul knows that within the order of sacred violence desire and the prohibition interact deceptively so as to produce rather than to curb mimetic desire. The serpent, deciphered in context of the narrative, symbolizes both the temptation to and the realization of this deceptive possibility. The moment of sin occurred when inveigled Eve allowed herself to be constituted by the call of mimetic desire rather than the command of God. Within this scheme of interpretation the command of God is the call to true responsibility that resists the seduction of insecurity and sacred self-alienation.

Sin is, therefore, an act of unbelief in the sense of a distrust of the constituting call of the divine transcendence that arises out of the mimetic instability of the ego. The voice of desire tells of the insecurity of existence as response, and the self takes measures to secure itself by becoming its own mimetic other. That is, the self seeks to possess itself as it is in the other, either by becoming the other or absorbing the other into the self. In any case, as an allegory of the unstable ego, the Genesis story portrays the attempt to locate the structuring power of the ego within itself rather than in the divine transcendence, to become God to oneself, self-generating and self-sustaining. Since the serpent represents the temptation to mimetic rivalry, which is inherent in the unstable imitative structure of desire, one need not, in terms of the story, posit a pre-creational fall of the angels in order to account for the presence of temptation; it is given as a possibility along with desire. By the same token it is not inevitable that we succumb to mimetic temptation. Eve does not have to believe the voice of the serpent. The fact that she does is a free choice on her part, and so sin is a matter of history, not ontology, and emphatically not to be identified with desire as such. Sin is, rather, desire's decision to misuse itself, a self-abuse in the service of self-deception in the interest of self-sufficiency.

Desire in itself is good, and its imitative structure makes possible the vocation to imitate God in pro-creation (Gen 1:28-30, the first commandment in the Torah).[44] Sin, however, occurs at the moment we choose to imitate God enviously, when imitation turns to mimesis, at the point where violence begins, where the decision is made to resort to violence by treating the other as a rival. In this sense sin is violent desire, since it occurs at the moment when the self sees the other as a rival rather than as a benefactor or co-operator. Adam and Eve were the first to do this with respect to God. Their misprision of the divine desire led to the corruption of human desire; they fell into erotic concupiscence between themselves, and ever since we all have imitated them. Romans 5:12, ἐφ' ᾧ πάντες ἥμαρτον, is best taken in the sense of the imitation of Adam. Thus the *massa perditionis* consists in our mimetic enthrallment to Adam and to each other; and the way out is the *imitatio Christi*, the imitation of the last Adam (1 Cor 11:1; 15:45-48).

In conclusion we return to the theme of the antinomies.[45] We have presented a version of the *heilsgeschichtliche* solution to the antinomies of Paul's teaching on sin and the law. The Mosaic law produces the opposite of what it intends because of the context of sacred violence in which it is embedded in the old world. In the new world of the cross the primal prohibition (δικαίωμα) against envy comes into its own again and performs its proper non-alienating function as the principle of responsible restraint (Rom 8:1-4). In this sense the fundamental intention of the Mosaic law is fulfilled and the law itself rendered obsolete; it was ever only a distorted presentation of the prohibition in any case because of its embeddedness in the realm of the sacred. We have argued that the proper hermeneutic of these antinomies is the dialectic of violence and non-violence revealed by the death of Christ. Paul views the Mosaic law in terms of this dialectic. Mimesis uses the Mosaic law to deceive and manipulate desire and thus establish a regime (6:12-14). To be under the Mosaic law—that is, to live in the Jewish way—is to be in thrall to this regime, also called being "in the flesh" (7:5-6). The only way to escape from this domain is to die to its ruling power (7:1-6), and Christian faith is the death that effects this escape. In faith one dies metaphorically by an imaginative identification with (imitation of, 6:1-6) the dying Christ and in the same way rises with him to a new mode of life apart from the order based on the Mosaic law (χωρὶς νόμου, 3:21; 7:8-9; see also Gal 2:19-21). Life in Christ is a new regime constituted by grace, not by law (6:14), and free from the anguish of manipulated desire.

To summarize, Paul believed that the new creation had taken place with the death and resurrection of Christ. The cross and Paul's own persecuting zeal identified violence (defined as mimetic rivalry) as the essence of the old creation. He describes this aspect of the old creation in terms of the Adam story, which he reads as an account of the genesis of mimetic rivalry. Within this order, the primal prohibition as expressed in the the Mosaic law provokes the envy it was originally intended to prevent. This reading of Gen 2:15-17 and 3:1-11 followed the Jewish tradition in identifying desire as the cause of the first sin and in linking it closely with idolatry, but diverged decisively from the tradition when, because of his conviction that the best impulses of his Jewish religion had murdered God's Messiah, he came to see that the essence of desire is not erotic but mimetic, not lust but violence as rivalry, and that the most vicious expression of that violence is religion, an insight that he was well-prepared to appreciate, having been a zealous persecutor of the Christians (Gal 1:11-17). As a result of his conversion he came to understand Adam's transgression as an act of violent desire that founded a regime of mimetic rivalry on the misprision of the primal prohibition and the idolization of God. The death of Christ, understood in the light of the Damascus road event, showed him this and enabled him to see that the identification with Christ as victim restores the prohibition to its proper place within the heart of personal responsibility. Thus faith establishes the δικαίωμα of the law by relocating it outside the precincts of the sacred at the center of individual responsibility (Rom 3:27-31). This is Paul's disclosure to us, and Girard has given us a theoretical framework in which to interpret these treasures for our own time. The apostle saw into the heart of our darkness, and his vision is more pertinent than ever in the face of our capacity for unbridled violence. It is more than merely pertinent—it is true.

Notes

1. See D. Moo, "Paul and the Law in the Last Ten Years," *SJT* 40 (1987) 287-307; J. A. Ziesler, "Some Recent Work on the Letter to the Romans," *Epworth Review* 12 (1985) 96-101.
2. See J. L. Martyn, "A Law-Observant Mission to Gentiles: The Background of Galatians," *Michigan Quarterly Review* 22 (1983) 221-36; idem., "Apocalyptic Antinomies in Paul's Letter to the Galatians," *NTS* 31 (1985) 410-24. The most consistent presentation of this type of interpretation to date is F. Watson, *Paul, Judaism and the Gentiles: A Sociological Approach* (SNTSMS 56; Cambridge: Cambridge University Press, 1986). Watson characterizes Paul's attitude to Judaism as "an ideology legitimating separation, derived initially from other sources [than Judaism]" (48).
3. This is the unfortunate effect on at least one reader of H. Räisänen's *Paul and the Law* (WUNT 29; Tübingen: J. C. Mohr [Paul Siebeck], 1983).

4. D-A. Koch, *Die Schrift als Zeuge des Evangeliums: Untersuchungen zur Verwendung und zum Verständnis der Schrift bei Paulus* (BHT 69; Tübingen: J. C. B. Mohr [Paul Siebeck], 1986).

5. For a recent treatment of this theme, see G. Röhser, *Metaphorik und Personifikation der Sünde: Antike Sündenvorstellungen und paulinische Hamartia* (WUNT 2.25; Tübingen: J. C. B. Mohr [Paul Siebeck], 1987); J. Cohen, "Original Sin as the Evil Inclination: A Polemicist's Appreciation of Human Nature," *HTR* 73 (1980) 495-520.

6. The question about the center of Paul's thought is an old one. See H. Hübner, "Pauli Theologiae Proprium," *NTS* 26 (1980) 445-73. H. Weder, *Das Kreuz Jesu bei Paulus: Ein Versuch, über den Geschichtsbezug des christlichen Glaubens nachzudenken* (FRLANT, 125; Göttingen: Vandenhoeck und Ruprecht, 1981) is a compelling reassertion of the centrality of the cross as the founding event in Paul's thought; compare E. Käsemann, "The Saving Significance of the Death of Jesus in Paul," *Perspectives on Paul* (Philadelphia: Fortress, 1971) 32-59: "For Paul, that death incontestably contained the inherent conflict which is a central characteristic of his theology, with its irreconcilable opposition of law and gospel" (36).

7. The meaning and importance of Gal 3:13-14 in Paul's thought is disputed. Recently C. Dietzfelbinger, *Die Berufung des Paulus als Ursprung seiner Theologie* (WMANT, 58; Neukirchen-Vluyn: Neukirchener Verlag, 1985), makes it the center of his interpretation of Paul's thought and sees the dominant role of the cross in Paul's christology as stemming from his conversion experience as the realization that the law had cursed the Messiah. See the criticism by B. R. Gaventa, *JBL* 107 (1988) 142-44.

8. G. Lyons, *Pauline Autobiography: Toward a New Understanding* (SBLDS, 73; Atlanta: Scholars Press, 1985), shows that, based on the evidence of Gal and 1 Thess, Paul's autobiographical statements are analogous to those in the ancient philosophical lives and, therefore, are closely linked to his vocation and "philosophy," rather than being merely reluctant responses to the need to defend himself. See also B. R. Gaventa, "Galatians 1 and 2: Autobiography as Paradigm," *NovT* 28 (1986) 309-26; idem., *From Darkness to Light: Aspects of Conversion in the New Testament* (OBT; Philadelphia: Fortress, 1986) 17-51. The fact that the experience on the Damascus road is central to Paul's theology, and that his understanding of the cross as the end of the law stands at its inception and is not a later development, has been argued convincingly by P. Stuhlmacher in several articles that are conveniently collected in *Versöhnung, Gesetz, und Gerechtigkeit: Aufsätze zur biblischen Theologie* (Göttingen: Vandenhoeck und Ruprecht, 1981). See especially "Die Gerechtigkeitsanschauung des Apostels Paulus," (87-116), "Das Ende des Gesetzes," (166-91), and "Actzehn Thesen zur paulinischen Kreuzestheologie" (192-208). We do not find convincing H. Räisänen's argument, in "Paul's Conversion and the Development of His View of the Law," *NTS* 33 (1987) 404-19, that Paul's negative attitude to the law developed gradually, in the sense of coming into being. The negative attitude that was there from the beginning developed as it was applied, but it did not come into being gradually.

9. His self-understanding was deeply conditioned by the fact that he had been a persecutor of the church (Gal 1:13; 1 Cor 15:9). There is an autobiographical allusion in statements like Rom 5:10, that we were reconciled to God when we were God's enemies, and 5:1, that we now are at peace with God. Paul had been a religiously violent man!

10. See C. K. Barrett, *From First Adam to Last: A Study in Pauline Theology* (New York: Charles Scribner's Sons, 1962) 14; W. Wink, *Naming the Powers: The Language of Power in the New Testament* (vol. 1, *The Powers*; Philadelphia: Fortress, 1984); W. Carr, *Angels and Principalities: The Background, Meaning and Development of the Pauline Phrase* hai archai kai hai exousiai (SNTSMS, 42; Cambridge: Cambridge University Press, 1981).

11. See J. Tyson, "Works of Law in Galatians," *JBL* 92 (1973) 423-31. C. K. Barrett, *A Commentary on the Epistle to the Romans* (New York: Harper, 1957) 84, writes on Rom 3:31 that the law "is not simply the written record of God's revelation to man, but the whole system of religious thought and practice based upon this revelation—in a word, the religion of Judaism."

12. See R. Girard, *Deceit, Desire, and the Novel: Self and Other in Literary Structure* (Baltimore:

Johns Hopkins University Press, 1965); idem, *Violence and the Sacred* (Baltimore: Johns Hopkins University Press, 1977); idem, *The Scapegoat* (Baltimore: Johns Hopkins University Press, 1986); idem, *Things Hidden Since the Foundation of the World* (with Jean-Michel Ourgoulian and Guy Lefort; Stanford: Stanford University Press, 1987); *Violent Origins: Walter Burkert, René Girard, and Jonathan Z. Smith on Ritual Killing and Social Formation* (ed. Robert Hamerton-Kelly; Stanford: Stanford University Press, 1987); *Violence and Truth: On the Work of René Girard* (ed. Paul Dumouchel; Stanford: Stanford University Press, 1988).

13. Girard uses the adjective *mimetic* as a technical term to describe desire's imitative propensity *in malam partem*—that is, as already involved in rivalry. Thus he can use the phrases *mimetic desire* and *mimetic rivalry* interchangeably.

14. If the model is far away in the sense of being exalted far above us, the tendency to rivalry is less than when the model is near to us in status. Girard calls these two possibilities "external" and "internal" mimesis respectively.

15. For general guidance to Romans we have used C. K. Barrett, *Romans*; C. E. B. Cranfield, *The Epistle to the Romans* (2 vols.; ICC; Edinburgh: T&T Clark, 1975); and E. Käsemann, *An die Römer* (3rd ed.; HNT 8a; Tübingen: J. C. B. Mohr [Paul Siebeck], 1974).

16. For Romans 1, see M. D. Hooker, "Adam in Romans 1," *NTS* 6 (1959-60) 297-306; idem, "A Further Note on Romans 1, *NTS* 13 (1967-68) 181-83; C. K. Barrett, *From First Adam*, 17-19; for Romans 7, see S. Lyonnet, " 'Tu ne convoiteras pas' (Rom vii 7)" *Neotestamentica et Patristica: Freundesgabe O. Cullmann* (Leiden: E. J. Brill, 1962) 157-65; and G. Theissen, *Psychologische Aspekte paulinischer Theologie* (Göttingen: Vandenhoeck & Ruprecht, 1983) 204-13; P. Perkins, "Pauline Anthropology in the Light of Nag Hammadi," *CBQ* 48 (1986) 512-22.

17. Apoc. Mos. 19, 25; Apoc. Abr. 23:6-8; 4 Macc 18:9. G. Theissen, *Psychologische Aspekte*, 207.

18. Even this account does not explain the cause of the lust. The watchers must have transgressed already to be watching women in such a way (compare "He that looks on a woman to lust after her has already committed adultery in his heart," [Matt 5:27]). In a more fundamental sense even than this dominical admonition the watchers had been distracted prior to the outbreak of sexual desire. See Jub. 5:2, 9; 7:21; 1 Enoch 6:1-2; 7:1-6; 10:9; 15:8, 11; 16:1. 1 Enoch 6–16 comprises a "Book of the Watchers." In it the chief sin of the Watchers is, however, that they revealed the secrets of heaven to humans, a form of the sin of Prometheus (see Jdt 16:7), which is clearly an allusion to the Adamic desire to know good and evil. Philo devotes a short treatise to the giants, in which he allegorizes them as the earth-born mind that is devoted to the pleasures of the senses.

19. 1 Enoch 7:4-8:1; 1 Bar 3:26.

20. C. K. Barrett, *From First Adam*, 16.

21. See W. D. Davies, *Paul and Rabbinic Judaism* (4th ed.; Philadelphia: Fortress, 1980) 27-31. Davies reminds us of the relationship between the thought of this passage and the Wisdom of Solomon. The significant passages in Wis are 2:24; 6:20; 6:23; 7:1ff.; 9:2; 10:1-2; 15:8; 13:1ff.; 12:23, 27; 14:12; 14:24-27; and 16:28-9. There is also a remarkable reflection on the origin of idolatry in 14:12-31 that is similar to Girard's theory of religion. It traces the origin of idolatry to the memorialization of a dead child by the father, whose excessive grief causes the remembrance to escalate into worship, with the result that τόν ποτε νεκρὸν ἄνθρωπον νῦν ὡς θεὸν ἐτίμησεν (v. 15). The transformation of a dead human into a God is the essence of the surrogate victim mechanism. This kind of religion leads to violent disorder, which nevertheless they call peace (ἀλλὰ καὶ ἐν μεγάλῳ ζῶντες ἀγνοίας πολέμῳ τὰ τοσαῦτα κακὰ εἰρήνην προσαγορεύουσιν, 22).

22. Barrett, *Romans*, 72, "one of the great turning points of the epistle"; Cranfield, *Romans*, 73, "the center and heart of the whole of Rom 1:16b-15:13"; O. Kuss, *Der Römerbrief* (2 vols.; Regensburg: Friedrich Pustet, 1957-59) 1.110, "theologische und architectonische Mitte des Römerbriefes."

23. On "righteousness" as world order, see H. H. Schmid, *Gerechtigkeit als Weltordnung:*

Hintergrund und Geschichte des alttestamentlichen Gerechtigkeitsbegriffes (BHT 40; Tübingen: J. C. B. Mohr [Paul Siebeck], 1968); idem., "Rechtfertigung als Schöpfungsgeschehen. Notizen zur alttestamentlichen Vorgeschichte eines neutestamentlichen Themas," *Rechtfertigung: Festschrift für Ernst Käsemann zum 70. Geburtstag* (eds. J. Friedrich, W. Pöhlmann, and P. Stuhlmacher; Tübingen: J. C. B. Mohr, and Göttingen: Vandenhoeck & Ruprecht, 1976) 403-14.

24. W. D. Davies, *Paul and Rabbinic Judaism*, 30. Davies interprets Rom 1:18ff. by means of the rabbinic categories of the *yetzer ha-ra* and the *yetzer ha-tob*, which are quite appropriate if one understands *yetzer* to signify desire as such. R. Yannai (200 CE) said: "He who hearkened to his evil impulse is as if he practised idolatry: for it is said, 'There shall no strange God be within thee: Thou shalt not worship any God.' " (y. Ned. 9.41b). Here idolatry is identified with every obedience to the *yetzer ha-ra*. The *yetzer* is, therefore, desire as such seen from two possible points of view; when it deviates to mimesis it is the *yetzer ha-ra*, and when it maintains its proper orientation to God it is the *yetzer ha-tob*.

25. Compare Wis 14:30, "They think evil of God in turning to idols." See also 2:24: "By the envy of the devil death entered the world." On the general theme of envy in the divine see Plato, Tim. 29e, Phaedr. 247a, quoted by Philo in Quod. Lib. 13, see also Spec. Leg. 2.249, Leg. All. 1.61, 3.7, Abr. 203-4. That the gods need nothing is a commonplace of Greek philosophy (see the evidence cited by H. Conzelmann, *Acts of the Apostles* [Hermeneia; Philadelphia: Fortress, 1987] 142, in commenting on Acts 17:25). The generosity of the divine was, therefore, a commonplace of Hellenistic philosophic and religious thought.

26. The RSV translates the two adjectives טוב and תאוה, and the Niph of חמד from the MT. The LXX adjectives καλός, ἀρεστός, and ὡραῖος are more aesthetic than their Hebrew equivalents, emphasizing the surface appearance of the fruit. In any case, although the word ἐπιθυμία is not used, the idea of desire is powerfully present, and the RSV translation fairly reproduces the thrust of both the Hebrew and the Greek.

27. Compare Philo, Sacrif. 32, which Colson and Whitaker call, "probably the most formidable catalogue of bad qualities ever drawn up" (Loeb 2, 89). See also Wis 14:25ff. Philo presents the list as the work of the "Cain" type of mind, whose characteristic is to think that it alone is the source of all its benefits (Cher. 57, 63-66, 83) and to refuse to give thanks to God.

28. In Hellenistic Jewish sources, desire (ἐπιθυμία) was often said to be the root of all sin: Philo, Spec. Leg. 4. 84, 130; Dec. 142, 173.

29. R. W. Thompson, "How Is the Law Fulfilled in Us?" *LS* 11 (1986) 31-41, referring to Rom 8:4, 13:8-10, and Gal 5:13-16, argues that δικαίωμα means primarily the love of neighbor as the "just requirement" of the law. In 1:32, therefore, we have the negative formulation of the same point: The interdiction of mimetic rivalry is the negative expression of the command to love the neighbor (13:10).

30. Compare τὸ κρίμα in 2:2, which means essentially the same thing—namely, the condemnation due transgression.

31. K. Donfried, "Paul and Judaism: 1 Thessalonians 2:13-16 as a Test Case," *Int* 38 (1984) 242-53; W. D. Davies, "Paul and the People of Israel," *NTS* 24 (1977) 4-39. A recent argument for interpolation that reports on the literature to that time is D. Schmidt, "1 Thess 2:13-16: Linguistic Evidence for Interpolation," *JBL* 102 (1983) 269-79. Donfried (250-53) relates the discussion of 1 Thess 2:16 to the occurrence of the term *wrath* in Romans.

32. See T. Donaldson, "The 'Curse of the Law' and the Inclusion of the Gentiles," *NTS* 32 (1986) 94-112, who says that for Paul the Jews, "the people of the law, thus functions as a kind of representative sample of the whole. Their plight is no different from the plight of the whole of humankind, but through the operation of the law in their situation that plight is thrown into sharp relief" (104). Donaldson says this apropos of Gal 3:13-14, but it is equally apt of Rom 1:18ff.

33. The term παράπτωμα, used in 11:12 to describe the act of sin of the Jews, is the same term used in 5:15-18 to describe Adam's act of sin, which we all imitated. In 4:25 it describes that on account of which Christ died; διά with the accusative here must be

understood as that which caused the death. Barrett's translation is apt: "... was delivered up because of the sins we committed, and raised up because of the justification that was to be granted us (*Romans*, 99).

34. Cranfield writes: "The reality of the wrath of God is only truly known when it is seen in its revelation in Gethsemane and on Golgotha" (*Romans*, 1.110).

35. A. T. Hanson, "Vessels of Wrath or Instruments of Wrath? Romans IX. 22-23," *JTS* 32 (1981) 433-43. Hanson argues that the unbelieving Jews were the instruments by which the wrath of God was revealed.

36. As for "temple robbery" there is nothing *outré* about that. Paul may even have in mind the collection of statues bought as stolen goods from temple robbers. See Sanday and Headlam, *The Epistle to the Romans* (ICC; Edinburgh: T&T Clark, 1895) 66.

37. G. Klein, "Sündenverständnis und theologia crucis bei Paulus," *Theologia Crucis—Signum Crucis: Festschrift für Erich Dinkler zum 70. Geburtstag* (eds. C. Andersen and G. Klein; Tübingen: J. C. B. Mohr [Paul Siebeck], 1979) 249-82. "Die von Gott gegebene Gesetz ist nicht einfach mit dem identisch, was der Jude zu erfullen trachtet" (257). He refers also to Stuhlmacher's argument that the spiritual intention of the law achieves its goal only when Christ liberates its life-preserving function. Stuhlmacher calls this new Torah the Zion Torah as distinct from the Sinai Torah ("Das Gesetz als Thema biblischer Theologie," in *Versöhnung, Gesetz, und Gerechtigkeit*, 136-65).

38. See 4 Macc 2:6; G. Theissen, *Psychologische Aspekte*, 207-8; R. Weber, "Geschichte des Gesetzes und das Ich in Romer 7, 7–8,4" *Neue Zeitschrift für systematische Theologie und Religionsphilosophie* 29 (1987) 147-79.

39. R. Weber, "Geschichte des Gesetzes, 156-58, reads the relationship between ἐντολή and νόμος in roughly the same way as we do. Specifically, he does not see them as synonyms as so many other commentators do.

40. On Adam in Romans 7 see Cranfield, *Romans*, 1.343, and Käsemann, *Römer*, 187-88.

41. On exclusionism as the main issue in the debate between Paul and the Jewish way of life, see J. Dunn, "Works of the Law and the Curse of the Law (Gal 3:10-14)," *NTS* 31 (1985) 523-42.

42. See Leg. All. 2.5,24,38,72,74; Opif. 157; Quaes. Gen. 1.47-48. G. Theissen, *Psychologische Aspekte*, 208-9.

43. M. Borsch-Jacobsen, *The Freudian Subject* (Stanford: Stanford University Press, 1988), shows the inner contradictions in Freud's arguments for the isolated, pre-social subject; compare E. Käsemann, *Perspectives*, 27: "His [the believer's] continuity and identity also rest outside himself, in his participation in the heavenly world and communication with the Word of his creator, which is always challenging him anew to leave his own past behind and which drives him forward into the future of his Lord . . . it means being involved in the world-wide conflict between *civitas dei* and *civitas terrena*."

44. R. Samuel ben Nahman understands our point completely, and his famous logion in Gen. Rab. 9.7 could be Girard in a nutshell: " 'And behold it was very good.' This is the evil impulse! Is then the evil impulse good? Yet were it not for the evil impulse no man would build a house, nor marry a wife, nor engage in trade. Solomon said 'All labor and all excelling in work is a man's rivalry with his neighbor (Ecclesiastes 4:4)" (Davies, *Paul*, 22).

45. On the antinomies see also H. Weder, "Gesetz und Sünde: Gedanken zu einem qualitativen Sprung im Denken des Paulus," *NTS* 31 (1985) 357-76. J. L. Martyn, "Paul and His Jewish-Christian Interpreters," *USQR* 42 (1988) 1-16, returns to the theme of the antinomies and responds to the accusation of Marcionism and incipient anti-semitism in a characteristically judicious and irenic way. Nevertheless he maintains the position that for Paul the cross meant "a fatal loss of cosmos," and that the apostle was serious when he said he had died with Christ (Gal 2:19). There is no "through-train" from the old covenant to the new. That Paul's Jewish-Christian interpreters would have read him this way, then, is confirmed by the fact that perceptive Jewish interpreters like Leo Baeck read him this way now.

THE RELATIONSHIP BETWEEN SIN AND DEATH IN ROMANS

J. Christiaan Beker

The relationship between the power of sin and the power of death is a vexing problem for Christian thought, especially when we view it from the perspective of its manifestation in suffering. Indeed, the power of death in the world raises the acute question of the meaning or meaninglessness of suffering.

In this context two recent, widely acclaimed books—Harold S. Kushner's *When Bad Things Happen to Good People* and Dorothee Soelle's *Suffering*—correctly castigate traditional Christian explanations as insufficient and cruel. These traditional explanations forge a bond between suffering and sin by deriving suffering *from* sin. This derivation of suffering from sin has the effect of heaping the suffering of guilt on top of the mental and physical suffering of people.

In the face of this profound hermeneutical issue, I want to explore Paul's response to the question of suffering, especially as it comes to the surface in Romans.

In the first place Paul draws important distinctions between several levels of suffering. There is deserved suffering, redemptive suffering, and the suffering of created life, which is in "bondage to decay" (Rom 8:21). *Just or deserved suffering* is the consequence of the wrath of God, God's judgment against human idolatry—that is, "God's decree that those who do such things deserve to die" (Rom 1:32). However, this type of suffering is quite different from the call of the gospel to *redemptive suffering* (Rom 5:3)—that is, the call to enlarge the domain of God's righteousness in a hostile world.

The question arises, however, whether Paul acknowledges the presence of *meaningless suffering* in the world as the consequence of the continuing reign of the power of death. In other words, is the creation's "subjection to futility" (*mataiotēs*, Rom 8:20), its "bondage to decay" (*douleia tēs phthoras*, Rom 8:21), the cause of "the sufferings of the present time" (Rom 8:18), and do these sufferings constitute the realm of meaningless or tragic suffering in the world?

I will proceed by discussing two interrelated issues: Paul's stance as an apocalyptic theologian and the question of Paul's consistency or inconsistency with respect to the relationship between sin and death.

Paul as an Apocalyptic Theologian

Paul is an apocalyptic theologian. This means that the problem of theodicy becomes especially acute for him, because apocalyptic theology hopes for the restoration of God's creation rather than for its annihilation. Thus apocalyptic theology affirms that God, the creator of a good creation, is the God who redeems us not out of the world, but rather in and with it. Paul claims, therefore, that the sovereign power of God will ultimately triumph over all the rebellious forces in the world that resist his will. However, Paul's anchorage in the Jewish-apocalyptic world view, which affirms a correspondence between *Urzeit* and *Endzeit*, yielded shortly after the apostolic period to a Platonizing world view, which interpreted the relation between the Creator and the creation in a very different manner. The Platonizing view of creation is based on a "tempered dualism," which sees creation at best as a material copy of the *kosmos noētos*, the heavenly model of creation, an ideal world, produced by a Demiurge and not by God. Thus creation—although not evil—belongs to the realm of transience-finitude and matter, which resists goodness and is incapable of perfection. Macrocosm and microcosm correspond to each other. The cosmological inertia of matter is duplicated in the anthropological sphere, where the *nous* is surrounded by the weight and passions of the *sōma*.

The differentiation between the divine world and the world of creation enables a Platonizing interpretation of Christian faith to come to terms with the issue of theodicy and suffering. Suffering is here inherent in the imperfections and transience of creation. Thus redemption must be seen as an escape from this world, or at least as a transcending of the world by means of the contemplation of the divine world. In other words, where creation is denigrated and where intermediaries between God's pure being and the created world are posited—as was the common view of the Hellenistic-Roman world from Plato's *Timaeus* via Middle-Platonism and Philo to Plotinus—suffering can be accounted for, either as a path of insight and wisdom or as a prelude to the final heavenly goal of human life.

For Paul, by contrast, such a solution is impossible. He affirms the power and goodness of both God the Creator and the creation, and he claims moreover that there is a solidarity among all the diverse components of God's creation. How then does Paul come to grips with the powers of sin and death, which seem to triumph in the world in the form of evil and affliction?

Sin and Death in Romans

In Romans sin and death form an inseparable alliance. They are the supreme powers of the old age, which in turn determine the function of the powers of the law and the flesh in the world. Both sin and death "reign over the old age" (Rom 5:12-21); sin is able to "deceive" (Rom 7:10); and "the sting" of death is sin (1 Cor 15:56). Indeed "sin reigned in death" (Rom 5:21), and "the body of sin" (Rom 6:6) is the equivalent of "this body of death" (Rom 7:24). Moreover, sin is the procreator of death: "Therefore as sin came into the world through one man and death through sin, and so death spread to all men because all men sinned" (Rom 5:12 RSV).

Paul's gospel proclaims that Christ has triumphed over the powers of sin and death: "The death he died he died to *sin,* once for all" (Rom 6:10 RSV, italics added) and "*death* no longer has dominion over him" (Rom 6:9 RSV, italics added). Because Paul—along with Jewish apocalyptic thought—posits a causal relationship between sin and death, his claim that Christ has triumphed over sin and death seems to push him logically to the statement that just as Christians participate in Christ's victory over sin, they likewise participate in his victory over death. In other words, if sin and death are causally related, then it follows that the *defeat of sin* by Jesus Christ on behalf of Christians entails as well the *defeat of death.* And indeed Paul states in Rom 6:13 that Christians are people "who have been brought from death to life."

But if this is the case, why are Christians still subject to death and suffering? How can death be defined by Paul as "the last enemy" (see 1 Cor 15:26)? To put it more sharply, why do Christians still have to suffer at the hands of the power of death in the world? If sin and death are so intimately related that the presence and absence of the one signifies the presence and absence of the other (Rom 5:12), how can Paul claim that although Christ has defeated both powers, death still continues to reign in Christian life? How can he simultaneously conjoin and disjoin the powers of sin and death? (See the disjunction in Rom 6:3-14, where the defeat of sin for Christians as a realized fact is paralleled, not by the defeat of death as a realized fact, but rather by the expectation of its defeat.)

The problem of why Christians must still suffer under the power of death in God's world after the triumph of God in Christ over the powers of sin and death is indeed addressed by Paul. However, his response to the problem seems to be different when we compare Romans with 1 Corinthians.

The relationship between sin and death seems utterly consistent in Romans. Sin has invaded God's good creation because of human idolatry (1:18-32). The human act of sin creates a sphere that overpowers the human situation, so that sin becomes an enslaving power (3:9; 5:12-21). The relationship is viewed by Paul in causal terms—that is, sin is the procreator of death (5:12). Although sin and death form an inseparable alliance (5:12-21), Paul emphasizes the primacy of sin as the true cause of death and suffering in the world. This is clear when we notice how Paul focuses on *the power of sin* in 5:12-21, 6:1-23, and 7:1-25.

Sin is here discussed in terms of its own power (6:1-23) and in terms of its various spheres of power—that is, in its relation to death (5:12-21) and to the law (7:1-25). The consistency of Paul's argument is apparent: Because death entered the world through sin, sin has not only "deadly" anthropological consequences, but also cosmic-universal consequences.

Christ's actual triumph over sin contains as well a promise: the promise of the imminent defeat of death. Death, indeed, still reigns over Christians and in the world, because although the power of sin has been overcome, the consequences of sin—its unleashing of death in God's world—still linger on. Therefore, when Paul, in Rom 8:18-39, speaks about the subjection of the creation "to futility" (8:20) and its "bondage to decay" (8:21), he actually speaks about the lingering effects of death in the creation, caused by God's reaction to the fall of Adam (8:20b).

It is important to notice, however, that "the sufferings of this present time" (8:18)—caused by the presence of death in the world—will soon be undone by the "glory [of God] that is to be revealed to us" (8:18b). In other words, the groaning of creation, along with that of the Christians, is grounded in the sure hope of the imminent defeat of death. Indeed, the imminence of the hope in Paul is motivated by the fact that since the power of sin has been defeated in Christ, the defeat of its ally—the power of death—must be imminent.

Romans, then, presents a consistent description of the relationship between the power of sin and the power of death. Because of the causal relation of sin and death, there is to be sure harsh suffering in the world, but there is no meaningless or tragic suffering. God's good creation has been poisoned by the twin powers of sin and death, which human idolatry (since Adam) has unleased in the world. Because of Christ's triumph over sin, however, Paul can claim not only that death has already lost its "sting," but also that the defeat of death is at hand. Therefore, he can proclaim that "neither death, nor life, nor angels, nor principalities, nor things present, nor things to come, nor powers, nor height, nor depth, nor anything else in all creation, will be able to separate us from the love of God in Christ Jesus our Lord" (8:38-39 RSV).

According to the scenario in Romans, Paul would probably have responded to the question of why there is so much suffering in the world in Anselmian fashion: *"nondum considerasti quanti ponderis peccatum est."*

The uniqueness of Paul's argument, with respect to the relation of sin and death in Romans, becomes clear when we compare Romans with his argument in 1 Corinthians.

The relation in Romans between sin, death, and the created order shifts to a different key in 1 Corinthians. The difference concerns not only the texture of the argument, but also its underlying premise.

In 1 Corinthians the vocabulary of *sin* as an apocalyptic power disappears almost completely (except for 15:56). And even when the term appears (twice), it occurs in the plural and means "transgressions" (15:3, 17). Moreover, the term *sarx*—so closely allied with *hamartia* in Romans—carries in 1 Corinthians nowhere the special pejorative meaning of "existence in rebellion to God."

In other words, a very different cosmological premise is operative in 1 Corinthians. Paul builds his argument here against the background of a Jewish-Hellenistic cosmology, which is characterized by a "tempered dualism." In Romans, however, the goodness of God's creation was perverted by human sin and sin's ally—the power of death—still ruled in the world, even after Christ had defeated the power of sin.

In 1 Corinthians, however, there is no speculation about the relation of sin to death. Death seems to be the signature of created life; at least, the creation has an inherently temporal, transient, and finite character (see especially the contrasts in 15:42-49: *phthora-aphtharsia; atimia-doxa; astheneia-dynamis; sōma psychikon-pneumatikon*). And although 15:21-22 alludes to the fact that Adam caused death to appear in the world (because of his sin?), we should notice the quite different emphasis in the argument of Rom 5:12-21, where sin and grace are the primary foci rather than "death" and "the resurrection of the dead" (1 Cor 15:21). Thus in 1 Corinthians Paul's argument stresses the contrast between the finite-transient character of the created world and the coming apocalyptic glory, when "the perishable" will have put on "imperishability" and "the mortal" immortality (15:53), when death—inherent in the created order—will have been overcome (15:54-55).

It seems, then, that Romans and 1 Corinthians present us with two different apocalyptic scenarios. In Romans, the triangular relation between sin, death, and the creation determines the stature of the created order and the nature of its redemption. God's creation is inherently good; its "fall" is due to the power of human sin, which has infected the created order by unleashing death in the world. Indeed, "the futility" of creation and its "bondage to decay" (Rom 8:20-21) was not due to "its own will," but to God's response to the power of sin (Rom 8:20).

But now, after Christ's victory over the power of sin, the lingering power of death in the creation will soon be overcome by God's coming apocalyptic triumph. Thus the creation will be restored to its original goodness. In other words, according to Romans, *Urzeit* and *Endzeit* will correspond to each other, and God's apocalyptic triumph will confirm the goodness of God's creation.

In 1 Corinthians, however, the emphasis does not fall on the triangular relation among sin, death, and the cosmos. The triangular scenario of Romans shifts here to a binary or bi-focal scenario. "What is sown is perishable, what is raised is imperishable" (15:42 RSV). The opposition here is between a transient-imperfect creation and a resurrection order of immortality (15:54) and pure spirituality (15:46-49). There is no reflection in 1 Corinthians about the relationship between sin and death, and we look in vain for an assertion like the one Paul makes in Rom 8:20 (see above).

Since the nature of creation is here—different from Romans—conceived in terms of a tempered dualism, the redemption of creation likewise undergoes a shift. Paul seems to stress in 1 Corinthians the apocalyptic-ontological *transformation* of a transient-finite and mortal creation rather than its *restoration* to its original goodness.

Conclusion

Therefore we may conclude that Romans and 1 Corinthians provide different answers to the question of human suffering in the world. Romans suggests that since all suffering is due to the power of sin, which has unleashed death in the world, there can be no question about the meaninglessness or tragedy of suffering.

However, 1 Corinthians permits a different perspective on the issue of suffering. Since suffering is the signature of the creation itself—because of its inherently mortal-transient nature—it is a necessary ingredient of life in this world. Although the necessary character of suffering in our world may not constitute a sufficient answer to its meaningless or tragic aspect, Christians in Corinth are assured that suffering in this world will cease when God inaugurates a different ontological world of eternal bliss and transforms our mortality into immortality.

Finally, a word about the coherent character of Paul's thought concerning the relationship between sin and death in the world. The crucial issue hinges on the question whether Paul's divergent responses are caused solely by the exigencies of the different contingent situations in Rome and Corinth, or of whether Paul has shifted his theological stance, with the result that he operates with different coherent frameworks in Romans and 1 Corinthians. Are we here dealing solely with different nuances and emphases of Paul, or with basic new formulations concerning the relations of sin, death, and cosmology? If the latter is true, how does this affect the continuity and overall coherence of Paul's gospel? Are we in this case forced to surrender the coherence of Paul's gospel and characterize him either as an opportunistic, *ad-hoc* theologian or as a developmental thinker? Or could it be that we must locate the coherence of Paul's gospel in a place that transcends the particularities of world views and cultures, of cosmologies and anthropologies?

The fact that the answer to these questions is until now—for me, at least—a *non liguet* demonstrates how much work still awaits the interpreter of Paul.

And it is not the least of the great qualities of the one we honor in these pages that he has constantly stimulated us to new openness and to chart new ways in New Testament scholarship.

THE WORM AT THE CORE OF THE APPLE: EXEGETICAL REFLECTIONS ON ROMANS 7

Paul W. Meyer

I

> First, it is a just principle of interpretation, that we should understand every writer, when this can be done in consonance with the laws of language, as speaking to the purpose which he has immediately before him. There are very many truths of the gospel, and many plain and important truths, which are not taught in this or that passage of Scripture. The question concerning [Romans] chap. vii. 5-25 is not, whether it be true that there is a contest in the breast of Christians, which might, at least for the most part, be well described by the words there found; but, whether such a view of the subject is congruous with the present design and argument of the apostle.[1]

These words were written over a century and half ago by Moses Stuart, one of America's pioneers in biblical exegesis. If the words bear the unmistakable marks of his time, their point is so contemporary and possesses such undiminished pertinence to theological discourse today that they may still serve as a kind of motto for exegesis. One of the major tasks of exegesis, in our day no less than in earlier ones, is to check the arbitrary exploitation of passages from scripture to score points in theological controversy, to inhibit their use for purposes alien to their original form and function, to prevent their being made simply subservient to the interests of those who use them. One might, of course, ask why such tendencies need to be restrained. Why should anyone not be free to make whatever one wishes of these familiar and fondly held texts? People will be found, after all, to do just that. But if these texts were composed initially to guide, correct, and reform the community's perceptions and understanding, to clarify and restore its identity and direction, and if this role was recognized and conceded to them in the process of canonization by the community that still uses them as scripture, then their own power to shape rather than to be shaped by contemporary interests must be respected. Whatever one may have to say about the failings and inadequacies of actual biblical exegesis in its practice, this continual search to recover and reinstate in the first instance the texts' own integrity must remain its ideal.[2]

In that search, the tools and methods of historical study—defined in the broadest sense as the attempt to understand these texts in their original historical, literary, and cultural contexts—take on growing rather than diminishing significance and urgency. Indeed, one may even redefine the major task of exegesis under discussion here as the purification of all anachronistic understandings from our reading of biblical passages. These anachronisms comprise more than the deliberate uses of texts for purposes that have nothing to do with their original composition. They are even more likely to be the unintended or even well-meaning interpretations that read back into the texts the lexical usages, the debates, the anxieties and designs, and the theological claims of later times in the church's life. It is ironic, but true, and amply documented in the history of biblical interpretation, that one of the major barriers to the recovery of the texts' integrity is often the accumulated freight of the church's own long history of the use of scripture, the sedimentation left behind by its own previous attempts to honor and appeal to these very texts! This surely does not mean that the texts have no integrity of their own. It is the situation and needs of those who take recourse to them that never remain the same. But the task becomes more pressing than ever of distinguishing carefully, in Stuart's words, between what "might, at least for the most part, be well described by the words there found" and what is "congruous with the present design and argument" of the writer. The power of a biblical text to transcend the subsequent tradition in such a way as to perform a regulative function upon it depends on this preservation of its historical distance and priority as much as it does on the continuities that bind the biblical materials to the church's life and thought, by virtue of which they remain "the church's book." This in turn requires giving heed in every particular instance to "the purpose which [the writer] has immediately before him."

Recovering that purpose, of course, is just the problem. To recreate the situation that called forth a New Testament text and shaped it requires all the resources and skills the exegete can muster: detailed familiarity with available sources, balanced judgment in their evaluation and use, knowledge of the complex processes by which tradition grows, but above all a sympathetic historical imagination that can use such information in a disciplined projection of the interpreter into another place and time. It requires the ability to sit loose to previous interpretations of a text rather than to let false modesty absolutize these;

a willingness to let issues of sometimes immense theological import take on unsuspected and unforeseen contours under the promptings of the text itself and its oft-unnoticed details, sometimes in defiance of what the interpreter or his community has previously held most dear; and a readiness to seek out the critical and reforming intent of the text without the defensive or manipulative reactions that so often distort both historical reconstruction and exegesis.

Simply to list these requisite qualities for recovering the setting of a biblical text is already, for those who know him and his work, to describe the gifts that Lou Martyn has brought in special measure to the interpretation, first, of the Fourth Gospel and, more recently, of the Pauline letters. Some of the most rewarding hours I have been privileged to enjoy have been those spent in unhurried conversations with him, exploring "the design and argument" of this or that Pauline text, especially from Galatians or Romans. What I offer here as a token of gratitude and respect is but an attempt to continue such conversation, now in a fashion more one-sided than usual, but more open to public perusal and discussion.

II

Romans 7 is a showcase of the issues in exegesis that have just been outlined for at least two major reasons. The first is clearly suggested in the passage quoted from Moses Stuart. It is a quality of the text itself: its location at a critical turning point in the general argument of Romans, its susceptibility to a variety of interpretations, and its seeming propensity to evoke from the reader analogy and comparison with one's own apparently similar experiences.[3] These characteristics of this particular text are well-known, and every commentary lays out to some extent the choices with which it confronts the thoughtful reader. Paul's extended use of the first person singular pronoun "I" is one of the features of the text that most notably imparts to it this ostensible multivalence. We need not review here the various proposals that have been made to identify more precisely the antecedent of this pronoun.[4] A fairly strong consensus seems to have emerged that the passage is not autobiographical in any sense that allows it to yield details about Paul's personal life, either before his conversion or after. Paul is employing rather a rhetorical style in which the self functions in a representative way as a type or paradigm for others.[5] At the same time, the pronoun is not used in a purely fictive way, as though Paul were excluding himself from its pattern. The closest parallels in his own letters to this intense and vivid device of casting fundamental religious affirmations involving the self into first person singular language are provided by Gal 2:18-21 and Phil 3:8-14. Both passages follow so closely upon obviously autobiographical references that it is impossible to dismiss all personal nuances from his use of "I."[6] Moreover, the closest formal literary analogies to this style are found in the individual laments and thanksgivings of the Hebrew Psalter and the Qumran hymns. These reinforce the view that Romans 7:7-25 is a theological description, cast in a retrospective and reflective mode, of the destructive power of sin—by one who has himself known it and been delivered from it—and that its antithesis—announced already in the contrasting phrases of v. 6b—is provided by Paul in 8:1-11[7] Yet, the question remains: Who is Paul describing? Who is embraced by this paradigmatic rhetorical style? The answer is not a function of the style itself, but must depend on "the present design and argument of the apostle." In other words, a correct answer cannot simply precede exegesis, but follows it and depends on it.

If one major reason why a consensus in the reading of Romans 7 has been so elusive lies in a certain quality of the text itself, the second lies in the accumulated freight brought to it by its interpreters. The literature on this text seems to offer some particularly striking examples of the anachronistic reading referred to earlier, and it is on these that I should like to focus. The barriers to understanding, thrown up by the legacy of past interpretations, are the hardest ones to identify because they are so intricately interwoven with the positive debts every exegete owes to those who have gone before. Indeed, it is sometimes precisely some insight that once opened up with fresh vitality the force of Paul's gospel that now, taken as self-evident in another situation and frozen into convention, impedes the interpreter's ability to cross the differences of historical space and time in order to approach again that elusive intent of the author. To remove these barriers requires something akin to the paradigm shifts of other disciplines. It can come about only when proposals that may initially seem outlandish can win their way to new acceptance.

III

What would be an example of such an apparent "dogma" that has once appeared in the course of the interpretation of Romans 7:7-25 but now has become an impediment to our understanding of Paul's words?

In one of the most well known and fateful shifts in the history of exegesis, Augustine changed his mind about Romans 7:7-25. In his own words, he at first understood Paul in these verses to be "describing the man who is still under the law and not yet under grace. Long afterwards I learned that these words could also describe the spiritual man and indeed in all probability do so."[8] There had been differences of opinion on these verses before Augustine,[9] but like so much else he wrote and thought, his later view is particularly significant for the influence it has exercised, first, on the Protestant Reformers and then, through them, on subsequent interpretation right up to some of the most recent commentaries. The reasons why the Reformers were so attracted to Augustine's interpretation are complex, and they are not by any means identical with the ones that moved Augustine to alter his view.[10] Nevertheless, on an attentive reading of a few of the key paragraphs, an important element in this line of exegesis emerges quite clearly. A few sentences will suffice.

First, from Martin Luther:

> First, this whole passage clearly reveals disapproval and hatred of the flesh and love for the good and the law. Now such an attitude is not characteristic of a carnal man [carnalis homo], for he hates and laughs at the law and follows the inclinations of his flesh.
>
> Yet a spiritual man [spiritualis] fights with his flesh and bemoans the fact that he cannot do as he wills. But a carnal man does not fight with it but yields and consents to it. Hence, this well-known judgment of Blessed Augustine: "The will to be righteous is a large part of righteousness."[11]
>
> The first word, then, which proves that a spiritual man is speaking here is this: But I am carnal (Rom. 7:14). Because it is characteristic of a spiritual and wise man [spiritualis et sapiens homo] that he knows that he is carnal . . . and that he praises the law of God because it is spiritual.[12]
>
> Certainly no one will declare himself wretched except one who is a spiritual man. For perfect self-knowledge is perfect humility, and perfect humility is perfect wisdom, and perfect wisdom is perfect spiritualness [perfecta spiritualitas]. Hence, only a perfectly spiritual man can say: "Wretched man that I am!"[13]

And then a comment by Philip Melanchthon: "For Paul is speaking here of the sort of person he was after his conversion. For before his conversion that conflict did not exist since an ungodly person [impius] does not will from the heart what the law admonishes."[14]

One is naturally drawn to concur with what Luther is doing here. A few sentences after the last words quoted from him, he moves directly into a reassertion of his characteristic claim, made familiar in the formula simul iustus ac peccator: "The saints in being righteous are at the same time sinners."[15] Faced with a "Christianized" society in which every citizen was also a baptized Christian, Luther was insisting with that formula that Christian perfection was not to be claimed as a quality of the self in this life, but belongs to it only by imputation in the gospel's promise of God's forgiveness. As Wilckens has pointed out, Luther was taking the experience of confession, the starting point of Christian conversion, out of daily monastic practice and making it the permanent center of personal piety.[16] The religious application of Luther's exegesis is explicit and unmistakable: "Indeed, it is a great consolation to us to learn that such a great apostle was involved in the same grievings and afflictions in which we find ourselves when we wish to be obedient to God!"[17] Nevertheless, from these last words one may begin to suspect that the pastoral end has captured and distorted the exegetical means. The suspicion hardens into certainty when one notes how Paul's anguished cry in v. 24a is turned into an expression of "perfect spiritualness." If Augustine's exegesis here constitutes a celebrated volte-face, Luther's is a no less notable tour de force. It does not just water down Paul's language (as do all attempts to make the words of v. 14b, "I am sold under sin," apply to life in Christ). It turns Paul's text on its head and makes it mean its own opposite. The disparity between text and interpretation is painfully manifest as well in the "judgment" or axiom (*sententia*) of Augustine to which Luther appeals: "The will to be righteous is a large part of righteousness." Not only is there no basis for such a claim in Romans 7, but also it is altogether un-Pauline and irreconcilable with Paul's argument in chap. 2 (especially vv. 3, 6, 13, 22, 25-27).

What shall one make of this disparity? Is this a case in which, to paraphrase what Wilckens says about Augustine, Luther has the substance ("Sache") of Paul's theology in his favor, even though he has Paul's text against him?[18] Is the meaning of Paul's passage to be accessible only at the price of doing such violence to the integrity of the text?

When one looks more closely at these sentences from Luther and Melanchthon, one discovers something else. In v. 14, Paul uses the contrasting terms *pneumatikos* ("spiritual") and *sarkinos* ("fleshly, consisting of flesh" or "belonging to the realm of the flesh") to mark the gulf between *God's* law and the *human* self confronted by it. These adjectives are not used again in this section, although *sarx* ("flesh") reappears by itself in v. 18 and in contrast to *nous* ("mind") in v. 25b. But under the influence of Augustine's language, these adjectives have been deflected from Paul's usage and their new meanings have come to dominate the exegesis. They are now made to differentiate two classes of *humans*: the religious person who is righteous, wise, understanding, re-born, perfect in self-knowledge and humility, on the one hand and the irreligious, the ungodly, and the sinner on the other, who is utterly devoid of genuine religious impulse. This is the language of binary opposites, used by triumphalist religion to separate humankind into two groups of people, the saved and the damned. This language has been perpetuated in Protestant commentaries with such generic terms as *regenerate* and *unregenerate*. Such language must have had a certain appeal in the sixteenth century to distinguish the "godly" denizens of

Europe from the non-Christian infidels pounding on the eastern gates of Constantinople. So it is not at all surprising that the Reformers, wishing to deflate such natural religious pretension in the apostle's name, should jump to the conclusion that Paul must be describing the tension proper to Christian existence in 7:7-25. He does speak of continuing conflict between flesh and Spirit "in the breast of Christians," to use Moses Stuart's words, most explicitly in the next chapter, in 8:5-8 (compare Gal 5:16-18). So well-intentioned commentators have continued, with the Reformers, to think that it is the part of true Christian humility and self-knowledge to find that conflict to be "the present design and argument of the apostle,"[19] even though there is not a syllable in Romans 7:7-25 about life in Christ, and even though Paul himself has signaled to his reader in both 7:6*b* and 8:1-2 that the rest of chap. 7 is to be understood as the antithesis to chap. 8 and not in simple continuity with it.[20]

The flaw lies in the binary language that has been imposed on Paul's text. The "I" of Romans 7 must be either a "godly" or an "ungodly" person; there is no third possibility. That this reading coerces a false alternative on the text is betrayed by the harsh anachronism that results. It leaves no room for the historical Paul or his kind, the deeply religious Jew devoted to the God of Abraham and Moses. There are complex historical reasons, no doubt, why no living Jew sat in that empty chair at the Reformers' exegetical table. But whatever the reason, this absence permitted the deeper misunderstanding. Like the perfectionist piety that produced it, this binary mode of thinking dismisses with scarcely disguised contempt the religious seriousness of any person outside its own group. Melanchthon's comment is particularly revealing: "An ungodly person [anyone prior to Christian conversion] does not will from the heart what the law admonishes." Its modern counterpart is Cranfield's comment: "A struggle as serious as that which is here described can only take place where the Spirit of God is present and active."[21] The clear assumption here is that the Spirit of God is not at work anywhere outside of the Christian church—even though Paul himself has just stated in unequivocal terms that the (Mosaic!) law is "spiritual"—and so the inference is drawn with Luther and Melanchthon that the "I" of Romans 7 can only refer to the Christian.

But this refusal to take seriously any religious vitality other than Christian, even the apostle's Jewish past, this inability to concede any consequence or substance to a religious existence other than one's own, which breeds that pernicious binary language and feeds on it, has bedeviled the discussion of Romans 7 even among those commentators who have concluded that this section of the letter is to be sharply distinguished from chap. 8 and is Paul's negative description of life under the Mosaic law. They, too, perceive that Paul is saying some positive things about the "inmost self" and the "mind." If Paul is referring here to the unredeemed, one is confronted with what Käsemann identifies as the central hermeneutical quandary of Romans 7: "How can the predicates and capacities of the *redeemed* person be ascribed to the *unredeemed?*"[22] What follows is one of the more opaque sections of Käsemann's magisterial commentary. He simply puts the problem in different words when he asks how it happens that "in some sense the Christian situation of Gal 5:16ff. is here transferred to pre-Christian existence."[23] No reason is given; instead Käsemann insists that the force of Paul's words "sold under sin" must not be compromised by finding something good said about the human will in these verses.[24] Only Wilckens, who singles out Käsemann's formulation of the quandary for quotation and comment, seems to have broken through the tyranny of that false dichotomy. All those positive things said about the "I" in Romans 7 can be taken at their face value because they actually redound to the glory of the *law* and not to the praise of the human self.[25] With that we reach a new stage in our reflections on Romans 7, to which we must return in a moment.

But before we take up the implications of this last move, another observation is needed to conclude the present line of thought. These binary categorizations of religious human beings existed, of course, in Paul's day as well; they were not invented by Luther or by Augustine or by other Christians. Indeed, the depth to which any reading of Paul that clings to such a division between the "godly" and the "ungodly" has misunderstood the apostle is sounded accurately only when one realizes that the whole of Paul's epistle is but a single massive argument against the conventional uses of this distinction. In his own religious tradition the division was between Jew and non-Jew.[26] Paul never erases this historical or cultural distinction completely, but the whole first part of Romans is aimed at showing it to be a distinction without a difference and without consequence. When it comes to accountability before God, possession of the law, around which all the prerogatives of the Jew in 2:17-20 revolve, or non-possession, which defines the Gentile as Gentile (so twice in one verse, 2:14), makes no difference, as circumcision or its absence do not (2:25-29), for there is no favoritism with God (2:11).[27] All have fallen short of God's glory (3:23). Since a right relationship to God cannot be brought about by the fulfilling of any conditions from the side of human beings, or by anything men or women have done or not done (4:4-5; 9:11, 16), but only by God's free and undeserved gift (3:24), the new terms on which God's power to save operates are that both Jew and non-Jew, "the Jew first but also the Greek," relate to God in trust, for only these terms put Jew and Greek on the same footing before God

(1:16, the statement of the theme of Romans). The central creed of Judaism, the acknowledgment that God is one, requires that one abandon the notion that God is the patron of one constituency against another (3:27-30). The definition of God's election as his calling of those who were not his people to be "my people" applies equally to both Jew and non-Jew (9:24-26); the cultivated branch and the wild branch belong to God's olive tree on the same terms (11:20-24). Abraham provides the inclusive patriarchal precedent for the way in which God deals with all human beings and the model for the way in which all human beings rightly relate to God—by trusting in what God has promised. God has not changed. In Christ God has done what Abraham trusted God to do: to give life where from a human point of view the only prospect is death (4:11b-12, 19-22). Nowhere in this argument does Paul draw a distinction between Jew and non-Jew that is not aimed at showing that there is no privilege before God on the one side or the other. Nowhere in Romans does Paul draw a distinction between an authentic Jew (2:28-29) and an authentic Christian (4:18-25; 9:24; 15:7-13). "The same God is Lord of all rich and generous to all who call upon him" (10:12). Nowhere does Paul draw a line through himself, to distinguish the authentic Jew from the non-Jewish Christian in his own person, or through God, to distinguish a God of the one from a God of the other (11:1-5). What Paul has found in Christ is not an alternative God to the God of Abraham and Moses, but God's own gift to restore integrity to obedience to the God of Abraham and Moses.

The problem with human religion rests not with the "ungodly" but with those who separate themselves as the "godly" and in that way seek to establish "a righteousness of their own" (10:3). These "do not submit to God's righteousness," which, since its terms are trust in God, puts all on the same footing. Not a failure to keep and obey the law, but the attempt by those who do keep it and think to have every right to condemn others as "ungodly" to escape their own accountability to God, is what "stores up wrath on the day of wrath when God's righteous judgment will be revealed" (2:3-5). The conclusive demonstration of the power of sin over all, not just the "ungodly" but most especially the "godly" as well, is its power to destroy that inner integrity of trust, to make every genuinely religious person deny that all stand on the same footing before the same God and in that way to blaspheme God's good name. To the extent that Christians for 1,900 years have continued to divide up the world into the "godly" (themselves) and the "ungodly," they have merely remained caught within the very problem that Paul diagnoses in his own religious tradition. Its only remedy is a fresh disclosure of God's righteousness as the undeserved vindication of the unrighteous. Only this eliminates the self-defensiveness Paul calls "enmity" toward God, and by the power of the life-giving Spirit sets men and women on the way to an obedience that the law itself has remained powerless to produce (8:1-11).[28]

IV

We come back to that difficult question of "the present design and argument of the apostle" in Romans 7. If the history of exegesis has imposed on Paul's argument the not uncommon pattern of conventional human religion to separate the "godly" from the "ungodly," what would an interpretation look like that takes its cue from Paul himself and eschews this elitism? Would it provide some relief from the quandaries and anachronisms sketched above? It will be the aim of this final section to explore this possibility.

Due to limitations of space, certain preliminary observations can be noted only briefly. First, the subtleties and complexities of Paul's argument in chaps. 5–8 have rightly led most commentators to abandon as overly simple the thematic proposal that Paul describes the Christian life as freedom from a series of powers: in sequence, freedom from wrath (chap. 5), from sin (chap. 6), from the law (chap. 7), and from death (chap. 8).[29] Instead, the argument advances by cues that it has itself generated, as points require clarification, as potential misunderstandings need to be deflected, and as objections are anticipated. While these movements and turns sometimes have the form of "digressions," they are indispensable stages in the argument, for which rhetorical questions are often the major literary markers.[30]

Second, I take Rom 6:1–7:6 to be one of these larger units, so that 7:1-6 belongs with the preceding more closely than with 7:7-25. The question of 6:1 ("Are we to continue in sin in order that grace might increase?") arose inevitably out of Paul's previous description of the lavish generosity of God's gift in Christ, which the "intruding" law showed to be as undeserved and gracious as it showed the death that otherwise has come upon all since Adam to be deserved and due. Whereas in chap. 5 justification as God's restoration of integrity and righteousness to human life is presented as "a matter of grace" (compare 4:16), 6:1–7:6 reverses the argument to show that God's grace involves a new righteousness and integrity that alter life's previous patterns. Employing the polarities of sin and grace, death and life, and disobedience and obedience that were set up by contrasting Adam and Christ in chap. 5, three separate trains of thought turn aside that essentially libertinistic deduction to answer the question "Why not sin?" (1) An irrevocable death (Christ's) has taken place, in which the destiny of all for whom he died is reshaped. It follows that justification involves a new life of righteousness because it is a death to sin (6:1-14). (2)

Justification is a change of controlling allegiance; it sets one free from sin only insofar as it makes one an obedient "slave" to God (6:15-23). (3) Both these aspects of justification are illustrated by an example from the general area of human social law: While living with another man before her husband's death brings upon a married woman the damning epithet of an adulteress, exactly the same action after her husband's death has no such result, and she is free to enter the new relationship. The marriage legislation is not abrogated, but a death has broken its power to condemn (the point resumed in 8:1). Just so, by the death of Christ all those for whom he died have been "vacated" from that power of the law, and a new allegiance and a new productive life have been legitimated for them (7:1-6).

This illustration from everyday legal experience provides one of Paul's most striking definitions of justification, explaining both how a person is put into a completely new situation by the death of another party (Christ) and how that change carries with it new social and moral obligations. It is the quintessential Pauline refutation of all the antinomian constructions that have been laid upon him from his own lifetime (3:8) until now.

Yet, the choice of this very example creates a grave difficulty. While it does not start out as a specific allusion to Mosaic law, its application pertains unmistakably to release from the condemning power that Paul's previous argument has consistently assigned to the Mosaic law, which impartially silences every human attempt to evade God's indictment, imparts to human conduct the dimension of transgression against God, and so discloses the presence and power of sin (3:19-20; 4:15; 5:13, 20). The flow of the argument has progressively confused the roles of the law and the sin it condemns and discloses, so that "dying to sin" in 6:10 has become "being put to death to the law" in Paul's little tableau (7:4), and "being set free from sin" in 6:18 has become a "being vacated from the law" (7:6). The confusion is complete in 7:6a. The grammatical antecedent of the relative clause *en hō kateichometha* ("what bound us" NAB) is the law. Ironically, an illustration initially intended to rebut an antinomian argument has suddenly become itself susceptible to an antinomian interpretation, as if God's law and the demonic power of sin are to be identified.[31]

From that result, Paul "draws back with a kind of horror,"[32] and it is to ward off such a misunderstanding that Romans 7:7-12 is written. Verse 12 is Paul's Q.E.D.: the Mosaic law is not demonic and not to be confused with sin, nor is it responsible for producing sin.[33] This demonstration, however, is not carried out by directly defending the goodness of the law but by giving an account of how it has been used by sin. The focus is on the other side of the mistaken confusion: the central protagonist in the whole of 7:7-25—not just in vv. 7-12—the adversary of that "I," is not the law at all but sin as a personified power.[34] Once this is seen, it becomes clear that 7:7-25 advances the main argument of Romans in a variety of ways. In addition to the manifest intention of answering the question in v. 7 and warding off a misunderstanding of the law, this unit forms the first part of an exposition of the contrasts between past and present with which Paul in vv. 5-6 has brought the whole preceding section (6:1–7:6) to its climax. The obsolete quality of life in "what bound us" is depicted and analyzed in 7:7-25 in preparation for the discussion of the eschatological quality of life in 8:1-11.[35] Paul calls the one "letter" and the other "Spirit." This contrasting word-pair has been used earlier in 2:29 to distinguish spurious religious identity from authentic (beginning with the Jew), and its introduction here signals another level of Paul's argument. Chapter 8 forms the second part of the exposition and returns to the theme of what God has done for the restoration of human life by means of the life-giving Spirit; 7:7-25 prepares for that by showing what the law, despite its being God's own holy and good commandment, has not been able to do (8:3), because sin's use of it has produced death instead of life.

Clearly 7:7-25 proceeds in two movements, the first being vv. 7-12. Here the greatest difficulty has been caused by Paul's use of the first person verbs in past tenses, particularly in vv. 8b-9. When was Paul, or anyone else, "once alive apart from law," and when did the commandment "come"? It is useless to look for some point in Paul's own lifetime, so increasingly commentators find in these verses allusion to the story of the Fall in Genesis 3, even though the "commandment" Paul has in mind here is patently the Decalogue (v. 7d).[36] Most of the difficulties disappear if one notices that Paul is resuming with dramatic juxtaposition and reversal the motifs of death and life in their association with sin already used in 5:12-14. That explains the "epic" use of past tenses here. "In the absence of law" (*chōris nomou*, vv. 8b, 9) picks up 5:13; the "entry" (*elthein*, v. 9) of the commandment repeats 5:20, presupposed already by the mention of Moses in 5:14, and thus fits naturally with Paul's quotation from the Decalogue. At the same time, one need not deny the presence of such an echo of the Fall narrative as the "deceived" of v. 11. But clearly the allusion is to the Mosaic Torah, which, as the example of the prohibition of covetousness shows, is not only powerless to prevent what it prohibits but in fact produces the very thing it is supposed to prevent. The climax and center of the whole paragraph is provided in vv. 10b-11: "The very commandment that was supposed to lead to life turned out for me to lead to death; for sin, by taking advantage of me through that commandment, tricked me and by using it killed me."

The point of these verses and this section is entirely lost if one understands Paul to be talking only about the "ungodly" Jew who "does not will from the heart what the law admonishes" (Melanchthon), or if one takes the point to be the effect of the *law*.[37] The clear meaning of these sentences is that the effect of *sin* on the genuinely religious person who looks to God's Torah for life has been to produce exactly its opposite, death. This is not because the law has not been obeyed or because there is something demonic about the law. It is not because looking to God's Torah for life is somehow a lower order of human religion. The transcendentally (*kath' hyperbolēn*, v. 13) demonic nature of sin is its power to pervert the highest and best in *all* human piety, typified by the best in Paul's world, his own commitment to God's holy commandment, in such a way as to produce death in place of the promised life.

What these much disputed verses bring to expression is not despair over one's inability to live up to a demanding requirement—such as Luther's experience in the monastery at Erfurt—nor is it the pain of discovering that one has oriented one's life around a lesser surrogate in place of God as one's highest good, which Augustine repeatedly describes in his *Confessions*. It is the realization that one has been deceived by a much more sinister power, capable of making the *best* and the most genuine devotion to the one true God produce, as in the case of God's own commandment in the Decalogue, the very thing it is supposed to vanquish. There is no contradiction between these verses and Paul's claim in Phil 3:6 that the life he came to count as "loss" was "as to righteousness under the law blameless."[38]

Such a reading of 7:7-12 puts us in a position to take a fresh look at the second movement in the rest of the chapter. The transitional v. 13 does two things. In emphatically repeating first the question of v. 7 and then the substance of the answer in v. 11, but adding two purpose clauses, it makes clear that even when it has been used by sin, the law has remained God's and has continued to serve the divine purpose of disclosing and intensifying sin, attributed to it earlier in the letter. In this way v. 13 rounds out what precedes. At the same time, it begins to shift categories in such a manner as to open up a new level of discussion in the next section. In very much the same way, a change of terms from "life" and "death" to "freedom" and "slavery" marked the break in chap. 6 from vv. 1-11 to vv. 15-23, while vv. 12-14 modulated the transition with language about obedience. This time there is a change from the words for "life" and "death" (both nouns and verbs) that have colored the imagery in 7:8-11 to the vocabulary of "good" and "evil," signaled by the fact that in v. 13 "the good" replaces the law. Of course, this is because Paul has just called the law itself "good." But there is more involved. In a brilliant exegetical observation, Bultmann noticed that "the good" in this new section is equivalent to "life" in the preceding verses.[39] "The object of 'willing' is not the fulfilling of the 'commandments,' but 'life' (zoē). What is really willed in all our doing is 'life,' but what comes out of all our doing is 'death' (thanatos)."[40] "Good" and "evil," then, are not labels for conventional moral values that Paul simply takes for granted. They are "the two eschatological possibilities" of "life" and "death."[41] As a result, "that which is good" (v. 13) is not simply the law itself, but *the good* that the law holds out "to me" (twice in v. 13) in its promise of life, exactly as in v. 10.

This is confirmed by the contrasting verbs that increasingly carry the argument in this next section. They are still in the first person singular of Paul's paradigmatic style, but they shift to the present tense as he describes the self's encounter with the power of sin, the perennial human quandary that is the consequence of that "epic" event of sin's "entry." Since the opposite of "to will" is now "to hate," it is clear that the verbs, too, are not to be understood in any narrowly volitional sense. The "common Greek meaning"[42] of *thelein* is "to prefer, to want, to desire," and this is retained in the LXX where it often translates *hāpēsh* "to delight in" (echoed in Paul's *synēdomai* in v. 22). In v. 15 "the good" becomes "what I want" and in v. 19 "the good that I desire." Its opposite in v. 15 is "what I hate" and in v. 19 "the evil that I do not want." In short, the verbs help to circumscribe "the good" as that which every genuinely religious person longs for. The appeal and attraction and promise of the law, especially since it is God's own instruction, is that it will lead to the life that human beings want and desire more than anything else. When Paul says that he "delights" in God's law in v. 22, he is giving clear expression to the devotion to this law that echoes throughout the Hebrew Psalter (see Ps 1:2; 119:16). In it the desire to find life and the desire to live by the good that God commands are fully merged, and that desire is the greater the more any religious person realizes that "the good" that amounts to life in this ultimate sense is not available in one's human resources taken by themselves (which is the meaning "my flesh" in v. 18). There is nothing at all in this paragraph to suggest that this longing and desire, exemplified at its highest in the Jewish allegiance to Torah in which Paul was raised from infancy, is either illegitimate or misplaced.[43]

But now something has happened to contradict this expectation. "What a person wants is salvation. What he creates is disaster."[44] What it means to this person to be "sold under sin" is manifested in the discovery that what one in fact "produces" by one's actions is not recognizable, because it is exactly the opposite of what was intended, just what one hoped to avoid in one's reliance on the law (v. 15); *katergazesthai* ("to bring about, or achieve") has the same meaning throughout vv. 15-20 that it has in v. 13. It is clear that the fault does not lie in the law. Instead, the self, no longer the agent of its own actions, is controlled by the alien power of sin (vv. 16-17). The thought in these verses is exactly the same as in vv. 10b-11, only now it is not the Mosaic Torah but the religious self devoted to it that is powerless to achieve what it longs for, that in fact produces the very thing that it is supposed to avoid. The early chapters of Romans have already unfolded this unexpected power of sin to reverse and subvert the integrity of the relationship all religious persons have to God, both Jews and Greeks (3:9), especially those who know God's commands and judgments (1:31; 2:2) but use that knowledge to exempt themselves from accountability and to deny that all stand on the same footing before God, and so abuse God's goodness and blaspheme God's name (2:4-5, 17-24).

Commentators have made many quite different proposals for understanding the structure of vv. 13-25 in detail. Most suggestions fail in plausibility because they are wedded to prior decisions regarding the subject matter of this section, especially to the effect that Paul is primarily concerned with the malevolent power of the law rather than that of sin, or that he is describing a divided self. Again it was Bultmann who clearly saw that the seemingly impressive parallels to Paul's language that can be found in Greek and Latin literature really have little to do with the purpose his words serve in the present argument.[45] Paul is not talking about the conflict between the rational and the irrational in the human self, nor about two selves at different levels, as though one were under the power of sin and the other not. Both "inmost self" (v. 22) and "members" (v. 23) are but two aspects of the same self that is "sold under sin." The symptom of this enslavement is not simple frustration of good intent, but good intention carried out and then surprised and dumbfounded by the evil it has produced, not despair but the same disillusionment so clearly described in v. 10: What should have effected life has produced death!

Close scrutiny of Paul's verses shows a striking progression that confirms this interpretation.[46] The leading clue is provided by the quite complete and precise parallelism between vv. 15-17 and vv. 18-20, running twice through the same sequence of ideas.[47] Each series begins with an essentially negative proposition introduced with the phrase "We/I know": vv. 14-15a ("I don't recognize what I am bringing about, the results of my own actions") and v. 18 ("To desire the good is within my capacity but I cannot bring it about"). In the second place, this is followed each time by a short description of the experience behind this proposition, in almost identical language ("For I do not do what I intend, desire or prefer, but do the very thing I do not want or wish to

14 Οἴδαμεν γὰρ ὅτι ὁ νόμος πνευματικός ἐστιν,
   ἐγὼ δὲ σαρκινός εἰμι πεπραμένος ὑπὸ τὴν ἁμαρτίαν.

15 ὃ γὰρ κατεργάζομαι οὐ γινώσκω.

   οὐ γὰρ ὃ θέλω τοῦτο πράσσω,
   ἀλλ' ὃ μισῶ τοῦτο ποιῶ.

16 εἰ δὲ ὃ οὐ θέλω τοῦτο ποιῶ,
   σύμφημι τῷ νόμῳ ὅτι καλός.

17 νυνὶ δὲ οὐκέτι ἐγὼ κατεργάζομαι αὐτὸ
   ἀλλὰ ἡ οἰκοῦσα ἐν ἐμοὶ ἁμαρτία.

18 Οἶδα γὰρ ὅτι οὐκ οἰκεῖ ἐν ἐμοί,
   τοῦτ' ἔστιν ἐν τῇ σαρκί μου, ἀγαθόν.

   τὸ γὰρ θέλειν παράκειταί μοι,
   τὸ δὲ κατεργάζεσθαι τὸ καλὸν οὔ.

19 οὐ γὰρ ὃ θέλω ποιῶ ἀγαθόν
   ἀλλὰ ὃ οὐ θέλω κακὸν τοῦτο πράσσω.

20 εἰ δὲ ὃ οὐ θέλω (ἐγὼ) τοῦτο ποιῶ,

   οὐκέτι ἐγὼ κατεργάζομαι αὐτὸ
   ἀλλὰ ἡ οἰκοῦσα ἐν ἐμοὶ ἁμαρτία.

21 εὑρίσκω ἄρα τὸν νόμον,
   τῷ θέλοντι ἐμοὶ ποιεῖν τὸ καλόν,
   ὅτι ἐμοὶ τὸ κακὸν παράκειται

22 συνήδομαι γὰρ τῷ νόμῳ τοῦ θεοῦ
   κατὰ τὸν ἔσω ἄνθρωπον,

23 βλέπω δὲ ἕτερον νόμον
   ἐν τοῖς μέλεσίν μου
   ἀντιστρατευόμενον τῷ νόμῳ τοῦ νοός μου
   καὶ αἰχμαλωτίζοντά με
   ἐν τῷ νόμῳ τῆς ἁμαρτίας
   τῷ ὄντι ἐν τοῖς μέλεσίν μου.

24 Ταλαίπωρος ἐγὼ ἄνθρωπος.
   τίς με ῥύσεται ἐκ τοῦ σώματος τοῦ θανάτου τούτου;

25 χάρις δὲ τῷ θεῷ διὰ Ἰησοῦ Χριστοῦ
   τοῦ κυρίου ἡμῶν.

   Ἄρα οὖν αὐτὸς ἐγὼ

   τῷ μὲν νοῒ δουλεύω νόμῳ θεοῦ

   τῇ δὲ σαρκὶ νόμῳ ἁμαρτίας.

avoid," vv. 15*b*, 19).[48] In the third place, now in even more striking repetition of linguistic detail, each sequence draws the same conclusion: "If this is my experience, it follows that I am no longer the one producing this result but rather the sin that dwells in me" (vv. 16-17, 20). By their repetition these conclusions forcefully declare what it means to be "fleshly, sold under sin." The parallelism is clearly visible if the two sequences are written out in Greek beside each other in parallel columns [see Chart A]. When this is done, two more features become at once apparent: (a) The opening proposition for the second sequence (v. 18) rephrases that of the first (vv. 14-15*a*) in language colored by the intervening verses; and (b) the detail that distinguishes the second sequence and marks its advance over the first is the addition of those "eschatological" categories "good" and "evil" in vv. 18 and 19, expanding the incidental remark in v. 16*b* about the law's being itself "good." This new ingredient continues into v. 21 and provides a bridge to the concluding verses of the chapter.

This conclusion comes in vv. 21-23. The last time the law seriously entered Paul's argument was v. 12, his emphatic repudiation of the suggested identification of the law with sin in v. 7*b*. The place of the law was taken in v. 13 by "the good" (which, incidentally, Paul equates with God's will in 12:2). A brief reminder of 7:12 reappears in v. 14, but it functions only as the foil for its opposite, "I am fleshly, sold under sin," which it has been the main burden of vv. 15-20 to elaborate. There is also a parenthetical remark about the law's goodness in v. 16*b*, but the parallel in v. 20 shows that it can be dropped without loss to the argument—it only anticipates v. 22—and that the real purpose of the conditional clause in v. 16*a* is to serve as a protasis to v. 17. But now that thematic undercurrent of the law bursts to the surface and dominates the discussion in the form of *two* diametrically opposed laws: (a) *ho nomos tou theou* ("the law of God"), vv. 22 and 25*b*, which is also "the law of the mind"—that is, the law I intend to serve, in v. 23; and (b) *heteros nomos* ("a *different* law," not just another law), which is also *ho nomos tēs hamartias* ("the law of sin") "which is in my members," vv. 23 and 25*b*. Verse 22 confesses allegiance and delight in the first. Verse 23 reports the discovery of the second. The contrast could scarcely be sharper. In sum, 7:13-25 culminates with a "cleavage," but it is in the *law* and not in the self.

Attention to this movement toward an antithetical climax helps to solve two perennial difficulties in the exegesis of these verses. One is v. 21, in which commentators struggle both with the meaning of *ho nomos* ("the law") and with the syntax. It strains credulity to read Paul's definite noun in this context as "a law" (RSV) in the sense of a perceived regularity of experience. Serious lexicographical difficulties stand in the way of this translation as well, despite its natural sound in English. It must, instead, refer to the same law that is called a "different" law, or "the law of sin" in v. 23.[49] But what law is that? The polarized duality of "laws" at the end of chap. 7 provides the bridge to chap. 8, and this "different law" must be the same as "the law of sin and death" in 8:2. But the transitional verses in 8:1-2 also serve as a parenthesis with 7:6b to enclose the whole of our passage. The phrase "the law of sin and death" in 8:2 can only be intended as a shorthand summary of the whole point of 7:7-25: It is the *law* that has been used by *sin* to produce *death*. But that means that not only the "law of God" (v. 22) but also this "different law" (v. 23) is the Mosaic law! We return to this in a moment.

In the meantime, the problem of the syntax of v. 21 is now also eased. The dative participle and its infinitive have been advanced for emphasis, but they belong syntactically to the *hoti*-clause that is the direct object of *heuriskō*.[50] To take *ton nomon* as an adverbial accusative of respect is not nearly as harsh as is commonly argued if one realizes that the present active *heuriskō* has simply taken the place of the deponential aorist *heurethē* of v. 10,[51] to fit the altered context and its present tenses, but without significant change of meaning. Just as Paul said there, "the law that was supposed to lead to life has turned out for me to lead to death," so also he now opens this final section of chap. 7 by writing, "So then, as far as the (Mosaic) law is concerned, the outcome [of the above experience] is that for me, the very one who wishes to do the good, evil is what I find at hand" (v. 21). He goes on:

> I delight in the law of God. . . but what I see is a quite different law, operative in my members [that aspect of my self that ought to be at God's disposal, 6:13]; it is in conflict with that law of God that I adhere to in my intentions, and keeps me imprisoned to the law that controls me and that is used by sin." (vv. 22-23)

The other celebrated crux of chap. 7 is v. 25b, which has created difficulty both by its position, which has seemed to interrupt or even reverse the natural and logical movement of thought from v. 25a to chap. 8, and by its content, which has seemed to betray an anthropological dualism uncharacteristic of Paul and out of place in this chapter.[52] Here, too, the difficulty disappears once one observes that the load-bearing words in v. 25b are not "mind" and "flesh," even though these have the article, but rather the contrasting datives at the end of each clause, "*God's* law" and "*sin's* law."[53] The verse not only fits the context but also confirms our reading of it. As a summary, it tightens the link with 8:1-4. The same contrast between God and sin reappears in the subject and direct object of 8:3.

The translation of vv. 21-23 we thus arrive at makes "the present design and argument of the apostle" plain. The experience of the demonic power of sin to use the Mosaic law to effect just the opposite of what its devoted adherents expect, even and especially when it is obeyed, manifests not only the sinister nature of sin itself (v. 13) but also how profoundly the religious self is "sold" under it and indeed possessed by it (vv. 14-20). God's own good law takes on a quality and character opposite to that which a person knows to be true, so that the religious self is put in the wretched position of serving sin in its very service of God. Two thousand years of Christian history have shown that in the presence of this power there is no distinction between the "godly" and the "ungodly." As the Latin maxim puts it, *corruptio optimi pessima*, "the worst evil consists in the corruption of the highest good." That is not depicted here simply as a private experience from Paul's Jewish past. It is all part of Paul's explanation of why God sent God's own Son, on behalf of all, to deal with sin as the law could not (8:3-4). In the end, as Lou Martyn has also argued, the guiding theme of Paul's theology is not the law but Christ.[54] A more adequate penetration of Paul's diagnosis of the condition under which all human religion suffers may lead to a more profound understanding of his gospel.

Notes

1. M. Stuart, *A Commentary on the Epistle to the Romans* (3rd ed.; London: Thomas Tegg, 1836) 610.
2. Bultmann's classic essay on the problem touched on here, "Is Exegesis Without Presuppositions Possible?" in *Existence and Faith: Shorter Writings of Rudolf Bultmann* (New York: Meridian Books, 1960) 289-96, starts from this need to respect "what the text actually says"; "exegesis must be without prejudice" (289). In her presidential address to the Society of Biblical Literature ("The Ethics of Biblical Interpretation: Decentering Biblical Scholarship," *JBL* 107 [1988] 3-17), E. Schüssler-Fiorenza probes the issue raised here and advocates the adoption of a "critical theory of rhetoric" for which "context is as important as text" (5). Unfortunately, despite a wealth of insight on the responsibilities of biblical interpreters, she does not give any guidance on the most pressing hermeneutical issue of our day: By what criteria can one determine where responsible attention to context ends and ideological manipulation of a text begins?
3. Of the seven reasons for the attention devoted to Romans 7 listed by W. G. Kümmel in his influential monograph *Römer 7 und die Bekehrung des Paulus* (Leipzig: Hinrichs, 1929; reproduced with unchanged pagination in *Römer 7 und das Bild des Menschen im Neuen Testament* [Munich: Kaiser, 1974] 1), this is the first.
4. The various suggestions are surveyed in Kümmel, *Römer 7*, 74-132, and C. E. B. Cranfield, *A Critical and Exegetical Commentary on the Epistle to the Romans* (ICC; 2 vols.; Edinburgh: T. & T. Clark, 1975-79) 1.342-46.
5. BDF § 281. Kümmel adds many examples (*Römer 7*, 126-32), but his list was drawn up before the discovery of the manuscripts at Qumran (see also n. 7).
6. When Käsemann, *Commentary on Romans* (Grand Rapids: Eerdmans, 1980) 192, pronounces that an autobiographical reminiscence in the "I" "is refuted by Phil 3:6," he must not have the first-person language as such in mind, which is patently autobiographical and supports such a self-reference in vv. 8-14, but the putative

contradiction in the content of what is said about this "I" in Romans 7 and Phil 3:6. This is another issue to which we must return.

7. See the more recent discussion in U. Wilckens, *Der Brief an die Römer* (EKKNT; 3 vols.; Neukirchen-Vluyn: Neukirchener, 1978-1982) 2.76-78, and G. Theissen, *Psychological Aspects of Pauline Theology* (Philadelphia: Fortress, 1987) 190-201. Theissen has a particularly instructive treatment of "The 'I' in Romans 7."

8. Augustine, *Retractations* 2.1.1, in *Augustine: Earlier Writings* (LCC; Philadelphia: Westminster, 1953) 370. Fuller documentation of Augustine's different views is given by Kümmel, *Römer 7*, 90-94.

9. For the patristic exegesis, see the bibliography in Kümmel, *Römer 7*, 75 n. 1, and more recently K. H. Schelkle, *Paulus: Lehrer der Väter* (Düsseldorf: Patmos, 1956) 242-58. The best recent review of the whole history of the exegesis of Rom 7:7-25, with bibliographical notes, is to be found in Wilckens, *Römer*, 2.101-17.

10. The reasons behind Augustine's change are discussed by Kümmel, *Römer 7*, 93-94, and especially Wilckens, *Römer*, 2.105-7. The shift is usually connected with Augustine's conflict with Pelagius and dated in 418-419 CE (Kümmel, 91; Wilckens, 102). Nobody, in this literature at least, seems to have noticed that the later position is already emerging in Augustine's *The Spirit and the Letter*, 26—that is, in 412 CE; this would seem to reinforce the view that the factors behind the shift are more complicated. This subject, and in particular the nature and quality of Augustine's exegesis of Romans in his treatise on *The Spirit and the Letter*, requires further discussion elsewhere.

11. Martin Luther, *Luther: Lectures on Romans* (trans. W. Pauck; LCC; Philadelphia: Westminster, 1961) 201. Luther's Latin words are taken from Martin Luther, *Vorlesung über den Römerbrief 1515/1516* (Latin-German edition; 2 vols.; Darmstadt: Wissenschaftliche Buchgesellschaft, 1960) 2.24, which reproduces the Ficker Latin text. The reference is to Augustine *Ep.* 127, 5.

12. Luther, *Lectures on Romans*, 201-2; *Vorlesung*, 2.24.

13. *Lectures on Romans*, 208; *Vorlesung*, 2.42.

14. Philip Melanchthon, *Römerbrief-Kommentar 1532* (Latin text ed. Rolf Schäfer; vol. 5 of *Melanchthons Werke in Auswahl*; Gütersloh: Mohn, 1965) 224, translation mine. In this context the terms used by Melanchthon to contrast with *impius* are *renati* ("reborn persons") and *sancti* ("saints").

15. *Lectures on Romans*, 208; *Vorlesung*, 2.44 (*simul sancti, dum sunt iusti, sunt peccatores*).

16. Wilckens, *Römer*, 2.109.

17. *Lectures on Romans*, 208.

18. Wilckens, *Römer*, 2.107.

19. See, for example, Cranfield, *Romans*, 1.246-47, who uses the flagrantly ad hominem argument that one should question the moral seriousness of anyone who finds it hard to believe that Paul was describing life in Christ with his words "sold under sin" (v. 14*b*).

20. "Not until we come to ver. 25 is there a single expression used which belongs to Christianity." W. Sanday and A. C. Headlam, *A Critical and Exegetical Commentary on the Epistle to the Romans* (ICC; New York: Scribners, 1986) 186. Dissenting interpretations rely heavily on equating what is taken to be Paul's use of fairly conventional Hellenistic distinctions within the human self (between *ho esō anthrōpos*, "inmost self," and *melē*, "members," in vv. 22-23, and between *nous*, "mind," and *sarx*, "flesh," in v. 25*b*) with his distinction between "spiritual" and "fleshly" in v. 14. Such an interpretation of "inmost self" cannot be supported from 2 Cor 4:16, where the context is entirely different; see Wilckens, *Römer*, 2.93-94, and Kümmel, *Römer 7*, 14-15.

21. Cranfield, *Romans*, 1.346.

22. Käsemann, *Romans*, 207, italics added. See also n. 20 above. The quandary produces elaborate—one may even say tortured—discussions of Paul's use of these predicates. Does the "inmost self" refer to the spirit-endowed persons ("pneumatic"), and if so, what kind of relapse into the idealistic motifs of Greek religion does this signal (Käsemann, *Romans*, 206-8)? What sorts of contradictions and inconsistencies is Paul generating with these concessions to the general moral capacities of human nature in view of his more pessimistic assessments elsewhere (Kümmel, *Römer 7*, 134-38)?

23. Käsemann, *Romans*, 208.
24. Ibid.
25. Wilckens, *Römer*, 2.94.
26. For non-Jews, Paul uses the terms *Gentiles* (*ta ethnē*, "the [non-Jewish] nations") and *Greeks*. Sometimes they are simply interchangeable, as in 1 Cor 1:22-24. In his letters the former is always a collective designation (the singular *ethnos* ["nation"] occurs only in an OT quotation in Rom 10:19). The latter is always used for the singular individual, and even in the plural the emphasis seems to be on the members of the group (Rom 3:9; 1 Cor 10:32; 12:13).
27. For further treatment, see Jouette M. Bassler, *Divine Impartiality: Paul and a Theological Axiom* (SBLDS 59; Chico: Scholars, 1982).
28. For a more sequential and comprehensive treatment of the argument of Romans, see my commentary "Romans," in *Harper's Bible Commentary* (ed. James L. Mays; San Francisco: Harper, 1988).
29. A clear example of an exegesis of this type is A. Nygren, *Commentary on Romans* (Philadelphia: Muhlenberg, 1949) 191-349, summarized on 265-67. This summary shows the extent to which this reading of these chapters is shaped by appeal to statements made by Paul in Galatians rather than by attention to the internal movement of the argument in Romans itself.
30. For fuller discussion, see N. A. Dahl, "The Missionary Theology in the Epistle to the Romans," *Studies in Paul* (Minneapolis: Augsburg, 1977) 70-94, esp. 82-83, and the work there referred to by Stanely Stowers, since published as *The Diatribe and Paul's Letter to the Romans* (SBLDS 57; Chico: Scholars, 1981).
31. Many of the difficulties attendant upon the interpretation of Romans 7 arise from a failure to respect the differences between Romans and Galatians and from importing elements from Paul's argument in Galatians into Romans—another form of anachronistic fallacy. The Galatians background makes the developing antinomian entanglement of Paul's exposition here in Rom 7:1-6 plausible and understandable, but his clear and emphatic repudiation of this logical consequence shows how he has changed since Galatians. There the law still seems to play an adversarial, not to say quasi-demonic, role (Gal 3:19, 23; 4:4-5; 5:18). Here that has been more clearly transferred to the personified power of sin that uses God's good law (Rom 7:12-14). That the condemning power of the law is now more firmly subsumed under a consistent theocentrism is apparent from the subtle, but clear, differences between Gal 3:22 and Rom 9:32.
32. J. Knox, "The Epistle to the Romans: Introduction and Exegesis" (*IB* 9; New York: Abingdon Press, 1954) 491.
33. See the excursus in Wilckens, *Römer*, 2.80-81, for a decisive refutation of the notion that in Paul's view the law produces sin because the very desire it awakens, to commit one's efforts to the fulfillment of its precepts, is itself sinful, whether these efforts actually succeed or not. This notion is a particularly harsh anachronism.
34. Two stereotypes about Romans 7 that are particularly hard to uproot are the conventional views that vv. 7-12 constitute an "apology for the law" (questioned by Käsemann, *Romans*, 192) and that in vv. 13-25 "everything focuses on anthropology" (ibid.) and the divided self. O. Michel, *Der Brief an die Römer* (5th ed.; MeyerK; Göttingen: Vandenhoeck & Ruprecht, 1978) 225 n. 7: "What is distinctive about our section [Rom 7:7-25] is its description of the cleavage of the human self" (my translation).
35. Many commentators have noticed that the statements of 7:5-6 are resumed and elaborated in what follows (for example, Dahl, *Studies*, 85). The problem lies in identifying just how that is done. Nygren (*Romans*, 275-76) finds the two complementary "panels" of the Pauline exposition in vv. 7-13 and 14-25 respectively, which lands one right back in the problem presented earlier.
36. For the general trend to appeal to Genesis 3, one may note Käsemann, *Romans*, 196; Wilckens, *Römer*, 2.79; Cranfield, *Romans*, 1.351-52; Theissen, *Psychological Aspects*, 202-11. There is strong evidence in Jewish tradition for taking the commandment of

v. 7d, "Thou shalt not covet," as representative of the whole Decalogue or the law as such (Käsemann, *Romans*, 196; Wilckens, *Römer*, 2.78-79; Michel, *Römer*, 226-27).

37. "[Verses] 7-13 have in view primarily people under the Torah . . . the apostle wants to illustrate the effect of the law concretely by using the example of the recipient of the law and of Jewish piety" (Käsemann, *An die Römer* [Tübingen: Mohr, 1973] 187, my translation; compare ET *Romans*, 197).

38. See n. 6 above. The immense pressure exerted upon the exegesis of Romans 7 by the perception that what Paul writes here cannot be reconciled with Philippians 3 is plain from Kümmel's discussion (*Römer* 7, 111-19; see also Wilckens, *Römer*, 2.76-77 and n. 292; Cranfield, *Romans*, 1.344). The degree to which this perception, in turn, has been kept alive by the influence of the Reformers' exegesis should now be clear. Theissen (*Psychological Aspects*, 234-50) seeks to resolve the putative contradiction by using the distinctions of depth psychology between the conscious and the unconscious, a recourse fraught with difficulties that is simply unnecessary if the conflict does not exist!

39. R. Bultmann, "Romans 7 and the Anthropology of Paul," *Existence and Faith*, 147-57, esp. 154-55. See also his *Theology of the New Testament* (2 vols.; New York: Scribners, 1951–56) 1.248. Bultmann's exegetical insights here have been neglected because they are buried beneath a debatable argument about theological anthropology. They are nevertheless recognized by Käsemann, *Romans*, 202-3, and Wilckens, *Römer*, 2.88, n. 358 (see also 114-15 for a comprehensive assessment of Bultmann's exegesis of Romans 7 in general).

40. Bultmann, "Romans 7," 152.

41. Ibid., 154.

42. *TDNT* 3.44; compare *LSJ* s.v. *ethelō*.)

43. It is at this point that Bultmann's exegesis seems to remain under the spell of that aspect of the Reformation tradition from which we have been proposing we need to free our reading of Romans. Paul's "fundamental reproach," Bultmann writes, is "that the *direction* of this way [of the law] is perverse, and this for the reason that it intends to lead to 'one's own righteousness' (Rom 10:3; Phil 3:9). It is not evil works or transgressions of the law that first make the Jews objectionable to God. Rather the intention to become righteous before him by fulfilling the law is their real sin, which is merely manifested by transgressions" ("Romans 7," 149; translation slightly corrected from the German, "Römer 7 und die Anthropologie des Paulus" [1932], in R. Bultmann, *Exegetica* [Tübingen: Mohr, 1967] 200). By thus leaving no room for an authentic religious motivation from the law for obedient action, Bultmann seems to eliminate the very distinction Paul is making between sin and the law. This is exactly the issue at stake in interpreting Romans 7. Another symptom of the continuing force of this Reformation legacy may be seen in Theissen's elaborate attempt not only to make *hamartia* ("sin") the replacement for *epithymia* ("covetousness") in vv. 7-8, but also to treat *thelein* ("to want") in vv. 15-21 as a functional equivalent to *epithymein* ("to covet") in the commandment of v. 7 (*Psychological Aspects*, 210-11). He can mount such an argument only by importing elements from Galatians and 2 Corinthians (209). But it is already circular. The equivalence is assumed, and when there is no evidence to support it ("Zeal for the law, *which is the nomistic sin*, is *never* interpreted as a manifestation of covetousness," 208, italics added), the very lack of correlation with Genesis 3 is taken to show that Paul is reading his own experience into the role of Adam when he does not find it there.

44. Käsemann, *Romans*, 203.

45. Bultmann, "Romans 7," 148; *Theology*, 1.248. Careful attention to the contexts of these "parallels" confirms his judgment. In Ovid, *Metam.* 7.18-21, one of the most frequently cited passages, the conflict is between reason (*mens*) and desire (*cupido*); in Euripides, *Med.* 1076-80, it is between resolution (*bouleumata*) and passion (*thymos*). See also Plato, *Prot.* 352D; Euripides, *Hipp.* 375-85; Epictetus, *Disc.* 2.26.1-2, 4-5. A recent discussion that collects and presents these texts and some secondary literature on them, even though it comes to entirely different conclusions, is found in Theissen, *Psychological Aspects*, 211-21.

46. Despite strong disagreement with his interpretation, my own observations have been whetted and refined by the "text analysis" in Theissen, *Psychological Aspects*, 186-90; see also 187 n. 11, for reference to other constructions.

47. The phenomenon is not an isolated one in Paul's letters. A close analogue in Romans is the parallelism in chap. 6 between vv. 5-7 and 8-10, pointed out by G. Bornkamm, "Baptism and New Life in Paul," *Early Christian Experience* (New York: Harper, 1969) 71-86, esp. 74-75.

48. If there is any point in these verses where Paul is appropriating conventional or stereotyped phrasing, it is here in the *first* sequence (that is, in v. 15*b*), and it is confined to the ordinary observation of a discrepancy between intention and action, without any moral complications. Of the "parallels" cited above (n. 45), only the wording that Epictetus repeats as a sort of refrain in *Disc.* 2.26.1-2, 4-5 ("he does not do what he wishes"; "he does what he does not wish") is really similar.

49. The decisive lexicographical arguments are noted by Wilckens, *Römer*, 2.89 and n. 371. Even Cranfield (*Romans*, 1.361-62), while he finds all explanations of the term as a reference to the Mosaic law so forced as to be "incredible," recognizes the continuity with the "different law" in v. 23.

50. BDF § 475 (1). See the examples listed by Cranfield in his discussion of 11:31, *Romans*, 2.583-84.

51. BDF § 313.

52. Almost every commentator discusses these problems. The two major solutions are transposition (see James Moffatt, *The Bible: A New Translation* [New York: Harper, 1935]) and excision (see Bultmann, "Glossen im Römerbrief," *Exegetica*, 278-79).

53. The articles with *nous* and *sarx* simply function in place of the possessive pronouns, "with *my* mind." See R. Kühner-B. Gerth, *Ausführliche Grammatik der griechischen Sprache: Satzlehre* (4th ed.; 2 vols.; Leverkusen: Gottschalksche Verlagsbuchhandlung, 1955) 1.555-56, 581. There is no discussion of this common phenomenon in BDF, but see H. W. Smyth, *Greek Grammar* (Cambridge, Mass.: Harvard University Press, 1956) § 1121. On the other hand, the omission of the article with the datives underlines the qualitative nuance provided by the modifying genitives; see BDF § 252.

54. J. L. Martyn, "Paul and His Jewish-Christian Interpreters," *USQR* 42 (1988) 3: "Paul was firmly of the opinion that the nub of the matter was not the issue of the law, but rather christology." Contrast Michel, *Römer*, 239: "An der Gesetzesfrage hängt das Verständnis des ganzen Urchristentums" ("The understanding of the whole of early Christianity hinges on the question of the law").

CHRISTOLOGY, SOTERIOLOGY, AND THE PRAISE OF GOD (ROMANS 15:7-13)*

Leander E. Keck

aul's letters surprise us repeatedly, partly because what has seemed relatively clear often turns out to contain problems that require a solution before the passage can be interpreted convincingly, and partly because pursuing them implicates themes whose construal determines the way the entire letter is understood. Romans 15:7-13 is such a passage. In it Paul puts an intra-mural Christian problem in the context of christology, soteriology, and the praise of God.

We expect this paragraph to be especially important because it concludes the letter's theological/ethical core. Just as 1:16-17 opens the argument and paraenesis, so also 15:7-13 closes it;[1] this core is "framed" by a discussion of Paul's relation to the readers (1:8-15; 15:14-33). There are other "concluding" paragraphs within this core (8:31-39 and 11:33-36 being notable examples); indeed, 15:1-6 is another, as we shall see. However, whereas their horizon is the subject matter that precedes immediately, the horizon of 15:7-13 is nothing short of the entire argument. Moreover, given this paragraph's function as the capstone of the argument/paraenesis, as well as the care with which the entire discussion is crafted, we also expect this paragraph to be free of problems that might inhibit its effectiveness. Yet, on closer examination, we are surprised that everything is not as smooth and clear as we expect.

I

More important than this paragraph's formal function in the structure of the letter is its material role in relation to the letter's occasion

---

*I want to use this occasion to express my profound gratitude for the strong friendship and colleagueship with Professor Martyn, a relationship that has endured for four decades and continues to nourish my own work.

and purpose, on the one hand, and to the question of its literary integrity (and therefore its history), on the other. The two issues are intertwined.

We are surprised, to begin with, by the fact that the content of this paragraph appears to have been anticipated, even in the sequence of theme, by the paragraph that precedes it (15:1-6).

exhortation	vv. 1-2	7
Christ	3a	8-9a
Scripture	3b-4a	9b-12
hope	4b	13
praise of God	6	9-11

Having written vv. 1-6 as the climax of the word to the "weak" and the "strong," why does Paul begin afresh to treat the same themes in vv. 7-13, especially having ended the previous paragraph with a hortatory benediction (vv. 5-6)?[2] Since a transition from v. 6 to v. 14 would have been just as smooth as between v. 13 and v. 14, it can scarcely have been Paul's concern for stylistic felicity that prompted him to add vv. 7-13. Either he had something else in mind to say, suggested by the greater attention paid to Scripture,[3] or someone else is responsible for the juxtaposition of these two paragraphs. In any case, one thing must be emphasized: The relation of these two paragraphs to each other is the same, regardless of who juxtaposed them.

Given the well-known and complex history of the text of Romans, one cannot exclude a priori either of the two ways of holding someone other than Paul responsible for the phenomenon before us—the one that regards vv. 7-13 as an interpolation, as do Pallis and O'Neill,[4] the other that sees the paragraph as part of a genuine Pauline letter placed here by the editor who created the letter we have, as do Schmithals and his predecessors.[5] Despite evidence for interpolation throughout the entire letter,[6] here one should hold Paul himself responsible until there is clear reason to judge otherwise.

Romans 15:7 begins with διὸ προσλαμβάνεσθε ἀλλήλους, which clearly requires of both the "weak" and the "strong" what 14:1, which opens the discussion abruptly, requires only of the latter: τὸν δὲ ἀσθενοῦντα τῇ πίστει προσλαμβάνεσθε. The identity of these two groups continues to be debated because Paul himself does not provide the information we deem essential. Commonly, the "weak" are viewed as scrupulous, law-observant Jewish Christians (at least predominantly) and the "strong" as Gentile, perhaps, Paulinist, believers who are hectoring the former to join them in developing an ethos based on freedom from the law. Given the prominence of the "Jew-Gentile" theme in Romans, this identification may well be correct—so long as one does not impose it rigidly. Still, the remarkable thing is that Paul himself neither states such an identification (strictly speaking the "we who are strong" in 15:1 precludes it), nor argues his exhortation on this basis. What makes our paragraph potentially important for the interpretation of chaps. 14–15 is the fact that here, and only here, does the text speak of Jews and Gentiles. Indeed, apart from the initial and final sentences (vv. 7, 13), the theme of Jew and Gentile dominates the whole paragraph. In other words, the juxtaposition of the Jew-Gentile theme in vv. 8-12 with v. 7, which links the whole paragraph to the preceding discussion of the "weak" and the "strong," warrants the inference that the ἀλλήλομς in v. 7 refers to the Jewish and Gentile Christians. But still, an inference, no matter how valid, is not yet evidence.

The inference, however, is consonant with a coherent interpretation of the whole. Romans 15:1-13 wants the reader to infer that the "weak" (Jewish) Christians will praise God among "strong" Gentile (Christians), and that the latter will join their Jewish fellow-believers in praising God, thereby overcoming the tension between them.[7] But this, too, is an inference, which Zeller calls "a nice idea" but not one stated in the text.[8] The frustrating fact is that apart from the repetition of προσλαμβάνεσθε in v. 7, nothing in our paragraph expressly links it with the foregoing discussion of the "weak" and the "strong."[9] The link is in the mind of the reader, and it is the juxtaposition of themes that suggests it.

If at this point the letter has literary integrity, then it was Paul who brought the discussion of the "weak" and the "strong" to its conclusion by implicitly relating it to the Jew-Gentile theme in the rest of the letter. Then, moreover, 15:1-13 as a whole can be brought into a discussion of the letter's occasion and Paul's purpose in writing. Otherwise, in making the inference the reader is fulfilling the desire of the editor (or interpolator), and then 15:1-6 might still be a clue to the occasion that prompted Paul to write, but 15:7-13 would disclose nothing of either his purpose in doing so or the context in which he placed his admonition. Schmithals sees this clearly. A closer examination of vv. 7-13 is required before that question can be adjudicated properly.

II

Romans 15:7-13 contains four types of material: (a) an exhortation with a soteriological warrant (v. 7); (b) a christological assertion (vv. 8-9a); (c) a fourfold scriptural warrant for the christological assertion (vv. 9b-12); and (d) a hortatory benediction (v. 13).[10] What is surprising is not this diversity but the unexpected rationale, or lack of it, that unites these materials.

Apart from the benediction, which is loosely attached grammatically to the preceding elements by a post-positive δέ (as also in v. 6), each element is linked explicitly to the one that precedes it by a series of terms whose function is to create a coherent flow of thought:

vv. 5-6	hortatory benediction
v. 7a	διό + imperative: προσλαμβάνεσθε
v. 7b	καθώς + soteriological warrant
vv. 8-9a	γάρ + christological warrant
vv. 9b-12	καθώς γέγραπται + scriptural warrant

This formal, grammatical coherence, however, appears to be poorly supported by the material content. (a) To begin with, since the content of the preceding benediction in vv. 5-6 and that of the closely linked imperative in v. 7 concerns the readers' unity (ὁμοθυμαδόν, προσλαμβάνεσθε ἀλλήλους), one expects the supporting warrants to say something like: Christ, too, welcomed diverse persons, and this accords with Scripture, which also speaks of God's welcoming diverse persons. Instead, vv. 7-13 pick up the theme of the benediction's purpose clause, the glorification of God (εἰς δόξαν τοῦ θεοῦ v. 7, δοξάσαι τὸν θεόν v. 9a; and all Scripture quotations paraphrase the theme of glorifying God). Nothing more is said of the attitude of one group to the other, and the focus shifts to Jews and Gentiles. (b) Moreover, the christological warrant in v. 8 does not continue the theme of what Christ did (προσελάβετο ὑμᾶς) but states his function vis-à-vis Jews and Gentiles. Furthermore, of the four quotations adduced in support of the Gentiles' praise of God, only the first three explicitly speak of this, and of these only the second and third actually summon the Gentiles to praise. The first has the speaker himself do the praising, and the fourth shifts to two other themes: the Davidic ruler of the Gentiles and their hope in him. (c) Finally, although the theme of hope in v. 12 is continued in the concluding benediction (v. 13), it speaks of neither Jew nor Gentile but of an unspecified "you." How does one account for such a strange paragraph, located at such a strategic place? Clear examination of each of its components should help us forward.

III

A. *The exhortation and its soteriological warrant.* Verse 7 is relatively free of problems. The reciprocal welcome urged here, while going beyond 14:1 where the "strong" are to welcome the "weak," has been anticipated negatively at 14:3 (μὴ ἐξουθενείτω, μὴ κρινέτω) and warranted by God's welcome (προσελάβετο), not by Christ's as here.[11] In v. 7 the readers[12] are not so much urged to imitate Christ's welcoming them as to act in a way that is consistent with it.[13] The concluding εἰς δόξαν τοῦ θεοῦ probably goes with the imperative (welcome one another for the glory of God[14]) rather than with the indicative (Christ welcomed you for the glory of God).[15]

Although the glorification of God is both a major theme of the paragraph and the link to v. 6, there are subtle differences in the ways in which it is expressed. In vv. 5-6, the glorification of God is homological, a verbal act (ἐν ἑνὶ στόματι) that is to result from a christomorphic common mind (τὸ αὐτὸ φρονεῖν ἐν ἀλλήλοις κατὰ Χριστὸν Ἰησοῦν), which God is asked to give (ὁ δὲ θεὸς . . . δῴη). In v. 7 it is the goal of a moral act that reflects the soteriological experience. In terms of Christian dogmatics, in vv. 5-6 it results from sanctification, but in v. 7 it reflects justification.[16]

B. The christological warrant (vv. 8-9a). The serious problems begin here, where a different theme is introduced formally by λέγω γάρ.[17] It is this γάρ that makes what is said about Christ the warrant for the exhortation in v. 7.

Exactly what is said about Christ depends on how one construes the syntax of the complex sentence. There are two major possibilities.[18] According to the first, λέγω governs two clauses that begin with accusatives, thereby making Paul say two things, one about Christ's relation to Jews and the other about the Gentiles' glorification of God.

λέγω γάρ (1) Χριστὸν διάκονον γεγενῆσθαι περιτομῆς
ὑπὲρ ἀληθείας θεοῦ
εἰς τὸ βεβαιῶσαι τὰς ἐπαγγελίας τῶν πατέρων
(2) τὰ δὲ ἔθνη ὑπὲρ ἐλέους
δοξάσαι τὸν θεόν.

On this basis, the two ὑπέρ phrases are emphasized and contrasted, and δέ is consequently regarded as "but."[19] However, this makes the purpose clause (εἰς τὸ βεβαιῶσαι κτλ.) virtually a parenthesis[20] (and it appears to be more important than that). The main difficulty is that this construal merely juxtaposes two assertions, with the result that it remains unclear how this statement as a whole warrants v. 7—a difficulty exacerbated by the initial quotation that follows. Indeed, Zeller (see n. 8 below) concludes that vv. 8-12 explain only 7*b*. In other words, it has Paul make a series of statements that, despite explicit connecting links, are in substance disconnected:

1. Welcome one another for the glory of God as Christ welcomed you,
2. because I declare
   (a) [that] Christ became a servant of the circumcision for the sake of God's faithfulness (in order to confirm the promises of the fathers)
   (b) but [that] the Gentiles glorify God because of his mercy,
   (c) as it is written, "I will confess you among the Gentiles," and so on.

The second possibility has its eye on neither the two clauses introduced by the accusatives Χριστόν and τὰ ἔθνη nor on the two ὑπέρ phrases, but on the three infinitives (γεγενῆσθαι, βεβαιῶσαι, δοξάσαι) and regards the latter two as explicating the first. Moreover, it assumes that εἰς τό governs two infinitives, thereby having Paul make one complex assertion:

> λέγω γὰρ
> Χριστὸν διάκονον γεγενῆσθαι περιτομῆς . . . θεοῦ
>   εἰς τὸ βεβαιῶσαι τὰς επαγγελίας . . .
>   τὰ δὲ ἔθνη . . . δοξάσαι τὸν θεόν

On this basis, Christ's becoming a servant of the circumcision has a dual purpose (δέ now regarded as "and"): confirmation of the promises and evocation of the Gentiles' glorification of God. On the whole, the second construal is preferable,[21] though a completely problem-free solution is not likely.

Some modern versions prefer to paraphrase Χριστὸν διάκονον γεγενῆσθαι περιτομῆς. The New Jerusalem Bible, for instance, has: "Christ's work was to serve the circumcised," thereby substituting a statement about the work of Christ for his person. More subtle is the result of adopting the aorist infinitive reading γενεσθαι (BC*D*G) instead of adhering to the more difficult (!) perfect infinitive (γεγενῆσθαι), thereby substituting a simple historical event for a more complex transhistorical perspective: Christ has become and continues to be a servant of the circumcision.[22] Why NAS, and now de Jonge,[23] have "a servant *to* the circumcision" (my italics) is neither clear nor convincing,[24] and KJV's "minister of the circumcision" is quite misleading and wholly unPauline. It is unlikely that the phrase means more than that Christ became a servant who belongs to the Jewish people.[25]

The next phrase shows what Paul took the clause to mean. The incarnation occurred in a Jew ὑπὲρ ἀληθείας θεοῦ, a clear cross-reference to 3:4, where the truthfulness of God refers to God's faithfulness.[26] To this faithfulness the purpose clause refers: εἰς τὸ βεβαιῶσαι τὰς ἐπαγγελίας τῶν[27] πατέρων. This confirmation, however, includes the Gentiles[28] as equal beneficiaries (as in 4:12-25): τὰ δὲ ἔθνη ὑπὲρ ἐλέους δοξάσαι τὸν θεόν (for Zeller's contrary view, see n. 12 below). In other words, Christ's Jewish identity is significant for the current positive Gentile response to the gospel. Had he not been a Jew, the promise that Gentiles would be blessed through Abraham could not have been kept, and this would have violated the integrity, the fidelity, and the truthfulness of God.[29] This understanding of the matter is said to be supported by Scripture.

C. *The scriptural warrant (vv. 9b-12)*. There follow four quotations, taken from Ps 17:50 (= 2 Sam 22:30); Deut 32:43; Ps 117:1; and Isa 11:1, 10, respectively, each distinguished from its neighbor by a form of καὶ πάλιν, not simply combined to form a single "passage" as in 3:10-18.[30] Only in the case of Isaiah is the source identified; deviations from LXX are minor.[31]

Still, there are problems. (a) Given the customary καθὼς γέγραπται, the reader expects that all of the quotations will speak of the Gentile praise of God. As already noted, this appears only in the second and third, while in the first it is the speaker who does so, albeit in a Gentile context (ἐν ἔθνεσιν). The fourth quotation says something quite different. There is one word, and one word only, that connects all four quotations: ἔθνη. (b) However, the appearance of ἔθνη throughout poorly conceals the lack of a coherent rationale governing either the sequence or the substance of all four quotations. The sequence of the first three is governed by the idea of the universalizing of the praise of God: confession and praise of God (by a Jew?[32]) among Gentiles leads to a summons to them to join God's people (λαὸς αὐτοῦ) in rejoicing, which leads to an exhortation to all peoples (πάντες οἱ λαοί) to praise God. These three quotations, in this sequence, support the Gentile praise of God in v. 9a, but not a syllable in them prepares the reader for the fourth, which abruptly introduces the idea of the Davidic ruler[33] of Gentiles, and the Gentiles' hope in *him* (not in God!).[34] Indeed, the parity between Jew and Gentile,[35] manifest in the first three quotations (albeit in accord with "to the Jew first") is displaced here by the subjection of the Gentiles to the Jewish Messiah. (c) Despite the internal coherence of the first three quotations, the connection between the series and v. 9a is awkward because it is not clear who is the subject of verbs ἐξομολογήσομαι and ψαλῶ. Käsemann's proposal that Paul alludes to himself[36] is difficult to accept, but the alternative—that it refers to Christ—is even less satisfactory if taken to refer to the ministry of Jesus.[37] In fact, the transition from v. 9a to Scripture would be smoother without the first quotation; yet, the three quotations have a clear rationale holding them together. (d) According to vv. 8-9a, the Christ event has a dual purpose (confirmation of the promises and evocation of Gentile praise), but the former theme is absent from the first three quotations. However, the chief promise (a Davidic messiah) appears in the fourth quotation. From the standpoint of "promise," the whole paragraph would have a clearer coherence without the first three quotations in vv. 9*b*-11, which dominate the whole.

D. *The hortatory benediction (v. 13)*. The formal structure of this benediction is virtually identical with that of vv. 5-6.[38] Interestingly, here the transition from v. 12 is smooth, for the benediction picks up the theme of hope. Equally interesting is the fact that it does not mention Christ at all (contrast v. 5).

One way of accounting for these puzzling phenomena has not, to my knowledge, been explored[39]—that they result from the use of two previously independent pieces of tradition. This possibility may prove to be the key to the passage. In fact, all the difficulties can be accounted for by this hypothesis.

IV

The hypothesis can be stated succinctly: It was Paul himself who created the text before us, and he did so by inserting the threefold quotation into a tradition that consisted of vv. 8 + 12, and by adding phrases designed to bind the resulting paragraph to its larger context—namely, ὑπὲρ ἀληθείας θεοῦ (v. 8) and τὰ δὲ ἔθνη ὑπὲρ ἐλέους δοξάσαι τὸν θεόν (v. 9), as well as by inserting καὶ πάλιν Ἡσαΐας λέγει (v. 12). The Pauline character of these phrases argues against the hand of an interpolator or editor.

One tradition, probably formed in Hellenistic Jewish Christianity, consisted of the following:

> Χριστὸν διάκονον γεγενῆσθαι περιτομῆς
> εἰς τὸ βεβαιῶσαι τὰς ἐπαγγελίας τῶν πατέρων,
> καθὼς γέγραπται.
> ἔσται ἡ ῥίζα τοῦ Ἰεσσαί,
>
> καὶ[40] ὁ ἀνιστάμενος ἄρχειν ἐθνῶν.
> ᾽επ᾽ αὐτῷ ἔθνη ἐλπιοῦσιν.

The tradition made the legitimacy of Gentile Christianity conditional on acceptance of Jesus' Davidic messiahship, not unlike what we find later in Matthew. This perspective is consonant with the christological tradition that Paul cites, and also modifies, at the beginning of the letter

(1:3-4). Paul probably assumed that both of these traditions were known in Rome.

All that remains of the other tradition[41] is the threefold quotation in vv. 9*b*-11, which probably had a prefatory statement that Paul omitted. The distinctive content of this threefold quotation now emerges more clearly. Unless Paul had previously assembled these texts to support his self-interpretation, it is unlikely that the "I" in ἐξομολογήσομαι and ψαλῶ refers to the apostle himself. Rather, it probably refers to Christ,[42]—that is, to the pre-existent Christ's declaring in advance the purpose of his impending incarnation.[43] Nowhere else does Paul write of the incarnation in the first person. In the New Testament only Heb 2:12-14 does so, and there too the author uses three quotations from Scripture. Whereas the quotations in Romans focus on the consequences for Gentiles of Christ's work, those in Hebrews express the three stages of the Christ-event itself. Outside the New Testament the gnostic Naassene hymn also presents the incarnation in first person, though without relying on biblical quotations.[44]

In using the threefold quotation, Paul's interest is not in the "I" but on the rationale of the whole: through Christ the Gentiles join in the praise of God. Consequently he writes τὰ δὲ ἔθνη . . . θεόν to connect the quotations with the Hellenistic Jewish Christian tradition, which asserts the confirmation of the patriarchal promise. Moreover, by inserting the triple quotation into the Jewish Christian tradition, Paul gives a new interpretation to its quotation of Isa 11:10 (καὶ ὁ ἀνιστάμενος ἄρχειν ἐθνῶν, ἐπ' αὐτῷ ἔθνη ἐλπιοῦσιν). He deprives it of its imperialistic messianism, on the one hand, and assures its universal religious/soteriological meaning on the other—that is, he takes ἀνιστάμενος to refer to Christ's resurrection,[45] and his ἄρχειν to his universal lordship. These hermeneutical moves are consistent with those made in Rom 1:3-4—the Christ-event is interpreted by incorporating its messianic/Davidic dimensions into a wider context based on the meaning of the resurrection.

V

The resulting rationale and content of this passage, despite its various difficulties, form a fitting and effective climax to the theological/ethical core of Romans. In the first place, whatever the exact ethnic identity of the "weak" and the "strong" may have been, v. 6 clearly sees the ultimate purpose of their requisite unity in Christ as their united praise of God. Romans 15:7-13, then, expands this unity by showing that it is not simply a mutual, intra-mural accommodation to be reached in Rome, but a local instance of God's saving purpose in Christ—the eschatological unity of

93

all people, concretely Jew and Gentile. By coming back to this theme, Paul draws a thread through the entire letter and shows that in Scripture God has indeed promised in advance the gospel for all humanity (1:2).[46] Second, the theme of the universal praise of God is, in Paul's view, much more than a rhetorical flourish. It is the actual material soteriological alternative to the root problem of humanity: not giving praise to God or honoring God. The indictment of the Gentiles in 1:21 (γνόντες τὸν θεὸν οὐχ ὡς θεὸν ἐδόξασαν ἢ ηὐχαρίστησαν) and that of the Jews in 2:23 (ὃς ἐν νόμῳ καυχᾶσαι, διὰ τῆς παραβάσεως τοῦ νόμου τὸν θεὸν ἀτιμάζεις;) is basically the same. Moreover, in the next verse the stinging indictment, quoting Isa 52:5 (the name of God is blasphemed among the Gentiles because of you) is precisely what is overcome when the Gentiles join the people of God in praising God as a result of Christ.

Notes

1. The paragraph is surely more than an addendum (Ahang, bzw., Nachtrag), as Dietrich-Alex Koch says (Die Schrift als Zeuge des Evangeliums. Untersuchungen zu Verwendung u.z. Verständnis der Schrift bei Paulus [BHT, 69; Tübingen: J. C. B. Mohr (Paul Siebeck), 1986] 281).
2. Sanday-Headlam (A Critical and Exegetical Commentary on the Epistle to the Romans [ICC; Edinburgh: T. and T. Clark, 1895]) is content to say that in vv. 7-13 Paul generalizes.
3. So Koch, Die Schrift als Zeuge, 282.
4. Alexander Pallis, To the Romans (Liverpool: Liverpool Booksellers' Co., 1920) 152; John C. O'Neill, Paul's Letter to the Romans (Harmondsworth: Penguin Books, 1975) 240.
5. Walter Schmithals's views about Rom 15:1-13 are an essential part of his imaginative (some would say imaginary) reconstruction of the literary pre-history of our Letter to the Romans, in Der Römerbrief als historisches Problem (Gütersloh: Gerd Mohn, 1975). He calls attention not only to formal similarity between vv. 5-6 and 13 but also to the fact that such benedictions normally appear near the end of a Pauline letter and are never duplicated (154-56). He also contends that 15:1-6 and 8-13, taken in themselves, have nothing to do with one another (157-58). He also thinks that the editor shifted v. 7 from its original position after 4a (4b being redactional) in order to provide a connecting link to vv. 8-13, which originally followed 11:36 (but continued the thought of 11:32). Thus Rom 12:1–15:4a, 7, 5-6 + 15:14-32 + 16:21-23 + 15:33 once constituted Paul's Second Letter to the Romans (157-62), written shortly before going to Jerusalem. The first letter consisted of 1:1–4:25 + 5:12–11:36 + 15:8-13. Rom 16:1-20 was originally destined for Ephesus. Our Rom also includes fragments of genuine letters originally sent to Thessalonica, as well as non-genuine passages and redactional comments. (See 210-11 for a summary.) Schmithals generally follows Friedrich Spitta, whose turn of the century views he summarizes. See also Rudolf Schumacher, Die beiden letzten Kapitel des Römerbriefes. Ein Beitrag zu ihrer Geschichte u. Erklärung (Münster: Aschendorff, 1929).
6. See, for example, Rudolf Bultmann, "Glossen im Römerbrief," Exegetica (ed. E. Dinkler; Tübingen: J. C. B. Mohr [Paul Siebeck], 1967) 278-84; Leander E. Keck, "The Post-Pauline Interpretation of Jesus' Death in Rom 5, 6-7," Theologia Crucis—Signum Crucis (E. Dinkler Festschrift; eds. C. Andresen and G. Klein; Tübingen: J. C. B. Mohr [Paul Siebeck], 1979) 237-48; idem., "Romans 15:4—An Interpolation?" Faith and History: Essays in Honor of Paul W. Meyer (eds. John T. Carroll, Charles H. Cosgrove, E. Elizabeth Johnson; Atlanta: Scholars Press, forthcoming).

94

7. See Paul S. Minear, *The Obedience of Faith* (SBT II, 19; Naperville: Alec R. Allenson, 1971) 10-11.

8. Dieter Zeller, *Juden und Heiden in der Mission des Paulus. Studien zum Römerbrief* (Stuttgart: Katholisches Bibelwerk, 1973) 218-19.

9. Schmithals puts it sharply: In 14:1–15:6 there is no mention of Jew and Gentile; in 15:8-13 we do not meet the "strong" and the "weak" (*Der Römerbrief,* 157).

10. See Robert Jewett, "The Form and Function of the Homiletic Benediction," *ATR* 51 (1969) 18-34.

11. This shift from God to Christ cannot be adduced as evidence of interpolation because in other places as well Paul has Christ do on one page what God does on another. See, for example, Rom 14:10 and 2 Cor 5:10. The same sort of pattern applies to Christ and the Spirit (see, for example, Rom 8:27, 34).

12. If in v. 7 one reads ημας with BD*P and so on, as well as with the pre-Vulgate b r and the Sahidic, then Paul would include himself. Better attested, however, is υμας (אACD² FG lat sy Bo), and is to be preferred. O. Michel (*Der Brief an die Römer* [5th ed.; KEK; Göttingen: Vandenhoeck and Ruprecht, 1978] 447 n. 19), however, follows Schlier (*Der Römerbrief* [HTKNT; Herder: Freiburg, 1977] 424) in thinking that ημας might be original, even though it sounds "doxological."
Zeller's restriction of the ημας to the Gentile Christians in Rome (even though they are not simply equatable with the "strong") is one wholly unconvincing result of his construal of v. 8.

13. Here καθώς does not have its usual comparative sense but indicates that what follows is a warrant for the imperative. So also C. E. B. Cranfield, *A Critical and Exegetical Commentary on the Epistle to the Romans* (ICC; 2 vols.; Edinburgh: T. and T. Clark, 1975-79) 2.799, following Käsemann, *Commentary on Romans* (Grand Rapids: Eerdmans, 1980) 385.

14. So also H. W. Schmidt, *Der Brief des Paulus an die Römer* (Berlin: Evangelische Verlagsanstalt, 1966); J. Murray, *Romans* (NICNT; 2 vols.; Grand Rapids: Eerdmans, 1967) gives no reason for rejecting this construction. Westcott-Hort inserted a comma before the prepositional phrase.

15. So Michel (who does not comment), followed by Cranfield, who finds this construal more appropriate.

16. Käsemann, who is sensitive to the problems of the passage, sees here evidence that justification by faith is "the theme of the epistle so that exhortation is sustained and surrounded by it (*Romans,* 384).

17. Cranfield rightly observes that λέγω γὰρ "here introduces a solemn doctrinal declaration" (*Romans,* 2.740).

18. Cranfield discusses four others in *ibid.,* 2.742-44.

19. So Lagrange, *Épitre aux Romains* (Ebib; Paris: J. Gabalda, 1922) followed by Zeller, *Juden und Heiden,* 219. Accordingly, Paul contrasts the *"economie de promisse"* with the *"economie de misericorde."* Zeller must, therefore, conclude that this passage shows how little the call of the Gentiles can be subsumed under God's covenant faithfulness—precisely opposite of the view being developed in this discussion.

20. As Käsemann admits, citing Zeller (who cites Lagrange).

21. Michel (*Römer,* 448 n. 22) thinks the second possibility has the advantage of style, the first the advantage of context. NEB follows the second.

22. For this very reason, Zahn's commentary prefers the aorist!

23. Marinus de Jonge, *Christology in Context* (Philadelphia: Westminster Press, 1988) 88.

24. Sam K. Williams gets it right. The point is not that the Jews were objects of Christ's service (as Bernhard Weiss's commentary says), rather the genitive points to origin (and, I would add, belonging), as in Rom 1:3; 9:5; Gal 4:4 ("The Righteousness of God in Romans," *JBL* 99 [1980] 286-87).

25. Cranfield denies the force of the contrary considerations he cites when he maintains that this alludes to the Isaianic Servant (*Romans,* 2.741 n. 3). In view of Cranfield's concession that "no word of the διακονεῖν group is ever used in the LXX in the Servant Songs," Michel's "διάκονος = עֶבֶד" must be rejected.

26. See Richard Hays, "Psalm 143 and the Logic of Romans 3," *JBL* 99 (1980) 107-15.

27. One expects "promises *to* the fathers." Does Paul use the genitive instead because in 9:4 he had written, "to them belong (ὧν) the sonship . . . and the promises"?

28. H. W. Schmidt is right on target in rejecting all interpretations that restrict the scope of the βεβαίωσις to the Jews (*Römer*, 240).

29. Zeller is surely wrong in saying that v. 8 has a concessive sense, even though Christ became a servant of the circumcision (*Juden und Heiden*, 221).

30. See my "The Function of Rom 3:10-18," in *God's Christ and His People* (Nils Dahl Festschrift; Oslo: Universitets Forlaget, 1978) 141-57.

31. O'Neill's claim that this use of the LXX shows that the passage is interpolated because Paul made his own translation (*Paul's Letter to the Romans*, 240) is not convincing.

32. Koch sees the first quotation as being concerned with God's relation to Israel in contrast with the concern of the second and third, which is oriented to Gentiles (*Die Schrift als Zeuge*, 282 n. 25).

33. Commentators agree that here ῥίζα (root) should be taken to mean "shoot"—that is, "scion."

34. Cranfield (*Romans*, 2.747), however, says that this last sentence "makes a fitting conclusion" to the whole series, and Koch claims that *only* the fourth quotation corresponds to the orientation of the quotations that precede it. "Beobachtungen zum christologischen Schriftgebrauch in den vorpaulinischen Gemeinden," *ZNW* 71 (1980) 175. Later, in *Die Schrift als Zeuge* (283), he claims that v. 12 states the presupposition of vv. 9-11, thereby obscuring the difference between the fourth quotation and the other three.

35. Zeller (*Juden und Heiden*, 221) rightly sees that the Gentiles are not incorporated into Israel. Did Paul overlook the tension between this passage and his analogy of the olive tree in 11:17-24?

36. Rolf Dabelstein thinks that Paul is the subject not only in v. 9 but also in vv. 10-11 (*Die Beurteilung der "Heiden" bei Paulus* [Frankfurt/Bern/Cirencester: Peter Lang, 1981] 108).

37. Bernhard Weiss's commentary regards the subject as Christ, present among Gentile Christians (*Der Brief an die Römer* (Meyer K; Göttingen: Vandenhoeck and Ruprecht, 1899). Adolf Schlatter (*Gottes Gerechtigkeit* [2nd ed.; Stuttgart: Calwer Verlag, 1952] 383) agrees that it is Christ, but says that the church's confessing and singing are the work of Christ. Koch (*Die Schrift als Zeuge*, 282 n. 24) rejects this identification because it is unlikely that Paul would have included Christ in the church's praise, but he also doubts that the subject is Paul. What Bo Frid ("Jesaiah und Paulus in Röm 15, 12," *BZ* 27 [1983] 241 n. 5) means by saying that it is as a Jew among Gentiles that Christ is a servant of the circumcision is not clear.

38. The variants πληροφορησαι εν παση χαρα και ειρηνη (B) and πληροφορησαι παση χαρα και ειρηνη (FG) are difficult to explain. The omission of εν τω πιστευειν (DFG bm) is probably accidental (so also Cranfield, *Romans*, 2.748 n. 4), as is the omission of εις το περισσευειν (B 945 2495).

39. Wilckens (*Der Brief an die Römer* (EKKNT 6; Zurich: Benziger Verlag, 1978] 108) mentions the possibility that vv. 9b-12 are an originally independent catena and observes that this would account for the fact that its scope does not agree with the dual purpose of the Christ-event in vv. 8-9a. However, he does not reckon seriously enough with the possibility that also vv. 8 and 12 constitute a piece of tradition. Koch thinks that in v. 12 Paul is following a Christian tradition (which rests on Jewish tradition) of interpreting Isa 11:10 christologically, but he does not pursue the matter ("Beobachtungen," 186). In *Die Schrift als Zeuge* (283 n. 27) he repeats this view and rejects Wilckens's suggestion as bereft of any evidence.

40. Frid ("Röm 15, 12," 239) rightly sees that καί is not a copula here, but represents the Hebrew אשר and should be rendered "even he who."

41. Although Barnabas Lindars assumes that Paul assembled the quotations, he calls attention to generally overlooked data that might be evidence that the compiler regarded all three quotations as coming from the Psalter. (A) in the Catena, Deut 32:43 (LXX) stands between Ps 17:49 and 117:1. (B) in LXX, Deut 32 (the Song of Moses) is included in the *Odae*, which follows the Psalms. Lindars infers that "it is

probable that it already stood in the previous Jewish text as an additional hymnary for liturgical use." (C) Heb 1:6 also cites Deut 32:42, but in a form "which has an exact parallel only in the reading on the *Odae*. There also the quotation occurs in a catena of Psalm verses" (*New Testament Apologetic* [Philadelphia: Westminster Press, 1961] 244-45).

42. One should not confuse this confession with the "good confession" Jesus made before Pilate, according to 1 Tim 6:13.

43. So too A. T. Hanson, who also says that for Paul the Psalms "are the vehicle by which the Messiah is to praise God in the church (Rom. 15:11)" (*Studies in Paul's Technique and Theology* [London: SPCK, 1974] 171.)

44.

> "But Jesus said, 'Father, behold:
> Pursued by evils here upon earth
> There roams the (work) of thine own breath;
> . . . .
> Therefore send me, Father;
> Bearing seals I will descend,
> I will pass through all the Aeons,
> I will disclose all mysteries . . .
> Awaking gnosis I will impart.' "

(From Werner Forester, *Gnosis* [vol. 1: *Patristic Evidence*; Oxford: Clarendon Press, 1972] 282.)

45. Why Cranfield (*Romans*, 2.747 n. 4) rejects this as "hardly likely" is not clear. Wilckens assumes that Paul sees here an allusion to Christ's resurrection, as does Käsemann. Dietrich-Alex Koch rightly asserts it ("Beobachtungen," 185).

46. Richard Hays sees this, too, and goes on to observe: "In Romans, Paul cites Scripture not as a repository of miscellaneous wisdom on various topics but as an insistent witness to one great truth: God's righteousness, which has now embraced Gentiles among the people of God, includes the promise of God's unbroken faithfulness to Israel. Virtually every text that Paul cites or alludes to is made to circle around this one theme" (*Echoes of Scripture in the Letters of Paul* [New Haven: Yale University Press, 1989] 73). Hays, however, does not see the inner tensions of the passage discussed here.

FURTHER REFLECTIONS
ON THE ORIGINS OF THE CHURCH
OF ROME

Raymond E. Brown, S.S.

In 1983 J. P. Meier and I wrote *Antioch and Rome: New Testament Cradles of Catholic Christianity* (New York: Paulist). In that book I argued that the Jewish followers of Jesus exhibited various attitudes toward observance of the law and that, while some were not interested in making Gentile converts, many were, and the resultant converts reflected the diversities of those who converted them. Accordingly the New Testament shows *at least* the following diversities. (1) Jewish Christians and their Gentile converts to Jesus who insisted on full observance of the Mosaic Law, including circumcision. This group would be exemplified by those "of the sect of the Pharisees" (Acts 15:5) or "false brothers" (Gal 2:4) who entered the discussions with Paul, Peter, and James at Jerusalem, and those who opposed Paul in Galatia. (2) Jewish Christians and their Gentile converts who did not insist on circumcision but did require some Jewish observances. The portrayal of James (the brother of the Lord) and of Peter in Acts 15 and in Gal 2:6-12 would fit this category, although James seems to have been more insistent than Peter on some of the observances. (3) Jewish Christians and their Gentile converts who did not insist on circumcision and did not require observance of the Jewish ("kosher") food laws. Paul's attitude toward his Gentile converts would fit this category. (4) Jewish Christians and their Gentile converts who did not insist on circumcision or observance of the Jewish food laws and who saw no abiding significance in Jewish cult and feasts. I suggested that the "Hellenists" of Acts 6:1-6 (interpreted through Stephen's speech) and the authors of the Gospel of John and of the Epistle to the Hebrews reflected this attitude.

With the recognition that an analysis of the beginnings of Christianity at Rome depends on indirect evidence, I proposed the following thesis. Christianity came to Rome in the 40s, probably from Jerusalem. Those who proclaimed Jesus at Rome were similar to Group 2, analyzed above, inculcating respect for Jewish laws and customs. The ensuing debates in the synagogue caused both Jews and Jewish Christians to be expelled from the city in 49 CE (probable date) by Claudius, but by the time Paul wrote Romans in the late 50s there were house churches of Christians at Rome. Whether or not the majority of the Christians at that moment were Gentile is not decisive theologically,[1] for I contended that the tone of Romans, much more moderate than that of Galatians, suggests that Paul recognized most of the Christians at Rome to be more attached to Jewish law and customs than were his own converts. After discussing Paul's letter to the Romans, I continued my analysis of Christianity in Rome in the first century by discussing 1 Peter, Hebrews, and I Clement. In chaps. 1 and 2, 1 Peter (written from Rome probably in the 80s) used the Old Testament motifs of the exodus desert wandering and promised land in order to describe Christian basics, thus showing a deep appreciation of the Jewish heritage. Both Paul to the Romans and 1 Peter exhibit a use of the cultic language of Judaism, a respect for Roman civil authority, and an interest in community order (charisms in Rom 12:6-8 and presbyters in 1 Pet 5:1-5). About the same time Hebrews may have been written *to* Italy (13:23-24) and to Rome in particular in order to discourage the attraction of Christians there to such a heritage from Judaism, especially in matters of cult. At the end of the first century *I Clement* (which shows an awareness of Hebrews and seemingly of 1 Peter) still frequently uses the cultic and priestly language of Judaism, shows great respect for Roman civil and military organization, and tries to persuade the church at Corinth to have greater respect for the presbyter-bishops. Thus I found some consistent features in Roman Christianity over a half-century from the 40s to the 90s.

These observations were advanced with an insistence on their tentative character and an invitation to scholars to improve on or contradict the proposal. Accordingly, reviews of the book constitute an important contribution to the discussion. (Meier's half of the book on Antioch has, of course, been the subject of debate as well, but here I shall concentrate only on Rome.) I list alphabetically at the end of this article some twenty-five reviews that I have read, a few simply reporting content, some quite favorable and intrigued, some quite negative. (References to them in the article employ the author's family name without periodical or page indication.) I shall attempt to glean from these reviews what can clarify and further the discussion. Since Professor J. L. Martyn, to whom this Festschrift is dedicated, has spent much of these last years studying the Letter to the Galatians, an essay on the church at Rome involving Paul's companion writing to the Romans seems an appropriate tribute. A reading of the reviews has convinced me that the challenge at the end of *Antioch and Rome* (213) has not been met: "If we cannot win acceptance for our own solution, we shall be happy if we have provoked someone to offer a better solution." This article is another effort at gentle provocation.

Besides the reviews, a major contribution to the study of the origins of the church at Rome is an excellent Bern dissertation (1983) by P. Lampe, *Die stadtrömischen Christen in der ersten beiden Jahrhunderten: Untersuchungen zur Sozialgeschichte* (WUNT 2.18; Tübingen: Mohr, 1987), a work done contemporaneously with and independently of my study. I cite initially some views of Lampe relevant to points made in my book and to the discussion below. Acts 28:13-15 is historical in describing the presence of Christians at Puteoli and at Rome itself by the time of Paul's arrival there. The earliest pre-Pauline Christians at Rome were synagogue-going Jews. Orosius' date (49 CE) for the expulsion of Jews from Rome over the Chrestus issue is most plausible. Lüdemann is wrong in interpreting Cassius Dio as dating it in 41—Dio was not referring to the Chrestus event. By the time that Paul wrote to Rome, as detectable from the names in Romans 16, the majority of Christians were Gentiles, even though some very important Jewish Christians were present. The Christianity of the Gentile Christians had been heavily influenced by elements from Judaism: "Christians (Jewish and Gentile) from synagogue circles had exercised in the beginning an astonishing influence on the theological building of Christianity in the city of Rome. These Christians from the synagogue ambiance were probably the majority. Most Christians of the first generation had contact with a synagogue before their conversion and—understandably in very different intensities—had, as sympathizers or adherents, received a wealth of thought from Judaism" (Lampe, 60; my translation). The continuing strong influence of Jewish Christianity in Rome is traceable well into the second century.

Lampe reports modern estimates of the first-century population of Jews in Rome as between 15,000 and 60,000, of whom many were citizens. The ease with which Nero persecuted Christians suggests that they were not citizens, but there is little clear evidence of social differences between Jews and Christians in Rome. While there were Christians from all classes, probably a fair number were of slave origin and poor; their dwellings were in the valleys between the hills of Rome. The latinity of works associated with Christian Rome reflects the poorer classes, but the fact that for several centuries the language of most Christians was Greek suggests that many were foreigners who had come to Rome. Romans 16 indicates the existence of plural house churches at Rome. Later evidence refers to the titular churches of Rome. Probably there was a continuity of relatively self-standing "parishes" with their own cult, clergy, and burial places. The emergence of a strong unified leadership was delayed at Rome, so that monarchical bishops did not emerge until after 150. This does not mean that Roman Christians did not feel themselves part of a church: they sent the eucharist to each other, and Rome could function as a unity in dealing with outside Christians and churches. But within Rome there was considerable separate identity. (A similar situation had existed for the Roman synagogues of the Jews.) This may explain why so many diverse teachers (Valentinus, Marcion, Justin, Tatian) were able to function for a time in Rome. Some of them eventually fell foul of the collegium of presbyters, but there was no overall bishop entrusted with doctrinal care through much of the second century. Indeed, it may have been the care of the many poor that was most influential in the development of the monarchical episcopate.

False Trails

I begin by pointing out inaccuracies on both sides of the picture—inaccuracies in what some reviewers attribute to me, and inaccuracies in the book. The former are reported only as a way of making clear where I stand on some crucial points.

Ferguson suggests that Meier and I chose Antioch and Rome because we considered them the representative Christian centers, and he asks whether there were not other important Christian centers. But we did not consider Antioch and Rome to be uniquely representative of Christianity, and we explicitly urged the study of other Christian centers where the components were different.[2] Freyne objects to our treatment of the two cities as only a literary treatment that does not consider the realia of the social world. We proposed our book as initial and probatory, not as a full treatment, so that the added social dimension demanded by Freyne would be a welcome addition to the discussion.[3] In any case the social realia of Christians at Rome have now been provided in ample detail by P. Lampe, and they present no serious challenge to my thesis of the origins of the church of Rome.

Further discussion of Murphy-O'Connor's trenchant review will be given below. Here I deal only with some of his statements that fail to clarify the issues, for example, that Brown is "inaccurate in claiming that there is no alternative to Orosius' date" for the edict of Claudius, expelling Jews from Rome. I mentioned Orosius' date on page 102, reporting only that, while he is not famous for impeccable accuracy, his date receives some confirmation from Acts and so might be accepted as reasonable.[4] Working from Cassius Dio, who seemingly associates the first year of Claudius (41 CE) with the emperor's attempt to stop the Jews from holding meetings (explicitly not an expulsion!), Murphy-O'Connor states: "It would seem that Christianity reached Rome some ten years earlier than Brown would allow." In fact, however, I allowed that Christianity came to Rome years earlier than the usual date (49 CE) of the edict of Claudius, specifically in the early 40s (89, 103) and posited a long establishment of Christianity by the year 49 CE (102). Another misapprehension may be created by Murphy-O'Connor's statement: "The assumptions that Roman Jews were active proselytizers with close political links with Jerusalem have been rightly questioned by Kraabel" (*JJS* 33 [1982]: 451-54). I made no point of active proselytizing,[5] and Kraabel's article is aimed at refuting a thesis that is not mine—namely, the thesis that almost every aspect of Roman Judaism was determined by Jerusalem. It does not deny that there were some connections between Jerusalem and Rome (including Roman Judaism; see below).

Balch criticizes my portion of the book as not being concerned with the *development* of Roman Christianity. He draws this conclusion (which I regard as wrong) from the fact that I argued for a Christianity in Rome, which in the period 58-96 CE was conservative toward Judaism (more so than Paul in Galatians)—a consistent attitude that I think came from Jerusalem. Balch knows that I posit other motifs in Roman Christianity, such as respect for imperial authority and concern for church structure. Unfortunately, he assumes that I think that they also came from Jerusalem. The respect for imperial authority most likely developed in Rome itself, as also the concern for structure. Thus I hold that there was a development of Roman Christianity.

Kraabel chastises both Meier and me for not having consulted material that would have assisted our investigation. For instance, he states: "A more convincing study would need to pay more attention to apocryphal and heretical literature and to the non-Christian evidence, Jewish and Gentile." It would have been helpful if he had identified this apocryphal, or heretical or non-Christian, evidence *about the first-century church in Rome* that I neglected. Similarly he insists that the fact that Diaspora Jews took no part in the war won by Titus in 70 CE should have told me something relevant to the relation between Jerusalem Jewish Christians and the (Jewish) Christians of Rome. I did discuss on page 151 the impact of Titus' victory, but again Kraabel needs to be more specific about the relevance to *Christians*. Part of the difficulty of the investigation of the church at Rome is the lack of material pertinent to the earliest Christian community.

If, as I think, some reviewers have misunderstood aspects of the book, others have helpfully pointed out my own mistakes.[6] I cited (94) Penna's suggestion that there were about 20,000 Jews in Rome as the lowest estimate I had seen; he correctly points out that he himself called attention to the proposed number 10,000 in the *Encyclopedia Judaica*. I used a late inscription (211 CE) as attestation for the name Chrestus at Rome (100). Penna points out that the Roman poet Martial already used the name in the first Christian century (*Epigrammata* 7.55.1). Although there were some dozen different synagogues of Jews in Rome (101), Penna would more precisely maintain that perhaps only five of them were functioning in the first century. With Logan's prodding I have reexamined what I said about the Muratorian Fragment (109) in terms of its selecting *one* Pauline letter (Romans) as envisaging the whole church. That is incorrect; it sees this issue in a number of Pauline letters.

Substantive Issues

More important than such minor corrections are clarifying developments of the basic thesis of *Antioch and Rome* that I summarized at the beginning of this article—clarifications to which I have been brought by constructive criticism and by Lampe's helpful study.

A. *The Varieties of Jewish/Gentile Christians*

The fourfold grouping of early Christians in terms of their relation to the Mosaic law[7] and my insistence that Jewish Christianity and Gentile Christianity were meaningless terms theologically (since, at least outside Judea, there were Jewish Christians and their Gentile Christian converts in every group) were recognized by some reviewers as a praiseworthy departure from and rejection of the F. C. Baur approach.[8] Meeks is an outstanding exception, since he finds my approach to be that of Baur, revived after a long sleep. In comment, let me spell out what I affirmed on page 2 of *Antioch and Rome*: "In what follows I am presenting only the simplest form of diversities based on the relations of Christians to Judaism. *Surely the situation was more complex with further subdivisions based on christology and other factors.*" The sentence that I have *now* italicized (in which the word *subdivisions* might better be "divisions") suggested that Torah observance, which was the key to the four Groups, would not have been the only divider in first-century Christianity. It was a factor in discussions among Christians in Jerusalem, Antioch, and Rome, whence the capital importance given to it in the book. (It is noteworthy that J. Neusner, *Judaism: The Evidence of the Mishnah* [University of Chicago Press, 1981] sees issues of legal purity as a central concern among different proto-rabbinical groups.) Yet, even if I might describe John's outlook on Judaism as belonging to Group 4, there is no reason to suspect that Torah observance was a major factor in the internal history of the Johannine community, as I described it in *The Community of the Beloved Disciple* (New York: Paulist, 1979).[9] The factor that caused the expulsion of the Johannine Christians from the synagogue and later divided them internally (I John) was christology, not any expressed attitude toward the demands of the law, especially in relation to food. Thus my view of early Christianity (of which part is described in *Antioch and Rome*) is complex and far different from the classic Baur hypothesis. As for the various attitudes of Christians toward Torah observance, where those views were an issue, I warned (2) that even four groupings were not sufficiently complex to cover the New Testament picture: "Within the 'Groups' spoken of, inevitably there would have been a spectrum." Penna points out a certain heterogeneity in my Group 2. That is because it involves such a complex figure as Peter, who is deemed an apostle to the circumcised (Gal), yet is open to the Gentiles (Acts) and has followers at Corinth (see 131 n. 277). The partially law-observant Christianity that I judge to have been very influential at Rome had closer relations to Peter, who stood at one end of the spectrum of Group 2, than to James, who stood at the other end of the spectrum of the same Group. Although I gave an indication of awareness of this problem (110 n. 229), it might have helped if in speaking of this influential Christianity at Rome I had referred only to a derivation from the Jerusalem Christianity "associated with Peter" rather than "with James and Peter." There is no clear echo at Rome of any aspect of Group 2 distinctively associated with James instead of with Peter. More should be done also with the spectrum in Group 4, even though in passing I acknowledged differences of views among the exemplars of that Group: the Hellenists of Acts, the Epistle to the Hebrews, and John. Because my primary concern was to emphasize that a significant element in Christianity at Rome, even if it had a Gentile majority, was of Group 2, I may have failed to emphasize sufficiently the spectrum within groups and may thus have given an impression of more rigid categories than I had in mind.

B. From Jerusalem to Rome

I sought in *Antioch and Rome* to establish the likelihood that the missionaries who brought Christianity to Rome were Jewish Christians from Jerusalem. Ferguson asks why we need think of a missionary endeavor—why not accidental transmission by travelers? The stress on mission in the Gospels, Paul, and Acts creates, in my judgment, the likelihood that the planting of Christianity in the capital city of the empire would not have been left to chance. But the evidence for merchant contacts in Rome among the Roman Jews may well mean that, so far as Jewish Christians were concerned, the missionary and the merchant could have had a combined role, even as Paul was a missionary and a craftsman.

As indirect evidence for the suggested Jerusalem-to-Rome route of Christianity,[10] I gathered details about the relationship between the imperial capital and (the Jews of) Palestine/Jerusalem. For three-and-half pages (93 to the top of 96) I offered pre-70 CE evidence for political and economic relations; in a short paragraph on page 96 I dealt with post-70 intellectual interchange between Palestinian Judaism and Roman Judaism. Meeks nowhere discusses the former (which might throw light on Christian origins in Rome), but challenges the latter (which clearly postdates Christian origins).[11] Because there are few Hebrew or Aramaic Jewish inscriptions at Rome, Meeks denies the claim (made by the Jewish scholar Leon) that most of the Jewish residents in Rome had originally come from the Palestine/Syria area. This question has little relevance to my thesis, since I am interested primarily in showing that there were frequent contacts between Rome and the Jews in Jerusalem, not in showing where most of the Roman Jews or their parents were born.[12] However, granted the strong component of slaves, former slaves, and merchants in Roman Jewry, their dominant use of Greek in inscriptions may reflect the practicalities of their lives and education rather than their ancestral homeland. Meeks also objects that I do not deal with what *kind of Judaism* was dominant in Jerusalem before 70 CE. I think that a totally irrelevant question for my purposes.[13] My goal is merely to show the possibility or likelihood that Jewish Christians traveled from Jerusalem to Rome.[14] For that goal, a discussion of the theology of the Jerusalem or Roman non-Christian Jewish population is not relevant. The question that concerns me is what *kind of Jewish Christianity* was dominant in Jerusalem before 70 and whether that came to Rome. After there were Christians in Rome (in the 40s) and after the disputes between Jews who believed in Jesus and those who did not, leading to expulsion by Claudius ("because of their constant disturbances impelled by Chrestus"), we know little or nothing about ongoing contacts between the Jews of Rome and the Christians there, Jewish or Gentile. Acts 28:17-25 gives the impression that there was not much local contact at Rome between the two groups.

C. Christianity at Rome

Although *Antioch and Rome* argued that the dominant Christianity in Rome was appreciative of Judaism and loyal to many of its practices (and thus within the spectrum of Group 2), it did not portray a monochromatic Christianity.[15] It was urged (106-9) that Romans 16 belongs to Paul's letter and contains the names of people known to Paul, many of them favorable to his thought (thus Group 3). The hints in Tacitus and *I Clement* that Christians betrayed other Christians out of zeal and envy were interpreted (126-27) to show the presence of Jewish Christians and their circumcised Gentile converts (Group 1), who continued at Rome to manifest hostility to both Peter and Paul. Since I contended that each of these Groups present in the Roman church would have had both Jews and Gentiles, a division of Roman Christianity into Jewish and Gentile would not be a meaningful theological description. Nevertheless, I recognize that Paul addressed his letter primarily to Gentile Christians at Rome, not simply because of the scholarly guesses about the ethnic makeup of Roman Christianity, but because Paul indicates such an audience in 1:5, 13-15; 11:13; and 15:16. This address to Gentiles would have remained diplomatically faithful to the agreement at Jerusalem that Paul had been entrusted with the gospel to the uncircumcised (Gal 2:7). Some of the Gentiles who were addressed shared Paul's view of freedom from the purity regulations of the law, and he appeals especially to them. They are "the strong" in Rom 14:1-15:6,[16] while the Jewish/Gentile Christians who think that food prohibitions of the Torah are relevant constitute the weak.[17] Even if Paul is addressing himself to *Gentiles* of Groups 3 and 4 when he writes Romans and speaks to "the strong," there are some Jewish Christian members who are also strong. "We who are strong" (15:1) includes Paul and at least those Jews mentioned in Romans 16 who were favorable to Paul, like Prisca and Aquila. To summarize, then, Paul writes primarily to the Gentiles at Rome because that is his apostolate, even if he has in view Jewish Christians as well, and among the Gentiles at Rome he primarily addresses himself to those who share his own theology about the law. Why? He is particularly concerned that those of "the strong" who have known him and could even be considered his disciples not alienate the others in the Roman community by an arrogance that springs from their sense of freedom in Christ. Paul's address in Romans to Gentiles sympathetic to his position does not mean that they are the dominant theological position at Rome; rather, in my judgment, they are a new minority, a minority through whom a Roman Christianity more conservative about Judaism might form its opinion of Paul. Paul has that larger, conservative segment in mind when he writes this letter, but rather than address himself *directly* to it—an address that might not be welcome—he hopes that the admonitions addressed to those friendly to his thought will show other Roman Christians that he is not an extremist.

My claim that Christians of Group 2 are the majority at Rome and have created a dominant atmosphere of loyalty to Judaism and appreciation of values in the law flows from my analysis of peculiarities in Paul's letter to the Romans. These include Paul's willingness to phrase his gospel in a formula that echoes the language of Jewish Christianity (118); his use of Jewish cultic language with much greater frequency than in his other letters and with the assumption that it would be understood sympathetically (136-37);[18] his stress in Romans 9–11 on the unique role and privileges of Israel and on the destiny of Gentile Christianity to be grafted on to the olive tree of Israel. *Antioch and Rome* mentions other factors that point in this direction, but let me concentrate on two that need further development: Paul's request to the Roman Christians to help him with their prayers in regard to the collection that he is bringing to Jerusalem, and the differences between Romans and Galatians as they can be accounted for by my analysis of Roman Christianity.

(1) *Help and Prayers with the Collection.* On page 110 I asked the question: "If Roman Christianity were characterized by Gentiles who boasted of their superiority over Jewish Christians, why should Paul think that Roman help and prayers would make acceptable his service to the Jewish Christian saints in Jerusalem?" Thus I used an analysis of 15:30-31 as support for the thesis that many of the Roman Christians were Gentiles influenced by a Jewish Christianity that had come from Jerusalem in the person of early missionaries who proclaimed Christ but remained loyal to much of the law. Criticizing that argument, Murphy-O'Connor states with assurance: "The only help that Paul asks for is prayer, not 'help and prayer' as Brown would have it. Nothing can be deduced regarding the relation between the two churches [Jerusalem and Rome]." Yet, besides *proseuchē* Paul uses the verb *synagōnizesthai*, for which BAGD offers the meaning "help, assist." V. C. Pfitzner (*Paul and the Agon Motif* [NovTSup 16; Leiden: Brill, 1967] 121-22) stresses that the *agōn* is not located in the prayer itself (wrestling with God) but in the coming visit of Paul to Jerusalem, in which he is calling on the Romans to struggle with him. Those who with some exaggeration treat Romans as "the Letter to Jerusalem" and as a dress rehearsal for what Paul will say there will be amazed by Murphy-O'Connor's affirmation in the opposite direction that "nothing can be deduced regarding the relations between the two churches." Paul writes to Rome *before* he goes to Jerusalem and urges the Roman Christians to take part in the struggle that he will face in Jerusalem. A plausible explanation is that there is a similarity between the Christianity that Paul will face in Jerusalem and a Christianity in place at Rome. Paul then has two practical goals. First, since he will visit Rome, he wishes to be sure that he will get a favorable hearing there from a community much of which is not inclined to agree with things he is reputed to have said about the law, and which may be troubled by

insensitive attitudes taken by his friends among "the strong." Second, he needs all the help he can get to be favorably received in Jerusalem, where Christianity has a strong attachment to Judaism and the law.[19] If he can convince the influential Christians of Group 2 at Rome that his gospel is not alien to theirs, the fact that they have friendly relations with the similarily minded Christian majority at Jerusalem may be of great service to Paul.

This does not mean that I think Paul is simply diplomatic or manipulative in this letter. Paul is at a moment of crisis in his life as he goes to Jerusalem. There is a danger that his proclamation of the gospel is being distorted and misunderstood, with the possible result that Christian *koinonia* will be broken. The Letter to the Romans is a deliberately pacific formulation of his gospel by a Paul who wishes to be all things to all persons so that all may be saved. He wants it to be clear to those who will listen that his gospel is not divisive; that he does not want a church simply of the strong if that means excluding the weak; that he has no contempt for the law, but rather sees positive values in the Judaism of his ancestors, so long as he can make clear the primacy of what God has done in Christ. His diplomacy in this letter is for the sake of a gospel that proclaims only one Christ, in whom his followers must be one. If that diplomacy is designed to win Paul a hearing and acceptance, his identity drawn from the proclamation of that gospel rules out what we normally mean by self-serving.

(2) *Differences between Galatians and Romans.* Reflecting on the diplomacy of Romans, I argued that the differences from Galatians were significant both as to tone and to emphasis, probably because Paul was aware that the strength of his sweeping statements about the law in Galatians was causing trouble for him in Jerusalem and in Rome. Now he was not only seeking to explain his mind more pacifically by avoiding exaggerations, but he was also reflecting subsequent experience of how people had understood his opposition to the law. On page 114 I stated:

> Of course, here I am proposing what is virtually a heresy in the eyes of many Pauline scholars: namely, that Paul was not always consistent in his major epistles; that Paul even changed his mind; that the defiant Paul of Galatians was exaggerated; and that something is to be said for the position of Peter and James over against Paul on the observance of some Jewish customs (so long as the observances were not looked upon as necessary for salvation).

I was quite right in whimsically diagnosing my position as constituting heresy in the eyes of many Paulinists. Freyne insists that Paul is not so Jewish as I portray him in Romans. Duling asks if we are robbing Paul to pay Peter. Murphy-O'Connor states: "I am not persuaded that Paul made any substantial modification of his view on Judaism between *Gal.* and *Rom.*"

At least Murphy-O'Connor is specific about where I have gone wrong. He quotes from my page 113: "If echoes of Galatians would have reached Jerusalem, and if Roman Christianity was influenced by the Jerusalem Christianity of James and Peter, it is not unlikely that Pauline phraseology similar to that in Galatians reached *Rome* as well." He handles this suggestion with disdain: "Comment on the quality of this sort of argument should be unnecessary." J. L. Martyn, who is preparing the commentary on Galatians for the Anchor Bible, has given in *The Books of the Bible* (a forthcoming volume from Scribners) a foretaste of the tone of his commentary. He states: "The circumcision party in the Jerusalem Church was almost certainly in touch with the Teachers [those who presented in Galatia a gospel different from Paul's], both before and after their work in Paul's Galatian congregations." Thus I am not alone in thinking that echoes of Galatians probably reached Jerusalem Christians. As for the second half of my hypothesis—namely, that word might have reached Rome—Martyn sees Romans as constituting an interpretation of Galatians made by Paul himself to clarify harsh interpretations of what he had written in the earlier epistle. In other words, what Murphy-O'Connor disdains may well seem sensible to others. (See also U. Wilckens' EKKNT commentary on Romans.)

In dealing with texts, Murphy-O'Connor admits that I am right in claiming that in Rom 7:7, 12, 14 Paul does not state that the law is sin, but Paul "explicitly says this in 8:2, which Brown ignores." However, does one find that explicit statement in 8:2, literally translated: "The law of the spirit of life in Christ Jesus has set me free from the law of sin and death"? In order to check my impression that this verse does not say that the law is sin, I consulted eight commentaries that I found on my shelf (Achtemeier, Barrett, Cranfield, Fitzmyer, Käsemann, Kuss, Lagrange, Sanday), and not one of them interpreted it to mean that the law is sin. The prevalent interpretation was that the law had been made the instrument of sin and death.

As for the general contention that Paul is more moderate and balanced in Romans than in Galatians, I find support for this in Martyn:

> We can easily imagine that on the eve of his last trip to Jerusalem, he regretted the harsh interpretations that had been placed upon the letter [Gal]. Such regret, in any case, is consonant with the fact that in writing to the Romans Paul clarified, supplemented, and perhaps even modified things he had said to the Galatians.

Others could be cited who move in the same direction.[20] At the August 1987 SNTS meeting at Göttingen, U. Schnelle delivered the paper

"Wandlungen im paulinischen Denken," arguing that a specific Pauline doctrine of justification took its shape in controversy with the Galatian Judaists and underwent strong modifications by the time Romans was written. I reject the idea that Paul had changed his gospel, but my "heresy" that he had changed his expression, tone, and conception seems to be shared by many. My proposal that the dominant character of the Roman community may have influenced Paul as he gave expression to this change remains reasonable.

D. Roman Christianity After Paul

Proportionately, the reviews of *Antioch and Rome* paid less attention to the post-Pauline period at Rome, for which I used 1 Peter, Hebrews, and *1 Clement* as evidence. In a friendly review Barton reports that I conclude that Pauline Christianity did not gain ascendancy at Rome. My precise phrasing would be that Paul's sharp views, critical of the law, expressed in Galatians, did not gain ascendancy at Rome. But I think that a theology similar to that expressed by Paul's Letter to the Romans was acceptable and was echoed in 1 Peter. Balch thinks that my thesis about the origins and makeup of Roman Christianity are refuted by the household structure described in 1 Peter, which came from Greco-Roman society and for which there is a similar pattern in Aristotle.[21] In my view, however, not every feature in Roman Christianity came from Jerusalem,[22] but only a respect for the law and cult, and an observance of certain Jewish purity rituals, especially as regards food. Much of Roman Christian life presumably was shaped by local influences, perhaps including the household arrangement.

The claims of Lampe that in Italy we know of early Christian settlements only at Rome, Puteoli (the port of Rome), and Aquileia makes it statistically likely that if Hebrews was addressed *to* Italy, Rome was in mind.[23] While Marshall thinks that I am certainly right in associating Hebrews and 1 Peter with Rome, he queries the precise attraction to the religious features of Judaism that I posited among the Roman recipients of Hebrews. I suggested a "return to the levitical sacrificial cult of the desert" (154). It was a guess, but I still hold that after the destruction of the Jerusalem Temple some Christians may have hoped for a restored cult more harmonious with the memory of a Jesus who is supposed to have wanted his Father's house to serve as a house of prayer. In a sense, both the author of Hebrews and his intended readers drew on the cultic heritage of Israel and spiritualized it. The difference between them may have been that in Christ the author of Hebrews sees all things replaced, whereas the addressees expected a continuing cult on earth, involving sacrifices and apparatus described in the Old

Testament. In any case, the author of Hebrews disparaged the wrong type of attraction to the cultic heritage of Judaism.

I think that Meeks misses my point here when he advances as a counterargument the statement: "Neither Hebrews nor *1 Clement* shows the slightest interest in what living Jews actually were doing, either on the site of the now destroyed temple or in their synagogue. The examples they refer to are entirely drawn from scripture." I agree (see 155-56). Hebrews was written to dissuade[24] Christians not from an attraction to Judaism (as if they were going to become Jews), but from an attraction to a Christianity very conservative of the Jewish heritage. The Roman Christians may not have known anything about what Jews were doing at the Temple site, but they knew the attractiveness of the cult described in the Pentateuch. The author of Hebrews believes that this attraction fails to recognize the enormous change wrought by Christ and is a backsliding—a laying again of a foundation of dead works (6:1). He thinks that the heart is strengthened by grace and not by foods (13:9).[25] If such phrases in Hebrews sound as if they came from Paul, am I not self-contradictory, then, in saying that the Paul of Romans could be accepted by the majority Jewish/Gentile Group (2) in that church, whereas Hebrews served to correct them? (Drane phrases this objection thus: "To claim that in Hebrews Christianity 'in a sense had become a new religion' while Paul was still thoroughly Jewish is to blur important distinctions.") I think that neither Paul nor the author of Hebrews would agree with Group 2's adherence to some Jewish food laws, but in Romans 9–11 Paul does not suggest that the covenant of God with Israel is finished (for God reckoned with infidelity when he made that covenant and ultimately will use that infidelity to save all Israel [11:25-27]). Hebrews speaks of a second covenant that replaces the first, a better covenant, replacing an obsolete and vanishing one (7:22; 8:7, 13). "New religion" is a debatable term for the first century, but the view of Christianity in Hebrews is much closer to predicating a new religion than is the view of Romans 9–11.

As for *1 Clement* and what followed at Rome in the second century, I have little to add other than to recommend Lampe's work, from which I have learned much, especially about the parochial units in the Roman church. Nothing there would cause me to think that a strong heritage from Judaism was not a feature in the majority Christian outlook of the capital in that period, even while at the same time a patterning on Roman imperial models of authority and structure grew apace. My view that some of this double heritage became a part of the life of the Great Church and enabled it to survive causes Weiss to think that I may be suggesting that apostolic succession, ecclesiastical hierarchy, and a preservation of the levitical priesthood in *1 Clement* and Ignatius reflect what is essential in the gospel.[26] No such thought was expressed or intended. Nevertheless, were I asked to phrase my thought in Weiss's terminology, I might claim that such structures were shown by *1 Clement* and Ignatius not to be contrary to the gospel and may have helped to preserve the gospel for the future; and that is what the Great Church, at its best moments, has claimed for such structures. The role of the church at Rome in such a preservation is part of what contributed to its eminence in the Great Church.

Notes

The following reviews of *Antioch and Rome* were read as part of the discussion in this article: J. Ashton, *The Month* (April 1984) 138; D. L. Balch, *JBL* 104 (1985) 725-28; S. C. Barton, *ExpTim* 95 (1983-84) 118; E. J. Ciuba, *CBQ* 48 (1983) 476-78; R. Collins, *LS* 10 (1984) 192; J. Drane, *EvQ* 58 (1986) 176-77; D. C. Duling, *USQR* 39 (1984) 243-50; D. G. Dunbar, *WTJ* 46 (1984) 424-26; J. Ferguson, *Journal of Beliefs and Values* 4, 2 (1983) 20-21, and *RelS* 20 (1984) 514-15; S. Freyne, *The Furrow* 35 (1984) 479-81; G. Greenfield, *Southwestern Journal of Theology* 27, 1 (1984) 65; D. G. Hunter, *TS* 45 (1984) 354-56; H.-J. Klauck, *BZ* 28 (1984) 122-25; A. T. Kraabel, *Int* 39 (1985) 325, 328; A. Logan, *SJT* 38 (1985) 266-68; I. H. Marshall, *JSNT* 25 (1985) 125-26; W. A. Meeks, *HeyJ* 27 (1986) 455-57; J. Murphy-O'Connor, *RB* 91 (1984) 146-49; G. O'Collins, *Greg* 65 (1984) 181-82; J. F. O'Grady, *Chicago Studies* 26 (1987) 88-90; R. Penna, *Bib* 66 (1985) 139-42; R. H. Smith, *CurTM* 12 (1985) 183-84; H. Weiss, *AUSS* 23 (1985) 297-99; R. L. Wilken, *BA* 49 (1986) 63-64.

1. Although I insisted that "Jew" and "Gentile" do not constitute distinguishing theological nomenclature, I specifically suggested that the majority of Christians at Rome may have been ethnically Gentile (111). I italicized this statement on 110: "The dominant Christianity at Rome had been shaped by the Jerusalem Christianity associated with James and Peter, and hence was a Christianity appreciative of Judaism and loyal to its customs." That some have read that as Jewish Christianity (such as Freyne) shows how hard it is to wean scholars away from what I regard as imprecise terminology.
2. Asia Minor and Ephesus are mentioned in particular (213-14).
3. "While no formal sociological analysis is attempted in this study, the results may prove of use for pursuing a sociological analysis of NT churches" (*Antioch and Rome*, 14).
4. Lampe also accepts this date. He thinks that Cassius Dio (*Hist.* 60.6.6), who mentions that at the beginning of his reign Claudius forbade the Jews to assemble, was not referring to the expulsion of Jews over the Chrestus issue. The revised Schürer-Vermes (3.77) holds that Dio did refer to the expulsion, but at this point was not writing chronologically. J. A. Fitzmyer, in his rewritten article on Paul in the *New Jerome Biblical Commentary* (Englewood Cliffs: Prentice Hall, 1990) 79:9, regards as the most certain extrabiblical datum for dating Paul's career the tie-in with Gallio at Corinth (Acts 18:12) in the year 52, which means that Paul arrived there in 51. In that context Acts 18:1-2 relates Paul's arrival to "a Jew named Aquila, a native of Pontus, lately come from Italy with his wife Priscilla, because Claudius had commanded all the Jews to leave Rome" (RSV). Clearly the year 49 fits that expulsion better than does 41.
5. The conversion of Poppaea is not "supposed" on 95; the statement there agrees with the revised Schürer-Vermes (3.78): "The empress Poppaea herself may have been attracted to Judaism."
6. On 110 the Ambrosiaster reference on the last line should be PL 17.48 not 17.46. On

206 the Hippolytus reference, *Philosophumena* 6.15, is correct for the ANF translation; it would be 6:20 for the Greek text (*Patristische Texte und Studien* 25.225).

7. In a helpful private letter Carl Holladay showed me how on the basis of Philo (and Josephus) one might divide Jews themselves into approximations of my four Groups of Jewish Christians: my Group 1 = extreme literalists on circumcision (Josephus, *Ant.* 20.2.4; #38-46); my Groups 2 and 3 = responsible allegorists; and my Group 4 = extreme allegorists (Philo, *Migr. Abrah.* 16; #89-94; also D. Hay, "Philo's References to Other Allegorists," *Studia Philonica* 6 [1979-80] 41-75). On the other hand, Balch's condemnatory judgment about *Antioch and Rome* is difficult to understand: "The fundamental categories used by these authors to interpret early Christianity are not theological. . . ." The four groupings based on relation to the law are the fundamental categories for these two cities—that is why we explain them in the opening pages of the book—and relation to the Jewish law is theological. Meeks objects that my "Groups" are more nearly ideal types than real historical entities. One can sketch types from them, but in each Group I named real, historical people who held the views described (as I do in the summary above). They are not pure scholarly reconstructions but are attested in the pages of the New Testament.

8. See O'Collins (*Greg* 65 [1984] 181-82) and Klauck (*BZ* 28 [1984] 122-25). Logan states: "Now and again one comes across a book which opens a whole new perspective on a much-worked field and makes one ask why no-one thought of doing it before" (*SJT* 38 [1985] 266-68).

9. I assumed that many readers of *Antioch and Rome* would have been familiar with this earlier book. Indeed, in *The Churches the Apostles Left Behind* (New York: Paulist, 1984) I describe the three books as companion volumes on early Christianity. They scarcely supply a monolithic Baur outlook.

10. On 104 I remark, "Tacitus seems to have thought Christianity came to Rome from Judea." Murphy-O'Connor corrects me: "Tacitus implies nothing of the kind." Here are Tacitus' words: "This pernicious superstition had broken out again not only in Judea (where the mischief had originated) but even in the capital city [Rome] where all degraded and shameful practices collect" (*Annals* 15.44).What would Tacitus' readers have concluded about where Christianity came from?

11. The evidence for this post-70 period came from the Talmud. I tried to show proper caution about its reliability, using expressions like "supposed to" and simply reporting that "the Talmud speaks." Yet, the Todos stories are more suspect than I had known, so that "constant interchange" (96) between Jerusalem and Rome may be too strong for post-70 Judaism. See now B. M. Bokser, "Todos and Rabbinic Authority in Rome," in *New Perspectives on Ancient Judaism* (eds. J. Neusner et al.; Lanham: University Press of America, 1987) 1.117-30.

12. Similarly not to the point is Murphy-O'Connor's contention that there is little evidence that the Roman Jews were active proselytizers. Yet, was the Jewish religion not part of the Eastern superstitions, the attractiveness of which annoyed the Roman authorities? Lampe insists there were many *sebomenoi* at Rome.

13. If I had to answer, I would assume that at Jerusalem there were at least Sadducees, Pharisees, some Essenes, and many religiously indifferent.

14. To the evidence given in the book, let me add the "Marcionite" Latin Prologue to Romans, which some would date to the late second century. It states that Roman Christians got their knowledge of Jesus Christ from false prophets who introduced them to the law and prophets. But Paul, writing from Athens, called them back to the true and evangelical faith.

15. Drane misunderstands me on this point, neglecting the references to Groups 3 and 1 at Rome. Nevertheless, I sometimes wrote too summarily of "the Roman church" and "Roman Christianity." I should have written "many in the Roman church" and "many Roman Christians" when I was speaking of the dominant mindset.

16. See p. 119, where I suggested that Christians even more radically estranged from Judaism (Group 4) might also be included. I have recently read in typescript the paper that J. Marcus gave at the 1987 SBL Meeting at Boston on the contingent character of Romans, where he treats of the weak and the strong in relation to circumcision and

uncircumcision. He is very convincing that in Rom 14–15 Paul is treating a real dispute in the Roman church and not simply theorizing out of past experience, as reflected in 1 Cor 8:7-13. (Notice that Rom 14–15 is not concerned with the idol issue, even as 1 Cor was not concerned with "the strong" or eating vegetables.)

17. Lampe, *Christen*, 56-57, insists that the weak cannot be simply Christians of Jewish birth but must include the *sebomenoi*. On 119-20 n. 248, I hesitatingly suggested that Rom 14:2, "The weak eats (only) vegetables," refers to the way in which some Jewish/Gentile Christians of Group 1 at Rome avoided eating meat that might be contaminated by ritual impurity. Independently, the Jewish scholar A. F. Segal, "Romans 7 and Jewish Dietary Law," *Studies in Religion* 15 (1986) 361-74, esp. 367, takes the same approach. For ancient evidence, see Dan 1:8, 12.

18. If a passage like Rom 3:25 should be pre-Pauline, as some contend, and known already to the Romans, that could strengthen my argument about the extent to which Roman Christianity was affected by the theological language of Judaism before Paul wrote.

19. From the book it is clear that I firmly reject the thesis that Paul knew little about Christianity at Rome (see also n. 16 above), but that is a more logical position than the thesis that he knew the situation and that it was one in which the church consisted mostly of Gentiles who held the same views he held. Why then would he explain his gospel so carefully and at length? Why would he use formulations redolent of Judaism and otherwise unusual for him? Why such a long defense of the privileges of Judaism and the grafted-branch motif?

20. Segal, "Romans 7 and Jewish Dietary Law," 372, sees in Romans "a softening of Paul's other positions on law. Previously Paul virtually equated law with both sin and flesh."

21. For my purposes I need not debate Balch's analysis of 1 Pet, but it has been strongly challenged by J. H. Elliott in *Perspectives on First Peter* (ed. C. H. Talbert; Macon: Mercer, 1986).

22. To hold (as Balch thinks I hold) that, after Christianity came from Jerusalem to Rome, nothing changed would be nonsense, granted the expulsion of some or many Jewish Christians from Rome in 49 CE in the dispute over Chrestus.

23. Ashton, too, simply discounts the relation of Heb to Rome, without debating the evidence given on 144-47. Writings associated with Rome show an awareness of Heb throughout the second century, long before we can detect knowledge of it elsewhere. The recent major commentary by H. W. Attridge (*Hebrews* [Hermeneia; Philadelphia: Fortress, 1989] 10) states: "External evidence tends to tip the scales in favor of . . . a Roman destination."

24. Meeks objects that I interpret Hebrews as *polemicizing* against the old Israelite cultus (although he admits that Hebrews disparages that cultus). I do not pretend to be rigidly consistent in vocabulary, but in rereading *Antioch and Rome* I found no use of the word *polemic* for Hebrews. On 143 and 155 I used "dissuasive" and on 154 "corrective," and those terms represent exactly my understanding of Hebrews. Meeks also concentrates correctively on a rhetorical sentence I wrote on 140, mostly involving a quotation from another scholar: "Even the literary form [of Hebrews] is a mystery since 'it begins like a treatise, proceeds like a sermon, and closes like an epistle.' " Meeks argues that the literary form of Hebrews is not mysterious; it is a hortatory speech. Excellent—so long as we can agree that the exhortation involves a corrective against too great a loyalty to the cult of Israel as enacted in ongoing sacrifices.

25. These and other passages cause me to resist as inadequate Meeks's view that Hebrews "is only an appeal to Christians who have become bored and slack." Seemingly the Christians addressed are not slack about some works that involve food laws. While, I believe, the first Jewish Christians who came from Jerusalem to Rome in the early 40s knew Judaism firsthand from their own experience, by the latter part of the century Roman Christians, loyal to some of the heritage from Judaism, knew it more by tradition and from Scripture than from personal experience with Jews.

26. While many authors (for example, Ferguson and Greenfield) seem to have found the book without Roman Catholic bias, Drane hints at "dogmatic presuppositions." Balch sees it as "a view from the bishop's chair"—curious, since the book argues that the

single-bishop structure did not come to Rome until around 140-150 CE (163) and denies that Peter was the local bishop of the Roman church, or for that matter of the Antioch church (98, 215). Duling wonders, "How historically appropriate is the Pauline trajectory that leads to the canon of orthodoxy?" The answer to that lies in part in whether one understands 1 Cor 15:11 to be Paul's own claim to "orthodoxy": "Whether then it was I or they [a 'they' that includes Cephas and James, 15:5-7], so we preach and so you believed." For an intelligent treatment of some of the more classic Roman Catholic positions (which were not in the focus of *Antioch and Rome*), see P. Grelot, "Pierre et Paul fondateurs de la 'primauté' romaine," *Istina* 27 (1982) 228-68.

"ONE AGAINST THE OTHER": INTRA-CHURCH CONFLICT IN 1 CORINTHIANS

William Baird

In the course of Pauline research, serious attention has been focused on the problem of the apostle's opponents. Johannes Weiss, writing in 1910, could complain of the "unendliche Literatur,"[1] and Christian Machalet, over a half-century later, could observe that "eine Einigung unter den Exegeten noch nicht in Sicht ist."[2] The purpose of this essay is not to offer a novel identification of the opponents, but to propose a reconsideration of the basic question. In the light of methodological observations and exegetical investigation, I shall contend that the search for opponents in 1 Corinthians may be misguided. The situation reflected in the letter seems to be more complicated, involving not simply Paul against Corinthians, but Corinthians "one against the other" (4:6).[3]

I

The history of research need not be rehearsed in detail.[4] Suffice it to say that the major actors in the drama are F. C. Baur and Wilhelm Lütgert. Baur, writing in 1831, argues that 1 Cor 1:12 does not describe four parties, but only two: the Paul-Apollos party and the Cephas-Christ party.[5] Thus 1 Corinthians is aimed at a single group of opponents whom Baur identifies as Judaizers. To make his case, Baur cites references from the entire Corinthian correspondence, especially 2 Corinthians. Indeed, he detects traces of the Judaizing faction throughout the authentic Pauline letters. The conflict between the two Corinthian parties provides the hermeneutical clue for Baur's understanding of early Christianity. That history can be summarized in the subtitle of his essay: "der Gegensatz der petrinischen und paulinischen Christenthums in der ältesten Kirche."[6]

Lütgert, on the other hand, argues that Paul's opponents are

116

"libertinische Pneumatiker," or "antinomistische Gnostiker."[7] To be sure, Lütgert acknowledges the presence of Judaizers in Corinth, "eine Petruspartei," as well as the wisdom-loving "Leute des Apollos."[8] The chief opponents, however, are to be identified with the Christ party. They are the enthusiasts who have distorted Paul's doctrine of freedom—Corinthians who embrace sexual license and inflate the value of visions and revelations.

In more recent times,[9] Lütgert's theme has been played with variations by Walter Schmithals. Schmithals defines the opponents as Jewish gnostics. Within the Corinthian church Paul faces only one front of opposition: the Christ party—that is, the gnostics. Schmithals grounds his hypothesis in extensive research into the nature of gnosticism and develops the theory by detailed exegesis of 1 and 2 Corinthians. On the basis of his analysis of the Pauline argument, Schmithals purports to reconstruct the theology of the opponents—their Christology, anthropology, and eschatology. He concludes that "*all* questions handled in the epistles"[10] must be investigated in relation to this understanding of the historical situation.

In the style of Baur, Schmithals finds evidence of the same opponents in all the Pauline churches.[11] "Thus," writes James Robinson, "Schmithals provides a sweeping solution to the problems of primitive Christianity, comparable to the Tübingen hypothesis of Ferdinand Christian Baur, who saw everything in terms of the struggle of Paul with the Judaizers—only that with Schmithals the Judaizers are replaced by Jewish gnostics, a variant already proposed by Wilhelm Lütgert half a century ago."[12]

Not everyone is convinced.[13] Some detect in Schmithals's approach a "pan-gnosticism," perhaps even a German plot.[14] Nevertheless, a large number of scholars who quarrel with the details of Schmithals's reconstruction agree that Paul's argument in 1 Corinthians is addressed to a group of hellenistic enthusiasts. As Conzelmann concludes, "It is certainly possible to detect clearly in the Corinthian community tendencies of a pneumatic, enthusiastic individualistic kind."[15]

Most significant, many recent interpreters consider 1 Corinthians to be directed against a homogeneous opposition. Schmithals's argument in support of the one-front hypothesis can be briefly summarized: (1) The time is too short for more than one heresy to have arisen; and (2) the Corinthian correspondence affords no evidence that Paul's polemic is directed against more than one front.[16] The latter point is affirmed by Gorden Fee, who notes that the letter is addressed to the whole church and that the style throughout is combative.[17] The conclusion is clearly articulated by John Hurd: "1 Corinthians was addressed by Paul to a single, more or less unified, opposing point of view."[18]

This argument presupposes a dialectical interpretation of history, which seems, unconsciously, to owe much to F. C. Baur.[19] According to this interpretation, history progresses by a series of conflicting encounters. Thus Hurd, who pays scant attention to the religious backgrounds or sociological stratification of the community, attempts to reconstruct the history of the Corinthian situation in terms of direct, diametrically opposed exchanges between Paul and the church. When he first came to town, Paul, according to this view, was an ardent liberal, declaring, "All things are lawful!" (6:12; 10:23). After receiving a copy of the Apostolic Decrees (Acts 15:23-29),[20] however, he reversed himself and became a religious and moral conservative. When the Corinthians read in Paul's "previous letter" (1 Cor 5:9) of this sudden transformation, they wrote to Paul (7:1) in disbelief, hurling his own slogans back in his face. Paul, in turn, wrote 1 Corinthians in response to this direct opposition. And who were the opponents? The whole church of Corinth.

Although this dialectical view of early Christian history functions as a presupposition that shapes the exegetical results, the hypothesis that Paul is facing only one front is attractive. We may suppose that the devotees of σοφία in chap. 1 are to be identified with the people who boast of γνῶσις in chap. 8—the same people who are depicted as pneumatics in chap. 12 and charged with denying the resurrection in chap. 15. Perhaps, we could facetiously propose that *the* opponent is a feminist (11:2-16), who is sympathetic to the practice of incest (chap. 5), who takes fellow Christians to court (6:1-8), who advocates both asceticism (7:1) and license (6:15-18), who gets drunk at the Lord's Supper (11:21), and who speaks in tongues (chap. 12). More seriously, in view of the variety of religious and social backgrounds of the Corinthians, the attempt to pour all of the problems of the church into a single mold seems unduly restrictive. Even Schmithals has difficulty fitting everything into his pattern.[21]

II

The difficulty of reducing all the issues to a single pattern recommends the reopening of the question. For one thing, the arguments of Schmithals and Fee in support of the one-front hypothesis are less than convincing.[22] Heresies can arise in a short period of time, especially if they are related to the previous religious and social experience of the converts. The exegesis of 1 Corinthians, as we shall see, provides evidence for a variety of factions within the congregation. The letter is addressed to the whole church because the various problems disrupt the essential oneness of the body of Christ. The recognition that some sections of the epistle are combative says nothing about the number of fronts on which Paul is fighting.

Indeed, the larger question can be raised: Should the exegesis of 1 Corinthians be dominated by the thesis that Paul is primarily addressing opponents?[23] The preoccupation with opponents has encouraged exegetes to embrace a methodology whereby texts are read as antithetical responses to that which hypothetical opponents are supposed to have said. If Paul denies something, the opponents must have affirmed it. If Paul affirms something, the opponents must have denied it. This method of "mirror reading"[24] has imposed on the interpretation of the epistles an oppressive rigidity. A fresh reading of 1 Corinthians is needed—a reading open to a more flexible analysis of the conflict within the Corinthian congregation.

In further consideration of methodological matters, the question of sources can be raised. "For the answering of the questions about Paul's adversaries in Corinth," claims Schmithals, "it is methodologically indispensable to take as a basis all the correspondence with Corinth."[25] However, as Georgi has shown, the arguments of 2 Corinthians address a different situation which has arisen after opponents have invaded the church from outside.[26] Although his description of these opponents is debated,[27] Georgi's basic theory is widely accepted.[28] Investigation of the problems of 1 Corinthians should be restricted to the text of 1 Corinthians.[29]

Related to the question of sources is the problem of integrity. If 1 Corinthians is a composite of two or more letters, then its content could relate to more than one situation. Parts of 1 Corinthians, therefore, could have been directed to different stages in the development of the conflict. Although partition theories about the composition of 1 Corinthians come in conflicting variety,[30] they are not without supporting evidence: material that seems out of place (chap. 9), arguments that are less than consistent (8:4 and 10:20), and instruction that seems to assume different degrees of understanding (11:18 and 1:11-12). However, as the various commentaries indicate, most of these difficulties can be readily explained. As a working hypothesis, then, the view of the majority can be accepted: 1 Corinthians is a single, unified composition.[31]

Related to the question of integrity is the problem of identifying the sources of Paul's information. As the epistle indicates, Paul has received a report from Chloe's people (1:11) and a letter from the Corinthians (7:1); he has also been visited by a delegation from the church (16:17). Hurd's effort to restrict the information to these three sources,[32] together with his ingenious attempt to distinguish those parts of the epistle that respond to oral information from those that reply to

119

written,[33] tends to oversimplify the issue. For instance, Hurd fails to note that Apollos, after his ministry in Corinth, has apparently visited Paul prior to the writing of 1 Corinthians (16:12). The Corinthian delegation, made up of three persons, may have supplied a variety of data. And, given the relatively short distance between Corinth and Ephesus, sources other than those mentioned in the letter may have brought information to Paul.

Another methodological problem relates to the procedure for identifying opponents. Although some exegetes have employed uncritical and subjective methods, others have attempted to delineate criteria. Schmithals, for example, identifies literary and stylistic features that betray Paul's concern with opponents, such as the use of κἀγώ (7:40)[34] or technical "non-Pauline" terms like γνῶσις.[35] Hurd posits two criteria whereby the slogans or quotations from the opponents can be detected: grammatical or stylistic indications (like the repetition of "we" in 8:1) and forms of argumentation (such as the qualifications of a statement; 8:1, 6).[36] Lüdemann believes the utterances of anti-Paulinists can best be identified when Paul directly quotes their statements and indicates that they are directed against him ("*der ideale Fall*"), but says that passages where Paul employs a polemic style in answer to an attack can also be used with caution.[37] Gunther, in a detailed analysis of the issue, lists twelve ways in which a biblical author reveals response to opponents.[38] These can be reduced to three main categories: (1) statements of obvious negative intention (7:5); (2) statements that appear to counter doctrines that are attacked in other texts (7:19); and (3) statements whereby the opponents' "thunder is stolen" (7:40).

A review of these criteria and the supporting examples suggest that the methods used for identifying opponents are less than satisfactory. The principle of "mirror reading" frequently intrudes, and the grammatical and stylistic indications are sometimes unconvincing. Except for incidents of Lüdemann's "ideal case," most of the examples are open to debate. Consequently, in the absence of unimpeachable criteria, the effort to identify opponents or factions will have to rely on historical exegesis of the text. In pursuing this exegesis, attention will need to be given to the religious and social backgrounds of the converts.

III

The majority of the Corinthian Christians were Gentiles. For them, Corinth offered a variety of religious options. Pausanias, who visited the city more than a century later, viewed shrines to a variety of deities, including Zeus, Apollo, and Aphrodite.[39] Apuleius' hero Lucius saw his vision of Isis near Corinth, and in the city he witnessed a sacred procession of the goddess.[40] Nearby Isthmia, which sponsored important games, was sacred to Poseidon.[41] A major temple complex of Asclepius, including dining rooms, was located north of the central city.[42]

Although we cannot specify the religions of the Gentile converts, we can detect evidence of their previous participation in hellenistic cults. In 1:13-17, Paul implies that some Corinthians felt an inordinate loyalty to the minister who had baptized them. This may reflect an experience in the cults where the devotee assumed a special association with the priest who had performed the initiatory rites.[43] In 8:7, Paul observes that those troubled by food that had been sacrificed to idols were people who were "hitherto accustomed to idols" (RSV). This suggests that they were persons who had participated in pagan cultic meals.[44] In 12:2, Paul refers to the religious experience of Corinthians ὅτε ἔθνη ἦτε. "When you were heathen," he says, "you were led astray to dumb idols, however you may have been moved" (RSV). In other words, some of Paul's readers, prior to their conversion, had experienced religious ecstasy within the hellenistic cults.[45]

Along with the Gentile majority, the congregation at Corinth included Jews. The presence of a Jewish community in Corinth is attested by an inscription found near the main entrance of the agora, which can be reconstructed to read, "Synagogue of the Hebrews."[46] Mention of the Jews is made throughout 1 Corinthians (1:22-24; 9:20; 10:32), most notably in 12:13: "We were all baptized into one body, whether Jews or Greeks." Evidence for the presence of Jews in the church is visible in the controversy regarding meat that had been offered to idols (chaps. 8–10). The question of eating εἰδωλόθυτα would scarcely have been raised in a pagan city like Corinth apart from the presence of people who had been ardently opposed to it—the Jews.[47]

In the diaspora, Judaism displayed a variety of expressions, including everything from asceticism to hellenistic wisdom speculation.[48] These extreme examples could help to explain the Corinthian concern with sexual abstinence in 7:1 and the preoccupation with σοφία in chaps. 1 and 2. Among Paul's converts from the synagogue may have been some God-fearers[49]—Gentiles attracted by Jewish monotheism (8:6), but reticent about cultic matters such as Jewish ritual food laws (chaps. 8–10).

On the basis of the currently popular sociological approach to biblical research, observations can be made about the social backgrounds of the Corinthian Christians. The city of Corinth, destroyed in the second century BCE, had been rebuilt as a Roman colony in 44 BCE Populated first by veterans and freedmen, Corinth was soon teeming with people from all over the empire. A new city, burgeoning with commercial activity, Corinth included a variety of social classes. From this varied populace, members were recruited for the church. The resulting stratification of the congregation encouraged the conflicts reflected in 1 Corinthians.

According to Theissen, Paul's mission was directed first to the upper strata.[50] Paul had a special appeal to the upper classes, since, as many scholars have concluded, he was from the upper class himself.[51] Actually, Paul's mission appealed to people from a variety of social classes. Compared with various sorts of guilds and associations that were popular in the hellenistic age, the church was distinguished by the fact that its membership displayed a greater degree of social variation.[52] 1 Corinthians 1:26 is frequently cited to prove that most of the Corinthian Christians were from the lower classes—not many δυνατοί (politically powerful), not many εὐγενεῖς (upper class).[53] However, the statement that not *many* were from the upper strata implies that *some* were.[54]

Individuals who belonged to the upper classes included Crispus and Erastus. The former, if he can be identified with the Crispus of Acts 18:8, had been the leader of the synagogue—a position that usually entailed financial patronage and power.[55] Erastus, whose greeting is conveyed in Rom 16:23, may be the same civil official whose name is commemorated in an inscription found near the theater. According to the inscription, the pavement in this prominent place was "laid at his own expense."[56] Galius, who has a house large enough to host Paul and the "whole church" (Rom 16:23) is surely a person of means.[57] Members like Stephanas (1 Cor 16:17) and Phoebe (Rom 16:1) can afford to travel.[58] 1 Corinthians 16:2 implies that some Corinthians are financially able to make contributions to Jerusalem, and 6:1-6 indicates that Corinthian Christians are taking other church members to court for βιωτικά—cases concerning property and income.[59]

Among the membership were people of the artisan class, folk like Prisca and Aquila.[60] This Jewish Christian couple, however, was not without financial resources, since they were able to host churches in their houses (1 Cor 16:19; Rom 16:3-5).[61] Some of the members may have been laborers in the busy docks or Corinth's famous bronze foundries.[62] According to Theissen, Chloe's people (1:11) must have been slaves or dependent workers. If they had been members of the family, they would have taken the father's name (even if he were dead), not Chloe's.[63] Slaves, who constituted about one-third of the city's population,[64] were members of the congregation (7:21). Although considered property rather than persons, most slaves in this period were economically secure, not badly treated, and confident of eventual manumission.[65] They may not have been as unfortunate as those members of the church "who have nothing" (11:22).

Women, who were viewed in hellenistic society as a subordinate class, played an important role in the Corinthian church. Chloe is apparently the head of a household,[66] and Phoebe is a διάκονος, and possibly the hostess, of the suburban house church at Cenchreae (Rom 16:1).[67] Movements for women's liberation were active in the hellenistic age.[68] Isis, noted as the goddess who empowered women, was especially revered at Corinth.[69] Perhaps Paul's concern with women who had discarded their veils (11:2-16) indicates the presence of a "feminist" movement in the Corinthian church. Fee believes the presence of "eschatological women"—women who adopt a spiritual, realized eschatology and see themselves already living as angels—contributes to the conflict at Corinth.[70]

The presence of different social classes within the church provides fertile soil for the growth of factions. Tensions between classes, particularly in view of the unusual diversity within the Christian community, make conflict seem inevitable. Some scholars, Theissen, for instance, believe that virtually all the problems faced in 1 Corinthians can be attributed to this kind of conflict.[71] Peter Marshall thinks the Corinthian tensions exist primarily between Paul and some upper-class members of the church.[72] According to Marshall, Paul's refusal to accept financial support from wealthy constituents is a major cause of the problem. The Corinthian offer of a gift, made according to the hellenistic conventions of friendship, assumed a position of prestige and required obligations that Paul did not want to concede.

This conflict, however, did not represent a single front of opposition. Some of the upper class remained loyal to Paul, so that he could commend the leadership of a person like Stephanas (16:15-16).[73] The conflict between the upper classes was no doubt encouraged by the existence of a number of house churches—small congregations, hosted by the wealthy, where feelings of pride and personal loyalty were bound to arise.[74]

IV

The presence of factions in the Corinthian church can be attested by a hasty survey of texts. Of course, no interpreter supposes that the church had split into separate sectarian groups. Paul is able to address a single letter to the whole church; the members continue to assemble as an ἐκκλησία (11:18; 5:4). Nevertheless, texts and terms indicate that factions exist, and overt division is a genuine threat. In 1:10, Paul exhorts the Corinthians that σχίσματα should not be among them.[75] Although he may be merely warning about the threat of division, Paul later says that he has heard that when the Corinthians assemble as a church there are σχίσματα ἐν ὑμῖν (11:18)—that is, actual factions within the congregation. The word σχίσμα can be used to describe cliques in a cultic association. A papyrus, reporting the rules of one of these cults, reads, "It shall not be permissible for any . . . to make factions (*schismata*) or to leave the brotherhood."[76]

In 11:19, Paul says that "it is necessary for factions (αἵρεσις) to be among you." Although this expression may be ironic, it is more likely the citation of a traditional, apocalyptic word of the Lord.[77] If so, Paul takes the actual existence of factions at the Lord's Supper to be the eschatological fulfillment of this dominical prediction. The term αἵρεσις is used nine times in the New Testament, mostly in Acts, where it describes "sects" of the Jews. Philo and Josephus use it in reference to the different schools of philosophy or parties of Judaism.

According to 1:11, Chloe's people have reported the presence of ἔριδες among the Corinthians. The term ἔρις is used in the New Testament only in Paul and the Pastorals. For Paul, it is a typical component of the vice-lists (Rom 1:29; 2 Cor 12:20) and is frequently employed, as in 3:3, along with ζῆλος (Rom 13:13; Gal 5:20). Josephus (*J.W.* 5.596) uses ἔρις to describe the dissension between Aristobulus and Hyrcanus, which encouraged Pompey's attack on Jerusalem. Philo (*De Ebr.* 99) lists ἔριδες among the hostilities that belong to the works of war.

The presence of factions in the church is also attested by Paul's discussion of sacrificial meat (chaps. 8 and 10). The question has been raised by the Corinthians, as the περὶ δέ formula (7:1) indicates. The problem has arisen because members of the church have occasion to eat εἰδωλόθυτον—the Jewish term for food that has been sacrificed to idols. Although not all the food sold in the market was contaminated in this way,[78] the Corinthians had various opportunities to indulge in sacrificial meat.[79] Some members took advantage of these opportunities, while others were scandalized. Opposition was axiomatic among Jews, and in time opposition became the position of the church (Acts 15:20-29; 21:25; Rev 2:14, 20; *Did.* 6:3).

Difference of opinion crystallized into factions. Slogans were pronounced: "we all have knowledge" (8:1); "an idol has no real existence" (8:4 RSV). These slogans, however, came from one faction. Observation of this feature of the text has led Hurd to suppose that the conflict involves Paul and a single group of opponents.[80] Hurd believes that Paul's reference to the "weak" is a mere hypothesis of the argument. To be sure, the "weak" do not constitute a clearly delineated party; yet, they do represent a real group of people in the Corinthian church, as texts like 8:7 and 8:10 indicate. Paul's warning that freedom can give offense to the "weak" (8:9) and that knowledge can destroy the "weak" presupposes the presence of Corinthians who can be designated the "weak." Paul's argument is directed to a single faction not because no other group exists, but because the so-called "strong" possess the freedom that allows obedience to Paul's advice—a freedom not available to the "weak."

The group to which the advice is directed is usually called the "strong," though Paul does not use the term in 1 Corinthians 8 and 10.[81] Since they claim to possess γνῶσις (8:1), they can be dubbed the "enlightened"—the "intellectuals" who know that an idol has no existence, that food cannot be spiritually tainted (8:4). In response to their claim, Paul insists that all people do not share this knowledge (8:7). Some Corinthians, in other words, are not enlightened; they are the "weak."

Is it possible to identify more precisely the "weak" and the "enlightened"? In response, scholars usually answer in terms of the Jewish-Gentile controversy in the early church. Data from Galatians is cited, and one of the food factions is sometimes identified with the Cephas party of 1 Cor 1:12.[82] However, most interpreters, following the Jewish-Gentile line of argument, identify the "weak" as Gentiles who formerly ate sacrificial meat, who "were accustomed to regard an idol as a reality" (8:7).[83] After their conversion, these Gentile Christians, probably influenced by the church's Jewish heritage, became conservative in regard to eating sacrificial meat.

Since the "enlightened" claimed γνῶσις, they have sometimes been identified as gnostics.[84] However, the γνῶσις of the "enlightened" shows little trace of the kind of esoteric knowledge that characterizes gnosticism. Instead, the γνῶσις of the Corinthians is based on clear understanding of the fundamental Christian confession of God as creator and Jesus Christ as Lord (8:6). Theissen, employing sociological insights, argues that efforts to identify the factions in terms of the Jewish-Gentile conflict are misplaced.[85] According to Theissen, the divisions are social: The "weak" are from the lower classes, the "strong" from the upper. Although Theissen's argument conveys helpful information—for example, that members of the lower class in hellenistic society rarely had opportunity to eat meat—his conclusion is less than convincing. Social factors may have been involved, but as the content of Paul's argument shows, the issue is primarily religious.[86]

In regard to the factions of 1 Corinthians 8 and 10, therefore, we cannot be precise about the identification of the "weak" and the "enlightened." The latter are apparently Corinthians who eat sacrificial meat without qualms of conscience, supposing their action to be a badge of Christian freedom. The former are probably people who are denigrated as "weak" by the "enlightened," ridiculed for their unenlightened conscience, which prevents them from enjoying the special benefits of the sacrificial food (8:8).[87]

Although the "enlightened" are plagued by the pride that permeates much of the Corinthian community, their relation to other factions in the church cannot be determined with confidence. A conflict between Paul and Cephas had occurred at Antioch in regard to Gentile-Jewish table fellowship (Gal 2:11-21), but since the "weak" are probably Gentile converts, they can scarcely be identified with the "Cephas party" of 1 Cor 1:10. The "enlightened," since they are devotees of knowledge, would seem to be one with those who boast of wisdom in 1 Corinthians 1–4. However, Paul uses the term σοφία sixteen times in 1 Corinthians 1–3, and not once in chaps. 8 and 10. He uses γνῶσις five times in chap. 8, and not once in 1:10–4:21. All we can know for sure is that the Corinthian church contained at least two factions in regard to the question of sacrificial food.

Evidence for factions in the Corinthian church can also be detected in Paul's argument concerning spiritual gifts. Again, the question has been raised by the letter from the Corinthians (περὶ δέ; 12:1). Paul's answer indicates that the problem has been created by the claim of some Corinthians to have a special endowment of the Spirit. The gift that they have received they perceive to be the exclusive or the best χάρισμα of the Spirit. This gift manifests itself in glossolalia—the gift of ecstatic speech.

In response, Paul insists that spiritual gifts come in variety (12:4). The shape of his argument shows that the Corinthians are quarreling among themselves about this issue. In developing the body metaphor, Paul argues that no member can say that it does not belong (12:15-16), and at the same time, no member can say it has no need of another (12:21). Paul's questions in 12:29-30—"Are all apostles? Are all prophets?"— suggest that some members are claiming exclusive roles. Paul's contrast between tongue-speakers and prophets (14:2-5) may also imply that a struggle between these two types of spiritual leaders is taking place.

In attempting to identify the charismatics, Schmithals detects the omnipresent gnostics. His exegesis of 12:3 is ingenious. Like the gnostics of a later time, the Corinthian heretics praised the spiritual Christ, but cursed the earthly Jesus.[88] Although most interpreters reject this kind of precise definition,[89] the majority describe the trouble makers as some sort of spiritual enthusiasts or exponents of individualism.[90] Actually, the text displays the obvious: Different persons express their religious experience in different ways. The behavior of the Corinthian charismatics had been prepared by their religious background and their psychological makeup.[91]

Paul's argument is primarily directed against one faction: the charismatics who have caused the trouble and who are also, of course, able to remedy it. Besides the trouble makers, the Corinthian church includes members who do not express their faith through ecstatic speech, as 12:30 indicates: "All do not speak in tongues, do they?" (NASB). The argument, as the use of the body metaphor and the plea for ἀγάπη indicate, is addressed to the factionalism that the charismatics have created. Paul does not oppose speaking in tongues per se (14:5, 18). He attacks an understanding of glossolalia that disrupts the unity of the church.

Are the charismatics of chaps. 12 and 14 to be identified with those who apparently claim to be πνευματικοί in chaps. 2 and 3? On the surface, some connection seems obvious. In 12:1 πνευματικῶν can be construed as masculine ("now concerning the spiritual person"), and in 14:37, Paul mentions the individual who may claim to be a "spiritual" (πνευματικός). Nevertheless, the problems appear to be different. The spirituals of chaps. 2 and 3 are devotees of worldly wisdom. The charismatics of 12 and 14 are captives of a particular spiritual gift. The common element appears to be pride—a pride that has produced factions that claim special possession of the spirit or the spirit's gifts.[92]

The presence of factions within the congregation is also attested by 1 Corinthians 15. In v. 12, Paul asks, "How can some of you say there is no resurrection of the dead?" Who are these Corinthians who deny the resurrection? Concerning this question, a wide measure of agreement exists: Those who deny the resurrection are gnostics or proto-gnostics of some sort. This view, espoused by Lütgert long ago, was later embraced by Schniewind.[93] According to Schniewind, the Corinthian heretics have much in common with Hymenaeus and Philetus, who believe the resurrection has taken place already (2 Tim 2:18). Others, for instance Schmithals,[94] call attention to 4:8-13, where Paul appears to attack a "realized eschatology." This would imply that the deniers of the resurrection are to be identified with the devotees of wisdom in chaps. 1–4.[95]

In spite of the current agreement, other interpretations have been proposed for 1 Cor 15:12, and voices have been raised to protest the majority opinion.[96] Recently, Gordon Fee has argued that the deniers of the resurrection are the πνευματικοί who reject the hope of the resurrection of the body.[97] Yet, regardless of the identification of the deniers of the resurrection, 1 Cor 15:12 fails to support the hypothesis of a single front of opposition in Corinth. Paul says that "some (τινες) of you say there is no resurrection of the dead." Therefore, not all, but only some, a faction within the congregation, deny the resurrection.

As we have seen, 1 Cor 11:18 indicates the presence of σχίσματα in the congregation. The divisions are in evidence when the church assembles to observe the Lord's Supper. Some members arrive early and go ahead with their meal. Others come late and go away hungry. As the different contexts indicate, the σχίσματα here have no direct relation to the factions of 1:12. There the issue is loyalty to leaders, while here the divisions are socio-economic.[98]

The socio-economic line of interpretation, which has been followed for some time,[99] has been diligently pursued by Theissen.[100] Theissen observes that the division within the congregation is acutely apparent in the variable times at which the meal is begun. The wealthy Christians begin first and eat separately. Division is also manifest in the different quantities and qualities of food consumed. Citing hellenistic sources, Theissen presents illustrations of dinner parties where varying amounts and qualities of food were served to different guests on the basis of their social status. Similarly, the rich of the Corinthian church who host the meal probably feel justified, in accord with contemporary custom, to eat first, to eat better, and to eat more.

Again, Paul's response is directed primarily to one group: the wealthy who are responsible for the problem and, at the same time, able to solve it. The attempt to detect a relationship between these wealthy Corinthians and the "strong" of chap. 8 is, as we have seen, unconvincing. Moreover, no evidence points to the identification of the wealthy of chap. 11 with the charismatics of chap. 12 or the deniers of the resurrection of chap. 15. In responding to the wealthy, Paul's main concern is their role in perpetrating the conflict within the congregation. Although he deals with the theology of the Supper, Paul's argument is aimed primarily at Corinthian factionalism. Thus his final admonition: "Wait for one another" (11:33).

Other evidences of factionalism may be found throughout the epistle. For instance, there was apparently a group favoring celibacy (7:1), who imagined that Paul was on their side, and another that condoned (5:1-2) or even practiced (6:15-18) sexual license. However, let us return to the question of the Corinthian parties—the issue that launched Baur and his successors on the quest for the Pauline opponents. In the history of research, one of the most intriguing proposals was made in 1911 by Richard Perdelwitz.[101] According to Perdelwitz, the notorious difficulty of identifying the Christ party can be resolved by a simple textual emendation. Instead of reading ἐγὼ δὲ Χριστοῦ, the text should read ἐγὼ δὲ Κρίσπου—a change of only two letters. The result: the so-called Christ party is actually the party of Crispus.

Crispus, once ruler of the synagogue, had been converted to Christianity by Paul (Acts 18:8). After the apostle had left Corinth, a vacuum of leadership occurred. Who should emerge to fill the gap but a person of proven ability—Crispus the ἀρχισυνάγωγος. Once Perdelwitz had solved the problem of 1:12, he proposed another minor emendation to 3:22—a verse that, according to the accepted text, presents an imperfect parallelism. However, when κόσμος is changed to Κρίσπος, the results are stunning:

> whether Paul or Apollos,
> whether Cephas or Crispus,
> whether life or death,
> whether things present or things to come.

Although no one has accepted Perdelwitz's theory, his work calls attention to a crucial issue in the investigation of the Corinthian parties: The grammatical structure of 1:12 (the exact parallelism of the phrases) implies the existence of a fourth party, but the designation of the fourth party as the party of Christ (a party with no ecclesiastical leader) indicates that the nature of the fourth party must be somehow different.[102] This difference has encouraged inordinate interest in the party of Christ and fostered theories that view it as the major front of opposition. Strange as it may seem, the party about which we know the least—which may not even be a party—has become the major preoccupation of a large mass of New Testament scholarship.

Moreover, the focus on the party named for Christ, together with the emphasis on σοφία in chaps. 1 and 2, has led many—for example, Wilckens[103]—to construe Paul's struggle with the Corinthians as an ideological battle. From this perspective, the question can be raised: Why, if Paul is merely concerned with party loyalty to leaders, does he expend so much effort refuting the Corinthian claim to σοφία? Paul gives more attention to wisdom here than anywhere else in his epistles. The term σοφία is used eighteen times in 1 Corinthians 1–3, once in 12:8, once in Romans, once in 2 Corinthians, and nowhere else in the authentic letters. This may mean that σοφία was a key term in the vocabulary of the Corinthians. Besides, when Paul counters their claim to wisdom by the word of the cross, he implies that christological issues are involved in the factional conflict.

One should be cautious nevertheless about concluding that the primary thrust of Paul's argument in 1 Corinthians 1–4 is directed against a single theological position. For one thing, the mention of the "scribe" along with the σοφός (1:20) and the "Jews" in contrast to the "Greeks" (1:22) does not fit easily into a pattern of mono-frontal hellenistic speculation. Most important, the issue of the inordinate loyalty to leaders persists throughout the argument of the first four chapters (1:12; 2:1; 3:4-6; 3:10-15, 3:22; 4:1; 4:6). What finally proves that the Corinthians are not τελείοι or πνευματικοί is not their loyalty to wisdom theology, but their continuing allegiance to party slogans: "I am of Paul; I am of Apollos" (3:4). The worldly wisdom manifest in Corinth is not so much a way of thought as it is a style of life—the egocentric pride of the Corinthian factions.

Some recent research has returned to the older way of reading 1:12. According to this approach, the claim to belong to Paul, Apollos, or Cephas indicates the presence of actual, distinguishable parties within the Corinthian church. The Apollos party, since its leader is mentioned throughout chaps. 1–4, draws considerable attention.[104] According to Gerd Lüdemann, the Cephas party represents a faction that fosters anti-Paulinism in Corinth.[105] The current sociological approach has made new contributions to the older way of identifying the parties. As we have seen, the leaders of the house churches are probably from the upper class. The party of Paul and the party of Apollos may represent households that had hosted their respective leaders during their missions in Corinth.[106] According to Peter Marshall, the parties do not represent theological factions, but social groups, divided along lines of friendship or enmity with Paul.[107] Welborn, in a suggestive article, has shown that the slogans of 1:12 find formal parallels in the political rhetoric of the day.[108] Thus the Corinthian factions have similarities to the political parties of the Greco-Roman world.

V

In conclusion, some implications can be drawn from this reconsideration of the problem of conflict in 1 Corinthians:

1. The hypothesis that Paul is fighting exclusively on one front has been shown to be inadequate. A fundamental weakness of most formulations of this hypothesis is the tendency to construe all the problems of 1 Corinthians as theological. Methodologically, the one-front, one-opponent hypothesis errs in a dialectical reading of early Christian history and a mirror reading of the epistles.

2. The conflicts reflected in 1 Corinthians have arisen out of a variety of situations. Most important, the membership of the church is marked by social stratification. Conflicts between the upper and lower classes are evident. Tensions within the various social strata—for instance, among the hosts of the various house churches—are also implied. As well as the social sources of factionalism, conflict within the congregation has been fostered by the various religious backgrounds of the members. A variety of expressions of religious experience is manifest, and Jewish and Gentile converts differ in their relationship to the surrounding culture.

3. The analysis of the conflict in 1 Corinthians should not be

130

restricted to a single method. The new insights provided by the sociological approach ought to be welcomed with enthusiasm. However, the notion that all the problems are social represents another methodological oversimplification, parallel to the earlier theological oversimplification. The conflict at the Lord's Supper is primarily socio-economic, but the problem of sacrificial food is religious, and the question of the resurrection is essentially theological.

4. Paul treats the conflict according to the problems that have been raised by his sources of information. Thus particular problems, not factions, order the argument, so that the factions must be detected in relation to the problems. In regard to the problems, Paul's argument is directed to the factions responsible. Thus there is usually one "opponent" in relation to each problem. Paul, however, does not attack these trouble makers as "opponents"; he admonishes them as "beloved children" (4:14). Moreover, Paul's argument is always grounded in a theological conviction: The wisdom of the world is countered by the wisdom of God; the spiritual gifts are evaluated in terms of a doctrine of the church; the Supper and the resurrection are measured by the gospel tradition.

5. Precise identification of the factions is not possible. The attempt to find three or four groups on the basis of 1:12 is mistaken. To be sure, the followers of Cephas may have played some role in regard to sacrificial food, but chaps. 1–4 are concerned primarily with the problem of loyalty to leaders. Moreover, Paul himself is not precise about the factions. He frequently uses the term τινες (4:18; 6:11; 8:7; 15:12, 34). Apparently, he does not describe his "opponents" by name. The Corinthians know who they are; the exegetes cannot be sure.

6. Some patterns may emerge. Perhaps the charismatics of chap. 12 are related to the pneumatics of chaps. 2–3. Those who are denying the resurrection (chap. 15) may be the same as those who advocate a realized eschatology (chap. 4). Nevertheless, the evidence simply shows a variety of problems and a variety of factions—factions that are quarreling among themselves. The interplay between social and religious backgrounds, together with theological issues in relation to the different problems makes the task of identification difficult.

7. The most common feature of the Corinthian character, however, is pride. Although Paul says "some are arrogant" (4:18), he indicates that many Corinthians are proud of everything from a case of incest (5:2) to possession of knowledge (8:1). This pride has fostered the factionalism that plagues the congregation. Against this factionalism Paul contends, for it is a factionalism that threatens the essential nature of the body of Christ.

Notes

1. Johannes Weiss, *Der erste Korintherbrief* (MeyerK; Göttingen: Vandenhoeck & Ruprecht, 1910) xxx.
2. Christian Machalet, "Paulus und seine Gegner: Eine Untersuchung zu den Korintherbriefen," *Theokratis: Jahrbuch des Institutum Judaicum Delitzschianum 2* (Festgabe für K. H. Rengstorf; Leiden: E. J. Brill, 1973) 190.
3. Although the context suggests that Paul is describing a conflict among Corinthians, many commentators believe he is referring to Corinthian arrogance, which pits Paul against Apollos. See, for example, Gordon D. Fee, *The First Epistle to the Corinthians* (NICNT; Grand Rapids: Eerdmans, 1987) 169-70. In either case, however, the text reflects an intra-church conflict.
4. E. Earle Ellis, "Paul and His Opponents: Trends in Research," *Christianity, Judaism, and Other Greco-Roman Cults: Studies for M. Smith* (ed. J. Neusner; SJLA 12; Leiden: E. J. Brill, 1975) 264-98; John J. Gunther, *St. Paul's Opponents and Their Background: A Study of Apocalyptic and Jewish Sectarian Teachings* (NovTSup; Leiden: E. J. Brill, 1973) 1-16; Walter Schmithals, *Gnosticism in Corinth: An Investigation of the Letters to the Corinthians* (Nashville: Abingdon, 1971) 117-24. For the history prior to Baur, see Ferdinand Christian Baur, "Die Christuspartei in der korinthischen Gemeinde, der Gegensatz der petrinischen und paulinischen Christenthums in der ältesten Kirche," *Ausgewählte Werke* (ed. K. Scholder; Stuttgart: T. Frommann, 1963) 1.3-24. For the history from Baur to the end of the nineteenth century, see W. Lütgert, *Freiheitspredigt und Schwarmgeister in Korinth: Ein Beitrag zur Charakteristik der Christuspartei* (Gütersloh: E. Bertelsmann, 1908) 41-47; Richard Perdelwitz, "Die sogennante Christuspartei in Korinth," *TSK* 84 (1911) 180-93; Ignaz Rohr, *Paulus und die Gemeinde von Korinth* (Freiburg: Herder, 1899) 103-57.
5. Baur, "Die Christuspartei," 24-76.
6. Although it is usually supposed that Baur developed his dialectical approach to Christian beginnings under the sway of Hegelian philosophy, Peter C. Hodgson has shown that Baur had not read Hegel at the time he wrote the essay (*The Formation of Historical Theology: A Study of Ferdinand Christian Baur* [New York: Harper & Row, 1966] 23-24). In his later book (*Ferdinand Christian Baur on the Writing of Church History* [New York: Oxford, 1968]), Hodgson revised his dating of Baur's acquaintance with Hegel from 1835 to 1833. Apparently, Baur had been influenced by the dialectical understanding of early church history that had been propounded by J. G. Fichte (see Colin Brown, *Jesus in European Protestant Thought 1778–1860* [Studies in Historical Theology, 1; Durham, N.C.: Labyrinth, 1985] 79-83).
7. Lütgert, *Freiheitspredigt*, 86 and 96, respectively.
8. Ibid., 59 and 99, respectively.
9. Since Lütgert, some exegetes have considered the problem in a more traditional fashion. Hans Lietzmann (*An die Korinther I-II* [HNT; 5th ed.; ed. W. G. Kümmel; Tübingen: J. C. B. Mohr, 1969] 6-7) and Hans-Dietrich Wendland (*Die Briefe an die Korinther* [NTD; Göttingen: Vandenhoeck & Ruprecht, 1954] 14) identify four parties. Mary E. Andrews ("The Party of Christ in Corinth," *ATR* 19 [1937] 17-29) finds four, but believes the Christ party to be the most important. J. H. A. Hart ("Apollos," *JTS* [1960] 27) and Gerhard Sellin ("Das 'Geheimnis' der Weisheit und das Rätsel der 'Christuspartei' [zu 1 Kor 1-4]," *ZNW* 73 [1982] 60-96) concentrate on the followers of Apollos. The Cephas party is emphasized by T. W. Manson (*Studies in the Gospels and Epistles* (ed. M. Black; Philadelphia: Westminster, 1962] 190-209), C. K. Barrett ("Cephas in Corinth," *Essays on Paul* [Philadelphia: Westminster, 1982] 28-39), Philipp Vielhauer ("Paulus und die Kephaspartei in Korinth," *NTS* 21 [1975] 341-52), and W. O. Fitch ("Paul, Apollos, Cephas, Christ," *Theology* 74 [1971] 21).
10. Schmithals, *Gnosticism,* 286-87.
11. See Walter Schmithals, *Paul and the Gnostics* (Nashville: Abingdon, 1972). See also his *Paul and James* (SBT, 46; Naperville, Ill.: Allenson, 1965) and his *The Office of the Apostle in the Early Church* (Nashville: Abingdon, 1969).
12. James M. Robinson, "Basic Shifts in German Theology," *Int* 16 (1962) 79.

13. See George W. MacRae, "Review of Schmithals's *Gnosticism in Corinth*," *Int* 26 (1972) 490.
14. See R. McL. Wilson, "How Gnostic Were the Corinthians?" *NTS* 19 (1972-73) 68.
15. Hans Conzelmann, *1 Corinthians* (Hermeneia; Philadelphia: Fortress, 1975) 34. See also Sasagu Arai, "Die Gegner des Paulus im I. Korintherbrief und das Problem der Gnosis," *NTS* 19 (1972-73) 436-37; James M. Robinson and Helmut Koester, *Trajectories Through Early Christianity* (Philadelphia: Fortress, 1971) 32-34, 42-43, 58-59, 149-50; John W. Drane, *Paul: Libertine or Legalist? A Study in the Theology of the Major Pauline Epistles* (London: SPCK, 1975) 99. Exceptions can be found. In a Yale dissertation of 1927, Frank H. Marshall identified the opponents as Judaizers (*The Judaizing Faction at Corinth* [Leizig: W. Drugulin, 1927]). Werner Bieder ("Paulus und seine Gegner in Korinth," *TZ* 17 [1961] 319-33) argues that the opponents are Jewish pneumatics. John Gunther (*Paul's Opponents*, 314-17) believes that Paul's opponents in Galatia, Corinth, and probably Philippi were Judaizing missionaries from Palestine.
16. Schmithals, *Gnosticism*, 113-14. Schmithals's interpretation of 1 Cor 1:12 is supported indirectly by Joachim Jeremias ("Chiasmus in den Paulusbriefen," *ZNW* 49 [1958] 151). According to Jeremias, 1 Cor 1:12-13 displays a chiastic structure: Paul/Christ/Paul. Therefore, Apollos and Cephas are not important to the argument.
17. Fee, *First Corinthians*, 4-15. Fee concludes that "the *historical situation* in Corinth was *one of conflict between the church and its founder*" (6). His view is that the majority of the church boast of a special spirituality related to an "overrealized" eschatology.
18. John Coolidge Hurd, Jr., *The Origin of 1 Corinthians* (New York: Seabury, 1965) 96.
19. See Johannes Munck, *Paul and the Salvation of Mankind* (Richmond: John Knox, 1959) 69-86.
20. Hurd's confidence in the Apostolic Decrees is surprising in view of his appraisal of Acts 15 as "largely the literary creation of the author of Acts" (*Origin*, 35).
21. See Schmithals, *Gnosticism*, 222, 287.
22. See Vielhauer, "Kephaspartei," 343; Bernhard Spörlein, *Die Leugnung der Auferstehung: Eine historisch-kritische Untersuchung zu 1 Kor 15* (Münchener Universitäts-Schriften; Regensburg: F. Pustet, 1971) 30. Wayne A. Meeks, *The First Urban Christians: The Social World of the Apostle Paul* (New Haven: Yale University Press) 117: "The extended correspondence between Paul and the Corinthian Christians has left us a picture of conflict on several levels, about several issues."
23. See Machalet, "Paulus u. seine Gegner," 195.
24. See George Lyons, *Pauline Autobiography: Toward a New Understanding* (SBLDS 73; Atlanta: Scholars Press, 1985) 76-83.
25. Schmithals, *Gnosticism*, 345.
26. Dieter Georgi, *Die Gegner des Paulus im 2 Korintherbrief: Studien zur Religiösen Propaganda in der Spätantike* (WMANT 11; Neukirchen-Vluyn: Neukirchener, 1965; English trans., *The Opponents of Paul in Second Corinthians* [Philadelphia: Fortress, 1986]).
27. See C. K. Barrett, "Paul's Opponents in II Corinthians," *Essays*, 61-63.
28. See Victor Paul Furnish, *II Corinthians* (AB 32A; Garden City, N.Y.: Doubleday, 1984) 48-54; Gerhard Friedrich, "Die Gegner des Paulus im 2. Korintherbrief," *Abraham unser Vater: Festschrift für O. Michel* (eds. O. Betz, M. Hengel, P. Schmidt; Leiden: E. J. Brill, 1963) 181-215.
29. According to Nils A. Dahl ("Paul and the Church at Corinth According to 1 Corinthians 1:10–4:21," *Studies in Paul: Theology for the Early Christian Mission* [Minneapolis: Augsburg, 1977] 44) consideration of the parties of 1 Cor 1:12 should concentrate on 1 Corinthians 1–4. However, when the investigation is directed to the larger problem of conflict in 1 Cor, attention must be given to evidence of factions throughout the epistle.
30. See Weiss, *Korintherbrief*, xl-xliii; Jean Héring, *The First Epistle of Saint Paul to the Corinthians* (London: Epworth, 1962) xii-xv; E. Dinkler, "Korintherbriefe," *RGG*[3] 4.18. Wolfgang Schenk ("Der 1. Korintherbrief als Briefsammlung," *ZNW* 60 [1964]

219-43) considers 1 Cor to be a composite of four letters. On the basis of Schenk's work, Schmithals revised his earlier theory (two letters) to conclude that the epistle was composed of fragments of five different letters ("Die Korintherbrief als Briefsammlung," *ZNW* 64 [1973] 263-88).

31. For a summary of the issues and a defense of the integrity of 1 Cor, see Werner G. Kümmel, *Introduction to the New Testament* (rev. ed.; Nashville: Abingdon, 1975) 276-78.
32. Hurd, *Origin*, 47-50.
33. Ibid., 61-94.
34. Schmithals, *Gnosticism*, 179.
35. Ibid., 146.
36. Hurd, *Origin*, 120-22.
37. Gerd Lüdemann, *Paulus der Heidenapostel, II: Antipaulinismus im frühen Christentum* (Göttingen: Vandenhoeck & Ruprecht, 1983) 103.
38. Gunther, *Paul's Opponents*, 14-15.
39. Pausanias, *Description of Greece*, 2.2-5 (LCL; Cambridge, Mass.: Harvard University Press, 1954) 253 ff.
40. Apuleius, *The Golden Ass*, 11 (LCL; London: Heinemann, 1925) 538 ff. See Dennis E. Smith, "The Egyptian Cults at Corinth," *HTR* 70 (1977) 201-31.
41. See Oscar Broneer, "Paul and the Pagan Cults at Isthmia," *HTR* 64 (1971) 169-87.
42. Mabel Lang, *Cure and Cult in Ancient Corinth: A Guide to the Asklepieion* (Princeton: American School of Classical Studies, 1977). See Jerome Murphy-O'Connor, *St. Paul's Corinth: Texts and Archaeology* (Good News Studies 6; Wilmington, Del.: Michael Glazier, 1983) 161-67.
43. See Richard Reitzenstein, *Hellenistic Mystery-Religions* (PTMS 18; Pittsburg: Pickwick, 1978) 40-41; Lietzmann, *Korinther*, 8; Apuleius, *Golden Ass*, 11.25-26 (LCL, 584-87); Hans-Josef Klauck, *Hausgemeinde und Hauskirche im frühen Christentum* (Stuttgarter Bibelstudien 103; Stuttgart: Katholisches Bibelwerk, 1981) 39-40.
44. C. K. Barrett, *The First Epistle to the Corinthians* (HNTC; New York: Harper, 1968) 194.
45. Ibid., 278.
46. See William A. McDonald, "Archeology and St. Paul's Journeys in Greek Lands, III-Corinth," *BA* 5 (1942) 41. Murphy-O'Connor, *St. Paul's Corinth*, 78-79, notes that the precise date of the inscription cannot be ascertained.
47. See C. K. Barrett, "Things Sacrificed to Idols," *Essays*, 49.
48. See Gunther, *Paul's Opponents*, 59-133; Martin H. Scharlemann, *Qumran and Corinth* (New York: Bookman Associates, 1962); Robin Scroggs, "Paul: ΣΟΦΟΣ and ΠΝΕΥΜΑΤΙΚΟΣ," *NTS* 14 (1967) 35-55.
49. Gerd Theissen, "Social Stratification in the Corinthian Community," *The Social Setting of Pauline Christianity: Essays on Corinth* (Philadelphia: Fortress, 1982) 102-4.
50. Ibid., 102-10.
51. See Robert Banks, *Paul's Idea of Community: The Early House Churches in Their Historical Setting* (Grand Rapids: Eerdmans, 1980) 153; Edwin A. Judge, "St. Paul and Classical Society," *JAC* 15 (1972) 28. Ronald F. Hock, *The Social Context of Paul's Ministry* (Philadelphia: Fortress, 1980) 35, 67, observes that Paul was born into the upper class, but chose to be identified with the lower artisan class.
52. Banks, *Paul's Idea of Community*, 113-21; A. E. Judge, *The Social Pattern of Christian Groups in the First Century* (London: Tyndale, 1960) 40-61; Meeks, *Urban Christians*, 72-73.
53. Against the majority, W. H. Wuellner ("The Sociological Implications of 1 Cor 1:26-28," *SE* 4, ed. A. Livingstone, TU 112 [1973] 666-72) argues on linguistic grounds that this text does not support the claim that the Corinthians were from lower classes.
54. Dieter Sänger, "Die δυνατοί in 1 Kor 1.26," *ZNW* 76 (1985) 285-91.
55. See Klauck, *Hausgemeinde*, 33.
56. See John Harvey Kent, *The Inscriptions: Corinth: Results of the Excavation* (Princeton: American School of Classical Studies, 1966) 8/3.99-100; Murphy-O'Connor, *St. Paul's Corinth*, 37; Theissen, "Social Stratification," 75-83.

57. See Floyd V. Filson, "The Significance of the Early House Churches," *JBL* 58 (1939) 111; Abraham J. Malherbe, *Social Aspects of Early Christianity* (2nd ed.; Philadelphia: Fortress, 1983) 73-74.

58. See Banks, *Paul's Idea of Community*, 168; Judge, "Paul and Classical Society," 28; Theissen, "Social Stratification," 97.

59. Theissen, "Social Stratification," 97.

60. See Hock, *Social Context*, 26-49.

61. Klauck, *Hausgemeinde*, 21-26.

62. See Murphy-O'Connor, *St. Paul's Corinth*, 30-31, 86-88, 90-92.

63. Theissen, "Social Stratification," 92-94.

64. See S. Scott Bartchy, *Mallon Chresai: First Century Slavery and the Interpretation of 1 Corinthians 7:21* (SBLDS 11; Missoula, Mont.: Society of Biblical Literature, 1973) 58.

65. Ibid., 37-120.

66. Chloe was probably a member of the Corinthian community, since Paul assumes that his readers know her.

67. See Klauck, *Hausgemeinde*, 30-31.

68. See William Tarn and G. T. Griffith, *Hellenistic Civilization* (3rd ed.; London: E. Arnold, 1952) 98-100; Jerome Carcopino, *Daily Life in Ancient Rome* (New Haven: Yale University Press, 1940) 85.

69. See John E. Stambaugh and David L. Balch, *The New Testament in Its Social Environment* (Library of Early Christianity; Philadelphia: Westminster, 1986) 159.

70. Fee, *First Corinthians*, 269-70.

71. Theissen's emphasis on the social at the expense of the theological is noted by T. Engberg-Pedersen, "The Gospel and Social Practice According to 1 Corinthians," *NTS* 33 (1987) 557-84.

72. Peter Marshall, *Enmity in Corinth: Social Conventions in Paul's Relations with the Corinthians* (WUNT 2.23; Tübingen: J. C. B. Mohr, 1987).

73. Marshall (ibid., 341-48) also shows that the non-naming of an enemy is a conventional feature of hellenistic rhetoric. Since Paul never mentions an opponent by name, Marshall concludes that all the persons named in 1 Cor are on Paul's side.

74. See Filson, "Early House Churches," 110; Stephen C. Barton, "Paul's Sense of Place: An Anthropological Approach to Community Formation in Corinth," *NTS* 32 (1986) 225-46.

75. See Max Meinertz, "Schismata und Hairesis im Neuen Testament," *BZ* 1 (1957) 115; Henning Paulsen, "Schisma und Häresie," *ZTK* (1982) 180-211.

76. C. Roberts, T. C. Skeat, and A. D. Nock, "The Gild of Zeus Hypsistos," *HTR* 29 (1936) 39-42.

77. See Paulsen, "Schismata u. Häresie," 180-211.

78. See Barrett, "Things Sacrificed," 48-49.

79. See Karl Maly, *Mündige Gemeinde: Untersuchungen zur pastoralen Führung des Apostels Paulus im 1. Korintherbrief* (SBM 2; Stuttgart: Katholische Bibelwerk, 1967) 96-99; Arnold Ehrhardt, "Social Problems in the Early Church," *The Framework of the New Testament Stories* (Cambridge, Mass.: Harvard University Press, 1964) 279-80; Wendel Lee Willis, *Idol Meat in Corinth: The Pauline Argument in 1 Corinthians 8 and 10* (SBLDS 68; Chico: Scholars, 1985) 265-66.

80. Hurd, *Origin*, 123-74; Hurd is refuted by Maly, *Gemeinde*, 99.

81. Romans 14:1–5:1, which deals with a different problem in regard to eating, describes the weak in faith (ἀσθενοῦντα τῇ πίστει, 14:1), and Rom 15:1 contrasts the δυνατοί and the ἀδύνατοι. Paul has said that there are not many δυνατοί in the Corinthian church, and the synonymous ἰσχυρός is used pejoratively throughout 1 Cor (1:27; 4:10; 10:22).

82. Barrett, "Things Sacrificed," 53, believes that Peter introduced the Apostolic Decrees into the Corinthian Church.

83. Archibald Robertson and Alfred Plummer, *A Critical and Exegetical Commentary on the First Epistle of Paul to the Corinthians* (ICC; 2nd ed.; Edinburgh: T. and T. Clark, 1914) 169. Maly (*Gemeinde*, 110-14) accepts the variant συνειδήσει in place of συνηθείᾳ and argues that the "weak" are Jews. A strong case against the variant is made by Jerome

Murphy-O'Connor, "Freedom of the Ghetto (1 Cor. VII, 1-13; X, 23-XI, 1)," *RB* 85 (1979) 551-52.

84. Schmithals, *Gnosticism*, 224-29. Richard A. Horsley, "Gnosis in Corinth: 1 Corinthians 8:1-6," *NTS* 27 (1980) 32-51, argues that the "strong" are not gnostics. Their viewpoint "can be found in that Hellenistic Jewish theology represented by Philo and the Wisdom of Solomon" (33).

85. Gerd Theissen, "The Strong and the Weak in Corinth: A Sociological Analysis of a Theological Quarrel," *Social Setting*, 121-40.

86. See Malherbe, *Social Aspects*, 84.

87. See Willis, *Idol Meat*, 92-96.

88. Schmithals, *Gnosticism*, 124-30.

89. See Birger Pearson, "Did the Gnostics Curse Jesus?" *JBL* 86 (1967) 301-5; W. C. van Unnik, "Jesus, Anathema or Kyrios (1 Cor. 12:3)," *Christ and the Spirit: Studies in Honour of C. F. D. Moule* (eds. B. Lindars and S. S. Smalley; Cambridge: Cambridge University Press, 1978) 113-26.

90. John Howard Schütz, "Charisma and Social Reality in Primitive Christianity," *JR* 54 (1974) 51-70; Conzelmann, *1 Corinthians*, 15-16. Fee (*First Corinthians*, 7-15) believes the Corinthian claim of super spirituality to be the fundamental problem of 1 Cor.

91. See John P. Kildahl, *The Psychology of Speaking in Tongues* (New York: Harper & Row, 1972) 48-75. I. M. Lewis (*Ecstatic Religion: An Anthropological Study of Spirit Possession and Shamanism* [Baltimore: Penguin, 1971] 190-99) observes that ecstatic religion is frequently experienced by persons from marginal and repressed social positions, often women.

92. See P. Marshall, *Enmity*, 182-218.

93. Julius Schniewind, "Die Leugner der Auferstehung in Korinth," *Nachgelassene Reden und Aufsätze* (ed. E. Kähler; Berlin: A. Töpelmann, 1952) 114.

94. Schmithals, *Gnosticism*, 179-82.

95. See Karl-Gustav Sandelin, *Die Auseinandersetzung mit der Weisheit in 1. Korinther 15* (Meddelanden från Stiftelsens för Åbo Akami Forskningsinstitut, 12; Åbo: Adami, 1976) 148-53.

96. See Jack H. Wilson, "The Corinthians Who Say There Is No Resurrection of the Dead," *ZNW* 59 (1968) 107; Spörlein, *Leugnung d. Auferstehung*, 190-96; Richard A. Horsley, "How Can Some of You Say There Is No Resurrection of the Dead: Spiritual Elitism in Corinth," *NovT* 20 (1978) 203.

97. Fee, *First Corinthians*, 713-17.

98. Günther Bornkamm, "Lord's Supper and Church in Paul," *Early Christian Experience* (New York: Harper & Row, 1969) 126.

99. Robertson and Plummer, *First Corinthians*, 241.

100. Gerd Theissen, "Social Integration and Sacramental Activity: An Analysis of 1 Cor 11:17-34," *Social Setting*, 145-74; Murphy O'Connor, *St. Paul's Corinth*, 153-61.

101. Perdelwitz, "Christuspartei," 193-204.

102. The problem of the identification of the "Christ party" has never been satisfactorily solved. The phrase has been read as an interpolation (Weiss), or as a feature of Paul's argument (Hurd), or as the designation of the major opponents as Judaizers (Baur, F. Marshall) or hellenistic pneumatics or gnostics (Lütgert, Schmithals). For a summary of the issues, see Conzelmann, *1 Corinthians*, 33-34; Hurd, *Origin*, 101-6.

103. Ulrich Wilckens, *Weisheit und Torheit* (BHT 26; Tübingen: J. C. B. Mohr, 1956).

104. See Michael Wolter, "Apollos und die ephesinischen Johannesjünger (Acts 18:24–19:7)," *ZNW* 78 (1987) 49-73; Francis Watson, *Paul, Judaism, and the Gentiles: A Sociological Approach* (SNTSMS 56; Cambridge: Cambridge University Press, 1986) 80-87.

105. Lüdemann, *Paulus*, 118-23.

106. See Klauck, *Hausgemeinde*, 39-40.

107. Marshall, *Enmity*, 263-64.

108. L. L. Welborn, "On the Discord in Corinth: 1 Corinthians 1-4 and Ancient Politics," *JBL* 106 (1987) 85-111.

ALL THINGS TO ALL PEOPLE: A STUDY OF 1 CORINTHIANS 9:19-23

Barbara Hall

In his essay "Paul and His Jewish-Christian Interpreters,"[1] J. Louis Martyn has argued forcefully that, for Paul, the advent of Christ means the loss of all "criteria of perception that have been developed apart from the gospel." This startling claim means that everything in the life now lived in the flesh (Gal 2:20) is passed through the prism of the gospel and thus seen in a radically different way. It is this radically different way of seeing things that makes Paul so puzzling and difficult for us. A case in point is 1 Cor 9:19-23. We occasionally say of someone, "She tries to be all things to all people," taking for granted the impossibility of success in the attempt. But in this passage, Paul emphatically claims that he has become all things to all people.

In this essay, I examine the passage and its literary context as well as other relevant material in Paul's letters. Are there criteria of perception derived from the advent of Christ that caused Paul to be all things to all people? I will suggest that a way to make sense of this passage is to see Paul's position here as resulting from his understanding of the new situation in which Christians find themselves. Those whom God calls in Jesus Christ constitute the eschatological community, "those upon whom the end of the ages has come" (1 Cor 10:11). They are empowered by God to witness to, exhibit, and make real in the world the new-age, reconciled community. In that community there is neither Jew nor Greek, neither slave nor free, neither male or female. This means, among other things, to be all things to all people.

I

I translate 1 Cor 9:19-23 as follows:

(19a) For being free of all people, (b) I enslaved myself to all, (c) in order to win the more; (20a) and I became to the Jews as a Jew, (b) in order to continue to win Jews, (c) to those under law as one under law, (d)—not being myself under law—(e) in order to continue to win those under law; (21a) to those outside law as one outside law (b)—not being outside (the) law of God but inside (the) law of Christ—(c) in order to continue to win those outside law; (22a) I became to the weak a weak person, (b) in order to continue to win the weak; (c) to all I have become all, (d) in order by all means[2] to continue to save some; (23a) and I continue to do all, because of the gospel, (b) in order that I may continue to be a co-sharer in it.

What follows is a series of observations based on the literary character and grammar of the passage. Questions to be addressed in later sections of the essay arise out of these observations. The questions will guide our search for relevant material in the passage's immediate context and elsewhere in Paul's letters. Our purpose is to understand Paul's intentions in this passage: why he writes as he does and what he wants to say to his Corinthian readers.

Paul begins by speaking of his self-enslavement. He makes it clear in two ways that his enslavement occurred when he was called to be a Christian and an apostle. He opens the paragraph, "For, being *free* . . . " (*eleutheros ōn*). His readers would surely recall 1 Cor 9:1.[3] There, Paul speaks of his call ("Am I not an apostle? Have I not seen Jesus our Lord?") by first asking "Am I not *free*?"

That his self-enslavement occurred at his call is shown also by the aorist tense of the verbs "enslaved" in v. 19b and "became" in vv. 20a and 22a, indicating punctiliar action.

Paul's self-enslavement is his radical identification with all people. He says, "I enslaved myself . . . *and* became. . . . " The two actions, linked by the simple "and" are parallel to each other. His identification with all people is not one example among others of his enslavement. Clearly, Paul wants to speak of identification with others under the drastic heading of slavery. This is strong language.

The final statement in the passage (v. 23) is somewhat different from the rest: "And I continue to do all because of the gospel, in order that I may continue to be a co-sharer in it." Paul might have ended the paragraph with v. 22, in which he reiterates what he said at the beginning. The repetition of "all" words is especially striking. To this dramatic and effective climax, he adds the final statement "in order that I may continue to be a co-sharer of the gospel," thereby introducing a note not yet sounded. He acts so that he will continue to be a co-sharer in the gospel. Radical identification with all people is what the gospel requires of him. His participation in the community created by the gospel depends on it. These are strong, even drastic, claims.

The paragraph, without the final statement in v. 23, has a chiastic structure, which may be presented as follows:[4]

A 19a For being free of *all*[5]
   b I enslaved myself to *all*,
     in order to win the *more*,

A₁ 22c I have become *all* to *all*,
    d *in order* by *all* means *to save some.*

B 20a and I *became to the* **Jews** as a **Jew**,
   b *in order to win* **Jews;**

B₁ 22a I *became to the* **weak, weak,**
    b *in order to win* the **weak;**

C   c *to those* **under** *law as* one **under** *law,*

   d *not being* myself *under* **law**—

C₁ 21a *to those* **outside** *law as* one **outside** *law*

   b —*not being* **outside** the *law of God,* but **inside** the *law of Christ*—

   e *in order to win those* **under** *law;*

   c *in order to win those* **outside** *law;*

Weiss observed[6] that vv. 20-22*b* (BC/C₁B₁ in the above outline) have the form of a chiasm, but in content constitute a parallelism of members—that is, there is a careful balance of opposites in B and B₁, in C and C₁. In content, however, B and C refer to the same people: Jews and those under law. The same is true, he claimed, of C₁ and B₁: those outside the law and the weak. The identity of these latter two groups is problematical. If "weak" refers to those in Corinth who have scruples about eating idol meat,[7] they are, as 1 Cor 8:7 suggests, Gentiles. But those on the other side of the debate, whom we may label the "strong," were surely also Gentiles.[8] The weak and the strong together make up those outside law. Why does he not mention the strong? Does he not identify with them as well?

Those elements in the chiasm that parallel or oppose one another are obvious. There are some points of non-correspondence worthy of note:

1. I called attention above to Paul's use of "I became" in vv. 20*a* and 22*a*: "I became . . . as a Jew"; "I became weak." The intervening statements contain no verbs. The repetition underscores the correspondence between B and B₁, Jews and weak. This is an even odder combination than those without law and the weak. One expects the contrast to be either between Jew and Greek or between strong and weak.

2. The two clauses set off by dashes at the center of C and C₁ (vv. 20*d* and 21*b*) do not balance perfectly. Paul could have written them so that the second repeated the form of the first: "not being myself outside law." One of his several points would have been clear—namely, that his self-identification with others, though radical, does not mean that he ceases to exist. Paul remains Paul. He becomes *as* those with whom he identifies.

Paul has other points to pack into these clauses, however. The oddity

139

of v. 20*d* ("not being myself under law"), indeed of the whole verse, is that Paul *is* a Jew. Neither original readers nor present-day readers are unduly puzzled by these statements, for we all know that Paul, the apostle to the Gentiles, understood himself to be a Jew by heritage but, under Christ, part of the new creation.[9] Why, however, does he make this comment here?

The lack of balance in the terms "under law," "outside law," and "inside law" is striking. The first, "under law," is not mysterious. It means simply to be a Jew. It is unusual in a chiasm to repeat oneself, as Paul does here. Why say first that he became a Jew and second that he became as one under law? The reader expects "to the Greeks as a Greek."[10] "Outside law" as the opposite of "under law" is appropriate. The term and its cognates are not often used by Paul,[11] but Rom 2:12 contains a rough equivalent to the contrast being made here. The addition "of God" in v. 21*b*, however, is ambiguous. Does "law of God" mean Jewish Torah or something else here? 1 Corinthians 7:19 gives the crucial clue: "For neither circumcision counts for anything nor uncircumcision, but keeping the commandments of God." Having just seen this statement, Paul's readers were aware that he was not using the term "law of God" to refer exclusively to Jewish Torah. We must inquire into his meaning below.

"Inside the law of Christ" is the more important anomaly. Used by Paul only here, the phrase is surely occasioned by the other two expressions, "under law" and "outside law." We shall look at these items again.

3. These two clauses set off by dashes ("not being under law," "not outside law . . . " vv. 20*d* and 21*b*) recall the other similar one in this passage: "Being free of all." The last, with which the paragraph begins, has no parallel in the chiasm. The three have the same form. We consider below what the three, taken together, are saying.

4. Verse 22*a* ("I became to the weak, weak") does not correspond to the preceding statements about Paul's identification with others. In the earlier statements, he has claimed that he became *as* one or another. But here in v. 22*a*, he says he became weak.

In a chiasm with an even number of members, emphasis normally falls on the first and last. So here, Paul's initial use of "free"/"enslaved," the repeated use of "all," and the repeated purpose statements all stand out. Especially together with the four purpose statements repeated in the central part of the paragraph, emphasis falls heavily on Paul's self-enslavement, his radical identification with others, *as his strategy for achieving his goal.*

To summarize: A careful look at the grammar, vocabulary and literary structure of 1 Cor 9:19-23 calls attention to the radical claims Paul makes here. In order to obey, fulfill, and complete his call to be a Christian and an apostle, Paul enslaved himself to all people. The gospel required him to identify in a radical way with his potential and actual constituency. They were a diverse lot, and the possibility of multiple problems caused by such a stance was surely obvious both to Paul and to his readers. Nonetheless, this strategy was not one option among others for Paul. It was an integral part of his call. It went with the territory. It was required by the gospel, and Paul's co-sharing of the gospel depended on it.

Several problems and questions raised by this analysis revolve around Paul's specification of those with whom he identifies. What does it mean that Paul, the Jew, became *as* a Jew, *as* one under the law? Why does Paul speak twice of the same group, Jews and those under law? Why does Paul not speak of "Greeks" rather than "those outside the law"? What are we to make of the parallel Paul seems to draw between those outside law and the weak? How shall we understand the curious contrast between Jews and the weak? Why does Paul say he became *as* a Jew, and so on, but that he *became* weak? What exactly does Paul intend by the unusual language in v. 21*d,* which I have translated "not being outside (the) law of God but inside (the) law of Christ?"

II

What statements elsewhere in Paul's letters may help to illumine these questions regarding 1 Cor 9:19-23? Texts that come to mind are the immediate literary context (1 Corinthians 8–10); 1 Corinthians 7, which is similar in form and content to our text in some interesting ways; and texts in which Paul uses the vocabulary "Jew and Greek" (and their equivalents) and "weak."

In the discussion that follows I shall argue that, in relation to the discussion of idol meat (1 Corinthians 8–10), Paul speaks in 1 Corinthians 9 of his own ministry as an example for his Corinthian readers to imitate, specifically with regard to the debate about eating meat that may have been sacrificed to idols. I will suggest that Gal 3:26-28 is in Paul's mind when he writes 9:19-23, as there is a clear allusion to it in 1 Corinthians 7, and that this text has major importance for an understanding of our text. With regard to the third set of texts, I will inquire into Paul's special understanding of weakness in 1 Corinthians.

The Text in Its Context

In the immediate context, 1 Corinthians 8–10,[12] the strongest verbal links to our passage are found at the conclusion of the idol-meat discussion in 10:31–11:1. "Jews and Greeks" in 10:32 recalls the contrasted groups in our passage. Paul adds to these "the church of God." Whatever is at stake in the argument affects both those in the church and those outside. The latter are designated, as often in Paul, Jews and Greeks.

The similarities in 10:33 are to the beginning and especially at the end of our passage: the multiple use of "all," "the many" recalling "the more," the use of the verb *to save*. "Just as I try to please all people in all things" and "not seeking my own advantage" recall Paul's identification with others. These connections suggest that Paul returns at the end of his long discussion of idol meat to what he has said in 9:19-23. Our passage is then of major importance in the idol-meat discussion.

1 Corinthians 9:18, which immediately precedes the passage under consideration, speaks of Paul's "right" (authority, *exousia*) in the gospel. Two points are to be noted. First, I would maintain, with many other scholars,[13] that in the discussion of idol meat, and especially for those who eat it freely in the Corinthian church, "authority" (*exousia;* "liberty" in 8:9; "right" in 9:18) is the virtual equivalent of "freedom" (*eleutheria* in 9:19). Paul uses the latter in 9:1 and 9:19, the former is prominent in his discussion of his apostolic rights in 9:1-18. This is not surprising, since 9:1-18 is intended as an example of the behavior he asks of the idol-meat eaters in chap. 8. They are claiming the authority/freedom to eat idol meat, a claim Paul grants. He counters with an example from his apostolic practice. He first establishes his own right (authority) and then voluntarily relinquishes it. "Voluntarily" is misleading, of course. However one interprets 9:15-18, there is no escaping the "necessity" (*anagkē*) of 9:16. Just as Paul's call requires and depends on his relinquishing a right that is his as an apostle called by God, so also the Corinthians' calling may require the same of them. Paul is not discussing simple choices among opposite possibilities, much less the right of someone to act, based on some prior custom, status, or correct theological belief.[14] He is talking about what God calls people to be and do in the gospel. The criteria used to discern what God calls people to be and do are emphatically not the freedom and authority God confers when calling someone, as the strong in Corinth understood these terms.

Second, Paul qualifies his reference to his "right" (*exousia*) in 9:18 by the phrase "in the gospel," because of this highly paradoxical argument. He might have spoken of his "right *as an apostle.*" The phrase "in the gospel" helps to keep the necessary perspective in view. Why would God confer a right (liberty, authority) on Paul when he was called and then make Paul's renunciation of it a condition for the fulfillment of that call? Paul's answer is that *in the gospel* the only real freedom is *crucified* freedom. He speaks in a similar way in 9:23, "And I do all because of the gospel, in order that I may be a co-sharer in it" (author's trans.).

The verses immediately following our paragraph, 9:24-27, need only a brief comment. The final statement recalls the end of our passage: "lest after preaching to others I myself should be disqualified" (v. 27b). It contains a strong note of possible judgment. No one is automatically *in*, as some of the Corinthians believed. Again, Paul intends his own stance and behavior to be an example for his readers to imitate.

When Paul again takes up the matter of idol meat in 10:23-11:1, after various digressions, there are echoes of our passage, apart from those already noted at the end of the discussion (10:31-11:1). One echo occurs in 10:24: "Let no one seek his own good, but the good of his neighbor." It builds on Paul's claim to be all things to all people.

Paul's initial discussion of idol meat in chap. 8 was directed to the strong. He has warned them in very emphatic terms that they endanger their weaker brothers and sisters by their behavior. He ended this section of his discussion by speaking in the first person: "*I* will never again eat meat unto all eternity" (8:13b, author's trans.).

In the final section of the discussion, 10:23-11:1, he addresses the weak, but keeps a weather eye on the strong. Verse 23 is directed to the latter (" 'All things are permitted,'[15] but not all things are helpful. 'All things are permitted,' but not all things build up") Then follows the general injunction to seek the other's good. That it is addressed to those on both sides of the debate can be seen from what follows: Paul addresses the weak. They are to eat whatever is sold in the market without raising questions "because of conscience/consciousness," (v. 25)[16]. This appears to be a shift from what was said in chap. 8 about their possible destruction. Why are they to eat anything from the market? Because (*gar*, v. 26) "the earth is the Lord's and everything in it" (Ps 24:1).[17] Then there is more advice: Go to dinner with friends and eat what is given, again without raising questions "because of conscience/consciousness" (v. 27). Paul has asked the strong to abstain out of deference to the weak. He now asks the weak to do something for the strong—namely, to begin to free themselves from their tyrannical scruples. Paul does not expect them to change overnight, but they are to begin.[18]

The RSV makes vv. 28 and 29a a parenthesis. Here Paul sees the need to take account of his address to the strong in chap. 8. Having instructed the weak to eat without demur what is given them, he guards against the possibility that the strong will use this instruction to undermine his comments to them in 8:10-12. He addresses the strong in the parenthetical vv. 28-29a: No one is to injure anyone else's conscience/

143

consciousness. In vv. 25 and 27, he makes it clear that those with scruples are to do some work on their own.

In vv. 29b-30 Paul ends his advice to the weak as he ended his advice to the strong in chap. 8. He speaks in the first person: "For why should my freedom be judged by another's conscience? If I partake (of sacrificial meat) with thankfulness, why am I defamed for eating food over which I have said grace?"[19] At the end of his advice to the strong Paul asserts emphatically that if his eating food was a stumbling block for anyone, he would never again eat meat as long as he lived. Here he speaks emphatically to the weak about the rights of the strong, again in the first person.

In these two first-person statements (8:13 and 10:29b-30), the attentive reader can see examples of Paul's identification with the weak and with those outside law, 9:21 and 22. While his identification with the weak is very clear from 8:7-13, 9:22a, and 10:28-29b, it is also the case that he is known in the Corinthian church not to share their scruples about eating idol meat. He belongs to the strong, and in his abrupt challenge to the weak he speaks not only for himself but also for those who see themselves as the strong in Corinth. The result is a very difficult passage, one that has misled many and has sometimes been used to tyrannize others. It is an excellent example of the kind of trouble one can get into when one tries to be all things to all people.

What does it mean to be a co-sharer of the gospel? In the idol-meat controversy, it means the strong defer to the weak and the weak do not tyrannize the strong. Paul does not say it directly, but indirectly,[20] using himself as the one to be imitated. What is to be imitated is his radical self-identification with others.

1 Corinthians 7

In 1 Corinthians 7, Paul responded to the first of a series of questions or issues the Corinthian Christians had raised with him by letter.[21] 1 Corinthians 8–10 takes up a second issue.[22] 1 Corinthians 7 is, therefore, an important part in the literary context of 9:19-23, the passage under consideration here. The recipients of his letter hear Paul turn to the issues they have raised with him and deal, first, with questions about marriage and celibacy, and second, with the idol-meat debate.

Chapter 7 has a clear literary structure:

vv. 1-16 introduced by the formula "Now concerning" (*peri de*)
vv. 17-24 a digression
vv. 25-40 introduced by the formula "Now concerning"

Although simpler than 1 Corinthians 8–10, chap. 7 is similar to it.[23] Moreover, the digression in 7:17-24 has close parallels to 9:19-23. It is dominated by the notion of one's call from God. The thrice-repeated injunction to remain in the calling in which one was called (vv. 17, 20, 24) is like the much repeated "in order to win . . . " in 9:19-23. There is a clear, but not completely balanced, chiasm in 7:17-24,[24] as there is in 9:19-23. These similarities are strong enough perhaps to cause Paul's readers to remember the digression in chap. 7 (vv. 17-24), when they reach the digression in chaps. 8–10 (9:19-23).

The similarities between the two paragraphs, however, go beyond literary form. The reference in 7:18-19 to circumcised and uncircumcised is the equivalent of "Jews"/"those under law" and "those outside law" in our passage. To begin our passage in 9:19 by speaking of "free" and "enslaved" surely recalls comments about slave and free in 7:21-22, and especially 7:23, where Paul says "Do not become slaves of people." In the discussion that follows, he speaks of enslaving himself to all sorts of people!

Other items in 1 Corinthians might be recalled by readers of our passage. One is Paul's use of the verb *to save* in 7:16. The subjects of the verb are Christian spouses of unbelievers. In 9:22 the subject of the same verb is Paul. Elsewhere in 1 Corinthians,[25] *God* is the one who saves, explicitly or implicitly. Only in these two places (7:16, 9:22) does Paul speak of one human being saving another.

More broadly, Paul's stance is similar in the two passages. In chaps. 8–10, while he agrees with the strong in Corinth that idol meat is not a threat to the Christian, he defends the weak whose scruples about eating it he does not share. In 1 Corinthians 7, although he is celibate and supports others who are celibate, he defends marriage and married people in the church.

In the digression in 7:17-24, Paul clearly alludes to the baptismal formula, known to us in Gal 3:26-28 and presumably known to the Corinthians from their own baptisms.[26] It cannot be a coincidence that "circumcision and uncircumcision" and "slave and free" are mentioned in a passage about sexuality, marriage, and celibacy. Whatever the issues in Corinth to which 7:1-16 and 7:25-40 respond, they must have been related to "neither male nor female." It seems probable that the issues were directly related to the *Corinthians'* interpretation of "neither male nor female."[27] Only so can Paul be sure that his digression about circumcised and uncircumcised, slave and free, would be readily understood.

Paul works here to interpret the baptismal formula, which is essential to his case. He may have discovered that it needed careful interpretation when he saw what the enthusiastic Corinthian Christians were doing with it. The case he is building has to do with what behavior is appropriate in the eschatological community at the turn of the ages.[28] The formula itself (Gal 3:26-28) and Paul's use of it in Galatians might lead one to conclude that the transformation of all relationships, willed by God in Christ, is already complete. The formula does not speak about a future, hoped-for reality, of which the church has received the first fruits. It speaks of the present. It has all already happened! Paul, in response to the Corinthians' enthusiasm, uses the formula they are using, but interprets it differently.

When Paul speaks in 9:19-23 of being all things to all people, he again alludes to the baptismal formula. Readers have just been reminded of the formula in the preceding discussions in chap. 7. The clue that confirms this thesis appears in the list of those with whom Paul identifies. They are Jews, those under law, those outside law, weak. The anomalies in this list were noted above, and several questions were raised. The first was "What does it mean that Paul, a Jew, becomes *as* a Jew?" Paul can say that he became as a Jew because he has in mind the baptismal formula: The Christian is now neither Jew nor Greek, but a new creation. Moreover, I suggest that he writes in this way because he intends to name those mentioned in the formula (Jew/Greek, slave/free, male/female) as those with whom he identified. Had he done so, he would have made clear his identification with all people.

After naming the first group, Jews, he sees a better way to make his case, a way that will tie this paragraph more closely to the idol-meat discussion. I asked above why Paul speaks twice about the same group, Jews and those under law. I suggest that he begins the list again, so to speak. He names the first two groups in the baptismal formula (Jews/Greeks) in a somewhat broader way, those under law and those outside law, in order to refer to those on either side of the idol-meat discussion. "Those outside law" might suggest the strong in Corinth, for whom all things are permitted (10:23; see also 6:12-14); "those under law" then might suggest the weak.

The third question raised above is also answered by this thesis: Why does Paul not speak of Greeks, instead of "those outside law"? Paul speaks this way because he wants his list to tie in directly with those involved in the idol-meat discussion. The term *Greeks* will not do in the idol-meat debate because those on both sides are Greek.

Another question raised above is how to understand the curious contrast between Jews and weak (9:20*a*; 9:22*a*). By the time Paul says "To the weak I became weak," he has moved away from the groups mentioned in the baptismal formula. He is dealing with those who stand on either side of the idol-meat debate. He wants to mention the weak specifically and is unconcerned that this disturbs the balance of his chiasm.

Would the Corinthian readers understand Paul as I have interpreted him? I think it would not have been clear to them that the list of those with whom Paul identifies refers specifically to those on either side of the idol-meat question until they read "To the weak I became weak." "Those under law" and "those outside law" are not obvious parallels to "weak" and "strong," to say the least. In addition, these paraphrases of "Jew" and "Greek" would not have surprised them. They have just read a similar paraphrase of "Jews" and "Greeks" in 1 Cor 7:18 and 19, where Paul speaks of "circumcision" and "uncircumcision." But once Paul says "To the weak I became weak," they could hardly understand the paragraph as anything other than a comment about the issue under discussion. They were expecting Paul to cite those groups mentioned in the baptismal formula. The appearance of "weak" in the list is *very* anomalous. Why is it there? Surely, the reference to the "weak" in 8:7, 9-12 is the clue. It refers to those who have scruples about eating meat sacrificed to idols.

Indeed, the strong in Corinth must have thought, after reading 9:19-23, that Paul had changed sides. There is a little, but only a little, in the argument thus far to encourage them to see Paul as being on their side. For this, they will have to wait for 10:25-27 and, most notably, 10:29*b*-30.

The use of the baptismal formula in the passage sets the idol-meat issue squarely in an eschatological context. The formula proclaims the reality of a new creation, the transformation of relationships. For Paul to use the formula is to call his readers to awareness of what time it is from God's perspective. What a Christian does or does not do about idol meat is to be decided in the light of the eschatological advent of Christ.

Vocabulary of 1 Corinthians 9:20-22a Found Elsewhere in Paul's Letters

In this section we look briefly at two sets of vocabulary. First we will ask how Paul employs the phrase "Jews and Greeks" and various equivalent expressions. We will then look at his use of the word *weak* and its cognates, especially in 1 Corinthians. Our purpose is to help answer the question: How did Paul's Corinthian readers understand these terms in 1 Cor 9:19-23?

Paul refers to Jews as "those under law" (*hoi hypo nomon*) only in 1 Cor 9:20 and Gal 4:4. In the latter text, the expression appears to be caused by the description of Jesus in the preceding verse: "born of a woman (*ek gynaikos*), born under law (*hypo nomon*)"—that is, the expression "those under law," occurs in order to stress the relationship of those under law to Jesus, who was born under law. As in 1 Cor 9:20, the term is used because it suits Paul's immediate purpose.

A number of texts in which Paul refers to Jews and Greeks, or the equivalent "circumcised" and "uncircumcised," are of interest in this study. Gal 5:6 and 6:15 are very similar in form and content to 1 Cor 7:19. To say that neither circumcision nor uncircumcision counts is to claim that the distinction between them is gone in Christ. More important, the positive way to speak is to say what has taken the place of the distinctive groups: a new creation. The eschatological community has come into existence.[29]

1 Corinthians 1:18-25 is noteworthy in this study both because it is at the beginning of the epistle and because it contains references both to Jews/Greeks and to weakness. This passage marks the beginning of Paul's use of weakness as a way to talk about God's work in Christ and especially in the cross, a theme very prominent in the whole Corinthian correspondence.[30] It is apparent that Paul's struggle in 1 Corinthians 1–4 is not with Jews. It is with those in Corinth who believe they have wisdom or knowledge. Why then mention the Jews? Presumably he does so because it was customary for him to refer to humankind as a whole by the phrase "Jews and Greeks."[31] There is no obvious suggestion here of the baptismal formula of Gal 3:26-28. 1 Corinthians 9:20*a* might be understood in the same way, except for 1 Cor 7:17-24, which occurs before our passage.

It is also not apparent in the beginning of the epistle why the weakness motif is introduced. The issue is wisdom: the wisdom of the Corinthians, for whom the gospel means that they have acquired the wisdom of Christ. Wisdom and foolishness, then, are useful terms for Paul's debate with them. But why speak of weakness? It is surely introduced by Paul because he wants to speak of God's power as well as God's wisdom.[32] Power suggests its opposite to Paul and so gives him two dramatic opposites to work with: wisdom/foolishness and power/weakness. It may also be that the designation of some in Corinth as "weak" (chap. 8) contributes to the development of thought in 1 Cor 1:18–2:5.

In 1 Cor 1:18–2:5, Paul begins an argument about the powerful weakness of God in the cross and its effects on Jew and Greek.[33] In 7:17-24, he appeals explicitly to the eschatological baptismal formula and interprets it in a way different from that of his readers. In chaps. 8–10, Paul first speaks of the weak as his Corinthian correspondents did (8:7, 9, 10, 11, 12). In 9:22 ("To the weak I became weak"), he again recalls the baptismal formula and, speaking of himself, fuses together the Corinthian meaning of "weak" and his own developing notion about weakness as God's instrument. To put it differently, when the Corinthians sent their letter to Paul, "weak" referred to those who had scruples about eating idol meat. When they heard Paul's reply on this matter, "weak" meant something else. It now has to do with God's action in the cross. We raised the question above: Why does Paul say he became *as* a Jew, and so on, but that he *became* weak? For Paul to become weak is not for him to side with one group in Corinth against the other. It is for Paul to accept his calling to be an apostle of Christ, whose weakness in the cross is the power of God.

III

Paul's description in 1 Cor 9:19-23 of the way he habitually functioned in response to God's call is not just problematic; it is outrageous, quixotic, impossible. As a general guideline or principle of behavior, it is hopeless.[34] As I said in the beginning of this essay, we use the expression as a criticism. When we say that someone *tries* to be all things to all people, we imply failure in the attempt.

There are suggestions in Paul's letter that he was criticized for inconsistent behavior.[35] One need go no further than 1 Corinthians for examples of his violating his claim to be all things to all people. In 5:1-13, Paul condemns a man in Corinth for sexual irregularities and the church for tolerating him. In 6:1-8, he expresses no sympathy for, much less identification with, people who believed they had been wronged. Chapters 1–4 are full of ironic criticism of the wise and Spirit-filled Corinthians.

Even granted that Paul overstates his case[36] and that his readers know him well enough to make proper allowances, the problem is not resolved. Why would Paul dictate this passage, when he must have known both that his own behavior gives the lie to what he claims and that he invites all kinds of trouble by saying it?

The clue that leads to an answer is Paul's appeal to the baptismal formula in Gal 3:26-29: "There is neither Jew nor Greek. . . ." In relation to the disagreement about idol meat, Paul addresses the following question: What sort of behavior is appropriate for those called by God into community with his Son (1 Cor 1:7) and thereby community with each other, those on whom the end of the ages has come (10:11), those who know that now in Christ there is no Jew or Greek, slave or free, male or female? He answers, in effect: "You do not decide what to do about those who disagree on idol meat by appeal to theological affirmations" ("an idol has no real existence," "there is no God but one" 8:4). You do not decide by appeal to your rights (*exousia*, 8:9) or freedom under God in Christ. Nor do you decide by appeal to the promptings of your conscience/consciousness. Rather, you work out the problem by giving attention to your eschatological situation, to what God calls you to be and do, given that situation." Any and every problem that arises in the eschatological community is an occasion to ask how people can be related and how life in the community can be ordered so as to exhibit, witness to, and live out the new creation.[37]

How did Paul develop his answer? What did his readers understand?[38] First, he begins his letter with 1:18–4:21. This long passage contains the beginning of Paul's theology of weakness: the weakness of God in the cross and the weakness of those whom God calls. In these verses, he says the following of himself: He was weak among them as the proclaimer of the gospel (2:1-9); he and Apollos are examples to follow (4:6 and 16); and he and other apostles as well are weak, humiliated, mistreated, blessing, and enduring (4:9-13).

The next thing Paul does, prior to taking up the idol-meat question, is to interpret the baptismal formula in chap. 7, where he discusses sexuality in the eschatological community. Paul has a more complex understanding of the eschatological situation than do the Corinthians. They can speak of living in Christ, where now there is neither male nor female. The turn of the ages has in some sense occurred and the church is the eschatological community. But, Paul reminds them (1 Cor 7:26, 29-31), they do not yet live fully in the new age. In the present ambiguous situation, the eschatological witness requires both married and celibate people in the community. One way is not the only right way for everyone.

When Paul takes up the issue of idol meat in chap. 8, he first grants the "strong" their case. They have knowledge. Idols are nothing. There is only one God. He then makes an emphatic appeal for their solidarity with the weak. The brother or sister in Christ is more important than anyone's right to anything. He says of himself, "If food is the cause of my brother's falling (RSV), I will eat no meat to all eternity (8:13)."[39] It is an outburst. Thus far in the discussion, Paul appears to be solidly on the side of the weak.

In 1 Cor 9:1-8, Paul first establishes his right as an apostle, then passionately renounces the use of his right. He goes on, in 1 Cor 9:19-23, to describe in a positive, yet paradoxical, way the sort of life appropriate to the eschatological community. The baptismal formula to which he alludes put it in negative terms: now you are neither this nor that. What, then, are you? Characteristically, he speaks not of general principles or guidelines for behavior, but of relationships. Life at the turn of the ages means self-enslavement to everyone: Jews and Greeks and members of the church, whether Jew or Greek. God's call in Christ, which grants freedom, wisdom, and power, is to radical identification with the other.

This is so because the eschatological reality is a community that God calls into existence to exhibit, live out, and proclaim the new creation.

Paul speaks of this radical identification with the other in the face of the Corinthian absorption with self (*my* freedom/authority, *my* conscience/consciousness). Identification with the other is the condition on which one can be a co-sharer in the gospel (9:23). The new creation *is* the community, a harbinger of the future of the cosmos. How the community orders its life and how members relate to one another are in and of themselves proclamations of God's reconciliation of the world. The community is part of the gospel it proclaims. In this connection, we must take very seriously Paul's statements about people saving other people (1 Cor 7:16; 9:22). In the eschatological community called by God, the partnership (*koinonia*) with God in Christ is so close that Paul can speak of people saving people. It is done by radical self-identification with others.

How does self-identification work? How does one identify with others, without losing oneself, without losing the liberating, empowering gospel? The full answer to these questions is not clear until one reaches the end of the discussion, 1 Cor 10:29b–11:1. But some things are clear in our passage.

First, Paul becomes *as* one under law, *as* one outside law. The "not being" statements (9:20d, 9:21b) come into sharp focus at this point. Paul says that he is not himself under law and that he is not outside the law of God, but inside the law of Christ. I suggest that "under," "outside," and "inside" are *spatial* terms.[40] They designate what Martyn often calls "spheres of power." God's action in Christ has called into being a community that can be understood as a *place*, the place where God's power becomes operative, effective in overthrowing the power that is the world in opposition to God.

How would the Corinthians have understood "under," "outside," and "inside?" "Under the law" and "outside the law of God" would have caused no problem. These are clear ways to refer to Jews and Greeks. I suggested above that, in the context of the discussion about idol meat, Paul's readers would have associated those "under law" with people who were uneasy about eating idol meat. Likewise, they would have associated those "outside the law" as the strong to whom all things were permitted. "Under" and "outside" are clear opposites. But what of "inside?" It is also clearly the opposite of "outside." What does it mean to say that one is not outside the law of God but inside the law of Christ? Characteristically, Paul is more cryptic here than one might wish.[41] Also characteristically, Paul is playing with words, manipulating terms in his ongoing attempt to speak about the eschatological reality in ordinary language.[42] Paul says "inside the *law* of Christ" here because he has been speaking about law and, as usual, expresses himself in parallelism. The phrase would surely recall his frequent use of the expression "in Christ." In fact, that is what he means here.[43] In the eschatological community, in Christ, one is neither under law nor outside law ("neither Jew nor Greek"). The old ways of designating oneself and others do not work in the new creation. One does not lose one's identity or one's freedom in the act of radical identification with others because one is in Christ. One can forget about self,[44] not worry about or defend one's authority or one's conscience/consciousness. This is freedom—the freedom to identify with others, a freedom that exists only in Christ.

There are three "being" clauses in our passage:

> 19a For, being free of all
> 20d not being myself under law
> 21b not being outside the law of God
> but inside the law of Christ

Taken together, the second and third clauses explain the first. Being free means being neither under law nor outside law, but in Christ. In Christ, one is free to become *as* anyone. To do so may be to win that one for Christ, for the new creation offered in Christ.

Second, Paul becomes *as* one under law and *as* one outside law, but he *becomes* weak. The difference between the latter statement and the former is important and would not have been lost on the readers. By "weak," the Corinthians mean those who are uneasy about eating idol meat, those who ought to and can become strong.[45] Paul, however, has begun to develop his use of "weak" to describe what God has done in Christ and the consequences for the Christian (1 Cor 1:18–2:5, 4:10). Weakness is seen from the perspective of the eschatological reality. Paul's clear bias in favor of the weak in the whole of 1 Corinthians 8–10 must be seen in the light of this development. He risks the tyranny of the weak in order to call the triumphalistic Corinthians back to reality. In the eschatological community, to be weak is to be conformed to the cross of Christ. The strong, who hold a position on idol meat with which Paul agrees, endanger the eschatological community, which is God's new creation and God's witness in the world to the reality of the new creation. Thus Paul identifies himself more closely with the weak than with the strong. What is at stake is the new creation itself.

Third, near the end of his discussion of idol meat, just before he concludes his argument (10:29b-30), Paul speaks for the strong: "For what good does it do for my freedom to be subjected to the judgment of

152

another's conscience/consciousness? If I partake with thankfulness, why should I be denounced for that for which I gave thanks."[46]

Finally, we say in relief, Paul gives us something with which to defend ourselves from the tyranny of the weak! These statements are grammatically difficult, and Paul's intentions in them are not obvious. I suggested above that this sudden outburst is intended to stress the responsibility of the weak toward the strong, just as chap. 8 and 10:28-29a express the responsibility of the strong toward the weak. Paul does not take the side of one group against the other, nor does he try to resolve the problem once and for all. Certainly, he does not enunciate a general principle and then apply it to this specific issue. He works instead on relationships. He asks something of both groups which he hopes will make it possible for all of them to move forward together. Paul does not ask or expect everyone to agree.[47] What he asks, rather, is that those on each side identify with those on the other side, to become *as* the ones with whom they disagree. They are not initially required to change their convictions; they are to act on behalf of those with whom they disagree. Paul knows that this is a difficult and complicated thing to do. It is, however, necessary if the eschatological community is to exhibit and proclaim the new creation, even as its members take diverse paths of obedience.

IV

Does Paul offer insights in 1 Cor 9:19-23 that might help us to live out our calling to be in Christ? In a situation of conflict, the way of the cross is for people on all sides of an issue to try looking at it from their opponents' perspective.

Such an eschatological strategy has the possibility of doing a number of things. Perhaps the most important is that it may help to set new terms for the conflict. New possibilities may appear. Flexibility and diversity will be introduced where only increased hardening of positions was before. God can and will work powerfully in such a setting, and something will happen to change the character of the conflict. There are a great many disputes in congregations and other church bodies that might benefit from such a strategy.

Christians can risk such a stance because they know that any real, effective power they have is from God. If it is *God's* power, the important thing is to remove the obstacles that prevent God's power from working. Christians do not have to ask how they can use their power to achieve God's purposes. They can ask, as it were: How do we get out of God's way and into a position to participate in the transformation God is bringing?

Martyn concludes his essay, "Paul and His Jewish-Christian Interpreters," with the following words:

> For Paul himself, however, the gospel, by setting us free from the perceptive criteria that belong to what he called "the present evil age," was the event of liberation to true life. Called by the God of liberation into the battle against this evil age, Paul knew very well the cross-like afflictions of Christ's soldier. He also knew God's life-giving power precisely in those afflictions: . . . always carrying in the body the death of Jesus, so that the life of Jesus may also be manifested in our bodies (2 Cor 4:11).
>
> In this liberating battle God called Paul to his life's task: to preach the powerful word of the cross, knowing that, in that word, God was destroying the wisdom of the wise, in order to give us our true wisdom, our true life, and our true future in Jesus Christ.[48]

Paul saw "perceptive criteria that belong to . . . 'the present evil age' " at work in the self-centered claim to have freedom/authority, defended by theologically correct affirmations ("There is no God but one"; "an idol has no real existence"). On the other side, there was the self-centered claim to have demanding pangs of conscience/consciousness, no doubt defended as good Christian piety.

What criteria are offered when the issue is examined from the standpoint of the cross-centered gospel? For one, Christians could be all things to all people. The ordinary, normal life in the world of the eschatological community could be ordered so that its members identified themselves with their opponents. If they could do this, attention would be shifted from the issue under debate to the church's calling to be the eschatological sign of hope in the world. In the process, the debated problem would be resolved—not easily, not automatically, but by means of "the cross-like afflictions" through which the community might be transformed, might become again and again the witness to God's offer of life to the world.

Notes

1. J. Louis Martyn, "Paul and His Jewish-Christian Interpreters," *USQR* 42 (1988) 1-15.
2. Or "in order to (continue to) save at least some." See BAGD, 609, who prefer this reading but allow the other.
3. Whether 1 Cor 9:1-18 was included in the original letter as it stands here is a matter of debate among scholars. Many have challenged the unity and originality of chaps. 8–10 as we have them now. See the discussion in Conzelmann, *I Corinthians* (Philadelphia: Fortress, 1975) 137-38. "For" in 9:19 certainly refers to what has been stated immediately before this paragraph. The reference to "being free" in 9:19 and to "am I not free?" in 9:1 causes me to think that we have chap. 9 as Paul dictated it.
4. As elsewhere in Paul (see, for example, the chiasm in 1 Cor 7:17-24), the structure of the paragraph can be seen in more than one way. An alternative to the chiasm I offer

might include v. 23. Verses 19 and 23 show some parallels: the use of *pas*, a conjunction introduces each, each contains a purpose clause. I limit the chiasm to vv. 19-22 because of the obvious parallels that emerge when it is set out as I have done. Paul's attentive readers would no doubt notice both structures.

5. I have not included here the additional English words in my initial translation, in order to make the chiasm as clear as possible. The italicized words represent identical elements in both chiastic pairs. Those printed in bold type are contrasting elements.

6. Quoted by Conzelmann, *I Corinthians*, 160 n. 20.

7. This is suggested by the fact that this passage, 9:19-23, occurs between the two discussions of the idol-meat controversy in chaps. 8 and 10:23–11:1. I take 9:19-23 to be a digression at the center of the idol-meat debate, whether or not the other literary units (9:1-18; 10:1-13, 14-22) are also digressions or interpolations.

8. This is not to claim that there were no Jews at all in the Corinthian church, but only that the terms for this issue were set by Gentile "enthusiasts" and other, more timid Gentiles.

9. See Gal 6:15; 2 Cor 5:16; and also Gal 5:6; 1 Cor 7:19.

10. See, for example, 1 Cor 1:22-23; 10:32; 12:13.

11. *Anomos* is not used elsewhere by Paul. *Anomia* is found in Rom 4:7 (quoting Ps 32:1); 6:19; 2 Cor 6:14; which I take to be an interpolation. *Anomōs* is found in Rom 2:12.

12. I believe a case can be made for the integrity of 1 Corinthians 8–10, but it is not essential to my thesis that each of the links to 1 Cor 9:19-23 be accepted. The thesis does depend on the interrelation of 1 Corinthians 8; 9:19-23; and 10:23–11:1—that is, I am claiming that Paul wrote the passage under consideration here specifically in relation to the discussion of eating meat sacrificed to idols.

13. For example, Conzelmann, *I Corinthians*, 154 n. 27.

14. "An idol has no real existence"; "There is no God but one" (8:4). "Food will not bring us to judgment before God" (8:8).

15. With many scholars, I take "all things are permitted" as a slogan of the Corinthian strong. I have translated *exestin* as "permitted," rather than "lawful," as in the RSV, because the latter is misleading. *Exestin* is not a cognate of *nomos*.

16. With many scholars, I believe the term *conscience/consciousness* (*suneidēsis*) to come from the Corinthians' letter to Paul.

17. Possibly cited by the Corinthian strong. Whether from them or Paul, the latter here speaks on the side of the strong.

18. Among many discussions, see Robert Jewett, *Christian Tolerance: Paul's Message to the Modern Church* (Philadelphia: Westminster, 1982).

19. The translation is Jewett's (ibid., 52). On the problem of the continuity of thought from 10:28-29a to 29b-30, see ibid., 53. The problem is that v. 29b begins with the conjunction "for" (*gar*). It must follow on the material preceding. But v. 29bf. is obviously a very abrupt reversal of vv. 28-29a. What then does Paul intend? The solution, it seems to me, is to take seriously the parenthesis of vv. 28-29a. "For" in v. 29b follows, not in the parenthesis but in v. 27.

The passage then reads (using the RSV translation):

To the strong:	23	"All things are [permitted]," but not all things are helpful. "All things are permitted," but not all things build up.
To both:	24	Let no one seek his own good, but the good of his neighbor.
To the weak:	25	Eat whatever is sold in the meat market without raising any question on the ground of conscience[/consciousness].
Why?	26	*For* "the earth is the Lord's and everything in it."
To the weak:	27	If one of the unbelievers invites you to dinner
(This is parallel		and you are disposed to go, eat whatever is set
to v. 25)		before you without raising any question on the ground of conscience[/consciousness].

155

Side glance at   28-29a Parenthesis
the strong:
Why?   29b-30 *For* why should my liberty be determined. . . .
(This is parallel
to vs. 26)

Admittedly the connections are not a model of syntactical clarity. This is hardly unique in Paul's writing.

20. Philemon is another example of Paul's indirect approach. He does not ask for, much less command, Onesimus's freedom. It is clear, however, that this is what he wants.
21. As suggested by the introductory "Now concerning" (*peri de*) in 7:1, 25; 8:1; 12:1; 16:1.
22. Chapter 7 has "now concerning" twice, vv. 1 and 25, but both questions or sets of questions were related to sexuality.
23. 1 Corinthians 12–14 is another example of the same form, in which chap. 13 is the digression.
24. The irregularity of form is caused by vv. 21 and 23. Paul does not say of slavery and freedom, as he has just said of circumcision and non-circumcision, that it does not matter which one has. Instead we have the problematic v. 21. In addition, there is no parallel in the chiasm to v. 23.
25. 1 Corinthians 1:18, 21; 3:15; 5:5; 15:2.
26. Many commentators have argued that this text is quoted by Paul from a baptismal liturgy. Paul appeals to the baptismal formula also in 1 Cor 12:13. See the allusion in Col 3:11 by someone in Paul's circle.
27. If the issues about sexuality in Corinth are related specifically to "neither male nor female," this accounts for the absence of this pair in 1 Cor 12:13. Paul has just dealt with the Corinthians' dangerous interpretation of this pair in chap. 7.
28. See vv. 26, 29-31.
29. Romans 10:12 makes the same point.
30. Paul does not employ the "weakness" vocabulary in this way outside the Corinthian correspondence. In addition to 1 Cor 1:18–2:5, see 4:8-13; 15:43; 2 Cor 10:10; 11:30; 12:5, 9, 10; 13:4. Paul uses "weakness" words in 1 Cor 11:30 and 12:12 in ways that are different from his description of God's action in the cross. The uses of "weak" in 1 Cor 8 are also different. They surely originated with the Corinthian strong as a designation of those who have scruples about eating idol meat.
31. See 1 Thess 5:14; Gal 4:9, 13; Rom 5:6; 6:19; 8:26; 15:1.
32. See especially 1 Cor 4:20.
33. See Martyn's stimulating discussion of this passage in "Paul and His Jewish-Christian Interpreters."
34. Nevertheless, commentators continue to describe vv. 19, 22c, and 22d as stating Paul's "general principle" and vv. 20-22b as his specific application of the principle. Conzelmann, *1 Corinthians*, is a happy exception.
35. See Henry Chadwick, "All Things to All Men (I Cor IX 22)," *NTS* 1 (1954-55) 261-75.
36. As he does, for example, in 1 Cor 13. Paul is not exactly "bearing all things, believing all things . . . enduring all things" from the Corinthians.
37. This is the reason Paul's letters contain *five* chapters on an issue (what to eat and not to eat) about which Paul is not personally exercised. In addition to 1 Corinthians 8–10, one ought to consider Rom 14–15.
38. For thorough attempts to reconstruct the issues that caused Paul to write 1 Corinthians 8–10, see, for example, Robert Jewett, *Christian Tolerance*; Jerome Murphy-O'Connor, "Freedom of the Ghetto," *RB* 85 (1979) 551-52; Wendel Lee Willis, *Idol Meat in Corinth: The Pauline Argument in 1 Cor 8 and 10* (SBLDS 68; Chico: Scholars Press, 1985). See also Gerd Theissen, *The Social Setting of Pauline Christianity: Essays on Corinth* (Philadelphia: Fortress Press, 1982).
39. Conzelmann's translation, *1 Corinthians*, 146. The RSV translation of the final clause is too tame. Paul's statement is very emphatic.
40. I have translated the difficult *ennomos* as "inside" because the simplest, most obvious meaning of the prefix *en* is "in." Conzelmann translated "within."

41. See, for example, 1 Cor 7:21.
42. See, for example, Gal 4:1-7, where Paul works with the distinction between child and (grown-up) son and Jesus as the Son. See also Rom 6:12-23 and especially vv. 18 and 19, where Paul's penchant for parallel opposites causes him to speak of "slaves of righteousness."
43. See, for example, the commentaries by Conzelmann and Murphy-O'Connor. Galatians 6:2 and Rom 8:2, which contain similar expressions, do not help to interpret the verse. Both expressions, like this one, occur because they are appropriate to the specific issues being addressed in the passage.
44. Paul is a prime example of someone who had the freedom to forget self. I once had a student who disliked Paul because "he was such an egotist. He was always talking about himself." On the contrary, Paul spoke with great freedom about himself precisely because his identity was secure and guaranteed by Christ (Gal 2:20, 6:14). He appeals unashamedly to personal relationships that sustained him (1 Thess 3:6-10; Gal 4:12-15; Phlm and elsewhere). He shares his deepest anxieties and worries (Gal 4:11; Rom 16:30-32). He risks being vulnerable and pays dearly for it (2 Cor 2:1-4 and 2 Cor 11). He uses himself as an example for people in his churches to follow (1 Thess 1:6-7; Phil 3:17, as well as 1 Cor 4:16 and 11:1) with no apparent thought that this practice will be used against him. Most of all (in 2 Cor 4:7-12 and 2 Cor 11), he exposes his weakness. There is no way these extravagant expressions of emotion can be calculated maneuvers to manipulate his readers. Having forgotten himself, because his self is guaranteed in Christ, he can use himself all the time to make whatever point he believes is needed. None of us would dare do the same.
45. See Jewett, *Christian Tolerance,* and Willis, *Idol Meat in Corinth.* There is a good bit to be said for the position of the strong. Surely most of us would stand with them in desiring that the weak overcome their scruples about eating idol meat.
46. The first sentence is Murphy-O'Connor's (*1 Corinthians* [Wilmington: Glazier, 1979]), the second Conzelmann's.
47. Rather he defends diversity, as he does also in 1 Corinthians 7 and 12–14.
48. Martyn, "Paul and His Jewish-Christian Interpreters," 15.

THE KNOWING OF GLORY
AND ITS CONSEQUENCES
(2 Corinthians 3–5)

John Koenig

M ore than twenty years ago J. Louis Martyn demonstrated to the satisfaction of many that the chief dynamic at work in 2 Cor 2:14–6:10 is properly named "epistemology at the turn of the ages."[1] Focusing on the difficult vv. 16 and 17 of chap. 5, Martyn showed from the context that the phrase rendered in the RSV, "from a human point of view" (literally *kata sarka,* "according to the flesh"), must be taken adverbially. That is, to paraphrase 5:16, "Once we saw or perceived in a fleshly manner the one called Christ, but now we do so no longer." Paul does not spell out a direct contrast to this fleshly means of perception, but according to Martyn, the line of the apostle's thought, particularly in chap. 4, makes it clear that he advocates a form of knowing determined by that juncture of the ages that he terms the "new creation" (5:17). One may characterize this knowing as an activity *kata stauron,* according to the cross, where strength comes to expression in the midst of weakness, wisdom in foolishness, renewal in affliction, and the like (see esp. 4:5-12, 16).[2]

In concert with a number of other modern interpreters, Martyn has taken 2 Cor 2:14–6:10 as a defense of Paul's apostleship to his Corinthian readers in the face of competition from new missionaries who introduced themselves to the congregation with letters of recommendation and exuded a kind of spiritual power that was drawing the Corinthians away from Paul's gospel and leadership.[3] It follows from the designation of this literary unit as an apostolic defense that what Paul wants the Corinthians to know *kata stauron* are the signs of the true apostle so that they will choose his gospel over that of his competitors.[4]

I

I find myself to be in fundamental agreement with this analysis of 1 Cor 2:14–6:10. Yet, I also believe that it is desirable to move the discussion forward by taking another look at the object of knowing as Paul lays it out here. Can we not say more about *what* one is expected to perceive *kata stauron*? My proposal is that the sub-text for Paul's apostolic defense, the common cognition of believers to which he appeals and on the basis of which he expects them to make a decision in his favor, is nothing less than the knowledge of God's glory, or, to be more precise, "the knowledge of the glory of God in the face of Christ" (4:6).[5] In a second part to this proposal I want to argue that the chief consequence of knowing God's glory, more important even than the Corinthians' rededication to Paul and the truth of his gospel, is their fuller participation in God's cosmic reconciling activity. To put it in Paul's own, more dramatic, words, the Corinthians are to become, in ways that they have not yet become, the very righteousness of God (5:21).

Before we proceed with this line of thought, however, I need to state some of my operating assumptions about the body of writing we now call 2 Corinthians. With C. K. Barrett and V. P. Furnish I find most plausible the view that chaps. 1–9 of our canonical letter were written by Paul as a single unit. The chief purpose of the letter was to build upon a recent but somewhat unstable reconciliation between apostle and congregation so as to prepare the latter for a visit from him in the near future. By the time Paul arrives, he hopes, the Corinthians' monetary contribution to the fund for poor believers in Jerusalem will be ready and waiting for him. Again with Barrett and Furnish, I take 2 Corinthians 10–13 to be a separate letter, composed after 1–9 when Paul has learned that the missionary apostles alluded to in chaps. 3–5 are winning over the majority of the congregation to their form of the gospel, with the result, Paul thinks, that his own proclamation and leadership are being rejected.[6]

Another assumption to be noted is that in the so-called Moses midrash of 3:7-18 we come upon some material from Paul's missionary opponents themselves, perhaps a confession of faith with which they introduced themselves to the Corinthians. Furthermore, I think that in chaps. 4 and 5 we may catch additional glimpses of the opponents by getting behind Paul's polemical statements against them (see 4:5; 5:12-13). Here I rely on the work of S. Schulz and D. Georgi, both of whom attempt to reconstruct the opponents' version of the midrash.[7] While it may not be possible to recover the opponents' statement in its entirety, there is strong evidence for the view that at least some of their own words occur in 3:7-18. This is as follows. First, the dual focus of the midrash upon the old covenant as a mediator of glory (3:7, 9) and the figure of Moses as a type for believers (3:12-13, 18) does not square with Paul's treatment of these entities elsewhere in his letters.[8] Second, as far as I can tell, Moses and the law had not previously been matters of serious controversy between Paul and the Corinthians. But here, suddenly, they are. Third, just before the midrash (2:17–3:1) and right after it (4:2) opponents are denounced. The most reasonable conclusion from all this data would seem to be that the appeals to Moses and the old (in the sense of "ancient") covenant came from the opponents themselves as part of their claim to missionary success. Paul quotes their midrashic confession, which is well known to the Corinthians, but alters it for his own purposes.[9]

A final assumption about 2 Corinthians on my part is that chaps. 3–5 may be treated as a literary unit within the broader scope of 2:13–6:10. I say this because I see in 3–5 a movement in the apostle's thought from the glory of God, introduced in 3:7, to the righteousness of God, which appears already in 3:9 but then again in the climactic, probably creedal declaration that God made Christ to be sin "so that in him we might become the righteousness of God" (5:21).[10] The shift then is from perceiving and acquiring glory (see 3:18) to becoming righteousness.

II

But that is simply to restate my hypothesis, so we need to backtrack in order to show that the alleged shift really happens. To begin, we may look at what Paul intends to convey by his use of the word *doxa* ("glory"). This expression occurs with great frequency in chaps. 3 and 4 (3:7 [twice], 8, 9, 10, 11 [twice], 18 [three times]; 4:4, 6, 15, 17). We do not find it at all in chap. 5, although it is implied in Paul's description of the "house not made with hands, eternal in the heavens" (5:1), which I take to be the resurrection body, the spiritual body "raised in glory" (1 Cor 15:43) that becomes like Christ's body of glory (Phil 3:21).

Clearly there is a piling up of references to *doxa* in 3:7–18, not to mention the double appearance of the verb *doxazein* in 3:10. In vv. 7, 9, 10, and 11 *doxa* is associated with the giving of the Torah on Mt. Sinai, which suggests that the opponents made something of this in their proclamation of the gospel. Indeed, it was probably their use of *doxa* in the midrash that prompted Paul to offer his own thoughts about it here. On the other hand, we would err in concluding from this that the apostle was simply reacting to the opponents' notion of *doxa*, or reluctant to use it himself, for the word occurs some fifty-six times in his undisputed writings, nearly always in a positive light and never, apart from 2 Corinthians 3, in a way that would lead us to posit that he picked it up from adversaries or addressees.[11]

How then does Paul understand *doxa*? I am persuaded by the 1929 dissertation of George Boobyer that for Paul the root meaning of the term was "light-substance"—that is, a radiant emanation from God, which was considered to be more real, more lasting, and more solid than what we customarily think of as matter. Boobyer cites Exod 24:16-17; Ezek 10:3-4; Isa 60:1ff.; and Wis 7:25-26, among others, to show that this materialistic notion of God's glory existed within some strains of Judaism prior to the Christian movement.[12] That Paul shared in such a conception is demonstrated by the passages noted above, concerning the glorious resurrection body (1 Cor 15:43; Phil 3:21; 2 Cor 5:1ff.). To these we may add Rom 8:21-23, where the redemption of bodies at the end of time is sketched in terms of a glorification that marks a release from all bondage to decay. And finally, in 2 Cor 4:17, which does not seem to be drawing specifically upon the language of the opponents, Paul tells his readers that the present *thlipsis,* or affliction of believers, is preparing for them an "eternal weight of glory." Almost certainly this is the same as the heavenly body-house of 2 Cor 5:1ff. It is that substance which swallows up all mortality from human life in the body.

There is much to be said for J. Tabor's view that Paul held to a particularly realistic conception of *doxa* because of his encounter with the glorified Lord during his ascent to the third heaven (2 Cor 12:1-5). Tabor writes concerning the apostle:

> He has had a taste of . . . power and glory, a special taste. This gives powerful conviction to all his statements about "beholding the glory of the Lord" (2 Cor. 3:18) or the slight momentary affliction which is to result in "glory beyond all comparison" (2 Cor. 4:17) or the sufferings of the present being unworthy of comparison with the "glory soon to be revealed" (Rom. 8:18).[13]

As far as I can tell, Paul's Jewish Christian opponents in Corinth, whose boasting in heavenly visions no doubt prompted his own (2 Cor 12:11-13), would have agreed with him on much of this conceptualizing.

Because *doxa* is God's radiant light-substance, a human being's primary contact with it must be through perception, especially some type of seeing. Thus the Israelites see the glory of God shining from Moses' face (3:7). Believers behold it, as through a mirror, in Christ (3:18). Those who do not believe have their minds blinded so that they fail to apprehend the light of the gospel of the glory of Christ, who is the image of God (4:4). In contrast, believers know in their hearts the light of God's glory in the face of Christ (4:6). By faith, by inner perception, they look upon heavenly glory, which cannot be seen with ordinary eyes (4:17-18; 5:7). Such a vision works discernible effects upon the beholder. As Moses received a portion of divine glory on his face, so believers are being presently transformed, in some sense glorified even now, prior to their resurrection (3:18).

Again, Paul and his opponents may well have found themselves in agreement about much of this, but it was probably just on the issue of the transformation, referred to in 3:18, that their convictions about the experience of God's glory diverged. The opponents must have claimed that glory was improving their physical bodies, changing them in ways that would be visible and attractive to the Corinthians. Otherwise, why does Paul have to lay such stress on his own earthen vessel body as a bearer of Jesus' death and life (4:7-12)? Why otherwise would the apostle attack those who preach themselves (4:5) and pride themselves on their position (literally *prosōpon*, "face") rather than their hearts (5:12)? Why does Paul contrast the bodily and psychic afflictions of the present time so sharply with the heavenly glory to come (5:1-8), unless he is up against people whose message and personal appearance combine to present the Corinthians with an offer of God's light-substance here and now in their bodily lives?[14]

From a different perspective, the issue between Paul and his opponents must have been about what form God's power takes. Indeed, one of the more common synonyms for *doxa* in hellenistic Jewish literature is *dynamis*.[15] Does the believer see this power and acquire it gradually by means of some disciplined practice, perhaps, as Georgi argues, through a special method of interpreting the Torah?[16] Does the believer in effect *become* the power of God (compare the response of the Samaritans to Simon Magus in Acts 8:10)? This, or something close to it, is what the opponents were probably saying and attempting to display through their personal appearance. Furthermore, they must have been telling the Corinthians: "You can become like us!" Paul's alternative message was, of course, the theology of the cross. There is power, yes, but power that remains transcendent because it comes in and through the proclaimer's vulnerability. Life abounds for others through the dying of Jesus in the body of the apostle (4:7-12).

III

However, if Paul's argument limited itself simply to an assertion that his sacrificial work as an apostle was producing power and life for the Corinthians, it would seem to have had little chance of success in convincing them. Why should they not choose attractive leaders over an unattractive one, especially when the former are offering a more tangible, more bodily, more presently available form of power and life? At some level Paul must have sensed that he needed to say more in order to establish the authenticity of his gospel.[17]

One element in what I take to be Paul's expanded argument about glory occurs in 4:15, where he reminds his readers that, through his ministry to them, he and they have become a network for increased thanksgiving to God. In turn, this burgeoning thanks, which multiplies as more and more people come to faith, is said to produce glory for God. Boobyer's work proves helpful again at this point, for it alerts us to the strangely materialistic notion of glory that Paul and his readers were assuming. For Paul, God's light-substance not only comes to human beings, but it is also returned by them, chiefly through thanksgiving, to its Creator. And the end result is that God's very being, or at least well-being, somehow increases.[18] Whether the opponents made use of this notion we do not know, but Paul had employed it previously with the Corinthians (1:11, 20) and then did so again in 8:19; 9:12-13.[19] To know glory rightly, Paul thinks, is to know its motions, its divine-human reciprocity. One must offer it up as well as receive it. Paul claims that this great "increase," which works to the benefit of all parties, including God, is now happening in his service to the Corinthians (4:15). Why would they want to resign from such a magnificent cooperation in grace?

Another feature of Paul's extended argument about glory occurs at the end of his discourse on the eternal body-dwelling (5:1-10). Throughout this passage Paul has been building a contrast between present existence in the body, characterized by groaning and longing and anxiety, and future bodily existence, where one is clothed with glory so that everything mortal is swallowed up by life (5:4; note the parallel with 1 Cor 15:42-57). Only such an existence in the glorious body is properly called being "at home" with the Lord—that is, sharing Christ's glory somatically (Phil 3:21; Rom 8:17-23). The effect of Paul's contrast between present and future is to relativize all talk about the bodily acquisition of glory now. Thus 3:18 takes on a new perspective. We are all being transformed from glory to glory, Paul says. But whatever that means to him, to the Corinthians, or to the opponents, the conclusion one must draw from 5:1-10 is that *doxa* in the present body, if any, amounts to little in comparison with the *doxa* of the future (see 4:17 and Rom 8:18).

And then in 5:9-10 comes a sober reminder. The somatic glory of the future, which far surpasses anything that one can presently have at one's disposal, will be distributed in varying degrees from the judgment seat of Christ according to what believers have done in their bodies on earth to please the Lord (see also 1 Cor 3:12-15). The glory that really counts depends on one's obedient relationship with Christ now. This naturally has moral connotations, but more basically for Paul it always means sharing Christ's cross, being conformed to his death. Thus the apostle declares in Rom 8:17 that believers are "heirs of God and fellow heirs with Christ, provided we suffer with him in order that we may also be glorified with him." 2 Corinthians 4:17 should probably be read in the light of this passage. Suffering with Christ is never just an apostolic vocation, but the calling of all believers.

The active side of that calling comes to expression in 2 Cor 5:15: "He died for all, that those who live might live no longer for themselves but for him." What Paul means by living for Christ is the taking up of Christ's mission. And with this thought the apostle's argument moves toward its climax at the end of the chapter. The primary consequence of knowing God's glory in the face of Christ is not the acquisition of personal power or bodily pleasure or a happy confidence in one's superiority over others (all of which benefits the opponents appear to have offered to believers), but a fuller incorporation into God's reconciling work on behalf of the world. Knowing Christ *kata stauron* (5:16) means being drawn ever more deeply into his saving enterprise. This is true for every believer. If anyone is in Christ, new creation (5:17)—that is, anyone who beholds the glory of the Lord, who walks by faith rather than by conventional sight, and, as a result, both perceives and joins up with God's renewal of the cosmos. I read in the words "join up with," thereby modifying Martyn's almost exclusive accent on perception, in the light of 5:21. God's will, Paul says there, is that in Christ all believers might *become* the divine righteousness. And this *dikaiosynē*, as Käsemann has taught us, consists most fundamentally of God's reaching out to make the world right.[20]

Additional evidence for Paul's efforts to stimulate a fuller participation by the Corinthians in God's saving activity can be found in the series of first-person plural pronouns stretching from 5:16 through 5:21. On grounds of logic and grammar, V. P. Furnish has concluded that virtually all of these pronouns should be understood in the inclusive sense. Thus when Paul writes "we" or "us" in this context, he considers the Corinthians to be co-participants with him and his apostolic associates. This means that the ministry of reconciliation (5:18) and the message of reconciliation (5:19) are entrusted to all believers.[21]

Only in 5:20 does Furnish see an exception to the inclusive use of the first-person plural. There, he suspects, Paul limits the phrase "ambassadors for Christ" to himself and his missionary co-workers. To his Corinthian readers, Furnish says, Paul makes the appeal: "You, be reconciled to God."[22] However, the Greek of 5:20 does not require this we-you contrast between author and readers. An alternative (and preferable) translation would be: "So all of us believers are ambassadors for Christ, God making his appeal through us. We are beseeching [the world] on Christ's behalf, 'You [world], be reconciled to God' " (author's trans.). One advantage of this translation is that it harmonizes better than the RSV with the distinction already made in 5:19 between believers (us) and the world (them). Moreover, such a translation continues the flow of thought from 5:18-19, where the ministry and message of reconciliation are entrusted to the Corinthians.

IV

Here we may summarize. The major thrust of Paul's discourse in chaps. 3–5, reaching its climax in 5:21, is that the chief and most desirable consequence of knowing God's glory in the face of Christ consists of an ever greater identification with God's righteousness, with that divine outreach that is reconciling the world to its Creator. According to Paul's vision of *diakonia,* the Corinthians resemble him in his vocation far more than they differ from him. Paul and his congregations must work together in Christ on the world's behalf.

If the Corinthians do not do so, if they concentrate their energies on the premature acquisition of glory or on discipleship to false apostles who advocate this effort, they will frustrate God's will for them, and the world will suffer loss. That is the nub of Paul's concern when he urges his readers in 6:1 not to accept the grace of God in vain. My paraphrase of 6:1 would be: "And since all of us are working together in Christ as God's righteousness, I am also exhorting you not to accept the grace of God in vain." Vanity or emptiness for the apostle means attempting to own God's glory now in the privatistic way taught by the opponents. Such an attempt creates divisions among believers, with some claiming superiority over others. This in turn works against God's redemption of the world. By contrast, the true knowing of glory, which requires conformation to Christ and his ministry *kata stauron,* brings about a greater unity between believers, between believers and their apostle, and between God and the whole church, so that the new creation can proceed to its glorious fulfillment.

When Paul quotes Isa 49:8 in 2 Cor 6:2 and then insists that the acceptable time and day of salvation referred to are occurring *now,* he means once more to draw the Corinthians deeper into God's righteous activity, into salvation as a process that requires their service. Thus in 6:3 he asserts: "We put no obstacle in any one's way, so that no fault may be found with [the] ministry" (not "our ministry," as in the RSV). Paul obviously thinks of himself as the Corinthians' special icon and expositor of ministry. He is the congregation's founder; they are to imitate him as he imitates Christ (1 Cor 4:14-15). But "the ministry" is by no means limited to him and the co-workers who travel with him. It is the *diakonia pneumatos* (2 Cor 3:8) for righteousness (3:9) and reconciliation (5:18). And Paul's chief task here is to help his readers to take their full part in it. As a letter from Christ, ministered to by the apostle, they are to be "known and read by all" (3:2-3; note the parallel with the vocation of "ambassadors for Christ" in 5:20).

V

Martyn observes that life at the juncture of the ages is understood by Paul to be both "painful and glorious."[23] One can comprehend the first adjective in this description easily enough, for Paul never lets the Corinthians forget the centrality of the cross in his life or theirs. But how is the new life glorious in any way that retains the meaning of *doxa* as "radiant substance"?

For Paul, the chief point of contact with glory is the human heart, since that is where a person comes face to face with Christ in the gospel (4:4-6).[24] This encounter may or may not involve an actual vision—Paul never insists that his call and conversion experience or subsequent "visions and revelations of the Lord" (12:1) become normative for other believers—but it surely implies some definable *seeing* of glory. What is it that Paul expects his readers to see when they "look . . . to the things that are unseen" (4:18)? Taking together all the information about *doxa* given in chaps. 3–5, I conclude that the best answer is God's future for the world, which is still in heaven but nevertheless so close in time and space that it reaches out, through the Spirit, to claim and transform the lives of those who behold it (3:18; 5:5).

For Paul, the present is a time of earthen vessels (4:7), of affliction (4:17), of being away from the Lord (5:6). But simultaneously it is also a time of confidence, hope, and freedom (3:4, 12, 17); of power (4:7); of resurrection life (4:11); and of expanding grace that increases thanksgiving to God's glory (4:15). It is a time characterized by the daily renewal of the inner person (4:16), by courage (5:6), and by the real possibility of pleasing the Lord in one's body (5:9-10). It is also a time of being held together by Christ's love (5:14) and committing one's life to him (5:15). Above all, it is a time of new creation (5:17), in which believers take up the ministry of reconciliation (5:18) and become the very righteousness of God (5:21).

How can all these things be true together? It is only when believers see and are grasped by the radiant substance of God's *doxa* that they can live the new reality and play their roles in it. Seeing God's glory in the heart initiates a reciprocity between the believer and heaven: God bestows *doxa* in the face of Christ, but through thanksgiving and ministry *doxa* is also retuned to God.[25] In service to the new creation, believers suffer with Christ, but this counts for something in the divine economy:

> For this slight momentary affliction is preparing for us an eternal weight of glory beyond all comparison, because we look not to the things that are seen

but to the things that are unseen; for the things that are seen are transient, but the things that are unseen are eternal. For we know that if the earthly tent we live in is destroyed, we have a building from God, a house not made with hands, eternal in the heavens. (4:17–5:1)

Even now believers "have" a building from God in the heavens. To the extent that they walk by faith and not by conventional seeing (5:7), they already derive benefits from their inheritance, already live from the solidity of the future.[26] This could be reason for pride, but Paul is convinced that the right vision of *doxa*, which is cosmic in scope, will crucify all sinful forms of self-concern and empower the believer's willing cooperation with God's saving plan (5:14–6:2). The grandeur of God is the great light that puts everything else in shadows. It invites, inspires, and commands, because it is the very substance of reality. All this, believers know in their hearts but must come to know, again and again through daily renewal (4:16).

VI

Today the word *glory* survives chiefly in the hymns and liturgies of the church, where it retains some of the meanings associated with it by Paul. Occasionally the term turns up in more secular contexts to depict a quest for power and status, as in "he's on a glory trip." The adjective *glorious* enjoys more general usage, surfacing rather frequently in descriptions of landscapes, sunsets, music, and works of art. All in all, however, one gets the impression that there is something rather pale and wan about the glory apprehended by our age, especially when it is contrasted with the various notions of *doxa* alluded to in 2 Corinthians 3–5. This may or may not be cause for regret, but among those, like myself, who claim some continuity with the New Testament believers, it is at least cause for serious reflection.

As I see it, the historical-critical approach to interpreting ancient texts proves a strong ally in such reflection, for it offers a disciplined framework in which differences between ourselves and the early believers can be identified and clarified. Moreover, in the hands of some interpreters, critical methodology creates a kind of personal space for pondering the value-laden question of whether or not the ancients have anything to teach us about the nature of reality. I have always found in the work of J. Louis Martyn a positive answer to this question. And that is especially true of his now classical essay "Epistemology at the Turn of the Ages."

The particular gulf that has opened up before me in the course of this exercise has to do with the place of glory in the Christian life. It is clear that in 2 Corinthians 3–5 Paul's distinctive theology of the cross stands over against and exposes as false the triumphalistic understanding of glory held by his opponents. But it is equally clear that Paul never considers cross and glory *as such* to be natural enemies, even in the present time. What I hope to have demonstrated in this short study is that we might do well to grapple more vigorously than we have so far with the considerable evidence that the apostle's everyday thinking and feeling, and specifically his practical guidance for ministry, were deeply shaped by his contact with an inwardly visible and always impinging *doxa tou theou.*

Notes

1. J. L. Martyn's "Epistemology at the Turn of the Ages: 2 Corinthians 5:16" originally appeared in a Festschrift for Martyn's colleague at Union, Professor John Knox. See *Christian History and Interpretation: Studies Presented to John Knox* (eds. W. R. Farmer, C. F. D. Moule, and R. R. Niebuhr; Cambridge: Cambridge University Press, 1967) 269-87.
2. Ibid., 272, 284-87.
3. Ibid., 275-84. See especially D. Georgi, *The Opponents of Paul in Second Corinthians* (Philadelphia: Fortress, 1986). Georgi in turn relies on E. Käsemann, "Die Legitimität des Apostels," *ZNW* 41 (1942) 33-71; G. Bornkamm, "Die Vorgeschichte des sogenannten zweiten Korintherbriefes," *Gesammelte Aufsätze* 4 (BEvT 53; München: Kaiser Verlag, 1971) 162-94; and S. Schulz, "Die Decke des Moses: Untersuchungen zu einer vorpaulinischen Überlieferung in II Kor. 3:7-18," *ZNW* 49 (1959) 1-30. More recently similar views of the opponents have been expounded by C. K. Barrett, *The Second Epistle to the Corinthians* (New York: Harper & Row, 1973), and V. P. Furnish, *II Corinthians* (AB 32A; Garden City: Doubleday, 1984).
4. Martyn, "Epistemology," 272-73. It needs to be stated that Martyn does not see the polemic in 2:14–6:10 as being limited to personal issues between Paul and his opponents. The heart of the matter is how anyone (5:17) knows and lives at the juncture of the ages. Martyn begins to develop this point just at the end of his essay (see 284-87).
5. In his *Psychological Aspects of Pauline Theology* (Philadelphia: Fortress, 1987), G. Theissen asserts that in 2:14–3:18 the motif of glory is regnant. See 117 n. 1, where Theissen appeals to I. Friesen, *The Glory of the Ministry of Jesus Christ* (Basel: Reinhardt, 1971).
6. See Barrett, *Corinthians*, 1-50; Furnish, *II Corinthians*, 29-55.
7. See note 3 above. The relevant pages in Georgi's work are 229-319, esp. 270-71, where the reconstructed midrash is presented.
8. See Gal 3:6–4:7, 21-30, where Moses and the law function as a foil to the promise borne by Abraham and extended to all believers in Christ through the Spirit. See also Rom 7:1–8:4, where the law, although holy, is pronounced incapable of bringing about the life and righteous behavior it commands. Never, apart from 2 Corinthians 3, is the law associated with glory. The only soteriological reference to Moses in Paul is 1 Cor 10:2, and there the apostle cites his role at the crossing of the sea rather than his reception of the law on Mt. Sinai.
9. For example, it must be Paul who has introduced the theme of the fading of Moses' *doxa* (3:7, 12). For a more complete exposition of how Paul alters the crucial verse 3:18, see my 1970 Union Seminary Th.D. dissertation, *The Motif of Transformation in the Pauline Epistles*, 119-59. The supervisor of this dissertation was J. L. Martyn.
10. See R. P. Martin, *2 Corinthians* (Word Biblical Commentary 40; Waco, Tex.: Word Books, 1986) 156-57.

11. This is not to deny that Paul makes use of traditional material relating to *doxa*. 1 Cor 11:2-15 probably illustrates such a phenomenon.

12. See George Boobyer, *Thanksgiving and the Glory of God in Paul* (Borna-Leipzig: Robert Noske, 1929) 10-14.

13. J. Tabor, *Things Unutterable: Paul's Ascent to Paradise in its Greco-Roman, Judaic, and Early Christian Contexts* (Studies in Judaism; Lanham: University Press of America, 1986) 124.

14. See Georgi, *Opponents*, 229-313; Martyn, "Epistemology," 279-88; Koenig, "Transformation," 135-43.

15. See Boobyer, *Thanksgiving*, 11, 13.

16. Georgi, *Opponents*, 263-64.

17. N. T. Wright's interpretation of the glory in 3:18 as something that Paul and the Corinthians see mirrored on the faces of one another undervalues the polemical character of the passage, which was probably a claim of the opponents to some quite distinctive power and beauty. See "Reflected Glory: 2 Corinthians 3:18," in *The Glory of Christ in the New Testament: Studies in Christology in Memory of George Bradford Caird* (eds. L. D. Hurst and N. T. Wright; Oxford: Clarendon Press, 1987) 139-50. Wright's view gives insufficient weight to the apocalyptic understanding of *doxa* as heavenly light-substance, which is dominant in chaps. 3–5. He concludes: "This glory [referred to in 3:18 and 4:6-11] *consists in* the fact that Paul does not despair in his sufferings, is not abandoned although persecuted, is not destroyed even when struck down" (149). Actually Paul agreed with his opponents that glory itself was something palpably other than this paradoxical strength in weakness (4:14–5:1).

18. Boobyer, *Thanksgiving*, 79.

19. Ibid., 79-84. See also H. D. Betz, *2 Corinthians 8 and 9: A Commentary on Two Administrative Letters of the Apostle Paul* (Philadelphia: Fortress, 1985) 118-19, which draws upon and confirms the work of Boobyer.

20. E. Käsemann, "The Righteousness of God in Paul," *New Testament Questions of Today* (Philadelphia: Fortress, 1969) 108-37.

21. See Furnish, *II Corinthians*, 317, 320.

22. Ibid., 339.

23. Martyn, "Epistemology," 285.

24. Martyn correctly points up the tension between 3:18 and 4:6. Paul can affirm that he is beholding the Lord's glory with an unveiled face, but "he is careful not to say that his own face is what is changed." See ibid., 282 n. 3. On the other hand, hearts do change because that is where glory touches believers (4:6, 16-17).

25. Is it merely a coincidence that in 2 Corinthians 8–9 Paul repeatedly names the collection for poor believers in Jerusalem *hē diakonia*—and always with the definite article (8:4; 9:1, 12, 13)? See also 9:13, where the apostle envisions that the Corinthians' help in this project will bring about a significant glorification of God by the Jerusalem church. It appears that for Paul the next step forward to be taken by the Corinthians in the ministry of reconciliation is the completion of their part in the collection. The knowing of glory is meant to be eminently practical!

26. In my dissertation I argued that the eternal weight of glory (4:17) was in some sense a part of believers now. Although it remains "essentially inaccessible to [them] on earth until it is 'put on' at the parousia (5:4) . . . it is nevertheless a feature of their pre-parousia identities" (see 155). Now I would want to qualify the phrase "essentially inaccessible." To be sure, Paul contends that glory is not at one's disposal in the earthly body. Yet, knowing it in the heart makes it somehow "available" to such an extent that one can offer it back to God.

JEWISH ASSOCIATION WITH GENTILES AND GALATIANS 2:11-14

E. P. Sanders

Introduction

This essay has two *Sitze im Leben*. My own work recently has been on Jewish practice in the period 63 BCE to 66 CE. For this volume in honor of my teacher and friend, whose commentary on Galatians is much awaited, I wanted to offer something on Galatians. Desire and preparation intersect in Antioch, where Peter, at the behest of James, led a Jewish withdrawal from common meals with Gentiles (Gal 2:11-14). We need to know what it meant to "Gentilize" and to "Judaize" (Gal 2:14). Fortunately, in 1983 James Dunn published an article on "the incident at Antioch"[1] which has three advantages from the point of view of a would-be essayist: It points out that the specific issue that was at stake has been too little discussed; and it clearly lays out the exegetical options; it gets the Jewish evidence quite wrong. This judgment requires two immediate qualifications, both of which soften it. One is that some of Dunn's views about Jewish food and eating laws are quite widely held by various scholars. The second is that Jewish food laws can easily be misconstrued even more seriously than they are by Dunn. This will shortly become apparent.

With regard to what the issue at Antioch was, I do not disagree with him at a very general level: It fell between two extremes. He quite correctly notes that it is necessary to consider James's point of view, and he offers three possibilities of what was wrong with eating together as James saw it. (1) The common meals at Antioch transgressed the biblical food laws and permitted either pork or meat from animals that had been improperly slaughtered, so that the blood remained, or they included meat offered to idols. (2) The Christians observed the biblical dietary laws and also "even some of the halakhic elaborations concerning tithes

170

and ritual purity," but James wanted more; full proselytization, including circumcision. (3) The meals did not transgress Jewish law so blatantly as in (1), but the Jewish customs were not so strictly observed as in (2); they fell short of *strict* Jewish practice with regard to "ritual purity and tithing" (29-32).

Dunn proposes that (3) is the most likely, and in very general terms one may agree. What was wrong with common eating lay between the two possible extremes. It is most unlikely that Paul and other Jewish Christians sat down to eat undrained and unsalted pork from pigs sacrificed before a pagan deity, and it is not likely that James was the one who would "compel" Gentiles to be circumcised (Gal 2:3; 6:12). An intermediate issue is needed. Because of numerous passages on the problems posed for Jews by Gentile food (some of which will be cited below), I had always thought that the problem must have been the food itself. Dunn has persuaded me to look elsewhere.

The question is what requirements would fall into an intermediate area. Dunn proposes "tithes and ritual purity," tying these to a supposed Pharisaic program that dominated Palestine and exerted pressure on the Diaspora (15). I regard this as an unsuccessful effort; he gets both tithes and purity badly wrong. More recently Philip Esler has addressed the question of Jews, Gentiles, and food. He thinks that Dunn was in error to think that Jews even sometimes ate when Gentiles were present and that Stephen Wilson also was mistaken when he doubted that complete separation was always practiced by Jews.[2]

Between them, Dunn and Esler offer four possibilities of what the problem might have been:

1. The food had not been tithed.
2. The food or the Gentiles were impure by a strict (Pharisaic) standard.
3. The food was abominable in Jewish eyes: either "meat offered to idols," meat with blood in it, or meat from forbidden creatures (such as swine, shellfish, vultures, tigers, weasels, and mosquitos: Leviticus 11; Deuteronomy 14).
4. Jews would not eat with Gentiles.

Of these, we dismiss 3, at least as just stated. What restrictions on food itself Jews in the Diaspora accepted is an interesting question, and I discuss it elsewhere (see below). Enough will be said in this essay to show that there may have been a problem with the food, even though biblical law was not being transgressed. With regard to the issue at Antioch, however, I now agree with Dunn that the problem was not a major biblical law. (The laws that affect food are the forbidden creatures of

Leviticus 11; blood and fat; meat or wine that had been offered to an idol.) Paul shows himself squeamish over meat offered to idols (1 Corinthians 8, 10), and we may safely suppose that he, Barnabas, and other Jews would have been put off by being offered donkey or hare.

With reluctance, I must omit 1 and all but a small part of 2 from the present essay. The question of what offerings Diaspora Jews sent to Jerusalem, and whether anyone thought the food they ate should have had temple dues taken from it, requires more than the number of pages allowed for the present purpose. It could have been squeezed in, but the result is entirely negative: No one anywhere ever thought that Antiochene Jews should not eat until they had sent some of the food to the temple. Over and above the temple tax, Diaspora Jews did send voluntary gifts—never called "tithes," but rather *aparchai* or *anathēmata*—but they were precisely that: voluntary. Pharisaic purity laws have nothing to do with Diaspora Jews, and Diaspora purity laws have nothing to do with the Pharisees. Again, these studies are interesting in their own right, but they lead to negative conclusions for the question at Antioch. Many Diaspora Jews (to take a very quick example) washed their hands while praying, and Philo seems to have sprinkled himself after being in the room with a corpse and after sexual intercourse. He nevertheless associated with Gentiles, and these rules are not Pharisaic. Diaspora purity laws do not unlock the door.

All these topics—offerings from the Diaspora, food and purity laws in the Diaspora, and Pharisaic purity laws—I treat elsewhere.[5] Here I shall turn to the surviving point, the one that seems most likely to have been at issue among Peter, Paul, and James: the general question of association between Jews and Gentiles. First, however, I shall offer a short and partial excursus on the topic of Pharisaic/rabbinic views of the impurity of Gentiles. This is not an account of Pharisaic purity laws, but it is intended to respond to a very specific question: Did Pharisees think that Gentiles were impure in such a way as to prohibit association with them?

Impurity of Gentiles

Dunn cited some rabbinic passages and an essay by Alon in order to argue that Pharisees thought that Gentiles were impure, and that the Pharisees would have campaigned in the Diaspora to convince other Jews not to associate with Gentiles. There are two things wrong with the argument.

First, most of the passages cited are post-135. Dunn writes: "In several Rabbinic sayings the uncleanness of the Gentile is axiomatic" (18). This is perfectly true, but the passages that most clearly express abhorrence of Gentile-impurity come after the two revolts. (One cited by Dunn,

Eliyahu Rabba, is from the eighteenth century, and it should be considered in another context.) Some nasty things get said about Gentiles after 135, and Dunn accepts all these and retrojects to the 40s and 50s. Dunn rejects evidence from the same period that proves that Rabbis did not expect tithes from the Diaspora. One should reverse his assumptions. It is unlikely that the post-70 Rabbis, who wanted the priesthood still to be supported, would have declined tithes from the Diaspora if pre-70 Pharisees had sought them. Here one *should* retroject: Second-century passages help prove that pre-70 Pharisees did not look to the Diaspora for tithes. One should not retroject to the pre-70 period, however, the full expression of antipathy to Gentiles that comes after the second revolt.

Second, to no small extent Dunn relied on an essay by Gedalyahu Alon on the impurity of Gentiles. This is one of a series of three essays that seem, to people who do not understand the subject matter, to prove things they do not prove. The three essays argue the conclusions that the idea that Gentile theaters were off limits is early; that the view that Gentiles were impure as such can be found in early sources; and that the opinion that laypeople should observe priestly purity laws is early.[4]

To a person who is himself a rabbinic sage—as Alon was—it matters not only whether something was officially "decreed," and by whom, but also whether the official view has early roots. Alon's essays are not social history, but arguments that a given halakah has some basis in the formative period of Rabbinic Judaism—that is, the period before 70. He most carefully distinguished this question from that of *what people actually did*. About this he was honest: Not all Pharisees—much less Jews, generally—agreed that theaters must be avoided; that Gentiles *qua* Gentiles were impure; that laypeople should eat ordinary food in purity.[5] Alon was happy when he found in an early source an indication of the coming full halakah, and then he would write: "It shows that the halakah was in existence" (and the like; see 166)—not, "It shows what people did."

The Christian scholar will understand that if I offer an analogy. Many New Testament, and some patristic, scholars look for the origins of christology, and when they have found the seed from which the fourth- and fifth-century formulations would grow, they retire from the field, happy that the later doctrine has some basis in the formative period. This does not prove that first-century Christians in general believed that two essences coexisted in Christ, without confusion, distinction, or mixture. Nor does it lead anyone to deny that the New Testament contains statements of "low" christology. The question is only: Is the subsequent dogma a development of an authentically primitive element?

Searching for primitive evidence was Alon's intention, but sometimes he was not quite critical enough of himself. If he found that a passage in Josephus implies that Gentiles were impure, he would say that this was proof that *the* halakah of Gentile-impurity existed (165-66), which is not the case. I shall explain the legal issue, which is rather a fine one.

With regard to Gentile-impurity, Alon posed a simple legal question: Were Gentiles subject to the same impurities as Israelites, or did they have their own special brand? This is a sub-topic of a larger question: How much of the biblical law should apply to Gentiles?[6] A lot of fairly early rabbinic passages say that Gentiles did *not* contract the biblical impurities, of which semen-impurity, menstrual-impurity, and corpse-impurity are the most common. If they were not impure on these grounds, were they pure? No, Alon showed, they were impure under a separate rubric: the impurity of being Gentile. Then there was the question of how serious this impurity was. As serious as touching a rodent? As serious as menstruation? As serious as touching a corpse? The Rabbis disagreed.[7]

Alon proved to his own satisfaction that *some* people before 70 thought that Gentiles were immune from biblical impurities, but impure because they were Gentiles. Others, however, thought they were impure under the biblical headings (164-65). To illustrate the issue, I shall quote one dispute between the Houses of Hillel and Shammai:

> The School of Shammai say: If a man became a proselyte on the day before Passover he may immerse himself and consume his Passover-offering in the evening. And the School of Hillel says: He that separates himself from his uncircumcision is as one that separates himself from a grave (*Pesahim* 8.1)

Alon read the view of the House of Hillel as being what the Mishnah "ordains" (151). Leaving this assumption aside, I shall explain the debate. The Shammaites thought that before conversion the Gentile was not subject to the biblical impurities. Thus a Gentile could convert and immediately eat Passover. The Passover meal may not be eaten by those with corpse-impurity, who must wait for the second Passover (Num 9:6-11); the removal of corpse-impurity requires a week (Numbers 19). In specifying the next day ("in the evening"), the Shammaites ruled, in effect, that the Gentile had been immune from the impurity—which most Jews had most of the time, and which the Gentile would have had if he had been subject to it. The Hillelites seem to have agreed that the Gentile had been immune from corpse-impurity, but maintained that nevertheless he had an impurity that lasted a week—Gentile-impurity.

Like a Jew who had been to a funeral, the Gentile would have to wait until second Passover.

None of this means that Pharisees would not associate with Gentiles because they were impure. All Jews, including Pharisees, were impure more or less all the time.[8] Impurity was removed to enter the temple, to eat Passover, and to eat second tithe. Otherwise it was the rule. Semen-impurity, for example, lasts until one washes and the sun sets (Lev 15:16-18). Thus having intercourse after sunset means that one is impure at least until the next sunset—that is, all day. Yet, the Pharisees associated with themselves, day in and day out. The very nice legal issue of the category of Gentile-impurity does not bear on the question of association.

The character of Pharisaic/rabbinic debates, as well as views on Gentiles and impurity, may be illuminated by one other Houses dispute:

> The School of Shammai say: An (ordinary) Israelite may not be numbered [in the same company] with a priest for [the consumption of] a firstling. And the School of Hillel permit it even to a gentile. (*Bekhoroth* 5.2)

This does not prove that priests ate with Gentiles, although they may well have done so, especially among the aristocracy. Rabbinic passages of this type do not constitute sociological evidence. The Pharisees and later the Rabbis often took arguments to their logical limit, and that is the case here. The argument is an academic and exegetical one, and to follow it one will best look at the text of Numbers 18.[9] The House of Shammai take the position that, since purity is required for eating first-fruits of produce (Num 18:13), the same rule should govern firstlings (of animals). The Hillelites note that the paragraph on firstlings (Num 18:17-19) does not include the requirement of purity. On the contrary, firstlings may be eaten by the priests and their sons and daughters. The Hillelites (*t. Bekh.* 3.16) urged that this meant that menstruants could eat firstlings (daughters are included, purity is not explicitly mentioned), and they extended their argument to its logical conclusion: Gentiles, too, could eat firstlings. While the debate is academic, we nevertheless see that one group of Pharisees was prepared to entertain in theory the idea that Gentiles could sit down at table with priests. Priests and their families were required by biblical law to eat sanctified food in purity (besides Numbers 18, see Lev 22:3). If the Hillelites wanted to drop this commandment wherever sharp exegesis allowed, we must suppose that they would not have extended priestly purity to laypeople (which is what scholars commonly say the Pharisees did). There is certainly no reason to suppose that either Hillelites or

Shammaites thought that laypeople should refuse to associate with Gentiles.

We may accept the fact that first-century Jews in general thought that Gentiles were impure. Foreigners were allowed to enter only the Court of the Gentiles, not to go further into the temple. This is not a biblical view. According to Num 15:14-16, Gentiles could bring sacrifices in the same way as Israelites. The view that they had to be kept outside—along with impure Israelites—developed well before the New Testament period. It is attributed to the time of Antiochus III in a letter quoted by Josephus (*Ant.* 12.145-146), and it was accepted by Herod, who had priests trained as masons so that they could build the inner courts (*Ant.* 15.390). Thus the Zadokite priesthood, before the days of the Hasmoneans, had thought that Gentiles were impure, and so did Herod's advisers, presumably the priesthood, surely not the Pharisees.[10] We do not know the legal reasoning. They could have thought that Gentiles were impure because they were Gentiles, or that they were impure with the *biblical* impurities and had to be assumed not to have followed the biblical requirements for removing them. In either case they were impure. All the impurity meant, however, was that they could not enter further into the temple. Jews on their way in could brush up against them, just as Jews on their way in might brush up against a Jew who had semen-impurity.[11] This does not mean that association was forbidden. We now turn to more pertinent evidence: Did Diaspora Jews hesitate to associate with Gentiles?

There Was Association with Gentiles

Dunn, we have seen, took Alon to have proved that because of impurity Jews hesitated to associate with Gentiles, but he did not rule out fraternization entirely. He was attacked by Esler for granting too much in thinking that an undiligent Jew might possibly sit at the same table as a Gentile.[12] Since Dunn had taken the view that "the dominant tendency within Judaism" was to avoid social intercourse with Gentiles as much as possible,[13] Esler's criticism shows that he took an extreme stand: They avoided it altogether. Dunn, proposed Esler, was wrong to think that "table-fellowship occurred between Jews and Gentiles in the first century CE."[14] I transfer my tender attentions to Esler.

While Dunn had very reasonably realized that passages about not eating Gentiles' food have to do with food rather than people,[15] Esler cited the same passages as proving that Jews would not eat *with* Gentiles. This is complete misrepresentation. Daniel 1:3-17; 2 Macc 7:1-2; Jdt 10:5; 12:17-19; Add to Esth 14:17 (LXX 4:17x); and Tobit 1:11 all have to do with the food itself, though Esler claims that these passages support his view that Jews would not eat with Gentiles. On the contrary, they show that the problem was the food, in particular Gentile meat and wine. Similarly in 3 Macc 3:4, 7, not cited by Esler, the problem is again the food (*trophē*). All these passages have at least the implied paraenetic purpose of advising Jews of what to do when in Gentile lands or at Gentile tables: Avoid the meat and wine, and preferably bring your own food. Of Esler's passages, the only one that might be read as supporting his view is the Add to Esth 14:17 (RSV). It contains two long prayers, one by Mordechai and one by Esther. Near the end of her prayer, Esther reminds God that she had not eaten at Haman's table, nor graced the royal drinking party (*symposion*) with her presence, nor drunk the wine of libations.[16] "Did not *eat* at" does not mean "did not *sit* at," and the point seems rather to be that, when at Haman's table, Esther did not eat, while she did not attend the drinking parties at all. The point of all these exemplary stories of how to eat with Gentiles is that Jews should sit and eat their own food or only vegetables.

There are two passages in Jewish literature that fix on the Gentiles rather than their food: *Jub* 22:16, "eat not with [Gentiles]"; *Joseph and Aseneth 7:1*, "Joseph never ate with the Egyptians." It is a curiosity of *Joseph and Aseneth* that the food itself is not mentioned, except indirectly: Joseph did not want to kiss Aseneth because her lips had uttered what they had uttered and had touched what they had touched (8:5). When he dined in her father's house, he sat at a separate table (7:1), but we are not told what he ate. Presumably his servants provided for him; possibly he ate vegetables and drank water.

What do these two passages prove? Neither *Jubilees* nor *Joseph and Aseneth* can be regarded as representative of many Jews. *Jubilees* is closely associated with the sectarian literature from Qumran, and it is extremist in every way. There is no more reason to think that Jews in general accepted its admonitions about Gentiles than to suppose that they accepted its solar calendar. *Joseph and Aseneth* represents an attempt to argue, against the evidence of Gen 41:45, that Joseph had not married a pagan. Aseneth's father is praised as being a good man (1:3) precisely in order to drive home the message: Keep your distance from Gentiles, even morally upright ones. The author wishes to convince the readers not to eat with Gentiles and (the main goal of the work) not to marry them without insisting on full conversion. This is not sociological evidence that Jews did not eat with Gentiles or marry them; on the contrary, the author was trying to check a practice he considered threatening.

Thus far we have learned that some Jews who wrote wished Jews not to eat with Gentiles, but from Jewish sources there is no direct evidence that this was generally accepted.

There is, on the other hand, good evidence that Jews would eat with Gentiles in the right circumstances. Here Esler's argument is either confused or deceptive. He cites some of the following passages and claims that they prove his case, since the Jews in question ate and drank their own food and wine. He obscures or forgets that he was attempting to prove that Jews refused "to dine *with* Gentiles."[17] In either case the evidence is misinterpreted.

The *Letter of Aristeas* depicts the Jewish translators of the Bible as dining with the king of Egypt each day for seven days (*Arist.* 181-294). Esler takes the strange view that this passage only appears to contradict his argument, but it does not do so, since the Jews ate Jewish food. Here as elsewhere he confuses the issue of the people with that of the food. Even more curiously he asks "whether food or wine were passed between the king and the Jews," and concludes that "he ate his and they ate theirs" (82). The passage says quite clearly that he ate theirs. They could share since they were all served Jewish food (*Arist.* 181; Esler's reading started with 182).

Though Esler's principal interest was the Diaspora, as is ours, he was aware of two Mishnaic passages on table-fellowship, taken from Dunn: *Berakoth* 7.1 and *Abodah Zarah* 5.5. The former, Esler properly notes, contemplates eating with a Samaritan, not with a Gentile. (There are other such passages, including a House of Shammai/House of Hillel debate, *Berakoth* 8.8.) The second deals with the problem of wine if one is eating at the same table as a Gentile. The Israelite is to take care not to drink the Gentile's wine, and the passage shows a concern lest the Gentile pollute the Israelite's wine when the latter goes aside. As Esler says, this is "table-fellowship in a very limited sense, if at all" (84). Certainly the topic of the passage is not *fellowship*; it envisages a situation in which the Jew and the Gentile are not friends. On the other hand, there is no objection to sitting side-by-side.

Mishnaic discussions will not settle the question of common practice in Diaspora Judaism. All the Jewish evidence thus far considered presents the *legal* situation perfectly clearly: There was no barrier to social intercourse with Gentiles, as long as one did not eat their meat or drink their wine. As an aside, I shall explain why wine ranks along with meat (the objections to which are well known). Greeks (and others) poured out a small libation whenever they drank wine.[18] Jews thought that all Gentile wine had been the source of a libation at some time or other. Since the custom was public and well-known, Gentile wine doubtless conveyed associations of idolatry, just as did Gentile meat. Thus the Mishnah simply forbids Gentile wine (*Abodah Zarah* 2.3); it does not give a list of questions that, if answered satisfactorily, would make it suitable for Jewish consumption. This left a deep imprint, and many Jews today still avoid Gentile wine, even though libations were not continued in Christianity.

As a further aside, I should point out that some Jews objected to Gentile food other than meat and wine. When Judith set out to ingratiate herself with Holofernes, she took her own wine, oil, parched grain, fruit, and bread (Judith 10.5). Avoidance of Gentile oil is attested elsewhere.[19]

We shall be better to consider reality rather than legal theory. In real life many Jews mingled quite freely with Gentiles. Travel is the most obvious occasion, but not the only one.[20] In some Diaspora cities, such as Sardis, there was no Jewish quarter, and so Jews and Gentiles lived side-by-side.[21] Human sociability would lead to social intercourse of some kind or other. This was also the case in the cities and some of the towns of second-century Galilee, which have been studied by Martin Goodman. He observes that the normal sorts of social relations are evidenced by second-century rabbinic literature. This extends even to use by Jews of the public baths.[22] Paul, whose views of behavior in all respects reflect his upbringing, put it precisely: To avoid the sexually immoral and the idolatrous (in the common Jewish view, the Gentiles), one would need to go out of the world (1 Cor 5:10). Jews did not become hermits to escape contact with Gentiles.

Philo advocated living strictly according to the law, and he observed some purity laws that are not in the Bible. Yet, he associated with Gentiles. As Alan Mendelson has shown, he and other upper-class Jews in Alexandria aspired to participation in Greek educational and social institutions, and Philo himself had witnessed athletic contests in the *gymnasium*.[23] The last is probably also true of the author of the *Testament of Abraham* (see *T. Abraham* recension A 10.2).

Alon argued that it was "the halakah" that Jews would not go to the theater. He cited in favor of this view a story in Josephus (Alon, 143), according to which Herod provided to pious critics that there was nothing idolatrous about attending the theater, despite the trophies on display—and proved it while he and one of the critics were in the theater in Jerusalem (*Ant.* 15.267-279). There is a similar story about Agrippa I (*Ant.* 1.332-334). They hardly prove what Alon claimed. One may also note that, though some doubtless protested when Herod built a theater in Jerusalem, people went to it. There are stories about public show-trials and other large gatherings in the amphitheater in Jericho, attended by thousands of pious Jews.[24] Even in Palestine Gentile institutions were not entirely avoided.

Jewish participation in the main socializing aspects of Gentile city life—theaters, gymnasia, and civil government—is attested by epigraphy. Tessa Rajak has recently surveyed this material. It is, of course, sporadic, and some of it is later than the first century. There is evidence of a first-century Jewish member of a city council in Cyrene, of Jewish attendance at the theater of Miletus in the second or third century, and of Jewish ephebes in Cyrene in the first century—to name only some of the major items. These activities included at least passive contact with idolatry, and they show willingness to overlook formal, civic idolatry in order to participate in the broader civilization.[25]

Thus Dunn's concession, which was attacked by Esler, is to be confirmed: In real life there was "a broad range of social intercourse," which depended on the strictness of the Jew in question (23). This was true not only privately but also publicly. Even strict Jews (such as Philo) managed to square their Jewishness with participation in some of the major aspects of Graeco-Roman culture: the public baths, the gymnasia, the amphitheaters and the theaters. I cannot agree with Dunn that the issues Jews thought about in mingling with Gentiles were tithing and ritual purity, or that the matter depended on the influence of a particular Rabbi (23-24), but the variety he proposed is correct. At the strict end, we noted *Joseph and Aseneth* (worried about neither ritual purity nor tithes, and not written by a Rabbi, but opposed to eating with Gentiles), while at the lenient end we have the evidence cited above, as well as the general considerations that show that intermingling of various kinds was necessary.

The Practice and Theology of Separatism

At the same time there is evidence of considerable Jewish separatism. In many Diaspora cities there *was* a Jewish quarter. Several pagan authors regarded the Jews as antisocial, and a few used the term *misanthropes*. Some singled out eating as an example of their exclusivism.[26] These passages are often discussed under the heading "antisemitism," which I take to be the wrong category. Beyond doubt, whatever the motive, they reflect some sort of social reality. To put the matter cautiously, Jews were in general less willing to mix than were the other peoples of the empire.

How things look to the outsider is of considerable interest and can be decisive on some points. Pagan comments, for example, may be taken as proving that Jews generally observed the sabbath. Yet, they do not show what was done on the day. Some Gentiles took the sabbath to have been a fast day, which was mistaken.[27] Similarly, pagan comments on Jewish exclusivism prove some kind of separatism, but they will not reveal how it was understood on the Jewish side. We have already seen enough evidence to answer this question in part: The principal impediment to social intercourse was general Jewish refusal to eat pagan meat and drink pagan wine. A harder line is seen in *Jubilees* and *Joseph and Aseneth*, but otherwise the bar to relations with Gentiles was the food and drink itself. Dunn (14) correctly notes that Jewish food laws permitted them to entertain Gentiles, but not to accept Gentile hospitality (unless the Gentiles could provide Jewish food and wine). The new result of this one-sided possibility would be very little entertaining of the one by the other. Social intercourse among equals involved reciprocity.

More important is the evidence that points to Jewish pride in separatism. Christian scholars habitually discuss the question under the implied heading "What was wrong with Judaism that Christianity corrected?" Exclusivism is considered to be bad, and the finding that Jews were to some degree separatist fills many with righteous pride. We shall all agree that exclusivism is bad when practiced by the dominant group. Things look different if one thinks of minority groups that are trying to maintain their own identity. I have never felt that the strict Amish are iniquitous, and I do not think that, in assessing Jewish separatism in the Diaspora, we are dealing with a moral issue. (The moral issue would be the treatment of Gentiles in Palestine during periods of Jewish ascendency. How well were the biblical laws to love the resident alien [Lev 19:33-34] observed?) On the present topic, willingness to participate in the larger surrounding culture, Christians would subsequently follow the same range of behavior as did Jews. They would hesitate to marry pagans, Jews, and even Christians who belonged to the wrong party; they would not participate in aspects of public life that included the trappings of idolatry, and so forth.[28]

Exclusivism is built into the basic covenantal conception of Judaism, and as such Jews took pride in it. They did not themselves take this to be "misanthropy," hatred of humanity. The author of the *Letter of Aristeas* was pleased with the king who (in the romantic narrative) commissioned the translation of the Bible. He is shown throughout as a gracious, kind and wise king. This is not misanthropy or even misbasileuity. The author favored cordial and warm relations between Jews and Gentiles. On the other hand, he despised idolatry, following the standard ranking: Graeco-Roman was less bad than Egyptian (*Arist.* 134-138). To prevent idolatry, he wrote, Moses, following divine revelation,

> surrounded us with unbreakable palisades and iron walls to prevent our mixing with any of the other peoples in any matter, being thus kept pure in body and soul, preserved from false beliefs, and worshiping the only God omnipotent over all creation (*Arist.* 139-40).

Gentile questions about meats, drink, and unclean creatures (128), he thought, were off the mark. The Jews were not concerned with these things in and of themselves, but only "with the sovereignty of God" (140-41). Monotheism is what led to separatism. It was to prevent corruption of worship that Moses "hedged us in on all sides with strict observances [purifications, *hagneiai*] connected with meat and drink and touch and hearing and sight, after the manner of the law" (142). The food laws are symbolic: "the cloven hoof, that is the separation of the claws of the hoof, is a sign of setting apart each of our actions for good" (150), and so on. The Jews are forbidden to harm anyone "in thought or in deed" (168). Their responsibility is to live among others as "wise and prudent companions" who help them to "rise above ignorance and achieve progress in life" (130).

Here separatism is accepted, in no contradiction to the story of banqueting with the king. The latter had shown respect for God's law, including the restrictions on food, and so dining with him was compatible with Jewish separatism. Separatism did not, in the view of thoughtful Jews, entail misanthropy. On the contrary, Jews, by standing apart and worshiping the one true God, might be a light to the Gentiles (help them to "rise above ignorance"). Full assimilation would mean acceptance of idolatry; some degree of separation might be of benefit to others.

According to Philo, Balaam, in refusing to curse Israel, predicted that they will "dwell alone, not reckoned among other nations." This does not mean physical separation, but rather that "in virtue of the distinction of their peculiar customs they do not mix with others *to depart from the ways of their fathers*" (*Moses* 1.278). Philo, too, opposed misanthropy: The law "stands pre-eminent in enjoining fellowship and humanity" (*Special Laws* 1.324). This summarizes the "second table," the laws governing relations with other humans, and it is balanced by commanding the love of God (*Special Laws* 1.299). Similar is *Special Laws* 2.63, where the law is taught in synagogues on the sabbath under two main heads: "one of duty to God as shown by piety and holiness, one of duty to humans as shown by humanity (*philanthrōpia*) and justice (*dikaiosynē*)."

In a splendid passage Josephus combines these points: separateness and *philanthrōpia*:

> The consideration given by our legislator to the equitable treatment of aliens (*allophyloi*) also merits attention. It will be seen that he took the best of all possible measures at once to secure our own customs from corruption, and to throw them open ungrudgingly to any who elect to share them. To all who desire to come and live under the same laws with us, he gives a gracious welcome, holding that it is not family ties alone which constitute relationship, but agreement in the principles of conduct. On the other hand, it was not his pleasure that casual visitors should be admitted to the intimacies of our daily

life. The duty of sharing with others was inculcated by our legislator in other matters. We must furnish fire, water, food to all who ask for them, point out the road, not leave a corpse unburied, show consideration even to declared enemies. He does not allow us to burn up their country or to cut down their fruit trees, and forbids even the spoiling of fallen combatants; he has taken measures to prevent outrage to prisoners of war, especially women (*Apion* 2.209-12).

Thackeray (the LCL *ad loc.*) noted that Juvenal had said that Jews would not point out the road (*Sat.* 14.103-4). Josephus here, and presumably throughout, wished to argue that Jewish separatism should not be taken as some Gentiles took it—as evidence of misanthropy.

Special interest attaches to the statement that "casual visitors" are not to be "admitted to the intimacies of our daily life" (*anamignysthai tēi synetheiai*). Thackeray notes that French commentator Reinach proposed that the reference was to Passover (Exod 12:43). There is no reason to make this limitation, for *synetheia* is a general term for what is habitual as well as for what is intimate. Thus Thackeray's translation, "the *intimacies* of *daily* life," is correct. In the same vein Josephus wrote that Moses regulated "with what persons [a Jew] should associate" (*peri tōn koinonesontōn tēs diaitēs*, "associate with regard to living," *Apion* 2.174).

According to Josephus, Antiochus Sidetes was urged by some to extirpate the Jews "because of the separateness of their way of life" (*Ant.* 13.245, *tēs diaitēs amixia*). In a learned note Marcus observed (LCL 7, 350-51) that Diodorus had charged Jews with both separateness and regarding others as enemies. Josephus, in effect, affirms the former and denies the latter: Jews were to some extent separate, but they did not harbor enmity toward others.

We cannot, of course, know how many Jews *felt* enmity toward Gentiles, just as we cannot know how many assimilated to some degree or other. There are enough stories of conflict in mixed cities to indicate that there was sometimes hostility on both sides (see *J.W.* 2.561). The same evidence shows that on the whole Jews did in fact remain separate and distinctive.

This was especially true of marriage. Endogamy is not precisely a biblical law. Exodus 34:11 forbids marriage with women of certain Gentile nations because of the fear of idolatry, and Deut 7:3 forbids marrying the sons or daughters of the seven conquered nations (see the complaint of Ezra 9:1-2). According to Deut 23:3, "no Ammonite or Moabite shall enter the assembly of the Lord." Yet, Ruth, ancestress of David, was a Moabitess, and clever exegesis could have voided the biblical passages. The prohibited nations no longer exist; existing nations are not prohibited. But many favored a total ban on intermarriage. The author of *Joseph and Aseneth*, we say, wished to require full conversion before intermarriage. *Jubilees* had taken a completely hard line against intermarriage (*Jub* 30:7, 14-17), and this is also true of Pseudo-Philo (*Biblical Antiquities* 9.5 and elsewhere) and Tobit (4:12). Addition to Esther 14:15 (LXX 4:17u) indicates that Jewish women should avoid intercourse with the uncircumcised. Most striking, Josephus wrote that it was "not in accord with the [Jewish] laws" to take a Gentile wife (*Ant.* 18.345). In Josephus's view Solomon had transgressed the law of Moses when he took Gentile wives (*Ant.* 8.191). Philo too attributed to Moses the prohibition of marriage with a person of another nationality (*Spec. Laws* 3.29). Even less pious Jews—if sufficiently prominent—observed the prohibition: When Drusilla, daughter of Agrippa I, married a Gentile king, he accepted circumcision (*Ant.* 20.139).

If, however, we ask about common practice, we shall arrive at a more nuanced view. The fierce denunciations of Pseudo-Philo and *Jubilees* virtually prove that some Jews intermarried, and *Joseph and Aseneth* is a much gentler attempt to persuade Jews to require full conversion of Gentiles before marriage. While these efforts prove some intermarriage, we may nevertheless accept that most Jews would have been very reluctant to marry an active worshipper of idols, someone who might bring home meat or wine that was tainted with idolatry, or even pour out a libation at home before drinking.

If it is true that most Jews would hesitate to marry a practicing worshiper of idols, we must also assume that social intercourse was restrained. One would not want the young people to get to know Gentile youths and maidens too well.

Yet, when they met sympathetic Gentiles—I mean, sympathetic to Judaism—we may be confident that Jews in general made them feel welcome.[29] This point is made in *Apion* 2.209-210, quoted just above, and elsewhere. According to *J.W.* 7.45 in Syria "multitudes of Greeks" were attracted to the "religious ceremonies" (*thrēskeiai*), and they were incorporated into Judaism "in some measure." *Apion* 2.123, 280-82 claim that many Gentiles imitated some Jewish laws, and the sabbath is specified. Philo makes the same claim. Although Athenians reject Spartan customs, and Spartans reject those of Athens, the Jewish law attracts "the attention of all, of barbarians, of Greeks, of dwellers on the mainland and islands, of nations of the east and the west, of Europe and Asia, of the whole inhabited world from end to end." The sabbath illustrates the point (*Moses* 2:17-21).

We may suppose that these claims are exaggerated, but we should also grant that, from the Jewish point of view, interest in their worship, and limited participation, were welcome. That there were such people is proved by pagan comments.[30] We should not suppose that Jews refused to mix at all with Gentiles who were interested and sympathetic. The existence of the category "God-fearers" shows that there was association.[51]

Separatism: Conclusion

I have tried and failed to draw the balance in one judicious sentence. Jews in general did not like idolatry. They avoided it and the things that went with it—including wine and marriage with practicing pagans. They also, in general, kept the major biblical dietary laws, and this restricted social relations even further, since it inhibited mutual entertainment. Yet, many rubbed shoulders with Gentiles because of their work. More significantly, many Jews admired Gentile institutions, education, and culture, and they sought to participate. Jews also prized their own culture, and they wanted others to appreciate it. To attract Gentiles, to make them sympathetic to the Jewish way of life, Jews had to be open to them. Most knew that the only *real* problems with associating with Gentiles were idolatry and the biblical food laws (especially not to eat pork, blood, and fat). Different people balanced mingling and separatism in different ways, and doubtless in most communities and families there were customs that removed the burden of anxious decision-making from the shoulders of individuals.

Antioch

I shall very briefly try to apply the results of this study to the controversy in Antioch. I shall include points that have been only hinted at in this essay and that are argued in full elsewhere (n. 3). We start with three items that probably were not at issue, and then press on to some that may have been.

1. It is not reasonable to think that laws of tithing and offerings were the problem.

2. The ritual purity of participants at common meals was also not the difficulty. Everyone there, it should be assumed, had corpse-impurity. If the meal was held before nightfall, most of the married couples had semen-impurity; on average one-fourth of the women had menstrual-impurity; and other women would have had childbirth-impurity. There is no indication that these impurities restricted dining companions— even among the Pharisees.

3. There is no reason to suppose that in Antioch Jews were under pressure from Pharisees to raise purity standards. The evidence is that Pharisees did *not* try to impose their special rules on others.

4. That is not to say that there could not have been any influence from Pharisees in the debate. It is quite possible that James was close to the Pharisees. Numerous scholars think that those who were "strict about

the laws," who protested when he was executed by the Sadducean high priest Ananus, were Pharisees (*Ant.* 20.199-203).[32] When he found Peter's behavior to be too lax, he may have been worried about how it looked to "the strict."

5. Being "strict" included reluctance to associate *too much* with Gentiles, since close association might lead to contact with idolatry or transgression of one of the biblical food laws. "Too much association" is not a law, but a worry about the results of fraternization. How much was too much would be judged differently by different people and groups, and it would also vary with the circumstances.

6. If specific rules about "table-fellowship" were at issue, the problem was probably the food itself. (a) Some foods are explicitly forbidden by the Bible, and Gentile wine is implicitly forbidden in Daniel. (b) Some people had a *general* reluctance to eat *any* Gentile food.

7. If the worry was the meat, it was probably not the direct fear of idolatry, since Paul himself would have been more than reluctant to eat meat that had been offered to an idol. A more probable concern about meat would be that the mode of slaughtering left blood in it.

My guess is that number 5 is the most likely. James worried that too much fraternization with Gentiles would have bad results, and that Peter's mission would be discredited if he were known to engage in it himself. As second choice, I suggest 6b—a general dislike on James's part of eating Gentile food, which led him to think that Peter was not being cautious enough. I doubt that biblical law was actually being transgressed. It is possible that Paul was literally willing to live like a Gentile in order to win Gentiles (1 Cor 9:21), but we must wonder whether that was true of Barnabas and the other Jewish Christians in Antioch. I am now inclined to doubt it.

It is more likely that the concern was *general*—too close to Gentiles too much of the time—while in another sense it was *particular* and *individual*—James worried about Peter's reputation, since he might be thought to be flirting with idolatry or food that the Bible calls "abomination." It was not the case that Antiochene Jews in general were persuaded by Pharisees not to eat with Gentiles, and probably not that James sent a message to the Jewish members of the church there, prescribing this behavior in general. He apparently sent a message to Peter—*You* should not eat with Gentiles—and the other Jewish members followed him. This particular message is best explained by a theory of general concern on the part of James. He feared that it might be said of Peter that he fraternized too much, and was thus generally suspect, not that he had violated some individual rule.

If number 5 (or 6b) is correct, it would mean that Paul's statement that Peter had been "living like a Gentile" (Gal 2:14) was exaggerated. He probably had not been doing anything as drastic as eating pork, shellfish, or hare. Exaggeration on this point fits perfectly since the charge that Peter was "forcing Gentiles to live like Jews" in the same verse goes beyond the story as he tells it. Paul very often used extreme or hyperbolic language to polarize a situation,[33] to make it black and white, and this seems to me to be the best explanation of the term "live like a Gentile" in Gal 2:14.

Notes

1. James D. G. Dunn, "The Incident at Antioch (Gal. 2:11-18)," *JSNT* 18 (1983) 3-57.
2. Philip F. Esler, *Community and Gospel in Luke-Acts* (Cambridge: Cambridge University Press, 1987). The reference is to Stephen Wilson, *Luke and the Law* (Cambridge: University Press, 1983) 70.
3. See my forthcoming book *Jewish Law from Jesus to the Mishnah* (London: SCM/Philadelphia: Trinity Press International, 1990). The relevant essays are these: "Did the Pharisees Eat Ordinary Food in Purity?" and "Food, Purity and Offerings in the Greek-Speaking Diaspora."
4. Gedalyahu Alon, "On the Halakhot of the Early Sages"; "The Levitical Uncleanness of Gentiles"; "The Bounds of the Laws of Levitical Cleanness," in *Jews, Judaism, and the Classical World* (trans. Israel Abrahams; Jerusalem: The Magnes Press, 1977) from *Studies in Jewish History* I (Jerusalem, 1967 [Heb.]). The third essay is discussed extensively in "Did the Pharisees Eat Ordinary Food in Purity?" and the other two in "Food, Purity and Offerings" (n. 3 above). Enough is said in the present essay, however, to show the direction of my fuller discussions.
5. With regard to the impurity of Gentiles, see the repeated statements that many did not agree with or follow what he calls "the halakah": Alon, "Levitical Uncleanness of Gentiles," 147-49, 165, 168, 189.
6. On the question of Gentiles who work on the sabbath on behalf of Jews, some sages took the line that they should be prevented from doing so, while others held the opposite view. See *Shabbath* 1.8.
7. See Alon, "Levitical Uncleanness of Gentiles," 179.
8. Louis Finkelstein (*The Pharisees: The Sociological Background of Their Faith* [2 vols.; 3rd ed.; Philadelphia: Jewish Publication Society of America, 1962] 1:26-28) argued that only Jerusalemites made an effort to be pure and that other Jews were always impure (except, of course, when they wished to make a pilgrimage to the temple).
9. As is usual in the Mishnah and Tosefta, the biblical passages are not referred to.
10. On Herod and the Pharisees, see *Ant.* 14.172 (conflict with Samaias, a Pharisee according to *Ant.* 15.3); 17.41-46 (they are implicated in a plot against him).
11. Since "brushing up against" is a fact of life, and Jews did not walk through Gentile streets without touching people, nor did the pious walk through the streets of Jerusalem while completely avoiding contact with other, we must doubt that passages that seem to say that there was complete physical separation should be taken literally. Two passages deserve special note: According to Acts 10:28, it is unlawful for a Jew to associate closely with or *come near (proserchesthai)* a Gentile; according to *War* 2.150 Essenes bathed after touching someone of a different degree of impurity, "as after physical contact with a foreigner." Some take this to mean that Jews in general bathed after touching Gentiles. In the Diaspora some may have washed hands when returning from public places (so Mark 7:4), and there is good evidence that they washed hands while praying, especially before the synagogue service or during it (see the essay referred to in n. 3 above). But that they bathed every time they touched a Gentile is simply not possible, and it is even more impossible that Jews in general would not come near Gentiles. This will become clear as we proceed. On Acts 10:28 see n. 20 below.
12. See Esler, *Community and Gospel*, 77, 83.

13. Dunn, "Antioch," 17-18.
14. Esler, *Community and Gospel*, 83.
15. Dunn, "Antioch," 18.
16. See Esther 4:17x in Rahlf's enumeration of the Addition. Esler states that Esther is apocryphal (81), but the term applies only to the Additions.
17. Esler, *Community and Gospel*, 80, italics added.
18. See Walter Burkert, *Greek Religion* (Oxford: Blackwell, 1985) 70-73.
19. See Josephus, *J.W.* 2.590-592//*Life* 74-75 (with some differences); *Ant.* 12.120.
20. F. F. Bruce, commenting on Acts 10:28, explains that Jews could not eat any Gentile food at all. "It was thus a very difficult thing for Jews to travel in foreign lands" (*The Acts of the Apostles* [2nd ed.; London: Tyndale, 1952] ad loc.). A majority of all the Jews in the world actually lived in foreign lands, and a lot of them traveled. Philo and other pious Jews went on an embassy to Rome. Paul went hither and thither persecuting Christians. Lots of Diaspora Jews made pilgrimage to the temple.
21. See A. Thomas Kraabel, "Social Systems of Six Diaspora Synagogues," in *Ancient Synagogues: The State of Research* (ed. Joseph Gutmann; Chico: Scholars Press, 1981) 79-91; here p. 85.
22. Martin Goodman, *State and Society in Roman Galilee, A.D. 132-212* (Towtowa, N.J.: Rowman and Allanheld, 1983) 44-45, 61, 83-84.
23. Alan Mendelson, *Secular Education in Philo of Alexandria* (Monographs of the Hebrew Union College, 7; Cincinnati; HUC, 1982) 25-33. This is a gentle but effective rebuttal of the view of H. A. Wolfson, *Philo: Foundations of Religious Philosophy in Judaism, Christianity, and Islam* (2 vols.; rev. ed.; Cambridge, Mass.: Harvard, 1962) 1:78-82.
24. *Ant.* 17.160f. ("theater" is a variant); *War* 1.666.
25. See Tessa Rajak, "Jews and Christians as Groups in a Pagan World," *"To See Ourselves as Others See Us": Christians, Jews, "Others" in Late Antiquity* (eds. Jacob Neusner and Ernest S. Frerichs; Chico: Scholars Press, 1985) 247-62.
26. Pertinent passages are given by Esler, *Community and Gospel*, 78-80.
27. See the passages collected by Molly Whittaker, *Jews and Christians: Graeco-Roman Views* (Cambridge Commentaries on Writings of the Jewish & Christian World 200 BC to AD 200, 6; Cambridge: University Press, 1984) 70.
28. See recently Peter Brown, *The Body and Society: Men, Women, and Sexual Renunciation in Early Christianity* (New York: Columbia University Press, 1988) 191, 285-86, 342, 358.
29. So Dunn, "Antioch," 19.
30. Dunn, "Antioch," 22.
31. I take it that the existence of sympathizers is proved from the literary sources (Acts 10:2; Josephus, *War* 7.45). The reservations of A. T. Kraabel, however, are not without merit (see "Synagoga Caeca: Systematic Distortion in Gentile Interpretations of Evidence for Judaism in the Early Christian Period," in Neusner and Frerichs, *"To See Ourselves as Others See Us,"* 219-46). The significance of the list of *theosebeis* in the synagogue inscription at Aphrodisias is hard to assess. When one notes that a large number of these were members of the city council, one must doubt that they had entirely forsaken pagan rites but had not become fully Jewish. This would have meant that, religiously, they were nothing. I think it unlikely that several city councillors would have been in such a position. We must reckon with the possibility that they only respected Judaism and contributed money to the synagogue, without converting to monotheism. For the purpose of this essay, the existence of sympathizers is all that is required. Jews would have associated with them even though they were not "spiritual" converts. On the inscription, see J. Reynolds and R. Tannenbaum, *Jews and Godfearers at Aphrodisias* (Cambridge Philological Society Supp. 12; Cambridge, 1987). They define God-fearers as accepting whatever parts of Judaism they like without giving up paganism (88). The definition is apt.
32. See S. Safrai in *The Jewish People in the First Century* II (Assen: Van Gorcum, 1976) 400; M. Stern in ibid., 370; A. I. Baumgarten, "The Name of the Pharisees," *JBL* 102 (1983) 411-28.
33. See Carol Schlueter, *Polemical Hyperbole*, unpublished Ph.D. dissertation, McMaster University.

THE MATERNITY OF PAUL:
AN EXEGETICAL STUDY
OF GALATIANS 4:19

Beverly R. Gaventa

T he title of this contribution will undoubtedly cause some
eyebrows to rise and some smiles to form. The laugh, however,
comes from within the text, for my title only reflects what Paul
himself says: "My little children, with whom I am again in travail until
Christ be formed in you!" (Gal 4:19). Surely we pause for a moment
when we read Paul's comment that he is in travail. The word that he
employs here, *ōdinein*, customarily refers to the physical labor, even
pain, that accompanies human birth. Paul's claim to be doing something
that is manifestly impossible—giving birth (again!)—immediately
attracts our attention.

Although Paul is the one who is in labor, and in labor with the
Galatians, the second half of Gal 4:19 seems to contradict the first. It is
not the Galatians who are being born but Christ: "Until Christ is formed
in you." How is it that Paul is giving birth, but it is Christ who is formed?
If we draw a picture corresponding to Paul's words in this verse, we
would have Paul concentrating in labor. Inside his "womb" we would
find the Galatians, and the object of the labor is Christ who is born
among the Galatians! The portrait is, to say the least, complicated.

No less troubling than these strange statements within the verse is the
context in which the verse occurs. In v. 12*a* Paul appeals to the Galatians
to imitate him.[1] He then recalls the way in which they received him,
despite his bodily affliction (vv. 12*b*-14). He reminds them of their
ardent desire to help him and asks whether he has become their enemy.
Referring to the Teachers[2] who have entered their churches and have
proclaimed a different gospel, Paul accuses them of making much of the
Galatians merely to lead them astray. Then he says this:

> It is always good to be made much of in a good way, and not only when I am
> present with you. My children, with whom I am again in travail until Christ be

189

formed in you! I could wish to be present with you now and to change my tone, for I am perplexed about you. (author's trans.)

Grammatically, v. 19 follows closely on v. 18 and seems to be in apposition to the *hymas* at the end of that verse.[3] The transition at the end of v. 19 is an awkward one, however. In fact, if v. 19 were removed, the whole section would read more easily; that observation again raises the question of the function of v. 19 in its context.

When this text and its accompanying problems first began to provoke me, I cast a casual eye on the commentaries to see what help they might offer. Surprised to find little attention given to the verse, I looked further into the secondary literature. I am aware of one article on the second part of v. 19 and a few brief remarks in the commentaries and monographs. It fascinates me to find so little written about a text in which there are so many interesting problems. Why is it, for example, that we could find perhaps dozens of articles about an issue like the nature of Paul's thorn in the flesh, but scarcely one devoted to this passage with all its complexities?

The reason that first comes to mind for the strange silence about Gal 4:19 is that, until recently, few women have been involved in the scholarly exegesis of biblical texts. Perhaps Gal 4:19 is simply one of the texts in which the anomalies strike women with particular force. The last two decades of biblical scholarship have produced many studies of Paul instigated by the questions of women, however, and to my knowledge none of those studies deals with this text.

I suspect that the more decisive factor in the silence about Gal 4:19 arises from its location in what is usually regarded as Paul's personal appeal. This portion of the letter, 4:12-20, concerns Paul's relationship with the Galatians and is thought to have little to do with the important theological matters of the letter itself.[4] In fact, what most commentaries suggest about our text is that Paul is here overcome with emotion and that he plays on the relationship he has had with this community. This line of interpretation goes back at least to Chrysostom, who wrote regarding Gal 4:19: "Behold his paternal tenderness, behold this despondency worthy of an Apostle. The cry which he utters is far more piercing than of a woman in travail."[5]

We shall explore in more detail below H. D. Betz's attempt to move beyond this reading of 4:12-20 by suggesting that all of 4:12-20 employs the friendship topos in order to rectify the relationship between Paul and the Galatians.[6] Betz also suggests, although tentatively, that 4:19 may draw upon regeneration or rebirth motifs such as are widespread in the ancient world.

In what follows, I shall argue that Gal 4:19 is not merely an emotional outburst or an example of a typical rhetorical feature. Galatians 4:19 associates Paul's apostolic vocation with the anguish anticipated in an apocalyptic era and recalls to the Galatians their own crucifixion with Christ. As such, Gal 4:19 employs a conventional metaphor—that of the anguish of a woman in labor—to identify Paul's apostolic work with the apocalyptic expectation of the whole created order. The goal of Paul's anguish, in this instance, is that Christ be formed within the communities of believers in Galatia. This reading of 4:19 suggests that it is not an emotional outburst but an important theological link between this section of personal appeal and the remainder of the letter.

Galatians 4:19a

What can it possibly mean for Paul to say that he is in labor with the Galatians? There is no mistaking the word *ōdinein,* translated in the RSV as "travail." This is not travail in the sense of the English verbs *toil* and *work,* but refers to the process of giving birth. Clearer, if somewhat archaic, is the expression "birth pangs." Paul refers unmistakably to the period that immediately precedes birth itself.

Because Paul prefaces this statement about his travail with the affectionate address "my children,"[7] commentators normally identify this text with those passages in which Paul describes himself as the father of believers. For example, in 1 Cor 4:14-15 we find:

> I do not write this to make you ashamed, but to admonish you as my beloved children. For through you have countless guides in Christ, you do not have many fathers. For I became your father in Christ Jesus through the gospel.

Similarly, Paul compares his role with that of a father in 1 Thess 2:11: "For you know how, like a father with his children, we exhorted each one of you and encouraged you and charged you to lead a life worthy of God, who calls you into his own kingdom and glory."[8] Placing Gal 4:19 within the context of these statements about Paul's relationship to believers supports the contention that what Paul presents in this verse is an emotional personal appeal based on the relationship he had earlier established with Galatian Christians.

While there are perhaps connections between Gal 4:19 and Paul's sense of being the father of believers in his congregations, to beget a child is not the same thing as to give it birth, and we should not hastily equate the two.[9] Somewhat closer to our text is the statement in 1 Thess 2:7: "But we were gentle among you, like a nurse taking care of her children."[10] Even there, however, where Paul compares himself with a nurse who cares for her child, he uses the adverb *hōs.* He does not claim to *be* a nurse but to be *like* a nurse. Here, in Gal 4:19, there is no *hōs,* making the comparison even more unlikely and hence more provocative.

Perhaps the most extended attempt at understanding this image in Gal 4:19 is found in H. D. Betz. While Betz refers to the "somewhat pathetic" character of this verse and draws the customary comparison to Paul's use of the father imagery elsewhere, he does acknowledge the unusual character of the verse and attempts to understand it, first, as part of a conventional topos of friendship and, second, as part of the larger complex of rebirth imagery. Betz initially comments on the imagery of maternal relationship as a part of the friendship topos, but the texts he cites refer in a most general fashion to the nature of family relationships and have little in common with Gal 4:19.[11] In addition, Betz himself recognizes that Paul wants to accomplish more here than "merely *compare* himself to a mother."[12]

As I indicated above, Betz does go on to suggest that *ōdinein* may be associated with the language of spiritual rebirth that appears in many religious traditions.[13] Betz points to a text in the Nag Hammadi corpus in which the figure Hermes explains rebirth to his spiritual son. The son asks whether those who are so reborn have mothers as well as fathers. The response is: "My son, they are spiritual [mothers]. For they are potencies; they let the souls grow. Therefore I say, they are immortal."[14] Also in the Hermetic literature, Betz points to the conversation between Hermes and his son regarding the soul's rebirth through special knowledge. But these discussions of the hows and wherefores of the soul's passage to knowledge of its divine origins seem far removed from Paul, and Paul himself does not use the language of rebirth or regeneration.

For insight into Paul's strange claim to be in labor with the Galatians, we need to look more closely at the use of the word *ōdinein*. *Ōdinein* appears as early as the *Iliad*, which compares the pain of Agamemnon with the "throes a writhing woman suffers in hard labor" (11.268-72). In his treatise on biology, Aristotle employs *ōdinein* to refer to the actual pain of a woman in the process of giving birth (*Historia Animalium* 7.9[586b, 27-29]). Thus the term appears both in discussions of physical travail and in metaphors that compare various forms of pain to that of a woman giving birth.

For closer parallels to Paul's use of *ōdinein*, we must look to the Septuagint, where *ōdinein* often appears in metaphors having to do with situations of agony or pain. In fact, the Septuagint reserves the word and the related noun *ōdin* almost entirely for such metaphors. The verb *tiktein*, to give birth, occurs in the multitudinous references to the fact of a human birth (see Gen 3:16; 4:1, 2; Exod 1:16; 1 Sam 1:20). *Ōdinein*, however, never refers to the mere *fact* of a birth, but always to the accompanying anguish (see Deut 2:25, 1 Sam 4:19, Sir 19:11, Jer 4:31). Further, *ōdinein* usually appears in contexts having to do with the situation of the people collectively, rather than with the situation of an individual.

This use of *ōdinein* and *ōdin* is especially clear in the case of the prophetic passages that speak about the day of the Lord.

> Writhe [*ōdinein*] and groan, O daughter of Zion, like a woman in travail; for now you shall go forth from the city and dwell in the open country; you shall go to Babylon. (Mic 4:10)

> Wail, for the day of the LORD is near; as destruction from the Almighty it will come! . . . Pangs and agony will seize them; they will be in anguish like a woman in travail" [*ōdin*]. (Isa 13:6, 8)

> We have heard the report of it, our hands fall helpless; anguish has taken hold of us, pain as of a woman in travail" [*ōdin*]. (Jer 6:24)

This association between travail and tribulation occurs in a variety of places outside the Septuagint as well. For example, 1 Enoch 62:4 speaks of the pain that will come, at the last judgment, upon the rulers of this age as on a woman in travail (see also 2 Bar 56:6, 4 Ezra 4:42). In the library of the community at Qumran, a famous passage describes what appear to be the birth pangs of the new community:

> They caused [me] to be
>   like a ship on the deeps of the [sea],
> and like a fortified city
>   before [the aggressor],
> [and] like a woman in travail
>   with her first-born child,
> upon whose belly pangs have come
>   and grievous pains,
> filling with anguish her child-bearing crucible [1 QH 3.7-10].[15]

We find in these texts an established association between apocalyptic expectation and the anguish of childbirth. That association appears in the New Testament most explicitly in Mark and in Revelation. Mark 13:8 warns that "nation will rise against nation, and kingdom against kingdom; there will be earthquakes in various places, there will be famines; that is but the beginning of the [sufferings] birth-pangs [*ōdin*]" (see also Matt 24:8). Revelation 12, in its description of the woman whose child is to rule all the nations, refers to her cries in "her pangs [*ōdin*] of birth."[16]

Paul uses this word group only three times outside of Gal 4:19. Just after our text, in his treatment of the story of Sarah and Hagar, he quotes Isa 54:1: "Rejoice, O barren one that does not bear; break forth and shout, thou who art not in travail" [*ōdinein*].[17] When Paul discusses the parousia in 1 Thess 5:3, he warns against those who proclaim peace and security, for "sudden destruction will come upon them as travail [*ōdin*] comes upon a woman with child, and there will be no escape." In Rom 8:22, he speaks of the whole creation's "groaning in travail [*synōdinein*] together until now."

From this variety of evidence we may conclude that, by the first century, it was customary to speak of a coming cataclysm, however interpreted, as being accompanied by anguish like that of a woman giving birth.[18] It is widely recognized that Paul himself employs that theme in Romans 8 and in 1 Thessalonians 5. In my judgment, the best explanation of Gal 4:19 is that the same association is at work here as well.[19] Paul's anguish, his travail, is not simply a personal matter or a literary convention having to do with friendship or rebirth but reflects the anguish of the whole created order as it awaits the fulfillment of God's action in Jesus Christ.

This leaves us with the question of how Paul, an individual, can claim to be giving birth in this apocalyptically construed manner. That question can best be answered by turning to the second half of the verse: "until Christ be formed in you."

Galatians 4:19*b*

Earlier we noted the puzzling nature of this half of the verse. While Paul is in labor with the *Galatians,* it is *Christ* who is formed, and not the Galatians. Before dismissing this verse as another of Paul's incomplete analogies, we need to examine the expression "until Christ be formed in you."

What does it mean to say that Christ is formed? Commentators have posed a variety of answers to this question, but the answers do not adequately reflect the context of this expression in Galatians. For example, E. D. Burton argued that the formation of Christ referred to the spiritual maturation of the Galatians, "the full development of the Christ begotten in them."[20] Aside from the absence of this motif elsewhere in Paul, which Burton himself acknowledged, the difficulty with this interpretation is that the present context does not suggest that Paul views this formation as a natural progression toward spiritual maturity.[21] Instead of spiritual formation, Lietzmann suggested that Paul had in view here moral formation, so that the invisible Christ would be made visible in each believer.[22] But the language here is not moral language, at least not in the sense that Paul refers to the behavior of individual Christians as reflecting the behavior of Christ.[23] Hermann and Müssner regard the "formation of Christ" as the formation of the right image or understanding of Christ. The phrase then signals the need for the Galatians to return to right doctrine regarding Christ.[24] However, while Paul surely wants the Galatians to return to the gospel he preached among them (1:6-7), there is little indication that 4:19 refers narrowly to a correct christology.

In order to move beyond these suggestions, we need to examine Paul's reference to the formation of Christ within a larger context. Paul uses *morphoun* only here, but he does employ some closely related verbs. For example, in 2 Cor 3:18, he speaks of the transformation (*metamorphousthai*) of believers into the likeness of the Lord. In Phil 3:10, he refers to his hope of being conformed to the death of Christ (*summorphousthai*). And in Rom 12:2, he urges Christians at Rome to be transformed (*metamorphousthai*) by the renewal of their minds. While none of these texts refers specifically to the formation *of Christ*, each reflects the conviction that the Christ event issues in a profound shaping and reshaping of human perceptions.[25]

With this constellation of usage in mind, we return to Galatians and notice several passages that may shed light on the formation to which Paul refers in 4:19. First is 2:20, which commentators frequently associate with our text:

> I have been crucified with Christ; it is no longer I who live, but Christ who lives in me; and the life I now live in the flesh I live by faith in the Son of God, who loved me and gave himself for me.

Paul experienced the crucifixion with Christ, and now Christ lives in Paul. What comes to expression here is Paul's conviction that Christ has overtaken him. Everything that preceded, even his status among his Jewish peers, to which he refers in 1:13-14, counts for nothing. The gospel has eclipsed Paul's life.

That this crucifixion with Christ is not to be a characteristic only of Paul or only of Paul and his apostolic colleagues becomes clear in 3:27-28. Because of the prominence of this text in contemporary Christian discussions regarding pressing issues of justice and equity, we may overlook the repetitious references to Christ here: "You were baptized into Christ"; "You have put on Christ"; "You are all one in Christ Jesus." Whatever Paul says about the nullification of divisions among human beings he says because and *only* because of the prior claim that all believers are in Christ and, by implication, nowhere else. The Christ who overtook Paul overtakes all believers.[26]

That this change goes beyond even the corporate life of the believing community becomes clear in 6:15, where the cosmic implications of this claim are made: There is neither circumcision nor uncircumcision, but new creation. As J. Louis Martyn has shown, what is at stake in this letter is the apocalyptic antinomy between cosmos on the one hand (which include both law and "unlaw") and the New Creation ushered in by Jesus Christ on the other.[27]

If we look at the words in 4:19b again in this larger context, we see that they begin to take on a different meaning. For Christ to be formed in the Galatians is not simply for them to develop spiritually or morally or christologically. The formation of Christ among the Galatians is simultaneously their crucifixion with Christ.[28] It means that the eclipse of the old occurs among them. The letter reflects Paul's conviction that the Galatians were called, that they had heard the gospel, and that they responded in faith. But he also believes that they are in danger of turning again, of converting back to their earlier views. For that reason he speaks of his own labor with them and the need for Christ to be formed.[29]

The phrase *mechris hou* ("until") gives us pause. It is unclear whether Paul regards this formation as one that will have a completion date in the near future or whether the formation is continuous. We find in his letters both the expectation that the believer is really changed by the gospel (Rom 6:1-4) and the common-sense awareness that such change is ongoing (1 Cor 3:1-4). Here those two expectations seem to be held in tension. What creates Paul's dilemma in this letter, after all, is that believers are in danger of being led away from that birth (he is in labor again!)—but these people have been called (1:6), have received the spirit (3:2), and have been baptized into Christ (3:27). It is difficult for him to imagine such a development. On the other hand, the apocalyptic setting of the first part of the verse indicates that the formation of Christ continues until the fulfillment of the Christ event in God's final triumph.[30]

The formation of Christ is *en hymin* ("in you"), and the plural pronoun requires comment. Formation does not belong to individual believers, as a personal or private possession only. Instead, formation refers to the community of those who are called to faith, what Paul elsewhere refers to as the body of Christ.[31]

Now we may ask again how the two parts of this verse work together: "My children, I am in travail with you again until Christ be formed in you." The first part of the verse invokes not only Paul's apostolic role, but also the apocalyptic stage on which that role is played. At stake here are not the birth pangs of an individual apostle, but the birth pangs of the cosmos itself. Paul's labor is that of an individual who knows that the world has been invaded by a new reality: a crucified Lord who confronts and overturns the world.

The flaw that appears in the second part of Paul's analogy occurs, not because his imagination is defective, but because he does not wish to carry the analogy through to its logical conclusion. It is not believers who are born. That reflects the attitude of the philosophical schools of Paul's day, in which a premium was placed on the full development of the individual. Paul's point, by contrast, is that it is Christ who is formed, and the apocalyptic maternity is completed only when Christ is formed.

Still the analogy seems flawed, for we might expect Paul to say, "until *I bring forth* Christ in you." But that is not to be said for two reasons. First, God and God alone brings forth Christ. God is the one who sends Christ (Gal 1:4); it is not Christ who authorizes himself. Second, neither Paul nor any other believer wills Christ into existence or forms Christ within himself or herself. Paul's use of *morphoun* here and related verbs elsewhere is consistently in the passive voice—that is, the formation of Christ occurs as a gift, not as an achievement.

So the analogy is flawed, but for a very specific set of reasons. It is not that Paul is unable to make the analogy work, but that he is unwilling to do so.

Now we return to the larger context of v. 19 in Gal 4:12-20. I noted at the outset the awkward way our text stands in relation to the larger passage. Galatians 4:19 seems, at first glance, to be an aside in a passage that appeals primarily to the earlier warm personal relationship Paul had established with the Galatians. However, we have discovered that 4:19 is not simply an appeal based on the friendship Paul and the Galatians established. It is, instead, a theological claim that Paul's work as an apostle occurs within an apocalyptic framework that is created by God's revelation of Jesus Christ and that looks forward to the full incorporation of all believers—indeed of the cosmos itself—into Christ. This theological claim provides the grounding for the personal appeal of earlier lines, not merely in the person of Paul but in the action of God.

Conclusion

Far from being merely an emotional appeal from a man whose argumentative powers have temporarily escaped him, Gal 4:19 occupies a pivotal place in the argument of 4:12-20.[32] This verse also touches on a variety of significant issues in Pauline theology. While none of these issues can be addressed here in any detail, it is important to signal ways in which further exploration of this text might prove beneficial.

The first of these issues arises from the presence in Gal 4:19 of apocalyptic language. Lou Martyn has argued that the theology of Galatians is bound up with a set of apocalyptic antinomies between the old world—characterized by circumcision and uncircumcision, Jew and Gentile, slave and free, male and female—and the new world, or New Creation, disclosed in Jesus Christ. Despite the difficulties surrounding the term *apocalyptic,* it helpfully identifies Paul's conviction that the Christ event constitutes an invasion of the world. The antitheses that characterize this letter make it clear that the revelation (the apocalypse) of Christ is not simply one more act in a string of revelations. It is, rather, a new creation, and there is (to borrow an image from Martyn) no "through-train" connecting the old creation with the new.[33]

While Paul's use of apocalyptic language in Gal 4:19 does not in itself resolve the question of whether his theology is to be characterized as apocalyptic, the use of such language does argue for further reflection on the issue and especially for reconsideration of other texts that may have apocalyptic overtones.

Another issue emerges from the way in which the commentaries virtually dismiss Gal 4:19 by labelling it "personal." We make a serious mistake when we separate the so-called theological sections of Paul's letters from his personal or autobiographical comments. This study of Gal 4:19 confirms the need to understand the way in which Paul's theology informs even those passages that seem to be merely personal or apologetic.[34] Paul's ministry (in this case his pastoral relationship with believers in the Galatian church) is not separable from his theology. In fact, his theology shapes his responses at every turn.

A third issue raised by this study pertains to Paul's understanding of his apostolic role and authority. While there have been several studies of this topic in recent decades, this text scarcely makes an appearance. When it does enter the discussion, it does so at the end of a string of references to Paul's use of *paternal* imagery. That imagery in turn is associated with a reading of Paul's understanding of authority as hierarchical and authoritarian. With the maternal imagery of Gal 4:19, however, as in other passages (such as 1 Thess 2:1-10), Paul sounds a different note, that of the apostolic role as one characterized by nurture. This motif needs further consideration in discussion of Paul's apostolic office.

Directions for Further Study

The final issue returns us to my initial observations about the unusual character of the maternal imagery Paul employs in Gal 4:19. Such imagery appears in other texts as well (see 1 Thess 2:7, Rom 8:22-23, 1 Cor 3:1-4, 1 Cor 15:8), and I hope to turn to those in due course.[35] Because of the unusual character of this issue, it is important to indicate what I think such a study might have to contribute to our understanding of Pauline theology. At the very least, I am interested in bringing the language of maternity out of the footnotes and into the text of Pauline studies. I am particularly eager to free this imagery from footnotes devoted to *paternal* imagery in Paul.

Beyond that task of moving from footnotes to text, this reclamation project may have a place in the continuing discussion of Paul and women. At least since George Bernard Shaw dubbed Paul the "eternal enemy" of woman, students of Paul have argued both sides of that issue. In our time the question has often taken the form, "Was Paul a feminist or a misogynist?" Apart from the obvious problem involved with applying such categories to someone twenty centuries removed from us and our presuppositions, the problem with this inquiry is that people on both sides of the issue line up texts and do battle over them.

While study of maternal imagery in Paul will not resolve this conflict, it may provide another avenue for thinking about the issue of Paul's attitudes toward women. Whatever his explicit comments about women and their roles, it is undoubtedly significant that he would apply to himself the language of maternity. Is maternal imagery a language that can readily be used by a man who has no underlying sympathy with or identification with the lives of women? Pressing a little further, I want to suggest that the physical struggle involved in giving birth and the vulnerability involved in caring for a child are images not readily used by a man so alienated from women and so hierarchical as Paul is sometimes assumed to be. These are not questions for which answers are readily available, but they do merit further research and reflection.

Notes

1. Verse 12 does not explicitly call for the imitation of Paul (compare 1 Cor 4:16, 11:1; Phil 3:17), but the implication is clear. See W. P. De Boer, *The Imitation of Paul* (Kampen: J. H. Kok, 1962) 188-96; B. R. Gaventa, "Galatians 1 and 2: Autobiography as Paradigm," *NovT* 28 (1986) 319-22; R. B. Hays, "Christology and Ethics in Galatians," *CBQ* 49 (1987) 281-82.
2. For the use of the term "Teachers," see J. Louis Martyn, "A Law-Observant Mission to Gentiles: The Background of Galatians," *Michigan Quarterly Review* 22 (1983) 221-36.
3. So J. B. Lightfoot, *St. Paul's Epistle to the Galatians* (6th ed.; London: Macmillan, 1880) 178; E. D. Burton, *The Epistle to the Galatians* (ICC; Edinburgh: T. and T. Clark, 1921) 248. However, a number of commentators identify v. 19 as an anacoluthon, placing a period at the end of v. 18 and a dash following v. 19. So Pierre Bonnard, *L'Épitre de Saint Paul aux Galates* (CNT 9; Neuchatel: Delauchaux et Niestle, 1953) 94; Heinrich Schlier, *Der Brief an die Galater* (Meyer K; 5th ed.; Göttingen: Vandenhoeck & Ruprecht, 1971) 213; Franz Müssner, *Der Galaterbrief* (HTKZNT 9; Freiburg: Herder, 1974) 312.
4. Typical of this line of thinking is the recent commentary of Ronald K. H. Fung: "This section [4:12-20] manifestly differs from the others in the present division (III, 2:15–5:12) in that whereas the others are directly doctrinal, this section is Paul's personal appeal to his Galatian converts and has little doctrinal content" (*The Epistle to the Galatians* [NICNT; Grand Rapids: Eerdmans, 1988] 195).
5. Note also Pierre Bonnard's comment that in vv. 19-20 Paul overcomes with love the bitterness revealed in vv. 16-19 (*aux Galates*, 94).
6. Since Betz finds discourses on friendship in the ancient world that compare friendship

with parental relationship, he takes 4:19 to be yet another part of the friendship topos (*Galatians* [Hermeneia; Philadelphia: Fortress, 1979] 233-34).

7. Reading *teknia* (with ℵ², A, C, D², Ψ) rather than *tekna*, (with ℵ*, B, D*, F, G) the RSV translates, "My little children." The manuscript evidence seems weighted in favor of *tekna*, but the difference in meaning is negligible.

8. See also Philemon 10.

9. The connections are probably to be found in the relationship between these metaphors and Paul's understanding of apostolic authority.

10. On this text, see B. R. Gaventa, "Apostles as Babes and Nurses in 1 Thessalonians 2:7," in *Faith and History: Essays in Honor of Paul W. Meyer* (eds. John T. Carroll, Charles H. Cosgrove, E. Elizabeth Johnson; Atlanta: Scholars Press, forthcoming).

11. For example, Betz (*Galatians*, 233 n. 150) refers to Plato, *Lysis* 207E), which compares the love of parents for their child with the respect people have for a wise man. In several passages from Aristotle's *Nicomachean Ethics* there are references to the nature of parental love, sometimes distinguishing maternal love from paternal love (8.1.3 [1155a, 15-20]; 8.8.3 [1159a, 28-34]; 8.12.2-3 [1161b, 17-34]; 9.4.1 [1166a, 6f]; 9.7.7 [1168a, 25-27]). Plutarch (*Amic. Mult.* 93F-94A) and Cicero (*Amic.* 27) also compare friendship with parental love.

12. Betz, *Galatians*, 233.

13. Ibid., 233-34. Albrecht Oepke (*Der Brief des Paulus an die Galater* [THKNT 9; 3rd ed.; Berlin: Evangelische Verlagsanstalt, 1973] 108) also points to the mystery religions, in which the mystagogue is called the "father" of the novices, but thinks that Paul's usage probably has its precedents in Old Testament traditions (see 2 Kgs 2:12, Num 11:12). While Oepke regards the notion of rebirth as generally absent in Paul, he thinks that it is distantly hinted at here.

14. Betz, *Galatians*, 233-34. Here Betz follows the translation of K. W. Troeger, "Die sechste und siebte Schrift aus Nag Hammadi-Codex VI," *TLZ* 98 (1973) 498-99. This translation is accepted also by Jean-Pierre Mahe, *Hermes en Haute-Egypte* (Quebec: Les Presses de L'Université Laval, 1978) 67, 93; but see *The Nag Hammadi Library in English* (New York: Harper & Row, 1977) 293.

15. The translation is that of Vermes, *The Dead Sea Scrolls in English* (Baltimore: Penguin Books, 1968) 157. This text has been the focus of much debate. Early discussions of this hymn identified the child with the Messiah, but that interpretation has largely been rejected in favor of the notion that the text portrays the birth of the community of the righteous. Thus Matthew Black writes in *The Scrolls and Christian Origins* (New York: Charles Scribner's Sons, 1961) 150: "The eschatological setting of the hymn suggests that its subject is the 'birth-pangs of the Messiah' in the sense of the emergence through trial and suffering of the redeemed Israel." So also Ringren, *The Faith of Qumran* (Philadelphia: Fortress, 1963) 193; Marinus de Jonge, "The Role of Intermediaries in God's Final Intervention in the Future According to the Qumran Scrolls," in *Studies on the Jewish Background of the New Testament* (eds. O. Michel et al.; Assen: Van Gorcum, 1969) 58-59; John J. Collins, *The Apocalyptic Imagination: An Introduction to the Jewish Matrix of Christianity* (New York: Crossroads, 1984) 136; Dale Allison, *The End of the Ages Has Come: An Early Interpretation of the Passion and Resurrection of Jesus* (Philadelphia: Fortress, 1985) 8-9.

Müssner denies that there is any parallel between 4:19 and 1 QH 3.7-10, because in Paul there are two pregnancies, but that is an overly precise reading of the metaphor (*Der Galaterbrief*, 312 n. 102). Betz also denies any relationship between the two texts, apparently appealing to the earlier notion that IQH 3:7-10 refers to the birth of an individual rather than a community (*Galatians*, 234).

16. See also Acts 2:24, which refers to God's raising of Jesus from the dead as "loosing the pangs [*ōdin*] of death." On the woman in Revelation 12, see Adela Yarbro Collins, *The Combat Myth in the Book of Revelation* (Harvard Dissertations in Religion; 9; Missoula: Scholars Press, 1976) 57-100; John M. Court, *Myth and History in the Book of Revelation* (Atlanta: John Knox, 1979) 106-21.

17. The suggestion is sometimes made that the image of birth in 4:19 anticipates the quotation from Isa 54:1 in 4:27. See, for example, Dieter Lührmann, *Der Brief an die*

Galater (Zürcher Bibelkommentare; Zurich: Theologische Verlag, 1978) 74. J. Louis Martyn has connected the birth imagery in the two passages in his argument that Hagar and Sarah in Gal 4:21-31 represent, not Judaism and Christianity, but two forms of Christian mission—that is, two births ("The Covenants of Hagar and Sarah," in Carroll et al., *Faith and History: Essays in Honor of Paul W. Meyer*).

18. Allison, *The End of the Ages Has Come*, 6 n. 6.

19. See Albrecht Oepke's comment that Paul "erlebt sozusagen im kleinen die Wehen des Messias" (*Der Brief des Paulus an die Galater*, 109).

20. Burton, *Galatians*, 248-49. Because of the birth imagery in the first part of this verse, it is reasonable to ask whether *morphoun* refers to the formation of an infant in its mother's womb. In fact, *morphoun* can connote gestation, but that usage of the word appears to have been quite limited. Pedro Gutierrez argues that *morphousthai* frequently refers to gestation, but the evidence is scanty (*La Paternité Spirituelle selon Saint Paul* [Paris: J. Gabalda, 1968] 217.

21. Ernst Käsemann rightly contends that Gal 4:19 is not a text about spiritual perfection but about "apocalyptic expectation" (*Perspectives on Paul* [Philadelphia: Fortress, 1971] 31).

22. Lietzmann, *An die Galater* (HNT 10; 4th ed.; Tübingen: J. C. B. Mohr [Paul Siebeck] 1971) 28.

23. The line between theological language and moral language is much less distinct than I may seem to suggest here, especially in Paul. See R. B. Hays, "Christology and Ethics in Galatians."

24. R. Hermann, "Über den Sinn des μορφοῦν in Gal 4, 19," *TLZ* 80 (1955) 713-26; Müssner, *Galaterbrief*, 313.

25. On Paul's use of the word group, see John Koenig, "The Motif of Transformation in the Pauline Epistles," (Th.D. dissertation, New York: Union Theological Seminary, 1970).

26. On this as a central theological issue in Galatians, see Gaventa, "The Singularity of the Gospel: A Reading of Galatians," *Society of Biblical Literature 1988 Seminar Papers* (ed. David J. Lull; Atlanta: Scholars Press, 1988) 17-26.

27. J. Louis Martyn, "Apocalyptic Antinomies in Paul's Letter to the Galatians," *NTS* 31 (1985) 410-24. Independent of Martyn's work, Charles Cousar comes to remarkably similar conclusions in an unpublished essay read at the 1989 meeting of the Society of Biblical Literature, "Galatians 6:11-18: Interpretive Clues to the Letter."

28. So also Koenig, "The Motif of Transformation," 112-19.

29. Similarly Morna Hooker connects "formation of Christ" with conformity to Christ; see "Πίστις Χριστοῦ," *NTS* 35 (1989) 342.

30. See also Phil 3:10-11. See also J. D. G. Dunn's comment that the process ends only when the body is transformed to be like Christ's body (Phil 3:21; Rom 8:11) ("1 Cor 15:45—Last Adam," *Christ and Spirit in the New Testament: Studies in Honour of C. F. D. Moule* (eds. Barnabas Lindars and Stephen Smalley; Cambridge: Cambridge University Press, 1973) 137.

31. So also Schlier, 214 n. 2. F. F. Bruce modifies this interpretation slightly, arguing that the community is born through Christ's growth in individuals (*The Epistle to the Galatians: A Commentary on the Greek Text* (NIGTC; Grand Rapids: Eerdmans, 1982] 212).

32. On the relationship between 4:19 and the following passage, see J. L. Martyn, "The Covenants of Hagar and Sarah."

33. J. L. Martyn, "Paul and His Jewish-Christian Interpreters," *USQR* 42 (1988) 6.

34. Compare the comment of Fred B. Craddock: "Paul understood all issues in the church to be theological, however practical they may have appeared, and so he addressed all issues theologically" (*Philippians* [Interpretation; Atlanta: John Knox, 1985] 43).

35. See now Gaventa, "Apostles as Babes and Nurses in 1 Thess 2:7."

SINGING AND SUFFERING IN PHILIPPI

A mong the many aphorisms that have come from the pen of Amos N. Wilder, a theopoet, none is more astute than this:

Before the message there must be the vision,
Before the sermon the hymn, before the prose the poem.[1]

That aphorism applies point by point to the prose and the sermon of Paul's letter to the Philippians. At the core of this letter one finds a literary construction that is certainly poetic, probably hymnic, and possibly the fruit of prophetic vision. I refer, of course, to Phil 2:6-11. In this essay I wish to sketch the possible influences of that hymn on the perspectives and structure of the letter as a whole. Among those influences I will include the possible results of the singing of that hymn.

Preliminary Theses

To mount the task as quickly as possible, I will state several convictions without pausing to marshall supporting evidence, for I am confident that readers of this volume are fully capable of providing such evidence. The first thesis is that the poetic construction in Phil 2:6-11 may be viewed as an early Christian hymn.[2] A second, less widely recognized, thesis is that throughout the ancient Mediterranean world the creation of such hymns, with their striking coincidence of vision, poetry, and song, characterized the gift of prophecy.[3] An excellent example of such coincidence is furnished by the Apocalypse of John.[4] Here one needs only to glance at the Passion chorales in chap. 5, those songs that celebrate in poetic rhythms the worthiness of the slain Lamb and that are set within the context of a heavenly vision.

A third thesis is that the native habitat for these prophetic hymns was the liturgical gatherings of early Christian congregations. Such was clearly the case in Gentile churches founded by Paul. In Corinth, for instance, the apostle urged every member, on coming to meeting, to bring along a hymn (1 Cor 14:26), even though the singing of those songs often produced bedlam. Of course, those Christians did not have the benefit of modern service books, so their songs must have reflected a spontaneity and flexibility that were evoked by the emergencies and excitements of the moment. There must have been a great variety of "psalms, hymns and spiritual songs" in the Gentile churches. The author of Colossians and Ephesians was confident that "the word of Christ" could be heard through such singing and that "the peace of Christ" could invade the church through its music (Col 3:16ff.; Eph 5:15ff.). In such singing, the voices of several singers were fused—the voice of God, of Christ, of the Spirit, along with the voices of the congregation. As one who had received the gift of prophecy,[5] Paul must have been keenly sensitive to the complex medley of convictions that were conveyed by congregational singing.

A fourth thesis is that when these poetic strophes are viewed as a hymn, that hymn must be viewed as originating earlier than the letter in which it is now found. It is unlikely that the author of the letter should have created so carefully balanced a poem simply for the purpose of inserting it within a prosaic dialogue dealing with other matters. As we shall see, Paul did indeed have good reasons for using the hymn in this letter, but the reasons for composing the hymn probably lie elsewhere. Hymns are usually composed for communal use in worship and not for a teacher bent on making polemical points or on enforcing moral imperatives. Those very stylistic features that mark this structure as hymnic presuppose an origin prior to the writing of the letter.

A brief detour is needed now before specifying a fifth thesis. The question of how the hymn was used in this letter can be separated from the question of its authorship. As scholars know, the matter of authorship is vigorously debated.[6] The origin of the hymn has been assigned to a Jewish-Christian church, to a Hellenistic-Christian church, and even to a non-Christian Gnostic cult.[7] However that may be, I am concerned with only one moment in the hymn's history, the moment when Paul was writing this letter. The only extant version of the hymn is found here, and it appears here only because Paul found it useful for his own purposes. Regardless of who composed it, it became Pauline here.

But can we now say anything about its origin before it was embodied in this letter? I think we can, and this is my fifth thesis. The hymn was used in a Christian congregation where every tongue was engaged in confessing "Jesus Christ as Lord, to the glory of God the Father." But can this context be made even more specific? Only by conjecture, but in

203

some situations conjectures are better than silence. In which Pauline church had it been used? Presumably Paul had been present, if not as author, at least as one of the singers. Two congregations offer the best options. One is the commune where Paul was writing, "the brothers who are with me," including such trusted workers as Timothy and Epaphroditus, and "the saints of the imperial household" (4:21, 22). In this case, the singing had been quite recent, and the libretto was fresh in Paul's mind. The words would have received emotional force from the fact of his imprisonment, whether in Rome, Caesarea, or, as I think is more likely, Ephesus.

The second option would be "the saints in Philippi." They had shared in Paul's suffering, first in Philippi itself (1:29, 30) and more recently in the prison from which Paul was writing. In this case, perhaps some months had elapsed since the apostle and converts had sung it together. But there had been frequent interchange between them, and the period would have been short enough for the words to be remembered by both the apostle and his church. It would have recalled the fabric of joint memories and affections. It would have brought to their minds three different times: the time of Jesus' crucifixion, the time of the earlier persecution in Philippi, and the present time of crisis for both apostle and congregation, whether in Ephesus or in Philippi. If this option is taken seriously, it would help to account for Paul's placing of the hymn at the very center of his letter. It is not irrelevant to recall that, according to the book of Acts (16:25), it was the singing of such a hymn at midnight that had triggered an earthquake in the Philippian jail.

A final thesis: Because a hymn fulfills distinctive functions, the interpretation calls for respecting those functions. This Passion chorale, like many other early hymns, had a confessional component. It voiced a prophetic disclosure ("Therefore God has highly exalted . . . ") and a communal response ("confess that Jesus Christ is . . . "). This creedal role was clearly vital; yet, interpreters should not mistake the hymn for carefully formulated doctrine or for a test of faith.[8] The hymn has often been distorted by an overemphasis on dogmatic substance; music is not the place to look for theological precision. So, too, early Christian hymns often fulfilled historical functions by epitomizing the story of Jesus, giving an overview of his vocation as a slave of God, from its invisible beginnings to its invisible ending. Yet, it would be a mistake to interpret the song as if it were historical in the same sense as the account in Acts of Paul's journey to Rome.[9] In similar fashion the hymn was designed to exert moral pressure on the singers. One can hardly read the urgent appeals in the preceding and succeeding paragraphs and deny the presence of this function. Yet, interpreters should not construe the moral injunctions in quite the same way as they view the *Haustafeln*. The hymn was much more than a bland suggestion that because Jesus had been humble his followers must become humble.[10] The hymn reminded this choir of the multiple meanings of its existence in Christ as a colony of heaven. The hymn functioned in such a way as to shape the *phronēma* of the congregation and to clarify its sense of vocation. Emerging from deep levels of communal experience, the song articulated in both verbal and musical terms a rich cargo of non-verbal affections and emotions. It elicited memories that were relevant to meeting current dilemmas and dangers. The hymn assumes that the story of Jesus is prototypical of the story of the Messiah's family. By singing it the congregation affirmed a hidden conjunction between God's exaltation of Jesus and God's design for all things. Interpreters must seek to do justice to multiple motifs, confessional, historical, moral, liturgical, existential. Like all authentic music, the hymn encouraged participation at a level beyond the reach of analysis, where the *phronēma* of Philippian saints was being shaped. To sum up, these are the theses that have impelled me to examine the letter for more specific links between the hymn and the perspectives and structure of the letter as a whole.

The Hymn and the Autobiography

The first step will be to examine the "grammar of correlations" that linked the hymnic story of Christ to the story of Christ's messenger. The singing of the hymn concentrated attention on the action of two subjects: first Christ and then God. The hymn first pictured the downward movement of Christ through two stages, his becoming a slave and then his obedience in death on the cross. (Even in this movement, of course, the command of God is implied, inasmuch as Christ's action was in obedience to God). The hymn then celebrated the action of God, first in exalting Christ and then in securing all creation's subjection to him. The hymn preserved a basic symmetry between a beginning that referred to equality with God, a center that pivots on God's *dio* (not to be read as an *alla*), and an ending in the glory of God. Only after it is recognized as a *theo*logical hymn should this be called a *christo*logical one.

Now we must ask where lie the correlations with the story of the apostle. First of all, Jesus' action in taking the form of a slave corresponds to Paul's view of himself as a slave (*doulos*) of Christ (1:1). In his salutation, Paul in fact stressed this role by omitting the usual reference to himself as an apostle. In this instance he refused to advance any claim to authority except as such a slave.[11] Furthermore, his movement downward passed through two stages. In the first he had divested himself of all advantages that had accrued to him in earlier life: "confidence in the flesh . . . a Hebrew born of Hebrews . . . as to zeal a persecutor . . . as to righteousness under the law blameless" (3:4-6). When he had become a slave he had counted all such gains as loss. There was, of course, a distinction between the *status quo ante* of the two slaves. For Jesus this was the *morphē* of God; for Paul it was "a righteousness of my own, based on law" (3:9). But there remained a significant correlation of direction, a downward movement from the highest conceivable status toward total voluntary deprivation, a *tapeinōsis* (2:8; 3:21) in which all former privileges and securities had been voluntarily surrendered in obedience to God.

The correlation extended to a second stage, where the two descriptions were virtually identical—that is, each slave carried obedience so far as to die. With regard to the obedience of the first slave, the comment of O. Hofius is justified: "The words, 'yes, to death on a cross' (v. 8c) belong to the original content of the pre-Pauline hymn and actually form the climax of the first strophe."[12] The second slave speaks unambiguously of his own death: "That I may share his sufferings, being conformed to his death" (3:10). Paul's death takes the same form (*morphē*) as Jesus' death. At the time of writing there was only one difference: Jesus had already died, Paul not yet. Even so, Paul considered it far better for him "to depart and to be with Christ" (1:23). He urged his readers to rejoice with him when the time should come for his life to be poured out "as a libation on the sacrificial offering of your faith" (2:17). So for Paul this second stage covered his vocation from the time he had become a slave to the time of his obedience to death. And this stage required continuing divestment of every conceivable advantage. He chose to forget everything that lay behind, including not only his status as a Pharisee but also every accomplishment as an apostle, all the results of the gift of the Spirit.[13] Such renunciation was seen as an intrinsic mark of maturity (3:13-15).

This distinction between the two stages in Paul's *tapeinōsis* may help to explain one curious feature of the hymn—that is, the repetition of the lines:

> being born in the likeness of men . . .
> being found in human form

One line focused attention on the first stage in Christ's slavery; the second pointed ahead to the second stage. That repetition seems unnecessary; however, it does make clearer the correspondence to the two stages in the apostle's vocation.

It is sometimes argued that the second strophe in the hymn (God's action in exalting his slave) has little linkage to the rest of the letter.[14] That argument, however, runs counter to extensive correlations to the autobiography. It was through this exaltation that God had issued the "upward call" to the apostle (3:14). It was through knowing the power of the resurrection that Paul would receive whatever strength would be needed for him to share in Christ's sufferings. And it was through becoming like Jesus in his dying that Paul expected to attain the resurrection (3:10, 11). God's action in exalting Jesus had given this slave both the power to die and the assurance of reunion through death with the other slave. Can one state the correlation more clearly than that?

The correlation extends even beyond such reunion. According to the hymn, the plan of God found its completion in the subjection of all things to Christ. Now it was in that very subjection that Paul expected his own story to end. "He will change the body of our humiliation to be like the body of his glory, by the power which enables him to subject all things to him" (3:21, trans. mine). To share the sufferings of Christ was to share in subjection and thus to form a single body with him. To gain Christ by dying was to be found in him. Unity in the one body was accomplished when one slave by his sufferings confessed the other slave as lord, to the glory of the one Father. So the subjection of the apostle became the sign of the subjection of *pan gony*. Nothing could be more congruent with the triumphant conclusion of the hymn.

Paul detected other signs of such subjection. Just as the hymn helped him to face his own death with courage and joy, so also it elicited similar courage and joy among the choir as a whole. Indeed, the singing itself became a way of expressing this courage and joy, a motif not at all rare among early Christian hymns. He detected also positive results of his own imprisonment. It had produced positive effects among his captors (1:13) as well as among his coworkers, including former members of Caesar's household. He hailed both of these reactions as signs of the advance of the gospel, evidence of God's power to subject all things to the slave-lord. To the extent that the hymn defined the core of the gospel, its singing by slaves and prisoners achieved a role in the strategies by which that gospel spread.

In a word, then, the letter discloses an extensive pattern of parallels between the libretto of the hymn and Paul's understanding of his own vocation, its beginning, its current form, and its end.[15] It is not out of order, then, to suggest that these parallels may have been clarified in Paul's own mind through singing that hymn. Scholars have long been aware of the biblical penchant for synonymous parallelism as a rhetorical form that was used widely in speaking and writing. This letter furnishes evidence that it was also often present as a pattern of singing and thinking, a pattern that served to disclose solidarities in action that would otherwise have remained hidden.

The Hymn and the Polemic

As Paul discerned various synonymous parallels between the hymn and his own story, so, too, he discerned various antithetical parallels between the hymn and the stance of his opponents. This letter is marked by an explosion of anger against those adversaries.[16] So we raise the question of whether the hymn exerted any influence on the ways in which Paul visualized that conflict. The antithesis reached its sharpest thrust in the double reference to the cross. In the hymn the nadir of the downward movement was death on the cross as a measure of the Messiah's slavery. In sharp contrast Paul spoke of his adversaries as "enemies of the cross of Christ" (3:15), presumably because they still viewed such a death as something to be avoided at all costs.

Paul's expletives (3:3-4) would not have been so vitriolic had those enemies not been Christians and apparently leaders within the Philippian church. They may have been included among the overseers and deacons who were greeted at the outset, and may even have included Euodia and/or Syntyche, who were mentioned near the end. At the outset the letter plunged its readers into the recognition of strong partisanship and jealousy among rival leaders (1:15), all of whom claimed a degree of authority over the fledgling congregation. It is entirely possible that these leaders had sung the hymn with Paul at previous meetings of the church. If so, that would have given Paul a special incentive for citing the hymn in his attack on them. He did not call them enemies of Christ, for, after all, they proclaimed him, and the apostle reluctantly accepted that as a commendation (1:18). Rather, he called them enemies of the cross, the cross that marked the decisive transition between the two strophes of the hymn.

We have noted the two stages in the descent of Christ and Paul. As Paul saw things, these leaders had failed to share fully in either stage. Unlike Christ, these enemies, on becoming believers, had stopped short of renouncing circumcision as conferring a degree of security and superiority over others. They had not treated as garbage their earlier achievements of righteousness under the law. They continued to cherish the glory inherent in their former status and required others to seek the same preferments. They did not accept complete self-humiliation as the mark of a slave, nor did they encourage others to begin their discipleship as slaves.

It is not strange, then, that they refused to share in the second stage of the Messiah's descent. In Paul's view, this disqualified them from exercising authority over other believers. Their mind-set was the test; by giving preference to self-interest they failed that test (3:19). The apostle considered suffering for Christ a gift from God: "It has been granted to you that for the sake of Christ you should not only believe in him but also suffer for his sake" (1:29). These leaders did not welcome shame as such a gift.[17] But for Paul the hymn signified that a voluntary sharing in suffering marked the boundary between salvation and destruction; enemies of the cross could not escape that destruction (3:9). They reversed the definitions of *tapeinōsis* and glory, which the hymn provided.

A case in point was their reaction to Paul's imprisonment. For one thing, Paul's absence gave them a welcome chance to enhance their own authority over the congregation. For another, they exploited the reports of Paul's disgrace as evidence of the superiority of their own wisdom and strategy. To them, his foolhardiness discredited the faith and impeded the work of evangelism, and they urged the church to forego such dangerous exploits. In response, Paul viewed their arguments as efforts to "afflict me in my imprisonment" (1:17). In all probability, these leaders had found added ammunition in the fate of Epaphroditus. In an earlier burst of loyalty to Paul, the church had sent this member to help Paul in his troubles, a move by which they accepted complicity in Paul's "guilt." We must remember that the charges against him were serious enough to threaten capital punishment (1:20). Sure enough, disaster had almost struck down this emissary from Philippi; he had narrowly escaped death (2:30). The reactions in Philippi were so intense that Paul felt it wise to send their deacon home, both to relieve the anxiety of his friends and to spike the guns of Paul's adversaries.

To sum up, then, because these leaders were unwilling to share the body of humiliation, they forfeited any claim to share in the body of glory (3:21). By their actions they denied the revolutionary force of the *dio* in 2:9. As a result they could share neither the courage nor the joy from the kind of obedience the hymn celebrated. They had challenged Paul's authority, and he returned the favor. To Paul, authentic authority stemmed only from sharing in the Messiah's suffering. The suffering that validated Paul's authority invalidated theirs.[18] The hymn focused attention on this choice, a choice incumbent not only on every leader, but also on every believer in Philippi. Had they sung the hymn? Then they had already decided on which side truth lay.

In this respect the issues in Philippi were not unlike those in Corinth, as described by the scholar whom this volume honors:

> The old standards for identifying an apostle are shown to be invalid. The true apostle is not powerful, but rather weak. He looks like an impostor. . . . One sees a man who is dying, being punished, in sorrow and in

poverty. . . . " [In the cross the church is granted] the new means to distinguish true from false apostles.[19]

So, in judging two types of authority, two kinds of knowledge must be employed, knowledge *kata sarka* and knowledge *kata stauron*.[20] In Philippians the singing of the hymn was an implicit commitment to this later knowledge.

This may become clearer if we trace the hymn to one of its scriptural sources: the Genesis stories of creation. From other letters we know that Paul found it congenial to contrast two archetypical figures, the first Adam and the last (Rom 5:12-21; 1 Cor 15:45-50). The hymn echoes an awareness of that basic contrast, as demonstrated by at least four correlations.

1. The two Adams had comparable origins: "God created man in his own image" (Gen 1:27); "He was in the form of God" (Phil 2:6).

2. Both Adams had been tempted by the desire to be like God, but only one had succumbed to that temptation: "You will be like God, knowing good and evil" (Gen 3:6); "He did not count equality with God a thing to be grasped" (Phil 2:6).

3. Moved in opposite directions by their responses to temptation, the two Adams had based their actions on different appraisals of death, one accepting it and one rejecting: "You will not die" (Gen 3:4); "He became obedient to death" (Phil 2:8).

4. Their contrasting actions justified contrasting verdicts from God, destruction and exaltation: "You are dust and to dust you shall return" (Gen 3:19); "Therefore God has highly exalted him" (Phil 2:9).

Again we notice the distinction between the two stages in the Messiah's downward movement. First the becoming like Adam, and then the becoming unlike him.

These subtle correspondences would have been more obvious to Jewish-Christians than to Gentiles, and therefore more relevant to those leaders in Philippi who continued to prize circumcision and the achievement of legal righteousness (3:2ff.). By recalling to their minds the familiar stories of creation and fall, the hymn would have buttressed Paul's polemic and his warning that their fears of suffering were an omen of their destruction (1:28; 3:19). By underscoring the bond between *tapeinōsis* and *doxa* as God defined them, the hymn clarified the essential contrast between the two Adams. To sing the hymn was to articulate the antithesis between Christ and these enemies of the cross, and thus to support Paul's claim to authority and to undermine their claim.[21] To sing the hymn was to repudiate the fears of death that barred enemies of the cross from receiving God's gift of life. The antithetical parallelism reinforced the polemic.[22]

The Hymn and the Paraklēsis

Neither the autobiography nor the polemic, however, constituted the central purpose of the letter. That purpose was better revealed by the number and force of the exhortations. More than thirty such imperatives may be counted, a remarkable number for so brief a letter. In them Paul showed an intense concern for the morale, or better still the *phronēma*, of the saints in Philippi. Both autobiography and polemic were clearly subordinated to that concern as positive and negative examples of the desired behavior.

Those imperatives were typically absolute and uncompromising. With few exceptions (for example, 4:2), the exhortations appealed to the entire congregation as a single unit. They presupposed an involvement by the congregation in the same struggle as that of Paul (1:30), a struggle entailing immediate risks of imprisonment and possible martyrdom. The hymn was strategically placed near the center of the longest series of imperatives. From 1:27 on, the injunctions pointed ahead toward the hymn, every command being designed for those to whom God had given the grace to suffer for Christ's sake. From 2:12 to at least 3:1, the injunctions were grounded in the hymn, governed by the conjunction *hōste* in 2:12. This literary context thus made explicit what was only implicit within the hymn—that is, to believe in this slave Messiah was to suffer for him (1:29). Both in preparing for the hymn and in drawing out its implications, Paul stressed the necessity for readers to choose between his acceptance of such suffering and his adversaries' avoidance of it (1:28-30; 2:17-21).

This orientation of the *paraklēsis* becomes clear when one analyzes the injunctions that are repeated most frequently. For instance, the recurrent calls for unity provide silent evidence that the adversaries' challenge to Paul's authority had threatened such unity. So, too, the frequent commands to rejoice reflect the fact that the adversaries had been successfully playing on the anxieties of the congregation. Pleas to stand firm in the face of persecution testify to the temptations to be frightened by opponents. The use of the verb *phroneō* (repeated ten times) makes it clear that the selection of one of two opposing mind-sets constituted the central issue of the letter. The radical collision between these two "minds" gave maximum force to the hymn, quite apart from the difficult question of how to translate the ambiguous 2:5.[23]

Now we should look more closely at the correlations between the two strophes of the hymn and the exhortations. Most obvious, perhaps, is the parallelism between the two downward movements; to share in Christ was to share in this movement. Motivation for such movement stemmed from Christ, from love, from the Spirit, and from the fountain

211

of mercies (2:1, 2). Saints must give absolute priority to the needs of others, doing nothing from private ambition or self-concern. Their minds must be united to Christ's by a common *tapeinōsis* (2:3, 8). Their descent had already plunged them into difficult obedience, for more than any other church they had been ready to share in Paul's dangers and hardships (4:14-16). This readiness had been embodied in the work of Epaphroditus (2:25).

Like the descent of Christ, theirs had two stages, the second of which still lay in the future (2:12-18). They had not yet carried obedience so far as to die. The prospect of death had tended to demoralize them and to make them vulnerable to the arguments of the adversaries. So it had become more and more difficult for them to choose between the two minds. The implications of working out their own salvation (2:12) had become more ominous; "fear and trembling" had become inescapable. Even so, confidence that God was at work at the roots of their desiring would enable them as God's children to hold firmly to the word of life as a word of salvation and not destruction.

In the definition of this salvation the letter established a linkage to the second strophe of the hymn. This linkage came to the surface near the end of chap. 3, after the autobiography had shifted from the singular *I* to the plural *we* (3:14, 15). The climax of thought was reached in vv. 20 and 21, which Lohmeyer recognized as a second hymnic construction.[24] As in the first hymn, a double thrust should be noted: *exaltation*—"he will change the body (*sōma*) of our humiliation to be conformed to the body of his glory"; *subjection*—God's power will bring everything into subjection to him. This solidarity in the single body of humiliation and glory marked the telos of the story for both Paul and the Philippians, in full accordance with the telos of the hymn in 2:6-11. Such solidarity provided the basis for their firmness, fearlessness and joy.[25] Exclusion from this *sōma* marked the destruction of enemies of the cross (3:18, 19). In this second hymn may be found the largest concentration of verbal links to the earlier hymn: *theos, doxa, phroneō, hyparchō, kyrios Iēsous Christos, schēma, tapeinōsis, morphē, pan, epigeia*. The conclusion is almost inescapable: The double movement of the christological hymn (two stages in obedience and two ways of viewing glorification) informed Paul's perception of the vocation of all believers. The *paraklēsis* simply spelled out the vocational implications of the hymn.

Readers of the Gospels will not find this thought pattern strange. There, too, God had sent the Son of Man into a path of obedience that led inexorably to suffering, death, and glorification. There, too, this Son of Man had called all followers to deny self and to carry the cross. There, too, the divine demand of obedience had reversed all calculations of wealth and poverty, greatness and smallness, life and death. When the

Philippians sang the hymn, they were epitomizing more than a single letter from their one-time leader.

Scholars have discovered in the hymn echoes of the songs of Second Isaiah. Some of these may be itemized:

ISAIAH	PHILIPPIANS	
the righteous one, my servant 53:11	taking the form of a slave	2:7
he was numbered with the transgressors 53:12	he emptied himself	2:7
he grew up before him like a young plant 53:2	being born in human likeness	2:7
he was despised and rejected 53:3	he humbled himself	2:8
He poured out his soul to death 53:12 He was cut off from the land of the living 53:8	he became obedient to death	2:8
I will divide him a portion with the great 53:12 my servant . . . shall be exalted and lifted up 52:13	God has highly exalted him	2:9
I am the Lord, that is my name 42:8 You shall be called by a new name 62:2	the name above every name	2:9
To me every knee shall bow 45:23 Princes . . . shall prostrate themselves 49:7	at the name of Jesus every knee shall bow	2:11

What inferences might safely be drawn from these echoes? Did the composer of the hymn have Isaiah in mind as he shaped successive strophes? Had the Philippian church sung both hymns? In writing the letter, did Paul want his readers to recall the ancient prophecies? On reading the letter, did they catch the rich resonances and deep nuances of the song? The earlier prophet had voiced his vision in poetry and song and had commanded God's people to sing a new song (42:10, 11; 54:1). Did the Philippians consider their singing to be a response to that command? We do not know the answers to such questions. But we can well suppose that to the degree that communal memories of this sort were evoked by the singing, to that degree those memories would have reinforced the *paraklēsis.* Those memories would have strengthened awareness of the linkage between the various biographies—those of Jesus, of Paul, of Timothy and Epaphroditus, of the Philippians, of the

213

entire chain of prophets since Isaiah. The singing of the hymn would itself have encouraged that unity, courage, joy, and *phronēma* which marked the reality of the one body.

The Hymn and the Letter

We have now completed the analysis of two examples of synonymous parallelism in thought and action, and one example of antithetical parallelism. We will now consider some of the implications of the study for a better understanding of the structure of the letter. It appears to be the dominant view of recent commentators that the present edition of the letter is a rather clumsy fusion of two or even three letters that were written by Paul at different times and later joined by some unknown editor. This view prevails in spite of the fact that no supporting evidence is provided by textual variants or ancient manuscripts. Major evidence lies in apparently radical discontinuities of thought. It must, of course, be recognized that rough transitions do exist. The question is whether those transitions require the theory of composite origin or whether more satisfactory explanations exist.

Much depends on what expectations readers bring to the letter. Do they expect to find a smoothly flowing stream of thought that moves logically from one idea to the next, as any good theological essay should? If so, their thought will strike many snags, not the least of which is the elliptical transition from 3:1 to 3:2 to 3:3. Here the sudden shifts in mood and idiom require some explanation. And there are other places where the apostle's thought seems to jump the track.

Perhaps, however, Paul's situation and objectives should prompt readers to alter their expectations. After all, he was trying to cope in emergency fashion with turbulent conditions in both Ephesus and Philippi. In Ephesus he was facing the very real prospect of a violent death, which he knew would deeply shock his followers and would simultaneously give ammunition to his adversaries. In Philippi he had been warned of sharp conflict between those adversaries and the saints, and he knew that his own strategy for spreading the gospel was a pivotal issue in that conflict. Given those conditions, it is natural that his thought would shift almost without notice from his own position to that of followers or adversaries. It would have been unnatural for his thought to move smoothly forward in step with the literary specifications of modern critics. So we must look again at those rough transitions with a different set of expectations.

Most important is the transition between chaps. 2 and 3, for here is where most theories find the clearest evidence of separate letters. (Scholars differ in the precise limits of the second letter, locating the first seam at either 3:1*b* or 3:2 and the later seam at 3:19; 4:1 or 4:3). By contrast we have detected the closest parallels, both synonymous and antithetical, between the hymn of chap. 2 and the contents of chap. 3. Does our approach make intelligible the sudden shift in the line of thought between the chapters? I think it does.

"Finally, brothers and sisters, rejoice in the Lord" (3:1)

The Greek *chairete* can, of course, be translated "farewell" instead of "rejoice," as if Paul were terminating the letter, but there is no compelling reason for that translation. The injunction to rejoice follows quite smoothly from the preceding paragraph. The singing of the hymn, with its focus on Christ's humiliation and exaltation, would tend to release such "joy in the Lord." So, too, would the steadfastness in danger as illustrated by Timothy, Epaphroditus, and Paul himself (2:19-30). Danger and joy belonged together. But the very mention of joy would call to Paul's mind the opposite reactions to danger on the part of more cautious leaders in Philippi, who were not only fearful of personal loss but who also argued that it threatened the spread of the gospel. When Paul moved from the saints of chap. 2 to the dogs of chap. 3, his mood changed because of the radical difference in their attitudes toward sharing the sufferings of Christ.

"To write these things to you is not irksome to me" (3:1)

The adjective *irksome* denotes reluctance, difficulty, and cautious fear, which were precisely the reactions to the situation on the part of the dogs. If they had been thrown into prison, they would have found it inconceivable to rejoice and even more difficult to call upon their friends to rejoice. What was impossible for them, however, was basic for Paul. To command joy in suffering came easy to him—that is, if we trust his confession in 1:20, 21. "Irksome? Yes, to my opponents, but not to me."

"To write these things . . . is safe for you" (3:1)

Here the key adjective denotes both security and certainty. The core issue is the question of where security is to be found for the Philippians. By holding on to life and liberty? Or by sharing in the humiliation of Christ? Which answer is more certainly a corollary of the gospel? Step by step, a reader can observe a natural progression from the acceptance of death in 2:20 to the injunction to rejoice in 3:1*a* to the confidence of the apostle and the security of the saints in 3:1*b*.

The progression leads to the sudden explosion, "Beware the dogs," in 3:2. These dogs have been present in Paul's mind from the beginning and are implicit in his argument. The transition may seem to be sudden and awkward in literary terms, but this awkwardness results from the head-on collision between the obedience of Christ and the suffering of Paul and Epaphroditus, on the one hand, and on the other the fear of such suffering and the inability to rejoice on the part of the adversaries. As Paul saw the issue, it was a conflict between two circumcisions, true and false. Or, in the light of the hymn, between enemies of the cross and its bearers. When a reader becomes aware of this issue, he or she may already detect the presence of the dogs in chap. 2 (2:21), and the transition between the honey of 3:1 and the vitriol of 3:2 becomes entirely intelligible.

Sometimes another bit of evidence is cited to support the existence of more than one letter: the double reference to Epaphroditus in 2:25-30 and 4:18. In one letter Paul acknowledged the gift from Philippi; a second letter he sent back with Epaphroditus after his recovery from a serious illness. Our interpretation, however, is equally cogent in explaining this double reference within a single letter. The reference to the Philippian gift in 4:18 belonged among the concluding remarks, next to the benediction and greetings. The earlier reference constituted part of the central argument growing out of the hymn. In Paul's mind, Epaphroditus had become with Timothy a prime example of what was required of a true co-worker and fellow-soldier, the courageous acceptance of danger and death in the line of duty—an acceptance that, in fact, put to shame the workers of evil (3:2). As Alan Culpepper has convincingly shown, Paul appealed in chap. 2 to these men as servants with "the mind of Christ," who acted in full accord with the hymn.[26] The fact that he sent these messengers to Philippi with the letter shows how seriously Paul took the struggle within that church between the saints and the dogs. So the two references to Epaphroditus offer little support for the theory of two letters.

A third bit of evidence supporting the fusion of two originally separate letters is often found in the presence of two commands to rejoice in 3:1a and 4:4. It is plausible to explain this repetition by assuming that the intervening material had a separate origin. A later editor, having inserted a fragment from another letter after the first command to rejoice, decides to return to the first document by repeating the command, "Again I say. . . ." But the picture is altered if we remember that to the author it was more important to deal with a pastoral crisis than to compose a literary essay. That crisis threatened not only the lives of leaders but the survival of the church. For Paul, the greater the danger, the greater the call for joy. For his adversaries, the greater the danger, the greater the call for caution and anxiety. Given this situation, it is not at all strange that his first command to rejoice should have prompted his warning against them. That warning led, in turn, to the second hymn (3:20, 21) with its multiple echoes of the first. The repeated assurance that all things would be subjected to Christ prompted the renewed call to stand firm (4:1) and to rejoice (4:4). It had now become clear that joy should no longer be made a hostage to external conditions, either in Ephesus or in Philippi.

We may enhance our understanding of the structure of this letter by recalling the movement of thought in worship when the singing of a Passion chorale, perhaps on Good Friday, reminds a modern congregation of linkages between the song and their own cumulative and communal experience. Unexpected consonances and dissonances may emerge from the subconscious mind as the sung story of the Passion throws fresh light on the lived stories of followers. So it is entirely in order to imagine the movement in Paul's mind as he pondered the hymn celebrating the slavery and lordship of the Messiah—from the hymn to his own experiences, including prison, in Philippi; from the hymn to the tests of obedience that had been successfully passed by Timothy and Epaphroditus; from the hymn to those adversaries whose fears of losing life were leading them straight to destruction. When we place the hymn, or rather its singing, at the core of the letter, we catch new glimpses of the conceptual integrity of the letter. Those glimpses, in turn, may convey a sense of literary integrity as well.

This essay at the outset recognized the creative work of E. Lohmeyer in his identification of 2:6-11 as a hymn. Many of his successors have acknowledged this debt, and a great debt it has proved to be. But there is also a debt to this scholar for a second discovery, one that is less frequently recognized. Lohmeyer was convinced that the central problem in this letter was the threat of martyrdom to both apostle and church. So convinced was he of this that he made the issue of martyrdom the organizing principle for a detailed outline of the letter.[27] In almost every verse he detected a justification for that outline. It is not necessary to follow his outline or to accept without qualification his word *martyrdom*. But later scholarship would have profited greatly if it had taken more seriously his emphasis on persecution as a central key to understanding the apostle's thought. To have observed that key would have inhibited the tendencies toward euphemistic perversions that have plagued interpretations of this letter. Paul's commands have been trivialized into moral attributes that are highly honored in conventional middle-class behavior. As a result, the command to rejoice has become virtually meaningless. Nothing so quickly insulates a reader from the steel-tough logic of this appeal sent from an Ephesian jail. Nothing so quickly reduces the range and power of the hymn. Lohmeyer's accent on martyrdom cuts through such perversities of interpretation.

But is *martyrdom* the best term? It is true that for Paul martyrdom was a direct implication of the *therefore* of 2:9 and the *wherefore* of 2:12. It is true that the parallelisms, both synonymous and antithetical, between the hymn and the letter described radical obedience to the martyr Messiah as the litmus test of discipleship. But as Paul interprets the hymn, the accent falls on the opposite reactions to the death of the Messiah. Given God's action in exalting this martyr, can the gospel be advanced by any other strategy than that of the Messiah? Does the prospect of suffering "in the Lord" evoke courage, firmness, and joy *or* fear, caution, and dread? Does sharing in "the body of humiliation" define destruction or salvation? Lohmeyer rightly focuses attention on the danger of martyrdom. But Paul focused attention on the opposite reactions to that danger. And the singing of the hymn in Philippi would have encouraged the reactions Paul favored.

* * *

Let me add now a more personal word, addressed solely to the scholar whom this volume honors. As I have written these lines, I have often recalled the first years of our association at Andover Newton Theological School. One of our mutual friends there was the dean, Vaughan Dabney. Of all the biblical books, and in fact of all literature, Philippians was Vaughan's favorite. I do not recall all of the reasons for this, but one of them was surely the transparent evidence of courage and joy on the part of a prisoner who faced probable, if not certain, execution. This strikes the perceptive reader as nothing short of a miracle. I surmise that it was this same miracle that served to attract the two of us into the field of New Testament studies. In those far-off days it would never have occurred to either of us that the time would come when I would be engaged in writing an essay on Philippians for Lou Martyn's *Festschrift*. But *mirabile dictu*, that very thing has happened! That it has happened is a tiny measure of our constantly growing indebtedness to the apostle. But that debt itself is beyond measure.

Notes

1. Amos N. Wilder, *Theopoetic* (Philadelphia: Fortress, 1976) 1.
2. The chief responsibility for the discovery of the hymn is generally accorded to E. Lohmeyer, *Kyrios Jesus* (Heidelberg: Carl Winter, 1928) 5ff.; idem., *Der Brief an die Philipper* (Göttingen: Vandenhoeck & Ruprecht, 1953) 90-99.
3. See D. E. Aune, *Prophecy in Christianity and the Ancient Mediterranean World* (Grand Rapids: Eerdmans, 1983) 28, 31, 38, 46, 146ff.
4. Ibid., 274-90.
5. See D. Hill, *New Testament Prophecy* (New Foundations Theological Library; Atlanta: John Knox, 1979) 110-40; M. E. Boring, *Sayings of the Risen Jesus* (SNTSMS 46;

Cambridge: Cambridge University Press, 1982) 30-36; D. E. Aune, *Prophecy*, 248ff., 422 n. 2.

6. On this matter I have yet to be convinced of the pre-Pauline or non-Pauline origin of the hymn. I believe with L. E. Keck that here "a goodly degree of caution is in order, in part because we are uncertain about what principles govern the strophic structure and in part because all authors freely inserted their own comments into that structure" (Paper presented to the American Theological Society, April 1986).

7. For the theory of Gnostic origin, see R. Bultmann, *New Testament Theology* (2 vols.; New York: Scribner's, 1951) 1.298.

8. In *an die Philipper*, Lohmeyer examined this issue with judicious care and decided that the text should be viewed more as a hymn than as a creed (5ff.). Had his successors followed him in this respect, their interpretations might have been less skewed by obsession with the concepts of pre-existence and kenosis.

9. The hymn takes the form of a narrative that points realistically to quite specific events, but it avoids the trap of making "history" the test of meaning and truth; see Hans Frei, *The Eclipse of Biblical Narrative* (New Haven: Yale University Press, 1973) viii.

10. See B. S. Childs, *The New Testament as Canon* (Philadelphia: Fortress, 1985) 337.

11. See I-Jin Loh and E. A. Nida, *A Translator's Handbook on Paul's Letter to the Philippians* (New York: United Bible Societies, 1977) 4. The emphasis on *doulos* calls attention to the presence in the hymn of the twin metaphor slave/lord, each twin deriving meaning in part from its antithesis.

12. O. Hofius, *Der Christushymnus Philipper 2, 6-11* (WUNT 17; Tübingen: J. C. B. Mohr [Paul Siebeck], 1976) 56.

13. See V. C. Pfitzner, *Paul and the Agon Motif* (NovTSup 16; Leiden: Brill, 1967) 149.

14. See J. T. Sanders, *The New Testament Christological Hymns* (SNTSMS 15; Cambridge: Cambridge University Press, 1971).

15. The extensive syntax of relationships is supported by multiple verbal links between the hymn and the autobiographical references, including: *hēgeomai, hyparchō, morphē, lambanō, schēma, kenoō, doulos, heurischō, tapeinoō, thanatos, pan, doxa, phroneō, kyrios, christos;* see R. P. Martin, *Carmen Christi* (SNTSMS 4; Cambridge: Cambridge University Press, 1967) 58 n. 2.

16. It has proved very difficult to get a clear picture of Paul's opponents. Did he have in mind a single group or more than one? If there were more than one, there is sufficient evidence to assume that both groups were composed of Christian believers and of leaders who claimed authority over other believers. And if there were more than one, Paul applied the same criteria for testing their authenticity. This essay is concerned only with the nature of those criteria.

17. See Lohmeyer, *an die Philipper*, 124-30.

18. See V. C. Pfitzner, *Agon Motif*, 142.

19. J. Louis Martyn, "Epistemology at the Turn of the Ages: 2 Cor. 5:16," in *Christian History and Interpretation: Studies Presented to John Knox* (eds. W. R. Farmer, C. F. D. Moule, R. R. Niebuhr; Cambridge: Cambridge University Press, 1967) 271, 273.

20. Ibid., 285.

21. A significant modern parallel to Paul's polemic against Christian leaders may be found in S. Kierkegaard's *Attack on Christendom* (Princeton: Princeton University Press, 1943) 5-33.

22. Among the verbal links between the hymn and the polemic may be mentioned the following: *phroneō, stauros, theos, epigeion,* and *doxa.*

23. See Martin, *Carmen Christi*, 84-88.

24. See Lohmeyer, *Kyrios Jesus*, 8 n. 1.

25. Soren Kierkegaard must rank among the finest modern interpreters of the Philippian hymn. Allusions to it may be found in no fewer than ten of his major works. Consult especially *The Gospel of Suffering* (Minneapolis: Augsburg, 1948) 5-64. "No school lasts so long as the school of suffering" (63).

26. A. Culpepper, "Co-Workers in Suffering. Phil. 2:19-30," *Review and Expositor* 77 (1980) 349-58.

27. See Lohmeyer, *an der Philipper*, 4-8.

PHILIPPIANS:
PAUL'S MOST EGOCENTRIC LETTER

Robert T. Fortna

S everal working assumptions about the Apostle Paul both underlie and suggest this study:

1. Paul's psyche, or—simpler put—his feelings, are both relevant to his written message and are recoverable.[1] His letters are filled with evidence of intense emotion, often not altogether noble.

2. Paul was a fallible sinner—a great Christian, yes. Paul was very likely the subtlest intellect in the early history of the Christian movement, and in many ways he was a good man. But he was not quite the selfless apostle we have been taught—docetically, quietistically . . . and with his help—to see in him. His writings reveal a complex, often difficult, sometimes self-deceptive genius.

3. Paul's theology—that is, his written thought—developed contextually over time. It shifted and altered with circumstance,[2] like that of any relevant mind, and in particular of a person chiefly concerned with action rather than idea. He was a reluctant theologian. As a missionary always on the run, he was forced to stay in touch mostly by letters with the embryonic communities of faith that he left behind. More often than not it was less a reflective impulse on his part that drove him to expand the basic credo he has preached than events in his own life and interaction with those churches. The questions put to him, as well as his own precarious experience, occasioned much of his thought and the paths it took.

4. Therefore, finally, Paul's theology is not to be synthesized. Were that possible, it would be useful, even though it would violate the fundamentally ad hoc, occasional, unsystematic character of his writings (with the partial exception of Romans). But his letters defy harmonization.

As an immodest beginning, these presuppositions obviously challenge a great deal of recent Pauline research.[3] Consider the letter to

Philippi—customarily viewed as one of Paul's late letters (and, therefore, undoubtedly one of his more mature, if his thought did develop[4]); remembered chiefly for the lofty christology of the so-called "Carmen Christi" of chap. 2; considered primarily a dispassionate letter of good will and affection for his addressees; and usually wholly unexplained as to its occasion.[5]

Instead, I find Philippians to belong with the earlier letters and to be eccentric, displaying Paul's theology at perhaps its least noble.[6] In it, after appearances to the contrary, Paul is primarily preoccupied with himself and not yet at all aware of the present fact of unconditional grace.[7] Rather, as in 1 and 2 Thessalonians and 1 Corinthians, he still looks to a future *parousia*, the Day of Christ, for the solution of all practical theological human difficulties (see 1:6, 10; 2:16; 3:20-21; 4:5*b*). As elsewhere, in Philippians Paul invents answers when he must, some of which he will later quietly abandon. As often as not, and sometimes for the least impressive of reasons, he stumbles across what will thereafter be recognized as true.[8]

Let us explore Philippians to see if this may be documented. In the midst of the usual complimentary opening remarks to his addressees (Phil 1:3-11), Paul's self-concern intrudes embarrassingly soon—concern with his ministry (v. 5) and especially with his own present adversity—namely, his imprisonment and the possibility, seeming to him at times like the certainty, of execution (v. 7). I propose that it is this predicament that really preoccupies him as he addresses a letter to his mostly loyal followers in Philippi—indeed, it has chiefly occasioned the letter.[9] We need hardly fault him for this concentration of his attention on himself. But the urgency, desperation, and chaos of his changing responses to these circumstances patently belie a widely prevailing view of Paul as the great other-directed hero of the nascent Christian movement.[10]

Before developing this case, I must state that I accept the integrity of canonical Philippians—that is, as more or less a single letter, however jarring the shift in mood and subject matter at 3:1*b*. The burden of proof, and certainly the presumption, for taking the text before us to be a composite of more than one of Paul's letters lies, of course, with those who advocate lack of integrity. One of the side products of this study will be to find that on the psychological level—that is, from the perspective of Paul's underlying focus on his own trying circumstances, there is a surprising unity between the two halves of the received text.

I suggest that in this letter, along with the somewhat distracted attention Paul pays to the Philippians and their needs, there prevails a parallel and more basic attention to his own situation and especially to the *theological* problem it poses for him. Not for the first time that problem is his own suffering. Such it had been in 1 Thessalonians, where he devoted three chapters out of five to his own persecution by opponents.[11] By contrast to 2 Thessalonians, if—as I hold—it is authentic and earlier than 1 Thessalonians,[12] it is significant that in the latter Paul does not apply to his own persecution the traditional apocalyptic reassurances he had earlier so effortlessly written to the Thessalonians, regarding their righteous suffering and certain vindication.

Nor, in Philippians, as he faces the possibility of his own imminent death, does Paul remember the neat answer he gave in 1 Thessalonians 4 about the hope of those who had "fallen asleep in the Lord." Not for Paul, evidently, is there to be any delay, even a peaceful rest until the End. Nor does the realization of 1 Corinthians 15 that all humanity,[13] in its empirical state, is physically incapable of inheriting immortality and must, therefore, either by a premature death or suddenly at the last moment, be reclothed in a "spiritual body," have any consolation for him as he imagines the possibility of his own abrupt end.[14]

Evidently none of these answers, innovative and adequate as they had been, even suggests itself to Paul as he contemplates his own immediate prospects.

Let us attend closely to his reasoning, amounting almost to pure rationalization, as he attempts to determine, in fact to decide—as if the matter lay in his control (1:22b)—whether he will escape his present incarceration or in fact be executed. The issue seems to lack all uncertainty. Despite his preference to "depart and be with Jesus" he becomes convinced that he will be released and so provide for his converts, in particular his devoted Philippians. Yet, the fear, almost the inevitability of his early death, pervades the letter.

In vv. 12-18 Paul first treats his imprisonment relatively casually. "What has happened to [him]" is primarily a good thing, for it calls attention to the fact that it is for the gospel that he is suffering, and if some use this against him, as he feared so desperately in 1 Thessalonians, others are moved and even converted by it. Paul has evidently come to realize that adversity as such does not necessarily cause his own converts to lose their confidence in him, and may in fact have a positive effect.[15]

But even as he is rejoicing that "this will result in deliverance for me [moi . . . eis sōtērian]" (v. 19b), he imperceptibly shifts from this unequivocal expectation of release to the confidence that also by his death, just as by his life, "with full courage . . . Christ will be honored in my body" (v. 20b). There is both a brave trust here and a rash self-confidence.

For the moment, then, Paul can weigh either possibility confronting him with a kind of equanimity: "To live is Christ for me and to die is gain [*kerdos*]" (v. 21).[16] He is in fact unable to "decide which [he] will choose," as if it depended on his balancing out the pros and cons (vv. 22*b*-23*a*), a kind of whistling in the dark. But he puts the best face on his dilemma. Now that he has faced the possibility, he can say that he even prefers to die "and be [immediately] with Christ, for that is far better" from his own standpoint (v. 23*b*). Yet, due to his importance, indeed his obligation, to his Christian followers, he is "convinced" that he will remain on earth to come and benefit them (vv. 24-25). Perhaps this can explain what Paul meant by saying that remaining alive "is Christ for [him]": it is both his own continuing fellowship with Christ and, still more important, his mediation of that fellowship to others.[17]

Then follows a passage (1:27-30) encouraging his readers in their own experience of adversity, but not with the same brave confidence he has just shown in facing possible death. Instead, he voices the rather mechanical apocalyptic hope by which he had earlier reassured those in similar straits (2 Thessalonians 1). The Philippians are not to be in the least frightened by their opponents, for this suffering is "a clear omen to them of their [eventual] destruction, but of your [deliverance]" (v. 28).

Here Paul uses again the term *sōtēria*, which he earlier applied to his own rescue from an otherwise pointless death, but the difference, both in the content of this "salvation" and its timing, is obvious, and all the more striking in the face of Paul's equating his own situation with that of the Philippians: "[You are] engaged in the same conflict which you . . . now hear to be mine" (v. 30). We have still, therefore, to account for Paul's confidence that if necessary he will be afforded a special and early resurrection.

No doubt such an expectation goes hand in hand with his own sense of calling, for how could God abandon this special apostle and the project to which God had called him, the conversion, all but single-handedly, of the Gentile world? The answer to this question, since to Paul it is purely rhetorical, is obvious. So far, then, if Paul seems to distinguish himself from all other Christians, it is not so much a matter of egocentricity as the conviction common to many of God's agents, the prophets in particular, that they are under both a kind of unique obligation and a special protection.

But how, apart from mere wishful thinking, does Paul come to expect that in the case of his own death he will be rescued immediately (or so shortly as not to require mention)? I believe the clue is to be found, reading between the lines, in chap. 2. And it is here that Paul's grandiosity shows most painfully.

At that chapter's opening, Paul continues for a moment to think of the suffering and persecution of the preceding verses, imagining an easing of it: "If there is any encouragement, any loving comfort . . . any kindness and sympathy" (2:1, author's trans.). But whose suffering does he have in mind? Is it the Philippians or Paul himself who most needs this comfort? Usually readers (and even translators) have assumed it to be the former and have taken it for granted that Paul's joy, which he says would ensue from the relieving of the suffering (v. 2a), is a typical instance of his altruistic concern. And on the uppermost, the conscious level of the text, that is perhaps true.

But in fact what will accomplish this joy for him, as he goes on to say in v. 2b, is not the Philippians' encouragement, but rather the resolution of a problem in Philippi of which we have not heard till now—some kind of disunity and selfish concern in the Christian community there (vv. 3-4).[18] Thus, evidently, in v. 1 Paul himself is seeking the encouragement his own circumstances need. To find harmony and love on the Philippians' part, instead of their lack, will only add to that support for which Paul longs.

It is only what follows this little opening section of the chapter—namely, the famous christological hymn of vv. 6-11—that can answer his theological need. He does not explicitly acknowledge this, or even perhaps recognize it. Instead he appears (piously?) to recommend to the disagreeing and thoughtless Philippians the model of Jesus' self-sacrifice: "Have this mind among yourselves." Take a lesson from Jesus' unselfish death.

Paul has spoken before this of Jesus' death, and always in an astonishingly casual way. He did so in 1 Thess 2:15-16, citing it as only one example of unjust persecution among several, of which the opposition he experienced in his work is the chief instance![19] Again, in 1 Cor 1:18-25, Paul treated the crucifixion of Jesus as a "foolish" idea, an example only, of Paul's claim that his evidently unimpressive preaching is nevertheless an expression of God's power and wisdom.[20]

But to suggest that he intends the Philippians to be more orderly and considerate because of Jesus' death is simply absurd. Rather, what this unique christology of the hymn fits and fits precisely is Paul's situation, not the Philippians'—that is, it pertains to the hidden agenda of the letter rather than to the overt one.[21] Jesus, too—Paul now recognizes—had faced premature and pointless death,[22] and done so presumably without hesitation, but possibly with "fear and trembling."[23]

And the resurrection of Jesus, which alone had been basic for Paul from the beginning, the one christological fact to which he could instinctively turn, here once again is the answer to Paul's quandary. It can be applied by Paul to himself not only because he had already seen it as an example of how those who die before the Parousia of Christ can also be raised (1 Thess 4:14) and as absolutely essential to Christian faith

(1 Cor 15:19-20), but especially because it fits his own circumstance. Jesus' resurrection was—necessarily!—preceded by death, a death otherwise unacceptable. Paul can imagine himself experiencing, before any of the other prematurely dying believers, the same answer to death that Jesus found—yes, even choosing it.

"Let this mind be in you," Paul in effect says to himself, perhaps remembering the old hymn that celebrated what Jesus had himself sacrificed. Consider it this way: Jesus sacrificed everything, not only a God-given purpose and meaning but also a unique status.[24] Instead of holding on to this privilege, this rationale for his very being, Jesus willingly rid himself of it and "emptied himself." Not only did he find himself "in human form," but he also further "humbled himself and became obedient to death"—yes, even the humiliating death of crucifixion.[25]

But it is what follows, the last part of the hymn (vv. 9-11) that especially speaks to Paul:[26] Jesus had (as Paul might put it) worked out his own salvation. He had forfeited everything, even the semi-divine standing he had before God. And as a consequence, as a richly deserved reward, he was given an even higher status than he had at first. His death had hardly been in vain.

If Paul were to paraphrase what he writes (and probably reproduces from a pre-existing hymn) in this way, it would be too unthinkably crass. He can be scarcely more fully aware of the analogy he draws between Jesus' experience in dying and his own possibly imminent death than he intends his readers to be. And so, once again, he seems to be thinking and speaking only of them. But what he says to them, the consequence of the hymn for them, is almost outlandish, certainly from the standpoint of the more mature and far more objective theology of 2 Corinthians, Galatians, and Romans: "Therefore . . . [begin *or* continue] to *work out your own salvation*" (v. 12, italics added).[27]

Taken in isolation from Paul's situation, these astonishing words might appear to be softened either by understanding "work out" to mean only something like "bring out in your life the salvation that has been worked for you by Christ"[28] or by the phrases that immediately follow in the text: "with fear and trembling"[29] and "since God is at work in you" (12c-13). But the Greek does not allow this conventional interpretation.[30] And even if Paul has somehow been too bold and so must quickly cover over what he has said with easily found phrases, they do not cancel what he so blatantly drew as the Philippians' lesson from the experience of Jesus.[31] It is too easy to assume, for example, that Paul speaks only of "the well-being of [the Philippians'] . . . community" and not really of their "responsibility for their [own] salvation."[32] Rather, I find it clear that Paul does not yet fully comprehend the total incapacity of humans in the accomplishing of redemption.[33]

225

To keep striving to accomplish his own rescue is just what Paul is preparing himself to do because Jesus, his Lord, his very Life, had done so before him. If Paul, on the uppermost level of his letter, still speaks of the Philippians' behavior in what follows (vv. 14-16), it is nevertheless significant that he ends his appeal with another direct reference to his own stake in their behavior (v. 16b), even the exaggerated fantasy of his sacrificing himself for them (v. 17a).[34]

Thus does Paul work out a theology of his own approaching death! In this theological advance, inadequate as it will soon prove to be, Paul for the first time considers Jesus' death as it had been experienced—the nightmare that one had preferred to forget—and thereby sees it as not just an unacceptable and foolish idea[35], but as an existential event with meaning and effect, if only for Jesus himself. In Paul's eyes it was, after all, only Jesus (and perhaps also Paul!) who needed to be redeemed from a death "before the time."

The illusion Paul has created for himself is that, like Jesus, he can and will sacrifice everything. But the fullest expression of this is to be found only in chap. 3. First we must treat the issue of the letter's integrity.

In the latter paragraphs of chap. 2 (vv. 19-30) Paul evidently intends to bring his letter to a close, turning to practical matters having to do with his assistants and their relation to Philippi, perhaps easing some concerns of his own, setting things in order in case he is soon to die.

So Paul's original letter[36]—if Philippians comprises two or more letters—would have concluded with the first verse of chap. 3, taking up again the theme of joy from the end of the theological heart of the letter (2:18).[37] The disjuncture to be found at 3:1 and the likelihood that at least one other extant letter of Paul's (2 Corinthians) is a combination of two or more letters originally distinct in occasion and message lead many to deny the literary integrity of canonical Philippians.

But that is a hypothesis only. In fact, the two halves of the present letter are strikingly coherent, especially if viewed beneath the surface, as we have been attempting, at the level of Paul's emotional life. It is only the new beginning in 3:1b or 2 that suggests a complexity of origin, and it can be explained in other ways just as well by positing a later joining of two distinct letters.[38]

What is striking in the letter's second half is that Paul is dealing with the same personal issue as in chaps. 1 and 2: the question of his own standing before God and the world and whether he can and must hold onto that or just let it go.

If in this next material Paul at first (3:3-4) uses ideas very close to those to be found in Galatians (and again in Romans), it is nevertheless to be noted that the ideas of circumcision and flesh versus Spirit are present in a most condensed form, either as a summary or (I would argue) *in nuce*

226

before there has been occasion to spell them out.[39] Paul can already foresee the vocabulary by which he can refute his opponents on these issues, but he has not yet understood in any existential way its meaning for him (and all believers). He still intends, in effect, to achieve his own justification by making a supreme sacrifice comparable to Jesus'. That, as I have called it, is his illusion.

Let us explore the passage in question more closely. After his outburst against false teachers (3:2), those who evidently would impose circumcision on Gentile converts, Paul then in highly condensed, formulaic language identifies his opposing position (v. 3). This involves the dichotomy of flesh and Spirit, the former being not so much fundamentally worthless as inferior to the latter.[40] So having said that he, unlike his Judaizing opponents, would "put no confidence in the flesh," he can enumerate (as we shall see in a moment) the fleshly aspects of his life in which he legitimately might have put confidence.[41] Thus does Paul detail the sacrifice he will make, all that he might have been excused for holding on to, in short his very life. And he will do all this, he tells us, *"in order that I may gain* [kerdēsō] *Christ and be found in him"* (3:8d-9a, italics added).

In comparison to his later thought, the outrageousness of this claim is chillingly clear.[42] And it is not to be blunted or ignored because of the brief use of what sounds like Pauline orthodoxy that follows, again formulaically. He insists: "the righteousness I have is not from the Law but according to *pistis christou*, the righteousness of God [that comes from] faith" (9bc, author's trans.).*

Paul's claim then resumes. He has given up everything, he says, "so

---

*This dense clause, not even an independent sentence, requires the following observations: (a) "The righteousness I have is not from the Law" (lit. "having my righteousness, not from Law") seems to me the clear meaning of the text; RSV overtranslates, almost expurgates: "Not having a righteousness of my own, based on law." (b) The basis for the righteousness that Paul claims is not Torah, but rather *pistis christou*. Here we have what I take to be the earliest instance of a chief crux in Pauline interpretation: Is it to be understood as "faith in Christ" or as "Christ's faith"?[43] In every other occurrence I am convinced that the latter is decisively to be preferred. It is the trustworthiness of Christ, *his* faithfulness, that is the sole foundation of the world's justification. The only role of sinful humans is in accepting this proffered righteousness by faith. Paul almost always expresses the two poles of this imbalanced dialectic, the divine and the human,[44] and in that order. Is that not the case here as well: "The righteousness I have . . . that is . . . [based on] the faith of Christ, the righteousness of God [only accepted by our] faith" (author's trans.)? Very possibly. The only reasons to question that Paul has yet fully understood this utterly profound, fundamental Christian truth as he will, are the context surrounding this statement[45] and the preposition (*epi*, "upon," unusual for Paul) with the second instance of *pistis* and hinting that human faith is still seen as providing an essential basis for righteousness,[46] an idea Paul will later totally reject. But the issue can hardly be decisively resolved, and quite possibly the usual and more orthodox interpretation is to be preferred even here.

that I may know [Christ] and the power of his resurrection" (v. 10a, author's trans.). Usually this affirmation is understood in a spiritualizing way.[47] A similar understanding of the next clause ("and [know] the sharing of his sufferings, becoming like [him in] his death," v. 10b) most often prevails as well.[48]

But such interpretations will not do, for Paul draws the whole astonishing passage to a close: "*that by whatever means*[49] *I may attain*[50] *the raising up*[51] *from the dead*" (v. 11, author's trans.).

This surely is Paul's illusion at its most grandiose: that he can finally contribute to his own salvation, forcing his way through to it. He will accomplish this—here we must return to the verses we have skipped over—by the sacrifice of absolutely everything he has and is, even the standing he has in the world and under God, what he has called his "confidence in the flesh . . . greater than anyone's" (3:4b, author's trans.). And he dares to enumerate the grounds for that confidence:[52] validly circumcised, a member of God's Chosen People and of no mean part of it (the tribe of King Saul himself, whose name he bears), a pure Hebrew (tracing his bloodline to ancient times), belonging to the most illustrious party as to loyalty to God's will, so committed that he sought to expunge the heresy of the young Christian movement, and finally "as to righteousness under the Law [I have] *become blameless*" (3:5-6, author's trans.).

The irony here is unmistakable, but perhaps not entirely apparent to Paul himself. If he had not sacrificed all of this, might he still have claimed it? In any case, he *has* given all this up, as he goes on to say: "But whatever gain [*kerdē*] I had, that I have now counted—for the sake of Christ—as loss; in fact I count even all [other] things to be loss" (vv. 7-8a, author's trans.). Paul has forfeited everything—with one exception. He still holds on to his ability—perhaps he would say even his right—to make a sacrifice worthy of salvation, one like that of Jesus,[53] dying on the cross.

Paul's goal in all this, and therefore if need be his justification, is that he may "*gain Christ and be found in him* [with him, raised from death and in heaven]" (vv. 8d-9a, italics added). Paul shows his hand, some buried awareness of the extravagance of this hope, in the vehemence of what just precedes these phrases. On the one hand he validates both his immense sacrifice and the great hope he holds. It is grounded in "the surpassing worth of knowing Christ Jesus my Lord" (v. 8b). Who can fault that expectation? On the other hand, his audacity becomes excessive: "For his sake I have undergone the loss of everything; I regard [it] as excrement" (v. 8c). Paul's choice of words reveals the daring, perhaps also the conflict at some level, beneath his illusion.

I have said that there is a very close parallel between the mentality of the letter's first two chapters and this third. A clear difference seems to be that Paul can speak more confidently and with greater ease about both present and future in the letter's second half, and in most ways[54] even more modestly, despite the astonishing claim that culminates in 3:11. He goes to say (by way of concession?): "Not that I have already received this or am already perfected" (3:12a). He speaks of pressing on, straining forward, like a racer waiting at the mark or already in the race (vv. 12b-14) and commends this "mature" attitude to his readers with the hope that he and they may "hold true to what we have attained" (v. 14). It seems possible that Paul, by the time he adds this long postscript to chaps. 1 and 2, if such it be, has already learned that he is not to be put to death and, therefore, is beginning to take up again the life that, in his theological imagination, he had been willing and even eager to leave behind. Once again he must trust in only an eventual answer to all he needs and hopes for at the coming of Jesus. Thus, a few verses later, we find the lyrical passage:

> Our commonwealth is in heaven, and from it we await a Savior, the Lord Jesus Christ, who will change our lowly body to be like his glorious body, by the power which enables him even to subject all things to himself (3:20-21).

Note that Paul here implicitly distinguishes himself altogether from Jesus and his status, and Paul can now include himself in the general human need for a change in physical makeup in order to inherit the new age. Yet, the expectation that he can still contribute substantially to his own salvation sits squarely alongside.[55]

The lesson Paul is still to learn from his "despairing of life itself" when he was in Asia,[56] and from his unexpected escape from the "sentence of death" that he at least imagined to be his, presumably took place only somewhat later and in retrospect. If this depiction in the first chapter of 2 Corinthians describes his experience in Philippians, we see how it finally was forced upon Paul that he need not simply resume his old apocalyptic perspective, as evidently he does momentarily in Phil 3:20-21. Rather, he was both threatened by death and released from the threat, without any contribution of his own (he will quietly drop the outlandish theology of do-it-yourself resurrection) but solely based on the free gift of God, for "one has died for all,"[57] therefore *all have died*" (2 Cor 5:14, italics added); Paul need not force his way through death to a sacrificially deserved resurrection like that of Jesus; in fact, he cannot. Now anyone (not just Paul) who is "in Christ" has died with him. That person has now been raised with him, become "a new creature; the old has passed away, behold, the new has come" (2 Cor 5:17).

This, then, is the great watershed in Paul's theology. The self-achieved redemption of Philippians is never heard of again. It represents the last gasp of Paul's attempt to take credit, to believe that one must take responsibility, for contributing to one's salvation. It is this existential realization that finally gives body to the hitherto merely logical argument he must make against redemption by works, specifically against justification (and circumcision) under Law. Without the extreme grandiosity of Philippians and its aftermath, neither 2 Corinthians nor Galatians could have been written, and then not Romans as well.

Paul's egocentrism does not altogether die after this letter, and it did not surface there for the first time. What the letter—the experience and emotions underlying it, rather—will lead to is Paul's discovery, like Augustine and Luther after him, that humanity can contribute nothing to the accomplishment of its salvation, not even the negative and still egocentric contribution of giving up everything.

Yes, Philippians is surely Paul's most self-centered letter, the most subtly arrogant of all—before God and the world. (The honesty of Paul's display of shamelessness is almost admirable.) But it is not to be discounted, certainly not ignored. Within it are passages of great power and truth. That is due to the grace of which Paul is not yet truly aware. The glory belongs not to Paul but to God. Paul is but the fragile human vessel, typical of us all, through whom that grace, all unwitting, is made known.

Notes

1. J. C. Beker, "Paul's Theology: Consistent or Inconsistent?" *NTS* 34 (1988) 364-77, strongly disagrees.
2. I adopt a point of view and a chronological order for the letters similar to those of Charles H. Buck and Greer M. Taylor, Jr., in *Saint Paul: A Study in the Development of His Thought* (New York: Scribners, 1969), a work largely ignored by scholars. The hypothetical order of the letters used here is (2 Thess); 1 Thessalonians; 1 Corinthians; 2 Corinthians 10–13, Philippians, 2 Corinthians 1–7 (8–9), Galatians, Romans, (Colossians).
3. In this I do not have in mind the work of J. Louis Martyn, to whom I boldly and affectionately offer the following attempt to take another look at one of the Pauline letters.
4. See, again, Beker, "Paul's Theology," who denies such development, as is typical of the majority of Pauline interpreters today. A major exception is J. C. Hurd, notably in *The Origin of First Corinthians* (London: S.P.C.K., 1965).
5. In contrast to the other letters, where particular circumstances impelling Paul to write are usually patent, the need to thank the Philippians for their material support (during his imprisonment?) can hardly account for anything but a few lines in the last chapter; see below, n. 9.
6. That is, with 2 and 1 Thessalonians, 1 Corinthians, and 2 Corinthians 10–13 (see above, n. 2), but at the end of that group and on the verge of a theological breakthrough even greater than his conversion, leading to the unquestioned mature letters 2 Corinthians 1–7, Galatians, and Romans.
7. In this respect, too, Philippians shows that it belongs with the Thessalonian and early Corinthian correspondence, where, although the term *charis* appears, it is always used

in passing and most often in formulaic phrases. See Phil 1:2, 7; 4:23. See also 2 Thess 1:2, 12; 2:16; 3:18; 1 Thess 1:1; 5:28; 1 Cor 1:3-4; 3:10; 15:10; 16:23; 2 Cor 12:9 (but see below, n. 15); 13:13.

8. See further n. 20 below. This view of the emergence of Paul's theology is in my opinion not in the least incompatible with a profound concept of revelation.

9. Whose somewhat delayed material support he will only in the end get around to acknowledging and with not so subtle grudging (4:4-17).

10. See also P. F. Ellis: "Under the circumstances, one would expect Paul to put aside other matters and concentrate on preparing himself for death. Instead, he writes . . . a letter that is to Pauline letters what Moses' farewell address in Deuteronomy is to the Old Testament and what the Johannine Last Supper discourse is to the Gospels" (*Seven Pauline Letters* [Collegeville, Minn.: Liturgical Press, 1982] 115-16).

11. Formally, this major block of material comprises but the "Introduction" to the letter. But the fact that in thirty-six of the forty-three verses of these three chapters Paul speaks explicitly of himself shows that there he is already addressing what is chiefly on his mind.

12. Accepting 2 Thessalonians as authentically Pauline is almost totally out of fashion today, as the consensus expressed in the papers and discussion at the 1988 Leuven Biblical Days made clear. (See the forthcoming publication in BETL, and see also John Knox's essay in this volume.) But despite some elements in the letter that might seem to suggest a forgery (see the usual commentaries), I am convinced that the theology displayed in the letter jibes closely with what must have been Paul's earliest understanding of the good news—namely, a kind of typically Pharisaic future apocalyptic, altered mainly by the incorporation of Jesus for the principal role in the scenario of the End. In any case, however, although from time to time in illustrating a point I shall take 2 Thessalonians to be early, the argument made in the present study does not hinge on that letter's authenticity.

13. That is, not just the few who happen to die before the End, as in 1 Thessalonians. All humans have a need that, Jesus' resurrection shows, can and will be dealt with. The need, however, is as yet conceived of only as a physical flaw in the makeup of the natural human body.

14. The idea will surface in the latter half of the letter (3:20-21), where it applies to all the faithful, including Paul himself. Presumably by that time Paul no longer feels in immediate and desperate need of rescue.

15. In 2 Corinthians 10–13 Paul had developed at length such an understanding of opposition and suffering. Thus he could realize for the first time that God's grace is sufficient (12:9). But what God's grace means, especially as Paul contemplates his own death, is not yet clear in Philippians.

16. A term that not accidentally will be of special importance in this letter.

17. What is clearly implied here is that Paul, as appears often in this and other early letters, views his relation to his followers as set in a God-given hierarchy: "Imitate me as I have sought to imitate Christ" (1 Cor 11:1; see also 4:16; 2 Thess 3:7, 9; 1 Thess 1:6; Phil 3:17; 4:9).

18. The common pietism that always reads into Paul the best of thoughts usually makes the translation of v. 1 into something quite different from what the Greek, awkward as it is with its fourfold use of the conditional clause (often merged into one "If" in English), clearly says. Paul is speaking of the comfort that can come from God or Christ and which the Christian can count on receiving in time of need (the conditional being only a rhetorical device, as most agree).

19. "[The Judeans] who killed both the Lord Jesus and the prophets, and drove us out, and displease God and oppose all [people] by hindering us from speaking to the Gentiles that they be saved."

20. This focal passage, with its astonishing profundity, is a prime example of the way Paul so often happens upon both language and teaching that come to have permanent value ever after, but are occasioned (necessarily) by his own self-preoccupied need. In this case he defends himself in the only way he can against the evidently accurate charge that he is no competitor with the philosophical wisdom and rhetorical power

current in Corinth. Paul cites Jesus' crucifixion as only an instance of how wrong human perspectives, left to themselves, can be. See further, n. 33 below. (In much the same way, the resurrection of Jesus in 1 Corinthians 15 is an example of an apparently foolish idea that is nevertheless both true and theologically necessary.)

21. Thus I paraphrase the opening verses of chap. 2 in this way: "As the lyrical hymn I am about to quote to you plainly shows, we can thankfully count on Christ's example for relief for our (read "especially my") problems. Therefore, it would only add to my joy if also you were to settle the many differences among you. Join me in taking Christ Jesus to be our model, who—in the words of the hymn—'Though he was virtually God.' "

Paul still, as he had from the start, looks for the *activity* of Christ only in the apocalyptic future. (And, as both 1 Thessalonians and 1 Corinthians show, this is true whether or not 2 Thessalonians is an authentic early letter.) Here, too, in Philippians Paul views the experience of Jesus on the cross, not as accomplishing anything (except for Jesus himself, of course), but chiefly as an illustration of a previously unrecognized theological idea.

22. Despite the elapse of time since the crucifixion, at this point in Paul's thought it could still be accepted only as an expression of the incomprehensible purpose of God. This, in fact, was an advance over the earlier view that Jesus' execution was a profound embarrassment, a fact to be avoided or even denied (as undone by the resurrection), at the least to be apologized for.

23. Is it only Paul's daring to put himself in the same place as Jesus that evokes his own fear and trembling? We would like to think so.

24. His status was one within reach of divinity (so the extravagant christology of the hymn runs). Paul's own view of himself, for the mere human, is almost as lofty. He alone is within reach of what Jesus experienced.

25. Perhaps Paul adds this second instance of Jesus' self-sacrifice to make explicit its reference to his death. The image of obedience in particular may be Paul's, connecting the hymn to his own sense of a call to die like Jesus and also to the more superficial, moralistic application of the hymn he will make to his readers' situation (v. 12a).

26. This is evident from the emphatic and otherwise unnecessary "Therefore" (*dio kai*) with which it begins, and what follows is no mere conventional doxology.

27. The imperative is in present tense and so probably has either inceptive or durative force.

28. R. P. Martin, *The Epistle of Paul to the Philippians* (Tyndale NT Commentaries, 11; Grand Rapids: Eerdmans, 1959) 111: "The verb . . . is better rendered 'work at.' "

29. See above, n. 23.

30. The verb used (*katergazesthai*) is the emphatic of *ergazesthai* and means "bring about," "effect"; so J. P. Louw and E. A. Nida, eds., *Greek-English Lexicon of the New Testament Based on Semantic Domains* (New York: UBS, 1988) 150-51; see also Abbott-Smith, *Manual Greek Lexicon of the Greek New Testament* (3rd ed.; Edinburgh: T. and T. Clark, 1968) 240: "Effect by labor, achieve . . . bring about."

31. That he has a lesson in mind for them explains his way of beginning: "Therefore [again, as v. 9, but not so emphatically], my beloved, as you have always obeyed [me], so now . . . " (v. 12a).

32. I-J. Loh and E. A. Nida, *A Translator's Handbook on Paul's Letter to the Philippians* (New York: United Bible Societies, 1977) 67. The authors are right that Paul does not speak of the Philippians' "complete" responsibility for their "personal" salvation. But Paul is projecting his own concern for rescue from death onto the Philippian situation, so he cannot be thinking of "salvation," or rescue, in any superficial way. And to argue, as Loh and Nida do, that "Paul always speaks of personal salvation as the act of God" is to harmonize Paul's thought, to fail to let the distinctiveness—and the immaturity—of this particular letter speak out in its historical context.

33. This is true in spite of the superficially more "developed" interruption to come in 3:9.

34. Paul appears to put it modestly: "Even if I am to be poured out as [merely] a libation

232

upon the sacrificial offering of your faith." But he is not at all thinking of their dying (his own, rather), only of the metaphoric holy offering their faith constitutes.

35. Whose proclamation could be chosen as an instance of the foolishness of God, which is wiser than humans—see also 1 Cor 1:23: "We preach Christ crucified." Or does Paul exaggerate, even deceive himself, when he claims: "I decided to know nothing among you except Jesus Christ . . . crucified" (1 Cor 2:2)? In the light of the problem that the death of Jesus caused Paul and other early Christian writers it is more likely that in his initial preaching Paul mentioned the cross, if at all, only as a concession. But once he had been challenged about it in Corinth, together with the criticism (real or imagined) that he lacks philosophic wisdom and rhetorical eloquence, he brilliantly—if not quite accurately—maintains that it is just what seems weak and foolish to the Corinthians that he has always deliberately preached. Note that here, in Paul's perception, Jesus' death has not accomplished anything in history; it is only an example of how human knowledge is limited. But Paul's advance is to recognize that the cross, an eloquent example, has shown this to be true. See also n. 20 above.

36. If Philippians is a composite, the first two chapters would necessarily be earlier than chaps. 3 and 4.

37. The word for joy resonates with the word for (greetings and) farewells; so Loh and Nida, *Handbook*, 89.

38. For example, as an extended postscript, added when Paul (perhaps now released from prison) heard of a new set-back in his ongoing battle with the "Judaizers" over the Law, or when he simply remembered its threat to all his congregations, including that at Philippi. As we shall see, it soon gives way to the same kind of grandiosity as we find in chaps. 1 and 2.

39. They reflect the long and growing conflict over the place of the law of Moses in the matter of admission of Gentiles to the Christian movement, a conflict that would erupt fully only at the time of the writing of Galatians and would chiefly occasion that most polemical of Paul's letters. The issue in this part of Philippians and the way Paul deals with it can hardly have been written after Galatians.

40. "Flesh" for Paul most often means not so much the physical as what is mundane—the earthly, the merely empirical. Its opposite is not another and higher aspect of the human makeup, but God, through the agency of the Spirit. See my article on the habitual mistranslation of Rom 8:10 and similar passages, "Romans 8:10 and Paul's Doctrine of the Spirit," *ATR* 41 (1959) 77-84.

41. This is one of several passages in Paul's letters where he claims not to boast, even condemns boasting, yet manages to boast by pointing out what he might boast of if he were to allow himself—a clever rhetorical ruse! 2 Corinthians 10–13 is different. There Paul, calling himself a madman, eloquently boasts only of his flaws and weaknesses. (See above, n. 15.)

42. Does Paul perhaps confess retrospectively to the invalidity of this way of thinking in 2 Cor 5:16 ("From now on, therefore, we know [RSV "regard"] no one according to the flesh; if we once knew Christ according to the flesh, now [we do so] no longer;" author's trans.)?

43. In technical terms, an objective or a subjective genitive? See now M. Hooker, "Pistis Christou," *NTS* 35 (1989) 321-42.

44. If both poles are human ("righteousness . . . through [our] faith in Jesus Christ . . . to be received by [our] faith") there is no polarity, only a redundancy—and in passages where otherwise Paul is extremely spare with words.

45. A statement so at odds with the fuller expression of the concept of justification to be found in Galatians and Romans. The long intrusive phrase (v. 9bc) may be a later gloss, derived from a more fully developed stage of Paul's theology, as its interruption of what surrounds it might suggest; see vv. 8-9a and their obvious continuation in v. 10. But there is no manuscript evidence to support this possibility.

46. So G. F. Hawthorne, *Philippians* (Word Biblical Commentary, 43; Waco, Tex.: Word Books, 1983) 129, who paraphrases 9c: "The righteousness that is given by God and is obtained through faith."

47. Thus Loh and Nida, *Handbook*, 104, citing Romans and Ephesians: "*The power of his*

233

resurrection does not mean . . . the power of Christ by which Paul would be raised from the dead. Rather it refers to the power of the resurrected Christ which is at work in the life of the believer, raising him from death in sin to the new life in Christ." One is tempted to say, along with the newer materialist exegetes, that Paul has been made bourgeois by interpretations like this. But in fact Paul had to a large extent already made the gospel of Jesus into a spiritual, other-worldly message. That is true here, but my point is that one ought to do justice to the quite empirical *origin* of Paul's theology.

48. *"To share in his sufferings* refers most probably to an inward experience" (ibid., 105). Contrast Martin, *Philippians*, 149: "The . . . koinonia *of his sufferings* describes . . . the lot of the apostle who . . . represented Christ so realistically that his apostolic sufferings were regarded as an extension of the 'dying of Jesus. . . .' There can hardly be any other meaning of these verses, which so dramatically set forth the significance which Paul gives to his sufferings for Christ's sake." Martin does not, however, connect this meaning to Paul's immediate circumstance while writing Philippians.

49. The rough Greek *(ei pōs)* is stronger than RSV's "if possible." Paul's unswerving determination is clear.

50. Or "reach." The verb *katantan* has the connotation of getting to the bottom of a matter, going so far as necessary.

51. The noun with the unusual prefix *ex-* may emphasize Paul's personal involvement—like that of Jesus—in the resurrection.

52. In short, he boasts, violating what he has just said of Christians ("who . . . boast [only] in Christ Jesus and put no confidence in the flesh," 3*bc*, author's trans.). The RSV misleadingly translates v. 3*b*: "Who . . . glory in Christ Jesus," but the verb *kauchoun* is Paul's usual term for boasting.

53. *Mutatis mutandis*, we at least would like to add. Paul makes no such distinction.

54. Only excepting the overdetermined language we just saw.

55. So far as I know, no one would divide chap. 3 into part of different letters.

56. We have left aside the question of Paul's whereabouts when writing to the Philippians, but I would agree with the suggestion that he was in Ephesus, from which he set out for Troy. There at least he met Titus, who brought the good news of a reconciliation with the Corinthians, whereupon Paul wrote the so-called joyful letter of 2 Corinthians 1–7. At its beginning (1:8-9*a*) he describes his recent brush with death in Ephesus, about which he had written the Philippians.

57. Paul has used this phrase before, with the same preposition, but until now it appears to mean something more obvious: Jesus has died for [that is, because of the sins] of all. For the first time it comes to mean that Jesus has died *on behalf of, in place of* all; he has done their dying for them.

THE HYMN
OF THE COSMIC CHRIST

Walter Wink

For many years scholars have debated whether Col 1:15-20 was originally an independent Christ-hymn incorporated into the body of the Colossian epistle.[1] Thanks to the discovery of the *Tripartite Tractate* at Nag Hammadi, we can now demonstrate that it was indeed a hymn and that it was still actually being sung at the time this Gnostic tractate was written (possibly by Heracleon himself, fl. c. 145–180).

There have hitherto been very few objective criteria for determining whether there really is a Christ-hymn in Colossians. The reconstructions of the hymn that scholars have proposed have seldom been in agreement with one another. Indeed, a great deal of the discussion turns on suggested emendations, deletions, and poetic theories so subtle—and so at odds with one another—that more than one scholar has either given up the attempt at reconstruction or abandoned the notion that such a hymn existed altogether. But a strong case can be made for a hymnic structure even without the *Tripartite Tractate*.

Twenty reconstructions are conveniently graphed by Pierre Benoit.[2] Half of these can be dismissed at the outset because they fail to take into serious account the heavy dependence of the entire passage on the Wisdom of Solomon. No one doubts Wisdom's formative influence, but that influence should logically extend *either* to the original version *or* to the additions, not to both. The parallels are: Wis 1:14a (Col. 1:16a); 6:22c (Col 1:15b); 7:24b (Col 1:16f, 19); 7:26b (Col 1:15a)—these verses are assigned to the original version by the scholars whose reconstructions I dismissed above. The rest they assign to the redaction: Wis 1:7b; 8:1b (Col 1:17b); 5:23d; 6:21; 7:8; 9:12 (Col 1:16d); 7:29c (Col 1:17a, 18d). It makes far more sense to assume that all the allusions to Wisdom would have been developed at the same time by a single author; they are too explicit and too frequent to be accidental.

On the strength of the Wisdom parallels we can safely suggest then that Col 1:15-18a (up to "the church") was a part of the original. At that point Nestle-Aland[3] ends the hymn, treating the rest typographically as commentary. Others think that the hymn continues through v. 20. If we translate literally and lay out the Colossian hymn in poetic form, the rhyming of structures and the repetition of terms (which I have italicized) make it unmistakably clear that the hymn runs all the way through v. 20. This way of arranging the hymn also supports the hunch of so many scholars that "the church" in v. 18a and "through the blood of his cross" in v. 20b are interpolations. They are the only lines in the entire hymn that are lacking in italicized terms.[4]

(15a) *Who* is the image of the *invisible* God

  (b) *firstborn* of *all creation*

    (16a) *because in (en) him was created everything*

      (b) *in the heavens* and *on the earth*

      (c) *things* visible and *things invisible*

        (d) *whether* thrones *or* dominions

        (e) *whether* principalities *or* powers

          (f) *everything was created through* (dia) *him* and

                              for (eis) *him*

            (17a) and he is *before everything*

              (b) and *everything* coheres *in (en) him*

                (18a) and he is the head of the body

                        [the church].

(18b) *Who* is the *beginning*

  (c) *firstborn* from the dead

    (d) that he might be *pre-eminent* in *everything*

      (19) *because in* (en) *him all* the pleroma was pleased to dwell

        (20a) and *through* (dia) *him* to reconcile *everything*

                          for (eis) *him*

        (b) making peace [through the blood of his cross]

          (c) *whether things on the earth*

          (d) *whether things in the heavens.*

              (author's trans.)

If we connect all the repeated expressions in the hymn to each other with vertical lines, the sheer density of repetitions becomes even more impressive:

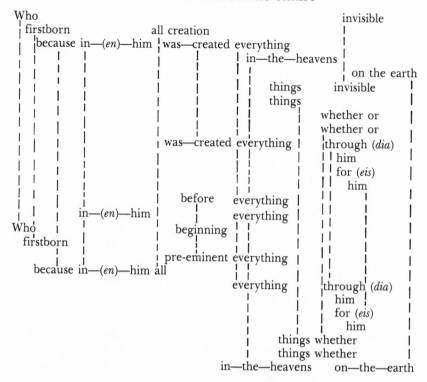

Without the *Tripartite Tractate*, this is about as far as sound exegesis can take us. Now we have stunning confirmation of all the essentials of the reconstruction proposed above. Sections 64-71 of the *Tripartite Tractate* appear to be an elaborate meditation on Col 1:15-20:

> and whom they speak about
> and the one toward whom they move
>   [compare "into (*eis*) him," Col 1:16-17, 20a]
> and the one in whom they are
>   [compare "in (*en*) him," Col 1:16a]
> and *the one whom they hymn*   (64:17-20)

As the last line indicates, the hymn was still being *sung* in this community. Indeed, the invisible Father has only become manifest in the one he has sent "so that he may be hymned because of the abundance of his sweetness" (63:26-28).

There are over a dozen other allusions to the Colossians hymn in this section of the tractate: "begotten" (64:23, 27; 66:7 = Col 1:15b); the first to exist (65:34; 66:11 = Col 1:15b, 17a, 18b); "the Totalities," equivalent to "thrones, dominions, principalities and authorities," over which the Father (= Christ in this section of the tractate) is exalted (64:29 = Col

1:16); archons and powers (66:23; 67:15; 71:5 = Col 1:16); all things are comprehended or encompassed by Christ (66:30; 68:36 = Col 1:17); they have come forth from knowledge and wisdom—that is, from Sophia or Christ (68:14-15 = Col 1:16); Christ is the "Father of the Totalities" (65:29-34; 67:11) which exist in a unified way in him (66:28-31; 67:33 = Col 1:16-18); the unknown Father whom the Son reveals is incomprehensible (64:30; 65:2-3 = Col 1:15). The Son (65:26 = Col 1:14) is "the preexistent" (65:34, 38 = Col 1:15*b*, 17*a*, 18*b*), "the face of the invisible" (66:14-15 = Col 1:15*a*)—unmistakable allusions to the Christ-hymn known to us in Colossians. The term *plēroma* appears in both (68:30; 70:1 = Col 1:19), and in both, more significantly, it is in the Son that the *plēroma* was pleased to dwell (67:7-11; 68:29-36; 69:41–70:1 = Col 1:19). Even the motif of "making peace" is shared (71:21 = Col 1:20), though there is, not surprisingly, no mention in this somewhat Gnostic treatise of the "blood of the cross." This may indicate that the community out of which the writer of this tractate came was still using the original form of the hymn, whereas Paul has altered it to adapt it to his own theology. Sophia is still remembered by the tractate (66:22; 68:13, 16), whereas she has been absorbed into the masculine Christ in the Colossians hymn; perhaps the hymn was originally sung to her.

Then, as suddenly as the tractate's allusions to the hymn began, they cease (end of 71). The author has exhausted this vein and turns elsewhere.

Further confirmation that the *Tripartite Tractate* is a self-conscious meditation on the same Christ-hymn that we find in Colossians is the fact that it draws its allusions from the hymn in largely the same order as the Colossians hymn, with only occasional anticipations and flashbacks. The order is as follows:

64:17-20	1:16*a*, 17, 20*a*	66:30	1:17
64:23	1:15	67:7-11	1:19
64:29	1:16	67:15	1:16
64:30	1:15	67:33	1:16-18
65:2-3	1:15	68:14-15	1:16
65:34	1:15*a*, 17*a*, 18*b*	68:29-30	1:19
65:38	1:17	68:36	1:17
66:7	1:15	69:41	1:19
66:11	1:15*a*, 17*a*, 18*b*	70:1	1:19
66:14-15	1:15	71:5	1:16
66:23	1:16	71:21	1:20
66:28-31	1:16-18		

Significantly, there are no references to "the church" and "through the blood of his cross" in the tractate's version of the hymn. Apparently they were not in the original, just as scholars had hypothesized.

We know from collections like the *Odes of Solomon* how important such singing was to the early church. The *Odes of Solomon* is a veritable hymnal, preserving forty-two odes or songs that extol singing as the most appropriate approach to God. A special class or charism existed for song writers (Odes 16:1-2: "My work is the Psalm of the Lord: my craft and my occupation one in His praises"[5]).

There are other such hymns to the principle of cosmic cohesion. One is the familiar Logos-prologue to the Fourth Gospel (John 1:1-18). Another has been interpolated into the apocryphal *Acts of John* (94:1–96:51), and here it is not only sung ("So he began to sing the hymn"), but also danced in the round with Jesus at the center, symbolizing synthesis and union with God incarnate:

> And we circled round him and answered him, "Amen."
> "Glory be to thee, Logos." (94:1)[6]

Such singing and circle-dancing was already a feature of the Jewish Therapeutae in Egypt in the early first century. Philo describes how they "seek wisdom" and "compose hymns and psalms to God in all sorts of metres and melodies which they write down in solemn rhythms as best they can" (*Vit. cont.* 28-29, LCL marginal reading). "Yearning for wisdom" (68), they study Scripture.

> Then the President rises and sings a hymn composed as an address to God, either a new one of his own composition or an old one by poets of an earlier day who have left behind them hymns in many measures and melodies, hexameters and iambics, lyrics suitable for processions or in libations and at the altars, or for the chorus whilst standing or dancing, with careful metrical arrangements to fit the various evolutions. . . . They all lift up their voices, men and women alike." (80)

They form "two choirs, one of men and one of women. . . . Then they sing hymns to God composed of many measures and set to many melodies, sometimes chanting together, sometimes taking up the harmony antiphonally, hands and feet keeping time in accompaniment." After choric dancing, they form a single choir and sing until dawn (83-89).

In the Nag Hammadi *Trimorphic Protennoia*, we find yet another rich lode of parallels to the Christ or Logos hymns in the New Testament. There is, however, no indication of hymnic form or usage in *Trimorphic Protennoia*, nor does it appear to be directly dependent on Colossians or John. Like the hymn in the *Tripartite Tractate*, it too is addressed to a female divine hypostasis, Protennoia, the "first thought" of the

Father.[7] Even though there is no direct evidence that the references to the cosmic principle in *Trimorphic Protennoia* were drawn from a hymn, they do give independent confirmation for the same kind of thought, and even expressions and turns of phrase, that we find in the hymns of Colossians and John. This suggests that *Trimorphic Protennoia* may be an exegesis or meditation on the same hymn-stock that lay behind the Christ-hymns of Colossians and John, though in the Gnostic document it is still centered on a female divine principle.

The new materials from Nag Hammadi show us worshipers devoutly praising the principle that holds all things together in unity. In a world in which local gods had been rendered ineffectual by the vastness of the empire, and where the cohesion of the polis had been replaced by the impersonal bureaucracy of a cosmopolis, such hymns affirmed that there was spiritual "glue" that would hold reality together against the threat of chaos.

Colossians 3:16 itself provides us an insider's view of the Colossian community itself at worship, singing hymns to the Logos-Sophia-Christ: "Let the word (*logos*) of Christ dwell in you richly, as you teach and admonish one another in all wisdom (*sophia*), and as you sing psalms (*psalmois*) and hymns (*hymnois*) and spiritual songs (*odais*) with thankfulness in your hearts to God."[8]

The theological consequences of our exegetical inquiry are crucial. The ancient Greek idea of the Logos congealing all reality around a single center of power is an essential presupposition of reason and science. Reality must be coherent if reason is to decipher it. But the Logos-idea has also been one of the chief instruments by which humanity has been rendered docile to the directives of its masters. In one of the earliest articulations of the Logos doctrine, Pythagoras asserted that a ruling principle was needed "in order to *control individuals* and offer to them and to the world in which they live a harmonious and just existence."[9] Notice how subtly Pythagoras shifts categories from a cosmic principle undergirding knowledge, to social structures capable of enforcing control. So quickly does knowledge become power!

Social control is necessary for any society, to be sure, but the institutional structures created to provide this control are seldom themselves subject to reciprocal controls. The very power they wield on behalf of all inevitably accrues to the benefit of but a few. The intuition of a principle of coherence all too easily translates into the political ideology of totalitarianism. The very intuition that seeks a harmonious and orderly universe all too often issues in a lust to totalize everything within a single hierarchical framework managed by an oligarchy. This is the spell of the cosmos, and under its thrall individuals are readily sacrificed to the good of the whole. "[It] is expedient for you that one man should die for the people, and that the whole nation should not perish" (John 11:50).

Even the God-image cannot escape the spell of the cosmos. Those who regard nature and society as an ascending hierarchy of power within an all-encompassing totality will inevitably conceive of God as a Being seated upon the pinnacle of this pyramid of power, justifying every evil as ultimately good and offering those who are crushed at the bottom a compensatory afterlife in a beyond for which the rulers themselves feel no need.

Paul (or whoever wrote the epistle) defeats this spell of the cosmos by two simple alterations to the hymn. The first is in a two word addition to v. 18a: "and he is the head of the body, *the church*." The second is his insertion of v. 20b: "making peace by the blood of his cross." He thereby changes Logos thought from a conservative legitimation of whatever-is-is-right, to a revolutionary image of total transformation.

The more fundamental of the two changes is Paul's reference to the blood of Jesus' cross. The principle of coherence has been crucified. The champions of law and order have crushed the bearer of cosmic order. The Logos is this finite, broken human. The meaning of the universe is this obscure Jew, living and dying among a subject people in a corner of a vast empire. The intelligibility of reality is not, then, abstract philosophical truths, but the drama of this peasant's execution by the Powers. If the Powers killed the living, breathing Logos-Sophia-Christ, then they are revealed to be, not defenders of the good, but demonic and rebellious usurpers. They are, in their essence, necessary and good; they have been created in, through, and for Christ (Col 1:16). But they are fallen, and they make their own self-interests the highest good. They are a "dominion of darkness" (Col 1:13). The crucifixion unmasks their idolatry and leads the Powers captive in God's triumphal procession (Col 2:15). They are still powerful, but they have been robbed of their unconscious compulsive power and their pretensions to sanctity. Now their works are out in the open, exposed for all to see.

It is not by chance, then, that the Hymn of the Cosmic Christ is flanked on either side by references to redemption (Col 1:14, 21-22). Fascination with the cosmos is thereby deliberately subordinated to the urgency of liberation. *The person is not subjected to the universe; rather the universe is subjected to a Person.* The ultimate value of the individual is now advocated and preserved in the One who was considered expendable by the Powers. Hence no one may be sacrificed to the whole. On the contrary, the whole suffers in the suffering of even its smallest part (see Luke 12:6-7). The Whole itself needed liberation from its proclivity to crush its parts. The Christ-image itself had to be cleansed of accrued dreams of domination and conquest, of kingship and revenge—a task that feminist and liberation theologians are finally helping us to complete. Wisdom as a divine hypostasis had to be rescued from prudential support of an autocratic status quo. The cold and heedless unity of the universe had to receive a heart, the cosmic process had to be given purpose, and the very image of God itself had to be humanized.

This brings us to Paul's other interpolation, the one in Col 1:18a: "and he is the head of the body, the church." This is his second thrust against the spell of the cosmos. Everything that has gone before this verse leads us to expect that the actual words in the original hymn ran, "He is the head of the body, the *cosmos*." The Logos would then be represented as the soul of the world, a theme frequently rehearsed in Stoicism. But if the real aim of the Logos, at least as far as it concerns human beings, is the emergence of true humanness, then what is needed is a matrix for the gestation of such people. The cosmos is no such matrix; only a human community committed to human emergence could be that. Making the possibility of true humanness known to those who do not recognize it, and liberation possible for those ready to receive it, and collective support against the continuing machinations of the Powers available for those who need it, requires something like a church.

The consequence of these slight emendations of the hymn are far-reaching. J. Christiaan Beker, for example, condemns the trend in the deutero-Pauline literature (he rejects the Pauline authorship of Colossians) toward cosmism, with its shift from eschatological to protological categories. He regards this as the abandonment of the radical dynamism of the hope of the imminent inbreaking of the triumph of God over the world's evil in the return of Christ.[10] That shift from eschatological radicalism to a focus on the orders of creation did indeed take place in Christendom. But it seems to me that the Colossians hymn brilliantly grounds the resurrection victory of God in Christ in the very fabric of the cosmos. Mythologically, it asserts that this was the *real* nature and intent of God from the very beginning of the universe, not an afterthought or a desperate expedient made necessary by creation's going sour. As such it *links* resurrection and creation, liberation and the very ground of being, protology and eschatology. If God is truly the Creator, these *must* be linked.

We cannot conclude without a final comment on the fact that this Hymn to the Cosmic Christ was sung. It was not composed primarily to inform, but to arm the faithful to carry their message to the very citadel of the Powers themselves. The early church sang its way through the Roman Empire, through persecution and estrangement and violent death. Theirs was a world no less derelict to its Center than ours, the evils they faced no less daunting. But they had songs that recalled them to a transcendent perspective so vast, so real, and so ultimate that not even the power of death could still their singing.

I remember hearing of a Native American woman who rejected an offer of companionship on her lonely walk home in the dead of night: "No, I won't be afraid. We have songs for this." There is another story, as well, of a man being crucified, crying out an old Israelite hymn sung by his people under duress:

> My God, my God, why hast
> thou forsaken me?

That hymn, sung to its close, ends in an affirmation of God's steadfast love:

> For [God] has not despised or abhorred
> the affliction of the afflicted . . .
> but has heard, when he cried to
> [God].   (Ps 22:24)

The Jew, too, could say, "We have songs for this."

We, too, even today—however evil the Powers may be, however resistant to change and violent they may be in their self-defense, however nimble and crafty they are in crushing opposition—we, too, thanks to the Colossians Christ-hymn, can say, "We have songs for this."

Notes

1. The bibliography on the hymnic structure of Col 1:15-20 is staggering. Pierre Benoit, O.P. ("L'hymne christologique de Col. 1, 15-20," in *Christianity, Judaism and Other Greco-Roman Cults* [Festschrift for Morton Smith; ed. Jacob Neusner; SJLA 12; 4 vols.; Leiden: E. J. Brill, 1975] 1:226-63) lists seventy-three titles, many of them monographs. Among the more valuable are D. von Allmen, "Reconciliation du monde et christologie cosmique, de II Cor. 5:14-21 à Col. 1:15-23," *Revue d'Histoire et de Philosophie Religieuses* 48 (1968) 32-45; J. M. Robinson, "A Formal Analysis of Col. 1.15-20," *JBL* 76 (1957) 270-87; Nikolaus Kehl, *Der Christushymnus im Kolosserbriefe. Eine motivgeschichtliche Untersuchung zu Kol 1:12-20* (Stuttgart: Verlag Katholisches Bibelwerk, 1967); Hans Jakob Gabathuler, *Jesus Christus: Haupt der Kirche—Haupt der Welt: Der Christhymnus Colosser 1:15-20 in der theologischen Forschung der letzten 130 Jahre* (Zurich: Zwingli Verlag, 1965); Frederic Manns, "Col. 1, 15-20: Midrash Chrétien de Gen. 1,1," *Revue des Sciences Religieuses* 53 (1979) 100-10; George E. Cannon, *The Use of Traditional Materials in Colossians* (Macon: Mercer University Press, 1983); A. Feuillet, "La Création de l'universe 'dans le Christ' d'après l'Epitre aux Colossiens (i.16a)," *NTS* 12 (1965-66) 1-9; R. Deichgraber, *Gotteshymnus und Christushymnus in der frühen Christenheit* (Göttingen: Vandenhoeck & Ruprecht, 1967) 143-55; Jack T. Sanders, *The New Testament Christological Hymns* (SNTSMS 15; Cambridge: Cambridge University Press, 1971); C. F. Burney, "Christ as the ARXH of Creation," *JTS* O. S. 27 (1926) 160-77.

2. See P. Benoit, "L'hymne christologique de Col. 1, 15-20." There is in Col 1:15-20 a remarkable number of *hapax legomena* in a mere six verses: seven unique terms plus two others used in a sense different from their meaning elsewhere in the NT. This is over twice the average for Paul (Romans: 269 HL in 433 vv.; 1 Corinthians: 226 in 437; Galatians: 83 in 149; Philippians: 67 in 104; Philemon: 10 in 25). John F. Balchin fails to do justice to the sheer density of HL here, though I agree with much of the rest of his debunking of the stylistic arguments for a hymn in Colossians 1 ("Colossians 1:15-20: An Early Christian Hymn? The Argument from Style," *Vox Evangelica* 15

[1985] 65-94). If Paul did not write Colossians, as many believe, these considerations of vocabulary become irrelevent. In other respects, however, the hypothesis that Col 1:15-20 is a hymn would stand no matter who wrote the epistle.

3. Nestle-Aland, *Novum Testamentum Graece* (26th ed.; Stuttgart: Deutsche Bibelstiftung, 1979).

4. The whole phrase, "through the blood of his cross," is actually omitted by both Basil and Chrysostom, which would make sense if they knew the whole passage by memory as a hymn better than they knew it as part of Colossians. J. C. O'Neill ("The Source of the Christology in Colossians," *NTS* 26 [1979] 87-100) argues that Col 1:15-20 is not a hymn but part of a series of excerpts from the public confessions of the community to which the author belonged. He overlooks the extent of parallelism in vv. 15-20, misinterprets the Powers in v. 16 as exclusively heavenly (see my *Naming the Powers* [Philadelphia: Fortress, 1984], Part 1), and unconvincingly excises all Christian references in Col 1:9-23 and 2:9-15 in order to ascribe them to a Jewish milieu. But these passages do seem to be patchworks of well-known exhortations and affirmations. Into precisely such a conglomerate it would be easy to read a hymn, and this appears to be what happened. Verses 18a and 20b are entirely lacking in italicized terms; perhaps they should be regarded as interpolations *in toto*. On the other hand, the logic of the hymn clearly builds toward the view that the Pantokrator is head of the cosmos, a common theme in Stoicism (Eduard Schweizer, *The Letter to the Colossians* [Minneapolis: Augsburg, 1982] 58 n. 9, 69 n. 37). And as to v. 20b, "making peace" is echoed in the *Tripartite Tractate*, as we shall see.

5. J. Rendall Harris's translation, *The Odes and Psalms of Solomon* (Cambridge: Cambridge University Press, 1909). See also Ode 6; 40:2-3; 41:16. Harris dates the Odes to the last quarter of the first century CE. Charlesworth places it anywhere from late first century CE to early second century CE (*The Old Testament Pseudepigrapha* [ed. James H. Charlesworth; 2 vols.; Garden City: Doubleday, 1985] 2:727). Apparently there was a virtual genre of hymns sung to the generative or unifying principle of reality, drawing on both Greek and Hebrew traditions and featuring Christ, Sophia, Logos, or the Son of Man. The Naassenes, for instance, "reverence beyond all others Man and the Son of Man. . . . A great many hymns of various kinds have been composed for him" (Hippol., *Ref.* V 6, 4-5 [trans. W. Foerster; *Gnosis*; Oxford: Clarendon Press, 1972] 1:263). That the hymn preserved in Colossians might originally have been addressed to Sophia is further suggested by the Nag Hammadi *Apocryphon of John*, where the divine Mother (2:14) is described as "the image of the invisible . . . the first thought, his image; she became the womb [or Mother] of everything, for she is prior to them all, the Mother-Father" (4:34–5:7).

6. E. Hennecke and W. Schneemelcher, eds., *New Testament Apocrypha* (2 vols.; Philadelphia: Westminster Press, 1964) 2:228.

7. I have supplemented my list of parallels to Col 1:15-20 and John 1:1-18 with those of Yvonne Janssens and Carsten Colpe, who, however, ignore the allusions to the Colossians hymn altogether. The Colossians parallels are italicized:

TriProt 35:2-6—"I am the movement that *dwells in the All*, she *in whom the All* takes its stand, the *first-born* among those who came to be, she who *exists before the All*" = Col 1:15b, 16a, 17a, 19 (reversed); John 1:3.

35:9—"the *Invisible One*" = Col 1:15a; John 1:18.

35:12—"I am the life" = John 1:4.

35:24—"*the Invisible One* within *the All*" = Col 1:16a, 19.

35:26—"*the All* exists *in it*" = Col 1:16, 17b, 19 (elsewhere, in 35:3, 11-20; 47:19-22, *TriProt* is pantheistic rather than, as here, panentheistic).

35:30-31—"I exist *before* the All, and I am *the All*, since I exist *before* everyone" = Col 1:15b, 16a, 17a.

35:33-34—"I exist *from the first*" = Col 1:15b, 17a; John 1:2.

36:5—"I shone down upon the darkness" = John 1:5.

37:4-14—"the Son . . . the Word . . . who was the first to leave the height . . . who is a

Light—(this Son) revealed the everlasting things . . . to those who dwell in darkness" = John 1:1, 5, 9; Phil 2:6.

37:19-20; 42:15-16; 49:25—"those who became Sons of the Light" = John 1:12.

37:32—(the Christ is) "the glory of *the Invisible* Spirit" = John 1:14.

38:10—"*the Invisible One*" = Col 1:15a.

38:11—"I am *the image of the Invisible* Spirit" = Col 1:15a.

38:12—"and it is *through me* that *the All* took shape" = Col 1:16-17.

38:17-18—"the Perfect Son revealed himself to his Aeons who originated through him" = Col 1:16 (the Powers).

39:12-13—"the Perfect Son, the God who was *begotten*" = Col 1:15b; compare John 3:16.

40:12—"I am coming down to the world of mortals" = John 1:14; Phil 2:6-7.

40:31, 36; 41:15-16, 27-28; 45:28-29—"I was with my own . . . to those who are mine" etc. = John 1:11.

41:32-33—"I went down to those who were mine from the first" = John 1:11.

42:6—"*the Invisible One*" = Col 1:15a.

45:6-7 (see also 38:15)—"I am *the Womb* that gives shape to *the All*" = Col 1:16a ("in him/her"), 19.

46:5, 14—"I am the Word" = John 1:1

46:30-32—"a Word . . . sent to illumine those who dwell in the darkness" = John 1:1-5.

47:14-16—"I revealed myself to them in their tents as the Word and I revealed myself in the likeness of their shape" = John 1:14.

47:18-19—"they did not know the one who empowers me" = John 1:10.

47:24—"And none of them (the Powers) knew me, although it is I who work in them" = John 1:10-11.

47:28-32—"I am the Light that illumines *the All*. I am the Light that rejoices in my brethren, for I came down to the world of mortals," etc. = John 1:4, 9b, 14; Col 1:19.

48:6-35 = Phil 2:9-10.

49:12-13—"I clothed myself as the Son of the Archigenetor" = John 1:14.

50:12-13—"I put on Jesus" = John 1:14.

50:15-16—"(they) did not recognize me" = John 1:10.

Total = 27 allusions to John 1:1-18, 14 to Col 1:15-20, 3 to Phil 2:5-11.

Unlike the *Tripartite Tractate,* the sequence of references to the cosmic principle in the *Trimorphic Protennoia* has no correlation with their use in the Colossians or Johannine hymns, except that the author does tend to draw on the hymn that lies behind Colossians first (of the thirty-eight allusions listed, parallels to Colossians appear in numbers 1-2, 4-7, 12-16, 23, 25, 33) and then shifts to the hymn underlying John's prologue. Otherwise, the order of their use appears largely random.

On the *Trimorphic Protennoia,* see the Berliner Arbeitskreis für koptisch-gnostische Schriften, "Die dreigestaltige Protennoia," *TLZ* 99 (1974) 731-46; Yvonne Janssens, "Une source gnostique du Prologue?" *L'Évangile de Jean: Sources, rédaction, théologie* (BETL 44; Gembloux: Louvain University Press, 1977) 355-58; Janssens, "The Trimorphic Protennoia and the Fourth Gospel," in *The New Testament and Gnosis* (R. McL. Wilson Festschrift; eds. A. H. B. Logan and A. J. M. Wedderburn; Edinburgh: T. & T. Clark, 1983) 229-44; Carsten Colpe, "Heidnische, judische und christliche Überlieferung in den Schriften aus Nag Hammadi III," *JAC* 17 (1974) 122-24. See also James M. Robinson, "Sethians and Johannine Thought," plus the helpful discussion in Bentley Layton, ed., *The Rediscovery of Gnosticism* (Vol. 2, *Sethian Gnosticism*; Leiden: E. J. Brill, 1981) 643-70.

8. In Col 3:16 the use of *logos* and *sophia* is only allusive, not titular, as also in 1:25-28: "to make the word (*logos*) of God fully known . . . teaching everyone in all wisdom (*sophia*)." See also Eph 5:19.

9. Arnold Ehrhardt, *The Beginning: A Study in the Greek Philosophical Approach to the Concept of Creation from Anaximander to St. John* (Manchester: Manchester University Press, 1968) 46.

10. J. Christiaan Beker, *Paul the Apostle* (Philadelphia: Fortress, 1980) 158.

DID THE THESSALONIANS
WRITE TO PAUL?

Abraham J. Malherbe

aul chose letters as the means by which to address the issues that engaged him and his churches. Other forms of literature that he could have used, such as treatises or epitomes, conceivably would have shown us how he treated subjects systematically or didactically rather than argumentatively. His letters, on the other hand, draw attention to him as a communicator as much as a theologian, and the epistolographic and rhetorical examination of his letters has attained a firm place in Pauline studies. Paul's conversation partners in his correspondence, by contrast, are generally regarded merely as the recipients of his letters, and with few exceptions are not viewed as communicators in their own right. This is not due to the myopia of Pauline scholars, but rather to the fact that Paul only seldom comments on communication he received from his churches.[1] The subject requires an imaginative approach, and 1 Thessalonians has been so approached.

1 Thessalonians is the earliest extant Pauline letter, and thus the earliest preserved Christian writing. It may in fact be the first letter Paul wrote to a church, but that is beyond proof.[2] Nevertheless, in 1 Thessalonians Paul is continuing a conversation with the Thessalonians that had begun with his arrival in their city months earlier.[3] This letter, however, does not only continue the conversation, but it has also been thought to provide information about earlier communication between Paul and the Thessalonians.

Correspondence Before 1 Thessalonians?

We should note at the outset that Paul mentions no communication, either oral or written, that had occurred between himself and the Thessalonians in the interval between his departure from Thessalonica and the writing of 1 Thessalonians. He had sent Timothy to Thessalonica from Athens (1 Thess 3:1-2), but he gives no indication that he had done so in response to anything that he had heard from or about the Thessalonians.[4] Rather, according to Paul, it was his anxiety about the Thessalonians' faith that compelled him to reestablish contact with them (2:17–3:5). His comments on Timothy's mission stress that he wanted, by means of Timothy, to strengthen their faith (3:2, 5) and ascertain whether they still looked to him as their teacher (3:6), but he provides no explicit information about any letter that he might have written or even any message that he might have sent them.[5]

Rendel Harris, however, surmised that already on this occasion Timothy carried a letter from Paul to the Thessalonians, traces of which Harris thought are discernible in 1 Thessalonians.[6] This letter would have stressed Paul's desire to see them (2:17; 3:2, 6) and his concern whether his work with them had been in vain (3:5). That such concerns were conveyed by Timothy is surely likely. In the absence of stronger evidence, however, Harris's suggestion of a letter has not met with favor.

Harris also advanced the hypothesis that the Thessalonians responded to Paul in a letter that was brought to him in Corinth by Timothy (Acts 18:5), to which 1 Thessalonians was the reply.[7] Harris found evidence of this letter in elements of epistolary form as well as the content of 1 Thessalonians. As to epistolary form, Harris considered "you always have a good remembrance of us" (3:6) and "we also [as you do in your letter] thank God constantly for this" (2:13) to be references to the thanksgiving period of the letter (see 1:2). As to the content of 1 Thessalonians, Harris thought that the repeated statements that the readers knew what Paul was saying (1:5; 2:1-2; 3:3; 4:2), and that they remembered (2:9), made it possible to reconstruct their letter to Paul.

Chalmer Faw regarded Harris's suggestion as ingenious, but judged his evidence elusive.[8] Faw thought that other elements of the form and content of 1 Thessalonians provided stronger evidence of a prior letter from the Thessalonians.

1. Faw held that the introduction of a series of comments with *peri de* (4:9, 13; 5:1) or *de* (5:12) compares with 1 Cor 7:1, 25; 8:1; 12:1; 16:1, 12, which are generally thought to introduce Paul's responses to written inquiries from the Corinthians (see 1 Cor 7:1). It is only in 1 Corinthians and 1 Thessalonians that Paul uses *peri de*, but elsewhere in the NT it also very specifically has to do with replies (Mark 12:26; 13:32; John 16:11; Acts 21:25).

2. Faw further argued that the transitions at 4:9, 13 and 5:12 would be very abrupt if they were not responses. More important, Paul is reluctant to discuss brotherly love and the times and seasons (4:9; 5:1)

and does so only because his readers had asked him for advice on these matters, but even then he goes on to tell them to continue in what they were already doing (4:1, 2, 10). The content of the Thessalonians' letter, which would have been written by their leaders (5:12), can be determined, according to Faw, primarily from chaps. 4 and 5, and dealt with brotherly love (4:9-12), Christians who had died (4:13-18), and the time of the end (5:1-11). The letter would have been supplemented by Timothy's report, echoes of which are found in chaps. 1–3, particularly in comments revolving around thanksgiving and personal defense, although it is not always possible to distinguish Paul's two sources of information.

The hypothesis of a letter from the Thessalonians has been accepted by some interpreters, regarded as possible by others, and as improbable by perhaps the majority.[9] The objections most frequently raised are that Paul would have mentioned such a letter at 3:6 and that too much weight is attached to *peri de* on the basis of 1 Cor 7:1: "one example of Paul's method does not create an essential pattern."[10] To these could be added the fact that Paul's references to what his readers knew are not allusions to a letter but belong to the paraenetic style in which 1 Thessalonians is written. Furthermore, the epistolographic conventions require closer investigation, especially in the context of ancient epistolographic practice, than they have received. I have elsewhere examined the letter's paraenetic style.[11] Here I wish to look more closely at epistolographic conventions.

An Earlier Letter to the Thessalonians?

An investigation of epistolographic conventions, especially in 2:17–3:10, which reflects the historical situation in which 1 Thessalonians was written, reveals significantly more such elements than have been identified perviously.[12]

We look first at Paul's comments about the sending of Timothy, thus at the occasion on which he may have written to the Thessalonians, as was suggested by Harris.

1. Paul's description of the letter's setting concludes the autobiographical section of the letter (chaps. 1–3) and constitutes its climax.[13] It is bracketed by statements lamenting Paul's involuntary separation from the Thessalonians and assurances that he wishes to see them face to face (2:17; 3:10). When Paul could bear this separation no longer, he sent Timothy (3:1). The themes of enforced bodily absence but spiritual presence and a desire to see one's correspondents were standard features in epistolographic theory and practice, as seen, for example, in

PLond Bell 1926, 17-18: "Even though in body I have not come to your feet, yet in spirit I have come to your feet."[14] These themes are also reflected elsewhere in Paul.[15] Such statements appear in correspondence between family members and friends, and 1 Thessalonians has much in common with such letters.[16] The reason for writing in this style was that writers thought "that nobody [would] refuse them when they [wrote] in a friendly manner, but [would] rather submit and heed what they [were] writing."[17] Paul has adopted features of the style of the friendly letter to express his feelings toward the Thessalonians and to set the tone for the advice he will give them in chaps. 4 and 5.

2. In friendly and family letters writers frequently emphasized their loneliness by drawing attention to their family relationships, as two examples illustrate.[18] In BGU 385, 4-6, a daughter writes to her father: "I want you to know that I am alone. Keep in your thoughts, 'I have a daughter in Alexandria,' so that I too might know that I have a father, lest I be regarded as without parents." In PSI 1161, 11-19, a woman bemoans her loneliness in a letter to her mother: "I have no one with me, neither sister nor brother nor son, no one but God. I urge you, my mother and lady, remember me even if (only) for one day, lest I die in a strange land without anyone." Paul conveys the same feeling of loneliness when he introduces this section of the letter by saying that he "had been orphaned [aporphanisthentes] by being separated from" the Thessalonians (2:17) and by calling attention to his having been left alone in Athens.[19]

3. Paul's reference to himself by name (2:18), which is unusual for him in the body of a letter (compare Philemon 9), also finds its counterparts in friendly letters, where such references express a particularly close relationship, although in these letters they appear toward the end of the letter.[20]

These epistolographic elements express Paul's emotional need for communication, as they do in other ancient letters.[21] They are precisely the kinds of statements that would have been natural in a letter written in Paul's circumstances, and may seem to lend further support to Harris's suggestion that Paul had sent a letter to the Thessalonians with Timothy. However, two facts speak against Harris's hypothesis. First, the epistolographic elements I have identified are not related to written communication, but to Timothy's mission. Second, these elements do not appear in a letter in which a writer attempts to reestablish contact, as they normally do, but in one that comments on how renewed contact had been effected. We should, therefore, ask how these statements function in 1 Thessalonians, but before we do so we must examine Paul's comments on Timothy's return.

A Letter from the Thessalonians?

Paul's account of Timothy's return (3:6) is confined to Timothy's report about the Thessalonians, and does not mention any sort of communication from them. It does, however, continue the pathos with which Paul had expressed his constant desire to remain in contact with the Thessalonians, and it contains epistolographic elements, only some of which have been noted before, that may support the hypothesis that Timothy had brought Paul a letter from them. There are two sets of epistolographic elements that come under consideration.

The Report About the Thessalonians

We turn first to the epistolographic elements that have been identified and to Paul's characterization of Timothy's report, which is also given in epistolographic terms.

1. Ancient letters teem with expressions of longing (*pothos*) for absent friends.[22] Timothy brought Paul the good news that the Thessalonians yearned (*epipothountes*) to see him, thus reciprocating Paul's longing for them (3:6).

2. A letter was proof that one had not been forgotten, and letters of friendship stress the constant remembrance in which friends were held.[23] Timothy brought the good news that Paul's converts constantly held him "in good remembrance" (3:6).[24]

These two epistolographic elements describe precisely the circumstances in which friendly letters were said to have been written, and they would have been perfectly at home in a letter written to Paul. That they appear in a letter written by Paul and not the Thessalonians does pose a problem, but that Paul uses epistolographic clichés to describe their mood and attitude supports the surmise that they had communicated with him by letter, particularly if it could be shown that he elsewhere appropriates clichés from his correspondents' letters. The surmise would be further strengthened if it could be shown that Paul elsewhere uses such language to describe a mediator's report about a church while remaining silent about a letter that the mediator had brought from the church. Paul in fact does so, and we shall consider such cases. For now, we note that, in addition to the description of Timothy's report, other epistolographic elements may point to a letter from the Thessalonians.

3. The strongest case for a Thessalonian letter, in epistolographic terms, has been made on the basis of the use of *peri de* (4:9, 13; 5:1). Taken by itself, this evidence is inconclusive. The main proof that *peri de* introduces a response to a written inquiry is derived from 1 Cor 7:1 and the assumption, generally held, that subsequent occurrences of *peri de* or

de in 1 Corinthians (7:25; 8:1; 12:1; 16:1, 12) refer to items brought up in the Corinthians' letter to Paul. That assumption itself should be called into question, however, particularly when it is observed that *peri de* is used in letters in a number of different ways: (a) It frequently occurs in papyrus and other letters as well as treatises simply to introduce a new topic.[25] This does not, however, decisively contradict, as is sometimes thought,[26] the possibility that Paul is responding to a letter. (b) While *peri* with or without *de* does not necessarily introduce a reply to a written request, it does so at times.[27] (c) It also introduces a response to an oral report.[28] On occasion it is not clear whether it introduces a reply to a written or an oral report. PEleph 13 provides an instructive example with parallels to 1 Thessalonians:[29]

> Andron to his brother Milon greeting. If you are well and everything is to your mind, it would be as I desire. I myself am in good health. On the arrival of Sanos I received your letter, and it was a pleasure to read it and hear your news.

Compare 1 Thess 3:6-9, Paul's joy over Timothy's arrival with good news. Andron continues by expressing his willingness to meet any need of the bearer of the letter, and matters are then taken up that may have been communicated in the letter or by the bearer:

> About the twenty drachmae [*peri de tōn eikosi drachmōn*], Phlion has not yet received them, for we have not found Pistocles. About the wine [*peri de tou oinariou*], Praxiades has not yet come in from the country, but from what his mother tells me. . . . "

Compare 1 Thess 4:9, 13; 5:1. It is not clear whether Andron uses *peri de* to introduce his replies to inquiries in Milon's letter, or whether *peri de* introduces topics of interest to Milon about which Andron had heard from Sanos or Praxiades's mother. The letter concludes with an assurance that the writer is prepared to render further assistance, which is equivalent to the polite formula offering to meet a friend's need:[30] "Now you will do me a favor if you take care of yourself and do not hesitate to write and tell me what I can do to please you." In correspondence, then, *peri de* can, but does not necessarily, refer to a written request. In the absence of supporting evidence, 1 Thessalonians cannot be read as proof that Paul is replying to a letter from the Thessalonians.

4. One bit of evidence that has received insufficient attention is the epistolographic convention of referring to a correspondent's needs. It was common for friends to express in letters their need (*chreia*) for advice—or for anything else, for that matter.[31] The preparedness to do

so was enhanced by epistolary clichés expressing the desire of friends to be helpful. Frequently little more than perfunctory expressions of politeness,[32] especially in official correspondence, such clichés nevertheless appear in genuine invitations to readers to make requests of writers. From countless examples, we note two: POxy 930, "do not hesitate to write me about anything of which you may have need [*peri hōn ean chreian echeis*]," and PSI 333, "And please write yourself if you ever have need of anything here [*ean tinos tōn kath' hēmas chreian echeis*]."[33] Either in reply to such an invitation, or simply because of a friendly relationship with the reader, a correspondent might write for something he or she needs, such as in PCairo Zen 59426: "For I have need [*chreian gar echō*] of it for my eyes." On two occasions Paul assures the Thessalonians that they have no need (*ou chreian echete*) to be written to about brotherly love and the last days (4:9; 5:1). In the light of the epistolographic practice of referring to one's correspondent's needs, it is not unreasonable to understand these references, as Faw did, as reflecting the Thessalonians' written requests for information. Thus Paul would be replying to a letter. Once again, however, the evidence is inconclusive, especially since these statements function paraenetically and are of a piece with other assurances in the letter that the Thessalonians already have knowledge of essentials.[34] Its value would be considerably enhanced if evidence were available that Paul did in fact recognize real needs and addressed them in 1 Thessalonians.

Paul's Reception of Timothy's Report

The epistolographic elements related to the Thessalonians' communication are supplemented by others relating to Paul's reception of their communication.

1. As it was standard to express joy upon the receipt of a letter,[35] so Paul says that he is overjoyed upon learning of the Thessalonians' attitude toward him and the condition of their faith (3:9).

2. As ancient writers thanked the gods that communication had been affected,[36] so does Paul thank God (3:9).

3. The most important evidence for a Thessalonian letter is found in Paul's statement at the end of his account of Timothy's return (3:10) that Paul prayed night and day to see the Thessalonians face to face and to supply what was lacking (*katartisai ta hysterēmata*) in their faith. His enforced absence made him turn to a letter to meet their needs, although he does not explicitly mention the letter he is writing. This opinion, held by all commentators I know, is supported by the fact that the preoccupation, night and day, with the inability to see one's correspondent in person, and a view of one's letter as a surrogate for one's physical presence, are well-known epistolographic conventions.[37]

What is noteworthy for our purpose is that Paul describes himself in these terms, which usually provide reasons for writing a letter, but does not mention a letter. It is this fact, which turns out not to be a lone occurrence, that suggests that the report Paul ascribes to Timothy in v. 6 could have been conveyed in a letter Timothy brought from the Thessalonians.

This possibility receives support from a closer examination of what Paul says about his intention in v. 10 and from two parallel passages. Rather than mention his own letter, Paul speaks of wishing to supply a lack in his readers' faith. The expression of a writer's desire to fill or meet a correspondent's need by means of a letter is, however, another epistolographic cliché that has not been introduced into the discussion. It requires more attention than I can give it here, but the following examples may be sufficient to demonstrate Paul's practice of not always mentioning letters, but rather of referring to individuals who carried letters between himself and his churches.

By means of a letter one was thought to satisfy or supply the want (*apoplēroun to endeon*) caused by one's physical separation from one's readers.[38] Stated in another way, a letter completes or substitutes for a writer's physical presence (*dia grammatōn plērō ta tēs parousias*).[39] Paul does not here use a form of *plēroun*, but *katartizein* is related and forms the same epistolary function. So does Seneca's *satis facere,* in his response to Lucilius's request for moral guidance: "I shall fulfil your want [*desiderio tuo satis faciam*], encouraging your virtues and lashing your vices" (*Epistle* 121.4). As we have seen, specific needs like these are frequently mentioned and described as *chreia.* The verb *chrēzein* is also used frequently, as is *hysterein,* which functions as an equivalent in letters.[40] PMerton 83, 23-24 illustrates how *hysterein* may function in an epistolary exchange. The letter concludes: "If you wish me to give (the money), write me and I shall send whatever you need (*chrēzeis*). . . . So as soon as you receive this letter, write back to us . . . so that you will not lack whatever you need (*hou ean chrēzeis mē hysterēsēs*).

Such conventional language supports the opinion that Paul in 3:10 refers to what he would write in chaps. 4 and 5 in response to the Thessalonians' needs. It does not yet, however, prove that those needs were expressed in a letter from Thessalonica. The objection that he does not mention such a letter is partly weakened by the fact that neither does he in 3:10 refer to his own letter. It is further weakened by two other texts in which Paul does not explicitly mention a letter although he has one in mind. These texts also happen to use the convention of supplying a readers' need, but they differ from 3:10 in that they express the intentions of Paul's correspondents, not his own. The reason for drawing attention to them is not to suggest that the Thessalonians had written to Paul with the purpose of fulfilling his needs. Rather, I introduce these texts into the discussion because they also leave letters unmentioned. That they use this particular convention is coincidental.

In 1 Cor 16:17 Paul expresses his joy over the arrival (*parousia*) of Stephanas, Fortunatus, and Achaicus, for they had supplied the needs of the Corinthians (*to hymeteron hysterēma . . . aneplērōsan*) by refreshing both his spirit and that of the Corinthians. Paul does not mention a letter, but the epistolographic formula suggests that he does have a letter in mind that they had brought him from Corinth. Indeed, on the basis of historical reconstruction, the view generally held by students of 2 Corinthians is that Stephanas was the bearer of the letter in which the Corinthians asked Paul for advice.[41] Yet, instead of mentioning the letter, Paul applies the epistolographic language to the bearer(s) of the letter. That letter thus performed two functions: First, it satisfied the need of the Corinthians that was caused by their separation from him. So Paul stresses the mutuality of affection that was strengthened by the delegation and probably their delivery of the letter. Second, the letter was also a means by which the Corinthians expressed their need for advice (7:1). Timothy's report to Paul about the Thessalonians accomplished at least the former, and probably the second as well.

The other text is Phil 2:25-30, which speaks of Epaphroditus, who is usually thought to have been the bearer of a letter from Paul to the Philippians, although that is not expressly stated.[42] The commendation of Epaphroditus is introduced with "I thought it necessary to send" (*anagkaion hēgēsamēn pempsai*), a phrase Koskenniemi has identified as an "*aphormē* formula," which was used to introduce an intermediary who was also a bearer of a letter.[43] Paul uses other epistolographic conventions in describing Epaphroditus and his mission: Epaphroditus yearned (*epipothōn*) for the Philippians and was distressed about them, and Paul sends Epaphroditus so that he and the Philippians might be reunited and so rejoice. So, once again, the bearer of a letter is described in epistolographic terms, while the letter is not mentioned at all.

Equally striking about Phil 2:25-30 is that two references to the correspondents' need frame the text, thus forming an *inclusio*, and both references deal with Epaphroditus's role as the Philippians' delegate to Paul. In v. 25, he is their messenger and minister to Paul's *chreia*, and in v. 30 the purpose of his mission is identified as fulfilling their need (*anaplēroun to hymōn hysterēma*) in their ministry to Paul. This is, then, another instance in which an intermediary's function is described in terms normally used of letters. It is not only possible, but highly likely, that Epaphroditus had brought Paul a letter, in addition to the contribution, from the Philippians.[44]

These texts clearly show that Paul on these occasions does not mention letters, although in each case the intermediaries he does mention carried letters between himself and his churches. They further show that Paul was in the habit of using epistolographic clichés, sometimes from letters he received from his churches, to describe the carriers and their reports.

Conclusion

Paul uses epistolographic clichés to an exceptional degree when he describes Timothy's work as an intermediary between himself and the Thessalonians. These clichés reflect the freedom with which friends expressed their needs to each other and the preparedness of friends to meet each others' needs. Although Paul does not mention earlier correspondence between himself and the Thessalonians, it is quite possible that he had written to them when he first sent Timothy to them, and it is highly probable that they in return wrote him for advice. That he does not mention these letters, especially the one from Thessalonica, should not be surprising, for he elsewhere does not mention letters where he could have been expected to do so.

An awareness of the clichés is important exegetically, for they impress one with the desire of both parties to remain in contact with each other. Despite being clichés, they are part of the pathos with which Paul, always on the run, could not let go of the little community he had founded in Macedonia, and they disclose that church's effort to hold on to Paul and his guidance. Paul, through Timothy's report and their letter, was well informed about their needs and addressed them in 1 Thessalonians.

Notes

1. For the difficulties in connection with 1 Corinthians, which provides more information than any other Pauline letter, see N. A. Dahl, "Paul and the Church in Corinth According to 1 Corinthians 1–4," in *Christian History and Interpretation: Studies Presented to John Knox* (eds. W. R. Farmer, C. F. D. Moule, and R. R. Niebuhr; Cambridge: Cambridge University Press, 1967) 313-35.
2. For discussion of 1 Thessalonians as the earliest letter, see: W. G. Kümmel, *Introduction to the New Testament* (rev. ed.; trans. H. C. Kee; Nashville: Abingdon, 1975) 257; W. Marxsen, *Der erste Brief an die Thessalonicher* (Zürcher Bibelkommentare: NT 11, 1; Zurich: Theologischer Verlag, 1979) 15; P. Vielhauer, *Geschichte der urchristlichen Literatur* (Berlin: W. de Gruyter, 1975) 82. For discussion of it as the earliest preserved Christian writing, see: E. von Dobschütz, *Die Thessalonicherbriefe* (KEK 10; Göttingen: Vandenhoeck & Ruprecht, 1909) 18-19.
3. For the ancient view of a letter as one-half of a dialogue, see, for example, Demetrius, *On Style*, 223; Cicero, *To His Friends* 12.30.1. The texts are available in A. J. Malherbe, *Ancient Epistolary Theorists* (SBLSBS 19; Atlanta: Scholars Press, 1988). Marxsen, *Der erste Thessalonicherbrief*, 9-11, stresses the ongoing conversation between Paul and his recent converts.
4. Paul had heard about their circumstances (see 1 Thess 1:7-10; 2:14), but he does not

relate Timothy's mission to this news. For the purpose of this essay, the account of Acts 17:10–18:5 may be left aside.

5. See the fuller discussion in my forthcoming commentary on the Thessalonian correspondence in the Anchor Bible. For a preliminary statement, see A. J. Malherbe, *Paul and the Thessalonians: The Philosophic Tradition of Pastoral Care* (Philadelphia: Fortress, 1987) 62-68.

6. J. R. Harris, "A Study in Letter-Writing," *The Expositor*, 5th ser., 8 (1898) 193.

7. Ibid., 167-73.

8. C. E. Faw, "On the Writing of First Thessalonians," *JBL* 71 (1952) 217-25. See also J. Moffatt, *An Introduction to the Literature of the New Testament* (New York: Charles Scribner's Sons, 1925) 67.

9. For example, accepted by J. E. Frame, *The Epistles of St. Paul to the Thessalonians* (ICC; Edinburgh: T. & T. Clark, 1912) 9, 107; C. Masson, *Les deux épîtres de Saint Paul aux Thessaloniciens* (CNT 11A; Neuchatel/Paris: Delachaux & Niestlé, 1957) 7-8, 66; E. Fuchs, "Hermeneutik?" *Theologia Viatorum* 7 (1960) 44-60; regarded as possible by G. Milligan, *St. Paul's Epistles to the Thessalonians* (London: Macmillan, 1908) xxx, 126; K. Lake, *The Earlier Epistles of St. Paul: Their Motive and Origin* (London: Rivingtons, 1911) 86-87; regarded as improbable by von Dobschütz, *Die Thessalonicherbriefe*, 19; B. Rigaux, *Saint Paul: Les épîtres aux Thessaloniciens* (EBib; Paris: Gabalda, 1956) 55-56.

10. E. Best, *A Commentary on the First and Second Epistles to the Thessalonians* (HNTC; London: A. & C. Black, 1972) 15.

11. For such reminders, see A. J. Malherbe, "Exhortation in First Thessalonians," *NovT* 15 (1983) 240-41. A longer discussion of the letter's paraenetic features appears in idem, "Hellenistic Moralists and the New Testament," *ANRW* 2.26, forthcoming.

12. See K. Thraede, *Grundzüge griechisch-römische Brieftopik* (Zetemata 48; Munich: Beck, 1970) 95-97.

13. P. Schubert, *Form and Function of the Pauline Thanksgivings* (BZNW 20; Giessen/Berlin: Töpelmann, 1939) 20-21; J. L. White, *The Body of the Greek Letter* (SBLDS 2; Missoula: Scholars Press, 1972) 119.

14. For the theory, see the sample of the friendly letter in pseudo-Demetrius, *Epistolary Types* 1 (Malherbe, *Ancient Epistolary Theorists*, 32-33); for practice, see BGU 4.1080, 6ff.; POxy 6.963; PSI 1261, 10ff., and for discussion, see H. Koskenniemi, *Studien zur Idee und Phraseologie des griechischen Briefes bis 400 n. Chr.* (Helsinki: Suomalainen Tiedeakatemia, 1956) 175-80.

15. See 2 Cor 10:10-11; 1 Cor 5:3, on which see G. Karlsson, "Formelhaftes in Paulusbriefen?" *Eranos* 54 (1956) 138-41; K. Thraede, "Untersuchungen zum Ursprung und zur Geschichte der christlichen Poesie II," *JAC* 5 (1963) 141-45; idem, *Grundzüge*, 97-102.

16. Thraede, *Grundzüge*, 95-97. On letters of friendship, see S. K. Stowers, *Letter-Writing in Greco-Roman Antiquity* (Library of Early Christianity 5; Philadelphia: Westminster, 1986) 58-70.

17. Pseudo-Demetrius, *Epistolary Types* 1 (Malherbe, *Ancient Epistolary Theorists*, 32-33).

18. See Koskenniemi, *Studien*, 110.

19. His use of *aporphanisthentes* to describe his deprivation of their fellowship is especially significant in view of the extraordinary concentration of kinship language in the letter. See Malherbe, *Paul and the Thessalonians*, 48-51.

20. Koskenniemi, *Studien*, 124. See Gregory Nazianzen, *Epistles* 64.5; 93; Chariton, *Chaereas and Callirhoe* 8.4.5-6; compare 1 Cor 16:21; 2 Thess 3:17; esp. Philemon 19.

21. See Koskenniemi, *Studien*, 73-75.

22. See Koskenniemi, *Studien*, 174-75; Thraede, *Grundzüge*, index, *s. v. pothos*, here, esp. 96-97.

23. See, for example, pseudo-Demetrius, *Epistolary Types* 1 (Malherbe, *Ancient Epistolary Theorists*, 32-33); Koskenniemi, *Studien*, 123-27. Basil, *Epistle* 271, provides a good example: "For how much would it have been worth to me to see the most excellent Eusebius, and to embrace him, and to return again in memory to our youth, and to recall those days when one home was ours, and one hearth, and the same teacher, and leisure. . . . Of how much worth do you think I consider it to renew all these things in

memory through meeting you. . . . But though the enjoyment of all this has escaped me, yet of the privilege of seeing your Excellency through the agency of a letter."

24. For the suggestion that, in addition to its epistolary function, this language reflects the paraenetic practice of recalling one's teacher as a paradigm for one's life, see Malherbe, *Paul and the Thessalonians*, 66-67.

25. For example, PSI 4.438, 10; PTeb 22, 15; PHam 1.27, 4; see E. Mayser, *Grammatik der griechischen Papyri aus Ptolemäerzeit* (Berlin/Leipzig: W. de Gruyter, 1934) 2/2, 449-50; Demosthenes, *Epistle* 3.1; Diogenes Laertius, *Lives of Eminent Philosophers* 8.80; Didache 7.1; 9.1; 11.3; compare D. Bradley, "The Topos as Form in the Pauline Paraenesis," *JBL* 72 (1953) 238-46.

26. See Bradley, "The Topos as Form"; H. Boers, "The Form Critical Study of Paul's Letters. 1 Thessalonians as a Case Study," *NTS* 22 (1976) 140-58.

27. See for example, PEdg 65; PLille 26, 7; POxy 1664, 9ff.; 1593, 14-15; 1766, 10.

28. See PHall 1.166.

29. The text and translation are published in *Select Papyri*, eds. A. S. Hunt and C. C. Edgar (LCL; Cambridge, Mass.: Harvard University Press, 1952) 1.280-83.

30. See the examples in H. A. Steen, "Les clichés épistolaires," *Classica et Mediaevalia* 1 (1938) 128-30.

31. See I. Hadot, *Seneca und die griechisch-römische Tradition der Seelenleitung* (Berlin/New York: W. de Gruyter, 1969) 166-67.

32. See Steen, "Les clichés épistolaires," 119-76.

33. See Koskenniemi, *Studien*, 68-69, and see PMich Zen 23, 8; 85, 5; POxy 1664; PCairo 59250, 5; 59251; PPetr 2.42b; 3.42⁹(g).

34. See 1:5, 8; 2:1, 2, 5, 9, 11; 3:3, 4; 4:2; 5:2, and see n. 11 above.

35. See, for example, PEleph 13, 2-3; PHamb 1.88, 3; see also Koskenniemi, *Studien*, 75-77.

36. See, for example, POxy 12.1481, 9-10; PVat A, 8.

37. For wishing to see one's correspondent, see: POxy 1676, 20-25; 1761, 6-8; PLond 1244, 3ff.; on night and day, see: PMich 203, 17ff.; POxy 528, 6ff.; PGiss 17; on a letter as a surrogate see: POxy 963, 1ff.; PSI 1261, 10ff.; compare Malherbe, *Ancient Epistolary Theorists*, 12. On these topics generally, see Koskenniemi, *Studien*, 170, 174-77.

38. See Basil, *Epistle* 297.

39. See Gregory Nazianzen, *Epistle* 68.1.

40. See PEnt 86, 3. 11; PZeno Cairo 59025, 2. 12.

41. See, for example, Dahl, "Paul and the Church at Corinth," 324-25. For Stephanas as the bearer of the letter, see J. C. Hurd, *The Origin of 1 Corinthians* (London: SPCK, 1965) 49-50.

42. This was already the view of the Marcionite Prologues and is still that of scholars who hold to the unity of the letter (see Kümmel, *Introduction*, 323) as well as those who favor a theory that the letter is a composite of fragments (see H.-M. Schenke and K. M. Fischer, *Einleitung in die Schriften des Neuen Testaments* [Gütersloh: Gerd Mohn, 1978] 1.127, and H. Koester, *Introduction to the New Testament* [Berlin and New York: Walter de Gruyter, 1982] 2.54).

43. For the exact formula, see PRyl 235, 2ff.; PLond Bell 1925, 3ff., and for a discussion, see Koskenniemi, *Studien*, 81-87, 122.

44. Philippians 4:10-11 confirms this suggestion: "I rejoice greatly" (*echarēn megalōs*) was a standard acknowledgment of receipt of a letter. See Koskenniemi, *Studien*, 75-76. On 3 John 2, see R. W. Funk, "The Form and Structure of II and III John," *JBL* 86 (1967) 424-30. Given what now appears to have been Paul's practice of reflecting in his own letters characteristic phrases from the letters he received from his churches, vv. 10-11 may also hint at the letter Epaphroditus brought to Paul. Commenting on the propitiousness of the time to write was part of the *aphormē* formula (Koskenniemi, *Studien*, 82) and suggests that their letter began with such a formula (compare *ēkaireisthe*). Further, it is not unlikely that Paul's denial that he is speaking *kath' hysterēsin* may reflect a comment in their letter that they wished to fulfill his needs (compare 2:25, 30).

ON THE PAULINE CHRONOLOGY: BUCK-TAYLOR-HURD REVISITED

John Knox

I n such writing as I have done on the subject of the Pauline chronology, major emphasis has been placed on what I have seen to be proper method in the use of our sources. This method has been to give exclusive attention to Paul's own letters until they have been "wrung dry" of biographical data; next, to construct on the basis of these data alone an outline of Paul's career as an apostle (as I believe can be done from its beginning to its end, however sparse in its detail the resulting sketch would be), and only then to consider what the book of Acts, critically examined, can yield by way of filling the gaps—having always in mind that materials from Acts can never have the certainty and authority that materials in the letters possess. Following this method as best I could, I have sought to construct a Pauline chronology.

I devoted little discussion in these writings to earlier chronologies. If—when my own proposal was first made in 1936-39, or even when my book was published in 1950[1]—I had been asked to justify this apparent neglect, I should probably have answered that previous chronographers, so far as I knew, had followed methods of using the sources so different from that just described and had therefore, inevitably and predictably reached chronological results so different from mine that there was little need for, or point to, my systematically comparing them, or even considering them severally. The differences among them were minor when considered alongside a chronology arrived at by an entirely different method. In other words, it seemed to me that unless the method I have briefly defined were adopted, chronologies of Paul's career were bound to be, from my standpoint, rather grossly inaccurate. And I have found in the years since no reason to revise that judgment.

But what if that method *were* adopted? Would a converse judgment be true? I confess that I was then bold enough to think so. I felt sure that once the proposed method was adopted, there could be only one resulting chronology, so far as basic structure was concerned, although minor variations could be expected. Thus, for example, my friend Donald Riddle, who almost at once adopted the method I had defined, reached at a number of points chronological results different from those I had earlier reached, but his conception of the fundamental outline of Paul's career was the same.[2] At that time it appeared to me almost self-evident that this kind of thing must inevitably be true.

But in this supposition I was mistaken, as I soon learned. I now know that there are scholars—and have been ever since my articles were published—as truly convinced as I that the corpus of Paul's genuine letters is not only the primary source but also the only absolutely reliable source for the chronology of Paul's career, and who have sought to be as faithful to that conviction as I have tried to be, but who have nevertheless reached significantly different chronological conclusions. Of these scholars I regard the three whose names are linked in the title of this essay as being by far the most important. Indeed, they and those who have followed their lead are the only such scholars I know. The first sketch of their chronology was offered by C. H. Buck.[3] It was given further statement by Buck and Greer M. Taylor[4] and, contemporaneously and in his own significantly different form, by John C. Hurd.[5] In this brief essay I cannot present or discuss in detail their common position and can give relatively little attention to the differences among them. I want only to comment on what seem to be the most important features of a shared view.

I

Perhaps the most conspicuous of these distinctive features is the insistence of all three scholars that one is not in position to use Paul's epistles in constructing a chronology of his career until one has determined the order in which they were written and thus the course of the apostle's theological thought. This process of determination starts from the references to the great collection for the poor of the Jerusalem church, which engaged Paul's attention for several years. Those references in 1 and 2 Corinthians and Romans make clear that these letters were written in that order, although not, of course, necessarily in uninterrupted progression. This being true, by carefully observing the theology of these three successive epistles, noting the stages in its development, the investigator will discern the directions in which Paul's thinking on such matters as eschatology, the believer and the law, the church, and the like was moving. The perception of these directions will in turn make it possible for one to determine where in the order of their writing other epistles should be placed. Thus, it is held, the investigator will see that Galatians belongs just prior to Romans and (by extension backward and forward, so to speak) that the Thessalonian letters were Paul's earliest and Colossians (with Philemon) the latest to be written.

Following this method of determining the chronological order of the letters, C. H. Buck and Buck-Taylor[6] arrived at this result:

2 Thessalonians
1 Thessalonians
1 Corinthians
2 Corinthians 10–13
Philippians
2 Corinthians 1–9
Galatians
Romans
Colossians–Philemon
Ephesians

John C. Hurd[7] reaches essentially the same conclusions:

2 Thessalonians
1 Thessalonians
Previous letter to the Corinthians (referred to in 1 Cor 5:9)
1 Corinthians
The Severe Letter (referred to in 2 Cor 2:3 and 7:6)
Philippians
2 Corinthians 1–9
Galatians
Romans
Colossians
Philemon
(Ephesians, if genuine)

An examination of these two lists—exactly alike except that Buck-Taylor identify Hurd's Severe Letter with 2 Corinthians 10–13 (surely not an unlikely identification) and that Hurd indicates some doubt as to the authenticity of Ephesians—will reveal that if we assume the post-Pauline date of Ephesians, it is only in the cases of 1 and 2 Thessalonians, Philippians, Galatians, and Colossians-Philemon that considerations of theological development (as over against external criteria) had for all three scholars the dominant role in determining the order. I should like to consider these five cases.

About 2 Thessalonians many scholars—perhaps most of the modern ones—have had their doubts for a long time, not about its order, but about its genuineness. Can any reader of that letter fail to be stuck by the strangeness on Paul's lips, as we know him from the other letters, of the eschatological language of 2:1-12?[8] I now find myself persuaded, after a fresh reading of Buck-Taylor and Hurd, that *if genuine*, 2 Thessalonians belongs to a period in Paul's career earlier than the time of 1 Thessalonians. Since, unlike these scholars, I cannot find such a period, my hesitancy about the letter's authenticity is ended, and I reject it as pseudonymous.

I have just said that I cannot "find" a period in Paul's apostolic career earlier than that of 1 Thessalonians when 2 Thessalonians could have been written, and perhaps some explanation of why I cannot is appropriate. As I have already indicated, it is not because I cannot conceive of Paul's having held at some earlier time the eschatological views expressed in 2 Thessalonians. This may be difficult, but it is not impossible. What I do not find possible is that he should have expressed these views to his *Thessalonian* converts—and this for the reason that I cannot see how he could have had Thessalonian converts at that earlier time. My conception of the beginning months and years of Paul's Gentile mission precludes such a possibility.[9] Absolutely nothing in Paul's letters even hints at a visit to Macedonia prior to the *one visit* to which he makes frequent and sole reference in the first three chapters of 2 Thessalonians as having occurred not long before. Nor does the Acts account allow for any earlier visit than this. It is true that this account tells of a missionary journey before the Macedonian one, but it extended no further than Galatia. I repeat, therefore, that since 2 Thessalonians, *if genuine*, must be the earlier of the Thessalonian epistles and since the evidence of both the letters and Acts strongly indicates that it was not the earlier, it must be regarded as *not genuine*. In this case, I recognize that theological considerations are the decisive ones.

I should regard such considerations as decisive also as regards 1 Thessalonians' early date if, as I have just said, that letter did not leave the impression, on this reader's mind at least, that the experiences in Thessalonica to which Paul refers occurred during his first visit and that the letter was written soon after this first visit, although it is worth noting that his references to Achaia in 1 Thess 1:7-8 suggest that he has gone beyond Athens by that time. And this impression is not without objective support. Gerd Lüdemann[10] calls attention to a very telling piece of external evidence which all but requires an early date for 1 Thessalonians—more particularly, its priority to 1 Corinthians. This is the fact that 1 Thess 4:13-18 clearly reflects a period in the church's history when very few Christians had died. Lüdemann points out that in the very beginning the Lord's return was confidently expected within a few months or at most years. The first Christian evangelists did not deal, and had no occasion to deal, with the tender problem created by the death of a believer before the Parousia. Would such a one witness and share in the glory of it? No one had need to ask. But this situation could not have lasted long. Yet, it was apparently still substantially unchanged when Paul first preached the gospel of the Lord's return to the Thessalonians. Lüdemann has no difficulty showing that the eschatological teaching of 1 Corinthians (esp. 15:51-52) reflects a different, and later, objective situation. I must say, therefore, that for me at least the weightiest evidence for regarding 1 Thessalonians as Paul's earliest extant letter is external, although the theological evidence alone would have sufficed to establish that precedence.

Although it means a slight digression, I cannot help pointing to a wider implication in Paul's silence at Thessalonica about the faithful dead than that with which Lüdemann is most concerned. May we not find here a very telling refutation of the traditional and prevailing chronology of Paul's career with its initial "silent years"? Paul has evidently reached Macedonia before any Christians—certainly before more than a few Christians—have died. Indeed, this consideration, if it stood alone, would suggest an even earlier date for the beginning of his European mission than other data (particularly the "after three years" of Gal 1:18) allow us to propose.

When we turn now to Philippians and note the place in the chronological order assigned by Buck, Taylor, and Hurd to this letter, agreement with them becomes for me far more difficult than in the case of 1 Thessalonians, and in the end impossible. I have read again Buck and Taylor's chapter on Philippians, giving careful attention to those passages from the letter that, in their view, require on theological grounds that we date its writing after 1 Corinthians and before 2 Corinthians, and I have no hesitancy in saying that I find the argument they make for this view quite impressive. But an indisputable external fact about Philippians stands in opposition to it, and, for me, the theological argument falls short of that absolute conclusiveness which alone would justify our denying to that fact decisive significance. This is the fact that there is no reference in that letter to the collection, with which Paul was intensively engaged from before the time of his writing 1 Corinthians until his writing of Romans. That Paul, in the very period of this activity (even though he was in prison at the time), in a letter to the Philippians, should not have made some references to this project—in which, we know, Macedonia was much involved—strikes me as being so improbable as to be almost incredible.

That being true, I am forced to think of the epistle as having been written either before 1 Corinthians or at least three or four years later, after Romans and thus during Paul's final internment. In the letter there are some pointers to the earlier of these periods, as for example, the apostle's hope soon to see the Philippians, his way of speaking of Epaphroditus's illness and the movements back and forth of news about him, his expectation of soon sending Titus, and the like. But, on the other hand, there are passages that sound valedictory, like an adieu (although with the wistful thought that things may not turn out so after all). My own conclusion is that although Philippians *may* have been written before 1 Corinthians, during some temporary imprisonment, it can with less difficulty be assigned to the final period, when Paul's imprisonment can be presumed to be more extended, probably more remotely located, and more portentous. But such a conclusion does not dispose of the chronological discrepancies within the letter, and my only really firm assurance is the negative one, that this epistle does not belong where it stands in the foregoing lists.[11]

Turning now to Galatians, I would concur with the authors of these lists that theological considerations predominantly determine its position next to Romans, where indeed most scholars place it.[12] But whether it was written *before* Romans or *after* it is, to my mind, far from settled. I read J. B. Lightfoot many years ago in my student days, and I have had occasion to reread him on this point several times since, but he has never convinced me that a comparison of the two letters established Galatians's priority. I can just as readily understand that letter as an echo of Romans, or more exactly as an impulsive letter written under the pressure of great emotion, created by an actual crisis in some of Paul's churches, a crisis involving a theological issue of enormous significance. In a calmer mood he had discussed at length this crisis in Romans not long before—so recently, indeed, that his argument in that letter and even some of its language are still in his mind, although he is too deeply stirred by the immediate circumstances to be consciously influenced by either language or argument or to speak always consistently with them. If ever he spoke *ad hominem*, and he often undoubtedly did, it was in this passionate letter.

He would now be in prison, probably somewhere in Judea, and could not go to Galatia as he surely would have wished. The total absence of any promise, or threat, to do so is evidence almost as convincing as an explicit reference to imprisonment would have been that some such circumstance rendered him helpless. That he does not speak of his situation more explicitly should not surprise us. Paul would not have needed to inform the Galatians that he was in prison. If they did not know it already, the carrier of the letter would at once have let them know. Actually, in all the so-called imprisonment epistles the references to imprisonment are invariably incidental, made usually in connection with some announcement of plans for further travel. But now, in writing

Galatians, it is clear that he cannot envisage the possibility of future travel. When news of trouble in the Corinthian church reached him, he could write: "I will come to you soon . . . and I will find out not the talk of these arrogant people but their power. . . . Shall I come to you with a rod, or with love . . ?" (1 Cor 4:19-21). Again, to the same congregation at another time he writes: "I write this while I am away from you, in order that when I come I may not have to be severe in my use of the authority which the Lord has given me" (2 Cor 13:10). But now, in Galatians, under incomparably greater provocation, he cannot threaten or even warn. All he can do is appeal. As he comes to the end of his passionate plea, he can only cry out, in effect: I have now done all I can do; the issue is out of my hands. Henceforth, let no one trouble me, for I bear in my body the marks of the Lord Jesus.

How is it possible—to me it seems hardly thinkable—that such a letter, expressing such frustration, with its tone of desperation sometimes close to despair, should be understood as having been written *by a free man* very shortly *before* his saying to the Romans (15:23): "I no longer have any room for work in these regions"?[13]

Quite incidentally, it might be observed that if Galatians is deemed to be one of Paul's last letters, and if the acute crisis in Galatia occurred near the very end of his career, perhaps we should see this fact as providing some support for the late dating of Philippians, where in 3:1b-3 Paul warns of the possible coming to Philippi of "those dogs . . . those mutilators of the flesh." It may also be observed that if Galatians is dated after Romans, its silence about the collection is fully explained and much of the ground for surmising that the Galatian churches did not participate in it disappears.[14]

We come finally to Colossians, the last of the five letters cited by Buck, Taylor, and Hurd whose relative dating is chiefly determined by theological considerations. On those grounds, they place this letter last on their list and, therefore, regard it as having been written during Paul's final imprisonment. Let it be agreed at once that Ephesians, if it is genuine, could not have been written earlier than this time and also that there are close and undeniable ties between Ephesians and Colossians. The same stage in Paul's thinking (again, if both epistles are genuine) is reflected in each—less clearly and fully in Colossians than in the other epistle, but manifestly in both. Stylistic, as well as theological, considerations have convinced the majority of scholars that Ephesians is not genuine, and many of these make the same judgment about Colossians, after which Ephesians, whether genuine or not, is obviously fashioned and upon which it to some extent depends. It would appear, then, that if Ephesians is genuine and late, Colossians is also.

At the same time, however, it must be recognized that the ties binding

Colossians to Philemon are far stronger than any bonds with Ephesians—ties so strong and intricate, so very improbable as the inventions of even the cleverest pseudepigrapher as to render it virtually impossible to decide that Colossians is not a genuine Pauline letter, as Philemon undoubtedly is.[15] How, then, shall we reconcile the two facts that Colossians is closely tied to the inauthentic Ephesians but is bound even more closely to the authentic Philemon? Almost by logical necessity the answer must be that only by recognizing that the author of Ephesians not only adopted Colossians as providing the model of his epistle, but also revised that letter to bring it into closer conformity with his own thought and style. This way of understanding the relationship between these two epistles is not merely the product of logical necessity. It was first called to my attention as a possibility by H. J. Holtzmann, who on quite different grounds ably defended it.[16]

Thus we must depend on the tiny, but stalwart, epistle to Philemon to establish the authenticity of the original Colossians, as well as to supply us with the probable circumstances of its writing—namely, while Paul is serving a brief prison term not very far from Colossae and his other churches in the Lycus valley, more probably than not in Ephesus. Since these circumstances indicate an earlier period in Paul's career than that of the writing of Romans, his final journey to Jerusalem, and his arrest, and internment, and since there is no hint in either Colossians or Philemon that the collection was in progress at the time of their writing, we must place the original, and alone authentic, epistle to the Colossians ahead of the Corinthian letters.

What does all of this add up to in the way of a list of Paul's letters in chronological order? Evidently to something like this:

LETTERS WRITTEN BEFORE COLLECTION

1 Thessalonians
Colossians (Original form)—Philemon

LETTERS WRITTEN DURING COLLECTION

1 Corinthians
2 Corinthians 10–13
2 Corinthians 1–9
Romans

LETTERS WRITTEN AFTER COLLECTION

Galatians
Philippians

Before we leave this matter of the chronological ordering of the letters it may be well to observe that, wide as the difference may appear to be between this proposal and that represented by the two lists previously presented, it is almost entirely accounted for by differing estimates of the importance of the collection in the determination of the order. Both proposals involve—as any proposal in the matter obviously must—close attention to the collection. Both of them recognize the significance in this connection of observable changes in the apostle's thought. They differ only—even if quite widely—as to the comparable degrees of importance they ascribe to these two criteria in the determination of the chronological order of the letters.

It will have been noted, perhaps, that in the preceding discussion of the order of the epistles and of the course of Paul's thought no notice whatever was taken of the book of Acts, either in the arguments of Buck, Taylor, and Hurd or in any counter-arguments. This is as it ought to be and indeed as it almost has to be, since Acts does not give the slightest indication of knowing that Paul wrote any letters at all, much less of understanding the thought expressed in them.

II

As we turn now, however, to a consideration of the events and circumstances of Paul's career itself, Acts comes inevitably into view, and all chronologers of the apostle, whatever their ideas about method, must take the evidence it provides into serious account. In this essay we are concerned only with the limited number of those chronologers who agree with one another that the evidence of Acts not only is less important than that the letters provide, but also that it has a different character and belongs to a different category. This fact separates these chronologers from most others. But none of these would think of denying that the testimony of Acts, particularly when it seems to be drawing on primitive sources, has significant weight. As to what the most primitive materials are, however, and as to how their weight is to be applied in the actual process of determining a chronology, there are notable differences. This is true regarding the differences between Buck-Taylor-Hurd and myself. The extent of these divergences, however, may be easily exaggerated. The fact of their existence appears unmistakably in the Buck article of 1950, but the total width of them has perceptibly narrowed in the writings of John Hurd.

So far as I know, the first outline of the progress of Paul's apostolic career as seen by those who rely primarily—and, in the absolute sense, only—on the letters was presented in 1939 as shown in the following brief sketch.

Conversion in or near Damascus.

First visit to Jerusalem ("three years later").

Evangelistic activity in Syria, Cilicia, Galatia, Macedonia, Achaia, Asia.

Second visit to Jerusalem ("fourteen years later" to confer with the church leaders there).

The taking of the collection requested at this conference and further evangelistic work in Greece and Asia Minor.

Third visit to Jerusalem (a few years after the Second) to deliver the collection; the arrest there.[17]

C. H. Buck in his 1950 article does not put his conclusions in tabular form, but I believe they could be accurately stated somewhat as follows.

First visit to Jerusalem ("three years later").

Preaching activity in Syria, Cilicia, Galatia, Macedonia, Achaia. Return to Antioch.

Second visit to Jerusalem ("fourteen years later") to deliver collection from Antioch (Acts 11:27-30).

At request of Jerusalem church, a revisit of churches from Galatia to Achaia (Asia?) to solicit further relief for the poor.

Third visit to Jerusalem to deliver additional funds thus raised; conference with "the pillars" about status of the Gentile converts.

Return to Ephesus; residence there with occasional visits to churches in his field until—

Fourth and final visit to Jerusalem.

Arrest and imprisonment.

It is at once apparent that this outline of the events of Paul's career reflects a quite different view of its course from that reflected in the other sketch.[18] Buck's proposal owes something to a hypothesis offered by several earlier scholars that an acceptable way to explain the discrepancy, as regards the timing of Paul's Jerusalem visit, between Gal 2:1-10 and Acts 11:27-30, 15:1-29 is to attribute to Luke the error of so reading his sources as to think of what was really one visit with two purposes, or at any rate two results, as having been two separate visits. Thus, it is argued, Paul's second visit to Jerusalem "fourteen years later" actually included both the delivering of the offering and the Conference with the "pillars." Luke mentions only the offering (11:27-30), and Paul only the Conference (Gal 2:1-10). Such is the earlier hypothesis. But Buck's version of it significantly differs, and perhaps I may be forgiven some repetition if I state it again in a more discursive manner.

After the Antioch gift had been delivered, but before Paul and Barnabas returned to Antioch, the Jerusalem church leaders asked that

Paul's churches in Galatia, Macedonia, and Achaia also be solicited for help in the emergency. In fulfillment of this request, Paul left Jerusalem at once for this field. His mission accomplished, he returned directly to that city and delivered the additional funds he had raised. It was then that he took occasion to confer with "the pillars"—James, Peter, and John—about the problems he was encountering among his Gentile converts about their relation to the Jewish law. The "pillars" generally approved the way he was handling these problems and expressed their hope that the largely Gentile churches would continue to "remember the poor." Paul then returned to Ephesus, where apparently his collection effort had ended, and resided there until he went again to Jerusalem (his fourth visit), where his arrest occurred and his active career was over. According to this understanding, then, the Thessalonian letters, 1 and 2 Corinthians, Philippians, Galatians, and Romans had been written and the collection had been finally delivered in Jerusalem before the Conference took place.

There are, it seems obvious to me, a number of difficulties in the way of accepting this scheme. I shall mention only the more serious.

First, the support of it in our sources is very weak. The letters furnish no support at all, although, it may be granted, nothing in them absolutely excludes the scheme as a possibility. The only ground for affirming two collections or a collection in two distinct parts, each entailing a trip to Jerusalem, is in Acts 12:25, where we read that "Saul and Barnabas returned to [*eis*] Jerusalem." This verse has virtually always been taken as concluding the story of 11:27-30. But, if so, it would appear that the preposition should be *ex* or *apo* (not *eis*), and there is not little textual evidence for each of them, but the great preponderance of evidence supports the *eis* reading.[19]

Buck accepts this reading and draws the necessary logical inference—namely, that the return *to* Jerusalem must have been preceded by a period of absence from it. Of this period Acts says nothing, but Buck sees it as having been spent in the continuing work on the collection, which, according to his hypothesis, the Jerusalem church leaders had requested. But this, I cannot help thinking, is a massive structure to build on the slender base of a somewhat problematical *eis*.

That *eis* is the true reading I have little doubt, and it seems equally clear that the source in which Luke found it was a primitive source. But is it to be assumed that 12:25 was *in that source* the conclusion of the narrative in 11:27-30? As we find it in Acts, this statement of a return to Jerusalem is completely detached, not related to its context in any way. It is separated from the 11:27-30 narrative by no fewer than 24 verses, concerned with Herod's beheading of James and arrest of Peter; with Peter's miraculous escape; with Herod's execution of the guards who had allowed the escape to happen; and with Herod's return from Judea to Caesarea, where he was struck down by the Lord for his arrogance. This series of rather lurid stories (Acts 12:1-23) is immediately followed by the generalization, "But the word of God grew and multiplied" (v. 24). There is not the slightest indication that 12:25 has any connection with 11:27-30. If 12:25 belonged to a primitive source of Acts, it may have stood in any number of connections. Only a pre-existing assumption of the coherency of Acts, which often elsewhere and in this very instance itself is convincingly disproved, would lead one to see in it the conclusion of the 11:27-30 episode.

But whatever is made of Acts 12:25 in connection with the Pauline chronology, let it be remembered that we are dealing with a statement not in our primary source, but in Acts, and that some degree of tentativeness attaches even to the most explicit statement in that writing which is not more or less explicitly supported by the letters. In this case the "statement" is certainly *not* explicit, and the letters give no support to it whatever.

A second and more serious objection is that Paul in Gal 2:1-10 gives an account of the occasion and circumstances of the Conference that is so different from the Buck-Taylor one as almost to contradict it. There is absolutely no hint there or anywhere else in the letters that the primary motive for Paul's visit to Jerusalem "fourteen years later" was to deliver an offering. On the contrary, Paul tells us very plainly that he went there "by revelation," to secure if he could the approval of the Jerusalem church leaders of his work among the Gentiles, or at the worst to make certain to himself that they were not disaffected, or perhaps in actual opposition, as some of his adversaries in the field alleged they were. This was manifestly a most important concern to him. He can even say that, for the moment at least, he felt that the validity of his whole evangelistic effort over many years was "on the line," going so far as to say "lest somehow I should be running or had run in vain" (Gal 2:2). That his Conference was the incidental result of his having gone to Jerusalem to deliver an offering is all but excluded.

A third objection to the Buck-Taylor chronology appears when we ask why Paul made a last or fourth visit to Jerusalem if the collection has already been delivered. Why does Paul feel, as he evidently did if we can trust at all Acts 20 and the following chapters (as I can, and I am sure that Buck, Taylor, and Hurd, who have shown more confidence in Acts than I can feel, would trust them, too—at least to this extent) that despite great risks to his liberty and even his life, he cannot escape making this visit? We are told its dire results. What could have been its urgent purpose? It may also be asked: How did Paul, this almost coercively motivated worker for the spread of the gospel, spend the immediately preceding time, an interval *ex hypothesi* of several years, between the third and the final visit to Jerusalem? The gospel had been preached from Jerusalem to Illyricum, and the work to which he had been specifically called had in that region been done (Rom 15:19). The collection had been completed and delivered, and, contrary to his earlier fears (Rom 15:31), it had apparently been thankfully received. Paul is residing, it would seem relatively quietly, in Ephesus. His former eagerness to go to Rome and other points to the west, which he had so strongly felt a few years earlier, had apparently disappeared. Why, I ask again, this dangerous trip to Jerusalem? These certainly are pertinent questions, and I do not find in Buck-Taylor or in Buck's earlier article any serious, and surely no adequate, consideration of them.

John C. Hurd, whose chronology has unmistakable resemblances to that of Buck-Taylor, nevertheless shows some departures from it. His latest statement of it, so far as I know, is this brief outline:

> First Jerusalem visit ("three years later").
> Missionary work from Syria to Achaia.
> Second visit to Jerusalem ("fourteen years later") (collection inaugurated).
> Collection journey to revisit churches.
> Third Jerusalem visit (collection delivered).
> Imprisonment and execution.[20]

Nothing is said in this outline about the talk with the pillars about the Jewish question, or what is usually referred to as the Conference, but it is to be assumed, and is indicated elsewhere in Hurd's writings, that, with Buck and Taylor and on the basis of his reading of the letters, Hurd associates this with the Antioch offering visit to Jerusalem (Acts 11:27-30). It is at this point, however, that Hurd makes what is perhaps his most important modification of, and advance beyond, the Buck-Taylor position: He softens Buck's hard statement that the collection took place before the Conference, not after.[21]

Departing from Buck, Hurd thinks of the Conference as occurring immediately after Paul, or Paul and Barnabas, placed the Antioch offering in the hands of the Jerusalem church leaders on what Hurd (at this point *with* Buck) regards as the second Jerusalem visit (Gal 2:1). "The collection," as Hurd uses the term, begins at this time as a result of the Conference and occupies much of the next decade. Thus its delivery can for him be the principal, or only, occasion for the third visit to Jerusalem, anticipated in Rom 15:25-29. The problem Buck's chronology raises for us of why Paul must make this dangerous final visit disappears.

So far we have been considering only the relative order of events in Paul's career and have given no attention to absolute dating. It has been a source of some perplexity to me that all three of the scholars, whose work on a relative Pauline chronology we have been examining, have seen fit to make their total proposal more difficult by attaching it to a questionable absolute date. There is evidence in Josephus and elsewhere that serious regional famines occurred in the Palestine area in or around 46 CE,[22] and these scholars adopt this date as that of Paul's second Jerusalem visit. But this conclusion involves several unproved assumptions: (1) the historicity of the "great famine" (Acts 11:28) and the correctness of its dating; (2) the truth of the Acts story that Paul made a famine-relief journey to Judea early in his career; (3) the fact that, if so, it was the famine of 46 CE which was its occasion (this assumption, despite the known penchant of Luke for dating happenings in his narrative by references to public events); and (4) that this was the "fourteen years later" visit. But if it is hard to understand the apparently unqualified assurance of Buck and Taylor of the accuracy of 46 CE as the date of Paul's second visit to Jerusalem, their willingness to tie its correctness as closely as they do to their carefully wrought relative chronology I find even harder to understand. Their doing so requires that they interpret Gal 1:18, 2:1 to imply a fourteen-year interval between Paul's conversion and the Conference, rather than allowing the seventeen-year interval, which most scholars regard as far more likely. Even so, they must date Jesus' crucifixion as early as 29 and the conversion no later than 32—admittedly possible dates, but surely not, on the other grounds, the most probable. The difficulty is not diminished by their naming of the year 53 as the time of Paul's last visit to Jerusalem, thus leaving something like five years between the completing of the collection and the related writing of Romans, and Paul's final Jerusalem visit.

John Hurd is more cautious than Buck-Taylor about absolute dating, apparently permitting the 46 CE date for Paul's second visit to Jerusalem only as "probable."[23] But given the serious difficulties even a tentative adoption of that date raises for his own chronology and given the fragility of the evidence supporting it, I am perplexed as to why he does not abandon it altogether.

Not long after *Chapters in a Life of Paul* was published, Professor Henry J. Cadbury wrote me: "I need not tell you again, as when I read some of your MS, that I feel sure you are right in putting the Judaizing crisis nearer the end than the beginning of Paul's work in the four Provinces, and much of the 14 years in that work, too. You and my friend Charles Buck agree in this, [but] I don't know which of you to follow in detail." This was high praise as coming from a senior scholar whom both Buck and I deeply revered, and Buck must have been as much gratified as I.

But there is also a warning, only half-hidden, in Cadbury's words for which we should have been equally grateful. He makes quite clear that, except for the matter on which he agrees with *both* of us, he is fully convinced by *neither* of us—a salutary reminder to us and perhaps to other workers on the problem of the Pauline chronology of the necessarily tentative character of many of our findings. Complete certainty will be possible only when we have documentary evidence far more ample than is now available or probably ever will be. As for myself, I feel very sure about what is proper method in using the two sources we do possess, and I am fairly sure of the basic outline of Paul's apostolic career, but I have, in varying degrees, less assurance about almost everything else. I have made clear that my disagreements with Buck and Taylor are, within the limits of a common methodology, wide and deep. But my differences from John Hurd, who now wears their mantle (but loosely!), are relatively minor. I do not doubt that, except possibly at a very few points, neither of us would insist that he alone has the right of it.

Notes

1. See my "Fourteen Years Later: A Note on the Pauline Chronology," *JR* 16 (1936) 341-49; "The Pauline Chronology," *JBL* 58 (1939) 15-29; *Chapters in a Life of Paul* (New York: Abingdon 1950; rev. ed., Macon: Mercer University Press, 1987); *"Chapters in a Life of Paul*—Thirty Years Later," *Colloquy on New Testament Studies* (Bruce Corley, ed.; Macon: Mercer University Press, 1980) 339-64.
2. See D. W. Riddle, *Paul, Man of Conflict* (Nashville: Cokesbury, 1940). See also "The Pauline Chronology."
3. C. H. Buck, "The Collection for the Saints," *HTR* 43 (1950) 1-29. This article appeared after my articles and also after my book had been written, but before it was published later in that same year; therefore, it could not be noted in my book. But in the revised edition of it in 1987 I should certainly have referred to Buck's article in the note on the collection on p. 36, and I deeply regret my failure to do so.
4. C. H. Buck and Greer M. Taylor, *St. Paul: A Study in the Development of His Thought* (New York: Scribners, 1969).
5. John C. Hurd, *The Origin of 1 Corinthians* (New York: Seabury, 1965); idem., "Pauline Chronology and Pauline Theology," in *Christian History and Interpretation: Studies Presented to John Knox* (Cambridge and New York: Cambridge University Press, 1967) 225-48; idem., "The Sequence of Paul's Letters," *CJT* 14 (1968) 188-200; idem., "Chronology, Pauline," in *IDBSup* (1976) 166-67.
6. Buck and Taylor, *St. Paul*, 145-46.
7. John C. Hurd, "Chronology, Pauline," 166-67. Because he is seeking in this very brief list to state a "consensus view," Hurd omits a reference to 2 Corinthians 10–13. But he regards it as belonging after Romans (but before the third and last visit to Jerusalem) and before Colossians. (See Hurd, "The Sequence of Paul's Letters," 198).
8. Chiefly because of this strangeness, but for other reasons also, I have always felt uneasy in affirming the genuineness of this letter—although some of the "other reasons" for doubt alleged by many scholars are, in my opinion, of dubious validity. See my "A Note on II Thess. 2:2," *ATR* 18 (1936) 72-73.
9. See my *Chapters in a Life of Paul* (rev. ed.), 56-59.

10. Gerd Lüdemann, *Paul, Apostle to the Gentiles: Studies in Chronology* (trans. F. Stanley Jones; Philadelphia: Fortress, 1984).

11. I have been assuming the integrity of Philippians. If, as has been proposed by several scholars, 3:1 marks the end of one letter and the rest of our epistle is a large fragment from another letter or perhaps an assembly of smaller fragments from several, it obviously becomes impossible to assign the whole to any one date or period. But even if one adopts such a partition theory—as, I gather, the three scholars we are examining are no more disposed to do than I—however fragmentary chaps. 3 and 4 may be, the first two chapters represent one substantially whole letter. And since any theological argument as to the relative date of Philippians must rest largely on the first two chapters, and since any argument from silence about the collection must rest there, too, the partition proposal would appear to be irrelevant so far as the present discussion is concerned. There are no references to the collection in the whole of Philippians, possible fragments and all.

12. One who accepts as true Acts 13–15 will almost certainly regard Galatians as Paul's first letter, although such a one can hardly call it an *early* letter since Paul will have been busy (or idle!) nearly fourteen years in Syria and Cilicia. It may also be said that such a one is likely to agree with J. Weiss and many others that no significant theological development is revealed in Paul's epistles. (But see Hurd, "The Sequence of Paul's Letters" for important exceptions, such as R. H. Charles and C. H. Dodd.) In this view, Paul's thought will have fully matured when he embarks on his mission to Macedonia, Achaia, and Asia, and any apparent changes in his theology are to be accounted for by variety in the situations and needs of the several churches addressed. One who believes Paul entered upon his major evangelistic work not long after his conversion will, almost necessarily, take a different view. To me it is an inescapable fact that the letters reflect real and substantial development in his thought. Buck and Taylor are most persuasive as to the fact of this development. They are perhaps not quite so persuasive in tracing it, but there are illuminating insights into Paul's theology throughout their book.

13. See also my "Galatians, Letter to," *IDB*, 2:338-43. The claim made by some scholars that the whole passage Rom 15:17-29 reflects, not a mood of satisfaction in accomplishment, but rather a recognition of failure is for me so patently false as hardly to deserve mention.

14. See Lüdemann, *Paul, Apostle to the Gentiles*, 86.

15. See my "Philemon and the Authenticity of Colossians," *JR* 18 (1938) 144-60.

16. H. J. Holtzmann, *Kritik der Epheser- und Kolosserbriefe* (Leipzig: Wilhelm Engelmann, 1872); see also Ch. Masson, *L'épître de saint Paul aux Colossiens* (Neuchâtel et Paris: Delachaux et Nestlé, 1950). Holtzmann finds the relationships between the texts of Ephesians and Colossians very complicated indeed. The acknowledgment of my indebtedness to him in suggesting the possibility of a shorter original Colossians must not be taken to mean that I was persuaded by his argument as a whole or in any other respect than this. As to Masson's case, I cannot but think that his hypothetical reconstruction of the original text of Colossians would have benefited from his taking into account the arguments of the article referred to in the preceding note.

17. This outline, virtually intact, is lifted from my article "The Pauline Chronology," but it does not now stand alone. It is not too much to say that Gerd Lüdemann, whose research on the subject of the Pauline chronology is immeasurably broader and deeper than mine, offers on pp. 262-63 of *Paul, Apostle to the Gentiles* an outline of Paul's career, which in its basic structure is essentially the same. He fills in this outline in ways that I can sometimes follow him and sometimes not, but there is nothing in his account that is not broadly comprehended in the outline I have just presented and to which I have adhered in every writing on the chronology I have published. And, as I hinted at the beginning of this essay, I believe this could be said of every other study of the chronology that is based on the letters, except for the Buck-Taylor-Hurd alternative. And as I have just been saying, that exception has become less markedly "exceptional" as we move from Buck-Taylor to Hurd.

18. I cannot forbear saying that in the statement and defense of his proposal, particularly

of those parts of it that chiefly distinguish it, Buck comes dangerously near to violating the basic idea of the absolute primacy of the letters as sources over Acts, if indeed he does not actually cross the line. I may also take this occasion to point out that this chronology of Buck, first proposed in his 1950 article, is reaffirmed in 1969, this time with Taylor's concurrence, in their *St. Paul* (see esp. pp. 175 and 213-15).

19. Many translators and commentators in an effort to relate 12:25 to 11:27-30 resort to what is not the most natural rendering of 12:25: "Barnabas and Saul, their task at Jerusalem fulfilled, returned." So the *New English Bible.*

20. John C. Hurd, *IDBSup*, 166-67. See also his "The Sequence of Paul's Letters." Hurd's very important book *The Origin of 1 Corinthians,* indispensable to interpreters of that epistle, also makes an important contribution to the formation of a Pauline chronology by making the Conference, as he understands its content (see esp. p. 269), central to the understanding of the earlier letter (1 Cor 5:9) and the resultant questions raised by the Corinthians, to which much of 1 Corinthians is Paul's reply. It also devotes not a little attention to defending most ably the methodological principle that the letters are in the fullest sense primary and to showing the failings of a chronology arrived at by the traditional harmonizing method. See especially pp. 3-45.

21. Buck, "Collection for the Saints," 27.

22. See esp. *Ant.* xx 5.2. But see also Lüdemann, *Paul: Apostle to the Gentiles,* 11, 35.

23. See Buck-Taylor, *St. Paul,* 162, and J. C. Hurd, "Chronology, Pauline," *IDBSup*, 167.

THE CONTRIBUTION
OF J. LOUIS MARTYN
TO THE UNDERSTANDING OF
THE GOSPEL OF JOHN

D. Moody Smith

I n the decades immediately after World War II the study of the Gospel and Epistles of John was dominated by theological questions, a state of affairs that was appropriate enough, for the controlling issues of the Johannine literature are clearly theological. The sharpest debates had to do with the historical setting and its bearing on the theological issues. In fact, Martyn's contribution lies precisely in the determination of that historical setting and its impact on the interpretation of Johannine theology, particularly in the Gospel. He called into question the view that the most relevant historical setting was Hellenistic, gnostic, or Christian by proposing that the primal context of Johannine thought was Jewish, or Jewish-Christian.

Johannine Interpretation in the Decades After World War II

The dominant modes of Johannine interpretation in the postwar decades were rooted in research going back much earlier. Fittingly, the era's two most notable scholars, in Great Britain and Germany respectively, capped lifetimes of scholarship with *magna opera* on the Fourth Gospel: Bultmann with his magisterial commentary;[1] Dodd with his two weighty books on the interpretation and historical tradition of the Gospel.[2] A third work should perhaps be put alongside them—namely, Hoskyns's *The Fourth Gospel*.[3] A kind of exegetical "Unfinished Symphony," it was brought to completion and published by Hoskyns's colleague Davey. In order to see Martyn's contribution in perspective, it will be useful to characterize each of the three, for in their approach and assessment of the issues they represented alternatives that differed, while sharing certain important presuppositions. All set the problem of Johannine interpretation against a horizon of Christian or more general religious or existential theological concerns.

Dodd's work was based on his wide-ranging and deep research in the Hellenistic cultural and religious world, as well as his appreciation of Judaism, its traditions and scriptures. *The Interpretation of the Fourth Gospel* (1953) set the Gospel of John against a wide range of Hellenistic and Jewish backgrounds, which Dodd deemed more or less relevant for its understanding. While Dodd saw important connections with Judaism, and particularly the Old Testament, he was satisfied to characterize the intended audience of the Gospel as those intelligent, literate, and religious readers who were fairly numerous in the Hellenistic world. Interestingly enough, Dodd did not dismiss the tradition of apostolic authorship, although it becomes quite clear in *Interpretation* that he placed little or no stock in it. That is, it was wholly unnecessary to the perspective and approach that work represents. The situation may change just slightly with *Historical Tradition in the Fourth Gospel*, for in that book Dodd clearly intends to trace the Johannine tradition, whether in written or oral form, to its historical roots. Moreover, he is strongly disposed to view it as standing in a significant and positive relation to Jesus himself. Nevertheless, he does not rest his case on apostolic authorship, but rather he analyzes the text with a view to establishing its traditional, and putatively historical, roots. Interestingly enough, the Johannine tradition's rootage in Jesus himself would be congruent with Dodd's view of Jesus' own realized eschatology. Thus the Fourth Gospel represents, not a development or departure from Jesus, but rather the fundamental eschatological perspective of Jesus, albeit dressed out in more hellenized form.

The hellenized form of the Fourth Gospel is roughly equivalent in meaning or import to its universal scope. Its message is adapted to cultured, literate readers with religious interests, be they Jew or Greek. Whether in Palestine, Athens, Alexandria, or Rome, the intended reader would understand and feel the appeal of the Gospel of John. Specific historical circumstances of the Gospel's setting are less important than general religious and cultural relevance and affinities in Dodd's view.

To a remarkable extent the same can be said of the equally influential perspective and theological interpretation of Rudolf Bultmann.[4] Of course, Bultmann had a quite specific and distinctive view of the Gospel's historical origin and literary development. Its origin lay close to the same baptist circles in Syria or Palestine from which John the Baptist emerged. In fact, the sign-source of the Gospel may have first been used as a missionary tract among disciples of John the Baptist, and the evangelist himself may have once followed John. These early baptists seem to have been heterodox Jews, from whom (or in near proximity to whom) the Mandaeans later developed or emerged. The Mandaean sources, with their dualism and terminological affinities with the Johannine literature, became for Bultmann extremely important documents for understanding the milieu and meaning of the Gospel and Epistles of John. The Mandaeans—whose name, of course, means "knowledge" (or gnostic)—provide the gnostic connection of the Fourth Gospel. One should recall, however, that the Gospel of John was written not to embrace or affirm a gnostic point of view, but rather to oppose it. It remained for his student Ernst Käsemann to espouse a much more positively gnosticizing interpretation of the Fourth Gospel. Of course, Bultmann assumed that the traditional view of Johannine authorship had long since been shown to be problematic. In fact, the ecclesiastical redactor of the Gospel was the first to equate the Beloved Disciple with the evangelist.[5]

While Bultmann's historical and literary theories are amazingly specific and detailed at some points, much more so than Dodd's, they too are at the service of a higher theological interpretation that tends to be universal or universalizing. The connection through Mandaeism with a largely hypothetical early oriental gnosticism developing at the fringes of Judaism is the key to this process. Bultmann, drawing upon the work of his student Hans Jonas, understood historic gnosticism to enshrine a classic understanding of existence as alienation, embodied in its typical dualism. It is this understanding of existence that is overcome in the Christian gospel as presented by John. The gnostic mythology becomes the vehicle for the Christian message. By the same token the Jews, who appear throughout the Gospel as Jesus' opponents, are not real, historic Jews, but symbolize unfaith's rejection of Jesus. Bultmann acknowledges almost incidentally that their presence in John may be rooted in a synagogue-church conflict.[6] Nevertheless, the Gospel of John can be properly read and understood without knowledge of its specific historical setting and purpose. At the same time, however, the Gospel can be appreciated in its theological purity only if Bultmann's various literary reconstructions are followed. Otherwise, one encounters a Gospel somewhat diluted, even corrupted, by later accretions and especially rearrangement accomplished by a process of ecclesiastical editing.[7]

Hoskyns differs from the interpretations of Dodd and Bultmann in that he placed the Gospel's development from beginning to end against a Christian background. That is, John knew, if not the synoptic Gospels, certainly the traditions they contain, and his purpose was to bring to the forefront their central and essential theological meaning and significance. Crucial for Hoskyns was the theological commensurability of John with the synoptics, indeed, with the other major New Testament witnesses also. This is the test of the Gospel's theological appropriateness and validity. Thus, not surprisingly, Hoskyns emphasized the indispensability and importance of the historical revelation of God in Jesus Christ for the evangelist. Fundamentally, Hoskyns agreed with both Bultmann and Dodd in this respect, although each exegete conceived of this historical dimension and emphasis on the Incarnation in his own distinctive way.

In setting forth the meaning of John's Gospel in the context of the earliest development of Christian dogma—that is, within the New Testament period, Hoskyns adopted a mode or horizon of interpretation most amenable to the classical Christian understanding of the document. Already, at the end of the second century, Clement of Alexandria spoke of John, in relation to the others, as a spiritual Gospel. The sixteenth-century reformer John Calvin, at the beginning of his commentary, characterized the Gospel of John as the key to the proper understanding of the others. In fact, making due allowance for the differences of historical understanding and circumstance, one could truthfully say that Hoskyns's perspective and commentary stand directly in the legacy of both Clement and Calvin, as well as many other Christian interpreters before and since. John embraces and brings to articulation the essence of catholic Christianity as it is found elsewhere in the New Testament and in other early Christian witnesses. Thus, in effect, John is perceived as paving the way for the kind of "New Testament" or biblical theology to which Irenaeus gave expression toward the end of the second century.

It is worth noting at this point that the obverse of Hoskyns's position on the place of the Johannine Gospel in the development of early Christianity is not represented by Dodd or Bultmann so much as by Ernst Käsemann, whose *Jesu letzter Wille nach Johannes 17* appeared more than two decades later.[8] In fact, the works of Käsemann and Martyn appeared at about the same time. Moreover, Martyn had studied with Käsemann in the 1950s. Interestingly, like Hoskyns, Käsemann saw the Fourth Gospel as a response to, or development of, distinctly Christian theological concerns or issues. He, too, attempted to place the Fourth Gospel in the history of early Christianity by analyzing the character and thrust of its theology. But there the similarity to Hoskyns ends. Whereas Hoskyns saw in John the paragon of what might be called orthodoxy in the development of dogma, presumably toward the end of the first century, Käsemann had already, since his famous article *"Ketzer und Zeuge,"* been accustomed to viewing the evangelist—or Elder, as he styled him—as both heretic and witness.[9] Far from representing the direction in which orthodox church doctrine would move, John was naively docetic, suspect in orthodox circles—if unfairly so—for its gnostic leanings. Only by human error and the providence of God did the Gospel eventually find its way into the Christian canon of holy scripture. Yet, despite the suspicion in which it once stood, Käsemann values John highly for its uncompromising emphasis on Jesus Christ as God's word, set forth at a juncture in church history when the gospel might easily have been overwhelmed or obscured by a suffocating ecclesiasticism and sacramentalism.

Bultmann's interpretation of John against a gnostic background lives on in Käsemann, but in drastically altered, if not inverted, form. No longer is John's kerygma to be demythologized in terms of an understanding of existence. Now the word of the quasi-docetic Christ calls human beings to uncompromising allegiance to himself, making claims that put his own humanity in question and that can only be described as dogmatic. Ironically, John's Spirit-inspired christology and ecclesiology in time came to undergird an ecclesiastical orthodoxy in which church office and sacrament tended to rein in, and perhaps override, freedom of the same Spirit.

Martyn's Proposal and Contribution

Just when the stage might have seemed set for a battle royal between Käsemann and his allies and the more orthodox position represented by Hoskyns, the terms on which such a discussion could go forward were radically questioned by the original, insightful, provocative contribution of J. Louis Martyn, *History and Theology in the Fourth Gospel.*[10] In setting John against a Jewish, rather than a Christian, background, Martyn had predecessors. But he rightly gets credit for a sea-change in Johannine studies for somewhat the same reason that the Wright brothers got credit for the airplane. Others may have gotten off the ground, but Martyn—like the Wright brothers—achieved sustained flight. To extend the metaphor, his vehicle may not have been perfect, but it has proven good enough to maintain itself and to stand correction.

This is not the place to summarize Martyn's position. That has been done often enough, with variations on the theme, by myself and others. Suffice it to say that Martyn, unlike the dominant interpreters antecedent to him, took seriously the tension and hostility between "the Jews" and Jesus as the key to the historical life-setting and purpose of the Gospel of John. His entire proposal is based on two fundamental assumptions or insights. First, the prominence of the Jews and their hostility to Jesus and his disciples likely represents a genuine historical setting (that is, it is not an exercise in theological symbolism). Second, this historical setting can scarcely be that of Jesus and his actual, original disciples and opponents.[11] Therefore, one is not only justified, but also impelled to look for a historical setting and state of affairs corresponding to the nature and direction or thrust of the Gospel's tensions and conflict. Martyn is actually invoking the modern, form-critical principle that the Gospels bear testimony primarily to the life-setting in which they were produced, and only secondarily to their subject matter.

As is well known, Martyn finds the major key to that setting in the thrice-repeated reference to the expulsion from the synagogue of those who confess belief in Jesus (9:22; 12:42; 16:2), and more particularly in the evangelist's statement that "the Jews had already agreed that if anyone should confess him to be Messiah, he would become an excommunicate from the synagogue."[12] This agreement is traced to the Jamnian Academy under the leadership of Gamaliel II (80-115 CE) and to the reformulation of the Twelfth Benediction of the Eighteen (*Shemoneh Esre*) by the legendary Samuel the Small. According to Martyn, this malediction against Nazarenes (Christians) and Minim (heretics) was used to smoke out followers of Jesus in the synagogue service, for they could not in good conscience recite it, much less lead it. Martyn daringly reconstructs a dramatic scene in which the Christ-confessor would be identified and excluded. His reconstruction is based principally on *Berakoth 28* (see also *y. Berakoth* 8a) of the Babylonian Talmud (54; see also 61), and secondarily on such data as the instances in Justin's *Dialogue with Trypho* (16, 110) in which Jews are said to curse in their synagogues all who believe in Christ (16) or to expel Christians from their property (60 n. 81).[13] *Berakoth* 28 describes how making a mistake on the Twelfth Benediction brings down upon the reader the suspicion of being a Min, and suggests, but does not say, that the recitation of the Benediction was intended as a test for heretics, possibly Christians. Martyn's dramatic reconstruction has made his thesis all the more alluring, as he evokes the synagogue and city of the evangelist.[14]

Wayne Meeks, who has made his own distinctive contribution to the definition of a Jewish milieu for John, has noted the difficulty of establishing some aspects of Martyn's thesis and rightly observes that the Twelfth Benediction has become a kind of red herring of Johannine scholarship.[15] For one thing, it is unclear that within the first century the Jamnian Academy had the kind of general authority that Martyn's thesis attributes to it. For another, the date of the Twelfth Benediction is uncertain, and since Martyn first published a number of scholars have strongly contested the view that it was composed as early as the 80s of the first century. In the third place, there is no direct or unambiguous evidence that the Benediction was formulated for the purpose of smoking Christians out of the synagogue or that it was ever actually used in that way. It should be added, however, that despite Meeks's reservations about the specifics of Martyn's thesis, he is far from dismissing it as unfounded and is inclined to believe that the evidence

Martyn has adduced on the Johannine side bespeaks some such controversy as Martyn has proposed. Moreover, his hesitations with regard to the Rabbinic and other evidence on the Jewish side do not amount to a rejection, but to a series of cautions.[16] Meeks would prefer to think of a linear development in which the promulation of the *Birkath ha-Minim* was a culmination rather than the beginning point of a development, a position that Martyn does not regard as devastating to his own.[17]

Nevertheless, in the revised edition of *History and Theology* Martyn sees no reason to retreat from what is from any point of view a murky swamp in which his opponents' views can be grounded no more securely than his own. The evidence is itself incomplete and demands a coherent theory if one is to make sense of it. In fact, he earlier on declared that the correlation between the *Birkath ha-Minim* and the expression "to be put out of the synagogue" is one of the relatively secure points in the history of the Johannine community.[18] Meeks's assessment, like that of other experts, is typical: "Louis Martyn's ingenious 'two-level' reading of John 9 and other conflict stories in this Gospel has been widely accepted in its general outline if not in all its details."[19] Meeks's discussion of the Johannine community makes clear that he himself is a part of this general consensus, although he would make some qualifications and introduce some important nuances. As many questions as one may have about the daringly bold formulation of Martyn's thesis, it is difficult to reject the evidence and Martyn's construal of it as without foundation.

Perhaps the issues have become exacerbated in view of Martyn's belief that John 16:2, when linked to the Jews' mortal opposition to Jesus in the Gospel, suggests that some Johannine missioner(s) had been put to death by Jews as a beguiler (*mesith*). At this point the possible implications of Martyn's thesis for modern Jewish-Christian relations are obvious enough, although Martyn himself has been careful to keep the discussion on the plane of historical investigation and to make clear that his findings have no direct implications of modern inter-faith relations in the sense that they could legitimately be used by anyone for or against anyone else. About 16:2, Martyn writes:

> In light of the fact that the horrible and heinous and centuries-long persecution of Jews by Christians has sometimes been "justified" by the theory that the Jews did the first persecuting, it is understandable that a number of Christian interpreters have wished to see this verse as a reference to the persecution not of Christians by Jews, but by Roman authorities. Yet the Greek word rendered "act of (worshipful) service" refers elsewhere in the New Testament to Jewish worship; and the other experience referred to in this text, excommunication from the synagogue, points to the action of Jewish authorities. Modern relations between Christians and Jews are not helped by an antihistorical interpretation of Biblical texts.[20]

To leave the impression that Martyn's work on John was mainly accomplished by the publication of one book, as important as it may be, would be misleading. Martyn's 1957 Yale Ph.D. dissertation, "The Salvation-History Perspective in the Fourth Gospel," was in large part a study of the historical setting of the Gospel, in which he found the key in the role played by "the Jews." As in *History and Theology in the Fourth Gospel,* Martyn argues that the original setting of the Fourth Gospel (or its antecedent tradition) was the synagogue, in which followers of Jesus incurred the hostility of their fellow Jews. One sees here already even the imaginatively constructed dramatic scenes in and around the synagogue that appear in *History and Theology in the Fourth Gospel.* What is missing is any reference to the *Birkath ha-Minim* on the Jewish side. Thus while the relevance of *aposynagogoi* is noted, it plays a somewhat less important role in the book. Nevertheless, the indications of setting in the Gospel led Martyn to look for a corresponding situation in post-70 Judaism, which in his further research he finds in the promulgation of the Twelfth Benediction.

Shortly after the publication of this major book, Martyn presented "Source Criticism and Religionsgeschichte in the Fourth Gospel" to the first Gospels Seminar of The Society of Biblical Literature (November 1969) and also before the Pittsburgh Theological Seminary Festival on the Gospels.[21] In that paper he correlates his own thesis with Robert Fortna's source criticism (see below), with side glances at the works of Käsemann and Meeks in particular. His subsequent book *The Gospel of John in Christian History* (1978), which draws together with some revision essays offered in the years intervening, appeared just a year before the revised edition of *History and Theology in the Fourth Gospel* (1979). In these essays Martyn advances three separate but related theses. He proposes that the evangelist has suppressed the identification of Jesus with Elijah found in his source. He analyzes the so-called *Ascents of James* in the Pseudo-Clementines and shows how it reflects a Jewish-Christian synagogal setting with real affinities and relationships with that of the Fourth Gospel. Finally, he draws together his earlier work by presenting "Glimpses into the History of the Johannine Community." In this essay, as well as the one on Elijah, Martyn's basic agreement with, and appropriation of, the source criticism of Robert Fortna is very much in the forefront.[22]

Although Fortna was Martyn's student at Union Theological Seminary, his work had an independent beginning point. Fortna undertook a source-critical analysis of the Fourth Gospel on the basis of convictions growing out of his careful and detailed study of earlier source theories, particularly Rudolf Bultmann's. Initially forgoing theological criteria, which are easily suspect of being subjective, and stylistic criteria, which are at least initially indecisive, Fortna undertook a careful study of the text of the Gospel, looking for tell-tale contextual traces of an author's annotating or supplementing an earlier text. It was Fortna's belief, which he tested by exegetical analysis, that the evidence of such redactional use of an earlier source could best be explained on the basis of a rather simple two-layer hypothesis, *Grundschrift* and later redaction and elaboration. As it turned out, the *Grundschrift* was discovered primarily in the narrative portions of John (signs and passion), and the evangelist's elaborations not surprisingly in the discourse that follow, or are interlarded among, the narrative portions.

Fortna's source theory might have become one of a rather large library of such efforts, which might—but need not—be true, had it not been integrally related to such an overall view as has been worked out by Martyn. The Gospel of Signs in the Martyn-Fortna proposal becomes the evangelistic tract that formed the basis of the missionary efforts by believing Jews in synagogues. That it consisted of miracles and passion corresponded perfectly with Martyn's scenario, for precisely the miracles are signs demonstrating the truth of the claim that Jesus was prophet Messiah. Moreover, the death of the messianic claimant would of necessity have been dealt with in the context of the synagogue, where it caused offense, and belief in the resurrection could not be assumed. That the miracles of Jesus are not signs in the synoptics, but only in John, further strengthens the linkage of Fortna's source analysis with Martyn's overall theory. While Martyn's thesis does not require Fortna's source-critical results precisely, it does require some cogent explanation of how the content of the Gospel of John, particularly the narrative content, is linked to the synagogue controversy. Fortna's work supplies that link, and Martyn has continued to regard it as essentially correct. Moreover, it has the virtues of coherence and plausibility. The Johannine narratives do not seem to be drawn from the synoptic Gospels. At the same time they stand out from the rest of the Gospel and, on Fortna's reading, form a coherent whole.

Interesting, as Martyn builds upon the essential correctness of Fortna's source-critical work, so Fortna now views Martyn's thesis as congruent with his own work. This is evident in his recent book, where he writes: "I find highly persuasive the detailed reconstruction of Martyn in his *History and Theology*, in particular his proposal that expulsion of the Evangelist's Christian community from the synagogue has occasioned many of the differences between source and extant Gospel."[23] Nevertheless, Fortna indicates that his own focus continues to be on the texts themselves, particularly on the theological shifts that can be observed between the Signs Gospel and the Gospel of John.

Less explicit, but no less intriguing is the question of the relationship of Martyn's thesis about Jamnia and the Gospel of John to his Union colleague W. D. Davies's proposal linking the Gospel of Matthew to the sequence of events that led to the emergence of the Jamnian Academy or College.[24] Suffice it to say that the parallels are broad and general, but both Martyn and Davies see the respective Gospels as Christian responses to a crisis brought on by the retrenchment of Jewish thought and life that "Jamnia" represents. While for Martyn John is more a crisis document than is Matthew for Davies, the latter nevertheless rests his case on the view that Matthew was a Christian response, and an alternative, to Jamnia. Thus its halakhic character. In fact, it was Davies who first described how the Twelfth Benediction might have applied to, or been used against, Christians who were seeking to remain within the synagogue. Obviously, Davies and Martyn share similar views of when the *Birkath ha-Minim* was composed (in the 80s) and where its focus and purpose lay, as Martyn acknowledges. Davies's book antedates Martyn by five years, but while there are affinities and points of contact, Martyn does not deal with Davies's thesis. By the same token, although Davies could not have taken account of Martyn when writing *The Setting of the Sermon on the Mount,* to the best of my knowledge he has not since commented on Martyn's thesis regarding the Johannine community in any formal way.

The question of such relationships is more than a matter of a possibly interesting scholarly connection, for substantive issues are involved. Can it be that such different Gospels arose out of parallel or closely related circumstances? If one Gospel arose out of the post-Jamnian rivalry between Judaism and the movement that was becoming Christianity, is it likely the other did as well? It is not impossible to think they both did, especially in view of the fact that they would represent different sorts of encounter and response. But just the differences posited are intriguing.

Although, as we have observed, Martyn does not deal with or react to Davies's thesis, in a most significant observation he points out that John refuses to engage in argument with his Pharisaic opponents on their terms. That is, he eschews midrashic debate on terms laid down or presupposed by Jewish opponents.[25] (Nevertheless, John is convinced that scripture, rightly understood, supports his cause.) Just such midrashic debate would seem to be what Matthew was engaged in, albeit in a different, narrative genre. From Davies's standpoint, Matthew undertakes debate with post-Jamnian, Pharisaic Judaism on terms they largely share. With John it is precisely the case that the most crucial terms are *not* shared. John 7:40-42 illustrates the point very well. Does John not know Matthew or Matthew's (and Luke's) tradition of Jesus' birth in Bethlehem, which is set forth precisely and explicitly as the fulfillment of Old Testament prophecy (Mic 5:1-3) and Jewish expectation? Or if he knows, does he simply pass it up because he does not want to engage in debate while conceding this common ground? Whatever one makes of John's relation to Matthew, his silence is telling. It is possible to maintain that John expects the reader to know Matthew and to appreciate the irony of the Jews' ignorance. If so, the evangelist is quite subtle on this point, and never reveals to the unknowing reader (or modern scholar!) that he is engaging in such subtlety. In any event, he chooses not to point out the Jews' (or the disciples') failure to understand, as he does elsewhere (such as 2:21-22). In fact, Martyn's assessment of John's rejection of a common basis for midrash seems to fit this pericope perfectly. Of course, we cannot here attempt to resolve this exegetical issue, much less the problem of John's relation to the synoptics. But the question of how to understand John 7:40-42 points up how fruitful a discussion over these matters between Martyn and Davies (from the standpoint of their respective positions) might be.[26]

The Continuing Influence of Martyn's Work

Perhaps Martyn's closest and longest scholarly and collegial relationship has been with Raymond E. Brown, who was in effect Davies's successor at Union Theological Seminary. Already in his Anchor Bible commentary (the first volume of which was published two years before Martyn's work appeared, but too late to influence it) and before they were colleagues, Brown had suggested that John's Gospel was written after and as a response to the situation of expulsion from the synagogue, brought about by the publication of the Twelfth Benediction of the *Shemoneh Esre*.[27] Of course, Brown's suggestion, which was quite important to him in fixing the date and establishing the purpose of the Fourth Gospel, was not developed in the detail and with all the nuances of Martyn's proposal. Nevertheless, Brown continued to work on the matter in conversation with Martyn, but in some ways also independent of him. Brown extended his analysis and description of the setting and development of the Johannine literature backward to the Beloved Disciple (and ultimately Jesus) and forward to the Epistles and their relationship to the Gospel (first in his *Community of the Beloved Disciple* and more definitively in his Anchor Bible commentary on the Johannine Epistles[28]). For Brown, as well as most other interpreters, the letters of John reflect a different, presumably later, setting in which the sharp conflict with representatives of the Jews has given way to other problems.

It would be misleading, however, to leave the impression that Brown simply accepted Martyn's construction of the historical setting of the Gospel and moved on to deal with the letters. His view of the origin of the Gospel is in some ways more complex than Martyn's and in others different. Already in the first volume of his commentary Brown had set forth the thesis that the Gospel arose in five stages of composition, beginning with the earliest oral preaching and culminating with the present canonical text, which is the product of editing by a hand later than the evangelist's. In *Community of the Beloved Disciple,* Brown refined, and complicated, his thesis of Gospel origins as he discerned various interests, such as the Samaritan mission, conservative Jewish Christians, apostolic (Petrine) Christians, each playing a role at different points in the development of the Gospel. Thus as Brown developed his own reconstruction it differed with Martyn's in more than one respect. But while the series of literary stages seems more complex, it is actually also more comprehensive. Martyn is concerned only with Fortna's Gospel of Signs, the *Grundschrift,* and the subsequent controversy that leads ultimately to its expansion into the Gospel we now know. (Thus there are three stages against Brown's five.) But Martyn actually deals only with the middle of the spectrum of development as Brown sees it and not at all with a putative development from Jesus to the original Johannine tradition or with any final redaction of the Gospel and the publication of the Letters.

In addition, Brown saw the initial conflict between Christ-confessors and Jewish authorities as breaking out over theological issues at a point at which Samaritan Christian influence began to assert itself in the Johannine community. For Martyn the tensions arose as the Johannine preacher(s) vigorously prosecuted the mission to other Jews, whether through the Gospel of Signs or otherwise, and threatened to draw increasing numbers of synagogue members to belief in Jesus. Only subsequently did doctrinal considerations—that is, ditheism (chap. 5)—become the paramount issue. Brown apparently sees the tensions arising precisely with the introduction of a "high" christology that appears to threaten monotheism and under the influence of the Samaritan Christian element of the Johannine community. The differences between Martyn and Brown are of less weight than the agreements, but they are not insignificant. Obviously, they reflect both the collegiality and the independence of two longtime friends and colleagues, even as they set an agenda for further discussion.

Just as Raymond Brown, the leading commentator on the Gospel of John in America, found himself in basic agreement with Martyn's thesis, something similar was happening across the Atlantic. In 1978 C. K. Barrett brought out a considerably revised and expanded version of his commentary, long regarded as the standard English-language commentary on the Greek text.[29] Barrett did not manifest much agreement with divergent views (the independence of John from the Synoptics; the close relationship of John and Qumran) that had gained increasing support since the initial publication of his commentary. But he tacitly acknowledged that research had advanced in at least one significant respect, for he indicated his basic agreement with Martyn's view of the circumstances of origin of John's Gospel. It was initially the product of the sharp disputation and hostility within the synagogue between Christ-confessors and other Jews. The influence of Martyn's thesis on Barrett's actual commentary is less pervasive than one might expect, but that is in large part a function of the character of the commentary as a series of erudite and exceedingly useful notes on the Greek text. Nevertheless, Barrett's agreement with Martyn's basic thesis was significant in itself, and also as an indication of which way the winds of informed scholarly opinion were blowing. (It should be noted, however, that Barrett had already suggested the possibility of a link between the Gospel and the *Birkath ha-Minim* in commenting on 9:22 in the first edition of his commentary.)[30]

Scholarly work, of course, advances but often reflects Martyn's influence at a quite fundamental level and in interesting ways. For example, the recent monograph of Klaus Wengst, *Bedrängte Gemeinde*, takes for granted the basic correctness of Martyn's proposal and proceeds to move beyond it in determining the geographical site and place of origin of the Johannine community and Gospel.[31] In a brief allusion to the matter of place of origin, Martyn had more or less dismissed the traditional site of Ephesus, but had left the door open for Alexandria.[32] Now Wengst, on the basis of research principally in Josephus and Rabbinic sources, proposes Batanea (the present Golan Heights) as the locus of the community that produced the Gospel of John. His reasoning actually begins from Martyn's thesis, as he asks where in the latter half of the first century one would find an area in which Jews were the dominant, but certainly not the only, group. It would be an area in which the designation "the Jews" would be intelligible as indicating one religious and cultural grouping over against others. Wengst argues that in such an area expulsion from the synagogue would involve genuine social, religious, and perhaps economic, penalties or loss. Perhaps it goes without saying that only after 70, and especially outside Palestine, would synagogue membership be the decisive mark of Jewish identity. Wengst believes, moreover, that connections and communications can be traced between Judaism in the Transjordanian highlands and Jamnia in the period soon after the Roman war. All this involves a considerable amount of inference from sources not intended to supply such information—the Gospel of John included! The thesis is, however, quite plausible, as Wayne Meeks has already observed.[33] Although it may fall into that rather large body or category of research that presents conclusions that are possible and plausible without being demonstrably true, Wengst's monograph nevertheless demonstrates how fruitful and seminal Martyn's work has been in stimulating further creative investigations.

Other instances of Martyn's influence could easily be multiplied. I shall mention only two works, both of which appeared even as this article was being completed. Jerome S. Neyrey, in *Ideology of Revolt: John's Christology in Social Science Perspective*,[34] seems to assume as generally correct a picture of the conflict setting of John's Gospel as Martyn has portrayed it. On that basis he then pursues his own new and distinctive analysis. Similarly, David Rensburger, *Johannine Faith and Liberating Community*,[35] moves forward on the basis of Martyn, indicating his own position even as he accurately describes the present state of scholarship on the Gospel:

> Subsequent studies have fully confirmed the rightness of this [Martyn's] basic insight. While few have accepted Martyn's delineation of the action behind the Fourth Gospel in all of its details, the fundamental conception that he outlined has been elaborated in a variety of directions and has become the cornerstone of much current Johannine research.[36]

Thus Meeks can say confidently and rightly:

> The rupture between the followers of Jesus and "the Jews" is at the center of attention. It has manifestly shaped the Johannine groups' language and their perception of the world. These features of the Johannine universe have become so widely recognized in recent scholarship that there is no need for me to rehearse the evidence.[37]

Needless to say, not all recent Johannine research has followed Martyn's lead. Quite legitimately, new questions are raised, and the Gospel of John is approached from fresh perspectives. Typical of the newer literary-critical or narratological approach is Alan Culpepper's *Anatomy of the Fourth Gospel*, a ground-breaking work as far as the Gospel of John is concerned.[38] In that Culpepper deliberately refuses to regard the Gospel of John as a window for looking beyond the text into some atextual historical reality, whether the Jesus the text describes or the community that produced this highly distinctive account of him, he would seem to run counter to Martyn's work. Yet, Culpepper explicitly indicates that his purpose in this regard is heuristic rather than eristic. That is, he is not disavowing historical research or its relevance, but simply setting it aside for the time being to take another tack.

In fact, Culpepper's earlier *Johannine School* was quite congenial with Martyn's perspective and approach, and the results of *Anatomy of the*

Fourth Gospel may be as well. Culpepper's literary analysis of John as such does not, of course, stand or fall with whether or not it makes John conform to anything beyond the document itself. Quite the contrary. Yet, when one reads Culpepper with Martyn in mind, some remarkable convergences or congruities appear. The implied readers of the Gospel need not be actual, ancient, historical readers. Nor need the implied author reflect, or address himself to, an actual historical setting or crisis such as Martyn posits. Yet, Culpepper's analysis of the implied author's role and interest, as well as those of the implied readers, actually fits rather well a historical situation in which a threatened or oppressed community (Wengst) draws upon its perception of its founder and master to find resources to face the present threat. Although the symbolic role of the Jews as foes of Jesus' disciples, not to mention Jesus himself, need have had no genuine historical counterpart, the existence of such referenced historical counterparts is certainly not excluded by viewing the Gospel from a literary-critical perspective, as Culpepper has done.

It would be unfair to Culpepper's own worthwhile project to imply that its value lies in confirming Martyn's contribution. But just the fact that by pursuing a different goal, from a different perspective, and with different methods, Culpepper has produced an analysis of John's Gospel that is in many respects congruent with Martyn's historical reconstruction is something that needs to be considered carefully in further historical investigations, whatever may be done on the literary-critical side.

Important work done outside the "Johannine school" may also reflect Martyn's influence or have bearing upon his work. Another scholar who studied with Martyn at Union, E. P. Sanders, has within the past decade produced two impressive and important works, *Paul and Palestinian Judaism* and *Jesus and Judaism*.[39] I wish to focus briefly on only one aspect of the latter work—namely, Sanders' contention that the Gospels (and Sanders actually deals only with the Synoptics) vastly overplay Jesus' conflict with the Pharisees. For Sanders the conflict between Jesus and the Pharisees over fasting, sabbath-breaking, purity, and the like is principally the product of later Jewish-Christian tension, retrojected upon the ministry of Jesus. What is the basis for this seemingly daring contradiction of what most readers have taken to be the weight and thrust of the Gospel's portrayal of Jesus?

Certainly Matthew's Gospel, even more than Mark or Luke, puts the Pharisees in a poor light and suggests that some such a later conflict was or had been in progress. It is worth observing that in Luke's Gospel the Pharisees do not always appear in a negative role (13:31), while in Acts the seat of Jewish opposition to Jesus' disciples is to be found in

Jerusalem among the high priests, the Sadducees, and temple authorities, rather than among Pharisees. Paul, who was a Pharisee, does not identify his Jewish, or Jewish-Christian, opponents as Pharisees or Pharisaic per se. When he refers to himself as a Pharisee (Phil 3:5; compare Acts 23:6) it is in an entirely positive way, even though he may be speaking of a past from which he has departed. Elsewhere in the New Testament Pharisees are scarcely mentioned—except, of course, in the Gospel of John. John's Pharisees are quintessential Jews. They represent the essence of Jewish opposition to Jesus—that is, to early Christians.

Thus if one asks for evidence of sharp conflict between early Christians and specifically Pharisaic Jews, the weightiest witness would be the Gospel of John, understood along the lines that Martyn suggests. As Martyn understands it, this conflict is not—or is not only—symbolic, literary, or theological. It represents the culmination of a long struggle, first within the synagogue and then between synagogue and church, developing over many years. Certainly Martyn himself does not think this struggle began with the publication of the *Birkath ha-Minim*. It goes back at least to the period following the end of the Roman War (70 CE), probably before.[40] Whether it has earlier roots might be important for Sanders. Perhaps the fact that Martyn did not trace the roots into the pre-war period, and differentiated the Johannine situation from the tensions spoken of in Acts and Paul has something to do with the fact that Sanders does not make much of the Fourth Gospel or of Martyn's proposal. If the Johannine conflict is more or less post- or extra-synoptic, it would have relatively less positive bearing on Sanders's thesis about Jesus and the Pharisees than if it could be traced to a time contemporary with the development of the synoptic tradition. (In that case, John might shed light on what was going on in the synoptics or the synoptic tradition.) To speculate further on such matters is intriguing and suggests the possibility of fruitful dialogue between Martyn and Sanders—who was actually Davies's doctoral student at Union—as well as between Martyn and Davies.

It is worth observing, however, that Martyn's proposal of two levels of Johannine conflict, one in the time of Jesus and one in the time of the church, stands in interesting relationship to Sanders's recent work on Jesus. Martyn is quite careful to distinguish his analysis of these two levels from John's own self-awareness or intent. That is, he does not claim that the two levels constitute a deliberate and conscious technique. Indeed, the evangelist would have insisted upon the unity of the two levels.[41] The Johannine church's struggle with its Pharisaic Jewish opponents toward the end of the first century is, in the evangelist's view, the same struggle as Jesus' struggle with Pharisees in the first half of the same century. If John knew of historical differences, they were irrelevant or unimportant to him. It is striking that on Sanders's terms John would have been, historically speaking, wrong about the identity of the two levels of conflict. The historical Jesus had no principal conflict with the Pharisees. This conclusion would presumably be less damaging to Martyn's point of view, which does not require the historicity of the *einmalig* level, as he calls it, than it would be to the evangelist's. The latter presumably took for granted that he wrote about a real conflict with real Pharisees with which Jesus, as well as his own community, was involved.

Obviously, we have now raised possibilities that go beyond Martyn's thesis in order to reflect, in what may turn out to be a suggestive and useful way, on its implications. Hopefully, such reflections stimulated by Martyn's work show how enormously fructifying his creative imagination and research have been, not only for the study of the Fourth Gospel but for other and related matters of New Testament history and interpretation as well.

Notes

1. Rudolf Bultmann, *The Gospel of John: A Commentary* (trans. G. R. Beasley-Murray et al.; Philadelphia: Westminster, 1971). The German original, *Das Evangelium des Johannes* (Göttingen: Vandenhoeck & Ruprecht, 1941) was first published in fascicles, 1939-41, and has been supplemented through the years with several *Ergänzungshefte*.
2. Dodd, *The Interpretation of the Fourth Gospel* (Cambridge: Cambridge University Press, 1953); *Historical Tradition in the Fourth Gospel* (Cambridge: Cambridge University Press, 1963).
3. Hoskyns, *The Fourth Gospel* (ed. F. N. Davey; 2nd ed.; London: Faber & Faber, 1947).
4. As well as the commentary, note also Bultmann's *Theology of the New Testament* (trans. Kendrick Grobel; 2 vols.; New York: Charles Scribner's sons, 1955) 2.3-92.
5. Bultmann, *The Gospel of John*, 716.
6. Bultmann, *Theology of the New Testament*, 2.5.
7. Bultmann's source theory is well known. The evangelist worked with several literary sources, a sign source, a revelation-discourse source, and a passion source as well as other more fragmentary sources or traditions. In a real sense he interpreted and even demythologized them as he wove them into the Gospel he was creating. The original form of this Gospel was unaccountably lost, but it has been the object of at least two serious efforts at restoration. The first was undertaken, according to Bultmann, by the ecclesiastical redactor, but with only limited success. The second was the work of Bultmann himself, who in a real sense created the text he was commenting on. His reconstruction entailed both large-scale and minuscule rearrangements of the traditional text as well as the elimination of some passages (such as 6:51-58; chap. 21), deemed the creation of the redactor. For further details, consult the English translation of Bultmann's commentary, for which a table of contents has been helpfully provided, enabling the reader to locate passages Bultmann has repositioned, or my *Composition and Order of the Fourth Gospel: Bultmann's Literary Theory* (New Haven and London: Yale University Press, 1965). In that monograph I call attention to the fact that Bultmann never offers an explanation for the destruction or, indeed, the defective restoration of the text as a deficiency in his work. I have since come to question the significance of such a historically based criticism, given Bultmann's hermeneutic. The text stimulates the interpreter, but the interpreter with the proper *Vorverständnis* then understands better than the (author of the) text what the text is

about. Why should the interpreter not then improve upon the text—within the resources provided by the text—to bring its *Sache* to clear expression? I do not seriously suggest that Bultmann actually or explicitly thought in this way, only that such a procedure is the logical extension of his hermeneutical program.

8. Ernst Käsemann, *The Testament of Jesus: A Study of the Gospel of John in the Light of Chapter 17* (trans. Gerhard Krodel; Philadelphia: Fortress, 1968).

9. Ernst Käsemann, "Ketzer und Zeuge," *Zeitschrift für Theologie und Kirche* 49 (1951) 292-311.

10. J. Louis Martyn, *History and Theology in the Fourth Gospel* (New York: Harper & Row, 1968). A revised edition, in which the author engages criticisms and questions appeared in 1979 (Nashville: Abingdon). References in this essay are to the revised edition.

11. Ibid., 39.

12. Ibid., 38.

13. Ibid., 54, 60-61.

14. As is well known, Kenneth L. Carroll related *aposynagogoi* to the *Birkath ha-Minim* in his article "The Fourth Gospel and the Exclusion of Christians from the Synagogues," *Bulletin of the John Rylands Library* 40 (1957-58) 19-32. At almost the same time, T. C. Smith, *Jesus in the Gospel of John* (Nashville: Broadman, 1959), made the same connection. Curiously, Carroll continued to think of the author of the Gospel as a Gentile Christian and did not make his insight productive for an understanding of its setting and purpose. Already William Wrede, *Charakter und Tendenz des Johannesevangeliums* (Sammlung gemeinverstandlicher Vorträge und Schriften aus dem Gebiet der Theologie und Religionsgeschichte 37; Tübingen: Mohr, 1903), had observed that the Jews in the Fourth Gospel reflected a Johannine conflict with contemporary Judaism. Shortly after the appearance of Martyn's book, but still independent of it, Göran Forkman, *The Limits of the Religious Community: Expulsion from the Religious Community Within the Qumran Sect, Within Rabbinic Judaism, and Within Primitive Christianity* (Coniectanea Biblica, New Testament Series 5; Lund: Gleerup, 1972) connected the *Birkath ha-Minim* with expulsion of Christians from the synagogue (90-92) and found that the experiences reflected in John 9:22; 12:42; and 16:2 are in all probability related to its promulgation. Forkman cites as important for his own work the unpublished Göttingen dissertation of Claus-Hunno Hunzinger, "Die jüdische Bannpraxis im neutestamentlichen Zeitalter" (1954), also cited by Martyn, which I have not seen. Forkman does not, however, cite Martyn, nor does he apparently know the works of Carroll or T. C. Smith.

15. See Wayne Meeks, "Breaking Away: Three New Testament Pictures of Christianity's Separation from the Jewish Communities," in *"To See Ourselves as Others See Us": Christians, Jews, "Others" in Late Antiquity* (eds. Jacob Neusner and Ernest S. Frerichs; Studies in the Humanities 9; Chico: Scholars Press, 1985) 93-115; pertinent discussion is on p. 102. Meeks's contribution began with his important monograph *The Prophet-King: Moses Traditions and the Johannine Christology* (NovTSup 14; Leiden: Brill, 1967).

16. See Martyn, *History and Theology*, 54-55 n. 69, and 56-57 n. 75, for Martyn's summary of discussions with Wayne A. Meeks and Morton Smith.

17. Much more negative, however, is Reuven Kimelman, "*Birkat ha-Minim* and the Lack of Evidence for an Anti-Christian Jewish Prayer in Late Antiquity," *Jewish and Christian Self-Definition* (vol. 2; eds. E. P. Sanders et al.; Philadelphia: Fortress, 1981) 226-44; also Stephen Katz, "Issues in the Separation of Judaism and Christianity after 70 C.E.: A Reconsideration," *JBL* 103 (1984) 43-76. Peter Schäfer, "Die sogannante Synode von Jabne," in *Studien zur Geschichte und Theologie des Rabbinischen Judentums* (Leiden: Brill, 1978) 45-55 (reprinted from *Judaica* 31 [1975]), argues that the Benediction was directed as much against political oppression as against heretics, and in any case was not intended to separate Christians from Jews. A balanced treatment with ample bibliographical citation is William Horbury, "The Benediction of the *Minim* and Early Jewish-Christian Controversy," *JTS* 33 (1982) 19-61. Horbury's judgment, p. 60 ("The

Jamnian ordinance belongs to this more systematized opposition of the late first century, and probably reinforces an earlier exclusion attested in John, although uncertainties of dating leave open the possibility that these two measures may be contemporaneous."), expresses approximately the same proportion of agreement and qualification as do those of Meeks and Morton Smith. But while also allowing for the Johannine persecution to antedate the Jamnian formulation, Horbury is inclined to continue to date the Twelfth Benediction within the first century.

18. See J. L. Martyn, *The Gospel of John in Christian History: Essays for Interpreters* (New York: Paulist, 1978) 92; see also 103-4.
19. Meeks, "Breaking Away," 95; see also 94-104.
20. Martyn, *Gospel of John in Christian History*, 56.
21. Published in the proceedings of that conference, *Jesus and Man's Hope* (vol. 1; A Perspective Book; Pittsburgh: Pittsburgh Theological Seminary, 1970) 247-73.
22. See Robert T. Fortna, *The Gospel of Signs: A Reconstruction of the Narrative Source Underlying the Fourth Gospel* (SNTSMS 11; Cambridge; Cambridge University Press, 1970).
23. Robert T. Fortna, *The Fourth Gospel and Its Predecessors: From Narrative Source to Present Gospel* (Philadelphia: Fortress, 1988) 224.
24. See W. D. Davies, *The Setting of the Sermon on the Mount* (Cambridge: Cambridge University Press, 1966) 256-315, esp. 275-86. [Editor's note: See also the article by Davies in this volume.]
25. Martyn, *History and Theology*, 128.
26. Meeks, "Breaking Away," 94-104, 109, apparently finds both Martyn and Davies largely convincing about the Gospels of John and Matthew respectively.
27. See Raymond E. Brown, *The Gospel According to John (i-xii)* (AB 29; Garden City: Doubleday, 1966) lxxiv-lxxv.
28. See Raymond E. Brown, *The Community of the Beloved Disciple* (New York: Paulist, 1979); *The Epistles of John* (AB 30; Garden City: Doubleday, 1982).
29. See C. K. Barrett, *The Gospel According to John: An Introduction with Commentary and Notes on the Greek Text* (2nd ed.; Philadelphia: Westminster, 1978).
30. Evidently, Barrett's influence will not end with the English-speaking world. A German translation of his commentary is projected for the renowned Meyer series, in which the John commentary has been Bultmann's famous *Das Evangelium des Johannes*. (Apparently Vandenhoeck and Ruprecht will also keep Bultmann in print, but Barrett's commentary will fill the need for a standard, up-to-date work.) If it would be excessive to say that, through Barrett, Martyn's work becomes canonical in Germany as well as Great Britain, the important point is nonetheless clear. Martyn's thesis has become a paradigm, to borrow from Thomas Kuhn. It is a part of what students imbibe from standard works, such as commentaries and textbooks, as knowledge generally received and held to be valid.

For example, in *Anatomy of the New Testament: A Guide to Its Structure and Meaning* (New York: Macmillan, 1989) 170-79, Robert A. Spivey and I present Martyn's thesis as providing historical perspective for the treatment of the Fourth Gospel. Something similar might be said of my book, *John* (Proclamation Commentary; 2nd ed.; Philadelphia: Fortress, 1986) 38-51, or of John Painter's excellent introduction, *John: Witness and Theologian* (London: SPCK, 1975) 13. That none of these works represents original scholarship is exactly the point. Insofar as they are successful in accomplishing their goals, they reflect the state of the art in Johannine research, and Martyn's work rightly stands at their center. One might add that these books are more or less typical of works of this genre.

31. See Klaus Wengst, *Bedrängte Gemeinde und verherrlichte Christus: Der historische Ort des Johannesevangelium als Schlüssel zu seiner Interpretation* (Biblisch-theologische Studien 5; Neukirchen: Neukirchener Verlag, 1981), esp. 30ff. n. 82.
32. See Martyn, *History and Theology*, 73 n. 100.
33. See Meeks, "Breaking Away," 102-3.
34. Jerome S. Neyrey, in *Ideology of Revolt: John's Christology in Social Science Perspective*, (Philadelphia: Fortress, 1988) see 3, 9-15, 35, 122-48, 196, 211.

35. David Rensburger, *Johannine Faith and Liberating Community* (Philadelphia: Westminster, 1988).

36. Ibid., 22.

37. Meeks, "Breaking Away," 94.

38. Alan Culpepper, *Anatomy of the Fourth Gospel: A Study in Literary Design* (Philadelphia: Fortress, 1983).

39. E. P. Sanders, *Paul and Palestinian Judaism* (Philadelphia: Fortress, 1977); idem., *Jesus and Judaism* (Philadelphia: Fortress, 1985).

40. See Martyn, *The Gospel of John in Christian History*, 99.

41. See Martyn, *History and Theology*, 137.

THE THEOLOGICAL CONTENT OF THE PROLOGUE TO JOHN IN ITS PRESENT FORM*

Oscar Cullmann

I had intended to deal more extensively with the subject I had chosen to contribute to this Festschrift, but circumstances thwarted my plan. Indeed, I had begun to fear that I should have to withdraw completely from participation in this work. I should have regretted this, since I feel particularly close to the one being celebrated. Years ago I had the pleasure of being his colleague during several guest professorships at Union Theological Seminary, and I share with him some fundamental views on the Gospel of John. Consequently, I am grateful to the editors for expressing the wish to include a short article by me. Without this willingness I should have hesitated to appear alongside the more substantial contributions of my other colleagues with so few pages of my own. I am pleased after all to be able to participate in honoring J. Louis Martyn, albeit in a modest way.

Nowadays, the subject, whose treatment I will briefly sketch here, is in this form seldom the object of academic research into John's Gospel. Although I primarily and especially inquire into the theological significance of the text of the prologue available to us today, I do not in any way want to underestimate or treat as superfluous the numerous important studies on the various stages of its development, such as the pre-Christian tradition or hymn on the Word (the Wisdom) of God, or the intermediate stages one may perhaps assume to have existed.

For now, I shall leave open the question of authorship of the Gospel,[1] although at least as regards the prologue, answers may be found in the following discussion.

When the final form of a text is examined, one usually concentrates

---

*Translated by Ulrike Guthrie, with revisions by R. T. Fortna.

too exclusively on the question of its *literary* development. If in so doing a theological tendency that motivated this literary process is uncovered (as is the case with so-called "redaction criticism"), one tends more or less to undervalue this tendency as a distancing from or even an abrogation of the original meaning of the text. I have in mind here the stance of New Testament studies on the Lucan writings.

Redactors have admittedly often diluted a text out of literary considerations or through a combination of various sources. Some redactors may be harmless, some inferior theologians, and they are not to be taken seriously. But this is by no means always true, and it certainly does not apply to the one who bears the responsibility—I should say deserves the credit—for the version of the prologue to John handed down to us. We have here a significant theological achievement, whether it is ascribed to a redactor or the evangelist.

It is true that even today the prologue as we have it before us is sometimes interpreted theologically—namely, by preachers who choose this text for their Sunday sermons. But I believe that academic exegesis should also be engaged with it. Of course, this was done in the commentaries of past centuries. But it is precisely research from the historical-critical school that ought to number this passage among its concerns. Only preliminary attempts are present in the commentaries by R. Bultmann and his successors.

In what follows I shall limit myself to *one* idea, which to my mind is the main theological point of the prologue. It is expressed in the *alternating juxtaposition* of the assertions about John the Baptist as the historical "beginning" (to use the modern term *historical*) and about the absolute "Beginning," *en archē*. From a *literary* perspective this juxtaposition is explained, in creditable arguments, by the adoption of a combination of various sources: a pre-Christian or Christian hymn and traditions from the Baptist sect and from the primitive Christian movement. But in the prologue transmitted to us it is precisely this juxtaposition that has the deep theological meaning characteristic of all biblical salvation-history.

The combining of historically unobservable occurrences with historical accounts is, of course, characteristic of the presentation of divine events in the Old Testament: the God who reveals himself in the story of the people of Israel is the same as the one who created heaven and earth.[2] In both cases his action derives from the *self-communication* to the world grounded in his being—it derives from the Logos. This revelation reaches its decisive high-point in the Christ event of the Incarnation, which is ushered in by the testimony of John the Baptist.[3] This is the grand idea of the prologue. But it is important that at the same time the *parallel* of this to the Creation event is constantly kept in view. The juxtaposition of phrases, seemingly unconnected and occurring on different levels and in alternating "strophes," is apparently haphazard, in the light of opinions concerning the literary development. But it gains its *theological* meaning in the very expression of this parallelism.

Thus the Creation story, closely dependent on Genesis 1, is retold anew. The prologue begins exactly like the First Book of Moses: *en archē/bēreṡît*. The new story is the same as the old, but everything leads back to the divine *communication* at Creation: the self-disclosure of God, the "Word." All of God's activity is seen in this way, as proceeding from the Being of God. Every work of the Divine Word enumerated in the Creation account is directed to the Word's highest goal: Incarnation. The first verses speak of Light and Life, as in the Genesis account and in the late Jewish texts inspired by it. But whereas in the latter the Logos appears in its transcendent form, here it is spoken of so that its incarnation is from the outset kept in sight. What is first said explicitly in v. 14, *sarx egeneto*, is already implicit in every expression of the first verse: It is the Word who became flesh who "is in the beginning."

Similarly, even vv. 9-13, whether taken from a strophe of a pre-Christian hymn or given a Christian interpretation at an interim stage, clearly refer in the present prologue to the one of whom the powerful comment is made in v. 14. The question, often asked and never completely resolved, of which verses speak of Christ and which are quotations from the pre-Christian hymn, does not arise for our prologue. Here, it is a case of the parallel between the words of Creation and the Word made flesh. Admittedly, the order of the verses indicates a temporal succession [Nach*einander*], but it is decisive that the order expresses a continuity of the divine "speaking" through an alternating juxtaposition [Neben*einander*], which is an interpenetration [In*einander*].

"God said, Let there be light, and there was light." God's speech is God's action. This identity is after all contained in the Hebrew equivalent for "Word" (*dabar*). The momentous phrase, "the Logos was God," which was determinative for all later christological explanations of the divinity of Christ and of christological dogma, in the framework of the whole Johannine prologue means: He was God in his communication to the world.

The action of becoming flesh is not limited to the moment of the incarnation, but rather refers to the *whole life of Jesus*, which is told from v. 19 following and begins with the testimony of the Baptist. *The life of Jesus, the Gospel according to John, is Logos.* The last sentence of the prologue, v. 18, flows smoothly into the following narrative: "No one has seen God; the only begotten, God [namely, the Logos], has 'explained' him [made him known (*exēgēsato*)]." He is the true "exegete" of the divine being. In the life of Jesus he reveals God's characteristics "in grace and truth." It is often assumed that the prologue was only later added to the gospel. As an integrating element in the theological framework of the Gospel of John lying before us it is in fact indispensable.

Notes

1. I treated it in my book, *Der johanneische Kreis* (Tübingen: J. C. B. Mohr, 1975 [*The Johannine Circle* (Philadelphia: Westminster, 1976]), which unfortunately did not evoke the discussion that I believed could be expected.
2. I have shown how through such linking myths have become demythologized—that is, historicized—in my essay "The Connection of Primal Events and End Events with the New Testament Redemptive History," in *The Old Testament and Christian Faith* (ed. B. H. Anderson; New York: Harper, 1963) 115-23 [German version in O. Cullmann, *Vorträge und Aufsätze 1925-1962* (Tübingen: J. C. B. Mohr, 1966) 159-65].
3. W. Baldensperger, and following him R. Bultmann (who even reckons with a hymn to the Baptist as an early version of the prologue), has shown that the claim of the Baptist sect, which sees John as the goal of all divine revelation and not just a witness and precursor, is under attack. This polemical defense is, however, only a subsidiary concern of the prologue. See my *Johannine Circle*.

JOHN THE BAPTIST AND ELIJAH IN THE FOURTH GOSPEL

Marinus de Jonge

I n the spring of 1975 J. Louis Martyn, then on sabbatical in Jerusalem, gave a number of guest lectures at Dutch universities, leading to interesting discussions with his colleagues and their students. In August 1975 he gave a major paper at the Colloquium Biblicum Lovaniense, which in that year was devoted to Johannine problems; again there was a lively discussion on what he had to say. These lectures were subsequently rewritten and published in the Festschriften for W. D. Davies and N. A. Dahl as well as in the Louvain conference volume.[1] They were finally brought together in Martyn's book *The Gospel of John in Christian History: Essays for Interpreters*, published in 1978, a year before the second revised edition of his influential *History and Theology in the Fourth Gospel*.[2]

I had the pleasure of being one of Louis Martyn's hosts during his lecture tour and of being President of the Colloquium at Louvain, to which he contributed. At the time I was engaged in Johannine studies myself. A year before *The Gospel of John in Christian History*, I published a collection of essays entitled *Jesus: Stranger from Heaven and Son of God*.[3] Anyone comparing these two volumes will notice many points of agreement and disagreement. Needless to say, the discussions between the two authors at Leiden and Louvain were stimulating and fruitful.

Having been invited to contribute to this Festschrift, it is appropriate for me to engage in a renewed discussion on a topic on which we clearly disagree. It is a pleasure to enter into a debate with Louis Martyn because he always states his case clearly, never conceals the points on which he himself is not quite clear, and is always willing to listen to arguments put forward by others. This characteristic certainly also applies to the first essay in his *The Gospel of John in Christian History* entitled " 'We have found Elijah.' A View of Christ Formulated Very

Early in the Life of the Johannine Community,"[4] in which at a certain point he declares that he is not convinced by a hypothesis put forward in my article "Jewish Expectations About the 'Messiah' According to the Fourth Gospel."[5]

The point under discussion is: Why does John the Baptist in John 1:21 solemnly deny that he is Elijah? After an emphatic "he confessed, he did not deny, but confessed," the Fourth Gospel records three denials. John declares that he is not the Christ, not Elijah and not "the prophet" (1:20-21). The three terms recur in 1:25 where John's interrogators ask why he is baptizing, if he is neither the Christ nor Elijah nor the prophet.

Not John, but Jesus, is the Christ—as the Prologue says: "He was not the light, but came to bear witness to the light" (1:8). Also the designation "the prophet" plays an important role in this Gospel. In fact, we may say that Jesus' messiahship (closely linked with his kingship) and his prophetic mission are both acknowledged and redefined in terms of the unique relationship between Son and Father, as portrayed in their gospel.[6] John's denial that he is the Christ and the prophet is part of his witness to Jesus. But what does his declaration that he is not Elijah add to this? Jesus is not referred to as Elijah in the Fourth Gospel, as it seems. When people in Jerusalem discuss Jesus' identity there seem to be only two major options: "This is really the prophet" and "This is the Christ" (7:40-44).

Because of possible implicit polemic in the Fourth Gospel against followers of John the Baptist exalting their master, it has been thought that John's denial that he is Elijah aims at contradicting such a claim by this group. But nowhere do we find evidence that these people regarded John as Elijah, and when the Fourth Gospel returns to the episode in question in 3:28 it makes John say: "You yourselves bear me witness, that I said, I am not the Christ, but I have been sent before him."[7]

In "We have found Elijah" Louis Martyn attempts to overcome the impasse along two lines. First, he combs the Gospel for possible Elijah-like traits in the portrait of Jesus. Second, he asks whether "the absence of an explicitly positive sequel to the Baptist's second negation may be a riddle that has resulted from the evangelist's editing of one of his sources."

The search for Elijah-like traits in the Fourth Gospel's portrait of Jesus is inconclusive. On the one hand 3:13 ("No one has ascended into heaven but he who has descended from heaven, the Son of Man") clearly discourages thinking of Jesus as Elijah. As Son of Man he has ascended into heaven, not as a new Elijah. On the other hand there are a number of reminiscences of the Elijah (and Elisha) stories: in 2:1-11; 4:46-54; 6:1-14; 9:1-7; 11:1-44. We may question the importance of these "hints" in the total picture of Jesus in the Gospel, but in Louis Martyn's opinion the evangelist, while emphatically excluding an explicit identification of Jesus as the eschatological Elijah, allowed some minor Elijah-like traits to remain in a number of miracle stories.

From this point Martyn follows his second line of approach. John the Baptist's three denials and all the Elijah-like traits in Jesus' portrait are found in sections of the Gospel assigned by a number of critics to a pre-Johannine source.[8] According to Martyn and others this source was a kind of rudimentary Gospel circulating in Johannine circles, intended not only for members of the church but also for potential Jewish converts. Now in 1:35-51 the disciples of John who follow Jesus find the fulfillment of their (typically Jewish) messianic hopes in Jesus. In v. 41 one of them, Andrew, says to Simon: "We have found the Messiah"; later, in v. 45 Philip tells Nathanael: "We have found him about whom Moses wrote in the law." Martyn takes the latter reference to be to "the prophet like Moses."[9] But where is Elijah? In answer to this question Martyn attempts to solve the difficulties presented by v. 43 by a very careful and ingenious reconstruction of the wording of this verse in the source, followed by an equally conscientious answer to the question why the evangelist would have altered it.

To cut a long story short: According to Martyn the original v. 43 must have contained a reference to Andrew finding Philip and saying to him: "We have found Elijah," followed by a meeting between Jesus and Philip, with Andrew as intermediary. The evangelist, taking over the source, wanted to break "the chain of witness/discovery so fundamental to the source's christological trajectory, which arches from traditional expectations to discovered fulfilment" (p. 49). In the present v. 43 it is Jesus who takes the initiative. In many other instances in this Gospel people approaching Jesus with their expectations are not able to penetrate into the real secret of his mission and his status; this is only revealed to those whom he elects. As Martyn aptly remarks, the source-material is imbedded in the evangelist's presentation of Jesus beginning with the Prologue (with, at the end, the very emphatic v. 18) and ending with the highly impressive Son of Man logion in v. 51. "We may note," he says, "that the Elijah identification is, so to speak, squeezed out of the picture between the pre-existent logos on the one side (1:18), and the pre-existent Son of Man on the other (1:51)" (p. 53 n. 89).

I find myself in agreement with much in Martyn's analysis of the christology of the Fourth Gospel as a whole, as presented in the essays in *The Gospel of John in Christian History,* and earlier in *History and Theology in the Fourth Gospel.* I appreciate that he is not content with reconstructing the wording of the supposed source material but also tries to explain why the evangelist could not take over the source as he had it before him. But I remain very skeptical about the possibility of distinguishing between source material and late redaction with any degree of certainty. It is one thing to say that the Fourth Gospel presupposes earlier written and oral traditions (and will also have known material preserved in the Synoptic Gospels), but it is quite another matter to claim that we are still able to determine beyond reasonable doubt what the source employed in 1:19-51 contained.[10] Although Martyn is of the opinion that his hypothesis enjoys "a considerable degree of probability," he will be the first to admit that his reconstruction of the source's version of v. 43 remains hypothetical. And I fail to understand why the evangelist who removed the reference to Jesus as Elijah in v. 43 found it necessary to retain John's explicit negation in 1:21 and its echo in 1:25.[11]

If any convincing solution to the problem at hand is to be found, we shall have to operate on the level of the present redaction and composition of the Fourth Gospel. In my essay "Jewish Expectations About the 'Messiah' According to the Fourth Gospel"[12] I attempted to explain 1:21 first of all in connection with the other statements on John the Baptist found in the Gospel as it lies before us; but as this analysis failed to convince my esteemed colleague and friend I shall have to try again!

John is a man sent by God (1:6; 3:28). His duty is to bear witness to the light (1:7, 8). His witness starts with the solemn triple negation in 1:19-21, includes the declaration that he saw the Spirit descend as a dove from heaven and remain on Jesus (v. 32), and culminates in the equally solemn and emphatic v. 34: "I have seen and have borne witness that this is the Son of God." His witness serves to bring people to faith in Jesus (1:7). In the end he witnesses to the truth (5:39). Those who give heed to his word will be saved (5:34).

He is not the light, only a witness to the light (1:8). He is "a burning and shining lamp," and even Jesus' opponents in Jerusalem "were willing to rejoice in his light" (5:35). Jesus himself in no way depends on John's witness (5:34). As 5:31-32 and 5:36-40 make clear, it is God who has borne witness to him. The very works that the Father has granted to the Son to accomplish bear him witness that the Father has sent him, and so do the Scriptures. John's witness is important to people, but not to Jesus himself.[13]

John, though sent by God, is thoroughly human. In the present arrangement of pericopes in chap. 3, vv. 31-36, which are clearly to be connected with Jesus' speech to Nicodemus (vv. 1-21),[14] now follow the pericope about John's witness to Jesus in his discussion with his disciples (vv. 25-30). The result is that v. 31 ("He who comes from above is above all; he who is of the earth belongs to the earth, and of the earth he speaks; he who comes from heaven is above all") refers, at least implicitly, to the relation between John the Baptist and Jesus. We may add here that John himself acknowledges that the one who comes after him was, in fact, before him (see 1:15, using the word μαρτυρεῖν again, and 1:30) as the word that became flesh (1:14; compare v. 18).

This "for he was before me" in 1:15, 30 is typically Johannine; it is not found in the Synoptic Gospels. With the Synoptics, John makes the Baptist emphasize that he baptizes with water (1:26, 31, 33) and that he is not worthy to untie the thong of the sandal of the one who comes after him (1:27). The coming one will baptize with the Spirit (1:33), but nowhere does the Johannine John announce him as "the one who is stronger than I." This expression is replaced by "he was before me," which was clearly regarded as more suitable. After all, John had to be depicted as the trustworthy witness to Jesus he really was. Therefore, John announces Jesus' death and its effects on the sin of the world (1:29, 36).

Strikingly, the Fourth Gospel does not record that John baptized Jesus; obviously because this action would suggest dependence on the part of Jesus. The Baptist does describe, however, one important event on this occasion as part of his witness in vv. 32-33. He saw the Spirit descending as a dove and remaining on Jesus, but did not really know who Jesus was (see also v. 31). Nor would he have known the meaning of what happened, if God, who sent him to baptize with water, had not told him: This is he who baptizes with the Holy Spirit.

Jesus, the Son of God coming from the Father, was present among the Jews, but they did not know him—as Jesus told them (v. 26). John, the witness sent by God, came to baptize with water in order "that he might be revealed to Israel" (v. 31), but he himself did not know him (as he says twice); from the beginning to the end he was dependent on his Divine Sender. In fact God was the one who revealed his Son to Israel (Φανερωθῇ as *passivum divinum*), not John.

John, then, is a reliable witness to Jesus, completely loyal to the one who comes after him. The latter in no way depends on the former; John himself is totally dependent on God, who sent him. The people do well to give heed to what he has to say—the next day two of his disciples become the first two followers of Jesus.

This witness calls himself "the voice of the one crying in the wilderness, 'Make straight the way of the Lord,' as the prophet Isaiah said" (1:23). This designation is taken over from the Synoptic tradition (Mark 1:2; Matt 11:10; Luke 7:27) by the Fourth Gospel. It rejects, however, the identification with Elijah that is found there, clearly because it regards that identification as unsuitable.

We may remark, of course, that only Matthew explicitly identifies John as Elijah (11:14; 17:13). Mark does so only implicitly (Mark 9:11-13, par Matt 17:10-13). Luke only records the announcement of the angel to Zechariah: "He will go before him in the spirit and power of Elijah" (1:17). Yet, the Fourth Gospel's explicit denial that John was Elijah comes as a surprise. Why was it not appropriate to identify John with this great prophet whose return was expected? Because in the view of the Fourth Gospel this identification suggested that Jesus was dependent on John! This, at least, is the theory I tried to substantiate in "Jewish Expectations About the 'Messiah,' " referring to a number of interesting statements in Justin's *Dialogue with Trypho*. It failed to convince Louis Martyn, not so much because I quoted a mid-second-century text (I shall return to this problem presently), but because he could not find clear points of contact between the Fourth Gospel and Justin's *Dialogue*.

The essential element in Trypho's statement (objected to by Justin) in *Dial.* 8:4 is that the Christ, even if he has already been born and lives somewhere, remains unknown (ἄγνωστος; he does not even know himself!) and powerless until Elijah comes to anoint him and to make him manifest to all (καὶ φανερὸν πᾶσι ποιήσῃ).[15] There is a parallel here with "among you stands one whom you do not know" in John 1:26, and it is not far-fetched to suppose that the avoidance of the identification of John with Elijah, the emphasis on his complete dependence as a witness on God's revelation, and the use of the divine passive in 1:31 go back to the desire to avoid any suggestion that Jesus, the Christ, would be dependent on John. Of course, it was not John who revealed him to Israel but God, who also sent his Spirit to remain on him[16] and thereby gave him power and authority. The unique relationship between the Son and the Father who sent him excludes any other role for John than that of "voice," of "witness."

In Trypho's second statement about Elijah (49:1) a significant new element is added. This view on the "hidden Messiah" implies that he is thoroughly human καὶ γὰρ πάντες ἡμεῖς τὸν χριστὸν ἄνθρωπον ἐξ ἀνθρώπων προσδοκῶμεν γενήσεσθαι, καὶ τὸν Ἡλίαν χρῖσαι αὐτὸν ἐλθόντα (see also 67:2; 68:5). Justin, who defends the Son's pre-existence and incarnation, disagrees, though in chap. 48 he insists that Jesus should be accepted as the Christ of God, even if he seemed to be a human being elected by God to be Christ. His own christology, he claims, is that of the great majority of Christians—implying that there were others who thought differently.

The Fourth Gospel repeatedly emphasizes that Jesus is "from above:, "from heaven," "from God" (3:31; 6:38; 8:23, 42; 13:3; 16:28; 18:36) and stresses the fundamental opposition between heaven and earth, for instance in 3:31-36, mentioned above, where Jesus is said to come from above, but John belongs to the earth. There is no doubt that this central point in Johannine christology was developed in discussions and debates with Jewish groups from which the Johannine Christians separated (in this issue I agree with Martyn). It also presupposes, I think, discussion with other Christians, particularly with those who try to counter Jewish objections to Jesus' messiahship differently.[17]

But is Justin's *Dialogue with Trypho* a reliable source for our knowledge of Jewish expectations concerning Elijah? In a recent article[18] Moris M. Faierstein mentions only one anonymous *baraitha* in *b. 'Erub* 43a-b where the idea of Elijah as forerunner of the Messiah is found. But it is a halakic passage that does not give any details about this belief. To Trypho's statement that the Messiah would be anointed by Elijah there is no rabbinic parallel. Then was not this statement put into Trypho's mouth by Justin, wanting to explain Jesus' baptism by John?

This is extremely unlikely. In *Dial.* 8:3-4 Trypho urges Justin to obey God and to observe his commandments instead of putting his hope in a man. Justin and the other Christians have invented a Christ of their own and will perish because of him, for the true Christ will be different—unknown and without power, until Elijah comes to anoint him and to make him manifest.[19] This is taken up in *Dial.* 49:1 where Trypho concludes "And because Elijah has not yet come I declare that also Christ is not there yet."

In the long discourse that follows in 49:2–54:2, Justin does not try to convince Trypho that Elijah has come in the person of John the Baptist. He quotes the well-known text Mal 3:23 but applies it to the second advent. At the occasion of the first advent of Jesus Christ on earth the Spirit of the Lord that was in Elijah operated in John, a Jewish prophet (compare Luke 1:17). Justin then tells what John did and how he was killed, and quotes words of Christ similar to those found in Matt 17:10-13, where it is stated that Elijah has already come. Justin includes v. 13, stating that the disciples understood that Jesus referred to John the Baptist. A discussion with Trypho on the possibility of Elijah's spirit being in John follows.

Interestingly, we do not hear that John baptized Jesus. What John did to Jesus is not important, but rather what Jesus did to John. He caused him to stop prophesying and baptizing (51:2). All along John is portrayed as the last Jewish prophet (49:3; [50:2;] 51:2-3; 52:3-4). Justin states that "the Spirit in the prophets anointed and appointed kings for you" (52:3) but does not connect this with John's baptism of Jesus.

He returns to this subject in *Dial.* 87-88 where the expression ἀναπαύσεται ἐπ᾽ αὐτὸν πνεῦμα θεοῦ in Isa 11:2 is explained as a reference to the end of the distribution of spiritual gifts among the Jews (87:1–88:2). Here John the Baptist appears as a κῆρυξ αὐτοῦ τῆς

THE CONVERSATION CONTINUES

παρουσίας καὶ τὴν τοῦ βαπτίσματος ὁδὸν προιών. There is again no reference to Jesus' baptism by John. What John did and said "had to be a token (γνώρισμα) for the people in order that thy might recognize who is the Christ" (88:6). When Jesus came to the Jordan people thought he was a son of Joseph the carpenter, but the divine voice at baptism (repeating what David had already said in Ps 2:7) declared him to be God's son (88:8). This declaration, as well as the visible descent of the Spirit, occurred because of the people; Jesus himself had no need of baptism or of the Spirit descending on him in the form of a dove—just as he need not have been born or crucified. He underwent all this on behalf of the human race (88:4).

This complicated picture of the relationship between Jesus and John the Baptist will need a more detailed analysis.[20] However, one thing is clear: Because for Justin the Christ is Son of God from eternity he has to avoid any suggestion that Jesus became Son of God only when he was baptized by John, received the Holy Spirit, and heard the voice from heaven. For the same reason he cannot clearly and straightforwardly identify John with the Elijah of Jewish expectation mentioned by Trypho. There is no reason to think that Justin is dependent on the Fourth Gospel in this matter.[21] All the more striking are the parallels between the two authors; the silence about Jesus' baptism by John; the reduction of John's role to that of a herald, a "voice," one who helps the people to understand who Jesus really is; and finally, the avoidance of an identification of John as Elijah—that is, an Elijah whose activity is indispensable for the Messiah's appearance in power.

Justin handles the Synoptic references to John as Elijah very carefully; it is unlikely that he would have invented Trypho's statements because they were in line with the Synoptic notions he is at pains to qualify. This means that the tradition to which Trypho refers existed before Justin—if not in Jewish then certainly in Jewish Christian circles[22]—and that he considered it necessary to take it seriously. And if this view on the relationship between Elijah and the Christ existed among Jews and/or Jewish Christians in the period before Justin, then it may very well have been known already at the time the Fourth Gospel received its final form. The theory that the explicit negation in 1:21 and other features in the Fourth Gospel's picture of the Baptist aim at preventing wrong ideas about Jesus' dependence on John the Baptist is, therefore, not at all improbable. The Fourth Gospel wants to safeguard the unique relationship between Son and Father from eternity and to counteract the notion that Jesus the Christ needed John's intervention in order to take up his task on earth.

This essay, then, is my contribution to a debate that should be continued. I am looking forward to a lively discussion with my friend, Lou Martyn, next time we meet!

Notes

1. "We Have Found Elijah" was published in R. Hamerton-Kelly and R. Scroggs, eds., *Jews, Greeks and Christians: Essays in Honor of William David Davies* (SJLA 21; Leiden: E. J. Brill, 1976) 181-219; "Clementine Recognitions 1, 33-71, Jewish Christianity, and the Fourth Gospel" in J. Jervell and Wayne A. Meeks, eds., *God's Christ and His People: Studies in Honour of Nils Alstrup Dahl* (Oslo-Bergen-Tromsö: Universitetsforlaget, 1977) 265-95; "Glimpses into the History of the Johannine Community" in M. de Jonge, ed., *L'Évangile de Jean: Sources, rédaction, théologie* (BETL 40; Gembloux: J. Duculot/Leuven: University Press, 1977, ²1987) 149-75.

2. J. L. Martyn, *The Gospel of John in Christian History* (New York: Paulist Press, 1978); *History and Theology in the Fourth Gospel* (1st ed.; New York: Harper, 1968; 2nd ed.; Nashville: Abingdon, 1979.

3. M. de Jonge, *Jesus: Stranger from Heaven and Son of God* (SBLSBS 11; Missoula: Scholars Press, 1977). The sub-title is "Jesus Christ and the Christians in Johannine Perspective."

4. Martyn, *The Gospel of John in Christian History*, 9-54.

5. M. de Jonge, "Jewish Expectations About the 'Messiah' According to the Fourth Gospel," *NTS* 19 (1973) 246-70; now chap. 4 in *Jesus: Stranger from Heaven*, 77-116. Martyn's disagreement is expressed in n. 20 on pp. 14-15 of his essay.

6. See my essay "Jesus as Prophet and King in the Fourth Gospel" in *Jesus: Stranger from Heaven*, 49-76 (= *ETL* 49 [1973] 161-177), and, of course, chaps. 6 ("From the Expectation of the Prophet-Messiah, Like Moses . . .") and 7 (" . . . To the Presence of the Son of Man") in J. L. Martyn's *History and Theology*.

7. In *Ps.Clem.Recogn.* 1, 54, 8 and 1, 60, 1, going back to an early source (see J. L. Martyn's second essay in *The Gospel of John in Christian History*) we find the assertion on the part of the Baptist's disciples that John is the Christ. In the Syriac form of *Ps.Clem.Recogn.* 1, 54, 8 John the Baptist is said to be "in concealment" (presumably to return). This may or may not suggest a parallel between John the Baptist and Elijah. In 1, 60, 1 there is no difference between the Latin and the Syriac. On the disciples of John the Baptist, see also H. Lichtenberger, "Täufergemeinde und frühchristliche Täuferpolemik im letzten Drittel des 1. Jahrhunderts," *ZTK* 84 (1987) 36-57.

8. Martyn mentions D. M. Smith, R. Kysar, R. T. Fortna, J. Becker, W. Nicol, and G. Reim and indicates, of course, the great influence of R. Bultmann's theory about a Signs Source. He could not have known Georg Richter's very detailed essay, "Zur Frage von Tradition und Redaktion in Joh 1, 19-34," published posthumously in G. Richter, *Studien zum Johannesevangelium* (Herausgegeben von J. Hainz; BU13; Regensburg: F. Pustet, 1977) 288-314. The redaction mentioned here is that of the editor of the *Grundschrift;* according to Richter the evangelist only added the words "for he was before me" in 1:30.

9. This is not immediately evident. One should note that Martyn regards the words "and the prophets" in this verse as an addition by the evangelist (*The Gospel of John in Christian History*, 44 n. 75).

10. See also chap. 8 "Variety and Development in Johannine Christology," in my *Jesus: Stranger from Heaven*, 193-222.

11. It is very unlikely that he retains these statements to prepare his readers for the implicit references to Elijah in the miracle stories.

12. de Jonge, *Jesus: Stranger from Heaven*, 77-116. On John's witness in 1:19-34, see esp. pp. 85-90.

13. In contrast to Jesus, who performed many signs (see also 20:30-31) recognized as works of God by those who have real insight, "John did no sign," we are told in 10:41 by people staying in the place across the Jordan where John at first baptized. Yet, they add: "Everything that John said about this man was true." This verse, incidentally,

implicitly denies that John could be connected with Elijah, well-known as a miracle-worker (see J. L. Martyn, "We Have Found Elijah," 16-19).

14. See chap. 2, "Nicodemus and Jesus: Some Observations on Misunderstanding and Understanding in the Fourth Gospel," in my *Jesus: Stranger from Heaven*, 29-48.

15. See also *Apol.* 35:1 and, esp., 110:1 where Justin states that he knows that the teachers of Israel say that the Christ has not yet arrived; or if they say that he has arrived, they maintain that one does not know who he is; ἀλλ' ὅταν ἐμφανὴς καὶ ἔνδοξος γένηται, τότε γνωσθήσεται ὅς ἐστι.

16. The notion of *anointing* with the Spirit, present in Luke 4:18 and Acts 10:38, is not found in John.

17. See *Jesus: Stranger from Heaven*, 96-102, and my discussion of 7:40-44 on pp. 93-94.

18. Moris M. Faierstein, "Why Do the Scribes Say That Elijah Must Come First?" *JBL* 100 (1981) 75-86;, followed by Dale C. Allison, Jr., "Elijah Must Come First," *JBL* 103 (1984) 256-58, and J. A. Fitzmyer, "More About Elijah Coming First," *JBL* 104 (1985) 295-96.

19. Faierstein is simply wrong when he writes: "Justin has earlier identified John with Elijah (8:4), making it a natural progression from John's baptism to Elijah's anointment of the Messiah" (p. 86).

20. See also the interesting discussion of these passages in O. Skarsaune, *The Proof from Prophecy: A Study in Justin Martyr's Proof-Text Tradition: Text-Type, Provenance, Theological Profile* (NovTSup 66; Leiden: E. J. Brill, 1987) 195-99. Nowhere does Justin refer to notions or vocabulary special to the Fourth Gospel.

21. John's statement οὐκ εἰμὶ ὁ χριστός, ἀλλὰ φωνὴ βοῶντος reminds us of John 1:20, 23, but it is a reply to the supposition of the people that he is the Christ (compare Luke 3:15) and is followed by the announcement of the one stronger than John (compare Luke 3:16).

22. Skarsaune considers it probable that Justin suppressed material on messianic anointing found in one of his Christian sources.

EQUAL TO GOD

Wayne A. Meeks

J ohn 5:18 says that the plot to have Jesus killed began because Jesus was "making himself equal to God." This assertion can hardly be historical, so we must seek an explanation for it in the history of the Johannine circle. It was not only the Johannine Christians who made such connections, of course. Already in Mark hostility against Jesus is first aroused by his claim to exercise a prerogative—to forgive sins—that is God's alone (Mark 2:7), and the actual plot against his life springs, as in John, from a Sabbath healing (3:6). Christians prior to John had appropriated for Jesus biblical texts and phrases that originally applied to God—"the Day of the Lord," "the Word of the Lord," "the Name of the Lord," for example—and had attributed to him functions and honors that traditionally had been God's. In the liturgical poetry used in Pauline circles even the phrase "to be equal to God" had been applied to Jesus (Phil 2:6), though in a sense very nearly the opposite of that implied in John 5:18. Thus the central issue that would impel the great christological definitions and controversies of subsequent centuries was already emerging in several quarters. Yet, the Fourth Gospel is the first document we have that focuses so intently on this issue. No other first-century writing concerns itself so explicitly and extensively with the relationship between Jesus and God. That is the reason this Gospel was able later to contribute so disproportionately to the language of systematic christologies both catholic and heterodox. Another reason for its importance in later christology is that it spoke in such ways of Jesus and God in Greek.[1] Its Greek, moreover, evoked some familiar discussions in pagan traditions without quite fitting them, even as it called on specifically Jewish traditions but radically transformed them. The peculiar Johannine language would thus furnish major materials for the bridge to be built between a Bible newly construed and Christianly interpreted on the one hand and a philosophical tradition mostly Platonic on the other. It is important, however, if we are to understand this Gospel itself, that we separate it in our minds from those later uses of it. We should not too quickly adopt the shorthand of later controversies, like "subordinationist," "docetist," and "Gnostic," to name what seems to be happening in John.

The thematic importance of the charge attributed to "the Jews" in John 5:18 becomes apparent when we note the similar formulation of two subsequent charges: 10:33, "[We intend to stone you] for blasphemy, because you, being human, make yourself a god," and 19:7, "He ought to die, because he made himself God's son."[2] In each case the verb ποιεῖν with the reflexive pronoun signals Jesus' crime as his opponents see it but also shows the Gospel's audience how wrong the Jews are. Jesus has not "made himself" θεός or υἱὸς τοῦ θεοῦ; he *was* from "the beginning," and what he does in the world is only what the Father had commissioned him to do. The predicates of the three parallel sentences are different, but their parallelism suggests that ἴσος τῷ θεῷ, υἱὸς τοῦ θεοῦ, and θεός, as applied to Jesus, all have roughly the same force for the Johannine Christians or for their opponents. We are reminded that the Fourth Gospel is almost alone among first-century documents in insisting upon confessing Jesus as θεός (compare Heb. 1:8; other examples are not so certain). Its first verse affirms that θεὸς ἦν ὁ λόγος, and the confession of Thomas at the end is ὁ κύριός μου καὶ ὁ θεός μου (20:28).[3]

Returning to 5:18 we are faced with three questions. First, what is the accusation that "the Jews" were making? Why does calling God Jesus' "own father" make Jesus "equal to God"? In what sense is that blasphemy? Second, in what sense is the audience of this Gospel itself expected to understand Jesus to be "God" or "a god" or "equal to God"? Third, as knowledgeable Jews themselves, how could the shapers of the Johannine tradition have come to speak of Jesus in a way that Jews apparently took to be self-evidently blasphemous? These questions become acute precisely because J. Louis Martyn has helped us to recognize that "the history of the Johannine community . . . forms to no small extent a chapter in the history of *Jewish* Christianity."[4]

Let us begin with the second question, for our initial step toward understanding the statements about Jesus' claims to divine honor must be to discover their place in the evangelist's literary strategy. John 5:18, like v. 16, which it resumes and expands, is an aside to the readers by an omniscient narrator. That the form of v. 18 precisely recurs in the direct speech of the opponents in 10:33 and 19:7, as we have noted above, helps to confirm that this narrator is no glossator but the primary author of the Gospel. As Bultmann rightly observes, the imperfect tenses in both verses break out of the narrative situation "to characterize the long-term attitude of the Jews toward Jesus' customary (or repeated) actions."[5] Following Martyn, we further suspect that, "at a second level," these reports characterize the complaints that Johannine Christians heard from other Jews about the Jesus they confessed.

Was the perception by the Jewish opponents accurate? In one respect, as we have already seen, the evangelist insists that it was not: The Johannine Christians did not believe that Jesus had *made himself* equal to God. One purpose of 5:19-47 is to expose that misunderstanding. Thus v. 19 takes up again the form of the dialogue—though as so often in John the interlocutors are not permitted to speak again—but the "answer" that Jesus gives does not reply to anything the Jews in the narrative have said, but to the generalized complaint that the narrator has told us about in his aside. The answer is, to say the least, ambiguous. On the one hand, Jesus claims to do nothing "of himself" (vv. 19, 30). He is merely like a child who imitates "whatever he sees his father doing" (v. 19).[6] He is the perfect agent, who does not seek what he wants, but only "the will of the one who sent me" (v. 30). He does not come "in his own name" nor seek human "glory" but comes in the name of the Father and receives glory from the one God (vv. 41-44). On the other hand, he does what God does: raises the dead, conducts judgment, and has life "in himself" (vv. 21-22, 25-29). And the Father has granted him the authority to do these things precisely that "all may honor the Son as they honor the Father" (v. 23). No wonder Sundberg could conclude "that two christologies are at work in the Fourth Gospel," the one depicting Jesus as "the subordinate agent of God who does his will in obedience," the other "a new christology in which the Son has reached his majority and has been granted like rank, position and power with the Father." The "new christology" is just what "the Jews" say it is, "a binitarian theology."[7]

All this is true; yet, we sense that this unravelling of the Johannine discourses into "two christologies" does not enable us to hear the effective force of the evangelist's composition. One of the problems with much of our modern way of talking about ancient religious conceptions is our tendency, once we have found a useful category for sorting the data, to treat the category as if it were a thing. A "christology" is not a contraption that, once wound up, runs on its own. What we see happening in the Fourth Gospel's controversies about Jesus' identity is not "two christologies" struggling for dominance but an exegetical and interpretive process by which a new religious movement interpreted Scripture, interpreted Jesus, interpreted its own history, and interpreted the world in one complex dialectic. To enter imaginatively into that dialectic, we must find our way with the peculiar style and idiom of this

311

Gospel. It is not this writer's—or this community's—style to develop an idea in linear argument; instead the tradition and the writer have juxtaposed notions and images, using the forms of dialogue and controversy to expose some of their implications and limitations—and then repeatedly shifted the connections in a kind of verbal kaleidoscope. Does the Fourth Gospel make Jesus into "a second god"? To ask the question this way, in the language of Justin Martyr, immediately reveals the distance between John and the latter author. Somehow the kaleidoscopic worrying of the issue in John is less clear but at the same time more subtle, more profound than the second-century apologist's lapidary assertions. To make John talk like Justin is to impoverish this Gospel.

The Johannine controversies make it clear enough that it was precisely in arguments with other Jews that this circle of Jesus' followers had to work out the sense in which Jesus was for them "equal to God." The implication that there could be any being equal to God was an age-old worry in Israel, one that would not quite go away. "Two powers in heaven" was a thought that the rabbis would still be combatting centuries later.[8] To "think oneself godequal [ἰσόθεος], being mortal" is the arrogance (ὑπερηφανία) of an Antiochus Epiphanes (2 Macc 9:12). "The mind that thinks itself equal to God," writes Philo, is "both vain and godless" (φίλαυτος δὲ καὶ ἄθεος, *Leg. All.* 1.49). It is a little too glib, however, to say, as commentators routinely do, that to call a human person "godequal'" was no offense to pagan or syncretistic sensibilities, but self-evidently impossible for a Jew. In fact, one finds ambivalent statements on both sides.

To be sure, ἰσόθεος was an epithet that could be lightly used in the Greek world, from Homer's formulaic ἰσόθεος φώς for any of his heroic warriors[9] to the medical writers' praise of a really good cough remedy or sciatica medication as ἰσόθεος.[10] All this has, as Bultmann remarks,[11] nothing to do with the discussion in John 5. Yet, there is one point of contact: When the Greek sources call a human being ἰσόθεος, it is a question of honor—for example, in the oft-repeated gnome that one ought to show to one's parents "godequal honor."[12] So, too, in John 5 Jesus' discourse turns on the question of the τιμή that is to be given to the Son (v. 23), a motif that returns in the guise of δόξα in vv. 41-44.

The notion put forth here and elsewhere in John, that the Son is to be honored as is the Father because he does the *works* of the Father, is also immediately understandable to anyone familiar with the Greek gnomic and philosophical traditions—understandable, but quite different in its logic and mode of expression. "To be like God," said Isocrates, "is to be a benefactor and to tell the truth."[13] The ideal of resembling God by sharing God's attributes was a commonplace. At the heart of the idea of moral progress that becomes so important in the philosophical *koine* in the time of the principate is the belief that to be wise is to strive to be like God. Plato *Theaetetus* 176B is particularly often quoted and commented on in this connection.[14] Here we are obviously in a different world from that of the Fourth Gospel. A "Greek" coming to the Jesus of John 5 might initially think himself on familiar ground, but at the end his puzzlement would be as great as that of "the Jews."

Greeks, too, knew that there were claims by mortals to be godlike that were quite improper, impious, or simply ridiculous. Even Homer's Apollo can warn Diomedes:

Take care, give back, son of Tydeus, and strive no longer
to make yourself like the gods in mind, since never the same is
the breed of gods, who are immortal, and men who walk groundling.[15]

Nearer to John's time, Seneca's satire on "The Pumpkinization of Claudius" is a familiar example of a sophisticated send-up of divine honors given an all-too-human emperor. The post-mortem literary portraits of Seneca's own patron, Nero, and of the earlier Gaius and the later Domitian give further evidence for the distaste for such hybris, at least in circles who suffered under it, in the period of our concern. An author writing an encomiastic biography of a figure regarded by part of his audience (including perhaps the author's patron) as divine could face a dilemma, as we see throughout Philostratus' *Life of Apollonius,* a work composed about a century and a quarter after the Fourth Gospel. Philostratus undertook to portray Apollonius as a philosopher, but not only was his hero depicted in some of the traditions as a demigod and even called a god, but also there was actually a cult of Apollonius in some places. Philostratus was aware that the miracles attributed to his "philosopher" would be scorned by some as the works of a γόης, and the divine claims on his behalf could seem the height of impiety.[16] Philostratus' dilemma was in some respects like that of the Fourth Evangelist, and in a few passages his solution is comparable.

The most interesting of these passages is the defense of Apollonius before the emperor Domitian, who has asked him, "Why is that men call you θεός?" Philostratus, perhaps guided by the tradition before him, has supplied Apollonius with two replies: one very brief, before Apollonius demonstrates his divinity by vanishing from the scene, the other an elaborate rhetorical apologia that Apollonius is represented as having prepared in writing. The short answer to the emperor's question is, "Because every person who is deemed good [ἀγαθός] is honored by being named after God [θεοῦ ἐπωνυμίᾳ τιμᾶται]" (*V. Ap.* 8.5). This answer is elaborated in 8.7.7: "I say that the good among humans possess something of God [θεοῦ τι ἔχειν]." Then the speaker draws a parallel between the dependence of the κόσμος upon the demiurge and the dependence of "another world"—that is, the commonwealth—on

313

the ἀνὴρ ἀγαθός, for this human world "needs a man made in God's image." "Undisciplined souls" must have a governor, "a man who concerns himself about their world, a god who has come at wisdom's behest [θεὸς ὑπὸ σοφίας ἥκων]."

Although the diction and the range of ideas are different, the argumentative strategy of this passage is quite similar to that in John 10:31-39. In both, the reply of the accused first suggests that the title θεός is innocuous because there are accepted occasions when it is appropriately used of humans. To be sure, the occasions are special: Only the ἀγαθοὶ ἄνθρωποι may properly be called gods in Apollonius' theology; only the recipients of the Word of God (at Sinai?) in John. In each argument there is then a further claim. Every ἀγαθός has "something of God," but Apollonius claims to belong to a unique category of ἀγαθοί, "a man shaped in God's image," "a god sent by wisdom." Even stronger is the heightening of the initially innocuous claim in John, for there the form of the argument is explicitly a fortiori: "If [Scripture] calls those θεοί to whom the Word of God came . . . are you saying that I blaspheme because I said that I am God's son—I whom the Father consecrated and sent into the world as his envoy?" (vv. 35-36). To those of the Gospel audience who are equipped with good memories, the comparison is bolder still: If those to whom the Logos came can be called gods, how much more the one who *is* the Logos.

The issue of Jesus' "blasphemy" in John 10:33 is stated in terms different from 5:18, but the Hannukah controversy obviously represents a further facet of the christological dispute that the Johannine Christians have had with other Jews. The controversy begins (10:24) with the specific question of whether Jesus is "the Christ," a question he refuses to answer directly. Thus we have here as forthright a discussion as we are likely to hear in this Gospel of what it meant to "confess [Jesus] as Christ"—the charge that had led to expulsion from the synagogue (9:22). The issue was not the title χριστός as such, and certainly not the assertion that Jesus was (one of) the Anointed One(s) expected in Jewish tradition. It was the novel complex of beliefs about him that clustered around that title in Johannine—and other—Christian circles that had led to their speaking of him as though he were a god. Thus Jesus' claim that here immediately provokes the charge of blasphemy is his statement, "I and the Father are one" (10:30). The subsequent discussion shows that the claim is connected with the use of the titles θεός and υἱὸς τοῦ θεοῦ for him. Jesus' sarcastic answer to the Jews' intent to stone him (v. 32) reintroduces the topic of the "good works" that Jesus has done. This recalls both his statement in v. 25, "The works that I do in my Father's name witness on my behalf" and the miracles that occasioned controversy earlier, beginning in chap. 5 (compare

314

7:21-23). Thus the assertion of Jesus' identity with the Father, like the assertion of his equality with God in 5:17-18, is immediately complemented and modified by his portrayal as the obedient son-agent.

The closest parallel in John to 10:31 is 8:59. As in the Hannukah scene the mob that wants to stone Jesus comprises those who initially seemed ready to accept him as the Christ, so in the earlier passage it is "the Jews who had come to believe in him" (8:31), at least in the Gospel as we have it, who are so provoked by Jesus' strange responses that they want to destroy him. As in 10:30, where the immediate provocation is Jesus' statement, "I and the Father are one," so in 8:58 it is his cryptic remark, "Before Abraham existed, I am," that is taken to be blasphemy, as the stoning indicates. Why is it blasphemy and not merely insanity (see also v. 52)? Probably the knowledgeable reader is expected to hear in Jesus' ἐγὼ εἰμί an allusion to the Tetragram, as various commentators have argued (see vv. 24 and 28a and 18:6).[17] If so, the counterpart to the theme of "works" of God that Jesus does is the *name* of God that he "manifests" to those who are "given" to him (17:6). As godequal Son and envoy, he does God's deeds; as bearer of the secret Name, he reveals that Name to the chosen ones (see 1:18; 14:7-11).

Two of our three questions to John 5:18 have now been answered. The Johannine Christians did indeed speak of Jesus as if he were a god or equal to God and even as if the very Name of God could be used of him. Other Jews were bound to see that kind of talk as blasphemy—both in the general sense of hybristic claims (see 2 Macc 9:12; Philo *Leg. All.* 1.49) and in the specific legal sense of speaking out the Tetragram.[18] So we see that, although John's authorial dilemma was in some ways surprisingly close to that addressed by Philostratus, the dilemma was cast for the Christian writer in specifically Jewish terms. And for him the dilemma was more acute, because he was not writing for a royal patroness, but for a community whose very identity had been shaped around this debate over Jesus' "equality with God," the issue they portray as having distinguished them from the (other) Jews. Thus from the Prologue's θεὸς ἦν ὁ λόγος to Thomas' confession ὁ κύριός μου καὶ ὁ θεός μου runs the theme that what *this* messianic group sees in its messiah is something far different from what a messiah could mean to other Jews, and perhaps even to some other Christians. Yet, they have struggled, and this author struggles, to show that what they see is something a Jew or a Samaritan ought to be ready to see, something encrypted in Scripture from the first chapter of Genesis on.

Our third question remains: How could the Johannine Christians, who were evidently themselves Jewish and, moreover, steeped in the Scriptures and traditions of Judaism, ever have come to make such claims about Jesus? If it were simply a question of titles, it would not be difficult to collect a number of instances in which Jewish and Samaritan writers call biblical heroes "gods." After all, God had said to Moses (Exod 7:1): "See, I have made you a god to Pharaoh" (see also Exod 4:16). Philo, as well as the later rabbis, spent considerable energy discussing the implications of that passage and others in which God's name and other attributes as well seemed to be shared with Moses. The hellenistic Jewish dramatist Ezekiel has Moses describe a dream of enthronement in heaven, in which he was invited to take the place of a human figure (φώς) evidently representing God, who gave Moses his diadem and scepter.[19] Five or six centuries later the Samaritan priest Markah likewise pictured Moses' heavenly honors, which constituted his ascent to "deity" (אלהו).[20] Nevertheless, we must resist the temptation to think that a fixed ideology, say "Moses as divine man," was ready at hand for the Johannine Christians simply to "apply" to Jesus. Even the "Jewish Wisdom Myth," which has seemed since the work of Harris and Bultmann early in this century so readily to explain the basic pattern of Jesus' coming into the world, rejection, and reascent, does not solve all the problems.[21] If there really was a myth, and not merely a common metaphorical and exegetical pattern on which many changes were rung, we still cannot understand the christology of John as arrived at by simply substituting the masculine λόγος for the feminine σοφία and equating it with Jesus. No more can we simply equate John's Jesus with Philo's λόγος or the *memra* of the targums. The dialectic that we glimpse in the Fourth Gospel could only have emerged from a much more complicated process than that.

It was a process, indeed, too complicated to explore on this occasion. Nevertheless, our investigation of the Johannine Jesus' equality with God will not be complete until at least a few of the clues are noted that point to that process's exegetical and traditional roots and its social context. As for the latter, we have already affirmed with Martyn that the Gospel's controversies press us to look for the context of its theologizing in the same disputes that constituted the Johannine groups a separate religious community over against the Jewish communities to which they had belonged. For the exegetical connectives, we must first pay attention to the series of motifs that are integrally connected with the talk of Jesus' divinity in John.

First, Jesus is depicted as "god," "equal to God," and "God's Son," precisely as the one who came from God and returns to God in the "exaltation" of the crucifixion. It is perhaps significant that the only clear New Testament parallel to John 5:18's ἴσος θεῷ is Phil 2:6, ἴσα θεῷ εἶναι. In the Philippian poem, "to be equal to God" was a graspable status of the one "in the form of God," precisely in contrast to his "emptied" status "in human likeness," and thus rather different from John's depiction of Jesus as manifesting his divine glory even in his humanness.[22] Nevertheless the mythic pattern in both cases is the descent, obedient completion of a mission, and reascent to glorious enthronement of a divine being.[23] Second—and this is unique to John—the descent/ascent pattern is connected closely with the title "Son of Man."[24] It is precisely as the descending and ascending Son of Man that Jesus is equal to God. Third, the Johannine Jesus can be given not only the general appellative "god," but even (though more subtly) the specific "name" of God, the "I Am," which he has "revealed" to those whom the Father has given him. The key clue in our mystery, however, may be a fourth observation, made nearly thirty years ago by Nils Dahl. The divine δόξα of Jesus had already been seen by Isaiah (John 12:41). His "day," the day of his crucifixion = exaltation = glorification, was seen by Abraham (8:56). Dahl argues convincingly that these passages are allusions to the visions that Scripture attributed to certain of the Patriarchs and prophets, which were either explicitly theophanies or had been so interpreted by tradition. In John they become christophanies—perhaps one should say rather "doxaphanies"—visions of the divine Son of Man enthroned in heaven.[25]

The Johannine Christians, in an attempt to make intelligible their own emerging sense of who Jesus was, joined in an interpretive process that was already going on and that would continue among Jewish readers of Scripture, quite independent of the peculiar twist that the Christians gave it. The Johannine group's sense that what Jesus had done in the world was God's action, that their worship of him was worship of God, led them to an interpretive move that paralleled and probably borrowed from attempted solutions to an old dilemma faced by interpreters of the Hebrew Bible. "No man shall see me and live," said YHWH to Moses (Exod 34:20, a passage clearly alluded to in John 1:16-18). Yet, Exod 24:9-11 (RSV) says that "Moses and Aaron, Nadab and Abihu, and seventy of the elders of Israel went up, and they saw the God of Israel" without harm and eventually "ate and drank" in God's presence. What was one to make of Isaiah's flat assertion, "I saw YHWH" (Isa 6:1), and the similar report by Micaiah (1 Kgs 22:19)—not to mention the elaborate visions of Ezekiel (esp. 1:26) and Daniel (7:9-14)?[26]

The solution that emerges in later Jewish exegetical literature assumes that Scripture's visionaries did not really see God. What they saw must, therefore, have been some intermediary, either a representative or a representation of God. Two texts are likely to have suggested these alternative construals. In Gen 1:26 God speaks of "our image" and "our likeness." And in Exod 23:21 God tells Moses of the angel who would accompany the Israelites: "My name is in him." What Israel's prophets saw was thus either God's image, conceived perhaps as a statue

317

or a bas-relief on the throne, or that highest angel who bore God's name, whom later mystics and exegetes would call "the lesser YHWH."[27] The development of these lines of thinking is reasonably clear in later mystical literature, such as the Hebrew book of Enoch. Earlier allusions to these patterns are fragmentary and hard to trace, but there is enough evidence to make us confident that speculations of this kind were taking place already in John's milieu. After all, Philo, for all his Platonizing exuberance in interpreting the "seeing" of the "invisible God," follows in part a similar exegetical path. Those who Scripture says saw God really saw "God's λόγος," which Philo repeatedly identifies with both God's image and the chief angel who bears God's name.[28]

Further, the reader of the theophanic texts would naturally conclude that the image or angel of God that the visionaries had seen was a human form. It was "in [or by] the image of God" that God made the first human (Gen 1:27). The figure that Ezekiel saw "on the likeness of a throne" above the cherubim was "the likeness of the appearance of a human" (Ezek 1:26). And, of course, the one who is presented to the Ancient of Days to become his vice-regent in the vision of Daniel 7 is "like a son of man." This intermediate, human figure in heaven provided the connecting point for those traditions that occasionally produced for some Jewish and Samaritan interpreters the equivalents of what Greeks would call the apotheoseis of heroes—like Enoch and Moses, already mentioned—and the epiphanies of gods—like the Man of the sixth vision in the Ezra apocalypse, or Jacob in the Prayer of Joseph. The last named text, quoted in part by Origen and probably roughly contemporary with John, is particularly interesting for our purposes. Jacob reveals to the angel with whom he wrestles at the Jabok, here identified with Uriel, that he is himself an angel, and indeed the highest of those who attend God's throne.[29] This astonishing claim becomes a little clearer when we compare the way Gen 28:12 is interpreted in the Palestinian targums and in some rabbinic midrash. The targums explain the unusual order of the angels' "ascending and descending" like this: "Behold the angels that had accompanied him from his father's house ascended to announce to the angels of the heights: 'Come and see the pious man whose image [אֵיקוֹנִין = εἰκών] is fixed to the throne of glory, upon whom you have desired to gaze.' "[30] Perhaps texts like these, cryptic and diverse as they are, give some hint of the way the Johannine Christians reasoned through Scripture to explain and justify their conviction that "whoever has seen [the Christ depicted in this book] has seen the Father" (14:9).

What drove the Johannine Christians to make just these connections, in the face of the social pain that it obviously cost them? We must remember that the social pain was but the negative side of the process by which they had become a distinctive community. It is after he is expelled from the synagogue for his stubborn claims about Jesus that the healed blind man, in whom Martyn has taught us to see the paradigmatic Johannine convert, learns the identity of "the Son of Man" and comes truly to believe and to worship (John 9:35-38). In this Gospel, "abiding" in the truth about Jesus has positive and negative social dimensions: It entails stalwart "love" for fellow disciples of Jesus and brave separation from those who reject him. The claim that constitutes the identity of this special group of former Jews is that in their abiding in the Son of Man they have been granted what the whole of Israel's Scripture and tradition—both Jewish and Samaritan versions—pointed to. That was the δόξα that the ancient visionaries glimpsed ("from afar," as Philo would say), the vision of God through God's heavenly messenger that was adumbrated in Scripture but fully granted to "no one" until now. They alone are Israel in the sense so beloved of Philo, "the nation that sees God." They are epitomized in one of the first of those "given by God" to Jesus, Nathanael the ἀληθῶς Ἰσραηλίτης. Here we have the very model of a sectarian consciousness. To "Pharisees" and to ordinary Jews of all kinds, as the narrative makes clear, these claims did not fulfill but rather subverted the classical Scriptures and traditions. These claims broke the community with other Jews by their audacity, their exclusiveness, and their persistence; they constituted blasphemy. Smarting from the forced separation, the circle of the Beloved Disciple exulted in this subversion, which became the principal literary strategy of the Fourth Evangelist. The ultimate irony of this Gospel, whose author used irony so adroitly, is that its subversive prose was so successful that it enticed future generations of Christian readers, long separated from the intense and specific engagement with the Jews that had given it birth, into ever new subversions of its own language. It is these subsequent strong misreadings of the Gospel's own strong misreading[31] that have contributed so much to the church's christology.

Notes

1. Even if an earlier generation's hypotheses about an Aramaic *Vorlage* of John were to be revived, it remains true that it is only our Greek Gospel or its later translations that the Fathers read.
2. Translations in this essay are my own, unless otherwise indicated.
3. Kikuo Matsunaga, "The 'Theos' Christology as the Ultimate Confession of the Fourth Gospel," *Annual of the Japanese Biblical Institute* 7 (1981) 124-45.
4. See J. Louis Martyn, *The Gospel of John in Christian History* (New York: Paulist Press, 1978) 120-21, emphasis original.
5. Rudolf Bultmann, *Das Evangelium des Johannes* (KEK 2; Göttingen: Vandenhoeck & Ruprecht, 1959) 82.
6. C. H. Dodd, "Une parabole cachée dans le quatrième évangile," *RHPR* 42 (1962) 107-15.
7. Albert C. Sundberg, Jr., "Christology in the Fourth Gospel," *Biblical Research* 21 (1976)

319

29-37. Compare already Walter Bauer, *Das Johannes-Evangelium* (HNT 6; 3rd ed.; Tübingen: Mohr [Siebeck], 1935) 82: "Die Juden verstehen richtig, was der jo. Christus meint, dass nämlich der Anspruch, Gottes Sohn zu sein, in seinem Munde nichts anders als die Anerkennung seiner Wesensgleichheit mit Gott (1:1) fordert."

8. Alan F. Segal, *Two Powers in Heaven: Early Rabbinic Reports About Christianity and Gnosticism* (SJLA 25; Leiden: Brill, 1977).

9. See *Il.* 2.565; 3.310; 4.212; 7.136; 9.211; 11.428, 472; 11.644; 15.559; 16.632; 23.569, 677.

10. See, for example, Galen, *De compositione medicamentorum* (ed. Kühn, vol. 13) 65.12; 279.15; Paulus Aegineta, *Epitomae medicae libri* (ed. Heiberg; *CMG*; vol. 9.2) 7.16.48.1; Aetius Amidenus, *Iatricorum liber vii* (ed. Olivieri; *CMG*; 8.2); 11.12; 112.15; *liber viii* (ibid.) 60.44; 63.184; 73.116; 75.131; 77.55; 77.67. All these examples are, of course, later than the first century.

11. Bultmann, *Johannes*, 183 n.1.

12. Νόμος γονεῦσιν ἰσοθέους τιμὰς νέμειν: Menander fr. 805 (in T. Kock, ed., *Comicorum Atticorum fragmenta*, vol. 3); *Sent.* ed. Meineke 1.378 = *Sent. ex cod. byz.*, ed. Jaekel, 525 = fr. 600 in Körte and Thierfelder. See also Aristotle *EN* 9.2.8 (1165A, 24). Of course, heroes, too, were accorded "godequal honors," see, for example, Dionysius of Halicarnassus *Antiq. Rom.* 1.6.4.2; 1.44.1.9; *Ars rhet.* 7.7.1-8. Some of these Dionysius calls "demigods, whose souls after they had left their mortal bodies are said to have ascended to Heaven and to have obtained the same honours as the gods, such as Hercules, Aesculapius, Castor and Pollux, Helen, Pan, and countless others" (*Antiq. Rom.* 7.72.13.20-22, trans. Earnest Cary in the Loeb edition). Artapanus claimed that Moses was "deemed worthy of ἰσόθεος τιμή by the priests" of Egypt (Eusebius *Praep. Ev.* 9.27.6). Similarly Alexander the Great in ps-Callisthenes *His. Alex. Mag.* 1.46a.4 (ἰσόθεος κράτος); 2.10.7; 2.22.12 (ἰσόθεοι τιμαί). The notion that a human could receive divine honors because of power, wisdom, benefactions, or other excellence could also be expressed by calling the *person* "godequal," as in *Hist. Alex. Mag.* 2.22.11; *Vita Aesopi* 116.9-10; Apollonius of Tyana *Ep.* 44; see also Philostratus *Vit. Ap.* 5.24; 7.21. Homer could be called "godequal in wisdom," evidently a commonplace, for Dio Chrysostom could use it as a base of comparison in the self-praise of Phidias (*Or.* 12.63.4). This usage, too, could be trivialized. Origen *c. Cels.* 3.25.17 derides the ἰσόθεοι τιμαί given by the Phythian oracle to a boxer, while Athenaeus *Deipn.* 13.55.31-32 speaks of Greece's enslavement to "the godequal beauty of Lais," a famous prostitute. In comedy, this line of thought could produce an ethnic joke: The Egyptians think the eel godequal, for eels cost more than (the images of) gods (Athenaeus *Deipn.* 7.55.4-5, citing Antiphanes, "in the comedy of Lyko," = Kock, *Com. Att. frag.* fr. 147). An interesting parallel to the whole Johannine controversy occurs in ps.-Heraclitus *Ep.* 4 to Hermadorus, conveniently available in A. J. Malherbe, ed., *The Cynic Epistles* (SBLSBS 12; Missoula: Scholars, 1977) 190-93. Heraclitus answers an accusation that he erected an altar and inscribed it with his own name, thus "making myself, a human, a god." He cites the example of Heracles, who *was* a man and became a god by means of his καλοκαγαθία καὶ ἔργων τὰ γενναιότατα.

13. Isocrates *fr.* 34.

14. Albinus *Epitome* 28.1.1-10, 2.1, 3.1, 4.1; Alexander of Aphrodisias *In A.pr.* 6.7-8; *In top.* 243.25-26; 254.4-8; Galen *De prop. anim.* 5.11.8; Plotinus *Enn.* 1.2.1.3-7; 1.2.5.2; 1.6.6.20; Porphyry *Abst.* 2.43; 3.27; *Marc.* 13, 16, 17, 19; *In Platonis Timaeum comm.* fr. 2.28.14; Theon of Smyrna *De util. math.* 16.1; compare Diogenes Laertius 6.104; Epictetus *Diss.* 1.12.21; Plutarch *Ad princ. inerud.* (*Mor.* 780E-F); Philoponus *In mete.* 14.1.1.9.

15. *Il.* 5.440-41, trans. by Richmond Lattimore, *The Iliad of Homer* (Chicago: University of Chicago Press, 1951) 140.

16. For example, *V.Ap.* 1.2; 4.18; 7.17; 8.7.2.; 8.19 (accusations of being γόης or magician); 1.5 (temple to Apollonius); 3.50; 8.5 (called θεός). See further G. Petzke, *Die Traditionen über Apollonius von Tyana und das Neue Testament* (Studia ad Corpus Hellenisticum Novi Testamenti 1; Leiden: Brill, 1970) 187-94.

17. See, for example, C. H. Dodd, *The Interpretation of the Fourth Gospel* (Cambridge: Cambridge University Press, 1968) 93-96; C. K. Barrett, *The Gospel According to St John:*

An Introduction with Commentary and Notes on the Greek Text (London: SPCK, 1955) 282-83; Raymond E. Brown, S.S., *The Gospel According to John (i-xii)* (AB 29A; Garden City: Doubleday, 1966) Appendix IV; Rudolf Schnackenburg, *The Gospel According to St. John* (trans. C. Hastings et al.; New York: Crossroad 1982) 2:199-200 and Excursus 8, pp. 79-89.

18. Lev 24:16; *m.Sanh.* 7:5.

19. See Eusebius, *Praep.Ev.* 9.29; see translation and notes by R. G. Robertson in James H. Charlesworth, ed., *The Old Testament Pseudepigrapha* (2 vols.; Garden City: Doubleday, 1985) 2.811-12.

20. I have collected much of the evidence in "Moses as God and King," in Jacob Neusner, ed., *Religions in Antiquity: Essays in Memory of Erwin Ramsdell Goodenough* (Studies in the History of Religions 14; Leiden: Brill, 1968) 354-71, and "The Divine Agent and His Counterfeit in Philo and the Fourth Gospel," in E. Schüssler-Fiorenza, ed., *Aspects of Religious Propaganda in Judaism and Early Christianity* (Notre Dame: University of Notre Dame Press, 1976) 43-67. See also the recent discussion by M. J. J. Menken, "The Provenance and Meaning of the Old Testament Quotation in John 6:31," *NovT* 30/1 (1988) 39-56.

21. See J. Rendel Harris, *The Origin of the Prologue to St. John's Gospel* (Cambridge: Cambridge University Press, 1917); Rudolf Bultmann, "Die religionsgeschichtliche Hintergrund des Prologs zum Johannes-Evangelium," *Eucharisterion: Festschrift für H. Gunkel* (1923), reprinted in Rudolf Bultmann, *Exegetica* (ed. Erich Dinkler; Tübingen: J. C. B. Mohr [Paul Siebeck], 1967) 10-35. Important for recent discussion has been George W. MacRae, "The Jewish Background of the Gnostic Sophia Myth," *NovT* 12 (1970) 86-101; see also Henry R. Moeller, "Wisdom Motifs and John's Gospel," *Bulletin of the Evangelical Theological Society* 6 (1963) 92-100.

22. In this respect Käsemann is relatively correct over against Bultmann's tendency to read John too much in the light of Paul. Ernst Käsemann, *The Testament of Jesus: A Study of the Gospel of John in the Light of Chapter 17* (Philadelphia: Fortress, 1968).

23. Perhaps the same pattern is implicit in the other poetic passages in which what is said of Jesus resembles what is said elsewhere of God's Wisdom as agent of creation. See Col 1:15-20; Eph 1:3-14.

24. See E. M. Sidebottom, "The Ascent and Descent of the Son of Man in the Gospel of St. John," *ATR* 2 (1957) 115-22; W. A. Meeks, "The Man from Heaven in Johannine Sectarianism," *JBL* 91 (1972) 44-72.

25. N. A. Dahl, "The Johannine Church and History," in William Klassen and Graydon Snyder, eds., *Current Issues in New Testament Interpretation: Essays in Honor of Otto A. Piper* (New York: Harper, 1962) 130-36.

26. For a full discussion of these and other, similar exegetical dilemmas and their various solutions in traditional exegesis, see Segal, *Two Powers.*

27. Enoch 12:5; see also 30:1; Gerschom G. Scholem, *Jewish Gnosticism, Merkabah Mysticism, and Talmudic Tradition* (New York: Jewish Theological Seminary, 1960) 43; idem, *Major Trends in Jewish Mysticism* (New York: Schocken, 1961) 68-69; Ithamar Gruenwald, *Apocalyptic and Merkavah Mysticism* (AGJU 14; Leiden: Brill, 1980), 196-98; Segal, *Two Powers,* 65-66.

28. See, for example, *Somn.* 1.238-41; *Conf.* 145-47; *Heres* 205; *Fug.* 101; *Spec.* 1.81; cf. *Cher.* 3, 35; *Fug.* 5; *Mut.* 87. Segal, *Two Powers,* 159-81, discusses the most important passages in Philo and compares Philo's exegesis with that of both the later rabbis and the merkabah mystics.

29. See the brilliant exposition by Jonathan Z. Smith, "The Prayer of Joseph," in J. Neusner, ed., *Religions in Antiquity* (see above, n. 20) 253-94, and his introduction and notes to his translation in Charlesworth, ed., *Pseudepigrapha,* 2:699-712.

30. See the Paris ms. of the Fragmentary Targum, trans. by Michael L. Klein, *The Fragment-Targums of the Pentateuch According to Their Extant Sources* (Analecta Biblica 76; Rome: Biblical Institute Press, 1980) 2:20. Other texts, including Neofiti I, are similar. Compare *Gen.Rab.* 68.12; *PRE* 35 (82a, in Friedlander's translation, p. 265); *b. Hul.* 91b; and see Dahl's comments, "Johannine Church," 286-87 n. 51.

31. See Harold Bloom, " 'Before Moses Was, I Am': The Original and Belated Testaments," *Notebooks in Cultural Analysis* 1 (1984) 3-14.

"DO NOT WONDER!"
JOHN 5:28-29 AND
JOHANNINE ESCHATOLOGY
ONCE MORE

Nils A. Dahl

I n his posthumous commentary on the Fourth Gospel, E. C. Hoskyns made only a few brief and simple remarks about the controversial verses 5:28-29. In his view the evangelist argues: "Those who know that there will be a day of resurrection unto life and unto judgement, and that there will be a final separation of those who have done good from those who have done evil, ought not to wonder and be surprised that the voice of the Son of God even now separates good from evil, exercises judgement and gives life."[1] That is a straightforward reading of the text. Most modern commentators, however, feel obligated to complicate the exegesis at this point by discussing problems of redaction and sources[2] and of present and futurist eschatology in the Fourth Gospel. This often pushes the basic question of syntax and meaning into the background. Hoskyns's simple way of reading the text is often not even discussed.

A number of other suggestions have been made. Verses 28-29 can be considered a doublet of v. 26, perhaps a relic of an earlier, futurist eschatology that has not been brought into full harmony with the present eschatology of the evangelist. More often the verses are considered a secondary gloss, inserted either to interpret or to correct the preceding sayings in terms of generally accepted doctrine of a future resurrection of the body and a last judgment. Interpreters who defend the verses as an authentic part of the Gospel text tend to find a clue in the formula "the hour is coming and is now" of v. 52 and/or to find a dialectical tension between "already" and "not yet."

In this article it is unnecessary to discuss the manifold variations of these theories.[3] My thesis is that the simple reading is also the correct one. Reasons for an interpretation in line with Hoskyns's suggestion will be given, mainly from a similar type of argumentation elsewhere in the

Fourth Gospel and in Rabbinic writings. Moreover, I intend to show that this exegesis provides a better approach to the complicated questions of redaction and of eschatology than most current theories do. This will result in some concluding suggestions about what is going on in the fifth chapter and in the Fourth Gospel as a whole.

Forms of Argumentation

On Hoskyns's interpretation, the general resurrection of all who are in the tombs is considered to be even more wonderful than a spiritual resurrection of believers through the lifegiving words of Jesus. The argument *a maiori* does not have the logical force of a syllogism, but it can persuade even if it does not prove. To put it differently, vv. 28-29 serve as a warrant for the credibility of the preceding assertions. In more colloquial language, the pattern of the argument would run: This is so, and no wonder; something still more remarkable is indeed the case.

We find arguments of a similar type several times in the Fourth Gospel. In the dialogue with Nicodemus the formula μὴ θαυμάσῃς is used in the same way as μὴ θαυμάζετε in 5:28: "You ought not to wonder that I said to you, 'You must be born from above.' The wind (*pneuma*) blows where it wills" (3:7-8). Here the reason why Nicodemus should not wonder is stated as an argument *a minori*. If Nicodemus is unable to understand whence the wind comes and whither it goes, how much less will he be able to understand the whence and whither of the Spirit (*pneuma*) and of a person born by the Spirit. The continuation of the dialogue makes us realize that the amazed question, "How is this possible?" could have received a further answer, but only one that Nicodemus would have been incapable of understanding, since it would have to do with "the heavenly things" (τὰ ἐπουράνια) and the ascension of the Son of Man (3:9-14).

In the dispute in 7:21-24 there is another example of the same type of argumentation, even though an explicit exhortation not to wonder is missing. In the context, the remark of Jesus—"I have done one work, and all of you wonder"—does not simply describe a reaction of awe and marvel, caused by a wonderful healing of the lame man in chap. 5. We have rather to think of an amazed and hostile reaction to the violation of the sabbath. This is made clear by the response of Jesus, which here again is based on the rule of "How much more" or *kal waḥomer* (lit. "light and heavy"). If circumcision takes precedence over the sabbath commandment, how much more should the healing of a man's whole body do the same. Already in 7:15 the narrator has not simply suggested that the Jews were surprised that Jesus, without formal schooling, was literate and able to teach in the temple. Rather, their astonished question implies a suspicion of something uncanny. Jesus might, for example, be a false prophet, an illegitimate, possibly Samaritan, teacher, or he might be possessed by a demon. Jesus responds that both his teaching and his legitimacy are from God, whose agent he is; thus there was no reason for wondering (7:16-18).[4]

The First Epistle of John contains an example of the same type of argumentation, except that the warrant is placed first: Cain murdered Abel because his deeds were evil and his brother's righteous; no wonder the world hates the Christian brethren (1 John 3:12-13). Otherwise I am not aware of any close analogies in early Christian writings or in Jewish literature of Greek origin or translation.[5] The imperative μὴ θαυμάζετε and similar injunctions are commonplace in Greek, and there may well be many examples in which the formula introduces a warrant for an apparently incredible report or an astounding proposition.[6] But so far as I know, rabbinic texts provide the most striking parallels to the Johannine usage. Some characteristic examples may serve as illustrations of this.

As one could expect, the rabbinic terminology is highly stereotyped. The most common form is a cohortative, "You should not be astonished (at this)," but a conditional clause, "If you are astonished at this," and other variations can have the same function. The choice of wording, like the optional use of the formula *kal waḥomer*, seems to be due to the preference of various rabbinic schools or editors.[7] Our earliest sources use the formula in halakic exegesis: one should not be amazed at a proposed ruling, e.g. about what is permitted on the Sabbath, because a rule that might seem even stranger is generally accepted *halakah*, perhaps based upon a biblical commandment.[8] The defense for the Sabbath healing in John 7:21-23 is formally of the same type.

In haggadic exegesis, an exegetical difficulty may be explained by the assumption that something miraculous has happened or will happen; a natural phenomenon or some extraordinary incident is then adduced as a reason not to wonder. Thus in *Sifre Deuteronomy* 317 (ed. Finkelstein, 360; see also *b. Keth.* 111b) the strange collocation, *'im heleb kilyot hittah* (lit. "with the fat of kidneys of wheat"), is taken to speak about the fantastic crop in the future, when each grain of wheat shall be as large as the two kidneys of a big bull. There is no reason to wonder, as one can learn from reports about enormous turnip (or cabbage?) heads and other tales. Later midrashim contain several examples of the same type. The observation that the house grows with the snail, for example, lends credibility to the opinion that the clothes of the Israelites grew as they grew up in the wilderness.[9] In John 3:7-8 the unknown whence and whither of the wind provides the analogy.

The closest parallels to the argumentation in John 5:28-29 are some rabbinic passages in which a biblical miracle provides the warrant for another miracle that the rabbinic interpreters postulate. A story that occurs in *Mekilta*, Beshallah 1 (trans. Lauterbach, I 177) and elsewhere may serve as an example. The report in Exod 13:19, that "Moses took the bones of Joseph with him," created a problem because it could be inferred from Gen 50:26 that Joseph received an Egyptian funeral, so that the Israelites would not know how to identify his coffin. A story that illustrates the wisdom and compassion of Moses tells that while his compatriots were despoiling the Egyptians (Exod 12:35-36) Moses searched for the bones of Joseph. An old woman could inform him that the Egyptians had put him into a metal coffin that they sank in the Nile. Moses found the place and called upon Joseph to come up, otherwise the Israelites would be guiltless of their oath (Gen 50:25). Immediately the coffin came to the surface. The formula, "You should not be surprised (*'al timtah*)" then introduces a quotation from 2 Kgs 6:5-6, followed by *kal wahomer*: "If Elisha, the disciple of Elijah, could make the iron come to the surface, how much more could Moses, the master of Elijah, do it." The supporting argument is likely to be a secondary accretion; it is absent from the *Mekilta de Rabbi Ishmael* and some other versions of the story.[10]

To give the full context of another variant, I quote a comment on Deut 32:1 in *Sifre Deuteronomy* 306 (ed. Finkelstein, 333):

> In the hour that Moses said "Give an ear, O heaven and I will speak," the heaven and the heaven of heavens kept quiet (*domemim*); and when he said "And hear, O earth, the words of my mouth," the earth and all that is upon it kept quiet. And if you wonder at this look at what it says in Joshua . . . "Sun stand thou still (*dam*) at Gibeon" etc. (Josh 10:12-14). Hence, we learn that the righteous ones have power over all the entire world.

In other versions, the cosmic silence serves as a model for silent listening in the synagogue.[11]

The rabbinic form of argumentation and the more or less stereotyped terminology can be traced back to the mid- or even early second century. The Johannine form is somewhat earlier and more fluid, but both inner-Johannine and rabbinic parallels confirm that "Do not wonder" in John 5:28 introduces a warrant for the preceding statements. In view of the rabbinic materials, it is quite possible and even likely that vv. 28-29 were appended to sayings that had a prior existence of their own. But as Bultmann has argued, it is normally the language and style of the Evangelist that have some striking similarities to rabbinic usage.[12] Thus the form of argumentation makes it unlikely that vv. 28-29 are a secondary gloss, but it remains to be seen whether other reasons support the conclusion that the reference to the general resurrection was appended at a late stage in the history of tradition and composition.

Traditions and Redaction

The endless discussions of the sources and composition of the Fourth Gospel have yielded one result that is beyond reasonable doubt—namely, that a long prehistory lies behind the text that we read, with minor variants, in the early manuscripts and in modern editions. A number of editorial explanations and comments and several aporias make it likely that author(s) and editor(s) worked with written texts and not only with oral traditions at their disposal. But this insight must be held together with the other observation that the textual evidence makes it unlikely that the Gospel was ever published and circulated in a form that differed substantially from what we read. What existed in written form prior to the publication is likely not to have been edited literary works but *hypomnemata*, notes and drafts for inside use within a narrow circle, the "Johannine School," or whatever term may be most appropriate.[13]

The famous problems within John 5–7 may serve as an illustration. The Sabbath conflict in 7:21-24 deals with the healing miracle in chap. 5 as if nothing had happened in the meantime. Theories of a haphazard or intentional transposition do not really solve the problems, whether chap. 5 is placed immediately after chap. 6 or after 7:13. The aporia is better solved on the assumption that the author had two versions of the sabbath dispute at his disposal, 5:16-17 and 7:21-23. One of them was expanded and interpreted by means of the discourse materials in chap. 5. The other was used for the composition of chaps. 7–8, a sequence of events and disputes associated with the feast of Tabernacles. There is no need to postulate a later redaction, different from the general composition of the Gospel. The question is whether or not the content of 5:28-29, favors any different conclusion.

The saying about a coming general resurrection and a last judgment in John 5:28-29 is a variation of well-known eschatological themes. The form is modelled on Dan 12:2.

DANIEL 12:2	JOHN 5:28-29
Many of those who sleep	All who are
in the dust of the earth	in the tombs
shall awake:	will hear his voice and come forth:
those who have done good	some
to everlasting life,	to the resurrection of life,
and some	and those who have done evil
to shame and everlasting contempt.	to the resurrection of judgment.

The Johannine paraphrase draws on other biblical passages as well. The phrase "Those who are in the tombs" is derived from Isa 26:19 LXX (see also Ezek 37:12-13). A combination of Daniel 12 with Daniel 7 is likely in view of the preceding saying about the judgment given to Jesus as Son of Man, see also Dan 7:10, 13, 22. Most important, the particular resurrection of some, those who suffered unjustly and their wicked opponents, has been combined with the axiom that everybody will receive reward or retribution according to what they have done (see Ps 62:13; Prov 24:12; Rom 2:5-11). Thus John 5:28-29 states the doctrine, common to Jews and Christians, that there will be a resurrection of both the just and the unjust.[14]

In John 5:28-29, the doctrine of a general resurrection has received a Christian interpretation. The transfer of the last judgment to Jesus is well attested (2 Cor 5:10; Matt 16:27; Acts 10:42; 17:31). Jesus is less frequently described as the agent of eschatological resurrection, but see John 6:39-40, Phil 3:21 and Barn 5:7. It corresponds to the context, however, that the dead will be called forth from their tombs by the voice of the Son of God, who is also the Son of Man, not by the voice of the archangel (1 Thess 4:16), or by a divine promise mediated through a prophetic miracle (Ezek 37:12).

In other respects, too, the linguistic form of John 5:28-29 has a Johannine coloring.[15] The saying sets forth a widely accepted eschatological teaching, based upon Christian reworking of scriptural passages and formulated as a saying of Jesus in a Johannine environment, probably to provide a warrant for the credibility of the preceding sayings about the authority given to Jesus to make alive and to exercise judgment. The persuasiveness of the arguments depends on the assumption that the warrant is recognized as a true statement for which there is scriptural backing, as in other examples of the same form of argumentation.

The discourse in John 5:17-47 is caused by the accusation that Jesus makes himself equal with God, to which Jesus responds by claiming that as the agent of the Father the Son does what the Father does. The sayings in vv. 21-26 (and 27) are typical Johannine rhemata, affirming that because Jesus has received authority to make alive and to pass judgment, whoever listens to his word and believes has eternal life, will not see death, and does not come into judgment but has passed from death to life.[16] Taken by themselves, these rhemata do not allude to and, apparently, do not presuppose a bodily resurrection with a double outcome, either life or judgment. The Johannine tradition was shaped at a time when eschatological concepts were fluid and belief in eternal life was not necessarily linked to the concept of a future resurrection of the dead, which later became prominent in Judaism and Christianity. Various ideas about a transition from a state of death to true life immediately after or even prior to physical death are attested to by some Old Testament Pseudepigrapha, Qumran scrolls, and Hellenistic-Jewish writings, as well as by sayings of Jesus in the Gospel of Thomas and gnostic doctrines of a spiritual resurrection. Some such doctrine must lie behind the denial of the future resurrection at Corinth, and it is possible that the docetists opposed in 1 John stressed that "We have passed out of death to life" (1 John 3:14), to the neglect of the qualification "it does not yet appear what we shall become" (3:2).

In the Gospel of John the references to the future resurrection do not correct but rather support sayings about the presence of life and judgment. In chap. 5, the appeal to traditional doctrine in vv. 28-29 is best understood as an argument *a maiori*. In chap. 6 the repeated statement "and I will raise him up on the last day" points to an eschatological verification of Jesus' promise to the believers whom the Father has given to the Son (6:39-40, 44, 54); on the last day those who reject Jesus and his words are to be judged by the word that he has spoken (12:48).[17] In no case does the emphasis shift from the present to the future, and in the dialogue between Martha and Jesus it shifts the other way around. Typical Johannine sayings (11:25-26) have been placed in a context, a world view or "symbolic universe," in which future resurrection and judgment are taken for granted. Within such a context sayings about Jesus' power to give life, and about judgment in the past and present, are meaningful just because resurrection, life, and judgment are eschatological realities that will be manifested at the last day. The evangelist has read Johannine rhemata in this way, and his reading makes good sense. It is not the only possible way of reading, however, as the rhemata make good sense even apart from the doctrine of a general resurrection of the dead. The Johannine redaction has removed the ambiguity, apparently for the sake of persuasion rather than for polemical reasons.

Sayings about Jesus as the giver of present salvation play a very important role in the Fourth Gospel. They interpret the deeper meaning of the signs and are, in turn, illustrated by the stories. In several cases a saying to the effect that the believer shall not die, but live forever, causes a negative reaction to which Jesus responds by giving reasons for his assertion. Thus the saying in 8:51 causes the astonished question of whether he thinks himself to be greater than father Abraham; Jesus denies that he glorifies himself but goes on to say that Abraham rejoiced when he saw his day and adds, "Before Abraham was, I am" (*egō eimi*). In a similar way, the saying in 10:28 is warranted by the unity of Jesus and the Father and backed up by a *kal waḥomer* argument based upon Ps 82:6, which was understood as a saying addressed to the Israelites who received the Torah at Mount Sinai.[18] In chap. 6, the saying in v. 27 is undergirded by the discourse on the bread of life that has come down from heaven. The appended sayings about eating the flesh and drinking the blood of the Son of Man (6:51c-56) make the discourse even more offensive to the Jews but in turn make it sound more familiar and credible to the Christians, who were familiar with the eucharistic words of institution.

In chap. 11, the saying in vv. 25-26 is an integral part of the Lazarus story. The christological warrant, "I am the resurrection and the life," introduces the promise that believers shall live even though they die, and the actual raising of Lazarus serves as evidence that Jesus has indeed power to make the dead alive. Martha had misunderstood both the literal and the deeper meaning of Jesus' prediction that her brother should rise again. The reader has to understand that her declaration, "I know that he will rise again in the resurrection on the last day" was both correct and inadequate, as was her later confession that Jesus is the Christ, the Son of God (11:21-27, and see vv. 39-40). On the narrative level the resurrection of Lazarus becomes a cause for the plot against Jesus. At a deeper level it anticipates the manifestation of the glory of God and the glorification of Jesus through his own death and resurrection. There is a remarkable parallelism between christological and anthropological statements. Jesus is first to die and then to rise; yet, the Fourth Gospel, more characteristically, says that in dying Jesus is lifted up and glorified and goes to the Father. In a similar way the dead, like Lazarus, are to be raised from their tombs; yet the Gospel also affirms that those who believe in Jesus shall live forever and never die. They are to follow him and be where he is.[19]

This brief survey has shown that there is a discrepancy even if there is no strict contradiction between a redactional layer that presupposes a bodily resurrection and a last judgment and the rhemata tradition that does not. The problem cannot be solved by bracketing some sayings about the future resurrection and the last judgment as secondary glosses. One would at least also have to assign the present form of the Lazarus story to the same redaction. In all probability the redaction also includes the conflicts that are analogues to the argumentation in 5:17-30, either in form, by giving reasons not to wonder, or in content, by setting forth warrants and backing for rhemata about the eternal life that Jesus communicates through his words and work. This means, to use the current terminology, that the Evangelist himself is the "ecclesiastical redactor."[20] This conclusion is compatible with the assumption that the redactor-evangelist thoroughly revised an earlier work, a *Grundschrift*, but it is not necessary to assume that a "first edition" ever existed. The data are sufficiently explained on the assumption that no published writing but only drafts, notes, and oral traditions preceded the final composition that integrates signs, rhemata, synoptic-like traditions, and passion and resurrection narratives, adding subsidiary arguments and editorial comments.[21]

It is impossible here to go any further into the question of traditions and redaction in the Fourth Gospel. And an attempt to reconstruct the notes and draft that precede a finished literary product is in any case a hazardous enterprise. The question that still needs some consideration is the scope and pragmatic meaning of the argument in John 5:19-30.

The Argument and the Audience

Within the narrative context, the discourse in John 5 is addressed to Jewish opponents of Jesus, who may have believed in a coming resurrection and a last judgment but could not have agreed that the dead would be called forth from their tombs by the voice of Jesus. But if vv. 28-29 are read as a warrant for the credibility of the preceding sayings, even this is taken as a given presupposition. Only a Christian audience could find the argument persuasive, but this does not mean that it is out of place. The discourse in chap. 5 begins as a defense against the accusation of sabbath violation, but its effect is to cause increased hostility, and it ends with sharp accusations. In vv. 28-29 the author makes Jesus support his preceding sayings with a statement that is even more provocative to his Jewish discussion partners, but which the Christian audience of the gospel will recognize as true. The literary pattern is even clearer in the dialogue with Nicodemus and in the disputes in chaps. 6, 8, and in 9:39–10:39. A saying of Jesus causes astonishment, confusion or direct hostility, but Jesus proceeds to elaborate what he has said and to give reasons that are even more offensive. The narrative makes it only too clear that the Jews fail to understand because they are representatives of lies and falsehood, so that their negative reaction will help to persuade an audience that accepts Jesus and the narrator as true witnesses.

This understanding of the discourse in chap. 5 is further confirmed in the remark in 5:20b about the greater works that their Father will show the Son. The remark speaks only on a superficial level about miracles that will be even more marvelous than the healing of the lame man. The consequence of the Lazarus story, however, shows to what kind of action the astonishment at such miraculous works could lead. At a deeper level the greater works are identical with the activity that gives life to those who hear the words of Jesus and believe in him. They are associated with his own ascension to the Father; the hour that is coming and now is, when the dead shall hear the voice of the Son of God, is the hour of his glorification (5:25, see also 12:23-25, 32-33). The reverse side of Jesus' glorification is the judgment of this world, whose prince is cast out (12:31). Moreover, through the testimony of the Paraclete and of the disciples, the voice of Jesus will reach out to everywhere.[22] The amazement that the greater works will cause is, therefore, analogous to

330

the incredulity that Jesus expects his disclosure of "the heavenly things" to encounter and to the sharpening of the offense that may result from the ascension of the Son of Man (3:13; 6:61-62).

The coming hour of 5:25 is the hour of glorification and not to be identified with the hour of the general resurrection in v. 28.[23] The new introduction, "Do not wonder," sets vv. 28-29 apart from the preceding verses. Consequently, the identification of Jesus as the Son of Man in v. 27*b* does not mean that Jesus is "the apocalyptic Son of Man." Rather it must be understood in the light of Johannine sayings about Jesus as the (Son of) Man, who has come down from heaven and is to be glorified. Authority to exercise judgment has been given to the Son of God, a true human being who cannot receive or do anything except what the Father has given to him, and who does not seek his own glory (see 5:19, 30, 41; 8:54; and also 8:27). The allusion to Daniel 7 is fully compatible with this understanding, but the transition from the sayings in John 5:21-26 to the warrant in vv. 28-29 would be especially smooth if the author and audience were already familiar with the sayings about Jesus as the Son of Man who will come to repay everybody according to their deeds (see Matt 16:27).

The section in John 5:19-30 is a careful composition of Johannine rhemata, with a Johannine formulation of traditional Christian eschatology appended as a supporting argument in vv. 28-29. The simple interpretation with which this essay began has received ample confirmation. Nevertheless, things are not quite so simple as the quotation from Hoskyns might suggest. As a part of the narrative of the Gospel, the discourse in John 5 is addressed to the Jewish opponents of Jesus, but the supporting argument has persuasive force only if not merely the coming of a general resurrection and a last judgment but also the eschatological role of Jesus are taken for granted. As part of the entire Gospel, the discourse is addressed to Christians who share this presupposition and should, therefore, not be astonished that the words of Jesus already now give life and exercise judgment. They are called, like Martha, to move from correct but inadequate belief to a faith that sees the glory of God manifested in the glorification of Jesus and hears his words as words of eternal life.

The scope of the redaction was not so much to make the Johannine tradition more orthodox as to persuade prospective readers. Those who know that Jesus is the Christ and wait for a day of resurrection and judgment should not be astonished by sayings of Jesus about the presence of life and judgment but should accept the testimony of the Beloved Disciple, so that they, believing that Jesus is Christ, the Son of God, may have life in his name (see 20:31). Disciples who from the outset believe that Jesus is the Messiah about whom Moses and the prophets wrote, the Son of God and the king of Israel, are promised that they shall see greater things (1:41-51). The addressees of the Johannine testimony are in a similar position.[24] Apparently, they are Christians to whom Peter is the chief representative of the disciples and the appointed shepherd of the sheep. Peter's authority is not disputed in the Fourth Gospel, but the author introduces an anonymous disciple who is even closer to Jesus, is legitimated by his relationship to Peter and is the most authentic witness.[25] Peter's confession has the form, "You have the words of eternal life," and that is, even more than any one christological title, the response that the testimony of the Beloved Disciple calls all believers to give.

The Fourth Gospel has been said to be a book for insiders.[26] This apt characterization needs a double qualification. First, the author constantly gives his readers inside information. Whoever follows the narrative and listens to the testimony becomes initiated; the other possibility is to be amazed and take offense, like the many disciples in John 6:60-66 and the believing Jews in 8:31-33. Secondly, redaction and publication altered the social setting of what was regarded as the testimony of the Beloved Disciple and later became known as the Gospel according to John. As a literary text, the Fourth Gospel is Johannine Christianity gone public. At least the argument in John 5:28-29 and related features favor the assumption that the redaction, edition, and publication was primarily intended for what R. E. Brown calls "Christians of the Apostolic Churches," rather than for missionary purposes or for internal use in a Johannine circle.[27]

It is remarkable that Old Testament testimonies, anti-Jewish polemic, and the use of synoptic-like traditions—features that would all appeal to "Apostolic Christians"—are absent from the Johannine Epistles. They are addressed to insiders and deal explicitly with questions of false doctrine and wrong conduct. Especially 1 John presupposes a schism within the community and sets forth dogmatic and moral criteria to distinguish between true and false brethren. The heretics must have been some sort of docetists for whom "Christ" was the name of a heavenly redeemer who was not fully identical with Jesus as a human being. Some passages in the Fourth Gospel indicate that similar doctrines existed already at the time of the Gospel. It contains little, if any, explicit polemic against false doctrines, but the Beloved Disciple is represented as a witness to the glory of the Lord incarnate and to the factual death of Jesus (1:14; 19:32-35; see also 20:25-28; 6:52-56). The rhemata tradition and even pre-publication drafts must have been more open to a docetic interpretation than the published work. The split in the Johannine community is therefore likely to have occurred before the Gospel was published even if the docetists at the time of 1 John may have known the Gospel and used it to support their views, as gnostic interpreters did later.

Several scholars have recently attempted to reconstruct the history and pre-history of Johannine Christianity. There is wide agreement that its origins can be traced back to a special group of Christian Jews (and Samaritans?) and that the gospel reflects conflicts between this group and more strictly monotheistic and Law-abiding Jews.[28] To use later rabbinic terminology, the Johannine Christians must in the eyes of their opponents have appeared as sectarians who taught that there were "two powers in heaven."[29] The Gospel responds, or makes Jesus respond, to the charge that he made himself like God (see 5:17-23; 10:32-38; 19:7-15). It does not follow, however, that Christian-Jewish dialogue is a main purpose of the Gospel. I would rather suggest that the redaction and publication of the testimony of the Beloved Disciple mark the face of historical development at which the current of the originally inner-Jewish Johannine sect (or school) debouched into mainstream Christianity.

The development may very well have been gradual. Comparison with rabbinic exegesis and terminology makes it likely that the Evangelist was himself a Jew, perhaps a Palestinian, but he wrote at a time when those who confessed Jesus as the Christ were cast out of the synagogues (9:22; 16:2). There is no expectation that the Jews will be convinced by the arguments of Jesus (see 5:37-38; 6:44-45; 12:37-40). We have already treated several examples of an argumentation that can only appeal to those who already share basic presuppositions of Christian beliefs. The second part of the discourse in chap. 5 provides a further illustration. It adduces a series of witnesses in support of Jesus' own testimony to himself as the Son who does what the Father does, but the evidence can only persuade those who are already convinced that John the Baptist spoke about Jesus, that the miraculous works of Jesus were from God and that God is his Father, that the Scriptures witness to him and, we may add, that the relationship between Jews and Christians is one of polar opposition (5:31-47).

In the comprehensive literary context both the overt anti-Jewish polemic and the more veiled anti-heretical polemic are used as means of persuasion intended to support the credibility of the Johannine testimony. Christians, who already believe in one God, the Father, and his Son, Jesus Christ, are instructed that the high Johannine christology, which insists upon the unity of the Father and the Son, does not compromise strict monotheism, nor does it cast doubt upon the true humanity of Jesus and the reality of his death. At the same time, the Johannine testimony clarifies and deepens the common apostolic faith by showing how faith in God and faith in Jesus mutually condition one another. The Fourth Gospel does not assume that all who believe in Jesus are genuine believers, but all who believe are called to heed the voice of Jesus, the voice of the Son of God, the crucified King of the Jews, which now—through the testimony of the beloved Disciple and of the Paraclete—can be heard in the whole world, by Greeks as well as by Jews.

If my general approach to the vexed questions of the scope and setting of the Fourth Gospel approximates the truth, the special argument in 5:28-29 falls organically into place, and I may conclude by rephrasing and supplementing the quotation from Hoskyns with which this essay began: The Evangelist argues that those who believe in Jesus Christ and know that there will be a future resurrection and a final separation of those who have done good from those who have done evil ought not to be surprised that the voice of the Son of God even own gives life and exercises judgment. The form of argumentation has rabbinic as well as Johannine analogies. Its most striking feature is that a christianized version of the doctrine of future resurrection and judgment provides the warrant for the credibility of the preceding sayings. The argument appeals to the Christian readers of the Gospel rather than to the Jewish discussion partners of Jesus. This literary device is characteristic of the redaction that arranged and edited the testimony of the Beloved Disciple for publication and use among Christians outside the special circle in which it originated. The controversial passage is an authentic part of the Fourth Gospel as a literary composition. As such, it illustrates how the Johannine testimony was modified when its setting shifted from a special form of Jewish sectarianism to mainstream Christianity. The shift was probably gradual, but the only event about which we have fairly precise knowledge was certainly the event of greatest historical importance—that is, the redaction and publication of the book that later became known as the Gospel according to St. John.

Postscript

Apart from some minor revisions, the manuscript of the preceding article was completed in 1980. For various reasons, including my return to Norway, it was buried in my files and might have remained there if the editors had not asked for a contribution to a volume of essays in honor of Lou Martyn. It is due to Robert Fortna's assistance that the paper can finally appear. It will, no doubt, be my last contribution to Johannine studies, and I am most happy to present it to Lou Martyn as a token of gratitude and appreciation.

Notes

1. E. C. Hoskyns, *The Fourth Gospel* (rev. ed.; ed. F. N. Davey; London: Faber and Faber, 1947) 291. Similar opinions were also stated by earlier commentators, such as J. H. Bernard (ICC; Edinburgh: T. and T. Clark, 1928).

2. Editor's Note: See most recently J. H. Neyrey, *An Ideology of Revolt: John's Christology in Social Science Perspective* (Philadelphia: Fortress, 1988) 23-24, 32-33.
3. The theory of interpolation is today especially associated with the name of Bultmann, but it originated much earlier. It has been restated by various scholars, including R. Schnackenburg, *The Gospel According to St. John* (vol. 1; New York: Crossroad, 1968). Scholars have even used the secondary character of John 5:26-28 as a key to their reconstructions of various stages in the development of Johannine Christianity. The most impressive example is G. Richter, "Präsentische und futurische Eschatologie im 4. Evangelium," in his *Studien zum Johannesevangelium* (ed. J. Hainz; Regensburg: Pustet, 1977) 346-82. The whole theory is rejected by other scholars, like C. K. Barrett, *The Gospel According to St. John* (rev. ed.; Philadelphia: Westminster, 1978).
4. John always uses θαυμάζειν for a puzzled, bewildered, or even negative reaction (also in 4:27 and 5:20). The same usage occurs occasionally in Luke 11:33, 24:41 and, possibly, 4:22.
5. In *Test. Levi* 2:9, Levi is told not to wonder at what he sees in the third heaven as he will see more marvelous things when he ascends further. Other examples are even less analogous to Johannine usage, such as Eccl 5:7, Sir 11:21, 26:11; Josephus, *Life* 339; Philo, *Somn.* 2. 183; Hermas 67:4 (*Vis.* 8.1); *Diogn.* 10.4.
6. See, as random examples, Ps.-Crates, *Sp.* 26 (*The Cynic Epistles* [ed. A. J. Malherbe; SBLSBS12; Missoula: Scholars Press, 1977] 76-77; *Corp. Herm.* 11.17).
7. Most of my examples are taken from W. Bacher, *Die exegetische Terminologie der jüdischen Traditionsliteratur* (repr. Darmstadt: Wissenschaftliche Buchgesellschaft, 1965) 1. 202-203; 2.236-37. The relevance of the rabbinic usage for the Fourth Gospel was observed by A. Schlatter, "Sprache und Heimat des vierten Evangelisten" (1902), in *Johannes und sein Evangelium* (ed. K. H. Rengstorf; Darmstadt: Wissenschaftliche Buchgesellschaft, 1973) 62. R. Bultmann, *The Gospel of John* (Philadelphia: Westminser, 1971) referred to this work in his comments on John 3:7, where he found an example of the Evangelist's affinity to rabbinic style. Nevertheless, he ascribed 5:23 to the ecclesiastical redaction. Further examples can be found in concordances to rabbinic texts. A full investigation would have to extend to comparison with Greek usage; see preceding note.
8. In Mishnah, *Pesah* 6.2 and *Seb.* 7.4, the warrant precedes the case under discussion, as in 1 John 3:12-13. See also Toseftah, *Pesah* 3.6, *Sota* 4.3, *Zebah* 6.18.20; *Sifre Numeri* 1 on 5:5; and several examples in *Sifra* on Leviticus.
9. See *Deut. Rab* 7:11 on Deut 29:5.
10. For a full collection of the parallels, see G. Kittel, "Das Josephgrab im Nil (Joseph und Osiris)," in *Die Probleme des Palästinischen Spätjudentums und des Urchristentums* (Stüttgart: Kohlhammer, 1926) 169-94.
11. See *Deut. R.* on 32:1. For other examples of this type see Mekilta, *Pisha* 14 (Lauterbach I 107) on Exod 12:37; *Cant. R.* 1.1.5 on 1 Kgs 6:7.
12. Bultmann, *Evangelium des Johannes*, 29 n. 1, and index, s.v. Rabinismen.
13. On the use of hypomnemata in antiquity and the relevance of this practice for gospel criticism, see the remarks by G. Kennedy, W. A. Meeks, and R. Fuller, in *The Plurality of the Gospels* (ed. W. O. Walker, Jr.; San Antonio: Trinity University Press, 1978), 136-37, 147-48, 159-60, 167-68, 178-80.
14. For other examples of paraphrases of Dan 12:2 combined with other passages, see 4 Ezra 7:32-36; *Sib. Or.* 4. 176-90; *T. Benj.* 10. 6-8; *b. Ros. Has.* 16b-17a; Rev 20:11-15.
15. The hour is coming," 4:21, 16:2, 25; "an hour when," 4:52; "hear his voice," 3:8; 5:37, 10:3-4; people "who do evil," 3:20; "life" and "darkness" as antonyms, 3:16-19; 5:24.
16. See John 5:24-26; compare 3:18-21; 6:47-51; 8:51-52; 11:25-26, and so on. The Evangelist apparently had a number of thematically and, to some extent, phraseologically related sayings (*rhemata*) at this disposal and used, repeated, rephrased, and interpreted them in various contexts. See P. Borgen, *Logos was the True Light* (Trondheim: Tapir, 1983), esp. 49-66 (reprinted from *NTS* 26 [1979] 18-35). Like the Gospel of Thomas and other extra-canonical collections and quotations of the sayings of Jesus, the Fourth Gospel presupposes an ongoing and still fluid transmission. A comparative study needs to be pursued further, but see H. Koester,

"Apocryphal and Canonical Gospels," *HTR* 73 (1980) 105-30, and "Gnostic Sayings and Controversy Traditions in John 8:12-59," in C. H. W. Hedrick and R. Hodgson, *Nag Hammadi, Gnosticism, and Early Christianity* (Peabody, Mass.: Hendrickson, 1986) 97-110.

17. For the variability of Jewish concepts, see G. W. Nickelsburg, Jr., *Resurrection, Immortality, and Eternal Life* (Cambridge, Mass.: Harvard University Press, 1972), and H. C. C. Cavallin, *Life After Death* (Lund: Gleerup, 1974). As the doctrine of the bodily resurrection became generally accepted toward the end of the first century of the Christian era, a similar development may have taken place within the Johannine circle.

18. See my *Jesus in the Memory of the Early Church* (Minneapolis: Ausburg, 1976) 109. Further literature is given by R. Kysar, *The Fourth Evangelist and His Gospel* (Minneapolis: Augsburg, 1975) 107 n. 15.

19. "Follow Jesus," 8:12; 10:27; 12:26; 13:36-37; "be where he is," 12:26; 14:3; 17:24.

20. A similar conclusion is reached by several scholars. See H. Thyen's review articles in *TR* 39-44, esp. 42 (1977) 213-61. Thyen, however, assumes that the evangelist/redactor revised an earlier *Grundschrift*, as do other scholars.

21. Appended and inserted comments, parentheses, and "footnotes" have only recently received due attention in studies of the composition of the Fourth Gospel; see C. J. Bjerkelund, *Tauta Egeneto* (WUNT 40; Tübingen: J. C. B. Mohr [Paul Siebeck], 1987).

22. See, for example, John 10:16; 14:12; 15:20; 17:14; 18-21; 21:21; and 15:26-27; 16:7-11.

23. This is confirmed by the use of the phrase "the hour is coming and is now" in John 4:23 and 16:32. What is characteristic of the Fourth Gospel is not so much a tension between "already" and "not yet" as a telescoping of times and events, both within the narrative sequence and in the sayings of Jesus about the experiences of his disciples at and after his own departure.

24. It does not follow that the beginning of the narrative about the disciples reflects the faith of the originating group of Johannine Christians in Jesus as the Davidic Messiah, as R. E. Brown assumes in *The Community of the Beloved Disciple* (New York: Paulist Press, 1979) 27-29, 166, and 176. Brown refers to J. Louis Martyn but has unduly simplified the ingenious argument that Martyn presented in two articles, both republished in *The Gospel of John in Christian History* (New York: Paulist Press, 1979) 9-54 and 90-121. A discussion of Brown's views, however, is beyond the scope of this article.

25. Chapter 21 provides the clue to the earlier passages about the Beloved Disciple, which are all likely to belong to the same redaction as the "Appendix." See A. Kragerud, *Der Lieblingsjünger* (Oslo: Universitetsforlaget, 1959) and the perceptive evaluation of this work by H. Thyen in *TR* 42 (1977) 243-46. See also H. Thyen, "Entwicklungen der Johanneischen Theologie," in M. de Jonge, ed., *L'Évangile de Jean: Sources, rédaction, theologie* (BETL 44; Gembloux: Duculot, 1977) 259-99.

26. See esp. W. A. Meeks, "The Man from Heaven in Johannine Sectarianism" *JBL* 91 (1972) 44-72, one of the most stimulating contributions to Johannine studies in recent years. Meeks's use of the term *sectarianism* has caused some misunderstandings and objections. My main problem with the sociological use of the term is that it fails to distinguish the relationship of the Johannine "sectarians" to their Jewish environment from their relations to non-Johannine Christians.

27. Brown does not discuss how far the "Apostolic Christians" are envisaged as potential readers but finds clear signs of a Gentile component among the recipients of the Gospel (*Community*, 81-89, 55-58).

28. The wide consensus at this point is in itself an eloquent testimony to the importance of J. Louis Martyn's work, from the publication of *History and Theology in the Fourth Gospel* onward. See Kysar, *Fourth Gospel*, 76-84, 149-56; Brown, *Community*, 22-28, 172-74, and, more recently, D. Rensberger, *Johannine Faith and Liberating Community* (Philadelphia: Westminster, 1988) 22-29.

29. See A. Segal, *Two Powers in Heaven* (Leiden: Brill, 1977) esp. 213-17.

"NOR DO I . . ."
A CANONICAL READING
OF THE CHALLENGE TO JESUS
IN JOHN 8

James A. Sanders

The story about the woman caught in the act of adultery, with its challenge to Jesus concerning the application of law to the case, has, despite its uncertain canonical status, received considerable attention both before and since the beginning of Enlightenment study of Scripture.[1] The principal features of the passage that have commanded notice are its form, its place in the canon and in which Gospel, its function in the Gospel once those questions have been answered, and the question of what Jesus wrote with his finger in the ground. The story does not appear in the most ancient witnesses to the text, and yet it has clearly been very difficult to dismiss it totally or to set it aside. While Roman Catholics seem obligated to deal with it, Protestants exhibit uncertainty about what to do with it. Rudolf Bultmann, for example, omits consideration of it in his masterful commentary on John. But the Revised Standard Version, which in its early printings placed it in the lower margin, later included it in the text.

The present study intends to address the problems of the form of the pericope, its content and context. The overall question addressed is what understanding of these issues enhances the sense of the passage. The text of the pericope is reasonably stable in the manuscripts where it appears, whether in John or in Luke.

Genre, Content, and Scripture

The passage appears to be a mixture of two genres. Verse 6a marks the story as a controversy passage, while vv. 6b-8 mark it as a prophetic symbolic act within a story in the life of Jesus. Both textual signals need to be heeded.[2] The following simple observations about its structure may be helpful.

John 7:53–8:2. These verses provide the general setting. In John the pericope follows directly on the dialogue in the temple precincts during the Festival of Tabernacles among the Pharisees who want Jesus arrested, on the one hand, and the officers and Nicodemus who, having heard Jesus and seen the reaction of the people, question the plan. Nicodemus' question in 7:51 shows his concern for rule by law as over against the Pharisees who are presented, on the contrary, as concerned more about policy in Jesus' case than law (7:52). The understandable concern about Jesus' growing popularity, due to a well-founded fear of how Rome might react to it, would bring certain leaders to devise a policy designed to quash any such popular movement.

Thereupon follow statements about departures from the temple, everyone going home except Jesus, who went to the Mount of Olives. Herein lies the linkage of the story at Luke 21:38 in family 13 of Byzantine manuscripts—teaching in the temple by day but lodging at night on the Mount of Olives. Luke 21:38 and John 8:2a are, while similar, not identical, so that 8:2b is consistently omitted in all the f13 readings.[3] The general setting provided in the three verses in John picture Jesus back in the temple early in the morning, seated and teaching. One cannot help but be struck with the inappropriateness of the Lukan linkage as over against the setting in John 7 and 8 where the story, despite its synoptic aspects, is enhanced in a number of ways. To this we shall return.

The story proper seems to fall easily into three scenes: 8:3-6a, 8:6b-9a, and 8:9b-11.[4]

John 8:3-6a. Verse 3 provides the specific setting. Scribes and Pharisees bring a woman caught in the act of adultery and place her ἐν μέσῳ, a clear signal of a juridical setting, even though not institutional. In vv. 4 and 5 the men speak to Jesus about the indictment brought against the woman caught *in flagrante delicto* (ἐπ' αὐτοφώρῳ) and cite law on such a case. The crux is then reached in their asking Jesus his opinion of the matter. Verse 6a characterizes their action and speech as a testing of Jesus in order to bring an indictment against him. The indictment against the woman is interpreted as an attempt to find another, more important indictment against Jesus. The disappointment expressed in 7:45 that the officers had not yet arrested Jesus during the last day (7:37—*Shĕmînî 'Atzeret*) of the annual festival par excellence (*he-Ḥag*), celebrating the law, is intended to be resolved in this further attempt to indict him.

John 8:6b-9a. Within the controversy setting is then found a typical prophetic symbolic act. No such specific act from Scripture is midrashically alluded to more than another; one need but think of those in Isa 30:8, Hab 2:2, and Jer 32:10-12, where cursory writing takes place in public view as part of the prophet's message, specifically conveying an immediately relevant point. This symbolic act, like the one in Jeremiah 32, involves not only writing but also a bit of drama, such as that in Jeremiah 18 and 19. Silently Jesus kneels twice and writes something in the ground (εἰς τὴν γῆν), but between the two actions of kneeling and writing Jesus also speaks, in his turn challenging his challengers: "Let any of you who is sinless cast the first stone." The law is cited in v. 5 by the Pharisees, apparently referring to Lev 20:10, Deut 17:7 and 22:22-24, though the law involved is not clear from the Pentateuch alone. (See *m. Sanh.* 11:1, 6.)[5] Those bringing the indictment must initiate execution of the sentence. While Jesus knelt a second time those who "heard" began one by one, starting with the elders (some manuscripts add "overcome by their conscience"), to depart the scene. Hearing on the part of the Pharisees includes also seeing what Jesus wrote; it might be understood as heeding.

The third and concluding scene is recounted in 8:9b-11. It begins: "And Jesus was left alone with the woman standing before him [ἐν μέσῳ]." Only Jesus is left to support the indictment and cast the first stone. A pause at the end of v. 9 suggests suspense. John, of all the Gospels, presents Jesus as sinless. Surely the hearer of the tale would think that this included obedience to the law given by God to Moses—or so the story is cast. The silence is rather deafening at this point. Two people are left in the scene, the one indicted by the law, the other a target for indictment by policy. Neither is acceptable to those charged with administering the law or the policy. Verse 10 begins in silence still: Jesus gets up from his writing a second time. A slow, careful reading brings to mind the silence in another trial scene, the silence that will later serve as answer to Pilate's question (18:38). But then Jesus speaks once more and asks the woman where her accusers are and whether anyone indicts her now. Her answer (v. 11) is a simple, "No one, lord." Thereupon Jesus says, "Nor do I condemn you; go and henceforth sin no more."

A bare outline of the above would look like this:

Mis-en-scene	7:53–8:2	Jesus teaching in temple
Scene 1	8:3-6a	Indicted woman used to indict Jesus
Scene 2	8:6b-9a	Symbolic act; reaction of accusers
Scene 3	8:9b-11	Dialogue between Jesus and woman

The form is mixed. A prophetic symbolic act thwarts the controversy raised by the Pharisees. The Pharisees induce the controversy on the basis of what must have seemed like a certainty from their point of view. The story as received admits of no question about the validity of the indictment against the woman. In their raising the issue, in the light of the failure of Jesus' arrest narrated in chap. 7, they are presented as being sure of their case. Would he dare run counter to the law, even though he had the clear reputation of presenting God as willing to forgive sinners, particularly those who had no power in society and could not feign righteousness?

Jesus is presented as responding to the challenge not by debating law but by engaging in a symbolic act. Debating law would be expected; that is what will make up Mishnah and Talmud. But those debates, as between the houses of Hillel and Shammai, would not ostensibly contradict the law. In the story, Jesus elects to dramatize the point he makes by silent action, encasing an *ad hominem* challenge to those who have challenged him. Such a challenge might well be ruled out in an institutional setting, but in the setting the Pharisees have chosen it works. Jesus is back in the temple, where yesterday many people had believed in him, despite policy against him (7:15, 31, 40). And he had only yesterday made the point on which the prophetic symbolic act and challenge will build: "Did not Moses give you the law? Yet none of you keeps the law. Why do you seek to kill me?" (7:19).

The question of which Gospel context most enhances the point of the story seems almost to be a non-question. While it is true that the story is synoptic in tone and vocabulary, includes non-Johannine expressions,[6] and may well have circulated independently or in another now lost context before being attached either to John (after 7:36, after 7:52, or after 21:25), or to Luke (after 21:38 or after 24:53), or omitted from the New Testament altogether (the majority of manuscripts and early witnesses), one must say that nowhere else is the story's main point so enhanced as in the context of John 7 and 8. The prophetic charge in 7:19 that no one keeps the law would be contextually sufficient to highlight the story. That charge is variously complemented: in 7:24 by the challenge not to judge by appearances; in 7:51 by Nicodemus's question about a fair and just hearing before condemnation; in 8:13 by the charge that "you are your own witnesses"; in 8:15 by the charge that "you pass judgment by human standards; I judge no one"; in 8:18 by the affirmation that "I give testimony on my own behalf and the Father . . . gives testimony for me"; and finally in 8:21, 24 and 46 that Jesus' interlocutors, in contrast to himself, are sinful indeed.

A Prophetic Symbolic Act

The method of Canonical Criticism may be helpful at three points: the question of what understanding of Jesus' writing would most advance the thrust of the story; the question of the significance of a prophetic symbolic act as the response Jesus chooses to the challenge by the Scribes and Pharisees; and the issue of the canonical context and hermeneutics by which to understand Jesus' response.

There are three factors to note in the act of Jesus' writing: the writing itself, writing with a finger, and writing in the ground. The first and third factors could indicate a midrashic reference to Jer 17:13: "O Lord, the hope of Israel, all who abandon thee will be ashamed; those who turn away from me shall be written in the earth *(bā-āretz)*, for they have abandoned a spring of living water, the Lord" (author's trans.). The Septuagint has only minor variants. This is seen as the implied reference by Ambrose, Augustine, Jerome, Eisler, Jeremias, and Schnackenburg, among others.[7] The reference could, however, be easily countered, and thus lose its force, since the Scribes and Pharisees would certainly not see themselves as abandoning God; they would have felt themselves, on the morrow of having expressed their annual joy in Torah, to be God's most faithful champions.

Derrett's references to Exod 23:1*b* and 23:7 are even less pertinent, since these passages in the Book of the Covenant condemn unjust witnesses and false charges.[8] The pericope, as noted, is quite clear that the woman was caught in the act. The story, as the text stands wherever it appears, does not permit of the possibility that the accusation is false. The statement of her crime, according to the law, must be accepted at face value.

Derrett's suggestion is similar to that of Osborne and others, but also impertinent to the story.[9] Susanna, in the LXX Daniel (v. 43), claims, precisely in the terms of the LXX phrasing of the ninth commandment, that the two old men "have borne false witness against me"; and Daniel accuses one of them (v. 53) of violating the ninth commandment as well as the laws in Exodus 23, to which Derrett refers. But the story of Susanna is quite different in significant details from the story of the woman caught in adultery.

The only pertinence the ninth commandment has is that it brings their own human sinful condition to the minds of the Scribes and the Pharisees, who were not necessarily her accusers in the first place. On the contrary, while 8:3-4 uses only the passive "caught," the statement in v. 5 that Moses "commanded us to stone such" may be taken as indicating the commandment's legal standing for all generations of Jews, and not necessarily that they who spoke the words of vv. 4-5 were the witnesses who must throw the first stone. The challenge of Jesus in v. 7 was to all present in the temple/teaching setting, "Let any of you who is ἀναμάρτητος throw the first stone," whether witness or judge.

The references most likely to enhance the thrust of the story are Deut 9:10 and/or Exod 31:18, God's writing the two tablets of the law, the decalogue, with the finger.[10] The writing on the wall in Daniel (5:24) is by a hand, in some early versions a fist or a knuckle, but not a finger. The factor of word tally to the Exodus and Deuteronomy passages is satisfied in that the expression is precisely the same in both passages in the Hebrew. The LXX of Deut 9:10 has the "plus" of the preposition ἐν. God not only dictated the law, but God actually authored it as well.[11] These three passages (Exod 31:18, Deut 9:10, and our passage) are, in truth, the only three loci in Scripture where writing with the finger is stated. This would indicate that Jesus was scratching some form of the decalogue "in the ground."

How early the practice of abbreviating the Ten Commandments began is unclear.[12] There is a delightful little midrash in *Mekhilta Bahodesh* 8 in which each of the ten commandments of the decalogue is written in abbreviated form; the first is written opposite the sixth, the second opposite the seventh, and so on until the fifth is opposite the tenth. The tradition of the decalogue being written on two tablets already appears in the Pentateuch, but how early it was written or inscribed in abbreviated form is not known. The *Mekhilta* passage is undatable but encourages one to think that practice of such abbreviation of the decalogue may have been quite early simply because of the human tendency to abbreviate the very familiar which after all, by tradition, has 613 (or 620) words.[13] No one in a Jewish community would have needed more than the (now in modern times very typical and) simplest of abbreviations to indicate clearly the decalogue.

Yet, for our story it is not any one specific commandment that makes the point more than another.[14] The tradition of the two tablets would be indicated by Jesus' kneeling twice. And for the sake of the story one might imagine that none of the first five commandments would really induce self-incrimination on the part of the hearers and witnesses to the scene. All could escape such self-indictment when reminded of the first five—no polytheizing, no idolatry, no taking of God's name in vain, honoring parents, and observing the sabbath. But escape from realization of the sinful nature of humanity would be considerably more difficult when faced with the whole thrust of the ten, upon Jesus' second kneeling.[15]

The story is set on the morrow of celebration of *Shĕmînî 'Azeret*, the climax of the high holy days when both human sinfulness and joy in Torah are brought to mind in the most poignant of ways at *Rosh ha-Shānāh*, *Yōm Kippūr*, and *Succōt*. Consciousness raising about general human sinfulness precisely by contemplating Torah, as Jesus is presented as doing, would not be difficult; and this unbelabored, cursory, abbreviated reminder summarizes the significance of the whole season.

Canonical Controversies

What the Scribes and Pharisees were doing had to be done, both in terms of responsibility to the law and to the policy they thought best regarding Jesus' intolerable challenges to their understanding of Torah. For Torah itself shows a divine bias for the poor and powerless. Here is where the canonical context of "controversy" plays a very important, but so far unrecognized, role in understanding the import of the story. We have noted that the story is both a controversy passage and a story of Jesus' performing a prophetic symbolic act. Both marks of its formality indicate important canonical dimensions.

The Torah and the Prophets very realistically demonstrate time and again how those charged with administering law were themselves sinners. The thrust of the whole story from Genesis 12 through 2 Kings 25 is that God had often and betimes sent prophets who indicted kings, priests, and prophets responsible for administering Torah. They indicted the indicters whose misadministration of Torah, according to the Deuteronomic historians, had brought about the failure of the Abraham-Sarah venture in the destruction of both the northern (2 Kings 18) and southern (2 Kings 25) kingdoms, and hence the failure of the promise of the land and the reduction of the promise of progeny to a remnant in exile. In the Hebrew canon, 2 Kings 25 is followed by the prophetic corpus, in part to explain the failure as well as the divine conditions set (Deuteronomy 29–31) for any kind of restoration, including the resurrection (Ezekiel 37) of a combined Israel and Judah into the new Israel to be called Judaism. In this passage Jesus is saying no more than had already been said by the prophets themselves.

In a poignant symbolic act, and largely in silence, Jesus sets the stage for the current leaders charged with administering Torah to indict themselves. He thus neutralizes the indictment of the woman whose guilt, according to the story, was not in question. The story, seen in this light, reaches into the depths of the human experience shared by all societies. Those charged with administering law are themselves quite vulnerable to indictment by it. Jesus' symbolic act makes the universal human point that those whose responsibility it is to execute justice in any society may simply be unindicted trespassers themselves, not yet "caught" as the woman had been. Some of the most poignant stories that reflect the human scene from Homer, Hesiod, and the Bible[16] on down to modern times, Occident and Orient, have to do with how a society can bring judgment against judges when need be.

The ancient prophet never pretended to be without sin (ἀναμάρτητος); prophets identified with the people. The Gospels frequently show Jesus in a similar relationship of identity with sinners in the first century. He is frequently accused of being in their company, eating with them and attracting them to him (see, for example, Luke 7:48-49, or less dramatically, Luke 15:1-2 and John 9). This story, however, seems to leave Jesus more vulnerable than others: "Nor do I. . . ." Why? The story is open to the interpretation that Jesus, perhaps like Isaiah, was a man of unclean lips living among a people of unclean lips. Jesus, being himself without sin, according to the gospel tradition at this point in its development, still would not cast the stone. The balance between that danger, in the minds of the early churches, and the poignancy of the message that God forgives sinners, so consistent with the gospel generally, left the early Christian communities with variant opinions about its canonicity. But at least attaching it, on the one hand, to the dialogue between the officers and Nicodemus and to the expressed policy and concern of the Pharisees in John 7:45-52, and to that between Jesus and the Pharisees in 8:12-59, enhances its poignancy considerably more than if inserted elsewhere, especially after Luke 21.

Certainly, if one moralizes the story, as Calvin did in his commentary, accusing the Roman church of his time of using the story for immoral license, then it presents Jesus as does no other, perhaps, to be antinomian. Yet Jesus is no more "antinomian" than the prophets. Jeremiah's critique of those who manipulated Torah (probably the Deuteronomists) in his time could be wrongly construed as antinomian! Criticism of applying the law by those charged with its administration, and even criticism of points of the law itself, make up a good portion of prophetic literature.[17] The classical prophets were often just as *ad hominem* in their charges against the leaders of God's people in this regard as this passage presents Jesus to be. What the story does, if carefully read, is to present the pervasive human situation—whether in ancient society or in modern—of sinners judging sinners. Normal humans have to assume institutional office in society and to administer justice despite the fact that, being human, they probably are also indictable on some score or scores—the issue often raised today on the appointment of a judge whose record may be less than totally clean.

The current status of study of true and false prophecy is enlightening for study of the controversy passages in the Gospels.[18] While it has been shown time and again that there are no sure criteria whereby to distinguish, in the ambiguity of reality, true from false prophecy, there is a clear difference in the hermeneutics whereby the true or canonical prophets applied authoritative traditions, even Torah, to their contemporary situations as over against the so-called false prophets. Danger of falsehood lurked where the prophet did not stress God as creator as well as redeemer. What saved belief in God as redeemer from denominationalism and tribalism was seeing God also as creator of heaven and earth and of all peoples, even animals, on earth. In other words the true prophet stressed that God was free to judge God's own people, as well as all peoples, and that God was free to bless people other than God's own people, and indeed, like Balaam, to speak God's truth through them.

In the controversy passages in the Gospels, Jesus simply stresses the other side of the same coin: God is free to forgive sinners. God only is above law, not humans. As good theology has long recognized, from a human point of view grace may seem to be a form of divine injustice. While God's promises are sure, God is free to judge and forgive whom God wills. In the Prophets and the Gospels God's freedom to follow God's own agenda, and not the agenda of those charged institutionally with administration of law and tradition, is equally stressed. The story's poignancy is in part the presentation of Jesus as one who in his ministry refused to be put in the position of judging others but became the instrument whereby judges might judge themselves. The God whom the canonical prophets had said was free to judge God's own people is also free, said Jesus, to forgive sinners and hence once more to judge God's own.

In a comment on our story, Augustine makes the beautiful observation, *Relicti sunt duo, miseria et misericordia:*[19] at the end of the story only "two are left," the woman and Jesus—that is, "sin and grace." It is a moving observation and well worth note. But it may be misleading. Law has not been eliminated by this story, by the gospel, or by those responsible for administering the law, being but human themselves. Nor is it the intent of the prophets or of Jesus as presented in these texts, or indeed in either testament, to suggest that only sin and grace remain as bearers of truth, human or divine. Society and human intercourse rest on law and its just and fair administration despite the pervasive and universal problem of that administration's being the responsibility of humans themselves. Where policy conflicts with law, it is law that must be obeyed and administered even by those whose policies are at variance with law. Seen in the light of a pervasive canonical wrestling, in both testaments, with the realities of human life, this poignant story, without prejudice as to its actual provenance or historicity,[20] deserves inclusion—whether with or without brackets, asterisks, or obeli—in the Fourth Gospel right where Codex Cantabrigiensis and later manuscripts place it—both for its sake and for the sake of the message of the Gospel.

Notes

1. Commentaries, monographs, and studies consulted include Augustine's *Homilies on the Gospel According to St. John and His First Epistle* (vol. 1; Oxford: John H. Parker/London: F & J. Rivington, 1848) 472-80; C. K. Barrett, *The Gospel According to St. John* (2nd ed.; Philadelphia: Westminster, 1978) 589-92; Ulrich Becker, *Jesus und die Ehebrecherin* (Berlin: Alfred Töpelmann, 1963) esp. 84-87; Raymond Brown, *The Gospel According to John* (2 vols.; AB 29; Garden City: Doubleday, 1966–70) 1.332-38; John Calvin, *The Gospel According to St. John* (eds. D. W Torrance and T. F. Torrance; trans. T. H. L. Parker; Grand Rapids: Eerdmans, 1959) 206-09; Beverley W. Coleman, "The Woman Taken in Adultery," *Theology* 73 (1970) 409-10; J. D. M. Derrett, *Law in the New Testament* (London: Darton, Longman & Todd, 1970) 156-88; A. Guilding, *The Fourth Gospel and Jewish Worship* (Oxford: Clarendon, 1960) 110-12, 214; Z. C. Hodges, "The Woman Taken in Adultery (John 7:53–8:11): The Text," *Bibliotheca Sacra* 136 (1979) 318-32 idem, "The Woman Taken in Adultery (John 7:53–8:11): Exposition," *Bibliotheca Sacra* 137 (1980) 41-53; J. Jeremias, "Zur Geschichtlichkeit des Verhors Jesu vor dem Hohen Rat," *ZNW* 43 (1950/51) 145-50; T. W. Manson, "The Pericope de Adultera (Joh 7,53-8,11)," *ZNW* 44 (1952/53) 255-56; R. E. Osborne, "Pericope Adulterae," *CTJ* 12 (1966) 281-83; F. A. Schilling, "The Story of Jesus and the Adulteress [Jn 8:1-11]," *ATR* 37 (1955) 91-106; R. Schnackenburg, *The Gospel According to St. John* (vol. 2; trans. C. Hastings et al.; New York: Seabury Press, 1980) 162-71; A. P. Wikgren, "The Lectionary Text of the Pericope John 8:1-11," *JBL* 53 (1934) 188-98. My gratitude to Mr. Kenneth Pomykala for his scrupulous assistance in bibliographic searches.
2. Becker, *Jesus,* 84-87, has provided the most thorough form-critical study yet available, and Schnackenburg, *John,* 162-71, the most useful commentary.
3. My gratitude to Mr. Johaness Erasmus for work in the Ancient Biblical Manuscript Center film collection, collating the text of the pericope at Luke 21:38 in mss 13, 69, 124, 346, 543, 788, 826, and 983 in the Ferrar Group (f13). See J. Geerlings, *The Ferrar Lectionary* (Salt Lake City: University of Utah, 1959); idem, *Family 13: The Text According to Luke* (1961) 128-29; and idem, *Family 13: The Text According to John* (1962) 45; B. Metzger, *A Textual Commentary on the Greek New Testament* (New York: United Bible Society, 1971) 219-23; K. and B. Aland, *The Text of the New Testament* (Leiden: Brill, 1987) 240.
4. See the structure analysis in F. Rousseau, "La femme adultere. Structure de Jn 7,53-8,11," *Bib* 59 (1978) 463-80, esp. 465-66.
5. Schnackenburg, *John,* 164; Derrett, *Law,* 166ff.
6. Brown, *John,* 1.333.
7. See Schnackenburg, *John,* 165-66.
8. See Derrett, *Law,* 175-86.
9. See Osborne, "Pericope Adulterae," 281-83. For the suggestion that Jesus was simply doodling, see Brown, *John,* 1.334.
10. Though I arrived at this conclusion independently, using the method described, I am pleased to note that Guilding, *Fourth Gospel,* 110-12 and 214, and Coleman had already seen the relevance of the decalogue to the passage.
11. Note the indirect allusion in Luke 11:20 to the finger (law?) of God by which Jesus cast out demons because a time of such divine activity had once more come.
12. My gratitude to Dr. Laila Bronner of the University of Judaism for calling my attention to articles on the decalogue in the history of art: by Israel Abrahams, "The Decalogue in Art," in *Studies in Jewish Literature in Honor of Kaufman Kohler* (Cambridge: University Press, 1913) 39-55; Ruth Mellinkoff, "The Round-Topped Tablets of the Law: Sacred Symbol and Emblem of Evil," *Journal of Jewish Art* 1 (1974) 28-42; and G. B. Sarfatti, "The Tables of the Covenant as a Symbol of Judaism," (in Hebrew) *Tarbitz* 39 (1960) 370-93.
13. See Abrahams, "Decalogue," 41.
14. If the sixth commandment scratched by Jesus was against killing (see n. 15 below), then it might well relate directly to Jesus' saying in John 7:19: "Did not Moses give you the law? Yet none of you keeps the law. Why do you seek to kill me?"

15. The early period of textual fluidity is quite evident in the arrangement of the so-called sixth to eighth commandments. The order kill, adultery, steal is found in the MT Ex and Deut, 4QDt[m], 4Q Phyl[A,B,G,J,L], LXX[ALuc] Ex, LXX[A] Deut, Vulg, Pesh Ex and Deut, Matt 19:18, Josephus, and the Didache. The order adultery, kill, steal is found in the Nash papyrus, LXX[BLuc] Deut, Rom 13:9, James 2:11, Mark 10:19, Luke 18:20, Philo, Tertullian and Clement of Alexandria. The order adultery, steal, kill is found in LXX[B] Ex. Incidentally the order steal, kill, adultery is found in MT Jer 7:9, while LXX there has the order kill, adultery, steal! The order of the rest of the decalogue is relatively stable.

16. See, for example, 2 Sam 12 and 14, where Nathan and the wise woman of Tekoa provide court cases for David to judge as mirrors for David as king and judge to be able to see his own sins and failures. Like the Scribes and Pharisees in our story, David was "overcome by his conscience" (Textus Receptus at John 8:9) because of their symbolic actions—that is, by their bringing parabolic court cases to the king—the supreme judge of the land.

17. For example, the sacerdotal laws as in Jer 7:21-22.

18. See J. A. Sanders, "Canonical Hermeneutics: True and False Prophecy," in *From Sacred Story to Sacred Text* (Philadelphia: Fortress, 1987) 87-105.

19. Schnackenburg, *John*, 167 and n. 123.

20. See Schnackenburg's thoughtful comment on historicity, *John*, 170; also Metzger's, *Textual Commentary*, 220-21.

ΕΛΛΗΝ IN THE GOSPEL OF JOHN: TRADITION AND REDACTION IN JOHN 12:20-24

Kiyoshi Tsuchido

I n the very short five verses of John 12:20-24, and the problems they present, the evangelist[1] gives useful keys to understanding theology and history in the Gospel of John. One problem is the identity of the "Greeks" in 12:20, and another concerns the "hour of the glorification of the Son of Man. Further, there are problems as to the meaning and the role of the parable of the grain of wheat in the context of this narrative sequence. The purpose of this study is to present a solution to these problems by finding clues in the evangelist's redaction of earlier sources and in the historical situation out of which the Gospel was written.

12:20-22 and Ἕλληνες in 12:20

A number of scholars regard the Ἕλληνες in 12:20 as non-Jews who have converted to Judaism. Some of these regard them as Gentiles who had become προσήλυτοι.[2] Others view them as σεβόμενοι,[3] and some treat them as both προσήλυτοι and σεβόμενοι.[4] On the other hand, some regard the Ἕλληνες in this verse as "the Jews of the Dispersion."[5] Further, in maintaining that the Ἕλληνες are so-called proselytes, C. H. Dodd,[6] R. Bultmann,[7] E. Haenchen,[8] and others suppose that the evangelist used the word to denote "the representatives of the Greek world" within Judaism. Finally C. K. Barrett[9] argues that it is unnecessary to suppose John had clearly defined the status of these people, that is to say as προσήλυτοι and/or σεβόμενοι; it was sufficient that they were not Jews. The word Ἕλληνες then signifies not a Greek person, strictly speaking, but one of non-Jewish birth.

348

We, however, would point out the following. (a) If the evangelist had intended to denote Ἑλληνισταί by the word Ἕλληνες, in 12:20 he would have used the phrase ἡ διασπορὰ τῶν Ἑλλήνων, which is found in 7:35.

(b) J. L. Martyn[10] has correctly pointed to the Sitz im Leben out of which the evangelist wrote his Gospel—that is, the historical situation of conflict between the Johannine community on the one hand and the synagogue, the Jewish community, on the other, governed under the Gerousia of the evangelist's city, which adopted the *Birkath ha-Minim* revised by Gamaliel II in approximately 85 CE in order to detect Christian heresy. Therefore, it is not valid to regard the Ἕλληνες in this verse as the Greek-speaking Jews of the synagogue and to insist that the Gospel was written for such people. The evangelist would not primarily refer to such Jews with this word Ἕλληνες.[11]

(c) The opening passage in vv. 20-24, Ἦσαν δὲ Ἕλληνές τινες ἐκ τῶν ἀναβαινόντων, is similar to the style used by the evangelist in his editorial work, as shown, for example, in 3:1: Ἦν δὲ ἄνθρωπος ἐκ τῶν Φαρισαίων. It is almost always used in the editorial sections.[12] Moreover, the use of ἐκ to indicate derivation is typically Johannine.[13]

(d) The narrative sequence of vv. 20-22 shows that the Greeks ask Philip to introduce them to Jesus, and then Philip consults with his fellow townsman, Andrew. After that, both of them go to Jesus to deliver their request to Jesus. Verses 20-22 not only closely resemble the characteristics of the story of the gathering of the first disciples in 1:35-51, but also contain parallels in content and formulae. It must be noticed that most of the narrative in 1:35-51 was derived from a pre-Johannine source and that the evangelist inserted the typical Johannine words and phrases.[14] Through such a Johannine editorial device, it appears here to be the evangelist's intention to compose a narrative that leads his readers from faith in which Jews and Jewish Christians regarded Jesus only as a great prophet within the prophetic line to the evangelist's own faith, according to which Jesus is regarded as the glorified Son of Man. Further, in the narrative sequence created by the evangelist's literary device, the ministry of Jesus develops through the medium of the works of his disciples.[15] It appears, therefore, that the evangelist's overall editorial method, in which he indicates the historical situation of his church in describing the ministry of Jesus, is also expressed here. Moreover, the typical Johannine editorial device is clarified by linking vv. 20-23 with the "glorified Son of Man" passage in the following verses.[16]

Furthermore, in vv. 20-22, it is stressed that Philip came from Bethsaida in Galilee.[17] That region bordered on pagan areas, and most of the people who lived there were more strongly influenced by Hellenism than the people in the other areas of Palestine. It may be presumed that a great number of people spoke Greek in that area. As I have shown elsewhere, Jerusalem was meant by the evangelist not only as a geographical place, the capital of city, where Jesus was rejected as Messiah by the Jewish authorities and people, but also as the community center of Jewish society where the Christian community of the evangelist existed and from whose synagogue the Christian Jews of the evangelist's day were driven.[18] Therefore, vv. 20-22 clearly indicate not only the existence of non-Jewish Christians in the church where the evangelist seems to have been the great leader, but also the historical situation in which the Gospel is being transposed from the central area of Judaism, Jerusalem, to the borderland of Palestine and the pagan world.

(e) The phrase ἐν τῇ ἑορτῇ in v. 20b is typically Johannine, like the same Johannine editorial phrase, for example, in 11:55 and 12:12.[19] That is to say, the evangelist creates a new historical situation in which the event, the coming of the Greeks to Jesus, takes place during the Passover in Jerusalem (see 11:55). Consequently, through this Johannine editorial device the coming of the Greeks in vv. 20-22 plays a role in smoothly linking the raising of Lazarus, the entry of Jesus into Jerusalem, and the anointing at Bethany with the discourse in 12:23-36a, whose theme is the glorious death of the Son of Man. It is, therefore, possible to say that this narrative sequence evidently indicates Johannine composition, since it shows the characteristics of the Johannine concept that the death of Jesus on the cross is a death for the redemption of all the nations—that is, the saving work of drawing all people to Jesus as the glorified Son of Man (12:32; see further 12:23, 34-35) in the hour of glorification.

(f) The composition of the request of the Greeks in v. 21b closely resembles that of the Samaritan woman's question about the true worship of God.[20] Moreover, the word προσκυνέω in v. 20b (ἵνα προσκυνήσωσιν) is used to indicate characteristic Johannine thought. That is to say, most of the uses of προσκυνέω occur in the typically Johannine section or in the editorial phrases.[21] These facts support our argument that 12:20-24 is an editorial creation, freely composed by the evangelist.

The above analysis shows that the word Ἕλληνες is used by the evangelist to refer simultaneously to the προσήλυτοι or σεβόμενοι in Jesus' day and "the representatives of the whole pagan world" in the evangelist's time. Therefore, C. K. Barrett is not correct to regard Ἕλληνες simply as people who were not Jews, nor are other scholars right to treat Ἕλληνες as simply either the προσήλυτοι or σεβόμενοι. Also, it is not proper for J. A. T. Robinson to view Ἕλληνες as Ἑλληνισταί. Such conclusions do not deal with the whole intent of the composition by the evangelist, but with only part of it. Further, the editorial section 12:20-22 was composed by the evangelist in order to link the sequence narratives in chap. 11 with the discourse contained in the two passages on the Son of Man, as we have seen.

12:23

The saying ἐλήλυθεν ἡ ὥρα ἵνα δοξασθῇ ὁ υἱὸς τοῦ ἀνθρώπου in v. 23*b*, which is very similar to the expression in 7:39, 11:4, and 13:31, is almost always used in the evangelist's redaction.[22] This saying in Jesus' reply to the two disciples seems not to be directly addressed to the Greeks in this narrative sequence. As we have seen above (sect. 1d) through this saying the evangelist provides an understanding of his own missionary activity and indicates his own *Sitz im Leben*. It appears here to be consistent with the intent of the evangelist's composition that the "Ελληνες in vv. 20-22 are not given any important role in the following discourse, whereas they appear in v. 20 and in this context indicate the historical situation of the missionary activities in the evangelist's day. In these verses, the evangelist shows that it is necessary for the salvation of the Gentiles that the hour of glorification of the Son of Man should come. Such a typically Johannine idea conforms with other statements: (1) Caiaphas's assertion that Jesus "should die for the whole nation" (11:52), which the evangelist has inserted into the story of Lazarus; (2) "I, when I am lifted up from the earth, will draw all men to myself" (12:32); and (3) the *kleines Gleichnis* contained in the form of pre-Johannine material (see below), but with stress of the parable shifted by the evangelist (see below). Furthermore, we can assume that in this verse, the bright side of the "hour," which was presented in 7:30 and 8:20 as that of Jesus' death, is emphasized.[23] Whereas the statement "Jesus' hour had not yet come" (7:30, 8:20) has been repeatedly made up to this point, v. 23 emphatically proclaims that the hour of glorification has now come (ἐλήλυθεν: perfect tense).

Through such a statement, the meaning of the "lifting up" of the Son of Man (see 3:14, 8:28) is clarified. Here we find the Johannine "higher Christology" in which the evangelist denotes the hour of Jesus being lifted up on the cross as at the same time the hour of the glorification of the Son of Man and the hour of the salvation of all the nations.[24] Concerning this association, several points are relevant: (a) In the entire New Testament the expression, which includes a combination of the Son of Man with δεῖ and ὑψοῦν in one phrase, appears only in the Fourth Gospel; (b) the evangelist never refers, as do the Synoptics, to the Son of Man's heading toward passion and death as Jesus' obedience to God; (c) we find in John 3:14 a similar typological application of Num 21:8-9, in which Moses raised up the serpent in the desert. This typology, which was frequently echoed in post-Apostolic times, occurs only here in the New Testament. These observations suggest that the evangelist has created the combination of the Son of Man with ὑψοῦν and δεῖ.[25]

The evangelist regards the cross itself as the beginning of the salvific lordship of Christ[26] and also as the hour of Jesus' glorification (see 17:1-5). That is to say, the glory of Jesus, which is given to him on the cross, means the glory that Jesus had with the Father before the world was made (17:5)[27] and enables the saving of all nations through his own death on the cross. Thus to the evangelist the expression "lifted up on the cross" contains a theological interpretation of the crucifixion as the acceptance of his glorification.[28] Therefore, the evangelist uses the parable of the grain of wheat in 12:24 because the content of this parable describes his own unique christology, as we shall see below.

12:24

Only the evangelist uses the double ἀμήν (twenty-five times in John) whereas the single ἀμήν occurs in the Synoptics (thirty-one times in Matthew, thirteen in Mark, and six in Luke). Moreover, the uses of μένειν and φέρειν (to bear fruit) in the parable itself is unique to the evangelist.[29] The form of the parable, however, closely resembles that in the Synoptics (see, for example, Matt 5:13; 6:12-23; 18:12-14; Mark 3:24),[30] but at the same time there are differences in the details; for example, the omission of introductory words or any "moral," and the different way the application is suggested. As C. H. Dodd aptly points out,[31] the parable of the grain of wheat may have been drawn from the same reservoir of tradition as used in the Synoptics. The parable, as a traditional and symbolic pre-Johannine saying, had circulated to explain Jesus' death as the necessary event for the salvation of all the people.[32] The evangelist regards the metaphorical understanding of the parable, in which the death of the grain of wheat bears rich fruit, as the best expression of his theological view that the Son of Man must be lifted up (12:34), and so he creates a new scene in adopting this parable. Therefore, it may be asserted that through the evangelist's editorial work, the climax of the original parable itself is shifted from Jesus' death for the salvation of all the (chosen) people to the glory of Jesus for the salvation of all nations.

Several conclusions follow from the above analysis. (a) The section 12:20-24 must be regarded as a continuous unit within its narrative context, composed by the evangelist, who used some pre-Johannine fragments. Therefore, the attempt to reconstruct a narrative and to interpret it by separating vv. 20-24 from 12:34-36 and by rearranging it as R. Bultmann did,[33] fails to detect the evangelist's intention. It also fails to provide a key for examining Johannine thought and the historical situation out of which the evangelist wrote his Gospel.[34]

(b) Έλληνες, which appears in 12:20, denotes not only the προσήλυτοι and the σεβόμενοι in Jesus' day, but also "the representatives of the whole pagan world" in the evangelist's time. He thus describes the sayings and the works of Jesus and simultaneously reflects his own *Sitz im Leben*.

(c) The story that describes the Greeks' request to be introduced to Jesus by Philip, and Philip's consulting with his fellow townsman Andrew, and finally their delivering the Greeks' request to Jesus, very closely resembles the content of the gathering of Jesus' first disciples as well as of the literary structure in 1:35-51. Furthermore, the story refers to the missionary activities of Jesus in his day and to that of the evangelist and his church. The story of the Greeks' coming to Jesus shows the evangelist's understanding of Christ—namely, his faith in Jesus as a pre-existent and glorified Christ, finding the life of the Revealer in the earthly life of Jesus as the Son of Man. In doing so, the evangelist intends to lead his readers from the faith of the Jews and the Jewish Christians to the faith that the evangelist himself grasped. The Jewish Christians remained in the synagogue of the city in which the evangelist lived, and in the same city was also the church of the evangelist and Christian Jews. The Jewish Christians regarded Jesus only as a great prophet within the traditional Jewish prophetic line. The consistent redactional intent of the evangelist in these verses, therefore, is to show that the evangelist would lead his readers from the lower christology held by the Jews and Jewish Christians to his own and his Christian Jewish followers' higher christology.

(d) Verse 23 is typically Johannine. Through its linking with vv. 20-22 and 24-26 the evangelist creates a continuous content. That is to say, because Jesus raised Lazarus from the dead (11:1-44), he was crucified (11:53-54, 57; 12:16) and thus the hour of his glorification as the Son of Man has come (12:23). As the result of his crucifixion—namely, his glorification that he had before the world was made (17:5), becomes the hour in which the salvation of all nations is fulfilled. Furthermore, the brilliant side of the hour that has been previously announced is now stressed.

(e) The parable of the grain of wheat seems to stem from the same origin as the Synoptic traditions but was transmitted through different channels. The evangelist adapts the parable and uses it in this context as the metaphorical interpretation of the climax of Jesus' earthly ministry. This is the hour of the glorification of Jesus, since the parable clarifies

353

both the Johannine theology of salvation for all the nations (11:51-53; 12:32-33) and the incident of Jesus' being sought after by the Greeks. The evangelist has adapted the parable and incorporated it to function like one of his editorial explanations. It appears, then, that the whole of vv. 20-24 fits squarely into the overall redactional—that is, *theological*— intent of the evangelist.

Notes

1. In this article the evangelist is understood as the one who composed, by use of earlier sources, the greater part of the Gospel of John, except for chap. 21 and a few other passages, which seem to be added pericopae from the post-Johannine age.
2. See W. Bauer, *Das Johannesevangelium* (Tübingen: J. C. B. Mohr [Paul Siebeck], 1925) 156; J. H. Bernard, *A Critical and Exegetical Commentary on the Gospel According to St. John* (2 vols.; Edinburgh: T. and T. Clark, 1928) 430; R. E. Brown, *The Gospel According to John* (2 vols.; AB 29; Garden City: Doubleday, 1966) 1.314, 466.
3. R. Schnackenburg, *Das Johannesevangelium* II (2nd ed.; Freiburg/Basel: Herder, 1977) 478; Str-B 2. 548-49; H. Windisch, *TDNT* 2.511; E. C. Hoskyns and F. N. Davey, *The Fourth Gospel* (2nd ed.; London: Faber and Faber, 1947) 423; H. Strathmann, *Das Evangelium nach Johannes* (NTD; Göttingen: Vandenhoeck & Ruprecht, 1963) 130; B. Lindars, *The Gospel of John* (NCB; London: Oliphants, 1972) 427. Lindars regards the Ἕλληνες as "devout Gentiles" like Cornelius (Acts 10:1-2).
4. See J. N. Saunders and B. A. Mastin, *The Gospel According to St. John* (New York: Harper, 1968) 291. S. Schultz, *Das Evangelium nach Johannes* (15th ed; NTD: Göttingen: Vandenhoeck & Ruprecht, 1963), 166, only observes: "Ob es sich hier um Proselyten oder nur um Gottesfürchtige handelt, wird nicht gesagt." G. H. C. Macgregor, *The Gospel of John* (Moffatt Commentaries; Garden City: Doubleday, 1928) 264, argues that the Ἕλληνες are Greek proselytes or semi-proselytes (god-fearers, adherents of Judaism). See also K. L Schmidt, *TDNT* 2.102.
5. See J. A. T. Robinson, "The Destination and Purpose of St. John's Gospel," *NTS* 6 (1960) 117-31, now in *Twelve New Testament Studies* (SBT 34; London: SCM, 1962) 107-25, esp. 120-21, and see also *The Priority of John* (ed. J. F. Coakley; Oak Park, Ill.: Meyer Stone, 1985) 61-62.
6. C. H. Dodd, *The Interpretation of the Fourth Gospel* (Cambridge: Cambridge University Press, 1958) 371, points out that "in the dramatic situation we may suppose them to be proselytes, but in the intention of the evangelist they stand for the great world at large; primarily the Hellenistic world which is his own mission field. These Greeks are the vanguard of mankind coming to Christ."
7. R. Bultmann, *Das Evangelium des Johannes* (KEK; Göttingen: Vandenhoeck & Ruprecht, 1957) 323.
8. E. Haenchen, *Das Johannesevangelium, Ein Kommentar* (ed. M. Busse; Tübingen: J. C. B. Mohr [Paul Siebeck] 1980) 445. Haenchen argues that the evangelist uses the word Ἕλληνες to represent the Greek world in general, and thus also the pagan world. Insofar as H. B. Kossen, "Who Were the Greeks of John XII 20?" in *Studies in John* (Festschrift J. N. Sevenster; NovTSup 24; Leiden: E. J. Brill, 1970] 97-110, esp. 108) also insists that the Ἕλληνες of John 12:20 should be understood to be the representatives of the Gentiles rather than the representatives of the Greek-speaking Jews in the Diaspora, he seems to be correct. I, however, will criticize his argument. See below, n. 11.
9. C. K. Barrett, *The Gospel According to St. John* (2nd ed.; London: S.P.C.K., 1978) 421-22.
10. J. L. Martyn, *History and Theology in the Fourth Gospel* (2nd ed.; Nashville: Abingdon, 1979), passim, and "Glimpses into the History of the Johannine Community" in *L'Évangile de Jean, Source, rédaction, théologie* (ed. M. de Jonge; BETL 44; Leuven: J. Duculot Gembloux, 1977) 149-75, reprinted in *The Gospel of John in Christian History*

(New York: Paulist, 1978) 90-121. I basically agree with Martyn's hypothesis concerning the Sitz im Leben of the evangelist; see K. Tsuchido, "The Composition of the Nicodemus Episode, John 2.23-3.21," *Annual of the Japanese Biblical Institute* 1 (1975) 91-103, and "Tradition and Redaction in John 12.1-43," *NTS* 30 (1984) 609-19.

11. As to this point, Kossen, "Who Were the Greeks?" esp. 98-100, comes to the same conclusion. However, Kossen does not take into consideration Martyn's work, which was published two years before his, and does not distinguish the Christian Jews, who were expelled from the synagogue by means of the application of the revised *Birkath ha-Minim*, from the Jewish Christians, who remained within the synagogue. Furthermore, Kossen's hypothesis, citing the evidence of Polycrates, the Bishop of Ephesus, that the ῾Ελληνες in this verse are Greeks from Asia Minor and that the readers of the Gospel of John must be sought in the same geographical area, is not persuasive. This evidence refers to Philip as being highly esteemed in Asia Minor, and the evidence of Papias, Bishop of Hierapolis, refers to Andrew's high status among the apostles (both witnesses cited in Eusebius, *H. E.* III and IV). Even if Philip and Andrew appeared in v. 22 and if they had contact with ῾Ελληνες in this narrative sequence, it would be invalid for Kossen to make his hypothesis on such a basis.

12. For 3:1 as a product of Johannine editorial work, see my "Nicodemus," esp. 95ff.; R. T. Fortna, *The Gospel of Signs: A Reconstruction of the Narrative Source Underlying the Fourth Gospel* (SNTSMS 11; Cam bridge: Cam bridge University Press, 1979) 132; R. Schnackenburg, *Johannesevangelium*, 2.477; and J. Becker, *Das Evangelium nach Johannes* (2 vols.; Gütersloh: Gerd Mohn, 1979-81) 2.381ff.

13. See E. Schweizer, *EGO EIMI: Die religionsgeschichtliche Herkunft und theologische Bedeutung der johanneischen Bildreden, zugleich ein Beitrag zur Quellenfrage des vierten Evangeliums* (Göttingen: Vandenhoeck & Ruprecht, 1939) 92, and E. Ruckstuhl, *Die li terarische Einheit des Johannesevangeliums* (Freiburg: Universitätsverlag, 1951) 205.

14. Concerning the problem of tradition and redaction in 1:35-51, see my article, "Son of Man in the Fourth Gospel (I)," *Church and Theology* 4 (1973) 1-17; further, R. T. Fortna, *Gospel of Signs*, 179-88.

15. T. Onuki rightly points this out in *Gemeinde und Welt im Johannesevangelium* (WMANT, 56; Neukirchen-Vluyn: Neukirchener Verlag, 1984) 66-68.

16. See the discussion of 12:23 below.

17. See Schnackenburg, *Johannesevangelium*, 478.

18. See my "John 12.1-43," esp. 612-13.

19. For the view that such phrases referring to the Jewish Festival are typically Johannine, see Schulz, *Johannes*, 152; Barrett, *John*, 409; Dodd, *Historical Tradition in the Fourth Gospel* (Cam bridge: Cam bridge University Press, 1963) 152-53; Tsuchido, "John 12:1-43," 610.

20. See Schackenburg, *Johannesevangelium*, 479.

21. Thus ten out of twelve uses of προσκυνέω are concentrated in the story of Jesus and the Samaritan woman in chap. 4. This story has no parallel in the synoptic Gospels. Of the other two uses of προσκυνέω, one appears in v. 21*b* and the other in 9:39, part of a section (9:8-41) composed by the evangelist to enlarge the pre-Johannine material (9:1-7) and to show the higher Johannine christology. Concerning the tradition and redaction in chap. 9, see my "The Composition of Chapter Nine in the Fourth Gospel," *Church and Theology* 5 (1974) 21-42.

22. See below in this section.

23. Schnackenburg, *Johannesevangelium*, 479, aptly points this out.

24. See B. Lindars, *Jesus Son of Man* (Grand Rapids: Eerdmans, 1983) 145-57, esp. 155.

25. Concerning the use of the word ὑψοῦν in the Fourth Gospel, see "Nicodemus," esp. 94-96.

26. E. Haenchen, *Johannesevangelium*, 445, suggests this point.

27. See Schnackenburg, *Johannesevangelium*, 480; Schulz, *Johannes*, 166; Barrett, *John*, 423.

28. See "John 12:1-43," 614.

29. Whereas ποιεῖν and δοῦναι are used in the similar parable in the Synoptic Gospels, φέρειν is used in the Johannine parable to show the same meaning as in the Synoptic Gospels.

30. For a noteworthy analysis of the form of this parable, see Dodd, *Historical Tradition in the Fourth Gospel,* 366-69.
31. Ibid.
32. See Schulz, *Johannes,* 166; Brown, *John,* 1.467. It is probably impossible to determine whether the parable in v. 24 is one of the genuine sayings of Jesus or not. Lindars, *The Gospel of John,* 428, regards it as genuine. It seems to me, however, that most of the parable can be traced back only to the oldest post-resurrection stratum of the tradition of the sayings of Jesus.
33. Insisting that the section 12:37-43 is the conclusion of the first half of the entire Gospel and that 12:44-50 originally belonged to the discourse about "Light" that begins from 8:12 and includes 12:34-36, Bultmann does not regard 12:20-50 as a continuous narrative.
34. On the view that the whole section, 11:55–12:43, must be regarded as one continuous narrative composed by the evangelist, see my "John 12:1-43."

LOWER AND HIGHER CHRISTOLOGY IN THE FOURTH GOSPEL

Reginald H. Fuller

(An imaginary dialogue between J. Louis Martyn and the late John A. T. Robinson with Reginald H. Fuller as Moderator).

Moderator: It seemed to me a good way of honoring Professor Martyn in this Festschrift if we were to summon John A. T. Robinson *ek nekrōn* and have these two scholars, one a friend for over thirty years, the other a former colleague, enter into dialogue about Johannine christology. In particular I would like to confront the views expressed by Professor Martyn (JLM) in his *History and Theology of the Fourth Gospel*[1] with those of John A. T. Robinson (JATR) in his posthumously published Bampton Lectures, *The Priority of John*.[2]

You maintain, JLM, that the expulsion of the Johannine Christians from the synagogue in the 80s provided the occasion for the composition of the Fourth Gospel in its penultimate form—what I like to call the Discourse Gospel, in which the discourses were added to the earlier form of the Gospel, the Narrative Gospel as I like to call it.

JLM: Yes, I believe I demonstrated that an important clue to the composition of the Discourse Gospel is to be found in John 9:22, 12:42, and 16:2—namely, the effect of a general directive to expel Christians from the synagogue.

JATR: I disagree. As you know, I believe all the NT books were written before 70 CE. There is nothing in the wording of the *Birkath ha-Minim* to suggest a formal banning of Johannine or any other Jewish Christians from the synagogue. Expulsion could have happened, and indeed did happen, at any time during the period covered by the narrative of Acts. Paul himself alludes to such occurrences in 1 Thess 2:14-15. Note *ekdiōxantōn* in 1 Thess 2:15, a text to which JLM never referred. And what about Luke 6:22 (which again I believe was written before 70 CE) with its *aphorisōsin*?

Moderator: To me the term *aposynagōgos* suggests something more definitive, the kind of thing Paul and his companions underwent in the passages you, JATR, cite from Acts. They were able to reappear in synagogues elsewhere.

They were not permanently excommunicated. And as for *aphorisōsin* in Luke 6:22, that is clearly Lucan redaction since it is absent from the Matthean parallel. I do not want to argue with you about the date of Luke, but to my mind it undoubtedly was written after 70 CE. I agree that *aphorisōsin* could refer to the same sort of thing as *aposynagōgos*, but this means that Luke was reflecting a later situation, an actual banning from the synagogue. As for *ekdiōxantōn* in 1 Thess 2:15, the compound has no special force: it probably means no more than "persecuted." Once again, there is no evidence that when Paul wrote 1 Thessalonians he had been definitively banned from the synagogue. *Aposynagōgos* seems to refer to something much more definitive that happened after Paul's lifetime. Also *synetetheinto* (John 9:22) suggests a formal decision rather than *ad hoc* expulsion, as in Acts.

But I wonder whether you, JLM, have proved your case that *aposynagōgos* refers specifically to the *Birkath ha-minim*. Your discussion with D. R. A. Hare in the long footnote on page 60 is not too convincing, though you may be right in claiming that Justin Martyr associated the expulsion of Christians from the synagogue with the curse. But in any case I do not think JATR has proved his contention that *aposynagōgos* must refer to ordinary *ad hoc* expulsions such as occurred during the period covered by Acts. There are, however, other reasons for assigning the Discourse Gospel to a date toward the end of the first century CE, including external evidence to which you, JATR, are ready enough to appeal when it suits you (for example, for the traditional authorship of the Gospel). The expulsion of the Johannine community in the last decades of the first century CE provides a possible Sitz im Leben for John. One of my major criticisms of your treatment of John, JATR, is that you appear unconcerned to provide a concrete Sitz im Leben for the development of Johannine theology. Of course, there is always the risk in suggesting one—any proposal such as JLM's is open to the charge of being mere speculation.

Turning now to you, JLM, I note that you define the occasion of the expulsion of the Johannine community from the synagogue as the community confession of Jesus as Messiah. "If anyone should confess [Jesus] to be the Messiah, [that person] was to be put to death" (John 9:22).

JLM: And I would go further. It was confessing him to be Messiah in a particular Johannine way. Merely to confess anyone as Messiah was not enough to merit expulsion from the synagogue, still less execution. We must look for something more. This, I suggested, is to be found in the fact that the Johannine community had developed a high christology, in which (at least so it seemed to the continuing adherents of the synagogue) Jesus was being acclaimed as God. I base this on John 5:18b, "making himself equal with God." There is also the charge in 10:32, "you, being a man, make yourself God." In other words, the Johannine Christians, or so it seemed to the adherents of the synagogue, were guilty of that greatest of all sins: the breach of the *Shemah*, which every devout Jew recited daily, of recognizing another God besides the God of Israel. In a word they were guilty of "ditheism."

JATR: Wait a bit. The Johannine Christians were themselves Jews. They were subject to the "constraints of history," as A. E. Harvey expresses it, and one of those constraints was that of monotheism. And another point. You redaction critics (that's what I called you, JLM, in *Redating the New Testament*[3]) always read Gospel texts as if they were evidence only for the beliefs of the community in which they were written, rarely for the historical Jesus. Neither Jesus nor the Johannine author (for me, John bar Zebedee) could ever have been guilty of ditheism.

Moderator: How then do you explain John 5:18*b* and 10:33? Even if these passages represent a Jewish misunderstanding of the real position of the author of John (or of Jesus himself), what led them to that misunderstanding?

JATR: It is quite likely that this is part of John's Mosaic typology. Moses was "God" to Pharaoh (Exod 4:16, 7:1). I have quoted in *Priority* (374 n. 88) no less than six passages in which Philo boldly called Moses "God." As Philo explains, he meant God by analogy, only functionally, not ontologically. Neither John nor Philo would have broken from the constraints of monotheism, any more than the book of Exodus would have.

Moderator: First, one slight correction. In Exod 4:16 Moses is "as God" to Aaron, not to Pharaoh. But that makes it even more functional. As God was the source of the prophetic word to Moses, so Moses is the source of that word for Aaron. More important, this is beginning to make sense of the charge against Jesus (or against the Johannine community). The issue at stake between the Johannine community and the synagogue was not ditheism *vs.* monotheism, as you, JLM maintained. The issue is whether Moses or Jesus was the revealer of God. The Johannine community was making claims for Jesus that the synagogue was making for Moses. So it has nothing to do with ditheism, but is part of a thread running all through the Fourth Gospel—that is, that Jesus is all the synagogue (especially a synagogue with a more mystical bent) claimed for Moses. This synagogue was thinking of Moses less as the giver of the law and more as the bringer of revelation, of Torah in a revelatory, rather than in a nomistic, sense. The issue, therefore, was not monotheism *vs.* ditheism (all were Jews and all were monotheists) but Moses *vs.* Jesus. Which of the two is the bringer of God's definitive revelation?

JATR: I want to insist that such a claim is not just Johannine theologizing. It is rooted in Jesus' own self-understanding (though without the anti-Moses polemic). In *The Human Face of God* I quoted with approval Ernst Fuchs's statement that Jesus' conduct was neither that of a mere prophet nor teacher of wisdom, but of one who dared to act in God's stead.[4] I think this is important. JLM exhibits a fine understanding of the nature of John's Gospel as a constant reapplication of living tradition to new cultural contexts. However, in practice, JLM, you treat John's Gospel too one-sidedly as evidence for the theology of the Johannine community, and not enough as evidence *also* for the historical Jesus. While recognizing a two-level drama in the Johannine episodes—the Jesus level and the Evangelist's level—in practice you spend all your time on the Evangelist's level.

JLM: And you, JATR, spend all your time on the Jesus level, concerning yourself with John as evidence (albeit indirect evidence) for Jesus' self-understanding. You pay no attention to the Sitz im Leben of the Johannine development.

Moderator: In fact you are both right in theory and one-sided in practice. JATR deals with the "priority" to the practical exclusion of the posteriority of John, and JLM with the Johannine level of the drama to the practical exclusion of the Jesus level. If we would arrive at a true understanding of John, we must combine the approaches of JLM and JATR, not treat them as antithetical by opting for one and not the other. If they had done this, JLM would not have found ditheism in John, and JATR would not have neglected the successive Sitze im Leben of Johannine theology.

A member of the audience: Is there not more to this charge of ditheism? Jesus does say, "I and the Father are one" (John 10:30). Does that not mean that Jesus is God?

JATR: Let me quote from my comment on this verse in *Priority*: "It is not a distinctive metaphysical identity, but a moral and spiritual unity, potentially open to all."[5] This is clear from the way Jesus speaks of the unity of the believers as a unity like that of the Father and the Son *(kathōs)* (17:21-22).

Another member of the audience: Jesus says "Before Abraham was I am" (8:58). Does that not mean that Jesus knew he was God? And that John, by quoting it, shows he thought so, too? And then again, Thomas recognizes it after the resurrection, when he addresses the risen Christ as "My Lord and my God" (20:28).

JATR: Let's take the Thomas saying first. If I may quote again from my *Priority*: "This is the language, not of ontological identity nor simply of functional equivalent, but of existential embodiment."[6]

Moderator: Let me add that Thomas does not start out like fundamentalists by saying, "Jesus is God," as the presupposition for his understanding of Jesus' history, and then fit that history into it. Rather it is a confession of faith: Thomas arrives at it at the end of the story.

JATR: It really means no more than "He who has seen me has seen the Father" (14:9). It means what Paul meant when he said that "God in Christ was reconciling the world to himself."

Moderator: Now let's turn to the Abraham saying. I was not altogether satisfied with your treatment of this, JATR. You explain it to mean simply that Jesus was greater than Abraham and that "precedence implies priority."[7] Therefore, you say, it means no more than that Jesus is greater than Jacob (4:12) or, as in the synoptic tradition, greater than Solomon (Matt 12:42 and parallels) or greater than David (Mark 12:37 and parallels). I think there is more to it than that. It is one of those many passages, like the great "I am" sayings, where the Johannine Jesus is speaking as the embodiment of the divine Wisdom. It does not mean that the man Jesus was prior to Abraham, and therefore a divine person, but that the Wisdom of God, embodied or incarnate in him and whose spokesperson he is, pre-existed before Abraham.

First member of the audience: But what of all those sayings in the Fourth Gospel in which Jesus speaks of himself as being sent into or coming into the world, as descending, and as returning to the Father?

JATR: I have offered an explanation to each of these types of saying. They all refer to the historical mission of Jesus as a divine agent rather than to his transcendental origin as a pre-existent and divine being, invading this world from a world above. As I put it twenty-five years ago in *Honest to God*,[8] he is not an alien intruder from another world.

Moderator: I can readily accept that as the meaning of the sending and coming sayings. At least in origin, all of these probably referred to Jesus' historical mission, analogous to the historical mission of the prophets, though, of course, a mission greater than these, a mission that was unique and final. This was the original meaning of these sayings. Whether they acquire a different meaning later in the Johannine tradition is a question we will have to face later.

I have rather more of a problem with the descent/ascent sayings (3:13; 6:33, 41, 50-51, 58). Your interpretation in *Priority*, with its appeal to Peder Borgen's essay at the Louvain Colloquium, is not at all clear. You write: "I would agree with Borgen's persuasive discussion of it that implies that the Son of man has previously gone up to heaven as in Dan. 7:13-14 (LXX) for his installation, to receive his seal of office" (6:26).[9] When did he "go up"? You rightly reject Borgen's curious view that this ascent took place in heaven before the incarnation. Your reference to the sealing in 6:27 suggests that you think of the ascent as occurring at Jesus' baptism, as a historical commissioning analogous to that of Moses' going up to Mount Sinai to receive the commandments, as you mention a little later.

JATR: Yes, that's it.

Moderator: This would be intelligible enough and an attractive view that, as we shall see, fits in with my own understanding of the Prologue. The problem, however, is that in this interpretation the ascent precedes the descent, whereas in the Johannine texts the Son of Man's ascent occurs *after* the descent. I would think that the background for this pattern of descent/ascent lies not in the story of Moses, but in Jewish Wisdom speculation. In John 6 it is as the bread of life or the bread of heaven that the Son of Man descends from heaven. As Raymond Brown has demonstrated in his commentary, the bread discourse of chap. 6 has a sapiental background.[10] Brown cites Isaiah 55 for the pattern of descent/ascent of the Word of God, a concept closely related to Wisdom. The same descent/ascent pattern occurs with explicit reference to Wisdom in Ethiopic Enoch 42:

Wisdom found no place where she might dwell;
Then a dwelling place was assigned to her in the heavens.
Wisdom went forth to make her dwelling among the children of men,
And found no dwelling place.
Wisdom returned to her dwelling-place
And took her seat among the angels.

We find the same pattern of thought in these two passages we have cited as that we find in John 3 and 6, the pattern of descent/ascent and of going forth/returning. In each case it is the Son of Man who ascends and descends or who goes forth and returns. The use of Son of Man here is not drawn from any established meaning of the term (such as in Dan 7:14 and the Jewish apocalyptic tradition), but simply denotes the "ego of the speaker," as Mogens Müller has demonstrated in his recent book.[11] Thus the meaning of "Son of Man" is determined by the context, and in John 3 and 6 it means the earthly Jesus as the one who embodies the Wisdom of God. Jesus is at this stage of Johannine thought not in his human person one who pre-existed as a divine being and who came down from heaven, but one upon whom Wisdom descended and in whom Wisdom ascends back to heaven at the close of his career.

JATR: Unfortunately, Mogens Müller's work appeared in the year after my death, and I was therefore unable to use it for my Bamptons. Some of his views would fit in very well with what I was trying to say many years ago in *Jesus and His Coming*,[12] where I argued that the present Son of Man sayings were primary. I welcome this reaction against the notion of an apocalyptic Son of Man. I wonder if the Germans will stop plugging for that!

Moderator: I want to press you on a question that you, JATR, never really answer. If the "incarnation" is to be understood as the embodiment or incarnating of Wisdom by Jesus, what was the moment of the incarnation? In later orthodoxy that moment is identified as the conception/birth of Jesus. However, there is nothing about that in the Fourth Gospel. It seems to me that John 6:27 gives us the answer. Jesus is the embodiment of Wisdom because (*gar*) the Father has "sealed him " Brown notes that the aorist tense has led commentators to look for a specific moment when the sealing occurred. Spicq said that it was at the incarnation, by which I suppose he means the conception/birth, while Bernard thought it was at Jesus' baptism. I want to suggest that the moment of incarnation in John is precisely the baptism. The idea of sealing is connected elsewhere in the NT with the gift of the Spirit to the believers that takes place at baptism (2 Cor 1:22; Eph 1:13; 4:30). The noun *sphragis* (seal) is used in the Apostolic Fathers for baptism (*s.v.* in BAGD). There is nothing in the text of the Discourse Gospel to suggest that the birth of Jesus was the moment of the incarnation. I leave aside for later discussion the question of the Prologue, which I regard as the addition of the Johannine redactor. The only theologically significant reference to Jesus' birth is in 18:27, where he says before Pilate: "For this *I was born* and for this I have come into the world, to bear witness to the truth." Here Jesus' birth is interpreted not as the moment of incarnation but (as with the conception/birth of the OT prophets) as predestining him for a specific role in salvation history. This role in Johannine terms is to witness to the truth—which is tantamount to being the embodiment of divine Wisdom. Jesus was born for the role he embarked upon at his baptism. This is the same view of the conception/birth of Jesus that we find in the infancy narratives of Matthew and Luke, except that there the mission is defined in terms of Christ, Lord, and Son of God. John contains nothing of a virginal conception. John 18:37 is thus consistent with the view that for the Discourse Gospel the incarnation (in the Johannine sense) begins at Jesus' baptism, when the Spirit descended on him and he was declared Son of God, or Elect One, depending on the reading (John 1:33-34).

A member of the audience: But what of John 1:14, "The word became flesh"? Does that not speak quite clearly of the birth as the moment of the incarnation?

Moderator: Several years ago in a *Festschrift* to Canon Edward West[13] I took up a suggestion first put forward by A. Loisy and combined it with Boismard's theory that the Prologue of the Fourth Gospel was deliberately spliced by the final redactor into the original beginning of the Gospel in such a way as to connect the incarnation of the Logos with the baptism, not with the birth of Jesus as the Prologue is normally interpreted. It was at the baptism that Jesus began to be the Logos, the incarnation of God's expressive activity. This article did not receive much attention at the time, but its thesis has been taken up recently by two scholars. One is an English NT scholar, Francis Watson, who has contributed an essay in the Caird *Festschrift*, and the other, the Dutch systematic theologian Piet Schoonenberg, discusses my suggestion in his 1986 Bellarmine lecture.[14] I was a little hesitant about this thesis at the time, partly because I did not want to be associated with Loisy's modernism and partly because of its adoptionist implications. Watson finds further support for my suggestion in 1 John with its assertion that the Son of God "came by water" as well as by blood. Watson argues that the author of 1 John shared with his gnostic opponents the view that the self-expressive activity of God in Jesus began with his baptism ("came by water"), but held that Jesus' death on the cross was also part of that self-expressive activity of God, a point the gnostics rejected. Schoonenberg also agrees with my connecting of the Prologue with the baptism.

However, as J. D. G. Dunn[15] has argued, the verb *egeneto* suggests something more than the descent of Wisdom upon the man Jesus, as in the Discourse Gospel. "Became" implies personal identity between the pre-incarnate Logos and the man Jesus. This goes beyond a christology of inspiration to one of real incarnation. We can no longer say that Jesus "embodied" or "incarnated" the Logos. We must now say that the Logos became incarnate in him. It makes no essential difference whether this incarnation took place at the conception/birth or at the baptism. The so-called Athanasian creed later defined the incarnation as the "taking of the manhood into God." According to the theology of the Johannine Prologue, this taking of the manhood into God took place at Jesus' baptism.

JATR: But surely that still means that, as I put it in my *Priority*, this was a union of the *anhypostatic* Logos with the *hypostatic* Jesus, the Logos being no more than a poetic personification of the self-expressive activity of God.[16]

Moderator: That's just what Dunn thinks, and this time you, JATR, agree with him. But I have argued elsewhere that Hellenistic Judaism, already before the rise of Christianity, was beginning to think of the Wisdom or Logos of God as a hypostasis. Not that the Logos was a personal being distinct from the being of God (that would indeed be ditheism), but as a personal entity within the being of God. I put this argument forward quite tentatively and with some trepidation, but was able to appeal to certain OT scholars like Helmer Ringgren and Hartmut Gese for support. I am glad to say now that Schoonenberg, in discussing the difference between Dunn and myself about the personality of the Logos, recognizes that I have a legitimate concern. He goes on to say, "The whole question is whether Dunn could make more room for being in God's extensions. I think in this respect Fuller might be right. . . . Perhaps Hebrew thought did not make the distinction of being and action which has become dominant in Hellenistic and Western culture."[17] I wonder if you, JATR, could make room for such an extension of God's being in action. After all, if God is personal, an "I," the presence of God's self-expressive activity must surely be personal, too.

JATR: I am not fully persuaded that Logos in Hellenistic Judaism is any more than a poetic personification, but I will reflect more on Schoonenberg's contention. There is one problem I would like to raise. How, in your interpretation, does the incarnation christology of the Prologue relate to the inspirational Wisdom christology of the Discourse Gospel?

Moderator: I have puzzled a great deal over this. The answer, I think, must lie in a proper understanding of *sarx egeneto*. I have on previous occasions quoted Hoskyns's statement that *sarx* here denotes "the whole observable history of Jesus of Nazareth." The incarnation did not, for the Johannine redactor, happen once for all at Jesus' baptism. It was constantly happening throughout the ministry. It happened ever anew (*je und je*, as the Germans would say) as the Son responded in perfect obedience and surrender to the Father, so that the Son appeared again and again as the perfect manifestation of the personal self-expressive activity of the Father. The ego of the man Jesus was being constantly identified with the ego of the Logos.

Thus the Prologue of the Fourth Gospel elevates all the previous christologies of the Johannine tradition to a higher level without replacing them. The original self-understanding of Jesus, his Abba experience, his sending consciousness, and his speaking as Wisdom's envoy have all been successively reinterpreted in the Johannine tradition. First, we have the historical sending or coming-into-the-world christology. Then Christ is presented as Wisdom's final spokesperson, the one in whom Wisdom descended and ascended, the one who as Son of Man embodied or incarnated God's Wisdom. Finally, he is portrayed is terms of the Logos who continually became flesh from baptism to glorification. Johannine christology, as you, JATR, have so powerfully demonstrated, is rooted in the self-consciousness of the historical Jesus. But it has been subjected to a constant *relecture*, as the French so aptly call it. This successive reinterpretation of christology was a series of responses to the ever-changing situation of the Johannine community, as you, JLM, have so well demonstrated. The Gospel of John is, in JATR's words, both the Alpha and the Omega of the Jesus tradition, but in a more profound way than JATR has allowed. And as JLM has so strikingly put it, we have here an experience like that of listening to Dvořák's *New World Symphony*, in which the traditional folk melodies of the Native Americans have been not merely quoted but newly interpreted for later times.

Thank you, gentlemen, for your help in enabling us to understand the Gospel of John.

Notes

1. J. L. Martyn, *History and Theology of the Fourth Gospel* (rev. and enlarged; Nashville: Abingdon, 1979).
2. John A. T. Robinson, *The Priority of John* (Bampton Lectures; London: SCM, 1985).
3. John A. T. Robinson, *Redating the New Testament* (Philadelphia: Westminster, 1976), 269.
4. John A. T. Robinson, *The Human Face of God* (London: SCM, 1973), 191.
5. Robinson, *Priority*, 375.

6. Ibid., 393.
7. Ibid., 184.
8. John A. T. Robinson, *Honest to God* (London: S.C.M., 1963).
9. Robinson, *Priority*, 385; see also Peder Borgen, "Some Jewish Exegetical Traditions as Background for the Son of Man Sayings in John's Gospel (John 3, 13 & Context)," in *L'Évangile de Jean: Sources, rédaction, théologie* (ed. M. de Jonge; BETL 44; Leuven: University Press, 1977) 243-58.
10. Raymond Brown, *The Gospel According to John* (2 vols.; AB 29; Garden City: Doubleday, 1966-70).
11. Mogens Müller, *Der Ausdruck 'Menschensohn' in den Evangelien: Voraussetzungen und Bedeutung* (Acta theologica danica 17; Leiden: Brill, 1984).
12. John A. T. Robinson, *Jesus and His Coming* (London: SCM, 1957).
13. Reginald H. Fuller, "Christmas, Epiphany, and the Johannine Prologue," in *Spirit and Light: Essays in Historical Theology* (eds. W. B. Green and M. L'Engle; New York: Seabury, 1976).
14. Francis Watson, "Is John's Christology Adoptionist?" in *The Glory of Christ in the New Testament: Studies in Christology in Memory of G. B. Caird* (eds. L. D. Hurst and N. T. Wright; Oxford: Clarendon, 1987) 113-24; Piet Schoonenberg, "A Sapiential Reading of John's Prologue," *Theology Digest* 33:4 (1986) 411-21.
15. J. D. G. Dunn, *Christology in the Making* (Philadelphia: Westminster, 1980).
16. Robinson, *Priority*, 30.
17. Schoonenberg, "Sapiential Reading," 419.

THE BELOVED DISCIPLE:
A JUNGIAN VIEW

Schuyler Brown

I t was during the years 1970 to 1978, when I was teaching in New York at Woodstock College and General Seminary, that I came to know J. Louis Martyn, at first through the Columbia University Seminar in New Testament, and later by invitation to the Biblical Field meetings at Union Theological Seminary. During those years I also came to know Martyn's student and colleague, Walter Wink, who profoundly shocked me with his declaration of the "bankruptcy" of biblical criticism.[1] Although Wink had overstated his case, his book was a catalyst for prolonged reflection on the methodological and hermeneutical presuppositions of our discipline.

I have come to realize that the historical *Fragestellung* can indeed frustrate the immediacy that is characteristic of religious literature. Instead of being summoned to question and deepen the way in which he views himself and the world, the reader is allowed, and even encouraged, to take a detached, "objective" point of view: he analyzes what he thinks the author intended to communicate to the original readers; he himself does not stand within the hermeneutical circle.

Paradoxically, by focusing on the "original meaning" of the text, historical criticism frustrates the pragmatics of the biblical author. The religious motivation and transformative purpose of his writing are inhibited by the realization which historical criticism brings home to the modern reader: that *he* is not included in the act of communication of which the biblical text was once a part.

We realize that we are eavesdropping on a *past* conversation: *we* are not the ones whom the author is addressing. Consequently, no practical interaction in the actual world is possible between ancient writer and modern reader; the two worlds are inaccessible to each other. How, then, are we to experience the reality of Paul's affirmation: "Whatever

THE BELOVED DISCIPLE: A JUNGIAN VIEW

was written in former days was written for our instruction" (Rom 15:4)?

Historical criticism, I have been obliged to acknowledge, is related more to the agenda of the university than of the church, whose primary concern, as Wink recognized, is human transformation. Biblical studies are often pursued in a university context, and the historical method is one that the university acknowledges and respects.

Yet, the rationality of historical criticism, though in tension with the religious pragmatics of the text, can only be ignored by the modern reader at his own peril. Although historical criticism may inhibit the religious reading of religious texts, it is also a bulwark against religious fanaticism, the fanaticism that we find, for example, in the strident anti-Judaism of the Fourth Gospel, with its chilling climax in the charge by the Johannine Jesus that the Jews are children of the devil (John 8:44). Modern critical scholarship provides an essential compensation for the archetypal power of scripture, whose primary purpose is not to inform the mind but, in the words of D. H. Lawrence, "to change the blood."[2]

The human transformation of which Wink speaks requires constant dialogue and interaction between the conscious ego and the unconscious psyche. To surrender to the latter means archetypal possession or psychosis; to function as though the former made up the entire personality means spiritual stagnation and decay. The consequences of ignoring historical criticism are evident to anyone watching television on a Sunday morning. The consequences of allowing it exclusive dominance are evident in the sterility and irrelevance that we have all encountered in some New Testament scholarship.

Rationality, religious rationality included, can be used to evade an encounter with the unconscious, and when this evasion is continued over the course of a life-time, the resultant personalities are apt to be "hypochondriacs, niggards, doctrinaires, applauders of the past or eternal adolescents—all lamentable substitutes for the illumination of the self."[3]

The use of both historical and archetypal exegesis corresponds not only to the plurality of psychic levels within the reader, but also to the plurality of levels within the author and the text, which is the point of intersection between two complex processes: the process of composition and the process of reading. The author did not begin with the surface structure of the text, and the reader does not end with it.

To see in a text only the concretization of the author's conscious intention, which the reader retrieves intact by using the "right" exegetical methods, is a drastic misrepresentation of biblical interpretation, and it is refuted by both the history of interpretation and the phenomenology of the reading process itself.

The difficulty with limiting the interpreter's role to recovering the intention of the author is not peculiar to biblical studies. During the bicentennial of the American Constitution the same issue arose. In a speech of July 1985, former Attorney General Edwin Meese urged a "jurisprudence of original intention." The courts, in his view, could do no more than apply the law according to the intention of the nation's founders.

Interestingly enough, one of the founders, James Madison, was concerned not to assist such a restrictive use of the Constitution.

> Madison did not permit the notes that he made during the Constitutional Convention to be published until after his death, believing that the Constitution must stand alone, that the specific thoughts of individual framers were essentially irrelevant and might even be mischievous in later times.[4]

Although, in the case of the Bible, no extra-textual authorial commentary is available, Madison's restraint underlines the basic hermeneutical principle that the indeterminacies in a text are to be filled in by the reader.

> The convergence of text and reader brings the literary work into existence, and this convergence can never be precisely pinpointed, but must always remain virtual, as it is not to be identified either with the reality of the text or with the individual disposition of the reader.[5]

Besides the archetypal depths of the biblical text, it is this impossibility of "pinpointing" the convergence between text and reader that explains the Bible's ability to address ever new situations and the variety of interpretations throughout the history of synagogue and church.

As in a literary work, the effectiveness of the Bible does not depend on the reader's ability to infer the intention of the author. The passage of time has detached the text from the writer, so that its pragmatic effect is no longer subject to the writer's intention. The Bible is in the public domain and is measured against something beyond the control of those who produced it.

Biblical interpretation, then, cannot be restricted to the restoration of some originally intended message. The change effected in the reader is not necessarily equivalent to the change intended by the writer. The public character of the written text liberates it from any single meaning, even that of the author himself, and enables the interest of the reader to fill the indeterminacies of the text with present meaning.

As American jurists search the Constitution for answers to questions about which the founders could have had no notion, so readers of the Bible seek to hear "the word of the Lord" addressing them out of the sacred text, as they wrestle with the challenges of daily life. The social function of a foundational text renders futile any attempt to impose upon it a hermeneutic of original intent.

The capacity of a text to generate multiple, even contradictory, meanings lies not only in the social character of language but also in the nature of the text itself:

> Every text is an intertext; other texts are present in it, at variable levels, in more or less recognizable forms: the texts of the previous culture and those of the surrounding culture. Every text is a new fabric woven out of bygone quotations.[6]

The process of reading, therefore, corresponds to the process of composition. Just as a religious text arises out of an archetypal world of which the author may have been unaware, so also the reader may penetrate, through the surface level of the text, to deep structures that powerfully engage his or her unconscious feelings. Therein lies the power—and the danger—of religious literature.

When read at the archetypal level, the language of the biblical text is expressive, rather than communicative. The worth of an interpretation depends on its value to the reader, rather than on its conformity with some interpretive paradigm. The old idea of "edification" reclaims its rightful place in interpretation.

> Whatever explanation or interpretation does to it [the archetype], we do to our own souls as well, with corresponding results for our own well-being. . . . A bad explanation means a correspondingly bad attitude [to the archetype]. . . . But the ultimate sufferer is the bad interpreter himself.[7]

The relation between biblical interpretation and what C. G. Jung has called "the individuation process" is not without social significance. For "in the last analysis what is the fate of great nations but a summation of the psychic changes in individuals?"[8] The individual neglect of psychic hygiene can lead to catastrophic epidemics.

J. Louis Martyn has situated the anti-Judaism of the Fourth Gospel in a historical situation in which the Johannine community had recently been excluded from the Jewish synagogue (John 9:22; 12:42; 16:2).[9] But the perceived threat of persecution does not automatically engender the hate-filled rhetoric we find in the Fourth Gospel. In the synoptic Gospels, Jesus surrenders to his enemies with quiet dignity (Mark 14:42 par; contrast John 18:4-9).

Nor has Christian anti-Judaism ever needed the catalyst of an external threat during the period in Jewish-Christian relations when Christians, not Jews, have been the persecutors. Christian feelings of inferiority, since they are unconscious, must be projected onto a scapegoat, and the Jews, historically, have been made to fill this role.

The rationality that characterizes historical criticism is unable to prevent the archetypal possession that expresses itself in anti-Judaism. Unfortunately, the ranks of New Testament scholars have included a number of notorious anti-Semites. Indeed, the Nazi phenomenon itself illustrates how a one-sided rationalism can produce a pendulum-swing to genocidal tribalism.

> Progress and development are ideals not lightly to be rejected, but they lose all meaning if man only arrives at his new state as a fragment of himself, having left his essential hinterland behind him in the shadow of the unconscious, in a state of primitivity or, indeed, barbarism. The conscious mind, split off from its origins, incapable of realizing the meaning of the new state, then relapses all too easily into a situation far worse than the one from which the innovation was intended to free it—*exempla sunt odiosa!*[10]

What is needed, then, is not rationality but consciousness—consciousness of what is happening in the psyche: "I experience the other in myself and the other-than-myself experiences me."[11]

The importance of complementarity between rational (historical) and archetypal interpretation of the Bible is indicated by the psychic structure of the reader (conscious ego/unconscious psyche), the intertextual character of the Bible, and the complexity of the processes of composition and reading. But an alternative to rational criticism is also demanded by the *Wirkungsgeschichte* of the New Testament and, specifically, of the Fourth Gospel. Rational criticism alone cannot retrieve this canonical text from its tragic role in the history of Christian anti-Judaism.

The problem of the Fourth Gospel is not simply a matter of ecumenical diplomacy.[12] It is a serious hermeneutical problem. To draw spiritual sustenance from an anti-Jewish work is as impossible for a contemporary Christian reader as it is offensive to a contemporary Jewish onlooker. To attempt to circumvent the problem by expurgating the anti-Jewish elements in the work is not a responsible option.

Religion is not a spectator sport, and a religious reading of a religious text requires the reader to step inside the hermeneutical circle. The *pro nobis* of the biblical text is a hermeneutical presupposition to which the anti-Judaism of the Fourth Gospel, situated historically by Martyn's work, poses a serious threat.

An approach to the text must be found that turns off the anti-Jewish rhetoric of the surface structure and enables the reader to penetrate to the deep structure of the archetypal world out of which the text has arisen and which it is still capable of reflecting.

One might compare the contrast Wagner makes between the vocal line and the orchestra:

> There [in the orchestra] the primal urges of creation and nature are represented. What the orchestra expresses can never be clearly articulated, because it renders primal feeling itself.[13]

Commenting on this quotation, O. Lee observes:

> No wonder that when we are first exposed to Wagner, our attention goes to the orchestra. It puts us in touch with the very depths of our unconscious feelings.[14]

The historical method corresponds, I believe, to the extroverted attitude of Western Christianity, and this explains how it has come to be the predominant paradigm. Just as Christian soteriology looks to *Deus extra nos,* so also Christian hermeneutics seeks the key to the Bible's meaning in "history," whether this is the critically reconstructed history of the biblical scholar or the dogmatically posited "history" of the fundamentalist. In either case, the answer lies *extra nos* and *extra textum.*

> We in the West believe that a truth is satisfactory only if it can be verified by external facts. . . . It is only logical that extroversion, when carried to such lengths, cannot credit man with a psyche which contains anything not imported into it from outside, either by human teaching or divine grace.[15]

Whether by human error, divine providence, or both,[16] the New Testament canon has preserved a work in which the extroverted reliance on *Deus extra nos* is implicitly criticized. It is, therefore, particularly appropriate to apply to this work an archetypal or endopsychic hermeneutic.

Having put forward these general hermeneutical considerations, which I consider pertinent to the interpretation of the Fourth Gospel, I wish to focus on the figure of the Beloved Disciple in that work. Two features of this mysterious personage have stimulated the speculation of historical critics: his anonymity and the relationship in which he stands vis-à-vis other characters in the Gospel.

The fact that the Beloved Disciple seems to be contrasted with the Twelve, especially in the person of Peter, has led Johannine scholars, such as R. Schnackenburg and R. Brown, to question his traditional identification with John, the son of Zebedee. The Beloved Disciple's anonymity has led me to suggest that he may not even have been a contemporary of Jesus.

H. Köster has pointed out that anonymity is characteristic of the second generation of the Christian church,[17] and this observation has prompted me to propose that the Beloved Disciple is a second generation Christian leader, who has been written into the story of Jesus,[18] in somewhat the same way that Paul has made himself a

371

participant in the Easter experience by describing his reception of divine revelation with the same word (ὤφθη) used in the tradition of the first witnesses of the risen Lord (1 Cor 15:5-8).

In an endopsychic interpretation, the features of anonymity and relatedness have further hermeneutical potential. That which is without a name, or unknown, suggests the unconscious, whereas differential relations between characters suggest the complementarity between the conscious ego and the unconscious psyche.

In chaps. 13, 18, 20, and 21 of the Fourth Gospel, the Beloved Disciple is paired with Peter.[19] In Jungian dream interpretation, a figure of the same sex as the dreamer is often taken to be "the shadow." This archetype represents unconscious elements in the dreamer's psyche that are unacceptable to his or her self-image or *persona*. Such elements are not evil in any absolute sense. On the contrary, when incorporated into the individual's conscious standpoint, they are a source of energy and creativity.

The positive potential of the shadow is often experienced in dreams: When the dreamer turns around to confront the "evil" pursuer, the monster turns into a beautiful helper. However, when the shadow is rejected by the conscious ego, it seems to become malevolent: Unable to gain willing acknowledgment by the ego, the shadow seeks to trip up the ego's conscious functioning by provoking indeliberate lapses, which are highly embarrassing and thwart the ego's purposes. Indeed, if ignored long enough, the shadow can bring a person into situations that are truly life-threatening or even fatal.

The encounter with the shadow is an essential task in the individuation process: "The shadow is a tight passage, a narrow door, whose painful constriction no one is spared who goes down to the deep well."[20]

An interpretation of the Beloved Disciple in terms of the intra-psychic relation between the ego and the shadow may prove illuminating. But, unlike dream interpretation, where the dreamer is the ego and the "other" in the dream is an aspect of the unconscious in the process of becoming conscious, the application of a Jungian perspective to a narrative allows the reader to consider which of the related characters represents his or her ego standpoint and which the unacknowledged "other." On the one hand, the anonymity of the Beloved Disciple suggests the unknown side of the psyche. But, insofar as the Beloved Disciple is the expression of a Christian ideal, he may represent the standpoint of the ego.

A psychological interpretation of Peter and the Beloved Disciple will, therefore, stress the complementarity of these two figures. Peter, though named, is not an "insider" figure in the text, and so, to the extent that he is represented in a disparaging or condescending way, *he* is the "unknown other," in relation to the Beloved Disciple.

Of the scenes in which Peter and the Beloved Disciple appear together, the Johannine epilogue provides a particularly illuminating instance of complementarity. Presumably as a result of the miraculous catch of fish (John 21:6), the Beloved Disciple exclaims, "It is the Lord!" (v. 7). His insight (as in 20:8) results from an intuitive grasp of the meaning of signs. For Peter, the man of action, faith is *ex auditu*: When he hears from the Beloved Disciple that "it is the Lord," he springs into the water (v. 7) and swims to shore.

In chap. 20, Peter and the Beloved Disciple run together to the tomb, in response to the report of Mary Magdalene that "they have taken away the Lord" (v. 2).[21] When the two disciples enter the tomb, the Beloved Disciple, having seen the grave cloths (v. 5), "saw and believed" (v. 8). Although Peter had likewise seen the grave cloths (v. 6), no response of faith on his part is reported. This is particularly striking in view of the extra-Johannine tradition that Peter was the first male disciple to see the risen Lord (1 Cor 15:5; Luke 24:34).

In the Thomas story, another member of the Twelve, who, like Peter in the tradition, has seen the risen Lord, is compared unfavorably by Jesus himself with "those who have not seen (me) and yet believe" (John 20:29). The Beloved Disciple, who came to faith in the empty tomb, without the objective certification of a resurrection appearance, exemplifies the group upon which this blessing is pronounced.

From the perspective of Johannine Christianity, seeing the risen Lord is not an apostolic privilege, upon which all subsequent faith must be based. On the contrary, the extroverted need for such an experience, or for testimony to such an experience, expresses the deficiency of the faith that is based on it. The faith of the Beloved Disciple is exemplary, and what *he* saw in the tomb remained hidden from Peter and Thomas.

Such intuitive insight into the sign value of incidents connected with Jesus' life and death is characteristic of the introverted understanding of faith within the Johannine community. In this Christian church, the testimony of the Spirit guides believers into all truth (John 16:13), by revealing to them the true meaning of the scripture (20:9) and the deeper meaning of the sayings and actions of Jesus, preserved in the tradition, as well as of those mysterious signs narrated in connection with his death and burial.

From this type of knowledge Peter, as the representative of "apostolic" Christianity, remains excluded. For Johannine Christians, the Spirit, not some apostolic figure from the past, brings to remembrance all that Jesus has said (14:26). The community, following the example of the Beloved Disciple, perceives the true significance of

Jesus' words and actions by remembering, under the Spirit's inspired guidance, what Jesus has said (2:22) and the scripture's testimony concerning him (2:17; 12:16).

An infusion of the introverted spirituality of the Fourth Gospel, exemplified in the figure of the Beloved Disciple, would bring a much needed balance to the religious psychology of contemporary Western Christianity. Christian extroversion, to be sure, has done much to humanize our society, but a one-sided *efflusio ad exteriora*, illustrated in the churches' increasing preoccupation with social and political activism,[22] is spiritually impoverishing our Western religious tradition.

Jung, like many others of Christian upbringing, noted this development with concern. He was alarmed by the tendency of young people to seek enlightenment in the religions of the East. This trend, he felt, was psychologically dangerous for the Western mind, which gives paramount importance to the individual and his fate. A Johannine emphasis would counteract the driving force behind this eastward exodus: the perception that Western Christianity is spiritually moribund.

In the Johannine version of the Last Supper, the Beloved Disciple "lies on Jesus' breast" (13:23), even as the Word reclines eternally on the Father's breast (1:18). As Jesus is the revelation of God, so the ideal disciple is the revealer of Jesus. But this revelatory scenario is interrupted by Peter's extroverted preoccupation with discovering the identity of the traitor, who is characteristically assumed to be without, rather than within.

The shadow must be unmasked and expelled from the community of the righteous. The Beloved Disciple's question (13:25) and Jesus' response (v. 26), followed by Judas' exit (v. 30), are both occasioned by Peter's curious request: "Tell us who it is of whom (Jesus) speaks" (v. 24). It does not occur to Peter to ask, "Is it I?" (compare Mark 14:19 and parallels). His extroverted interest leads to the identification and exclusion of the "unknown other," who takes his revenge in Peter's own denial (18:17, 25-27).

Just before this denial, Peter appears in the presence of "another disciple" (18:15). Peter's naive desire to follow Jesus (13:37) is acted out in the company of this anonymous companion, who, we are told twice, "was known to the high priest" (18:15, 16). Historical critics have wondered how such familiarity with Jesus' enemies could be compatible with the loyalty of discipleship. In an endopsychic interpretation, however, the anonymous disciple's knowledge of the "other" contrasts with Peter's ignorance of himself, as he protests his intention of dying for the Lord whom he will shortly deny (13:37).

The Beloved Disciple, like Hermes in the *Iliad* (24.322-467), can lead the psyche, through enemy lines, into the camp of the "other." During the night-time, that rich and evocative symbol of liminality, the Beloved Disciple, slips between the false oppositions erected by the conscious mind. The impending catastrophe to which Peter can only respond by denial—first the denial of his own shadow and then the denial of his Lord—will bring about a new situation; indeed, a new state of consciousness.

Like Hermes, the Beloved Disciple is the psychopomp who leads Peter, all unwitting, into a strange territory in which denial leads to repentance (the abandonment of the ego's pretensions to autonomy), and repentance leads to new insight.

In John 19:25-27, the Beloved Disciple appears in the company of another important figure in the Johannine story: the mother of Jesus. Neither of these two characters is present in the synoptic accounts of Jesus' crucifixion (Mark 15:40-41 par.), and it seems unlikely that Jesus' executioners would have allowed them, even if they *had* been present, to be "standing near" the cross (v. 26; compare Mark 15:40: "looking on from afar"). These verses are, therefore, generally taken to represent an "ideal scene," and the relation between the Beloved Disciple and the mother of Jesus has been given a number of symbolic interpretations. Bultmann's suggestion that the two figures represent, respectively, Gentile and Jewish Christianity may serve as an example of such extroverted interpretation.[23]

Since none of these suggestions has been accorded much probability by historical critics, I need make no apology in offering an endopsychic interpretation, based on the second great archetypal encounter of the conscious ego with the unconscious psyche: the encounter with the contrasexual archetype, the *animus* in women or the *anima* in men.

Since the better-known writers in our culture have been men, this encounter usually finds literary expression through the perspective of masculine psychology. The feminine guide of the male psyche appears in the person of Beatrice in Dante's *Divine Comedy* and in the *Mater Gloriosa* of the concluding scene of Goethe's *Faust*: "Das ewig Weibliche zieht uns hinan!"

Where the internal feminine is not acknowledged, the male psyche falls victim to the *femme fatale*, upon whom the *anima* is projected, as in "Tristan and Iseult," when this story is read from the masculine perspective.[24] Just as the one-sidedness of the rational ego needs compensation from interaction with the shadow, so also the one-sidedness of male or female consciousness needs to meet the contrasexual "other" in a *coincidentia oppositorum*.[25]

When Jesus' male disciple takes Jesus' mother εἰς τὰ ἴδια (19:27), a union of opposites—the goal of the individuation process—is able to take place, and the rejection of *Sancta Sophia*, with which the Gospel began (1:11; see εἰς τὰ ἴδια) is finally reversed. The action occurs on Calvary, at Jesus' command (vv. 26-27*a*).

Jung once remarked that the individuation process was "major surgery without anaesthetic," and he considered Christ to be the symbol of the Self, the integrating τέλος of the psyche. The sequence of these two archetypal encounters in the Fourth Gospel—first the shadow, then the *anima*—is psychologically appropriate. Until the male ego has confronted the threatening aspect of the shadow, he cannot approach the mesmerizing *anima*.

To those to whom our interpretation of the Beloved Disciple seems arbitrary and subjective, I would point out the subjective starting-point of *all* interpretation: the interest of the interpreter.[26] A claim to objectivity or literalism that is unconscious of the interests actually motivating us as we "search the scriptures" (John 5:39) leads to the worst possible subjectivism—the worst, because it is invincible. Only when we acknowledge what we, as readers, bring to the interpretation of the text can the Bible function once again as a prism that refracts our interests, questions, and concerns in ways that not only gratify the intellect but also feed the soul.

Christological exclusivism has tended to favor methodological exclusivism, and the extroverted equation between "history" and "reality"—whether critically or fundamentalistically understood—will certainly cause resistance to our suggestion of a compensatory alternative to the prevailing paradigm. In its efforts to achieve scholarly respectability and academic acceptance, biblical interpretation often forgets that the Archimedian standpoint of objectivity is unattainable in anything that touches the human soul.

Like the Gnostic demiurge, who vainly boasts that he alone is God, the rational ego proclaims the sole sufficiency of the scientific objectivity that our one-sided rational culture has seen fit to canonize.

By contrast, the archetypal or endopsychic approach, which we have illustrated in this article, is "religious" in the etymological sense: It links the reader back to the archetypal past, which has been transmitted through the human psyche since the origins of our race, but which reveals itself only through the encounter with the unconscious.

> Even the best attempts at explanation are only more or less successful translations into another metaphorical language. . . . The most we can do is to *dream the myth onwards* and give it a modern dress.[27]

The Beloved Disciple is not only the disciple *par excellence*, but he is also the interpreter *par excellence*.[28] We claim no more for our interpretation of him than that it is coherent and interesting (at least to us!). But this, in my view, is also sufficient.

THE BELOVED DISCIPLE: A JUNGIAN VIEW

Notes

1. See Walter Wink, *The Bible in Human Transformation: Toward a New Paradigm for Biblical Study* (Philadelphia: Fortress Press, 1973).
2. Quoted in W. G. Rollins, "Jung's Challenge to Biblical Hermeneutics," in *Jung's Challenge to Contemporary Religion* (eds. M. Stein and R. L. Moore; Wilmette, Ill.: Chiron Publications, 1987) 114.
3. C. G. Jung, *Modern Man in Search of a Soul* (New York: Harcourt, 1933) 109.
4. Lance Morrow, "The Ark of America," *Time* (July 6, 1987) 28.
5. W. Iser, "The Reading Process: A Phenomenological Approach," *New Literary History* 3 (1971) 279.
6. R. Barthes, "Text, Théorie du," *Encyclopaedia Universalis* (Paris: Encyclopedia Universalis, 1985) 17.998; trans. by Schuyler Brown.
7. C. G. Jung, *The Archetypes and the Collective Unconscious* (Princeton: Princeton University Press, 1980) 160.
8. Ibid., 47.
9. J. L. Martyn, *History and Theology in the Fourth Gospel* (rev. ed.; Nashville: Abingdon, 1979). We must not, however, use the Fourth Gospel to generalize about Jewish-Christian relations around the turn of the century. See S. A. Katz, "Issues in the Separation of Judaism and Christianity After 70 C.E.: A Reconsideration," *JBL* 103 (1984) 43-76.
10. Jung, *Archetypes*, 174-75.
11. Ibid., 22.
12. See A. Reinhartz, "Examining the New Testament After the Holocaust," an address given at the Holocaust education colloquium held on Nov. 12, 1986 in Toronto.
13. Quoted in D. Stanley-Porter, "The Fascination with *Tristan und Isolde*," *Canadian Opera Company Magazine* (Sept.-Oct. 1987) 39.
14. Ibid.
15. C. G. Jung, "The Difference Between Eastern and Western Thinking," in *The Portable Jung* (ed. J. Campbell; New York: Penguin Books, 1977) 494-95.
16. See E. Käsemann, *Jesu letzter Wille nach Johannes 17* (Tübingen: J. C. B. Mohr [Paul Siebeck], 1966).
17. H. Köster, *Einführung in das Neue Testament* (Berlin/New York: de Gruyter, 1980) 717: "From the decades that followed the death of the first generation of Christian apostles, thus from the period of roughly AD 60-90, we know not a single name. The second Christian generation reminis completely anonymous" (Editor's translation).
18. S. Brown, *The Origins of Christianity: A Historical Introduction to the New Testament* (Oxford: Oxford University Press, 1984) 137-38.
19. We follow the prevailing view that the "other disciple" (John 18:15, 16) is to be identified with the Beloved Disciple. See K. B. Quast, *Peter and the Beloved Disciple in the Gospel of John: Figures for a Community in Crisis* (JSNT Sup; Sheffield: JSOT Press, 1989).
20. Jung, *Archetypes*, 21.
21. In the Lucan parallel, Peter alone is mentioned (Luke 24:12). This suggests that the Beloved Disciple has been written into the Johannine version of the story.
22. See E. R. Norman, *Christianity and the World Order* (Oxford University Press, 1979).
23. R. Bultmann, *The Gospel of John: A Commentary* (trans. G. R. Beasley-Murray et al.; Oxford: Blackwell, 1971) 673.
24. See R. A. Johnson, *We: Understanding the Psychology of Romantic Love* (San Francisco: Harper & Row, 1983).
25. See J. P. Dourley, *Love, Celibacy and the Inner Marriage* (Toronto: Inner City Books, 1987).
26. S. Brown, "Reader Response: Demythologizing the Text," *NTS* 34(1988) 232-37.
27. Jung, *Archetypes*, 160.
28. The assumption that "the witness" of the Beloved Disciple can only be "true" (John 19:35) if he was an *eye*-witness is a typical example of extroverted thinking.

A DIFFERENT APPROACH TO JAMNIA: THE JEWISH SOURCES OF MATTHEW'S MESSIANISM

W. D. Davies

A t first encounter the title of this essay might seem inappropriate for a volume dedicated to Pauline and Johannine themes. But indirectly this is not so. Professor Louis Martyn has put us all deeply in his debt by drawing attention—strikingly, with great imaginative originality—to the radical break between Johannine Christianity and Jamnian Judaism. However, the very effectiveness of his work has perhaps overshadowed other less dramatic reactions to Jamnian Judaism among Christians. The Gospel of Matthew in particular, it might be urged, points to an encounter and engagement with that Judaism more nuanced, and less polarized perhaps, than that dealt with by Professor Martyn. The consideration of the Matthean reaction to Judaism at Jamnia, therefore, may help to fill in something of the background—contemporary but possibly distant rather than immediate—of the developments in Johannine circles. Professor Martyn was working on John, and I was working on Matthew, when we were together at Union Theological Seminary. I offer here a partial parallel and foil to the Johannine encounter in paying tribute to a cherished former colleague with gratitude and admiration for his work and friendship.

The term "messianism" in the subtitle needs careful definition since it can easily be confused with "christology." Is Matthew's "messianism" a christology? Traditionally in Christian theology, in its strict sense, the term *christology* designates the doctrine about the way in which God became man "in Christ"—that is, the mode or, if one may so crudely put it, the mechanics of the Incarnation in Christ. Recently, an Oxford scholar has urged that the Messiah was regarded as a divine or divinely begotten being in some passages in Jewish sources. However, most of the evidence of those sources points unambiguously to the Messiah as being purely human. Is the same true of Matthew's understanding of Jesus? Certain verses have been taken to indicate that God became man in Jesus, his Son, in the story of the virgin birth in 1:18-25. But that story begins with τοῦ δὲ Ἰησοῦ Χριστοῦ ἡ γένεσις οὕτως ἦν not with τοῦ δὲ υἱοῦ τοῦ θεοῦ ἡ γένεσις οὕτως ἦν, and the role of the Son of God christology in the strict sense so emphasized by Professor Kingsbury[1] in his influential and important studies is not foremost in the birth narratives as a whole, and this should warn us against overemphasizing its significance. Similarly, to read any later Trinitarian significance into the Spirit in Matthew is unjustifiable. In the virgin birth narrative the "spirit," a term neuter in Greek and feminine in Hebrew, is best understood in terms of the invasive power of God; there is no suggestion of the Spirit as the Second Person of a Trinity. But what of 1:23: ἰδοὺ ἡ παρθένος ἐν γαστρὶ ἕξει καὶ τέξεται υἱόν, καὶ καλέσουσιν τὸ ὄνομα αὐτοῦ Ἐμμανουήλ, ὅ ἐστιν μεθερμηνευόμενον μεθ᾽ ἡμῶν ὁ θεός? There are those who have taken Matthew to equate Jesus with God in this verse. (see John 1:1-5; 20:28). This view appears as early as Irenaeus (Adv. Haer. 3.21.4: "Carefully, then, has the Holy Ghost pointed out, by what has been said, His birth from a virgin, and His essence, that He is God [for the name Emmanuel indicates this].") In recent scholarship, many have placed 1:23 in parallel with 28:20. It is claimed that the words "Lo, I am with you" at the end of the Gospel most naturally refer to God and recall the presence of God in Jesus in 1:23. The argument is that μετά with the genitive in Matthew usually means "in company with." But usually, in Matthew, God is referred to as being "in heaven" (2:9). To be "with men" would be more appropriate to the Son than to God, the Heavenly Father: the Son has here in 1:23 become God with us.

But all these considerations (and they are not very cogent) do not outweigh others. Apart from 1:23, even if by implication there, Matthew never refers to Jesus as God, as is the case with most of the New Testament.[2] If Matthew has intended to identify Jesus with God we should have found in 1:23 Ἐμμανουήλ . . . ὁ θεὸς μεθ᾽ ἡμῶν rather than μεθ᾽ ἡμῶν ὁ θεός. Here the order of words makes ὁ θεός adverbial. The passage is not a statement of the Incarnation—that is, it is not strictly christological—although in a general sense it does indicate that for Matthew in Jesus' coming God's Spirit has become uniquely present among men. The Trinitarian formula in the canonical text in 28:19-20 poses such textual difficulties that it cannot be taken to invalidate the rejection of a strictly christological aspect in the messianism of Matthew. The most that could be claimed is that the messianism of Matthew offers an inchoate christology, its raw materials as it were. Matthew's use of the term *Lord* for Jesus, important and possibly primary as it is, does not invalidate our position.[3]

We can now turn to the origins of the teaching about Jesus, the Messiah, in Matthew. But before we do so three other preliminary notes are necessary. First, we take Matthew to have been a Jew who had accepted the Christian belief that Jesus was the Messiah. Everything points to his having been a sophisticated sage, possibly a trained Pharisee, rooted in Judaism, although familiar with the Hellenistic mentality and language. Hellenism and Judaism had deeply intermingled in Matthew's day, but it is to the Jewish sources that we most naturally turn for the signs of his thought. "Messianic" ideas in the form of an expectation of a future deliverer were not peculiar to Judaism, but they were certainly prominent in the first-century Jewish world, and Hellenistic and other parallels, though interesting, are peripheral to our purpose: They cannot be allowed to govern our exegesis.

A second preliminary is that the title of this chapter speaks of sources in the plural. We are not seeking a single origin. If we were, our task would be concentrated in the historical Jesus of Nazareth. The ultimate origin of Matthew's messianism is the historical Jesus and the impact he had on those who first believed. He is the *fons et origo* of Matthew's messianism. In this sense, there is one origin to it, whether Jesus himself claimed to be Messiah or not. The elusiveness of that one origin, however, we need not emphasize.

Third, we can here only deal with broad central aspects of our theme. We cannot follow every twist and turn in the origins of Matthew's messianism. Because of this we shall concentrate on the beginnings of Matthew's Gospel, the prologue—that is, chaps. 1 and 2. Fortunately much that is most pertinent in the rest of the Gospel is there foreshadowed. To examine the prologue will provide a guide to most—though, as we shall see, not all—of Matthew's emphases and because the prologue is replete with quotations and allusions to their origins also.

What, then, are the broad outlines of Matthew's messianism and what their origins?

The New Creation

We begin where Matthew began. His messianism is from the beginning cosmic in scope: The coming of Jesus is comparable to the creation of the universe. The evidence is clear in the first verse. Scholars have treated Matt 1:1, βίβλος γενέσεως Ἰησοῦ Χριστοῦ υἱοῦ Δαυὶδ υἱοῦ Ἀβραάμ, as introducing either the genealogy in 1:2-17 or the genealogy and the virgin birth in 1:2-25; or 1:2–2:23 down to the coming of Jesus to Nazareth; or, again, the whole section from 1:1 down to 4:16, which ends with the settling of Jesus in Capernaum before he began his ministry. But as early as Jerome, the first verse was also referred to the entire Gospel: It is a title for the whole of the Gospel of Matthew. The word γένεσις was understood to mean either "genesis" or "history". This seems to us to be the intent of Matthew in this first verse; it is twofold, at least. In the first place he quite deliberately begins his Gospel with the words βίβλος γενέσεως to suggest a parallel with the first creation described in Genesis 1 and 2, a parallel with the creation of the universe and Adam and Eve, on the one hand, and the new creation brought by Jesus, the Messiah, on the other. In using the term βίβλος, which is anarthrous, he is doubtless following prophetic, didactic, and apocalyptic conventions. The evidence is abundant.[4] But there is more to it than this. Matthew intends his βίβλος γενέσεως to recall the first book of the Tanak. The title "Genesis" had already been given to the first book of the Tanak in the earlier MSS of the LXX and other sources. But when I wrote *The Setting of the Sermon on the Mount* I had not proved that it was used when Matthew wrote. However, Dale C. Allison has referred to passages where Philo uses "Genesis" for the first book of the Tanak. The word *genesis* in Matthew 1:1 would, we conclude, naturally evoke that book. Jesus is the initiator of a new creation parallel to the first: The genitive in 1:1 is subjective.[5] We might speculate further. Like the Hebrew Text at Gen 1:1, so Matt 1:1 begins with the letter *beth* or *beta*. Later sages made much of the initial *beth* in בראשית in Gen 1:1. Some interpreted it as indicating "blessing" (ברכה) some (because *beth* is the numerical 2) as connoting two worlds of space and time. One interpretation claimed that the first letter was *beth* because *beth* is not circular and, therefore, closed, but open-ended. The creation is open-ended and looks to the future (see *Gen. Rab.* 1:10 on Genesis 1:1). Did such speculation, which is not datable, but is apparently early[6], influence Matthew to begin his Gospel with *beta*? Such speculation, fantastic to us, would have been congenial to Matthew.

But even if this significance assigned to the initial *beta* is too speculative, there is much in Matthew besides the initial words to suggest a new creation. It has been claimed with some degree of probability that the role of the Holy Spirit in the virgin birth in 1:18 recalls the activity of the Spirit at the creation in Genesis 1. Matthew takes up from Q the reference to the Spirit of God descending as a dove on Jesus at his baptism in Jordan in 3:16. There have been differing interpretations of the dove, but the most probable is that which points to the new creation motif. The calming of the raging sea in 8:23-27 recalls passages in the Old Testament (Job 38:8-11; Ps 89:9), indicating God's cosmic control. The discussion of divorce in 19:3-9 directs Matthew's hearers to Genesis 1 and 2. As the synoptic parallels to some of the passages referred to indicate, Matthew was not alone in the New Testament in thinking in this way. There were Jewish-Christians before him who had thought so. The relationship between Matthew and the Pauline epistles is unresolved, but certainly Paul had understood the Christian dispensation in terms of new creation and Jesus in terms of the Last Adam. It was he who may have been the first to develop the interpretation of Jesus as the Last Adam. One of the direct sources of Matthew, Mark, implies the new creation probably in its use of ἀρχὴ τοῦ εὐαγγελίου in its very first verse and in the evocation of Adam in its account of the temptation. The prologue of the Fourth Gospel is no stranger to the notion of a new creation. Jewish and other Christians before and after Matthew were familiar with it (see *Barn* 6). Its ultimate source is clear: It is Judaism.

Gunkel long ago established the parallelism between the cosmic beginnings in Genesis and the anticipated Messianic beginnings: as he put it, *Urzeit* parallels *Endzeit*. This is given prominence in Matthew from the very first words of his Gospel. The interpretation of Jesus as the Messiah who inaugurates a new creation is fundamental for him. He embraced the conviction explicitly expressed in 4 Ezra 7:30, but with a long history before his day, that with the coming of the Messiah the world would once again be "as it was in the beginning." As did the sages, he connected the beginning, the *rēshīth* of Genesis 1:1, with the Messiah, and accepted the principle τὰ ἔσχατα ὡς τὰ πρῶτα, that messianism has a cosmic dimension. Jesus sets in motion a γένεσις, a new creation. I emphasized that the title of this chapter refers to origins, but there is a caveat to be uttered: There is one origin—in the inaugurator of the new creation, Jesus.

A scientific analogy may help here. Modern physicists and astronomers have sought to find a common center from which the totality not only of this universe but of all universes is to be derived. Through intricate mathematical calculations they have been able to locate this center in space and time. They concluded that there was a kind of ball of fire that originally exploded. There was a "Big Bang," an explosion, at or of this central core, from which all else has evolved. For Matthew, we may argue, Jesus as Messiah was comparable with this "Big Bang" in that he explosively inaugurated a new creation.

The Son of David

But the matter is not so simple. According to most scientists perhaps, we cannot go behind the "Big Bang" to any space or any time. Unimaginable as this is to common sense, before the "Big Bang" there was no space and there was no time; these are concepts relative only to the "Big Bang." Space and time came into being only in relation to each other with or as a result of the "Big Bang," which has no origin or origins. To speak of any purpose or will of God behind the "Big Bang" is inadmissible. Oddly enough some of the rabbinic sages *mutatis mutandis* said the same of the beginning of Gen 1:1. "Just as the *beth* is closed at the sides but open in front, so you are not permitted to investigate what is above and what is below, what is before and what is behind." "This is explained in *Hag.* 11a as referring either to space or time or both" (*Gen. Rab.* on 1:1 p. 9).[7]

But for Matthew's understanding of Jesus, as the inaugurator of the new creation, things are different. Certainly he is the Big Bang so to put it. But he emerged at a particular time and space and he has an origin and origins. Much as Matthew by implication emphasized the newness of the Messiah, Jesus is no novelty for him and the centrality of his initiatory power connects him with a past in time and space. We can and must go behind him to the history of his people in time and to the land of Israel in space. The very term "Messiah" is incomprehensible without that people and their understanding of their own existence and of the world's.

Again we turn to the title of the Gospel. The term βίβλος γενέσεως does not refer only to the creation in Gen 1:1. As elsewhere in Matthew, one word or group of words can have no more than one connotation and function. So here, βίβλος γενέσεως refers not only back to Gen 1:1 but also forward to the genealogy of Jesus. The term γένεσις in 1:18 refers to the birth of Jesus, and it can also refer to the history or life of Jesus. βίβλος γενέσεως recalls the first creation and past history and simultaneously points forward to the emerging new creation and new history, and Matthew finds in the first creation and in the past history of God's people, Israel, the type or pattern of events in the life of Jesus and his people, the church.

Let us first look at the genealogy particularly, but also at the whole of chaps. 1 and 2. Matthew inherited the belief endemic to Judaism that the creation embodied a divine intention and that God is the Lord of history. God is divinely sovereign over all things. History is in the hands of God, the sphere of his purposeful activity. Looking for redemption, to use Luke's prologue (2:38), rose out of this belief: Messianism for Matthew is simply the corollary of the Jewish certainty about God—that God was responsible for creation and committed to history and, if so, committed not only in the past but in the future—hence the Messianic hope. In fact, for Matthew history had a messianic pattern. Each stage of Jewish history suggested the Messiah to him. The pattern leading to Jesus, the Messiah, is threefold. Each of the three stages is constituted of fourteen generations. From Abraham to David the king in 1:2-6; from David to the deportation to Babylon and the Exile (vv. 7-11); from the Exile to

Jesus—in each of these divisions were fourteen generations. This is expressly stated in Matt 1:17. According to the tradition of *gematria*, well established in first century Judaism, fourteen, as a number, spells the name of David. By explicitly pointing to "fourteen" in 1:17 Matthew indicates that history is messianic in form and leads to Jesus as the Messiah. Objections raised to the use of *gematria* in the genealogy are not cogent, as I have argued elsewhere. There is precedence for the use of it in 1:1-7 in Gen 46:8-27, where it occurs in a genealogy. Knowing the the Old Testament listed fourteen names from Abraham to David, Matthew probably set himself to look for fourteens and constructed his own Davidic messianic genealogy on this pattern. In his text the name David stands immediately before the genealogy, is placed in the fourteenth spot in the genealogy itself, and twice at its conclusion. At the fourteenth spot David is uniquely honored with the title "King": τὸν βασιλέα. The very first name after Ἰησοῦ Χριστοῦ in 1:1 is David.

Historically the term Son of David as a standard messianic title is attested in the Rabbis in *b. Sanh.* 97a-98a and may already be present in the *Pss. Sol.*, 17:21-35 in the first century BCE. It developed out of Old Testament passages such as Isa 11:10 (the root of Jesse) and Jer 23:5; 33:15. By the first century it had become the dominant Jewish expectation. Possibly the short-comings of the non-Davidic Hasmonaeans furthered the process that led to this. The messianic king "who was to come" was perceived as a Son of David who would fulfill the promises of 2 Sam 7:16, where the prophet Nathan is commanded by God to tell David: "Your family shall be established and your kingdom shall stand for all time in my sight, and your throne shall be established for ever" (2 Sam 7:16, author's trans.). Already before Matthew wrote, Christian circles recognized the Davidic connections of Jesus (Rom 1:3-4; see also Acts 2:29-36; 13:22-3; 2 Tim 2:8; Rev 5:5; 22:16). But of all New Testament writers it is Matthew who most emphasizes that Jesus is of Davidic ancestry. "Son of David" occurs nine times in Matthew, over against three times in Mark; it never occurs in Luke. It was apparently Matthew's most characteristic designation for the earthly Jesus, the Messiah. In the prologue—which refers to Bethlehem, the city of David (2:8, 16)—there is a clear intent to set forth Jesus as qualifying, through his father Joseph (1:16) as the royal Messiah of the Davidic line. It agrees with this that in the genealogy in 1:2-17, unlike Luke in 3:31, Matthew traces the descent of Jesus through Solomon, a Son of David, who later became famous as a mighty healer, exorcist, and magician (Jos., *Ant.* 8:45-49). It is significant that Matthew precisely connects Jesus as Son of David with healings and exorcisms (9:27; 12:23; 15:22; 20:30-31).

So far we have noted two aspects of Matthew's messianism: It affirms a new creation, and it traces a pattern in history that leads to the emergence of a Son of David as Messiah. In all this he draws upon the Tanak and traditions within Judaism. But one thing already makes it clear that he draws upon both selectively. In view of the reference to Genesis one would expect a parallel to be indicated between Jesus and Adam in the genealogy, as was the case with Luke. One scholar has found Adam to be the key to the chiasmus he finds in 1:1-1:16.[8] But, although Adam probably is in Matthew's mind, as in Mark's, in the Temptation narrative, the name is not found in the genealogy and does not appear even once in Matthew's Gospel. Paul was probably an innovator here, but Matthew, did he know of Paul's thought, ignores it. His concentration is on the divine activity in so guiding history as to lead to Jesus as Son of David. Matthew's thought smacks of "determinism." History seems inevitably to have led to Jesus as Messiah. But it is a "determinism" that allows for human error and perversity. Persons are always free to dispute and thwart the divine purpose at least temporarily. As in the Joseph saga, humans may mean evil and do it, and God may mean it for good (Gen 50:20), so in Matthew's genealogy there are sinners, but they subserve the divine purpose. Matthew is Pharisaic in his understanding of the paradox that everything is determined and free will given *(Aboth)*, and for him the determination of history is messianically aimed. The emergence of Jesus, the Son of David, is its climax.

The Son of Abraham

In all that we have said about the Son of David, it is clear that Matthew has drawn upon the kingship ideology of ancient Israel. This was grounded on that of the ancient Near East, and Mowinckel urged that this was the source of the messianic idea as it emerged in Jewish sources, the Tanak and the extra-canonical literature. Notice that the Davidic messianic hope was essentially a hope of and for Israel: It was inextricably ethnic. As 2 Samuel 7 makes clear, the choice of David as king had been inextricably bound in the tradition to the choice of Israel as God's people. In 2 Sam 7:23 David asks:

And thy people Israel to whom can they be compared? Is there any other nation on earth whom thou, O God, hast set out to redeem from slavery to be thy people? Any other for whom thou hast done great and terrible things to win fame for thyself? (author's trans.)

In the Hebrew tradition on which Matthew drew, messiahship had grown out of a particular people's history. It could be read exclusively in terms of that people's history—it involved Israel's peoplehood and territory and history. The source and condition of the messianic yearning that Matthew had indicated were the words, "I will be their God and they will be my people." There was and is in the Jewish messianic hope what Kenneth Cragg has called the perspective of an "inherent privacy." It was the hope of God's own chosen.[9] With this "privacy"—or, to use the more usual term *exclusiveness*—Matthew had to come to terms. He does so in the very first verse by asserting that Jesus is not only the Son of David, but also the Son of Abraham. Here the meaning of "Son of Abraham" is probably dual. First, Jesus is Son of David and, through him, he is personally and biologically the Son of Abraham; he is Son of Abraham as are all Jews whose father is Abraham. The term "Son of Abraham" is not to be taken automatically as "messianic." In Matt 1:1 it certainly means that Jesus is one of Jewish blood or one worthy of the father Abraham. But, second, it may also be that "Son of Abraham" is here a messianic title or at least, is messianic in intent. Outside Matthew, in Luke (1:30-33, 55, 69-73; Acts 3:25; 13:23) the promises concerning the seed of David and the seed of Abraham are brought together. Paul takes Jesus to be of the seed of Abraham (Gal 3:16). And in the Tanak, Jer 33:21-22, and later in the targum on Ps 89:4, Gen 17:7, the promise to Abraham and his seed is associated with 2 Sam 7:12 (the promise to David and his seed). The first verse of Matthew, then, means not only that Jesus is Messiah as Son of David—indicating the fulfillment of the strictly private Jewish hope, but also as the Son of Abraham. What does this signify?

The figure of Abraham in Jewish tradition needs scrutiny. He is certainly, like David, of the highest significance for the Jewish people as such. It was with him that God had made a covenant with Israel (Genesis 12, 15). In the *Testament of Jacob* 7:22 he is the "father of fathers." Descent from him constituted the ground for membership in the Jewish people (Judg 12:24; 13:3; 4 Ezra 3:13-15). Thus as a Son of Abraham Jesus is in Matt 1:1 an Israelite indeed, a true member of the people of Israel. Matthew makes him bring to its culmination the history that began with Abraham; the genealogy underlines his Jewishness. But there is another side to Abraham and his significance. He had a particular relevance to those who were not Jews by birth—that is, to those not within the covenant made between God and Israel through him. God had called Abraham before God had established the covenant, before there were Jews. Another way of stating this is to claim that by birth Abraham was a Gentile, and the covenant that God had initiated through him was to be a blessing not only to Jews but to all nations (Gen 12:3; 18:18). Abraham came to be portrayed as the father of all nations as well (Gen 17:5; 1 Macc 12:19-21). The promise to Abraham could, therefore, be exploited to further the Jewish mission. One Tannaitic sage saw in him the first proselyte (*b. Hag.* 3a). Paul, therefore, could naturally use the figure of Abraham as the true father of all who have faith, both Jews and Gentiles (Rom 4:1-25; Gal 3:6-29). Likewise Matthew, in 8:11-12 and in 3:9 possibly and in 1:1, appeals to an Abrahamic strain in Judaism itself to serve his Gentile interests. Franz Rosenzweig defined Judaism as a life one possesses by birth in "the eternal self-preservation of procreative blood . . . through shutting the pure spring of blood off from foreign admixture. . . Descendant and ancestor are the live incarnation of the eternal people, both of them for each other. . . . We experience our Judaism with immediacy in elders and children."[10] We suggest that, while Matt 1:1 includes Jesus, as Messiah, in the people of Israel by calling him the Son of David and a Son of Abraham, at the same time by calling Jesus the Son of Abraham, Matthew intends to redefine that people to include Gentiles. And just as the motif of the new creation reemerged in the prologue in the story of the virgin birth (1:18-25), and the significance of the Son of David is pointed to 1:2-17, so too the evocation of the Gentiles in the term Son of Abraham in 1:1 finds confirmation in the introduction into the genealogy itself of women of foreign origin—Tamar, a Canaanite, or an Aramaean; Rahab, a Canaanite; Ruth, a Moabitess; and Bathsheba, a Hittite; and in the story of the Magi. In thus connecting Jesus, Son of David, the king of the Jews, with the Gentile Abraham, Matthew was not innovating. In some sources Abraham was regarded as a king, and the advent of the Messiah was to witness the incoming of the Gentiles.[11] There were elements in Jewish apocalyptic as well as in the Old Testament that provided a hope for the final redemption of Gentiles. Doubtless Matthew was aware of these, and doubtless they were being neglected in the renewed apocalypticism after 70 CE. And so he called Jesus, the Son of Abraham, one who was relevant to the crisis in Jewish-Gentile relations, which three centuries of the exposure of Jews to the Hellenism had produced, the Savior of the world "not only of Israel." Was he not opposing the narrow exclusiveness of the nationalism of his day even after the collapse of Jerusalem in calling Jesus the Son of Abraham?

The Greater Moses

We now go beyond the title and the genealogy in the prologue to another figure or presence that the birth narratives in chaps. 1 and 2 evoke quite unmistakably, though not explicitly, for the interpretation of Jesus, that of Moses. In his genealogy Matthew does not mention Moses at all as being among the ancestors of Jesus. The reason is simple. In the part of the genealogy that covers the period up to the Exile, Matthew largely follows the genealogy provided for him in 1 Chronicles.

Up to 1:13 he copies an Old Testament genealogy. All the names in 1:13-15 occur in the LXX. But after this for the 500 years between Zerubbabel and Joseph, the father of Jesus, Matthew has only nine names. The names in 1:2-6 occur in 1 Chr 1:28, 34; 2:1-15 (see also Ruth 4:18-22). The name Moses is not in these passages, and Matthew—while innovative in the formulation or pattern of his genealogy—does not choose to depart from the substance of the Scriptures where he is drawing upon them, and so he also omits Moses, or rather does not insert his name. However, the influence of the figure of Moses in Matthew's interpretation of Jesus as Messiah has long been recognized, although in different degrees. The evidence is clear. Here I note only the bare-bones.

1. The infancy narratives recall the circumstances at the birth of Moses, especially as recorded in Josephus, and the *Liber Biblicarum Antiquitatum.* I note only the peril at the births of Jesus and Moses, from Herod and the Pharaoh respectively, the exile of both into Egypt, and the flight at night.[12]

2. The events in chaps. 3 and 4, immediately following the birth narratives, recall the story of the Exodus from Egypt. The baptism of Jesus at the Jordan is parallel to the passing of Israel through the Red Sea. The sojourn for forty days in the desert to fast and to be tested is comparable with the forty years of Israel's wandering in the wilderness, where Israel was tempted. As Israel was tempted by the worship of the golden calf, so Jesus was tempted to idolatry. The temptations of Jesus are a reliving of the temptations of Israel and are understood by Matthew in the light of Deut 8:2-3.

3. Following on chaps. 3 and 4 comes the Sermon on the Mount. Probably most scholars have seen here a delineation of Jesus as a New Moses, giving his new Torah from a new Sinai. For many reasons, not the least of which was the desire not to read into Matthew what was congenial, I long resisted this direct parallel. In a recent study, T. L. Donaldson has dismissed the parallel with Mt. Sinai in favor of a parallel with Mt. Zion, which von Rad taught us to consider as the Mount of the assembly of the nations and of which Jeremias wrote so approvingly. After examining every mountain scene in Matthew, Donaldson comes to the conclusion that in Matthew "the mountain motif is a device used by the evangelist to make the christological statement that Christ has replaced Zion as the center of God's dealings with his people: in him all the hopes associated with Zion have come to fruition and fulfillment."[13] This fits into the de-territorializing of Judaism in much early Christianity, but it overlooks two things: the data to which I have elsewhere referred, pointing to a well-marked Mosaic motif in Matthew, and the very convincing data pointed out by D. C. Allison, regarding the

nature of the introduction to the Sermon on the Mount and its conclusion.[14] First, after Jesus has gone up to the mountain, from which he gives his "sermon," he sits down on it. His "sitting" has suggested to commentators that Jesus here simply assumes the role of a teacher. Teachers and sages and rabbis and others sat when they taught. In 5:1-2 Jesus has his *yeshiba* ("sitting") (see Sir 51:23). But this does not go far enough. 5:1-2 recalls Deut 9:9 (which may well have been alluded to in 4:2). Deuteronomy 9:9 reads: "When I went up to the mountain to receive the tables of stone, the tables of the covenant which the Lord made with you, I remained on the mountain forty days and forty nights; I neither ate bread nor drank water." The Hebrew word translated "remained" in the RSV is *wā'ēšeb* from *yāšāb*. To this verb the BDB gives three meanings. The second and third are "remain" and "dwell," but the first is "sit." The Jewish sages made much of this. In *b. Meg.* 21a we read:

> One verse says, "And I sat in the mountain" [Deut. 9:9], and another says, "And I stood in the mountain" [Deut. 10:10]. Rab says: He [Moses] stood when he learnt and sat while he went over [what he had learnt]. R. Hanina said: He was neither sitting nor standing but stooping. R. Johanan said: "Sitting" here means only staying, as it says, "And ye stayed in Kadesh many days" [Deut. 1:46]. Raba said: The easy things [he learnt] standing and the hard ones sitting?

The same text appears in *t. Sota* 49a. The verb *wā'ēšeb* was, then, ambiguous. The dating of the rabbinic texts is uncertain, but some sages took Deut 9:9 to refer to Moses *sitting* on Mt. Sinai, as Jesus according to Matthew did on the mount of the sermon. Matthew not only knew the Hebrew text of the Tanak involved, but he was probably also acquainted with the Jewish exegetical traditions about it. This is further indicated by another simple datum. Jesus in 5:1-2 "goes up to the mountain." The Greek is simple: ἀνέβη εἰς τὸ ὄρος. This phrase occurs in the LXX twenty-four times: Eighteen of these are in the Pentateuch, and most refer to Moses. The phrase ἀναβαίνω εἰς τὸ ὄρος occurs in Deut 9:9.

But further, the close of the sermon also recalls Moses on Sinai. In 8:1 we read: "when he had gone down from the mountain." This is a redactional verse. The Greek is καταβάντος δὲ αὐτοῦ ἀπὸ τοῦ ὄρους. This is identical to the LXX(A) at Exod 34:29 of Moses' descent from Sinai (see Exod 19:14; 32:1, 15). The construction cited occurs only once in the LXX (LXXB has ἐκ for ἀπό). The beginning and closing of the sermon linguistically recall Moses on Sinai. I have elsewhere indicated that the figure of Moses lurks behind the Matthaean Jesus in other passages outside the Sermon and the prologue; they cannot be discussed here. We can safely assert that the figure of Moses had drawn into itself messianic significance for Matthew and that his Jesus and his messianism have inescapable Mosaic traits. Even 11:27-30, usually interpreted in terms of Ecclesiastes 51, almost certainly should be understood in terms of Moses.[15] He refers to Exod 33:12-13, where there is reciprocal knowledge between God and Moses, which Jews took to be exclusive. This is implicit in the context in Exodus (see 33:7-11, 17-23); Deut 34:10 makes it explicit. Paul reveals echoes of Exod 33:12-13 in 1 Cor 13:12-13, and Allison finds the Exodus passage to be the background of 11:27. In addition, the reference to "rest" in 11:28 has its parallel in Exod 33:14, and Exod 33:12-13 sheds light on the order of the mutual knowledge presented: The order of "the Father knows the Son and the Son knows the Father" in 11:27 may have been influenced by the fact that God's knowledge of Moses comes first in the Exodus passage. Finally, the attribution of meekness to Jesus (11:29) has its parallel in Moses' characterization in Judaism. Numbers 12:3 reads: "Now the man Moses was very meek" (πραΰς σφόδρα in the LXX). If Allison is followed—and his case is strong—there is no need to go outside the Exodus tradition to any Hellenistic Jewish syncretism, to the Dead Sea Scrolls, to the mystical philosophical literature of the East or to the wisdom tradition to account for 11:27-30, as Professor Suggs has so forcefully urged.

Up to this point we have noted four strands in the messianism of Matthew. First, it is informed by the interpretation of Jesus in terms of a new creation. Second, it is Davidic. Matthew drew upon the kingship ideology of the ancient Middle East, which Mowinckel long ago argued was the source of the messianic idea. Third, there is the Mosaic strand: Jesus is the greater Moses, who has wrought a new Exodus, and brought a new Law—that is, Matthew's messianism drew upon the tradition of the Exodus, which Joseph Klausner had emphasized as the determinative element in messianism and had drawn to itself creation motifs. Then, fourth, there is the Abrahamic strand, which had struggled to break through the privacy of the Davidic and Exodus traditions to reach out to the larger world. But here I must issue a warning. The differentiation of these four strands I have suggested in Matthew is almost certainly too clear. As in much modern science, our messianic models tend to a conceptual clarity that belies the "fuzziness" of all the data with which we have to deal. The strands I noted are in fact inseparable; they intermingle and are evoked not in isolation but all together sometimes in apparent confusion. They combine to produce a complexity of messianic presentation that belies the clarity and simplification of our neat divisions. Of one thing we can be certain: All the strands have their ground in the Tanak. I have noted elsewhere Matthew's familiarity with the Tanak. The formula quotations, which are from his hand and not drawn from a distinct pre-existent source, alone establish that he knew the Hebrew Bible as well as the LXX. There is other massive evidence for this, but as has already appeared and will later appear, it was not the MT and the LXX in their isolation or textual nudity nor in their historical context that he knew. He knew them as they were understood and interpreted in the Judaism of his day. The Apocrypha and Pseudepigrapha and other Jewish sources here claim their inescapable due.

This leads to at least two other dimensions of Matthew's messianism that are most important. I can only touch upon them here. Matthew applies the title Messiah to Jesus of Nazareth, a person who had endured the most ignominious and painful death, crucifixion—a form of death the Jews especially regarded as being under the curse of God. Nor was the suffering of Jesus confined to the cross. It was foreshadowed with trials at his birth; the political opposition of King Herod; the calumny of his origin; the temptation narrative, which points to his encounter with unseen powers of evil and Satan; and the constant opposition from religious leaders. To use another scientific metaphor, Matthew has throughout fused the messianic with suffering. The crucified messiah seems a contradiction in terms; it constitutes a fusion. Was it a revolution?

It has often been claimed that it was, that Judaism knew nothing of a suffering Messiah. I would like here to refer to my discussion in *Paul and Rabbinic Judaism* and to note in addition certain facts.[16] Apart from the presence of the great enigma of Isaiah 53—so important for Matthew—in the Tanak, I suggest that the presentation of Jesus as the Greater Moses probably carries within itself the notion of suffering. Moses certainly knew suffering—in the flight from Egypt as a refugee and fugitive and in the suffering with and for his people in the wilderness, where he faced the difficulties of idolatry and rebellion. Moses was a man of sorrow and was acquainted with grief. Not surprisingly some scholars saw his lineaments in Isaiah 53. The first redeemer was a suffering redeemer. So, too, the prophets, especially Jeremiah, were suffering figures. Not surprising and not unrelated to all of this is the high evaluation of suffering in Judaism. The difficulties in connection with the place of Isaiah 53 in Matthew and in the rest of the New Testament, I can only refer to, but the fact that the Suffering Servant of Isaiah 53 informed Matthew's view of Jesus can hardly be denied.

And then there is the enigma of the meaning of the Son of Man and his relation to the Messiah. Some scholars have traced the figure to Ezekiel, others to Enoch, others to Daniel 7. The debate continues, even though some have refused to contemplate a definite figure, the Son of

Man, but simply a personal reference in the term. We prefer to look at Daniel 7 as determinative for Matthew. In that passage also the Son of Man is a suffering figure. For our purposes what needs to be emphasized is that for the sources of Matthew's messianism we have to consider not only the Tanak, but also the Apocrypha, the Pseudepigrapha, and extra-canonical sources.

With these bare statements we must leave the role of suffering and of the Son of Man in Matthew. Nor can I here deal with the alleged influence of the Wisdom tradition. Some concluding thoughts are in order. We have emphasized that the origins of Matthew's messianism essentially, informed as it was by the ministry of Jesus of Nazareth, are in the Old Testament as it was understood and interpreted in his day. The Old Testament was his chief quarry both in Hebrew and Greek. But now we have to recognize that his use of it, while governed by the interpretations of it current in his own day, was very selective. He took over much from the Jewish tradition; he cast off much. In two areas especially he may have abandoned or neglected what he found in Judaism. First, it is not clear that he retained the political territoriality of Jewish messianism. Second, he ignores the priestly elements in the Messianic hope. That he did not embrace the territorialism of Judaism is consonant with his emphasis on Abraham and the Gentiles. Despite 19:27, he is not governed by Jewish privacy. Moreover, his distance from the discredited Zealots and the apocalyptic fervor that was probably reemerging in his day would reinforce his aloofness from territorialism. Similarly his indifference to priestly elements in messianism, which could be speculatively exploited by Christians and were (as, for example, in the Epistle to the Hebrews) is also understandable. His dialogue was with Pharisaism. The Temple was in ruins; the priesthood had become unnecessary and survived only in the shadow of Pharisaism. In the dialogue with Judaism in its Pharisaic form, Matthew was immediately and chiefly concerned with the messianic Torah—a notion at least inchoate in first-century Judaism—and the greater Moses. There were elements, not obviously significant in the ministry of Jesus, that would have naturally fostered the notion of Jesus as Priest in Matthew, but given the climate after Jamnia, which was not conducive to this, they were either overlooked or ignored. Nevertheless, despite its emphasis on the new creation, Matthew's messianism, because of its restraint, is not utopian, but restorative. This is largely because its sources are not simply the Jewish tradition in the Tanak, the Apocrypha, and the Pseudepigrapha, but the actualities, political and religious, of the situation he faced after the collapse of Jerusalem and the rise of Rabbinic Judaism. The necessity to formulate a parallel attraction to Pharisaism at Jamnia was among the factors that led to his presentation of a New Moses with a new messianic torah. The necessity to break the chrysalis of an increasingly privatized Judaism brought forth the Abrahamic emphasis. The presentation of the Son of Man as judge and of the Suffering Messiah, whose words are in the Sermon on the Mount, was possibly not unrelated to a desperate recrudescent, triumphalist apocalyptic, which was finally to lead to Bar Kokba.

At the same time, Matthew's messianism was paradoxical. He was aware of the demands of Judaism and deliberately honored them through the emphasis on Jesus as Son of David. Simultaneously, at a time when many Christians were doubtless tempted to revert to Judaism, he also preserved the radical newness of the gospel in terms of the new creation. In sum, any treatment of the origins of Matthew's messianism must recognize three dimensions at least: the actuality of the messianic ministry of Jesus; the illumination brought to the presentation of that messianic ministry from Jewish sources in the Tanak, the Apocrypha, and the Pseudepigrapha; and the political and religious conditions within which the messianism of Matthew came to be formulated. This last element, the context, does not *determine* the content of Matthew's messianism; Jesus and Judaism did that. But we suggest that it does help to *define* the forms in which he presents it. Perhaps this is the best point at which to refer to a most significant final aspect of Matthew's messianism.

Messianism, as Scholem reminded us, often born of disillusion and despair, has its dark side. It can lead to unrealistic, visionary enthusiasms that prove destructive. Doubtless much in early Christian messianism was of this nature. Paul had to combat it, and even more did Matthew have to shy away from it. In my work *The Setting of the Sermon on the Mount* I traced a *gemaric*, cautionary note in Matthew in which he tempered the radicalism of the early Christian movement and began to adapt its more perfectionist, extreme expressions to the actualities. There is evidence, pointed out especially by Kingsbury, that Matthew's church was probably more comfortably situated than those in which Mark and Paul found themselves and that Matthew was better prepared than Christian enthusiasts to come to terms with the well-to-do and to adapt the tradition. How far early Christian thinking was under the constraint of the disappointment caused by the postponement of the Parousia is in dispute. Matthew at any rate seems to have come to terms with that postponement and seems to contemplate a future on earth for the church of an indefinite duration, although he retains the sense of urgency. In such a situation his messianism becomes tempered, not to say modified. His emphasis on the commandments of Jesus as the greater Moses is not unrelated to this as those aspects of his Gospel that might be labelled as traces of early catholicism. As compared with that of many early Christian enthusiasts, the messianism of Matthew is rabbinically sober: It is Mosaic. Matthew pricks the balloons of enthusiasts by fashioning a messianism in which the figure of Moses is as prominent as the figure of David, and the figure of the Son of Man is especially, perhaps, in judgment. His messianism, in short, is a corrective messianism, corrective of excesses and illusions within the Christian community, as it was corrective, in the light of Jesus, of the messianic hope in the Jewish tradition. More messianism, Matthew seems to be saying, is not enough.

Notes

1. See especially Kingsbury, *Matthew: Structure, Christology, Kingdom* (Philadelphia: Fortress, 1975) esp. 75, and *Jesus Christ in Matthew, Mark, and Luke* (Philadelphia: Fortress, 1981) 64-73.
2. The use of *egō eimi* in 14:27 is still problematic.
3. For details, see Kingsbury, *Matthew* and *Jesus Christ in Matthew, Mark and Luke*.
4. See the examples in W. D. Davies and Dale C. Allison, Jr., *The Gospel According to St. Matthew, i-vii* (ICC; Edinburgh: T. and T. Clark, 1988) 149-53.
5. See W. D. Davies, *The Setting of the Sermon on the Mount* (Cambridge: Cambridge University Press, 1963) 67-72.
6. In the passage referred to, the speculators, introduced by R. Jonah in R. Levi's name, were probably widespread.
7. I am aware of the dangers of using analogies from scientific theories in the discussion of literary and theological themes. The scientific theories deal with "tangible," physical actualities. Their use as metaphors in such studies as the present one can obliterate the difference between their subject matter and the metaphorical. I had thought of the analogy between the New Creation and the Prologue of Matthew and the Big Bang Theory before reading a brilliant essay by George Steiner on "Some Black Holes," in *The Bulletin of the American Academy of Arts and Sciences* 41.2 (1987) 12-28. In words he ascribes, in imagination, to Sir Karl Popper, had Popper been present at the lecture, Steiner writes, "Don't mix up the momentary sound use of metaphor by exact sciences with what it is they are really doing or looking for" (26). However, Steiner's other words deserve quotation even more, that "there are certain moments in history and culture when convincing metaphors and compelling images in the arts, in philosophy, and in the exact and applied sciences seem strangely congruent, when the force of these metaphors is such that they bend gravitationally the light of sensibility . . . on its passage out of highly specialized areas into the more diffuse but vital centers of feeling and thought" (26). The same awareness emerges in a remarkable passage in Walter Benjamin ("Some Reflections on Kafka," in *Illuminations* [ed. Hannah Arendt; New York: Harcourt, 1968] 142). Possibly for us to feel as Matthew felt about the advent of Jesus into the world, nothing would be more helpful than an initiation, however superficially and amateurishly, into modern scientific discussion of cosmology.
8. See Peter F. Ellis, *Matthew: His Mind and His Message* (Collegeville: The Liturgical Press, 1974).
9. See K. Cragg, *The Christ and the Faiths* (Philadelphia: Westminster, 1986) 99.
10. Franz Rosenzweig, *The Star of Redemption* (2nd ed.; Boston: Beacon, 1970) 341, 346.
11. For the evidence, see Davies, *Jewish and Pauline Studies* (Philadelphia: Fortress, 1984) 381.
12. For the evidence, see R. E. Brown, *The Birth of the Messiah* (Garden City: Doubleday, 1977) 111-16.

13. T. L. Donaldson, *Jesus on the Mountain* (JSNTSup 8; Sheffield: JSOT Press, 1985) 200.
14. D. C. Allison, "Jesus and Moses," *ExpTim* (forthcoming).
15. D. C. Allison has made this convincingly clear in "Two Notes on a Key Text: Matt 11:25-30," *JTS* 39 (1988) 477-85.
16. W. D. Davies, *Paul and Rabbinic Judaism* (4th ed.; Philadelphia: Fortress, 1980) 264.

INDEX OF SELECTED
BIBLICAL REFERENCES